I Want to Eat Your Pancreas

THE COMPLETE MANGA COLLECTION

Story by: *Yoru Sumino*
Art by: *Idumi Kirihara*

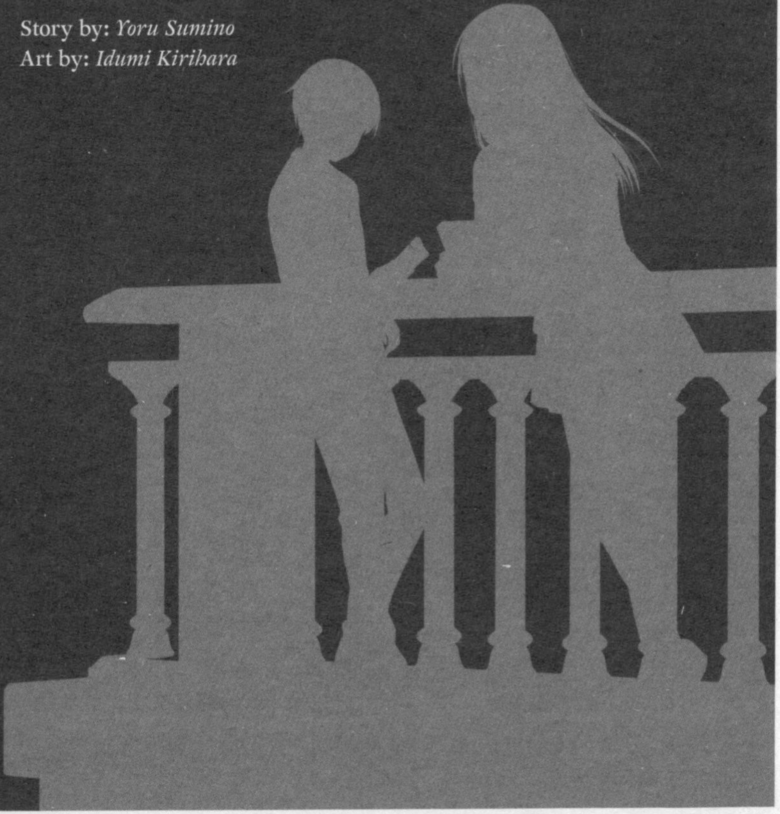

CONTENTS

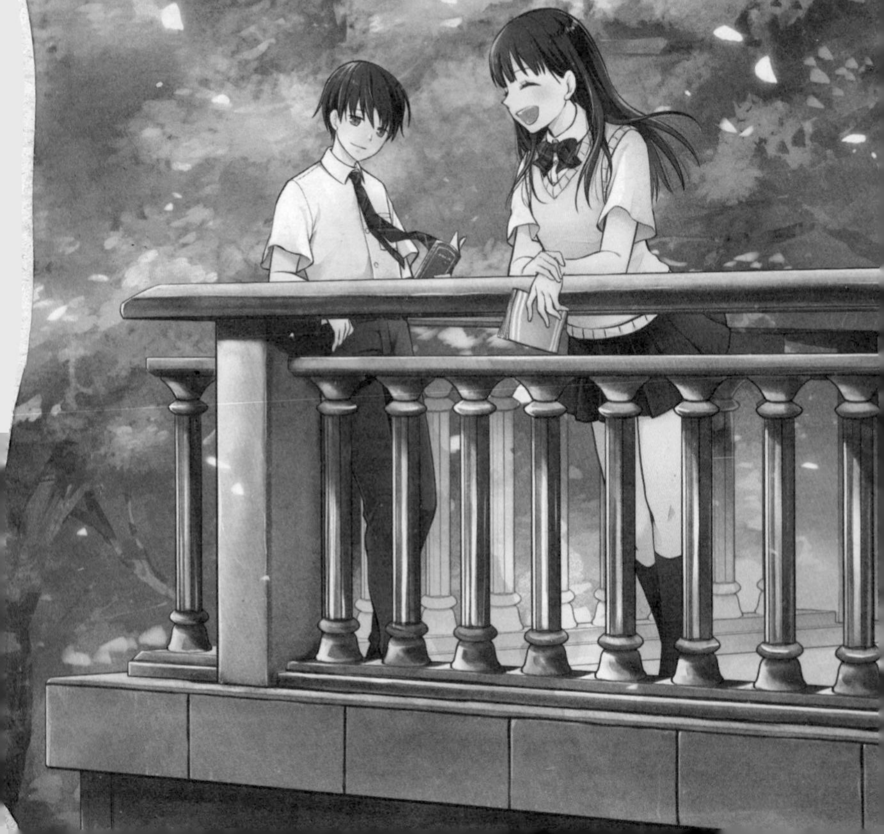

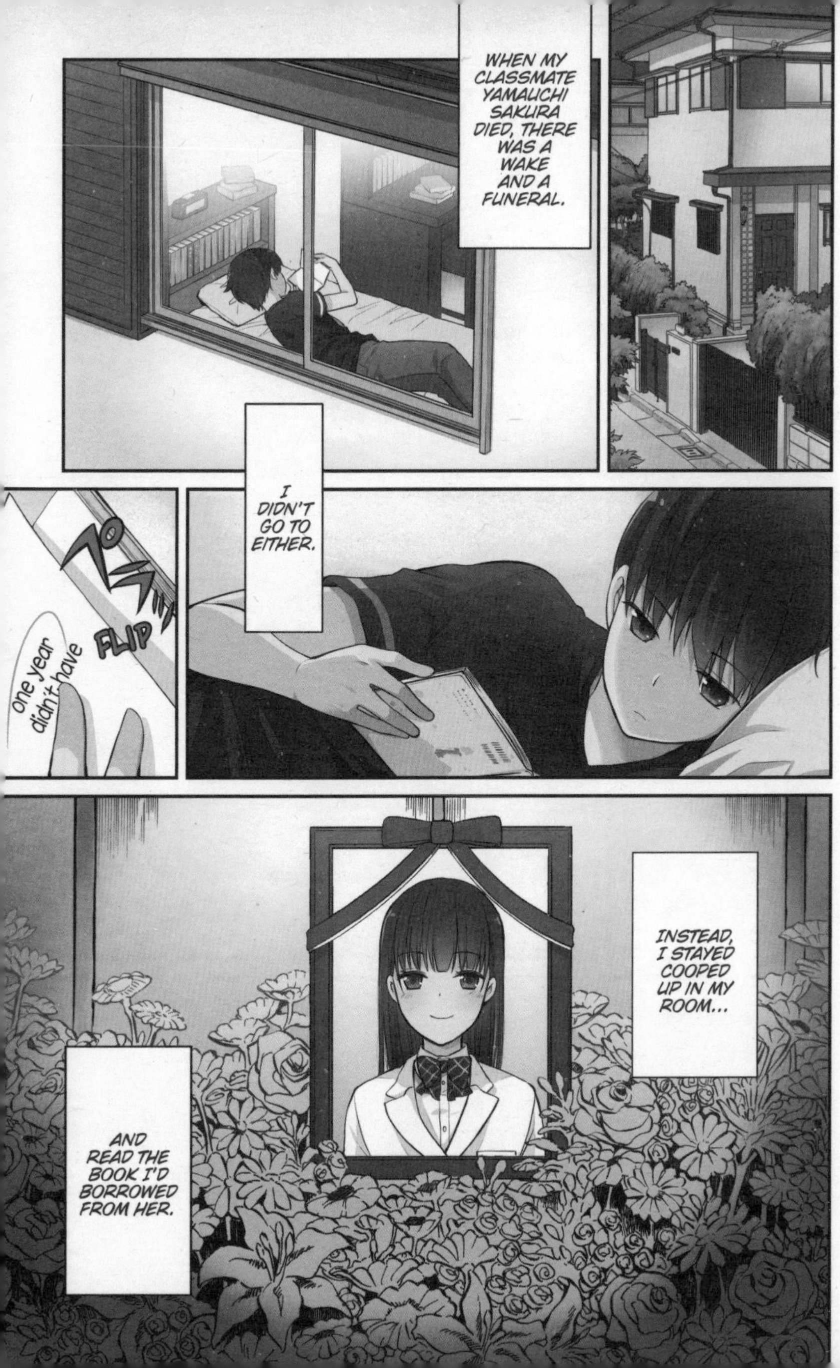

WHEN MY CLASSMATE YAMAUCHI SAKURA DIED, THERE WAS A WAKE AND A FUNERAL.
I DIDN'T GO TO EITHER.
FLIP
one year didn't have
INSTEAD, I STAYED COOPED UP IN MY ROOM...
AND READ THE BOOK I'D BORROWED FROM HER.

Ah... could you cook some rice, please?

WHAT IS IT, MOM?

SURE.

UH-HUH...

SHFF...

......

VRRZ VRRZ

VRRRN

I KEEP WONDERING...

FWMP

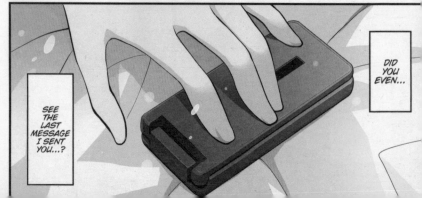

SEE THE LAST MESSAGE I SENT YOU...?

DID YOU EVEN...

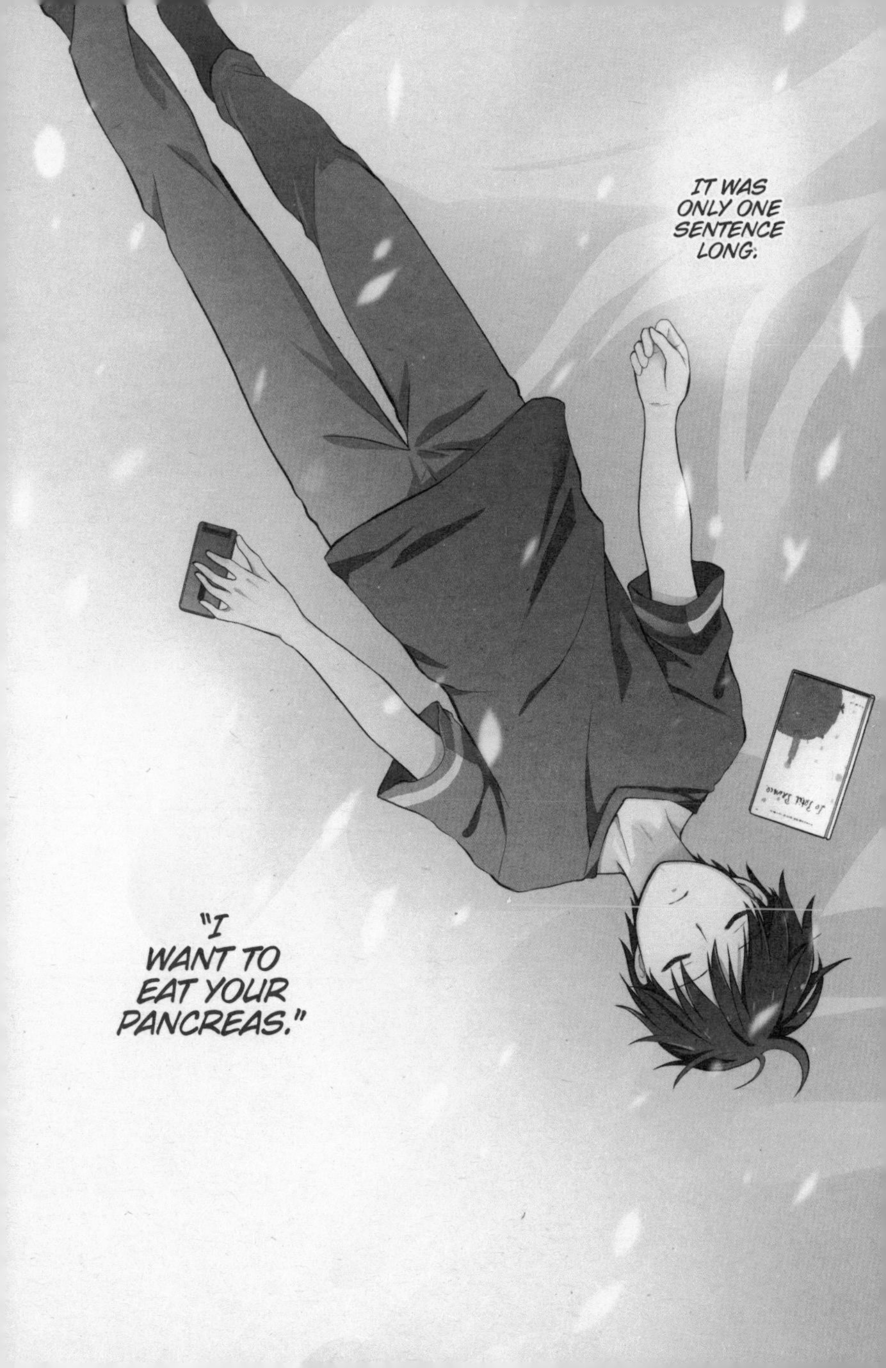
IT WAS ONLY ONE SENTENCE LONG:
"I WANT TO EAT YOUR PANCREAS."

Chapter 1 | [Introverted Classmate]

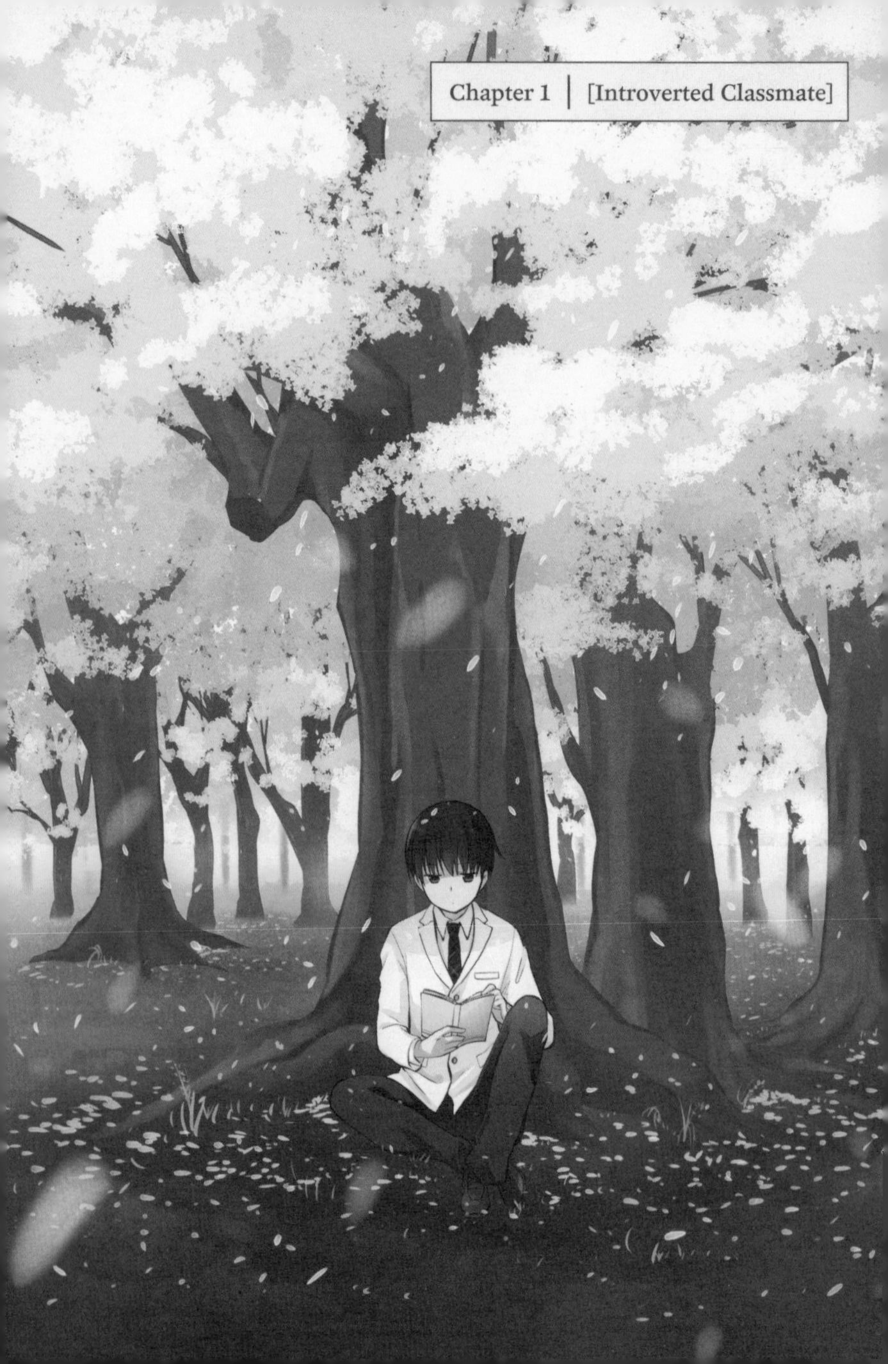

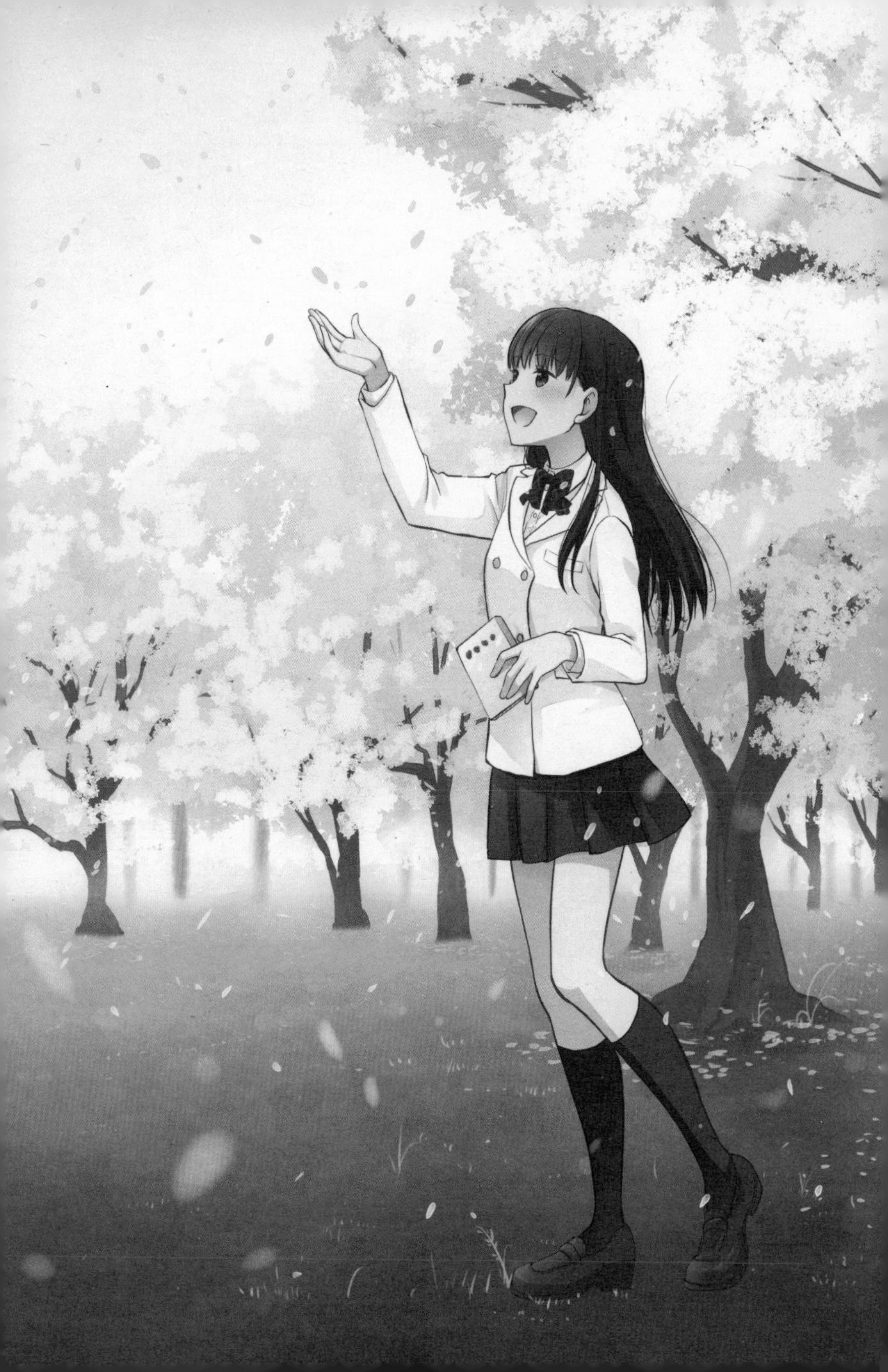

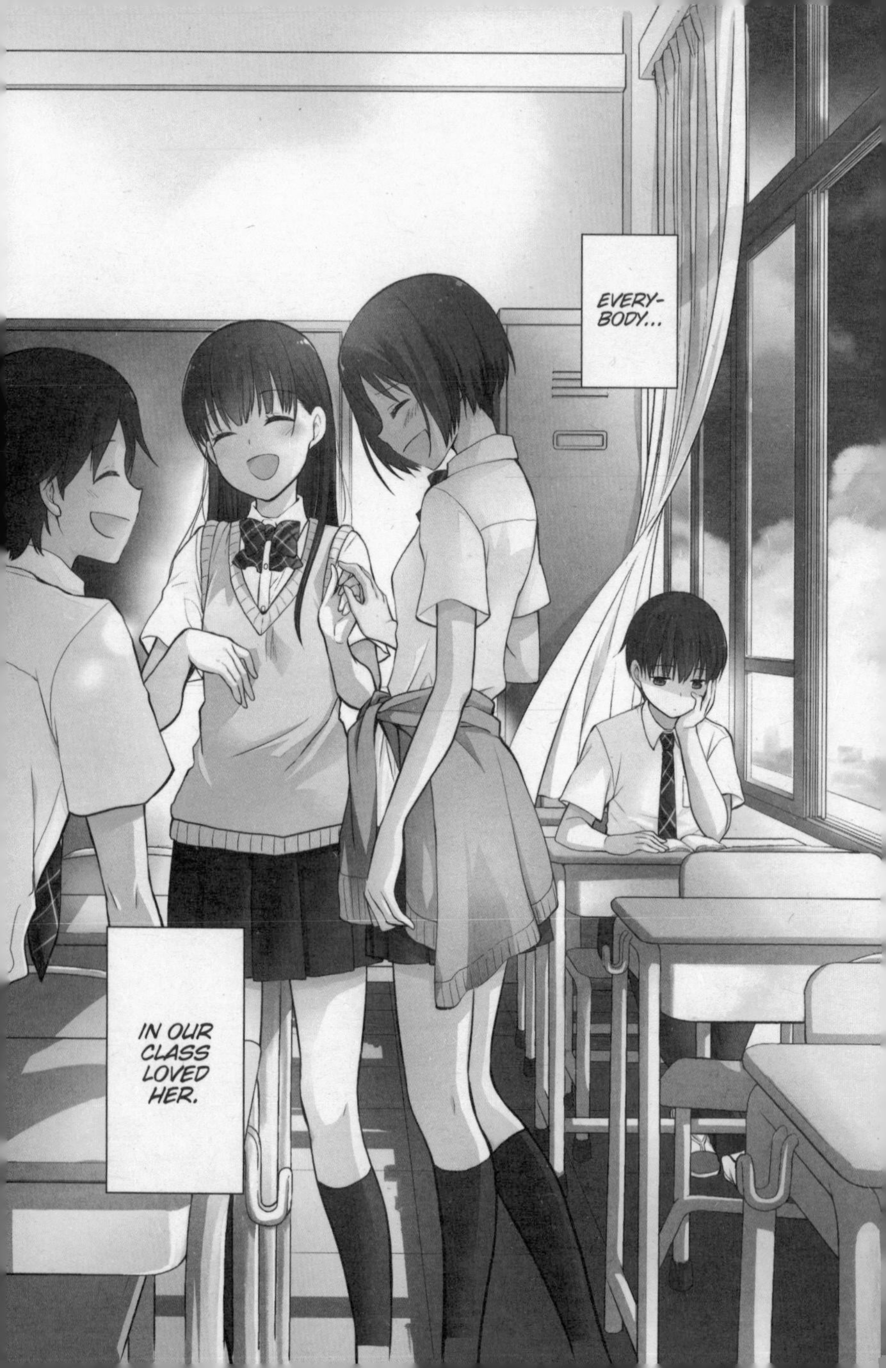
EVERY-BODY...
IN OUR CLASS LOVED HER.

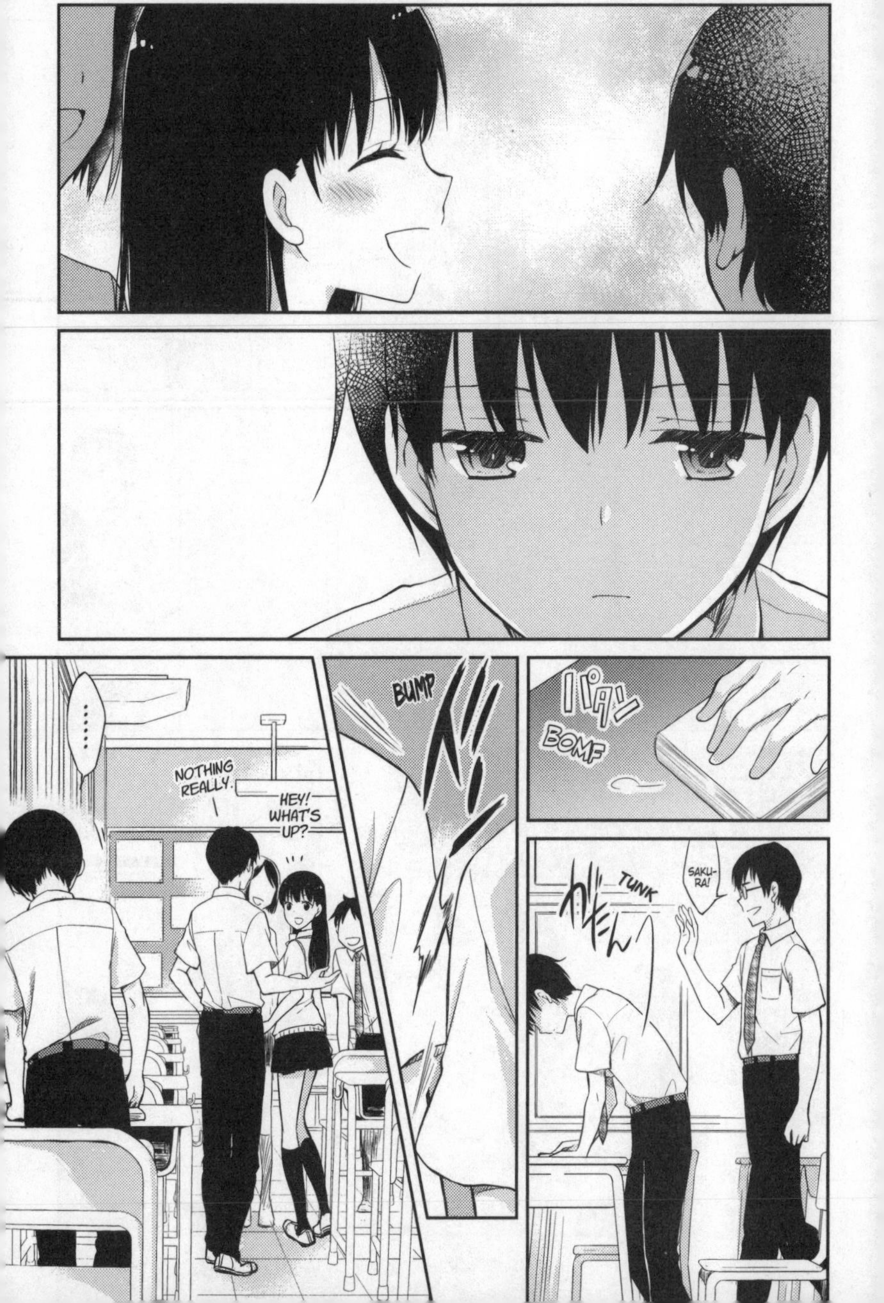
BOMF
SAKU-RA!
TUNK
BUMP
HEY! WHAT'S UP?
NOTHING REALLY.

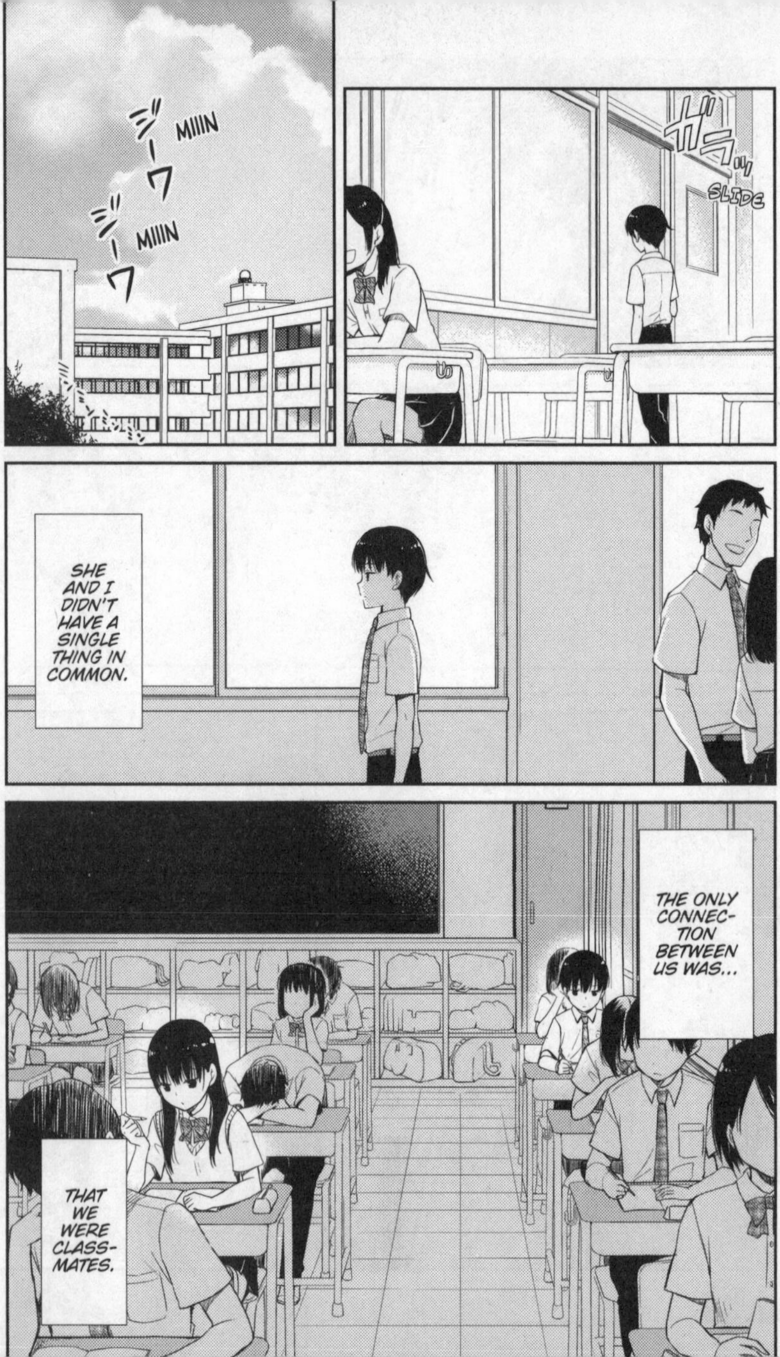
ジーワ
MIIIN
ジーワ
MIIIN
ガラッ
SLIDE
SHE AND I DIDN'T HAVE A SINGLE THING IN COMMON.
THE ONLY CONNECTION BETWEEN US WAS...
THAT WE WERE CLASSMATES.

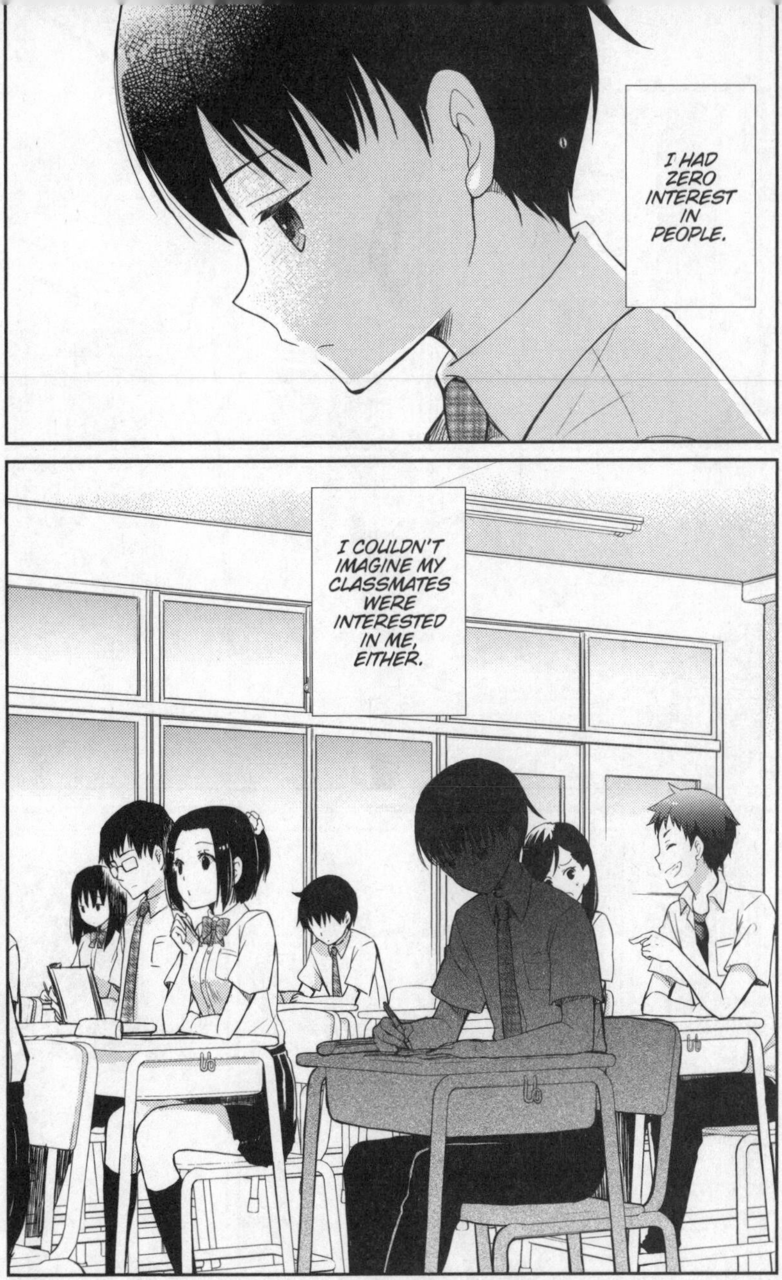
I HAD ZERO INTEREST IN PEOPLE.
I COULDN'T IMAGINE MY CLASSMATES WERE INTERESTED IN ME, EITHER.

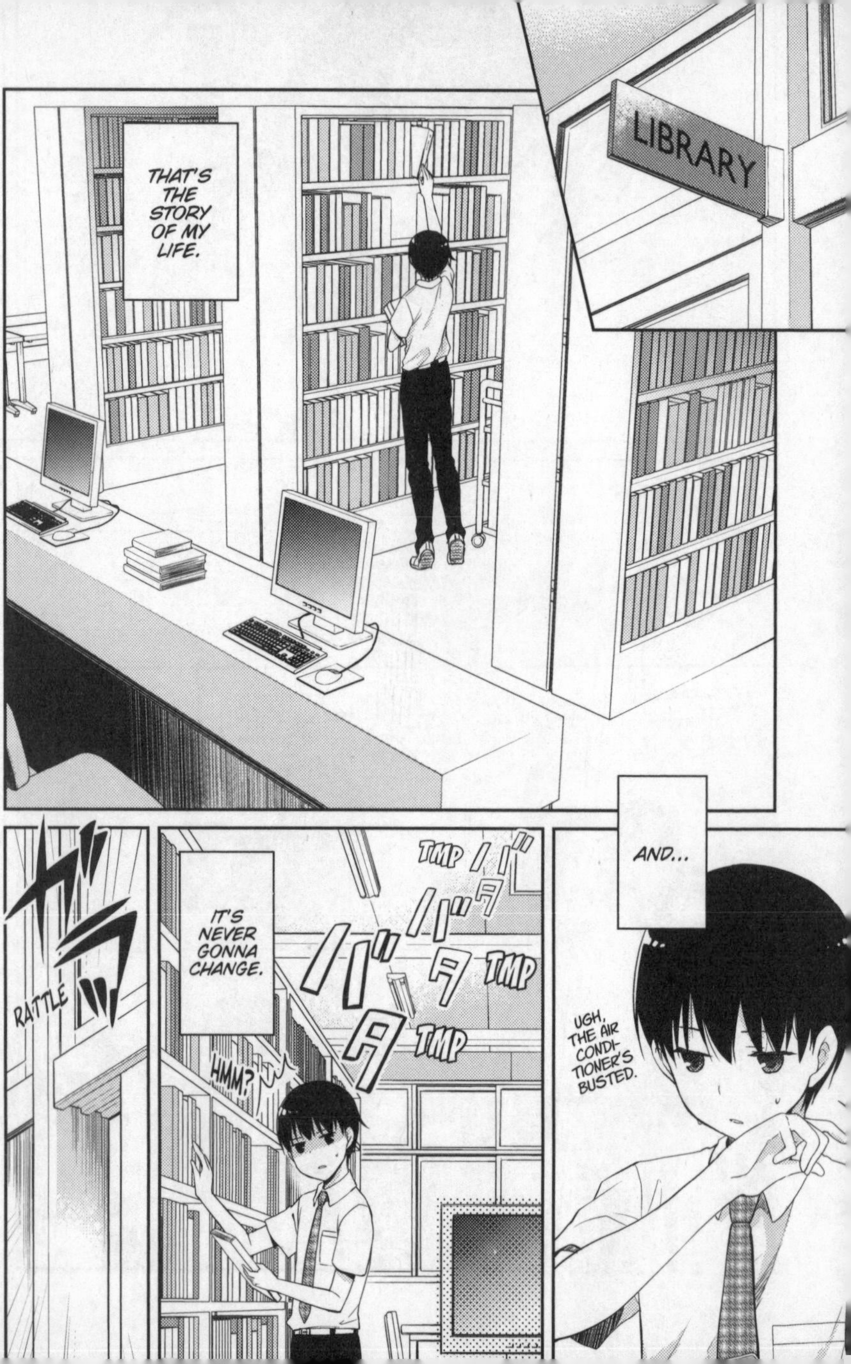
LIBRARY
THAT'S THE STORY OF MY LIFE.
AND...
UGH, THE AIR CONDITIONER'S BUSTED.
IT'S NEVER GONNA CHANGE.
TMP
バタ
TMP
バタ
TMP
バタ
HMM?
RATTLE

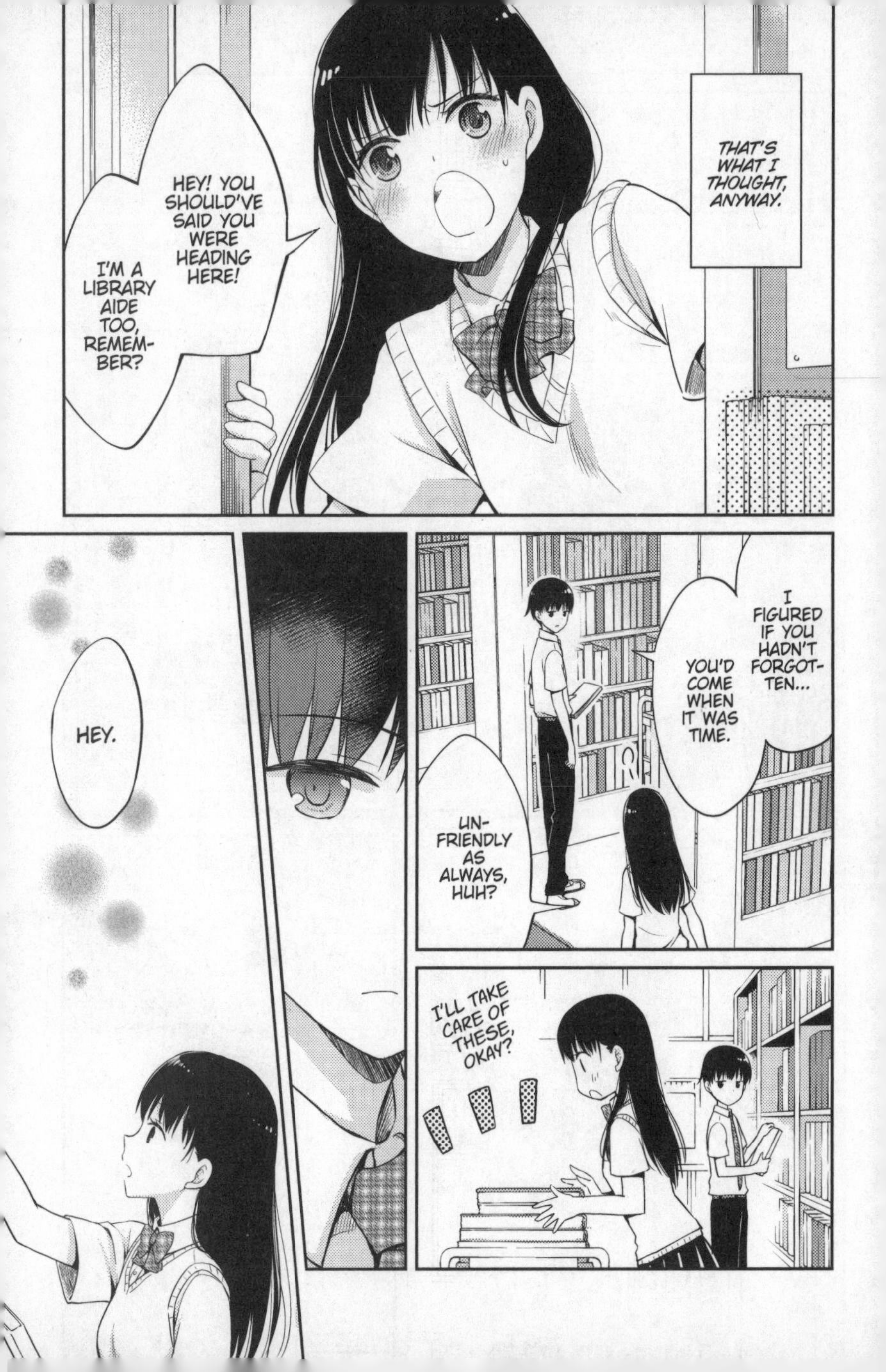
THAT'S WHAT I THOUGHT, ANYWAY.
HEY! YOU SHOULD'VE SAID YOU WERE HEADING HERE!
I'M A LIBRARY AIDE TOO, REMEMBER?
I FIGURED IF YOU HADN'T FORGOTTEN...
YOU'D COME WHEN IT WAS TIME.
UNFRIENDLY AS ALWAYS, HUH?
HEY.
I'LL TAKE CARE OF THESE, OKAY?

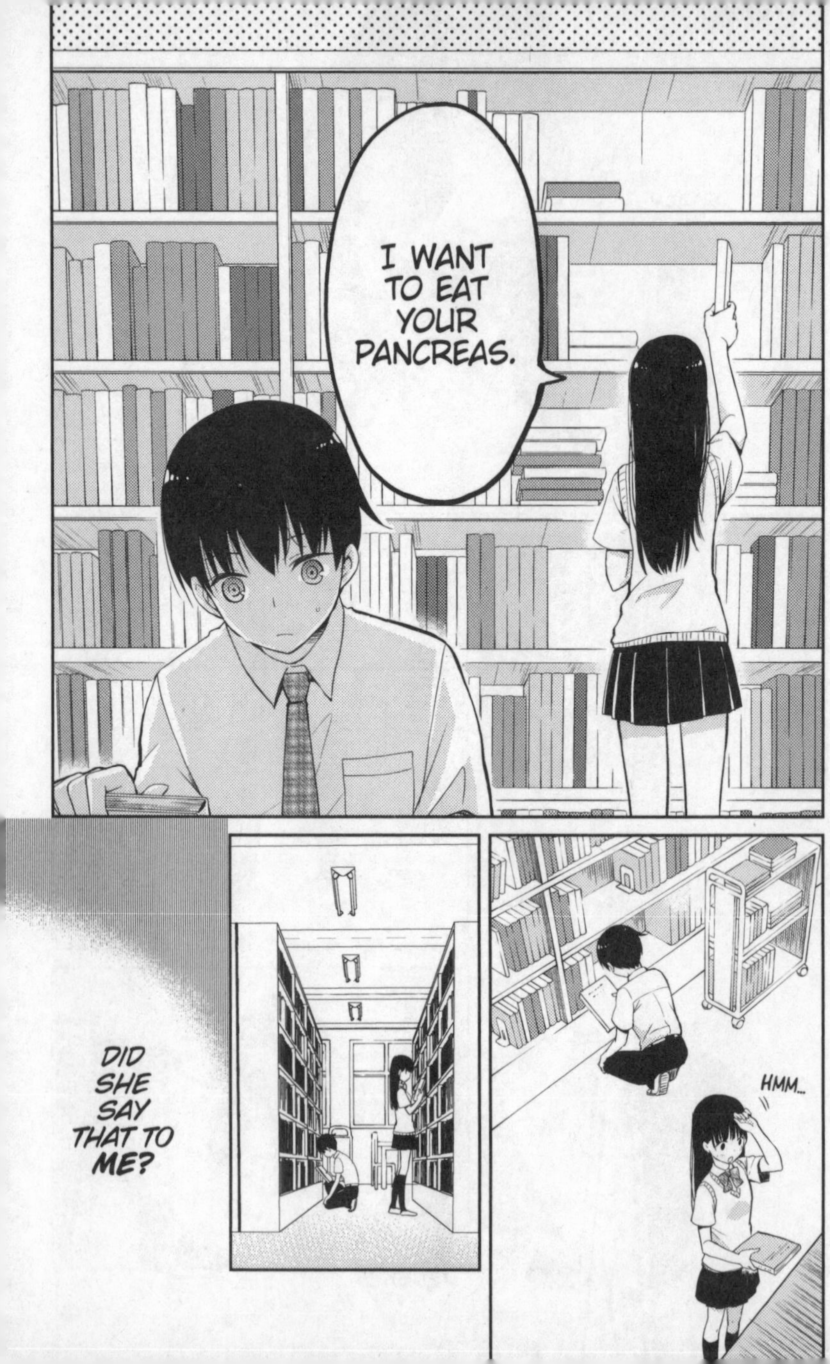
I WANT TO EAT YOUR PANCREAS.
DID SHE SAY THAT TO ME?
HMM...

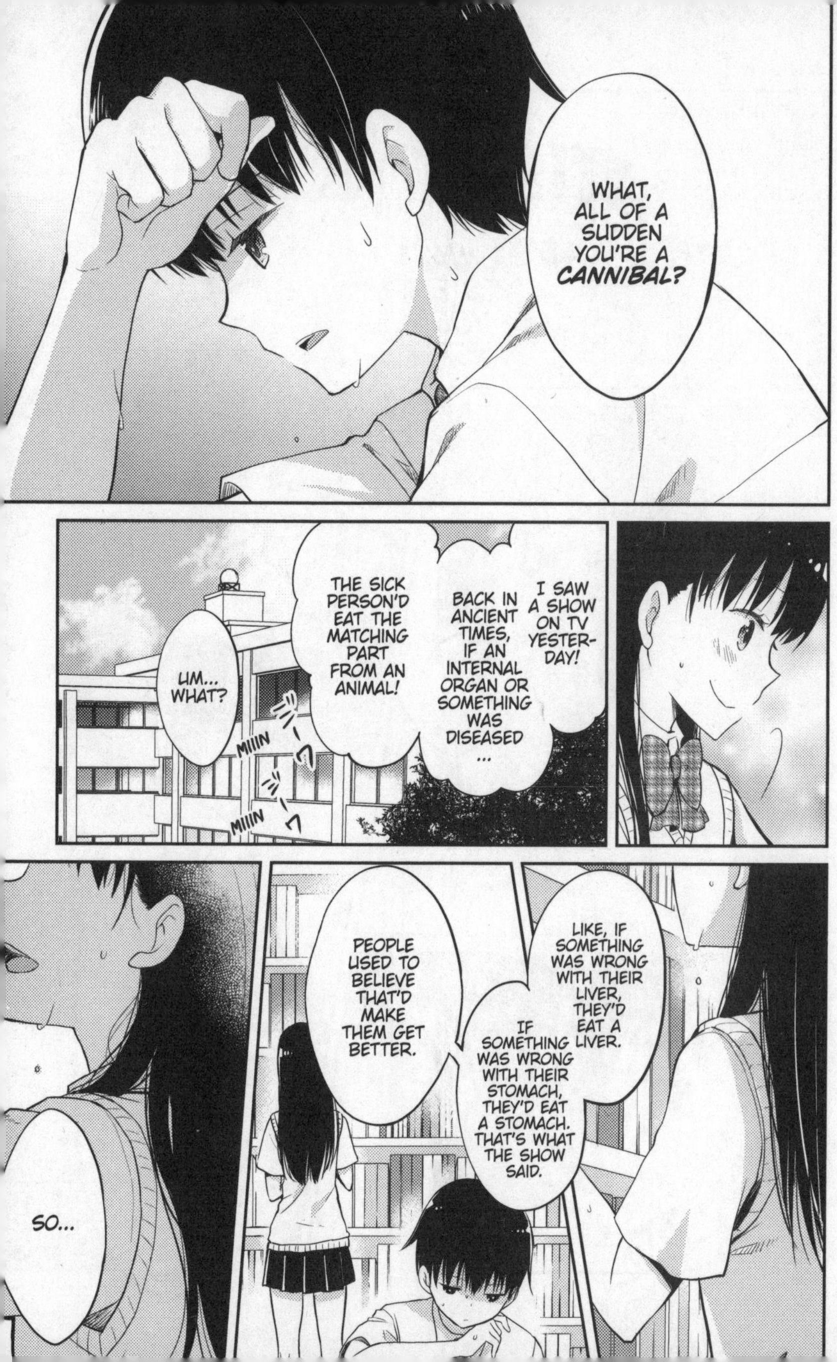
WHAT, ALL OF A SUDDEN YOU'RE A CANNIBAL?
I SAW A SHOW ON TV YESTER-DAY!
BACK IN ANCIENT TIMES, IF AN INTERNAL ORGAN OR SOMETHING WAS DISEASED...
THE SICK PERSON'D EAT THE MATCHING PART FROM AN ANIMAL!
UM... WHAT?
MIIIN
MIIIN
LIKE, IF SOMETHING WAS WRONG WITH THEIR LIVER, THEY'D EAT A LIVER.
IF SOMETHING WAS WRONG WITH THEIR STOMACH, THEY'D EAT A STOMACH. THAT'S WHAT THE SHOW SAID.
PEOPLE USED TO BELIEVE THAT'D MAKE THEM GET BETTER.
SO...

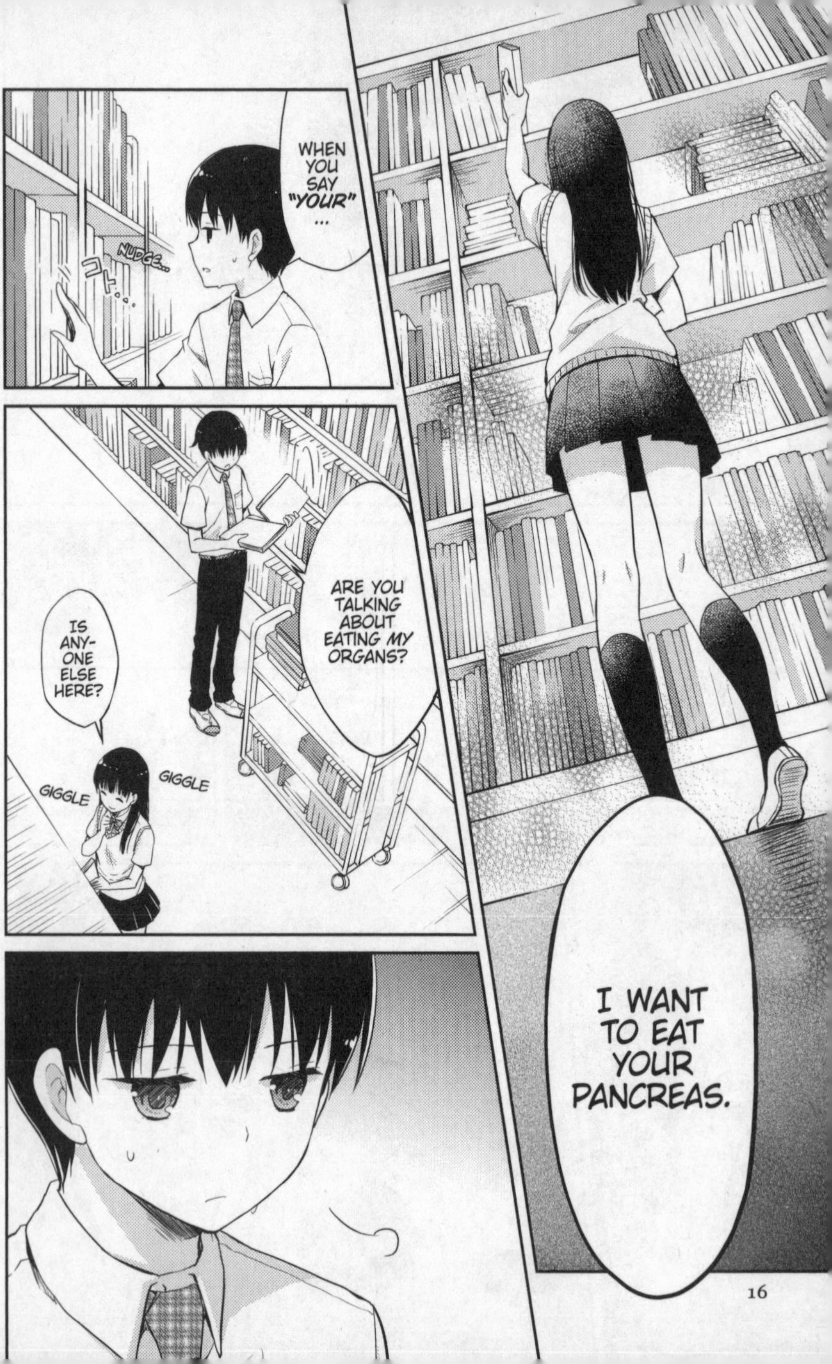

I WANT TO EAT YOUR PANCREAS.
WHEN YOU SAY "YOUR"...
NUDGE...
コト...
ARE YOU TALKING ABOUT EATING MY ORGANS?
IS ANY-ONE ELSE HERE?
GIGGLE
GIGGLE

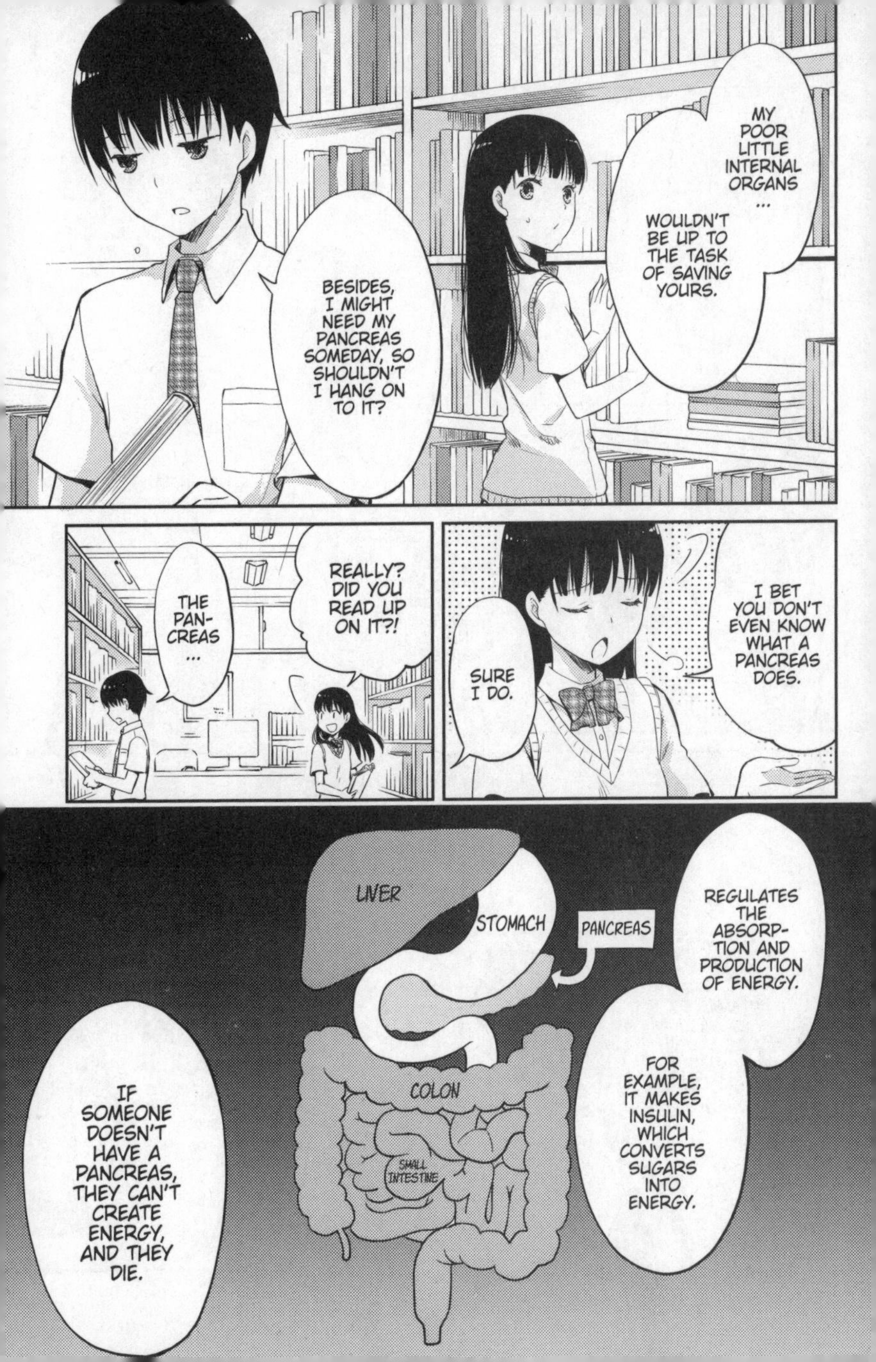
MY POOR LITTLE INTERNAL ORGANS ...
WOULDN'T BE UP TO THE TASK OF SAVING YOURS.
BESIDES, I MIGHT NEED MY PANCREAS SOMEDAY, SO SHOULDN'T I HANG ON TO IT?
I BET YOU DON'T EVEN KNOW WHAT A PANCREAS DOES.
SURE I DO.
REALLY? DID YOU READ UP ON IT?!
THE PAN-CREAS ...
REGULATES THE ABSORP-TION AND PRODUCTION OF ENERGY.
LIVER
STOMACH
PANCREAS
COLON
SMALL INTESTINE
FOR EXAMPLE, IT MAKES INSULIN, WHICH CONVERTS SUGARS INTO ENERGY.
IF SOMEONE DOESN'T HAVE A PANCREAS, THEY CAN'T CREATE ENERGY, AND THEY DIE.

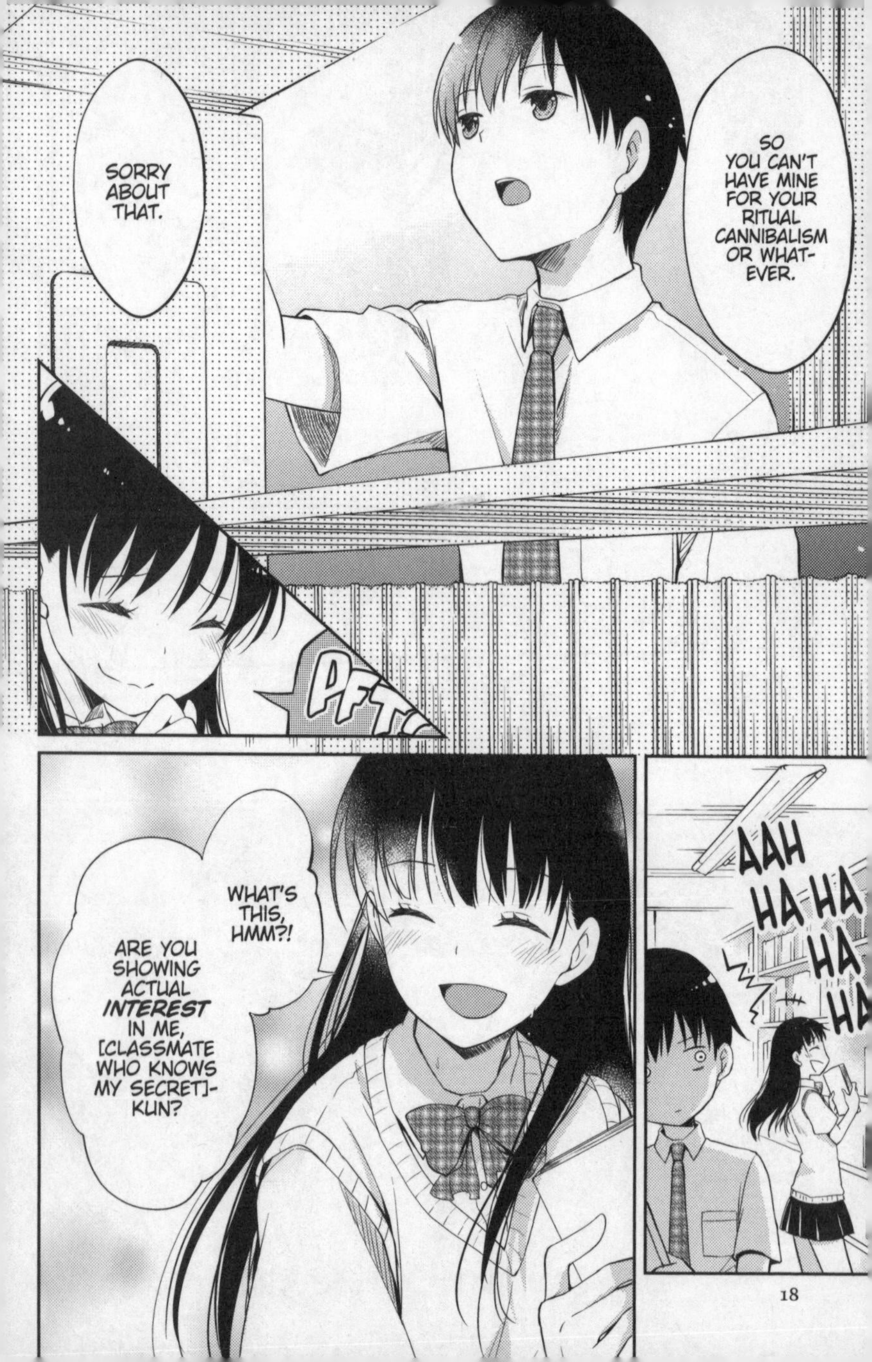
SO YOU CAN'T HAVE MINE FOR YOUR RITUAL CANNIBALISM OR WHAT-EVER.
SORRY ABOUT THAT.
PFT
AAH HA HA HA HA HA
WHAT'S THIS, HMM?!
ARE YOU SHOWING ACTUAL *INTEREST* IN ME, [CLASSMATE WHO KNOWS MY SECRET]-KUN?

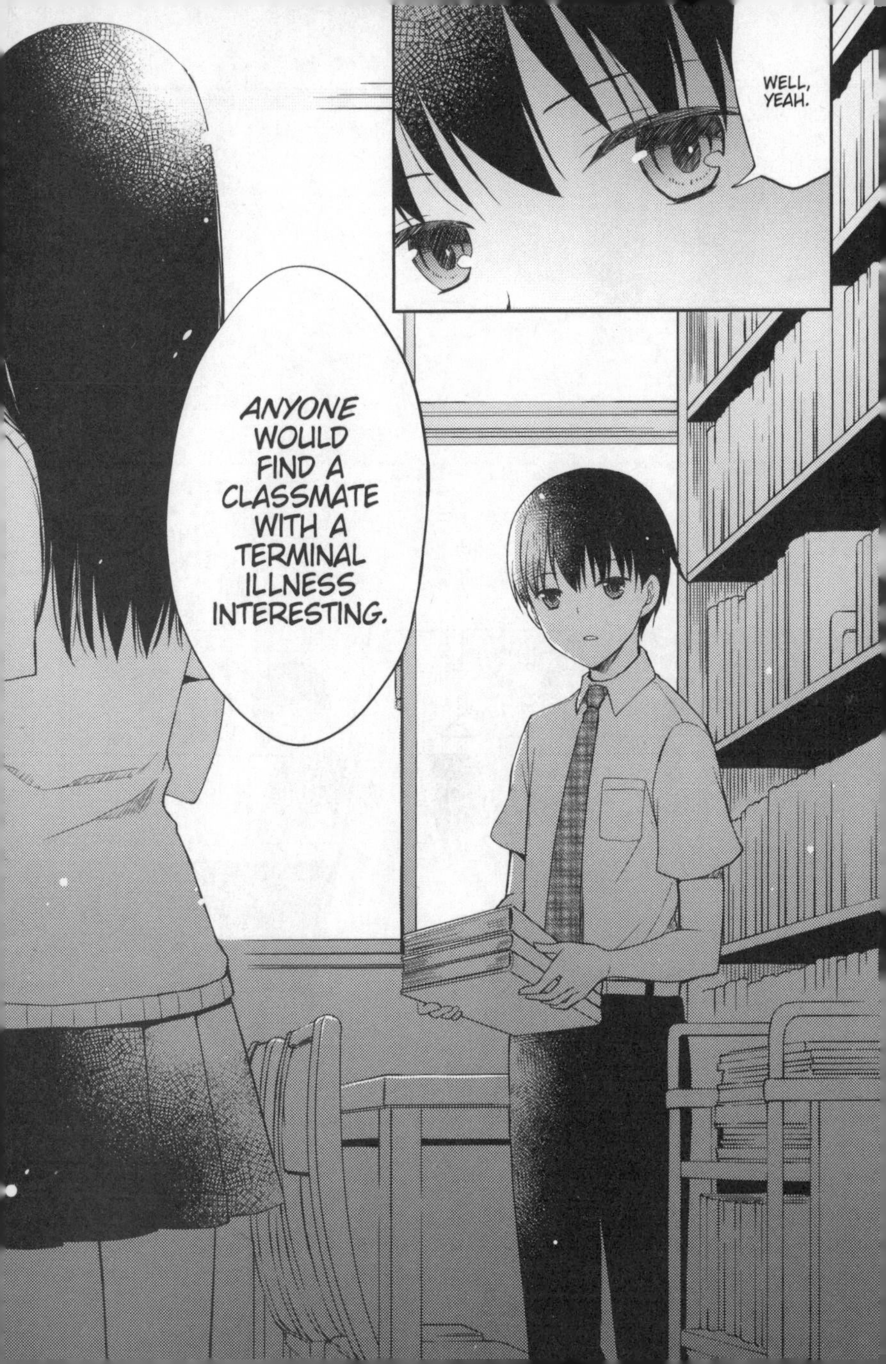
WELL, YEAH.
ANYONE WOULD FIND A CLASSMATE WITH A TERMINAL ILLNESS INTERESTING.

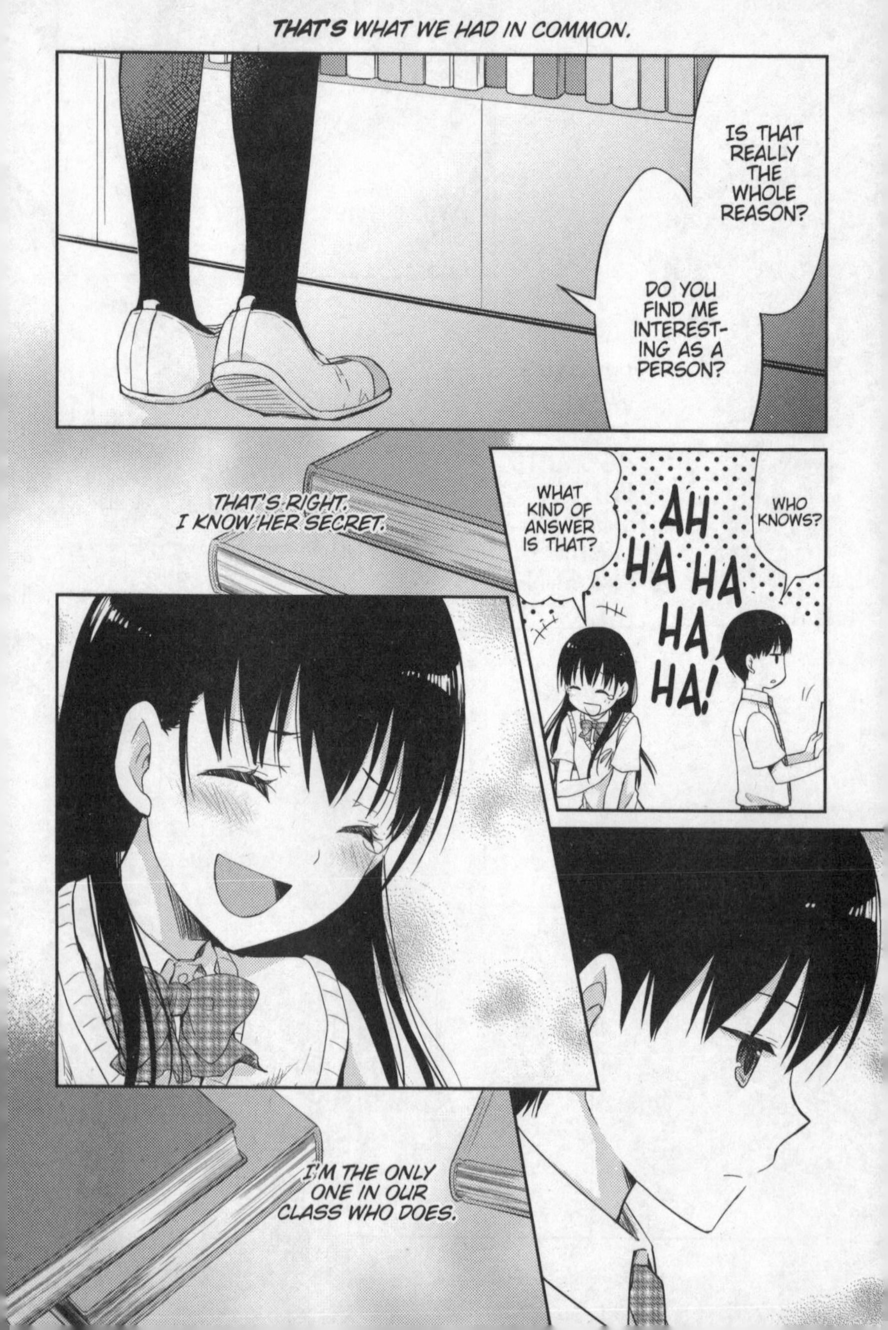
THAT'S WHAT WE HAD IN COMMON.
IS THAT REALLY THE WHOLE REASON?
DO YOU FIND ME INTERESTING AS A PERSON?
WHO KNOWS?
AH HA HA HA HA HA!
WHAT KIND OF ANSWER IS THAT?
THAT'S RIGHT. I KNOW HER SECRET.
I'M THE ONLY ONE IN OUR CLASS WHO DOES.

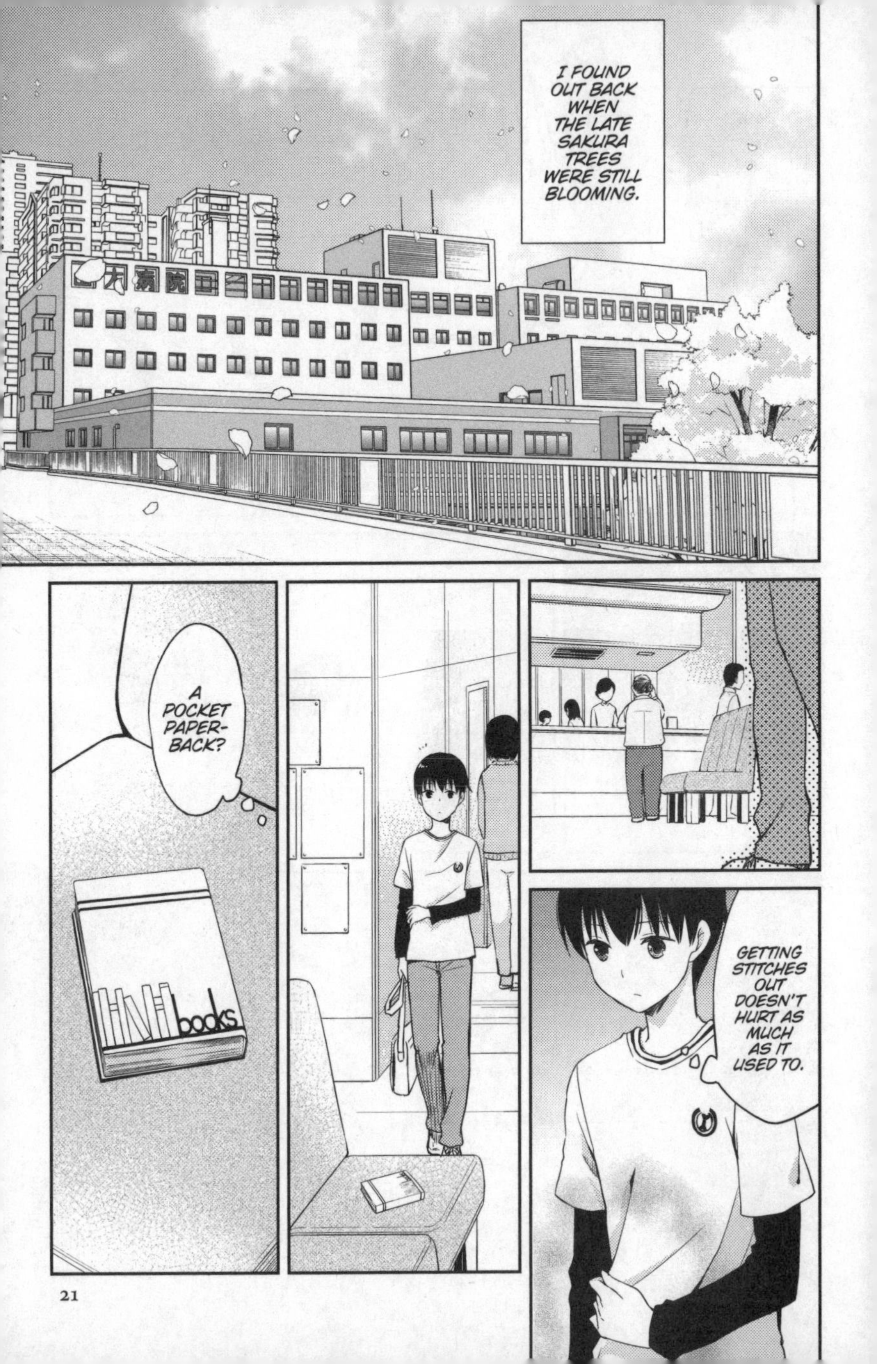
I FOUND OUT BACK WHEN THE LATE SAKURA TREES WERE STILL BLOOMING.
GETTING STITCHES OUT DOESN'T HURT AS MUCH AS IT USED TO.
A POCKET PAPER-BACK?
books

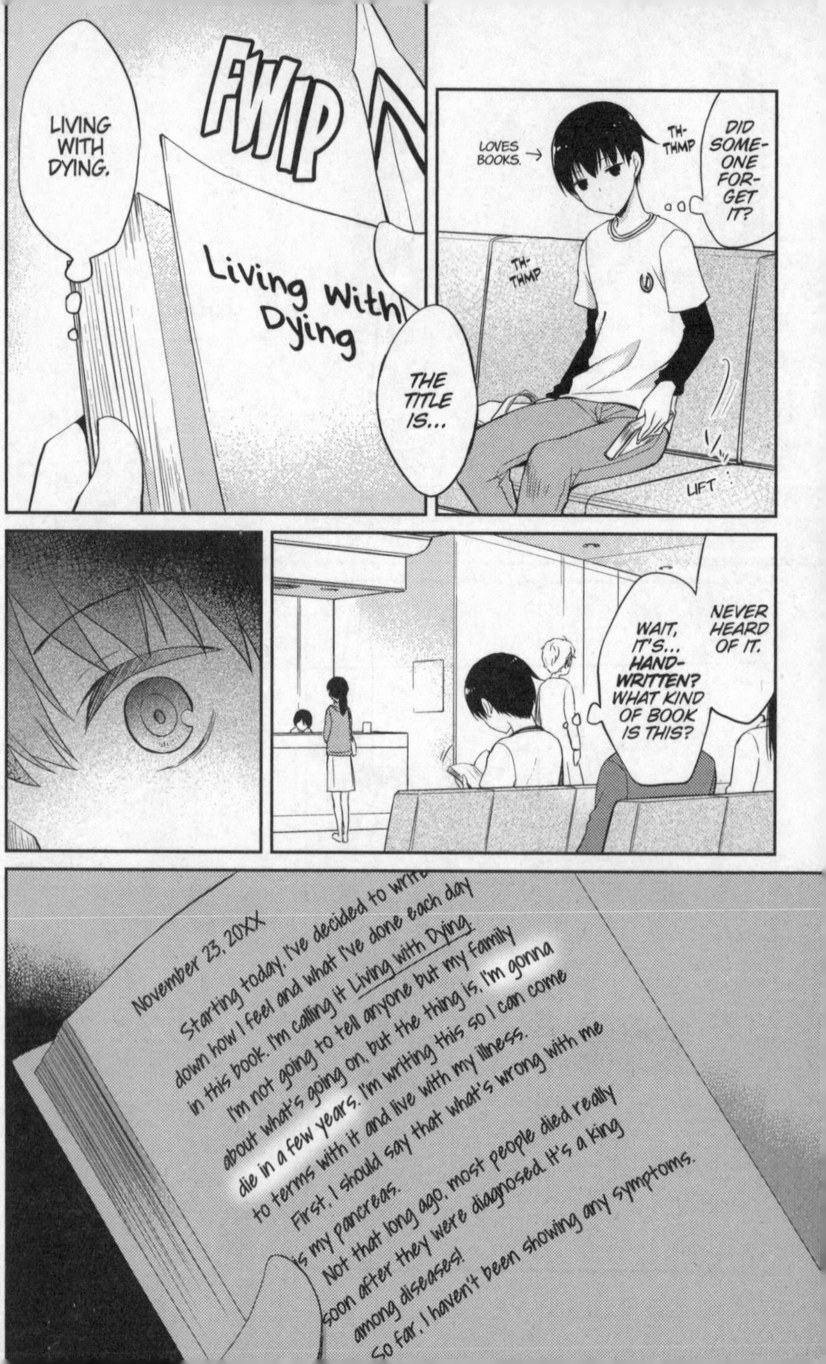

DID SOME-ONE FOR-GET IT?
TH-THMP
LOVES BOOKS.
TH-THMP
LIFT
THE TITLE IS...
Living With Dying
FWIP
LIVING WITH DYING.
NEVER HEARD OF IT.
WAIT, IT'S... HAND-WRITTEN? WHAT KIND OF BOOK IS THIS?
November 23, 20XX
Starting today, I've decided to write down how I feel and what I've done each day in this book. I'm calling it Living with Dying.
I'm not going to tell anyone but my family about what's going on, but the thing is, I'm gonna die in a few years. I'm writing this so I can come to terms with it and live with my illness.
First, I should say that what's wrong with me is my pancreas.
Not that long ago, most people died really soon after they were diagnosed. It's a king among diseases!
So far, I haven't been showing any symptoms.

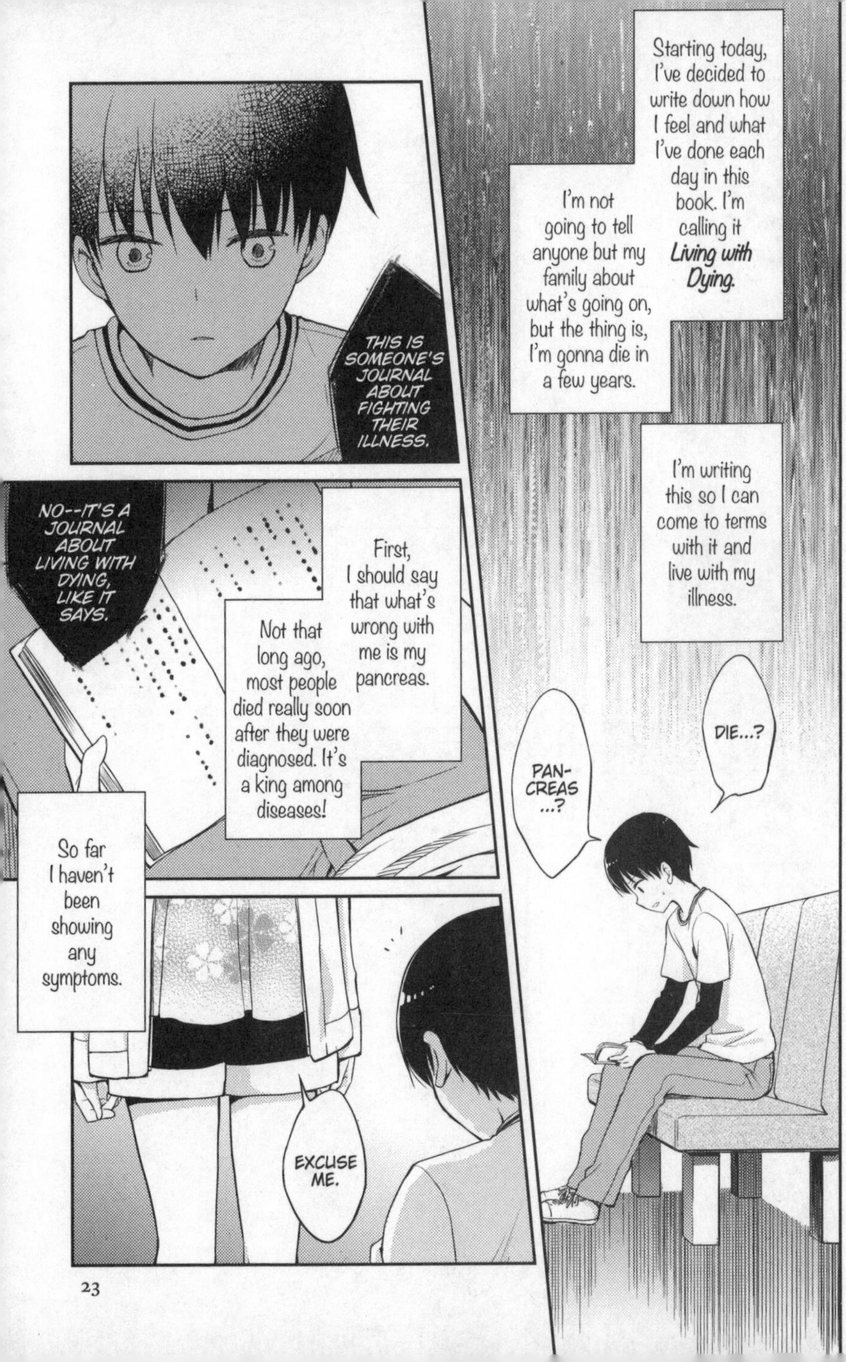
Starting today, I've decided to write down how I feel and what I've done each day in this book. I'm calling it *Living with Dying.*
I'm not going to tell anyone but my family about what's going on, but the thing is, I'm gonna die in a few years.
I'm writing this so I can come to terms with it and live with my illness.
DIE...?
PAN-CREAS ...?
THIS IS SOMEONE'S JOURNAL ABOUT FIGHTING THEIR ILLNESS.
First, I should say that what's wrong with me is my pancreas.
Not that long ago, most people died really soon after they were diagnosed. It's a king among diseases!
NO--IT'S A JOURNAL ABOUT LIVING WITH DYING, LIKE IT SAYS.
So far I haven't been showing any symptoms.
EXCUSE ME.

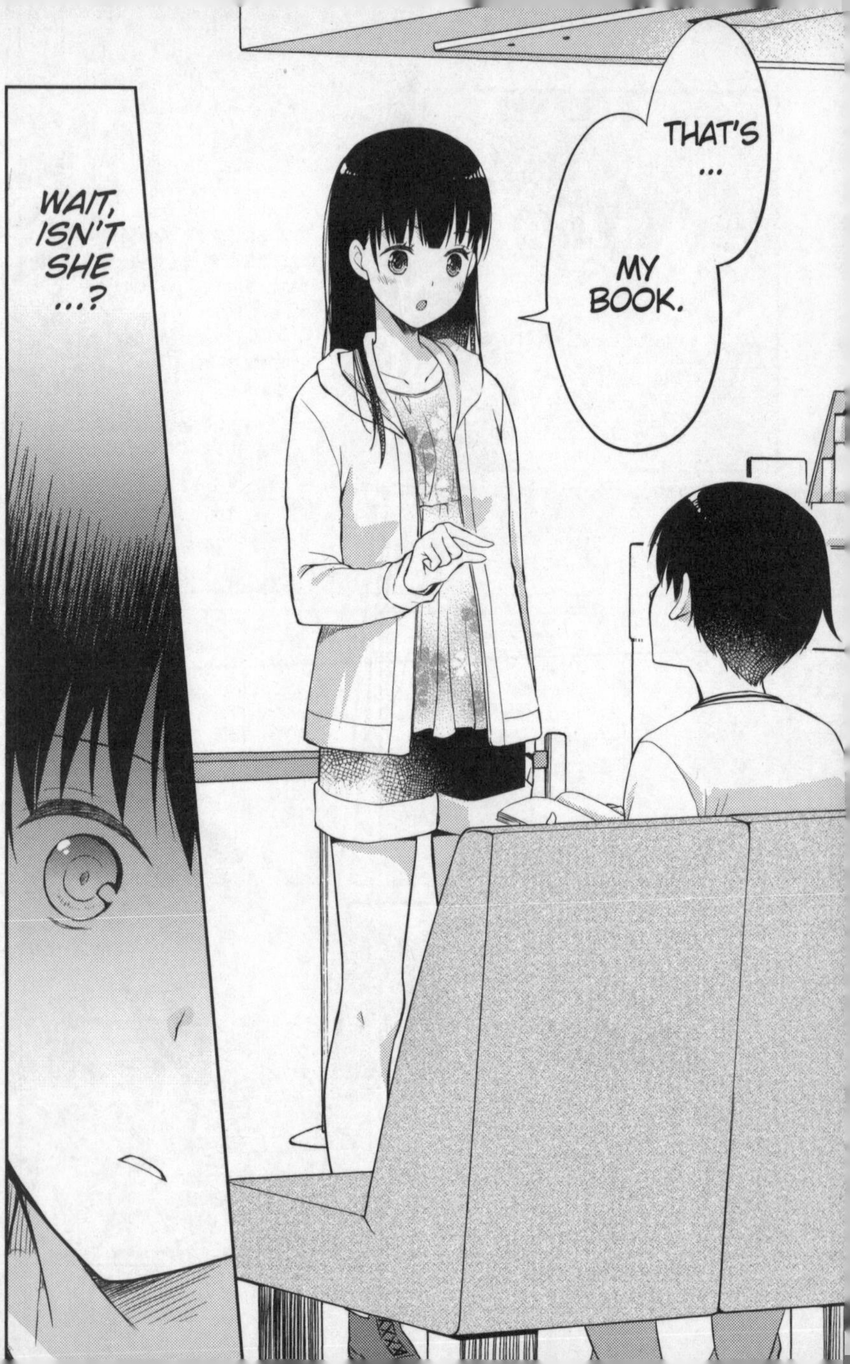
THAT'S ... MY BOOK.
WAIT, ISN'T SHE ...?

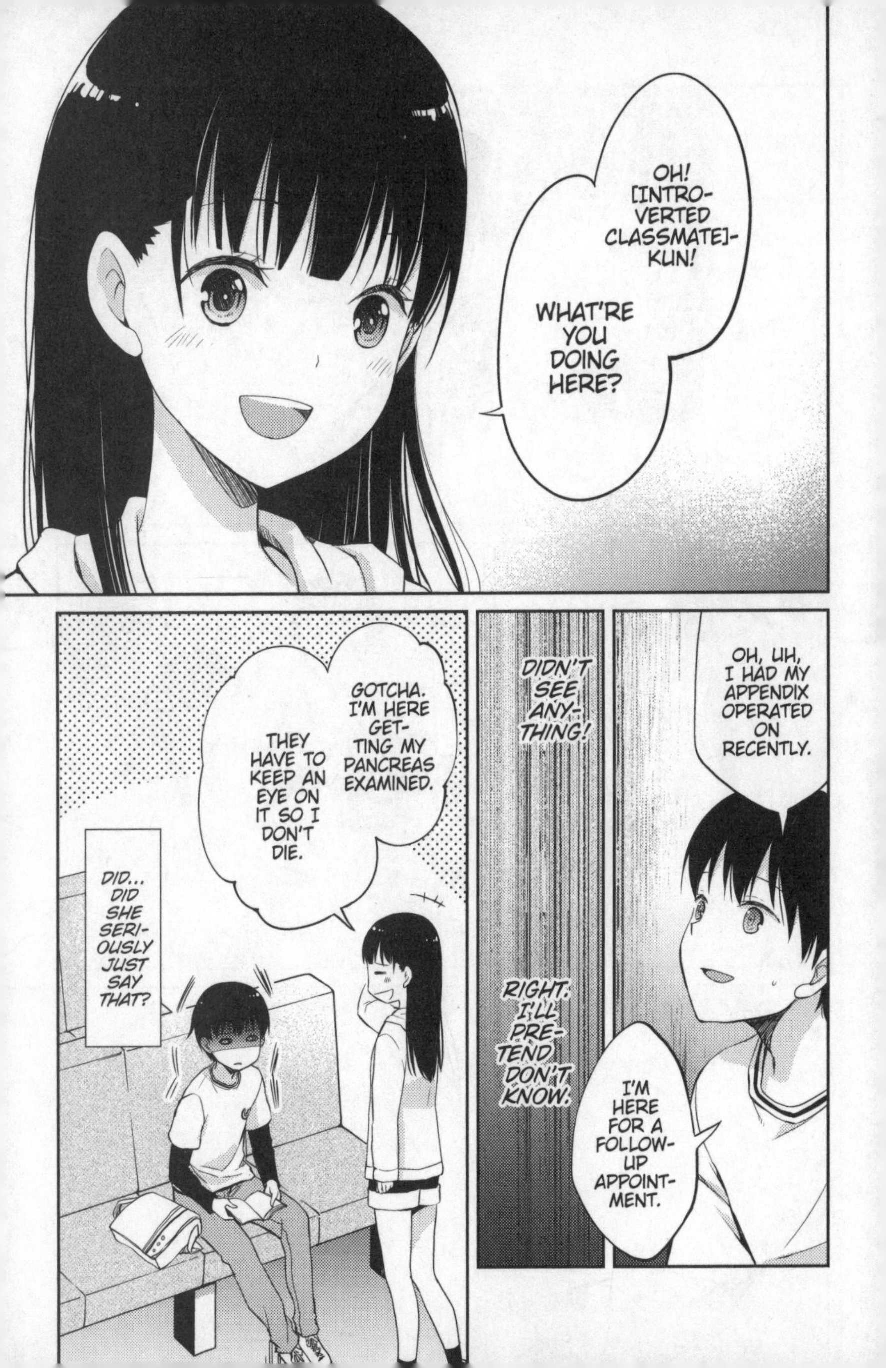
OH! [INTROVERTED CLASSMATE]-KUN!
WHAT'RE YOU DOING HERE?
OH, UH, I HAD MY APPENDIX OPERATED ON RECENTLY.
I'M HERE FOR A FOLLOW-UP APPOINTMENT.
DIDN'T SEE ANYTHING!
RIGHT. I'LL PRETEND DON'T KNOW.
GOTCHA. I'M HERE GETTING MY PANCREAS EXAMINED.
THEY HAVE TO KEEP AN EYE ON IT SO I DON'T DIE.
DID... DID SHE SERIOUSLY JUST SAY THAT?

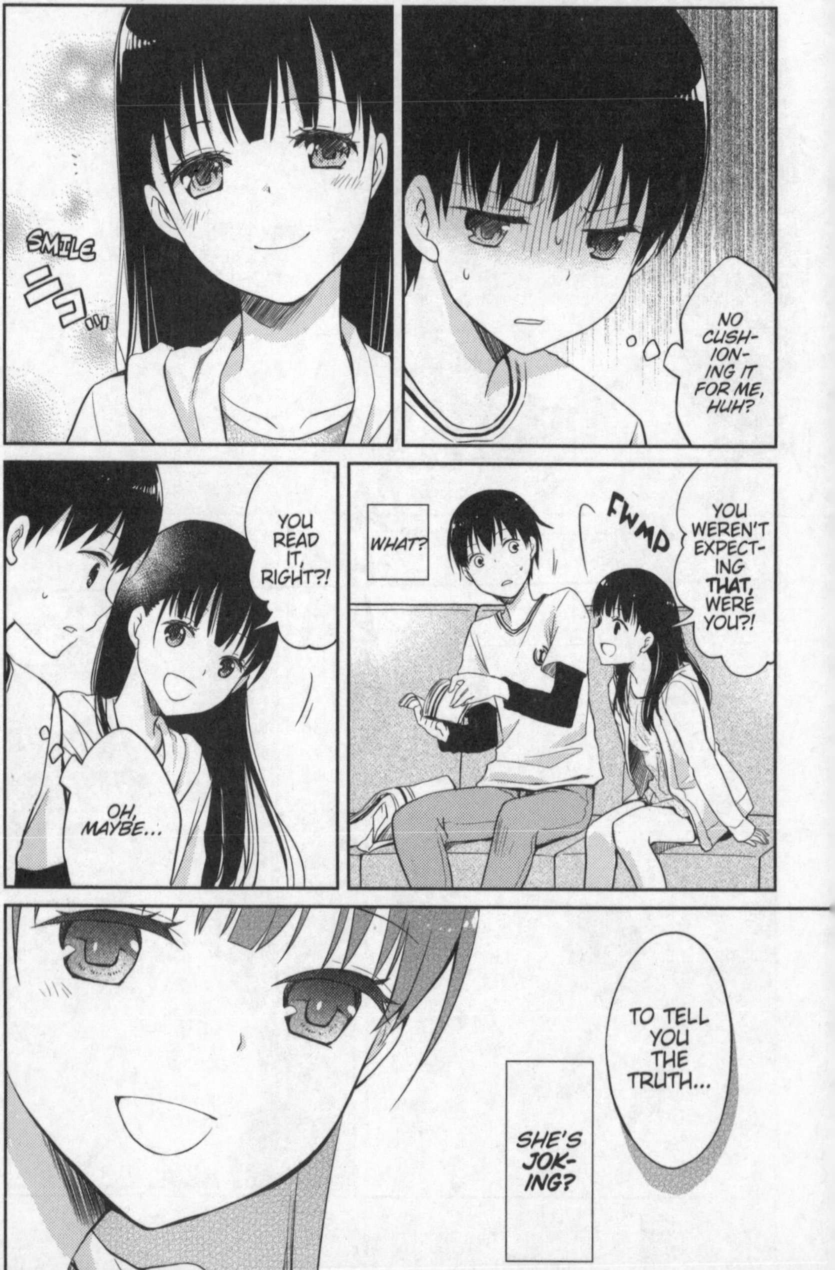
NO CUSHIONING IT FOR ME, HUH?
SMILE
YOU WEREN'T EXPECTING THAT, WERE YOU?!
FWMP
WHAT?
YOU READ IT, RIGHT?!
OH, MAYBE...
TO TELL YOU THE TRUTH...
SHE'S JOKING?

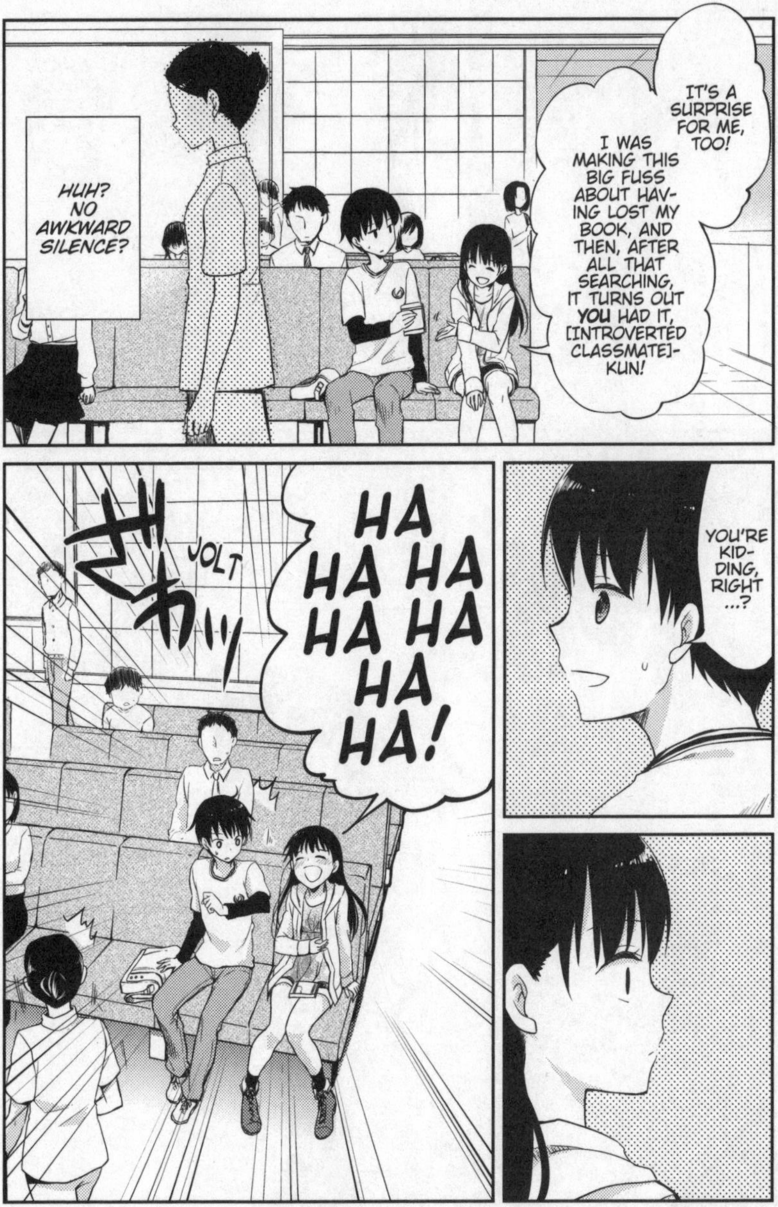
IT'S A SURPRISE FOR ME, TOO!
I WAS MAKING THIS BIG FUSS ABOUT HAV-ING LOST MY BOOK, AND THEN, AFTER ALL THAT SEARCHING, IT TURNS OUT YOU HAD IT, [INTROVERTED CLASSMATE]-KUN!
HUH? NO AWKWARD SILENCE?
YOU'RE KID-DING, RIGHT ...?
HA HA HA HA HA HA HA HA!
ざわッ
JOLT

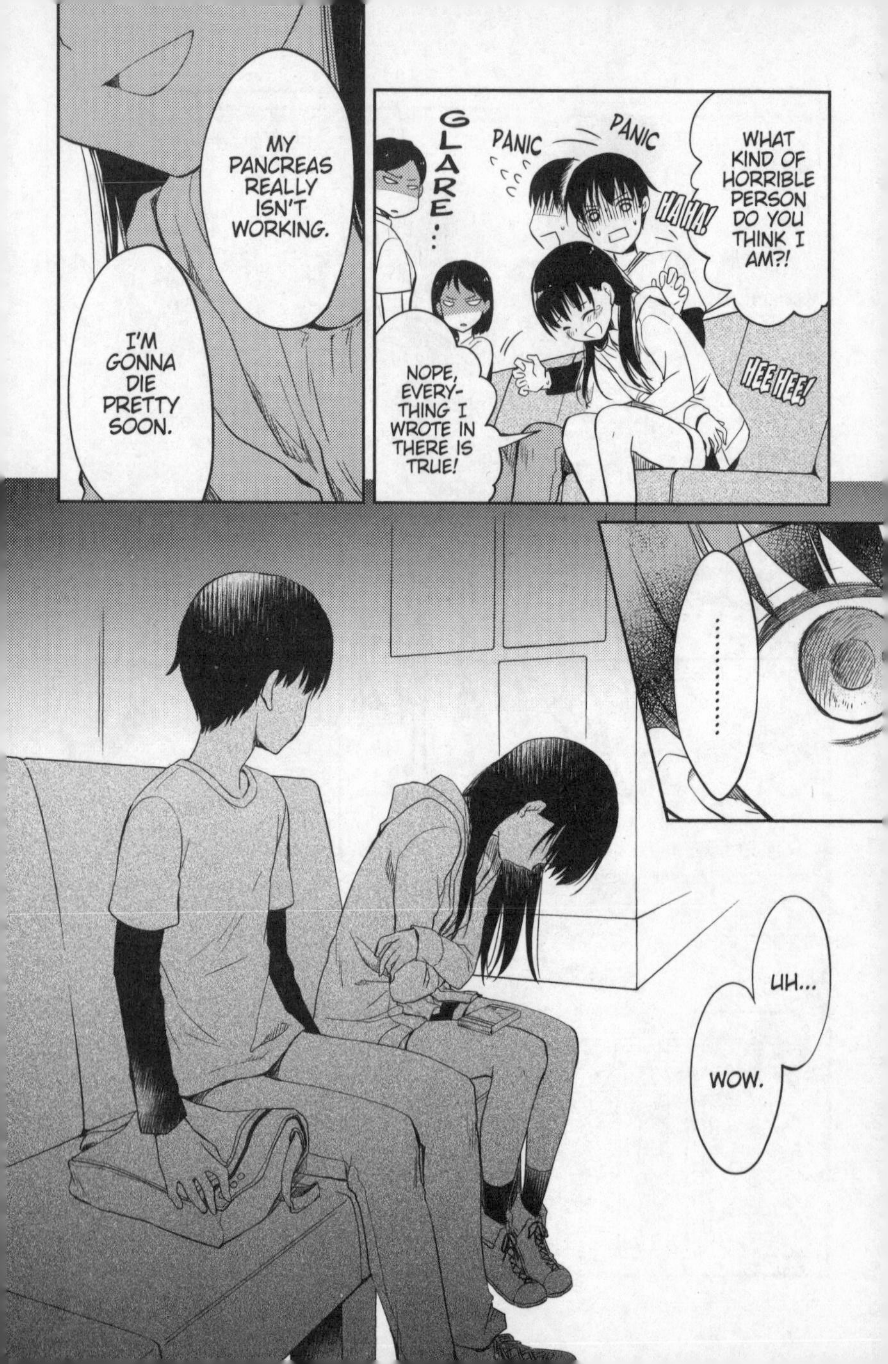
WHAT KIND OF HORRIBLE PERSON DO YOU THINK I AM?!
HAHA!
PANIC
PANIC
GLARE...
HEE HEE!
NOPE, EVERY-THING I WROTE IN THERE IS TRUE!
MY PANCREAS REALLY ISN'T WORKING.
I'M GONNA DIE PRETTY SOON.
......
UH...
WOW.

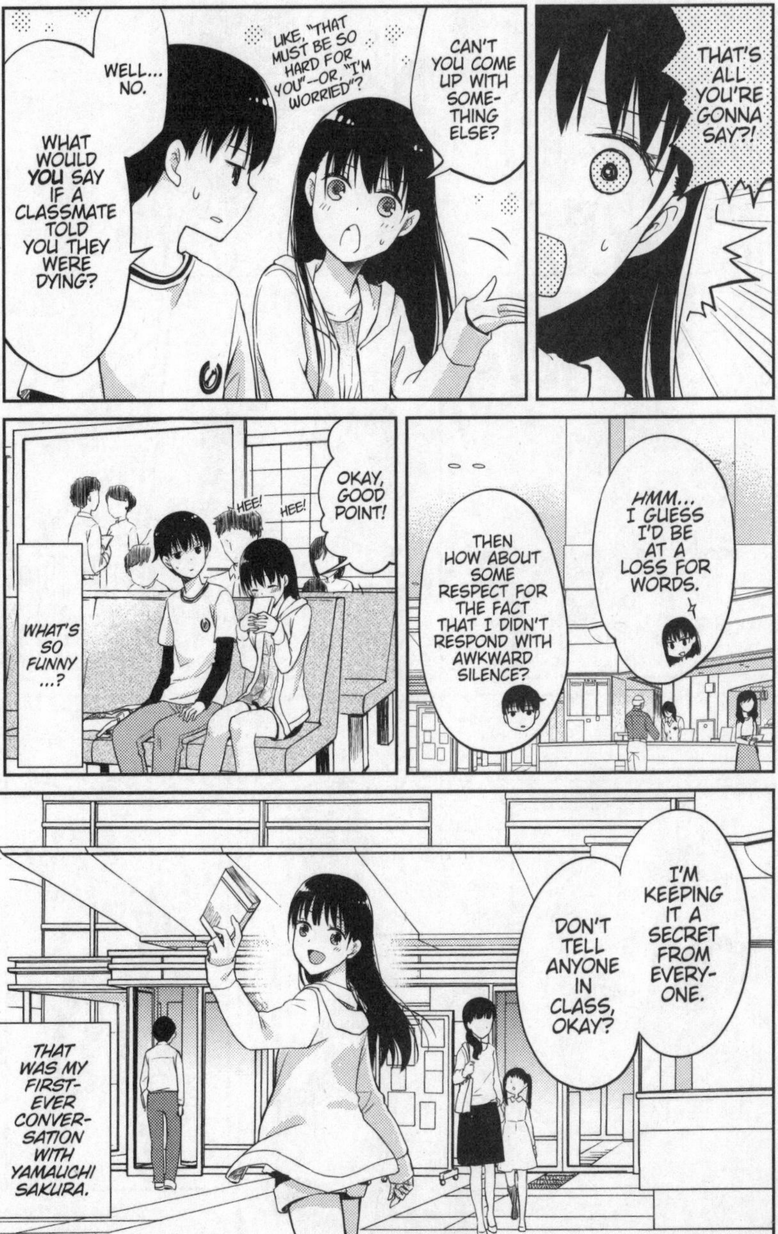
THAT'S ALL YOU'RE GONNA SAY?!
CAN'T YOU COME UP WITH SOME-THING ELSE?
LIKE, "THAT MUST BE SO HARD FOR YOU"--OR, "I'M WORRIED"?
WELL... NO.
WHAT WOULD YOU SAY IF A CLASSMATE TOLD YOU THEY WERE DYING?
HMM... I GUESS I'D BE AT A LOSS FOR WORDS.
THEN HOW ABOUT SOME RESPECT FOR THE FACT THAT I DIDN'T RESPOND WITH AWKWARD SILENCE?
OKAY, GOOD POINT!
HEE!
HEE!
WHAT'S SO FUNNY ...?
I'M KEEPING IT A SECRET FROM EVERY-ONE.
DON'T TELL ANYONE IN CLASS, OKAY?
THAT WAS MY FIRST-EVER CONVERSATION WITH YAMAUCHI SAKURA.

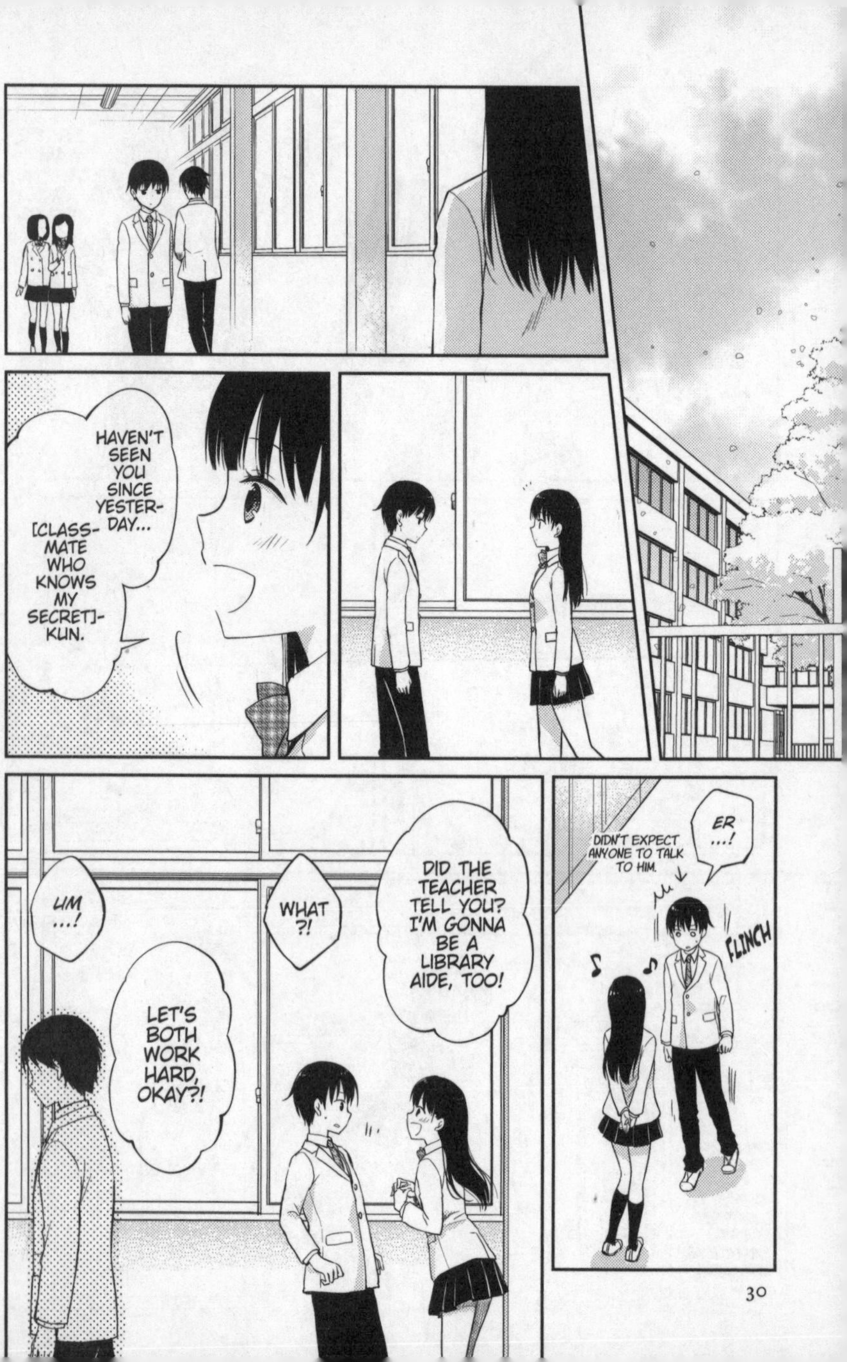
HAVEN'T SEEN YOU SINCE YESTERDAY... [CLASSMATE WHO KNOWS MY SECRET]-KUN.
ER ...!
DIDN'T EXPECT ANYONE TO TALK TO HIM.
FLINCH
DID THE TEACHER TELL YOU? I'M GONNA BE A LIBRARY AIDE, TOO!
WHAT ?!
UM ...!
LET'S BOTH WORK HARD, OKAY?!

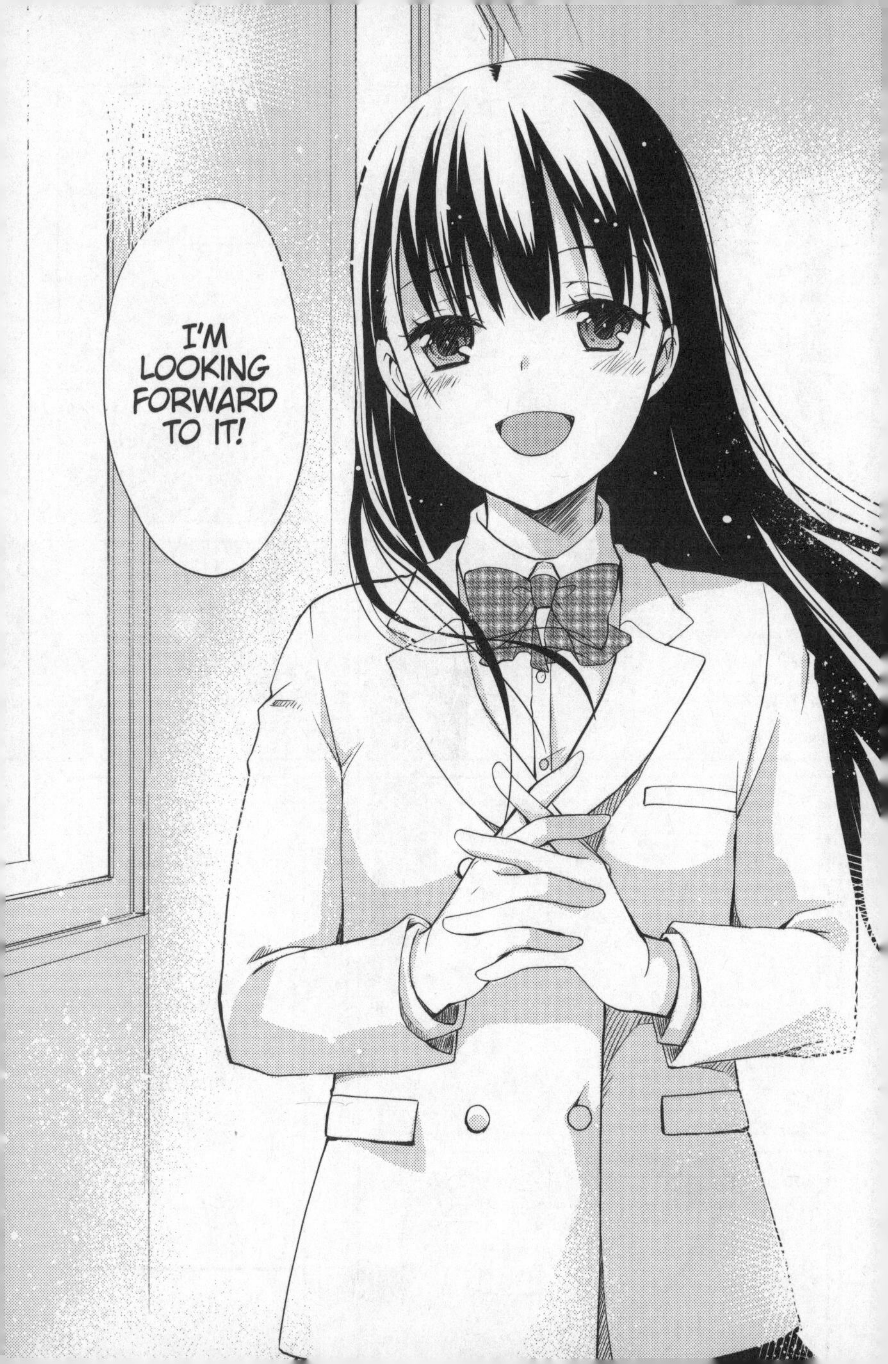
I'M LOOKING FORWARD TO IT!

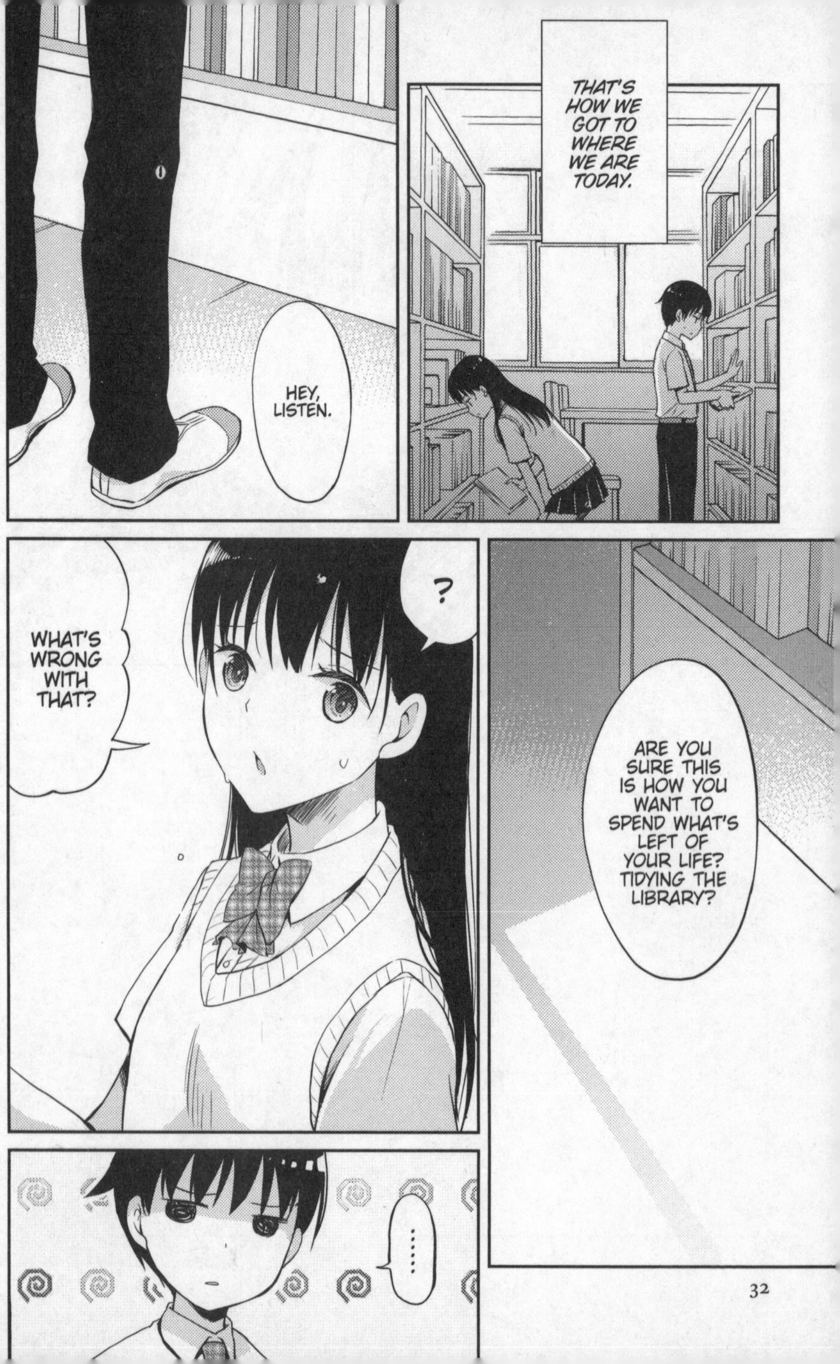
THAT'S HOW WE GOT TO WHERE WE ARE TODAY.
HEY, LISTEN.
ARE YOU SURE THIS IS HOW YOU WANT TO SPEND WHAT'S LEFT OF YOUR LIFE? TIDYING THE LIBRARY?
?
WHAT'S WRONG WITH THAT?
......

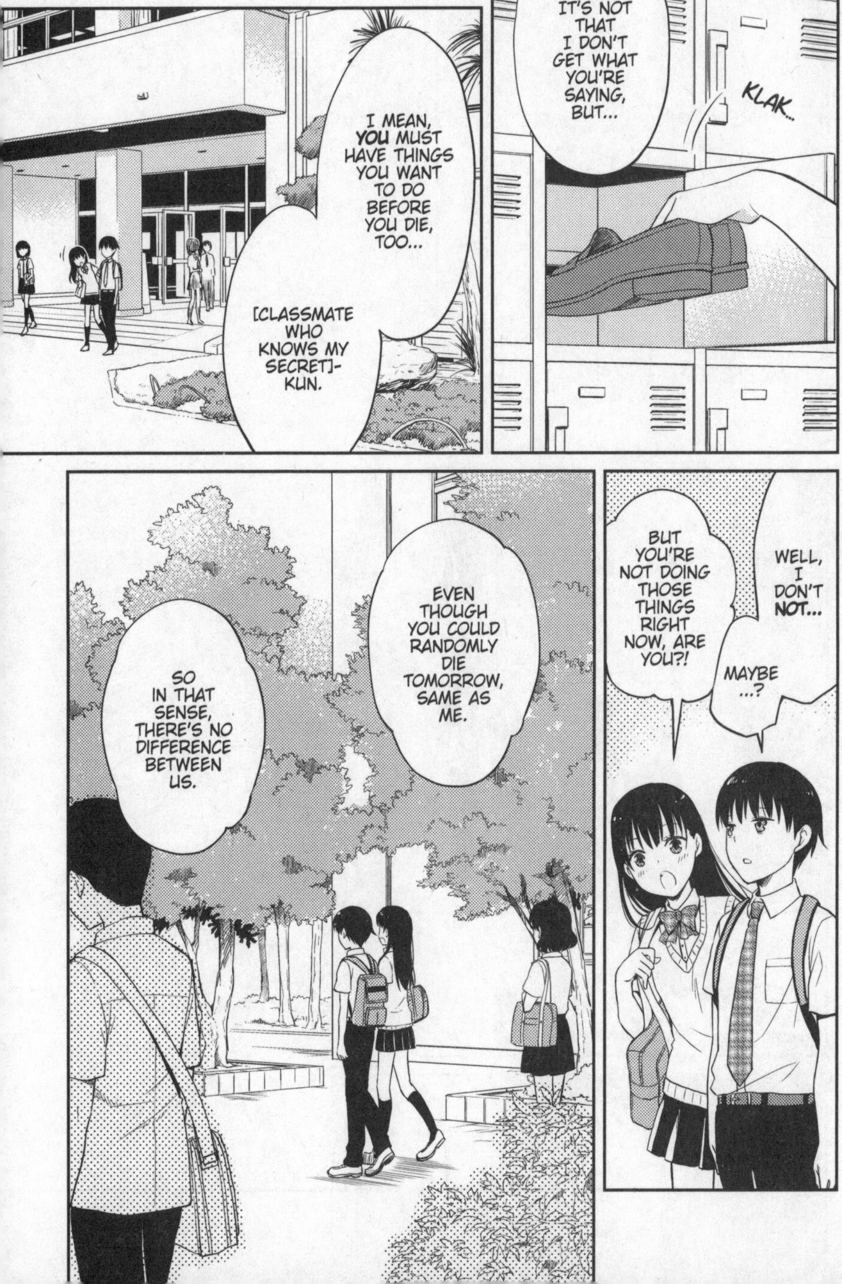
HMM... IT'S NOT THAT I DON'T GET WHAT YOU'RE SAYING, BUT...
KLAK..
I MEAN, YOU MUST HAVE THINGS YOU WANT TO DO BEFORE YOU DIE, TOO...
[CLASSMATE WHO KNOWS MY SECRET]-KUN.
WELL, I DON'T NOT...
MAYBE ...?
BUT YOU'RE NOT DOING THOSE THINGS RIGHT NOW, ARE YOU?!
EVEN THOUGH YOU COULD RANDOMLY DIE TOMORROW, SAME AS ME.
SO IN THAT SENSE, THERE'S NO DIFFERENCE BETWEEN US.

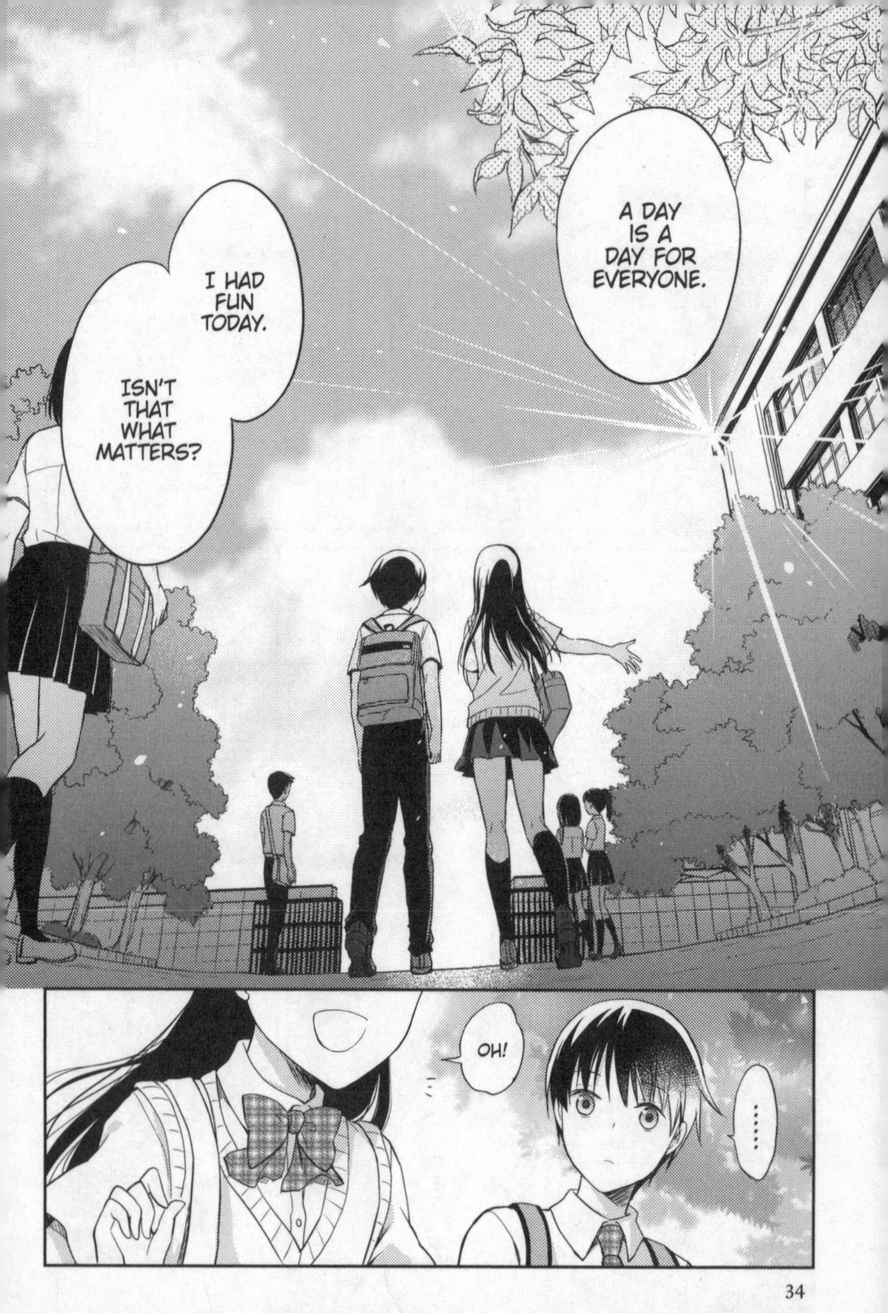
A DAY IS A DAY FOR EVERYONE.
I HAD FUN TODAY.
ISN'T THAT WHAT MATTERS?
......
OH!

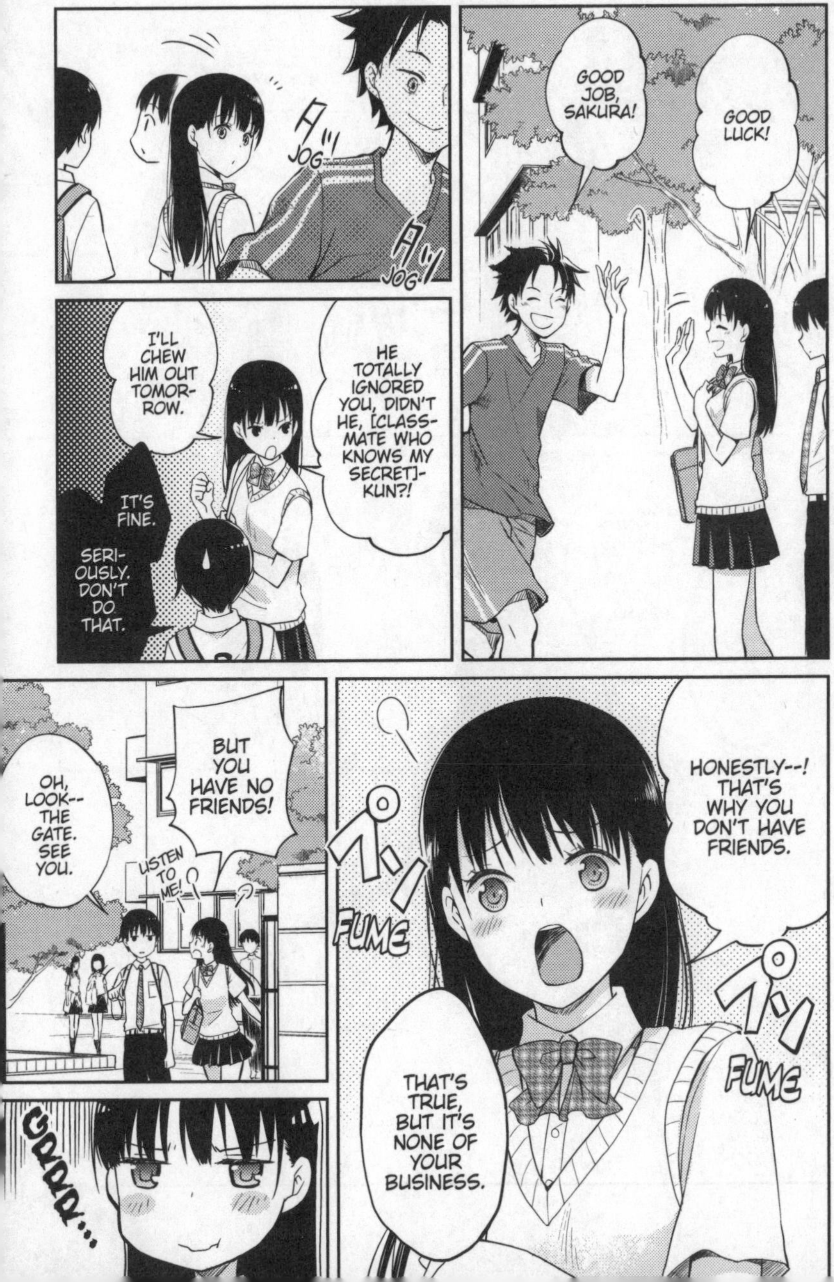
GOOD JOB, SAKURA!
GOOD LUCK!
JOG
JOG
HE TOTALLY IGNORED YOU, DIDN'T HE, [CLASSMATE WHO KNOWS MY SECRET]-KUN?!
I'LL CHEW HIM OUT TOMORROW.
IT'S FINE.
SERIOUSLY. DON'T DO THAT.
HONESTLY--! THAT'S WHY YOU DON'T HAVE FRIENDS.
FUME
FUME
THAT'S TRUE, BUT IT'S NONE OF YOUR BUSINESS.
BUT YOU HAVE NO FRIENDS!
OH, LOOK--THE GATE. SEE YOU.
LISTEN TO ME!
GRRRR...

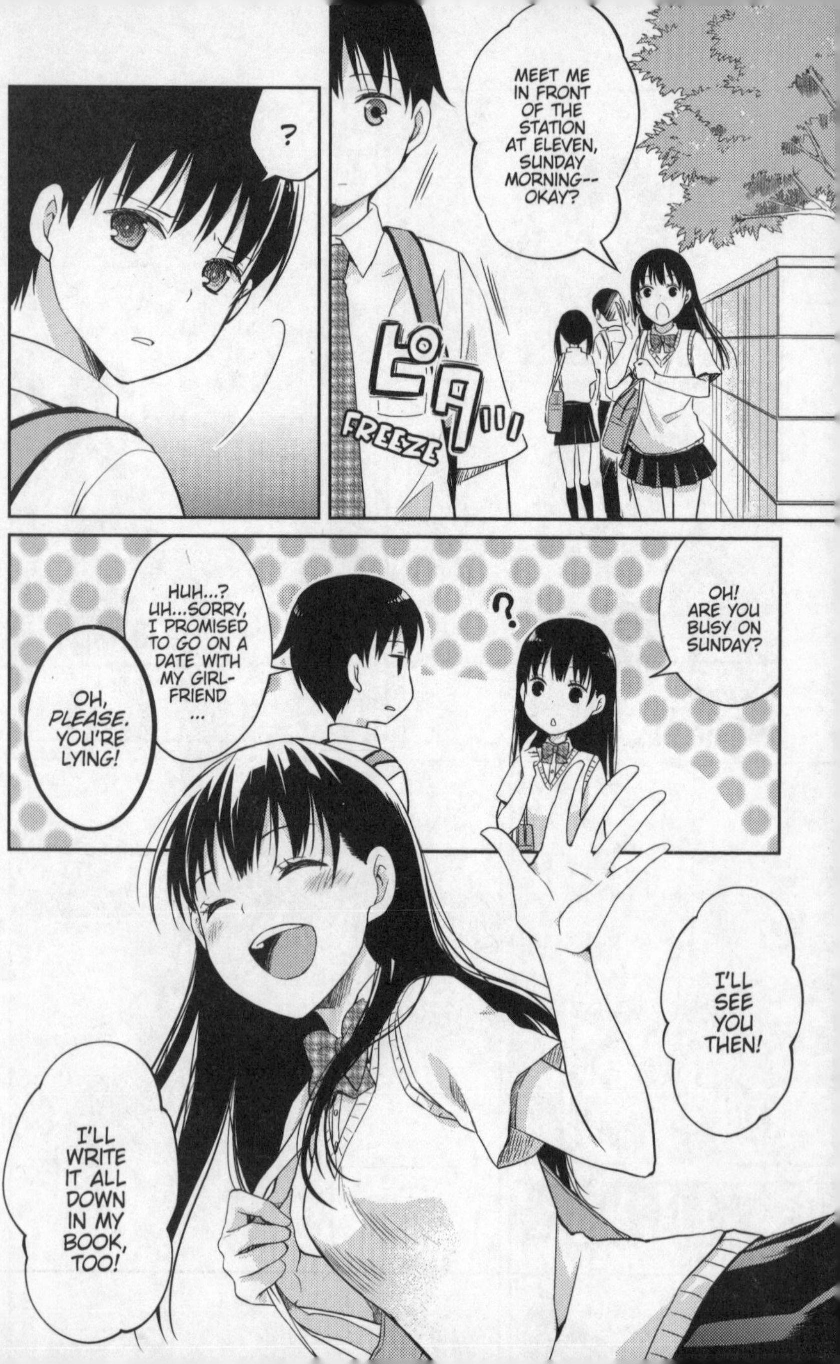
MEET ME IN FRONT OF THE STATION AT ELEVEN, SUNDAY MORNING--OKAY?
ピタ
FREEZE
?
OH! ARE YOU BUSY ON SUNDAY?
?
HUH...? UH...SORRY, I PROMISED TO GO ON A DATE WITH MY GIRL-FRIEND ...
OH, *PLEASE.* YOU'RE LYING!
I'LL SEE YOU THEN!
I'LL WRITE IT ALL DOWN IN MY BOOK, TOO!

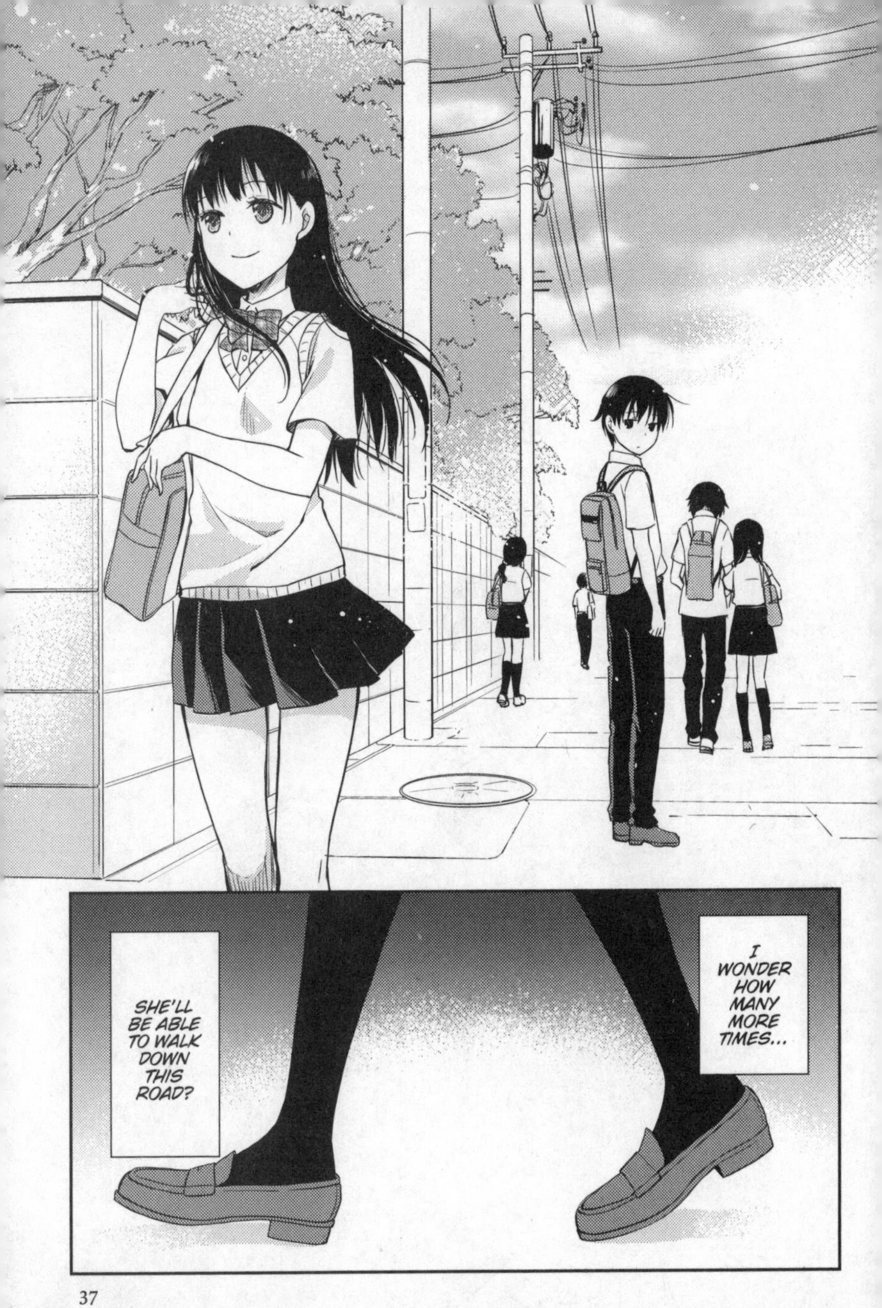
I WONDER HOW MANY MORE TIMES...
SHE'LL BE ABLE TO WALK DOWN THIS ROAD?

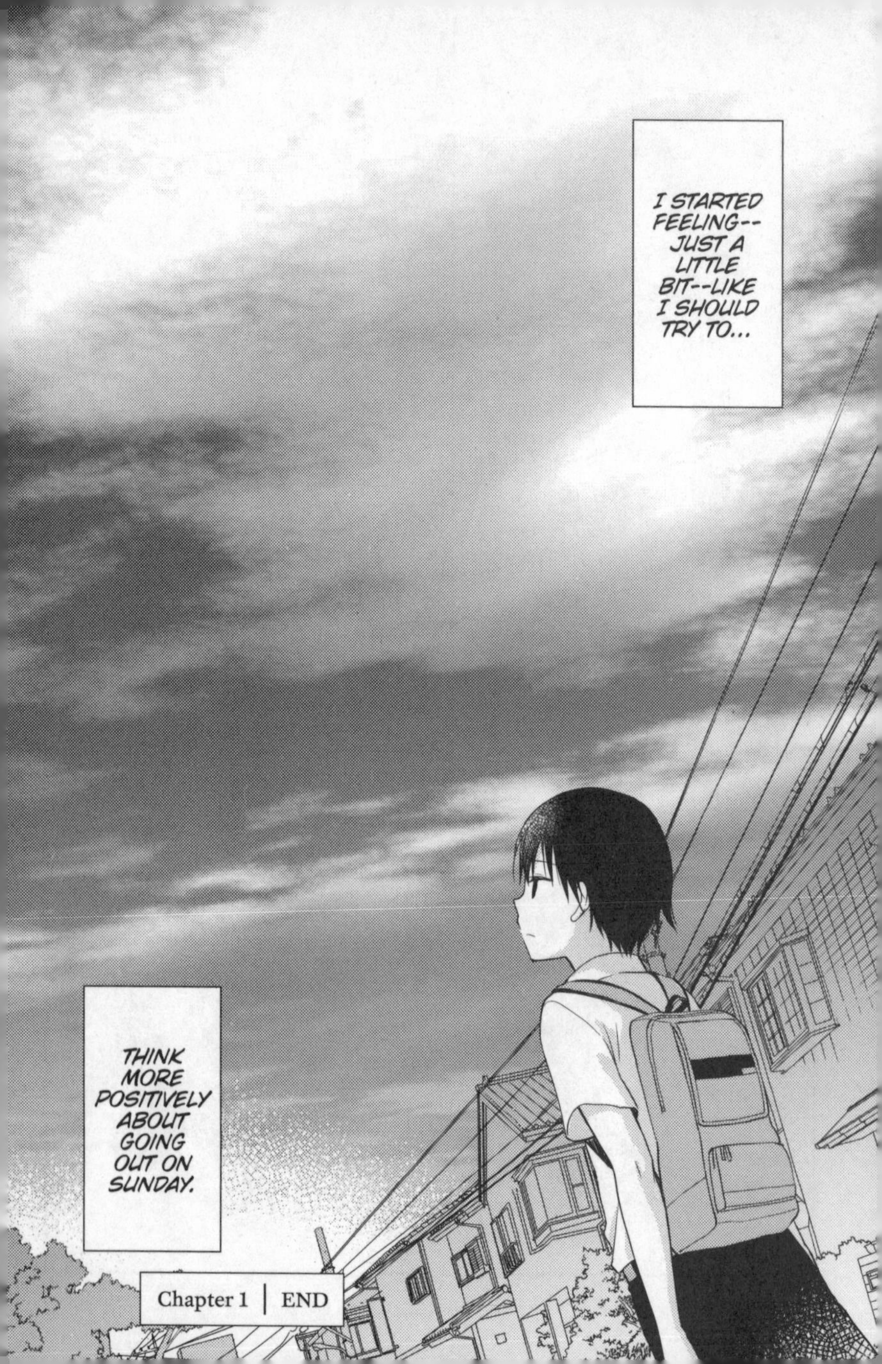
I STARTED FEELING--JUST A LITTLE BIT--LIKE I SHOULD TRY TO...
THINK MORE POSITIVELY ABOUT GOING OUT ON SUNDAY.
Chapter 1 | END

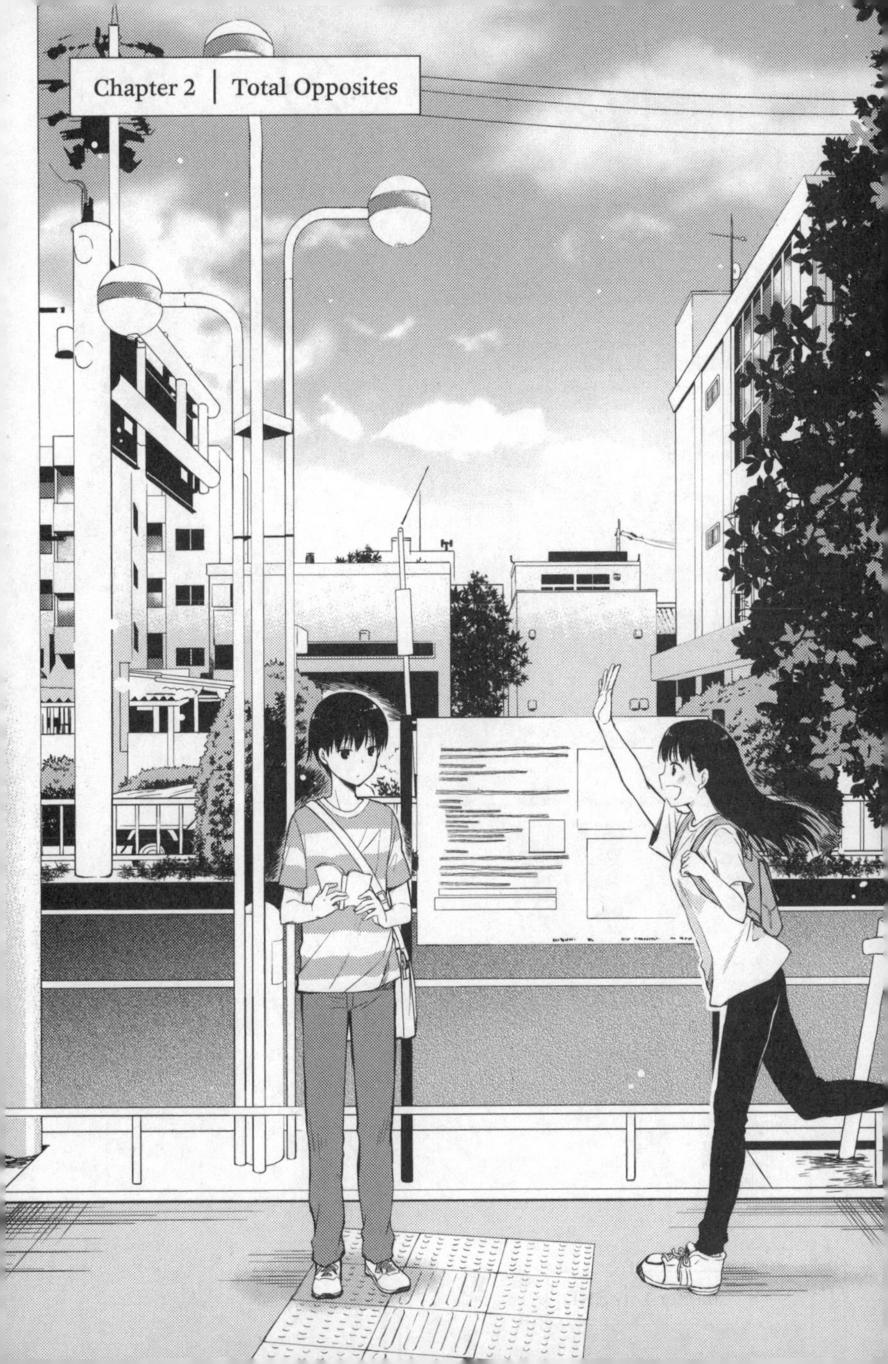
Chapter 2 | Total Opposites

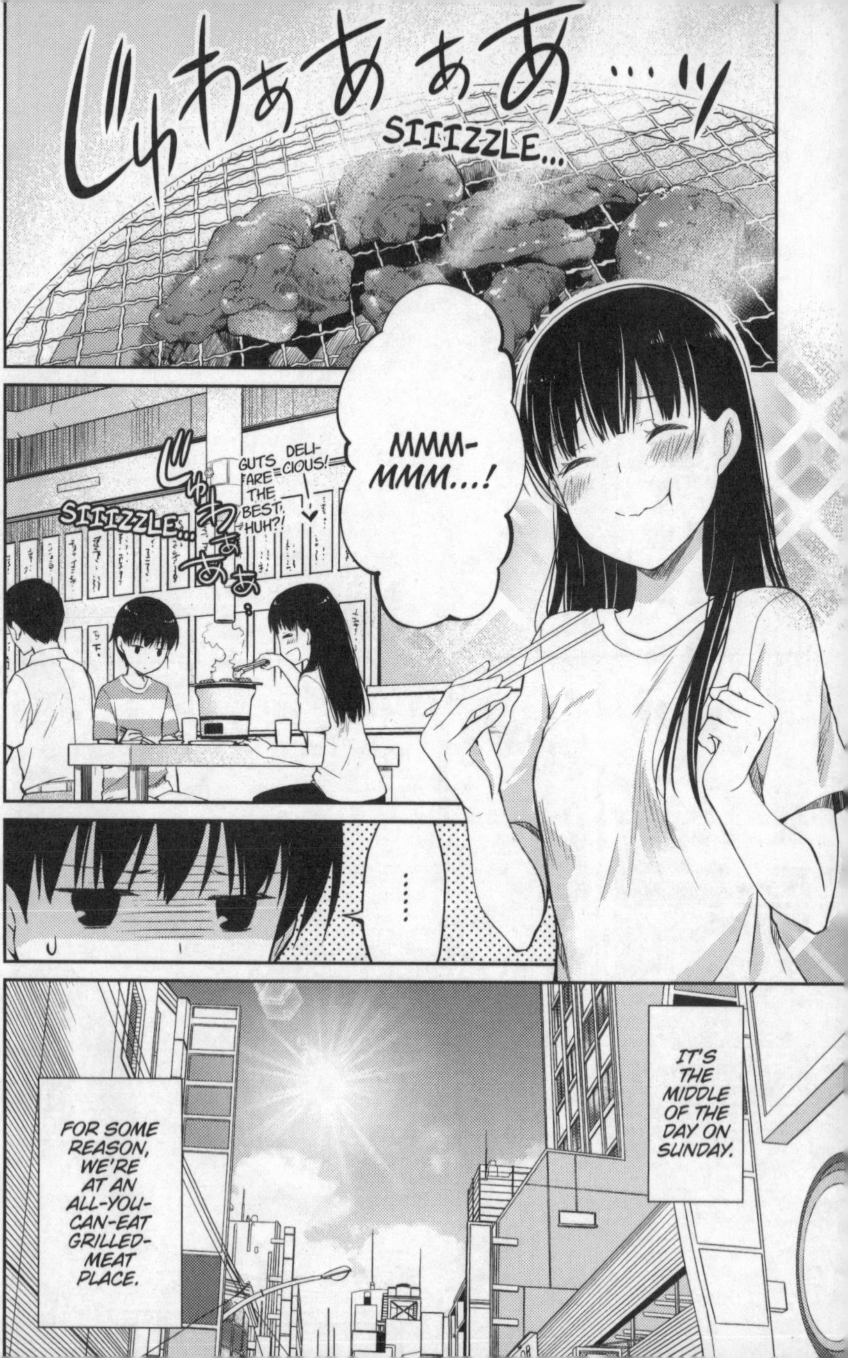
じゅわぁあぁあ…ッ
SIIIZZLE...
MMM-MMM...!
DELI-CIOUS!
GUTS ARE THE BEST, HUH?!
じゅわぁあぁあ
SIIIZZLE...
......
IT'S THE MIDDLE OF THE DAY ON SUNDAY.
FOR SOME REASON, WE'RE AT AN ALL-YOU-CAN-EAT GRILLED-MEAT PLACE.

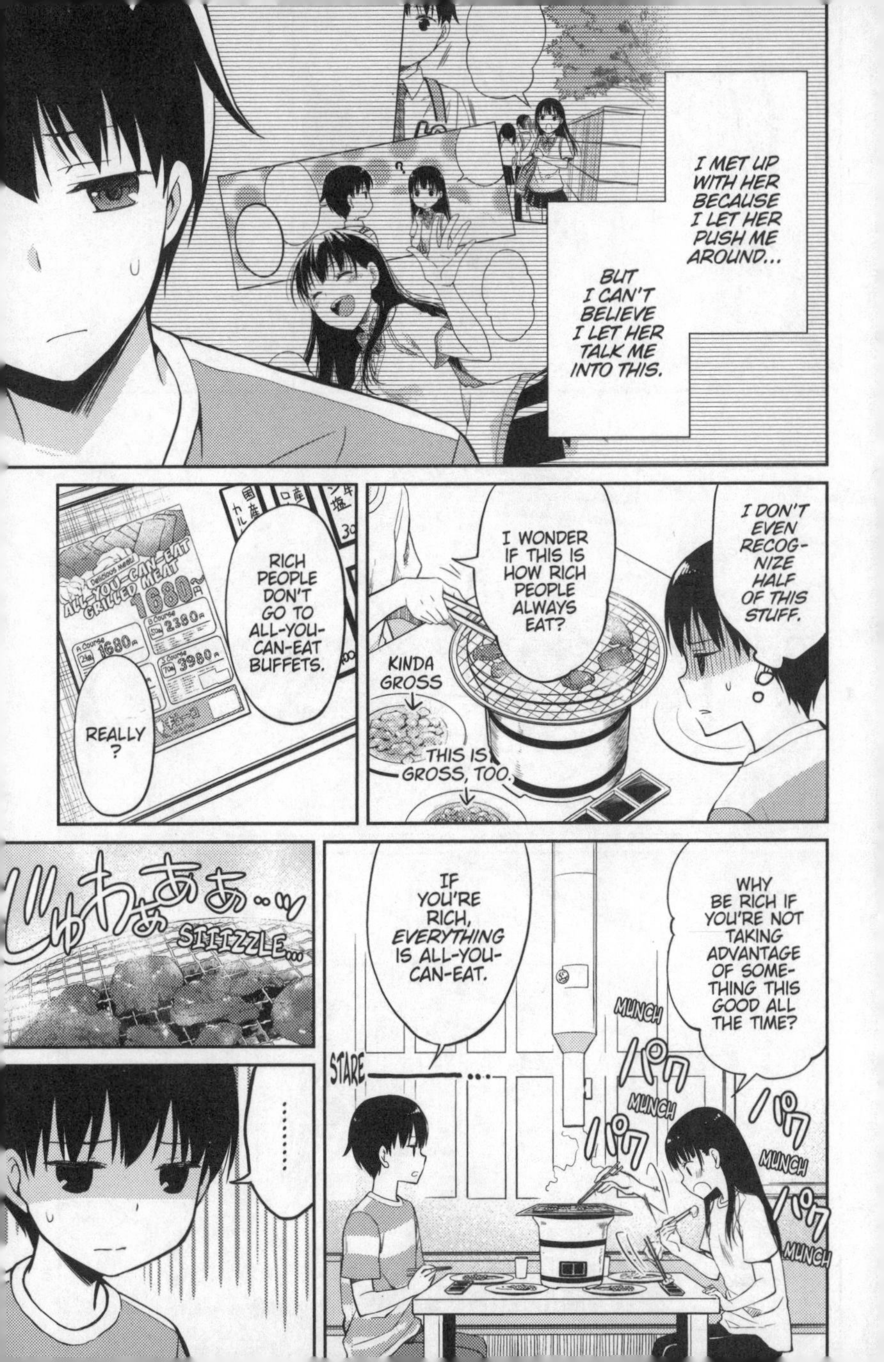
I MET UP WITH HER BECAUSE I LET HER PUSH ME AROUND...
BUT I CAN'T BELIEVE I LET HER TALK ME INTO THIS.
I DON'T EVEN RECOGNIZE HALF OF THIS STUFF.
I WONDER IF THIS IS HOW RICH PEOPLE ALWAYS EAT?
KINDA GROSS
THIS IS GROSS, TOO.
RICH PEOPLE DON'T GO TO ALL-YOU-CAN-EAT BUFFETS.
REALLY?
Delicious Menu
ALL-YOU-CAN-EAT GRILLED MEAT 1680円~
A Course 1680円
B Course 2380円
C Course 3980円
WHY BE RICH IF YOU'RE NOT TAKING ADVANTAGE OF SOMETHING THIS GOOD ALL THE TIME?
パク MUNCH
パク MUNCH
パク MUNCH
パク MUNCH
IF YOU'RE RICH, EVERYTHING IS ALL-YOU-CAN-EAT.
STARE——...
じゅわぁあぁ…ッ
SIIIZZLE...
......

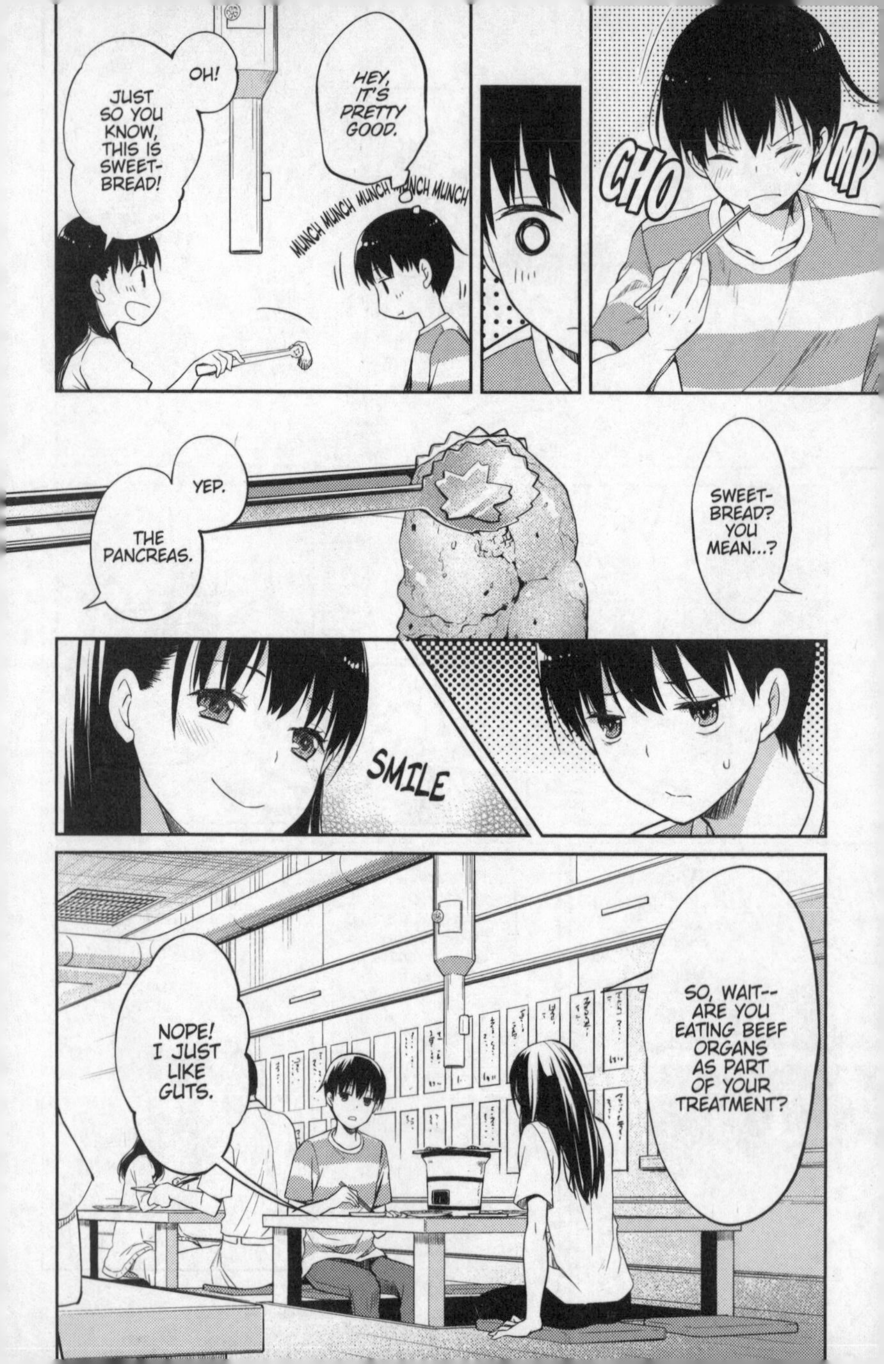
CHOMP
HEY, IT'S PRETTY GOOD.
MUNCH MUNCH MUNCH MUNCH MUNCH
OH! JUST SO YOU KNOW, THIS IS SWEET-BREAD!
SWEET-BREAD? YOU MEAN...?
YEP. THE PANCREAS.
SMILE
SO, WAIT-- ARE YOU EATING BEEF ORGANS AS PART OF YOUR TREATMENT?
NOPE! I JUST LIKE GUTS.

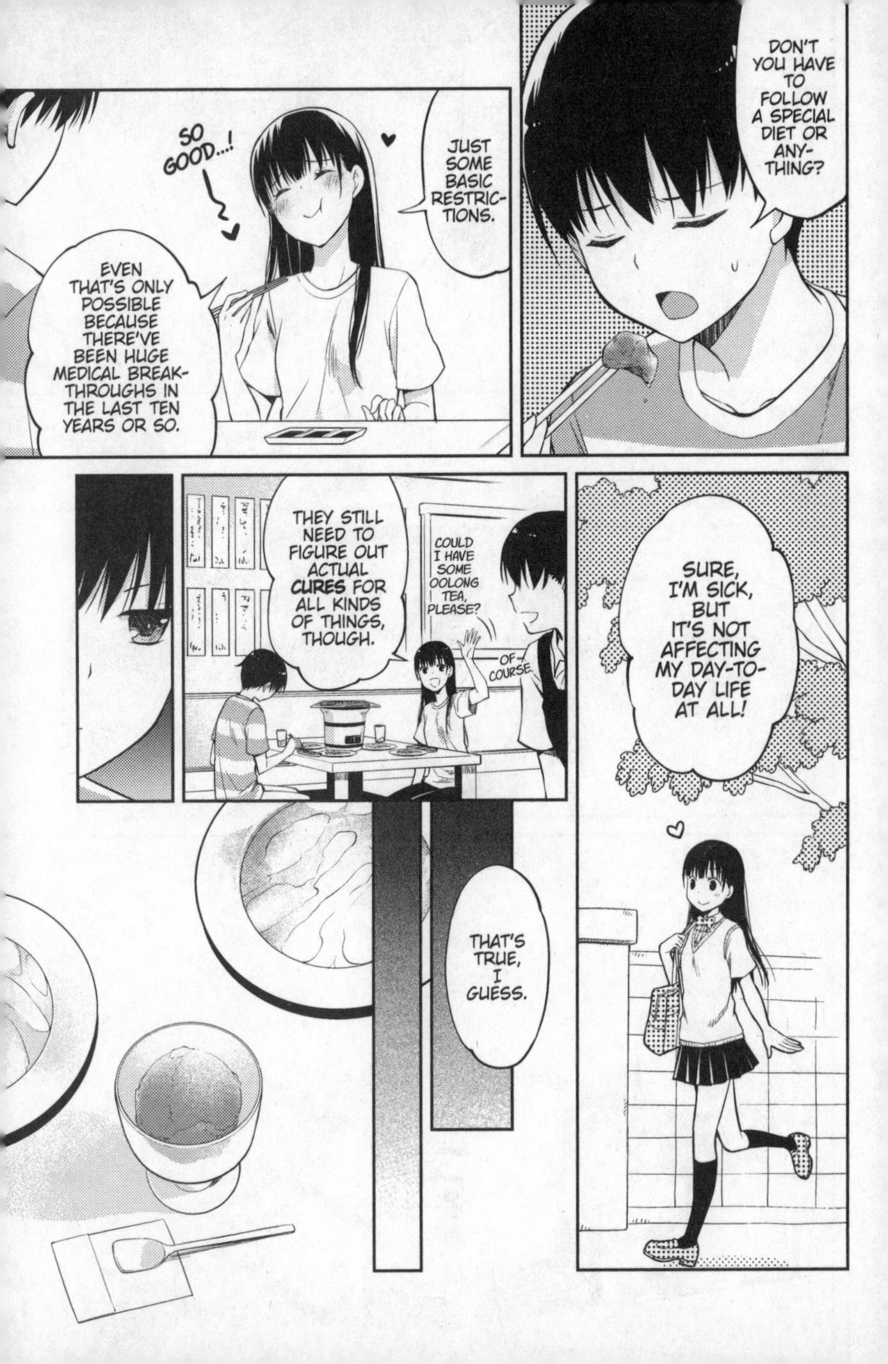
DON'T YOU HAVE TO FOLLOW A SPECIAL DIET OR ANYTHING?
JUST SOME BASIC RESTRICTIONS.
SO GOOD...!
EVEN THAT'S ONLY POSSIBLE BECAUSE THERE'VE BEEN HUGE MEDICAL BREAK-THROUGHS IN THE LAST TEN YEARS OR SO.
SURE, I'M SICK, BUT IT'S NOT AFFECTING MY DAY-TO-DAY LIFE AT ALL!
COULD I HAVE SOME OOLONG TEA, PLEASE?
OF-COURSE.
THEY STILL NEED TO FIGURE OUT ACTUAL **CURES** FOR ALL KINDS OF THINGS, THOUGH.
THAT'S TRUE, I GUESS.

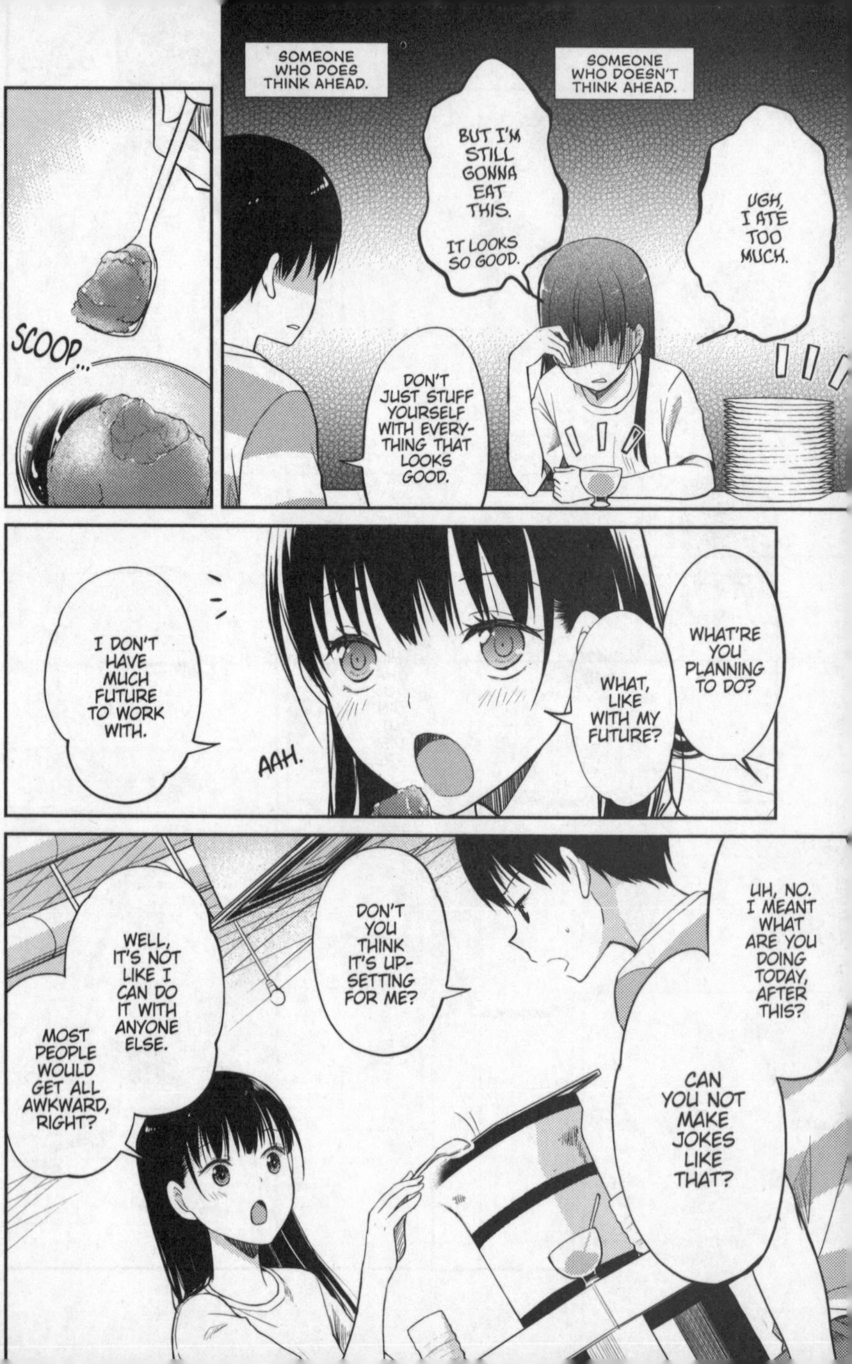
SOMEONE WHO DOESN'T THINK AHEAD.
UGH, I ATE TOO MUCH.
SOMEONE WHO DOES THINK AHEAD.
BUT I'M STILL GONNA EAT THIS. IT LOOKS SO GOOD.
DON'T JUST STUFF YOURSELF WITH EVERY-THING THAT LOOKS GOOD.
SCOOP...
WHAT'RE YOU PLANNING TO DO?
WHAT, LIKE WITH MY FUTURE?
AAH.
I DON'T HAVE MUCH FUTURE TO WORK WITH.
UH, NO. I MEANT WHAT ARE YOU DOING TODAY, AFTER THIS?
CAN YOU NOT MAKE JOKES LIKE THAT?
DON'T YOU THINK IT'S UP-SETTING FOR ME?
WELL, IT'S NOT LIKE I CAN DO IT WITH ANYONE ELSE.
MOST PEOPLE WOULD GET ALL AWKWARD, RIGHT?

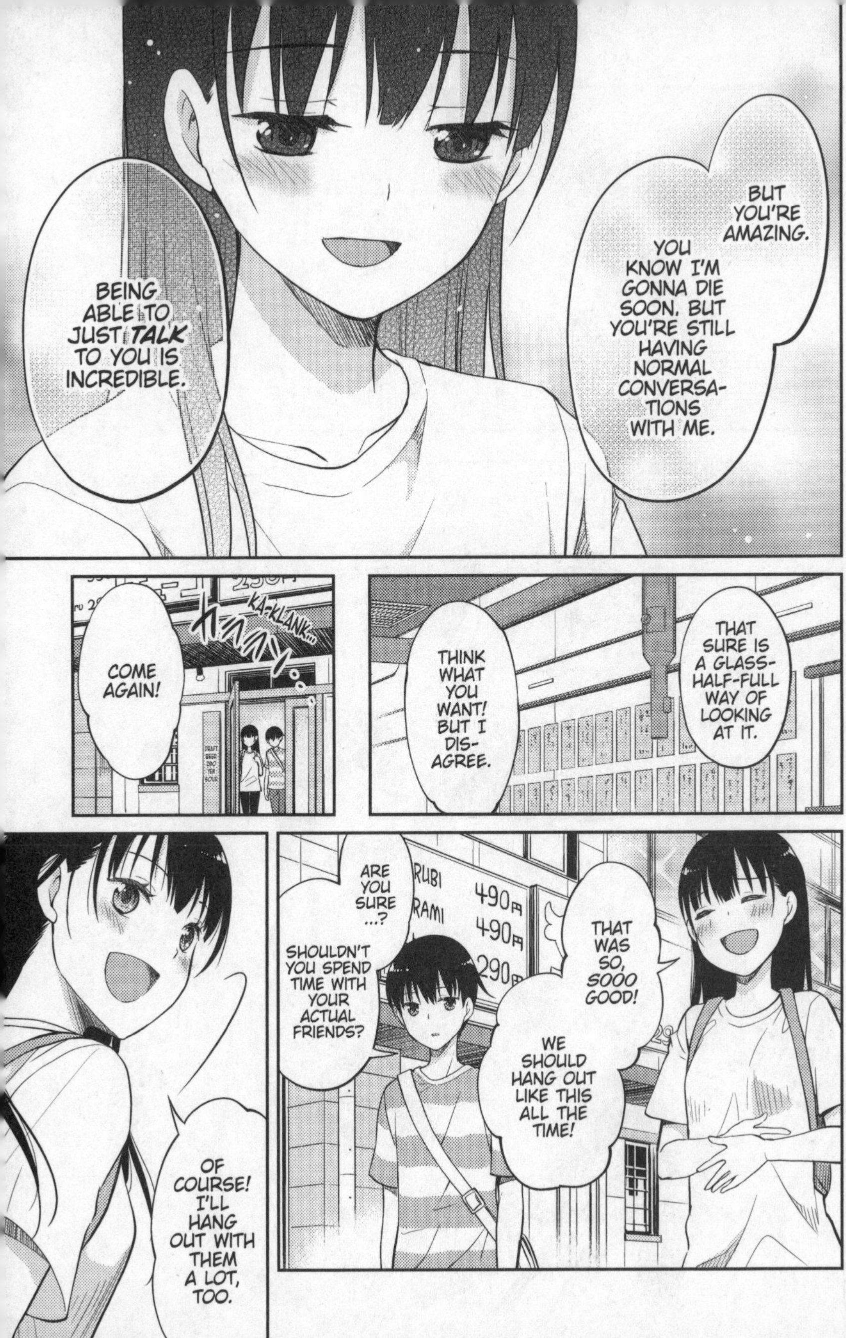
BUT YOU'RE AMAZING.
YOU KNOW I'M GONNA DIE SOON, BUT YOU'RE STILL HAVING NORMAL CONVERSA-TIONS WITH ME.
BEING ABLE TO JUST *TALK* TO YOU IS INCREDIBLE.
THAT SURE IS A GLASS-HALF-FULL WAY OF LOOKING AT IT.
THINK WHAT YOU WANT! BUT I DIS-AGREE.
KA-KLANK...
COME AGAIN!
THAT WAS SO, SOOO GOOD!
WE SHOULD HANG OUT LIKE THIS ALL THE TIME!
ARE YOU SURE ...?
SHOULDN'T YOU SPEND TIME WITH YOUR ACTUAL FRIENDS?
OF COURSE! I'LL HANG OUT WITH THEM A LOT, TOO.

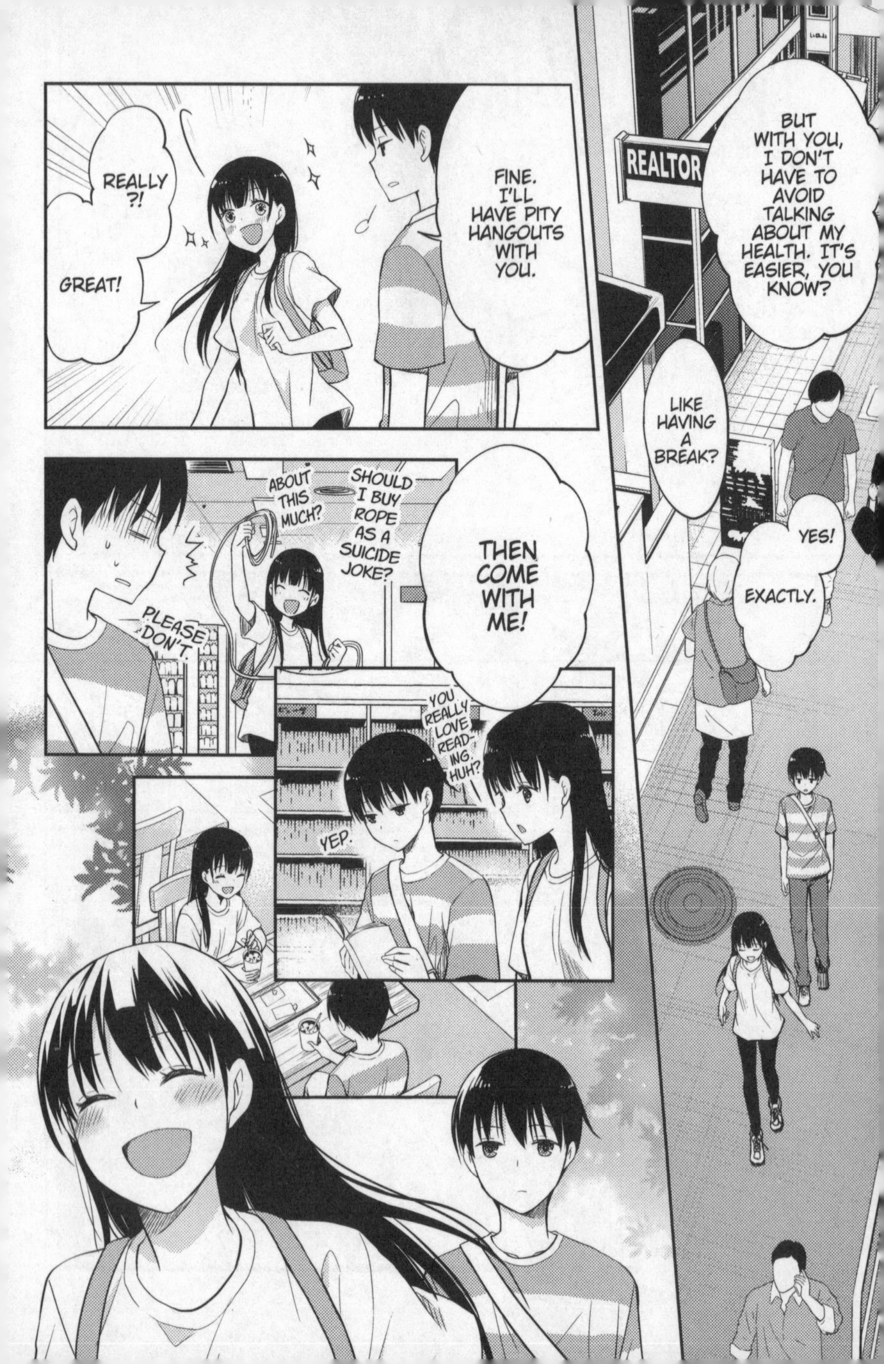
REALTOR
BUT WITH YOU, I DON'T HAVE TO AVOID TALKING ABOUT MY HEALTH. IT'S EASIER, YOU KNOW?
LIKE HAVING A BREAK?
YES!
EXACTLY.
FINE. I'LL HAVE PITY HANGOUTS WITH YOU.
REALLY?!
GREAT!
THEN COME WITH ME!
SHOULD I BUY ROPE AS A SUICIDE JOKE?
ABOUT THIS MUCH?
PLEASE DON'T.
YOU REALLY LOVE READING, HUH?
YEP.

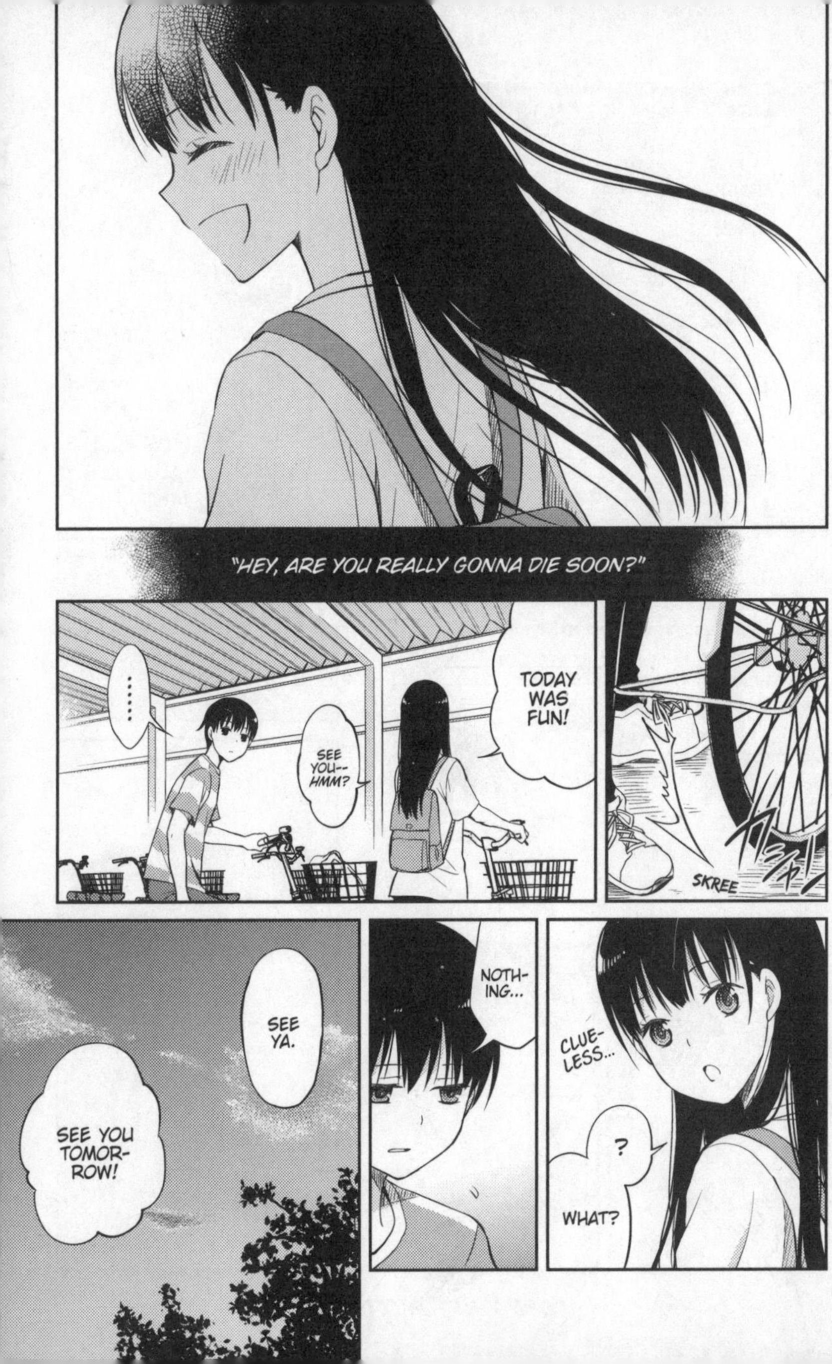
"HEY, ARE YOU REALLY GONNA DIE SOON?"
SKREE
TODAY WAS FUN!
SEE YOU-- HMM?
......
CLUE-LESS...
?
WHAT?
NOTH-ING...
SEE YA.
SEE YOU TOMOR-ROW!

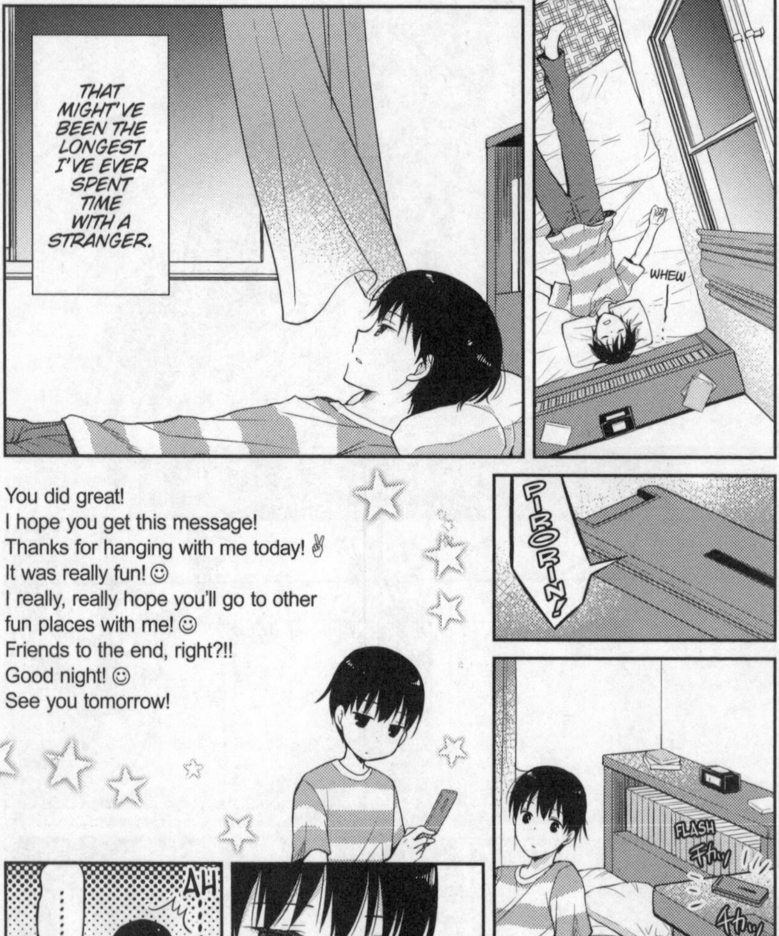
WHEW
THAT MIGHT'VE BEEN THE LONGEST I'VE EVER SPENT TIME WITH A STRANGER.
PIRORIN!
You did great!
I hope you get this message!
Thanks for hanging with me today! ✌
It was really fun! ☺
I really, really hope you'll go to other fun places with me! ☺
Friends to the end, right?!!
Good night! ☺
See you tomorrow!
FLASH
FLASH
AH...!
......
CHK...
YEAH, IT REALLY WAS FUN.

"SEE YOU TOMORROW."

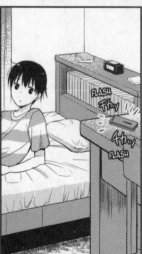

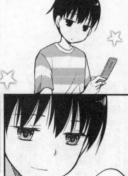

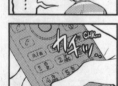

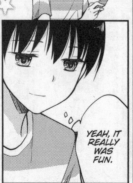

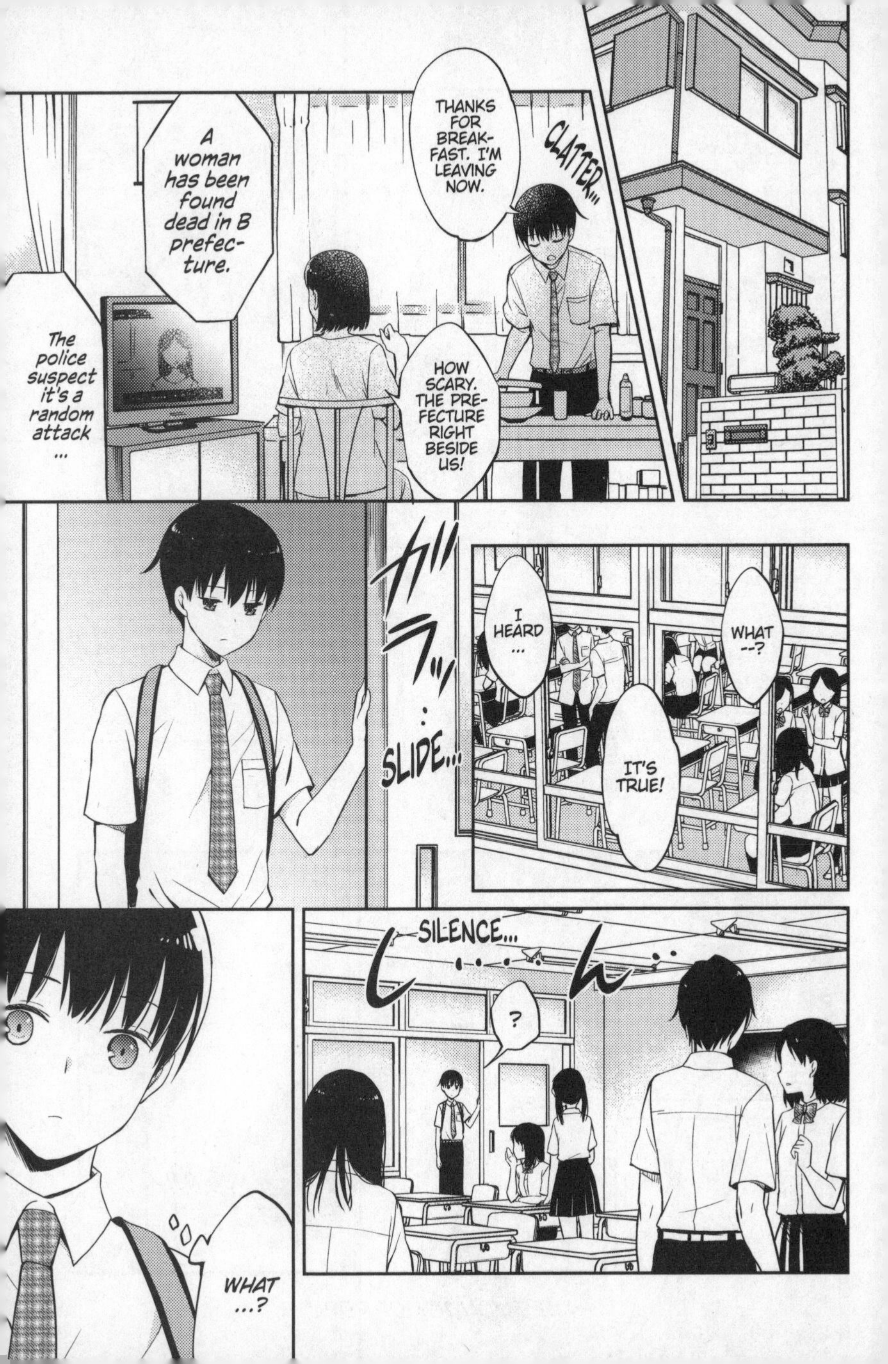
CLATTER...
THANKS FOR BREAK-FAST. I'M LEAVING NOW.
A woman has been found dead in B prefec-ture.
HOW SCARY. THE PRE-FECTURE RIGHT BESIDE US!
The police suspect it's a random attack ...
WHAT --?
I HEARD ...
IT'S TRUE!
ガラッ
SLIDE...
SILENCE...
しーん
?
WHAT ...?

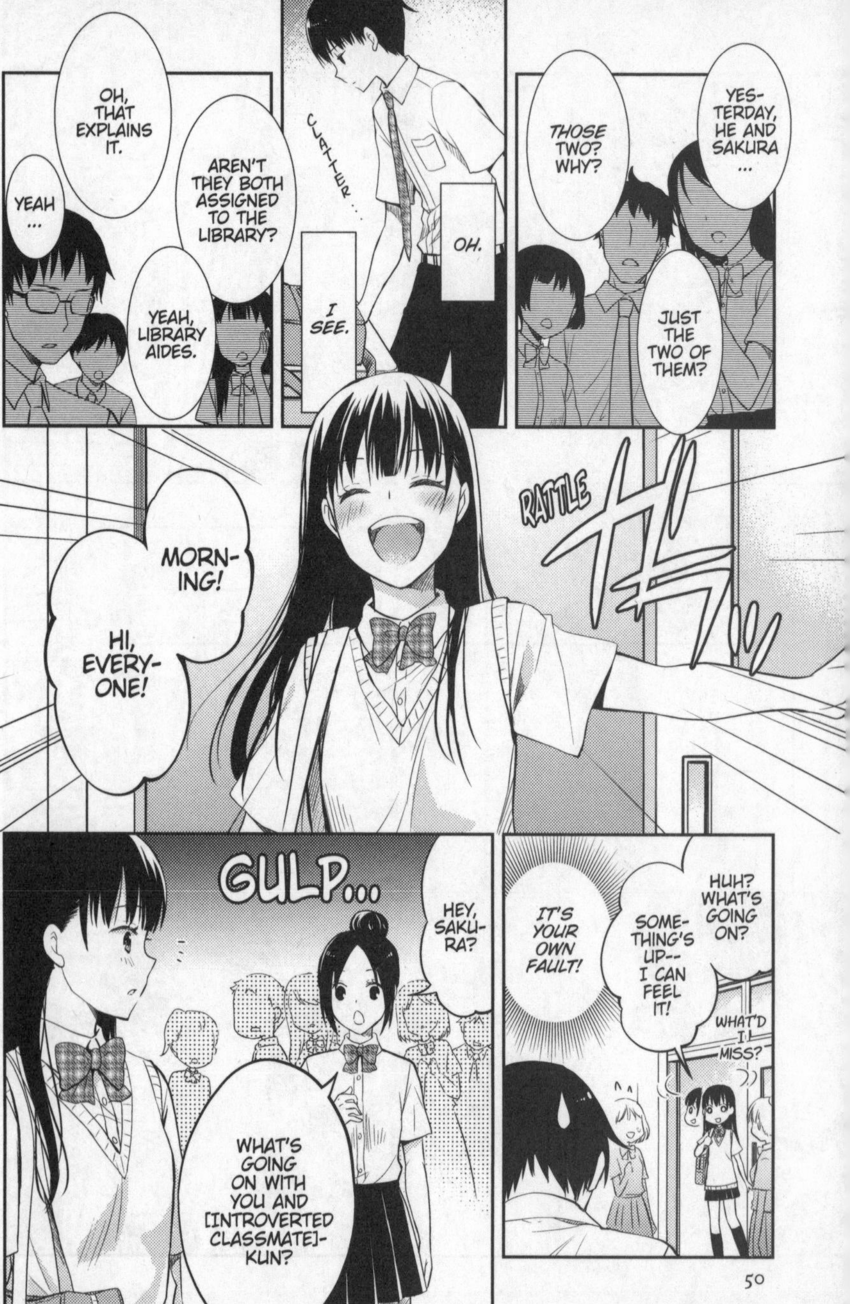
YES-TERDAY, HE AND SAKURA ...
THOSE TWO? WHY?
JUST THE TWO OF THEM?
CLATTER...
OH.
I SEE.
AREN'T THEY BOTH ASSIGNED TO THE LIBRARY?
OH, THAT EXPLAINS IT.
YEAH, LIBRARY AIDES.
YEAH ...
RATTLE
MORN-ING!
HI, EVERY-ONE!
HUH? WHAT'S GOING ON?
SOME-THING'S UP-- I CAN FEEL IT!
IT'S YOUR OWN FAULT!
WHAT'D I MISS?
GULP...
HEY, SAKU-RA?
WHAT'S GOING ON WITH YOU AND [INTROVERTED CLASSMATE]-KUN?

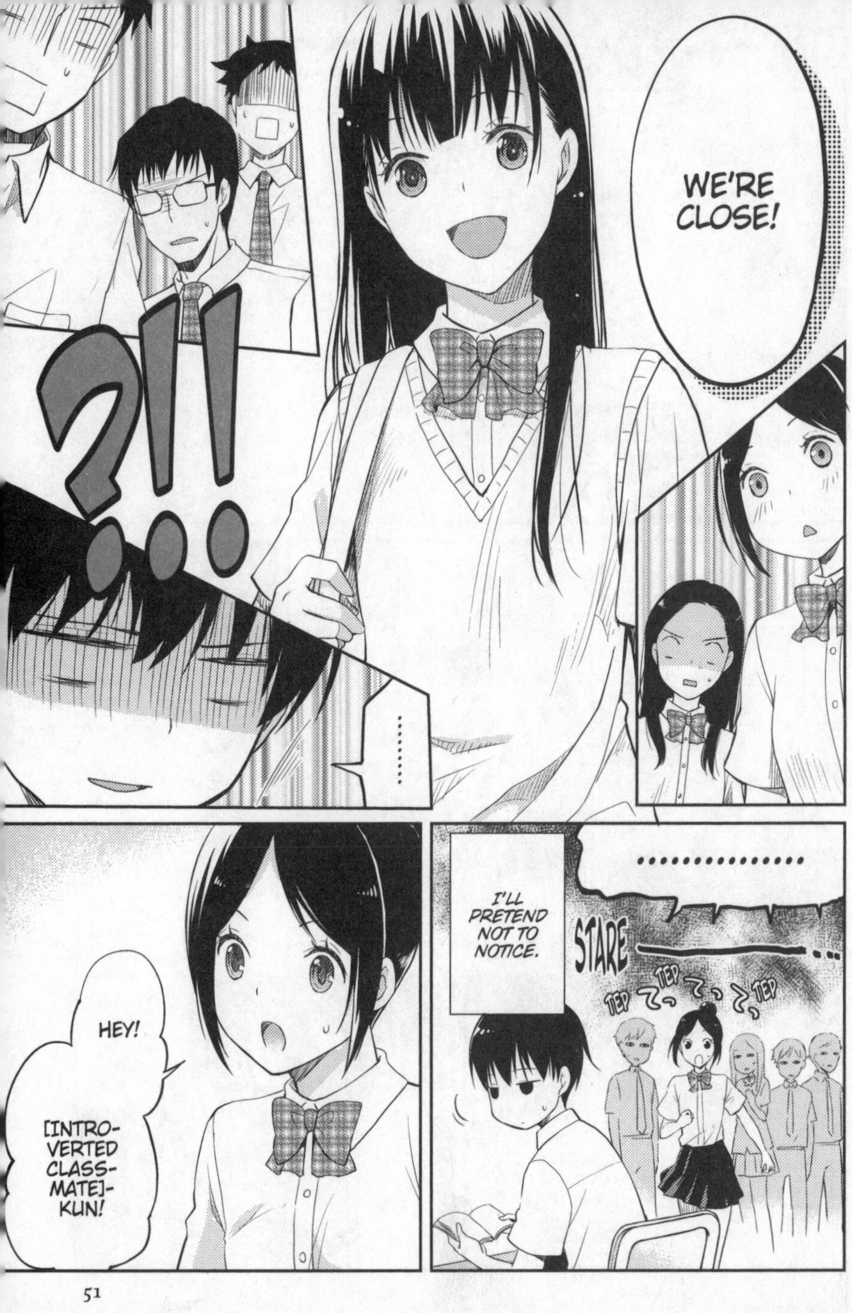
WE'RE CLOSE!
?!!
......
....
I'LL PRETEND NOT TO NOTICE.
STARE
TEP
TEP
TEP
HEY!
[INTRO-VERTED CLASS-MATE]-KUN!

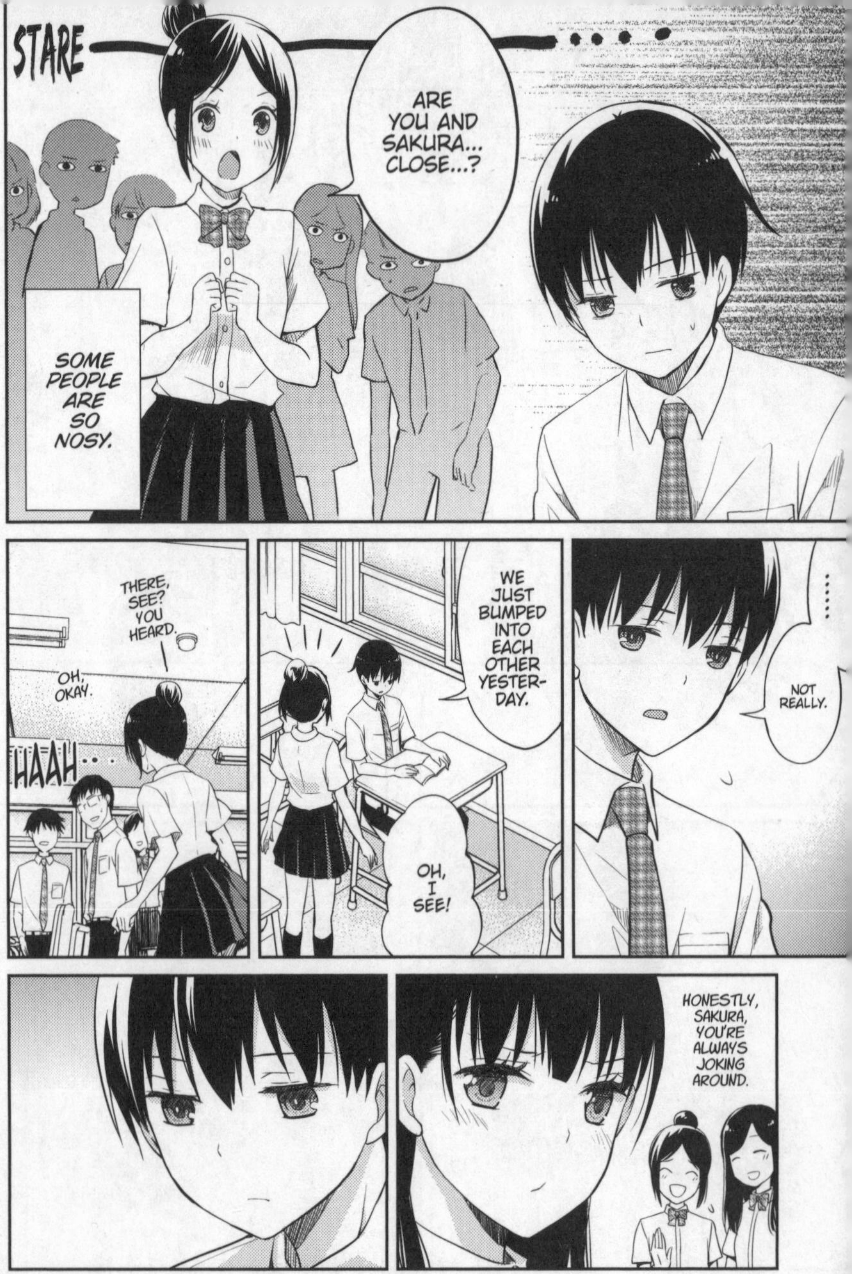
STARE
ARE YOU AND SAKURA... CLOSE...?
SOME PEOPLE ARE SO NOSY.
......
NOT REALLY.
WE JUST BUMPED INTO EACH OTHER YESTER-DAY.
OH, I SEE!
THERE, SEE? YOU HEARD.
OH, OKAY.
HAAH...
HONESTLY, SAKURA, YOU'RE ALWAYS JOKING AROUND.

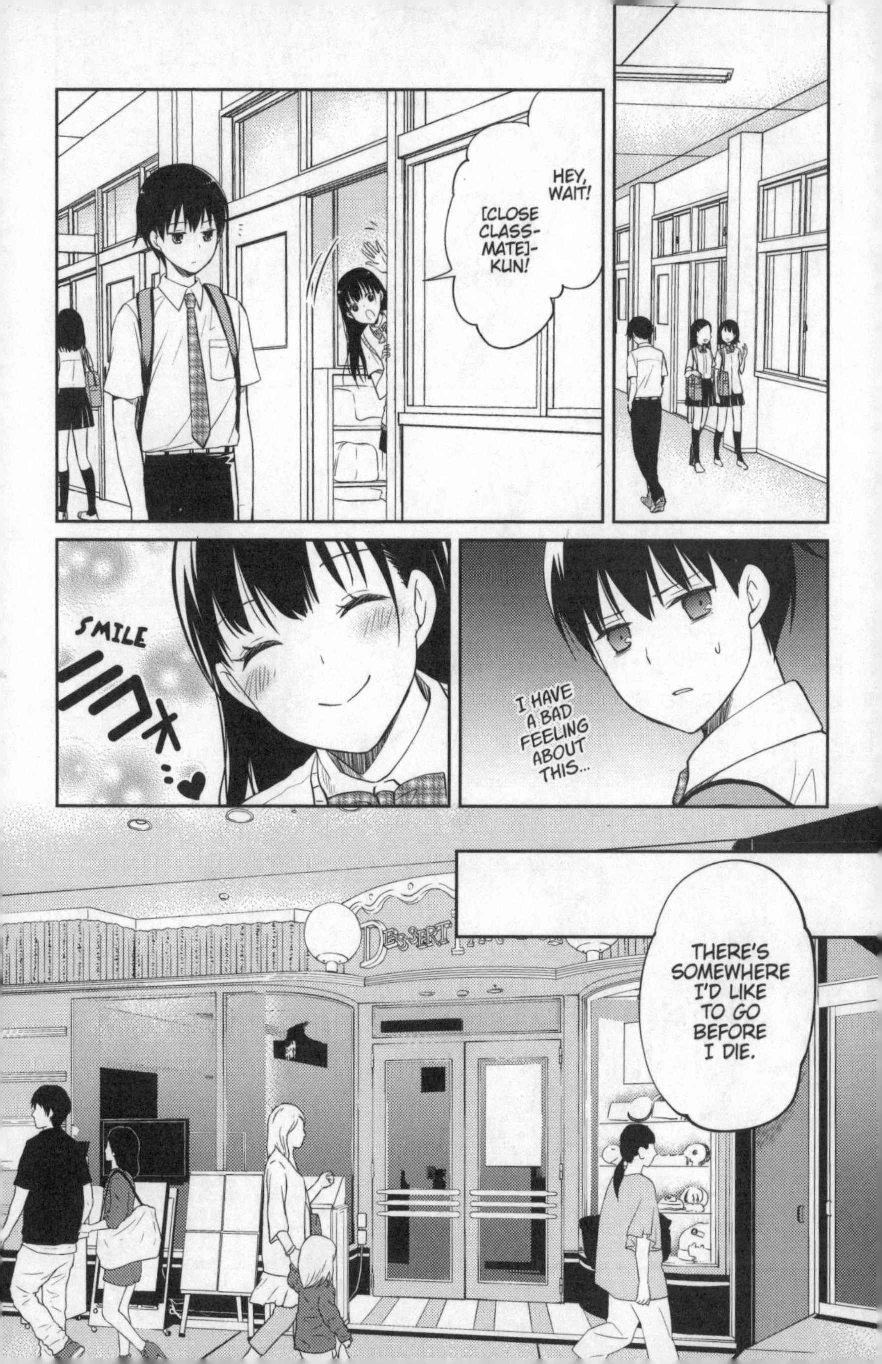
HEY, WAIT! [CLOSE CLASSMATE]-KUN!
I HAVE A BAD FEELING ABOUT THIS...
SMILE
DESSERT
THERE'S SOMEWHERE I'D LIKE TO GO BEFORE I DIE.

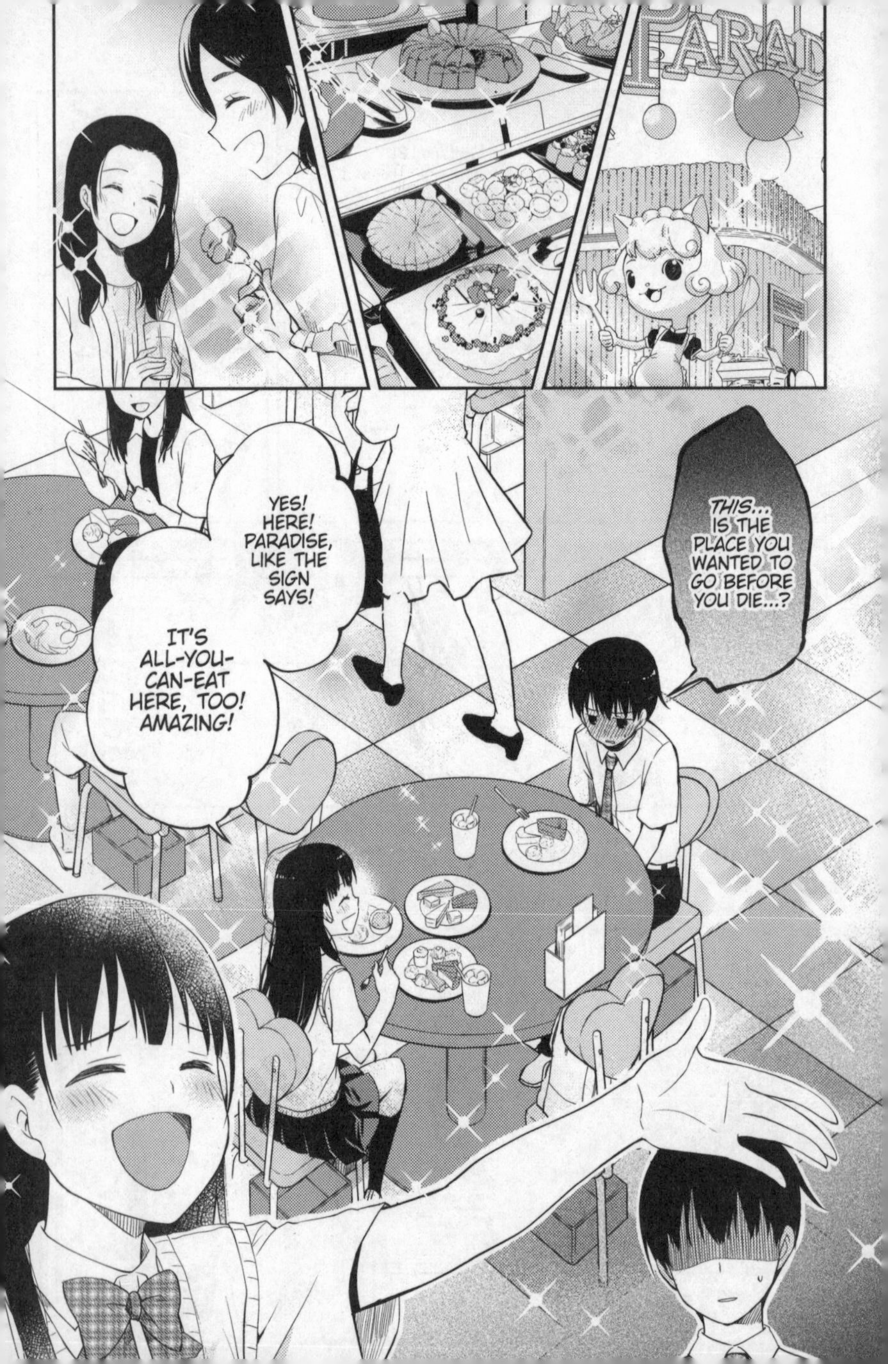
THIS... IS THE PLACE YOU WANTED TO GO BEFORE YOU DIE...?
YES! HERE! PARADISE, LIKE THE SIGN SAYS!
IT'S ALL-YOU-CAN-EAT HERE, TOO! AMAZING!

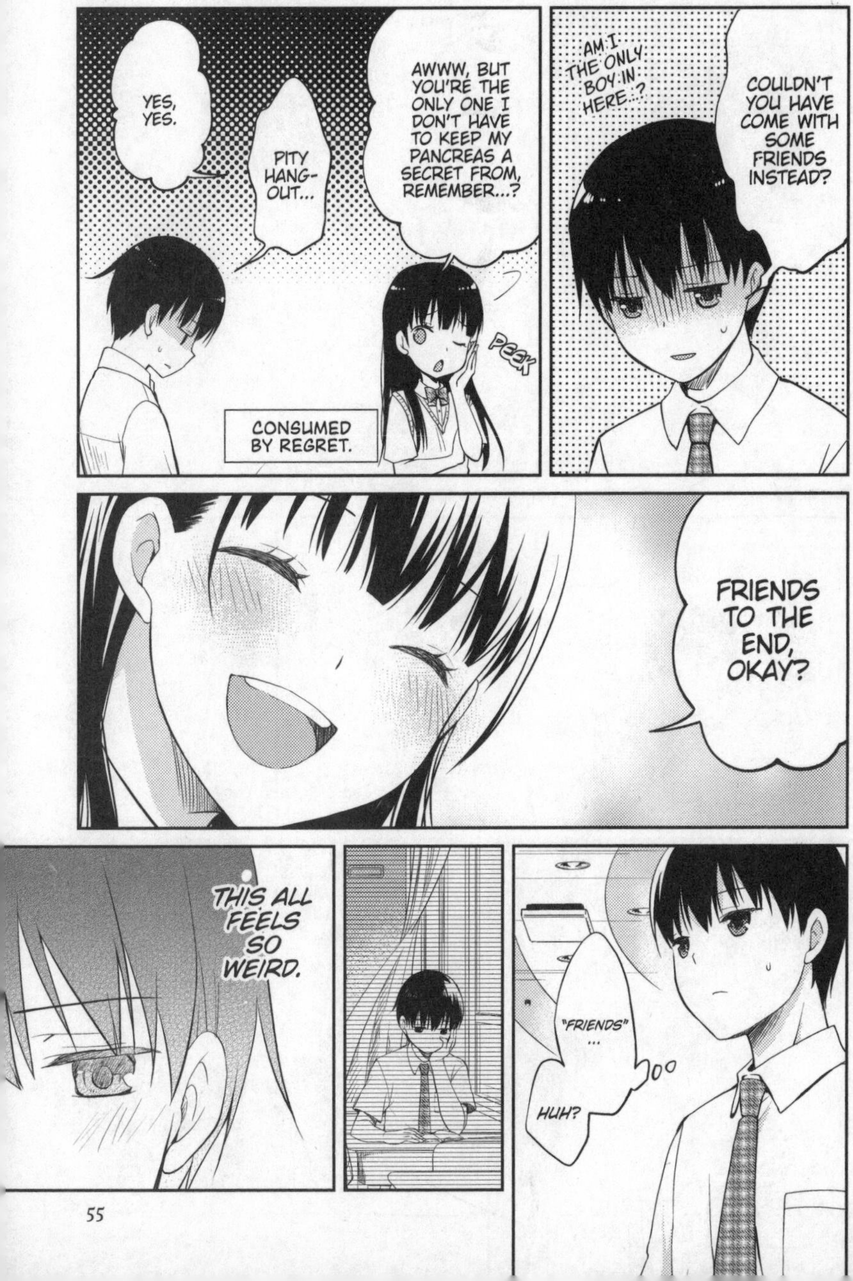
COULDN'T YOU HAVE COME WITH SOME FRIENDS INSTEAD?
AM I THE ONLY BOY IN HERE...?
AWWW, BUT YOU'RE THE ONLY ONE I DON'T HAVE TO KEEP MY PANCREAS A SECRET FROM, REMEMBER...?
PEEK
PITY HANG-OUT...
YES, YES.
CONSUMED BY REGRET.
FRIENDS TO THE END, OKAY?
"FRIENDS" ...
HUH?
THIS ALL FEELS SO WEIRD.

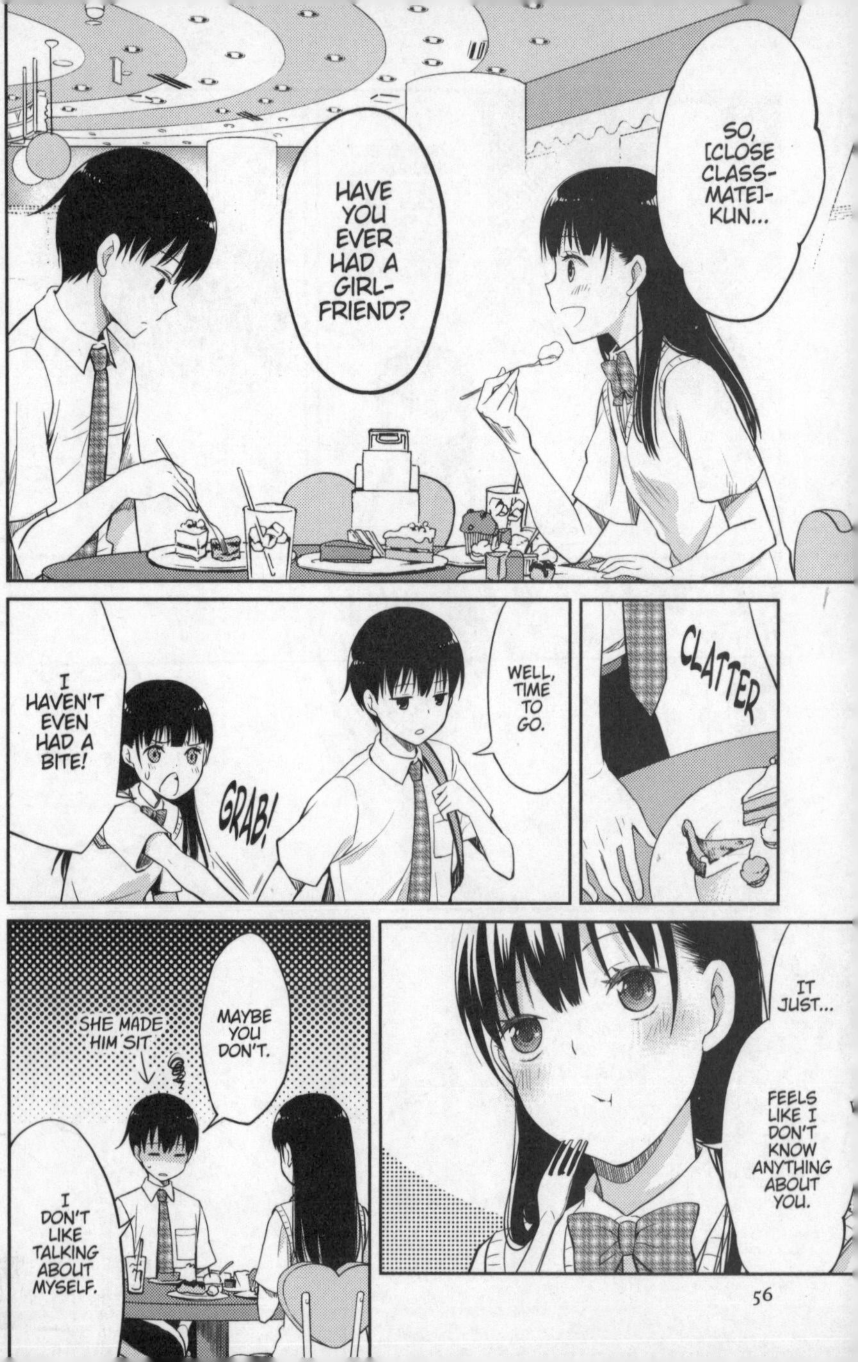
SO, [CLOSE CLASS-MATE]-KUN...
HAVE YOU EVER HAD A GIRL-FRIEND?
CLATTER
WELL, TIME TO GO.
GRAB!
I HAVEN'T EVEN HAD A BITE!
IT JUST...
FEELS LIKE I DON'T KNOW ANYTHING ABOUT YOU.
MAYBE YOU DON'T.
SHE MADE HIM SIT.
I DON'T LIKE TALKING ABOUT MYSELF.

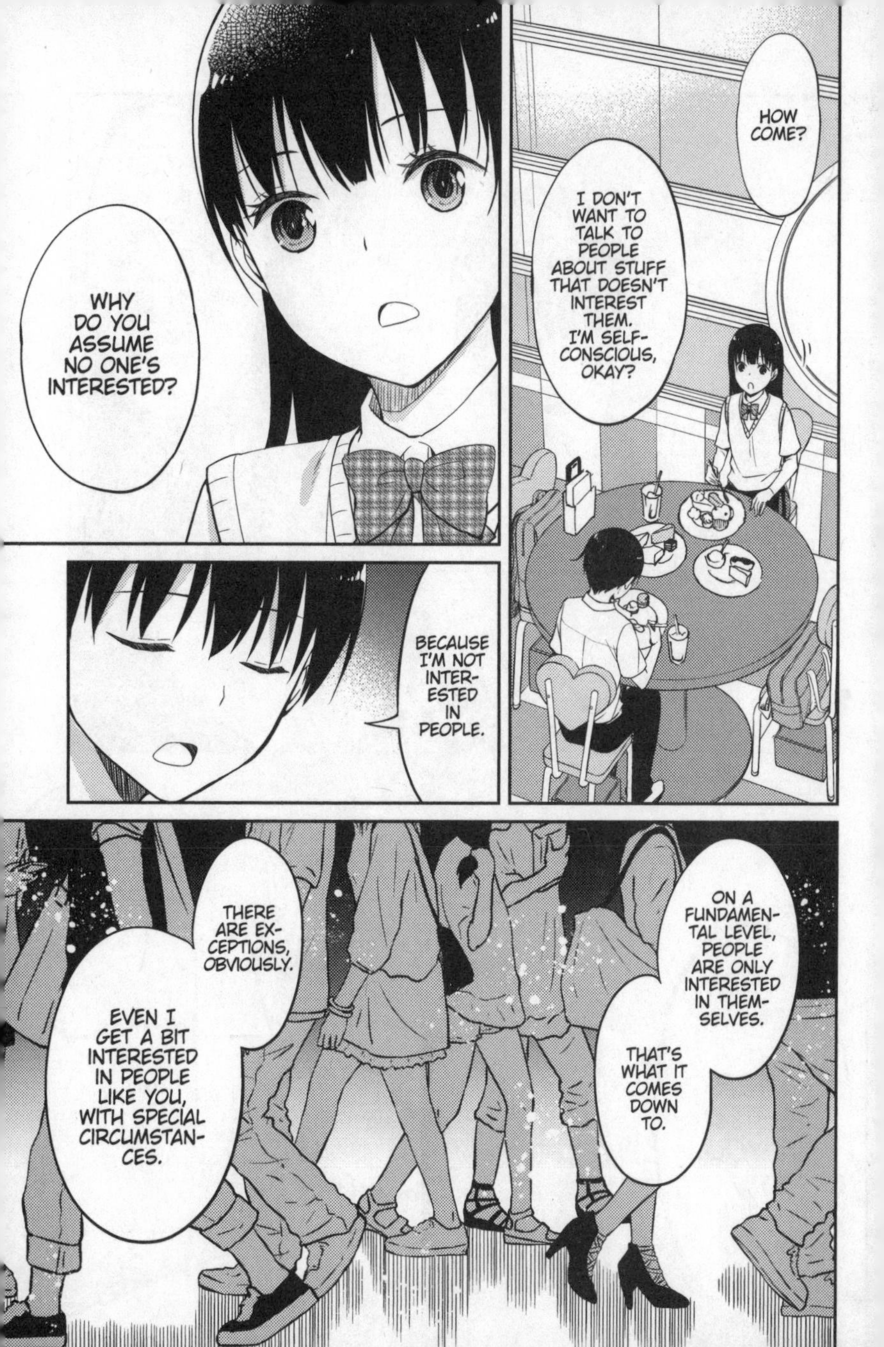
HOW COME?
I DON'T WANT TO TALK TO PEOPLE ABOUT STUFF THAT DOESN'T INTEREST THEM. I'M SELF-CONSCIOUS, OKAY?
WHY DO YOU ASSUME NO ONE'S INTERESTED?
BECAUSE I'M NOT INTER-ESTED IN PEOPLE.
ON A FUNDAMEN-TAL LEVEL, PEOPLE ARE ONLY INTERESTED IN THEM-SELVES.
THAT'S WHAT IT COMES DOWN TO.
THERE ARE EX-CEPTIONS, OBVIOUSLY.
EVEN I GET A BIT INTERESTED IN PEOPLE LIKE YOU, WITH SPECIAL CIRCUMSTAN-CES.

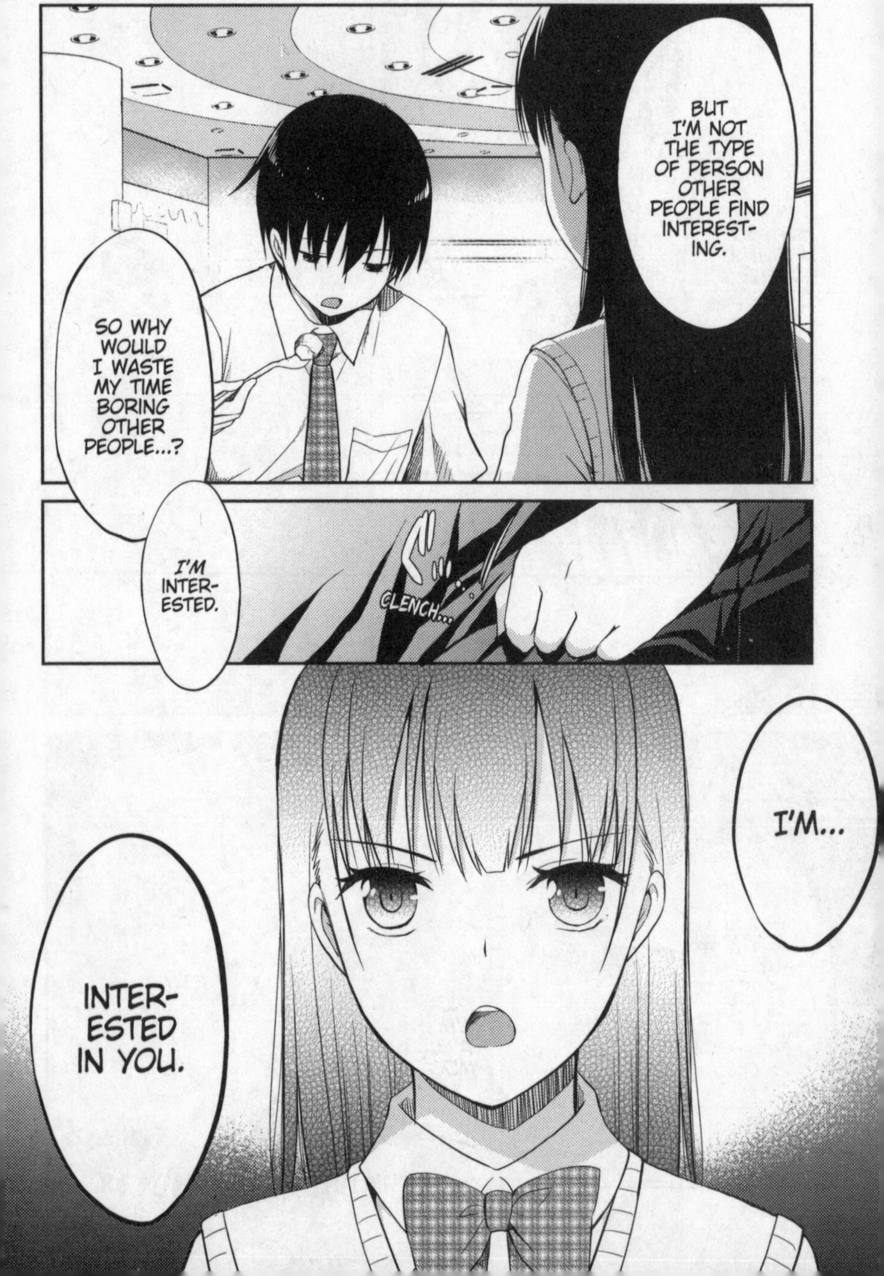
BUT I'M NOT THE TYPE OF PERSON OTHER PEOPLE FIND INTEREST-ING.
SO WHY WOULD I WASTE MY TIME BORING OTHER PEOPLE...?
CLENCH...
I'M INTER-ESTED.
I'M...
INTER-ESTED IN YOU.

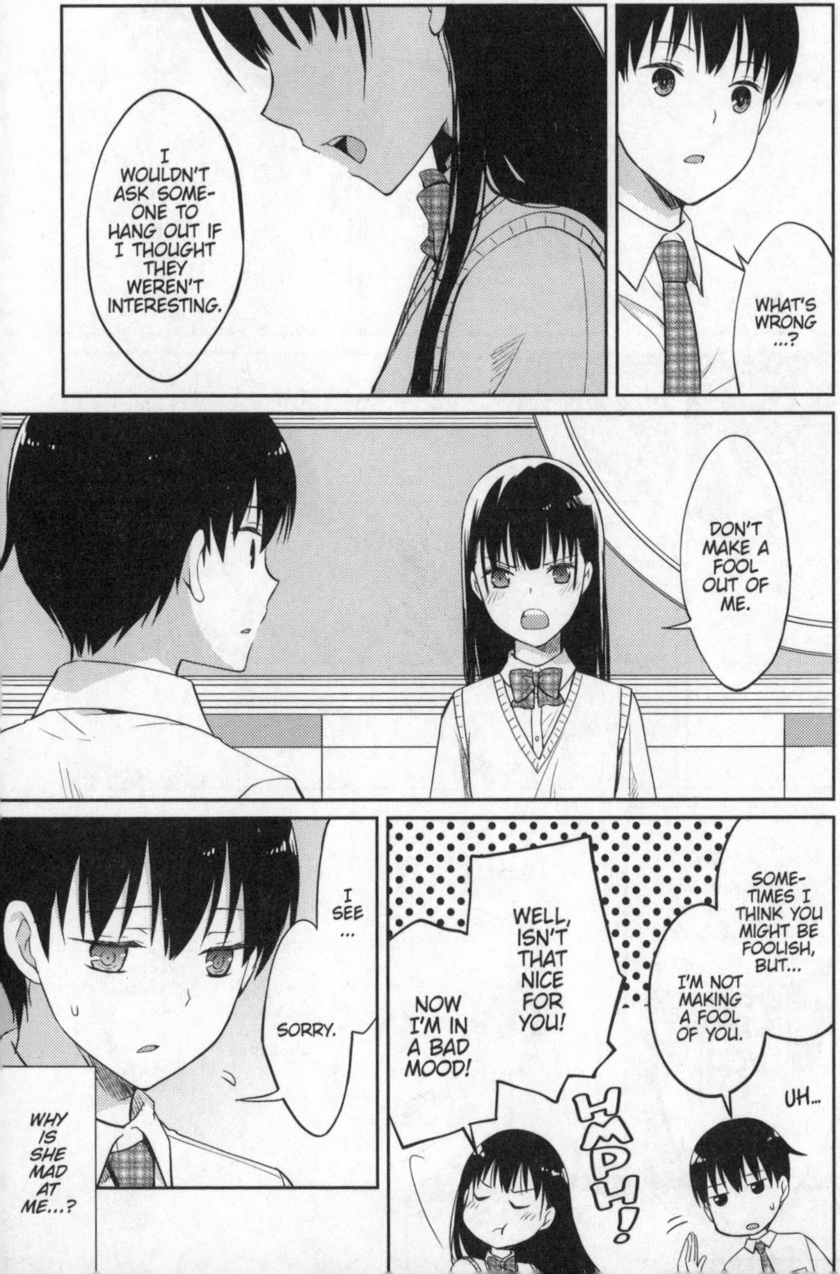
I WOULDN'T ASK SOME-ONE TO HANG OUT IF I THOUGHT THEY WEREN'T INTERESTING.
WHAT'S WRONG ...?
DON'T MAKE A FOOL OUT OF ME.
I SEE ...
SORRY.
WHY IS SHE MAD AT ME...?
SOME-TIMES I THINK YOU MIGHT BE FOOLISH, BUT...
I'M NOT MAKING A FOOL OF YOU.
WELL, ISN'T THAT NICE FOR YOU!
NOW I'M IN A BAD MOOD!
HMPH!
UH...

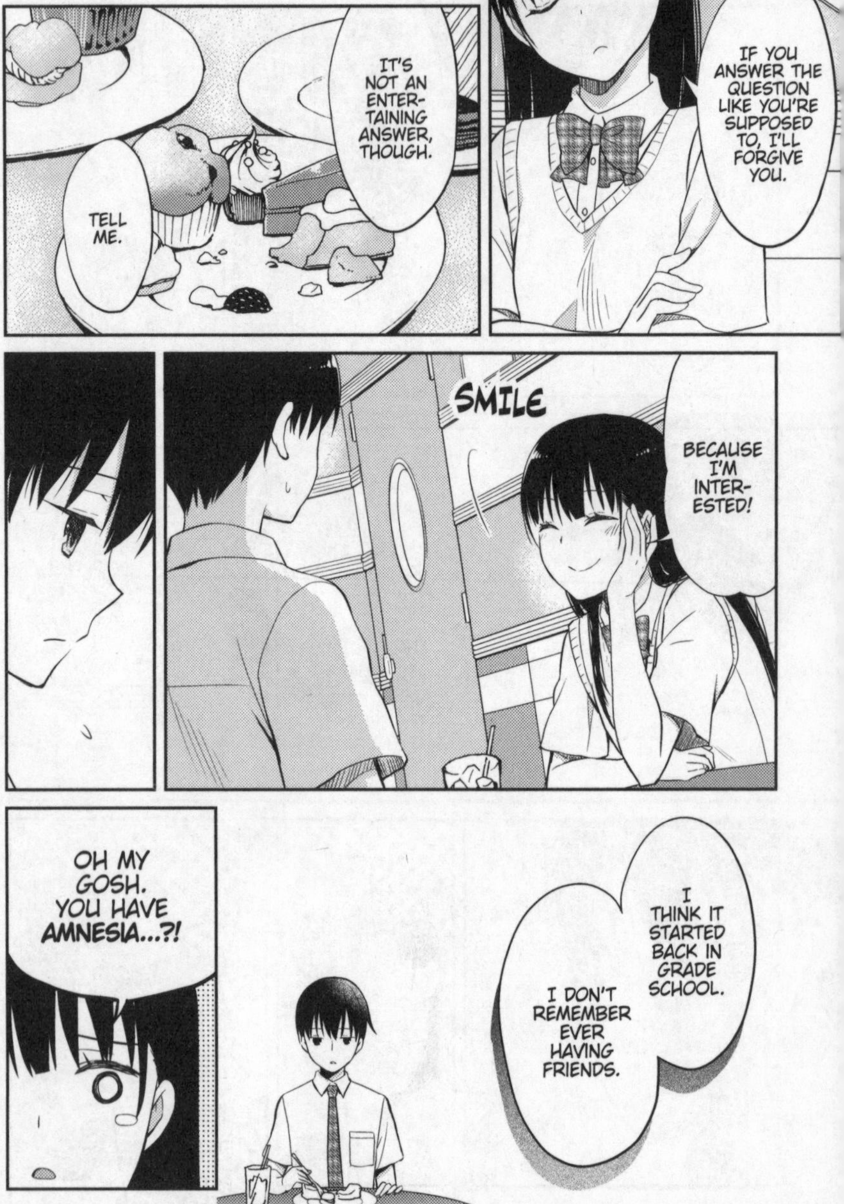
IF YOU ANSWER THE QUESTION LIKE YOU'RE SUPPOSED TO, I'LL FORGIVE YOU.
IT'S NOT AN ENTER-TAINING ANSWER, THOUGH.
TELL ME.
SMILE
BECAUSE I'M INTER-ESTED!
I THINK IT STARTED BACK IN GRADE SCHOOL.
I DON'T REMEMBER EVER HAVING FRIENDS.
OH MY GOSH. YOU HAVE AMNESIA...?!

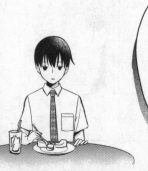

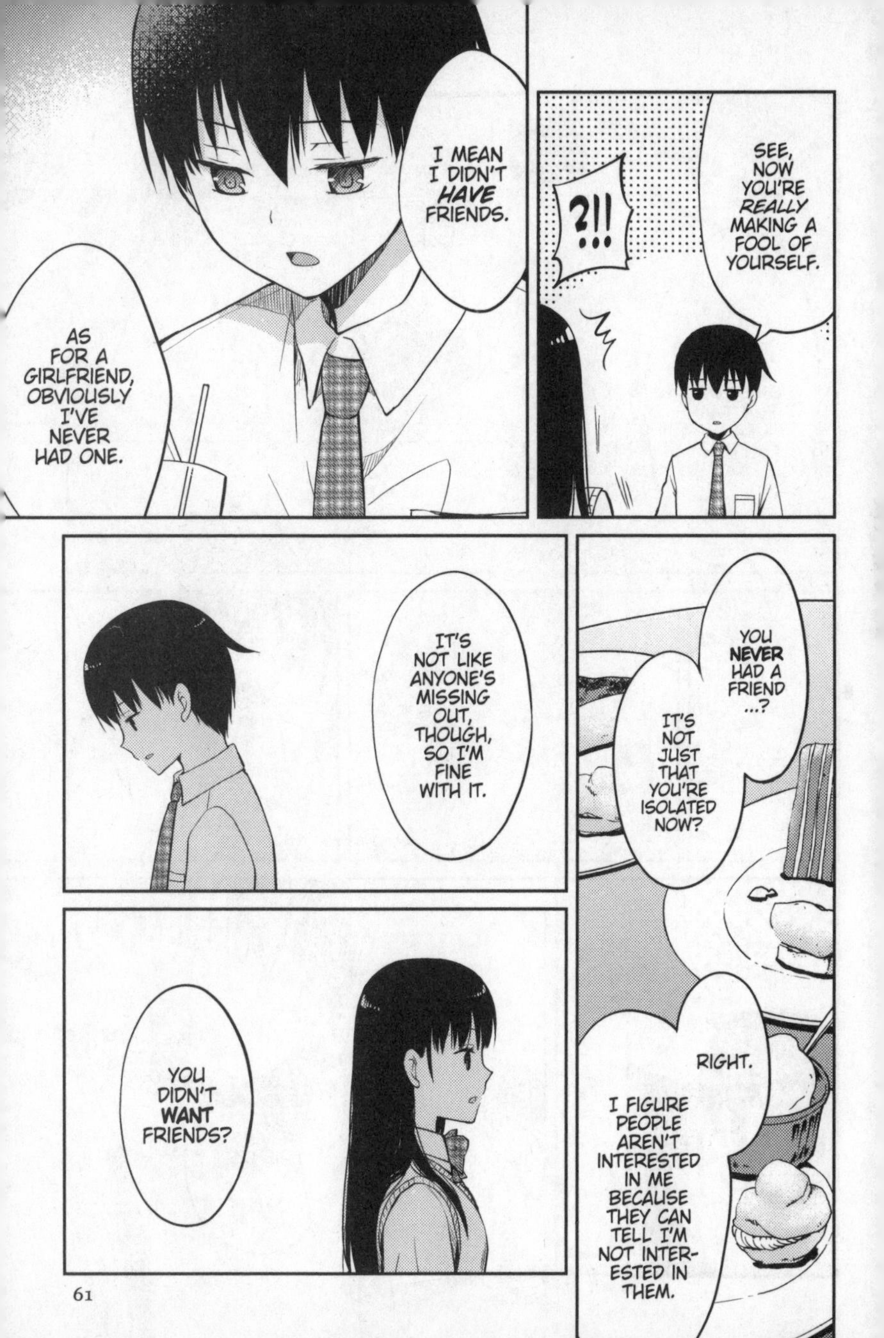
I MEAN I DIDN'T *HAVE* FRIENDS.
AS FOR A GIRLFRIEND, OBVIOUSLY I'VE NEVER HAD ONE.
SEE, NOW YOU'RE *REALLY* MAKING A FOOL OF YOURSELF.
?!!
YOU **NEVER** HAD A FRIEND ...?
IT'S NOT JUST THAT YOU'RE ISOLATED NOW?
RIGHT.
I FIGURE PEOPLE AREN'T INTERESTED IN ME BECAUSE THEY CAN TELL I'M NOT INTER-ESTED IN THEM.
IT'S NOT LIKE ANYONE'S MISSING OUT, THOUGH, SO I'M FINE WITH IT.
YOU DIDN'T **WANT** FRIENDS?

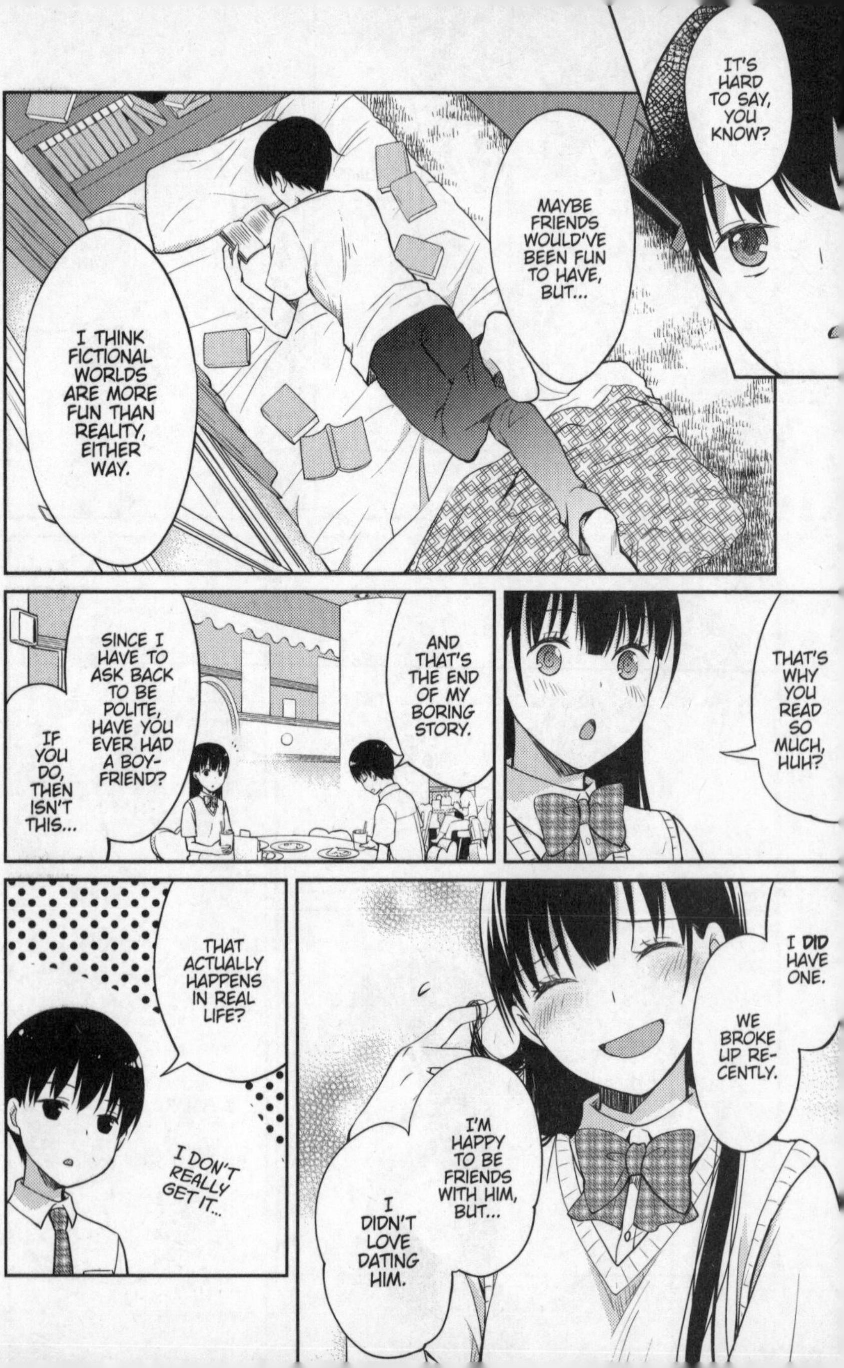
IT'S HARD TO SAY, YOU KNOW?
MAYBE FRIENDS WOULD'VE BEEN FUN TO HAVE, BUT...
I THINK FICTIONAL WORLDS ARE MORE FUN THAN REALITY, EITHER WAY.
THAT'S WHY YOU READ SO MUCH, HUH?
AND THAT'S THE END OF MY BORING STORY.
SINCE I HAVE TO ASK BACK TO BE POLITE, HAVE YOU EVER HAD A BOY-FRIEND?
IF YOU DO, THEN ISN'T THIS...
I DID HAVE ONE.
WE BROKE UP RE-CENTLY.
I'M HAPPY TO BE FRIENDS WITH HIM, BUT...
I DIDN'T LOVE DATING HIM.
THAT ACTUALLY HAPPENS IN REAL LIFE?
I DON'T REALLY GET IT...

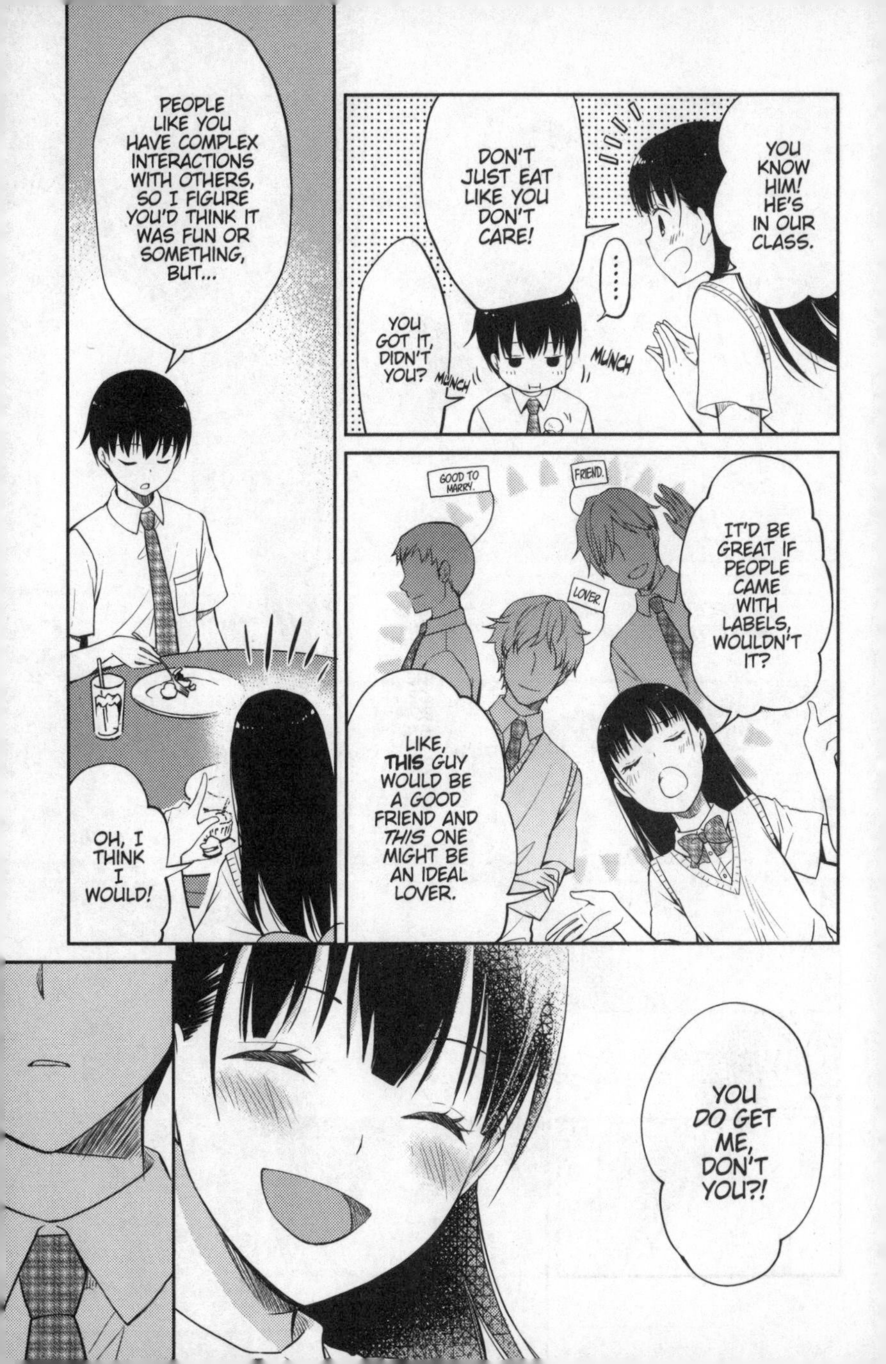
YOU KNOW HIM! HE'S IN OUR CLASS.
......
DON'T JUST EAT LIKE YOU DON'T CARE!
MUNCH
YOU GOT IT, DIDN'T YOU?
MUNCH
IT'D BE GREAT IF PEOPLE CAME WITH LABELS, WOULDN'T IT?
FRIEND.
GOOD TO MARRY.
LOVER.
LIKE, **THIS** GUY WOULD BE A GOOD FRIEND AND *THIS* ONE MIGHT BE AN IDEAL LOVER.
PEOPLE LIKE YOU HAVE COMPLEX INTERACTIONS WITH OTHERS, SO I FIGURE YOU'D THINK IT WAS FUN OR SOMETHING, BUT...
OH, I THINK I WOULD!
YOU DO GET ME, DON'T YOU?!

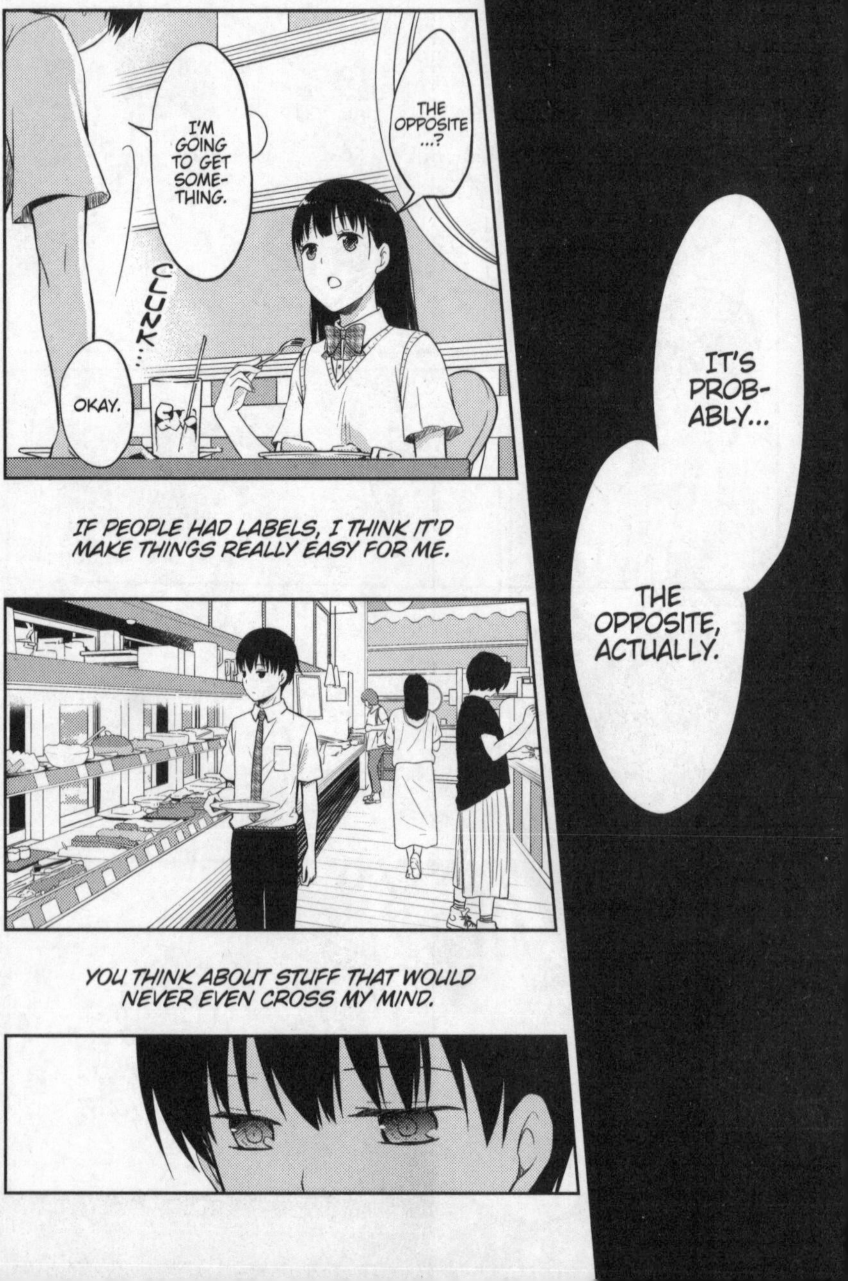
THE OPPOSITE ...?
I'M GOING TO GET SOME-THING.
CLUNK...
OKAY.
IT'S PROB-ABLY...
THE OPPOSITE, ACTUALLY.
IF PEOPLE HAD LABELS, I THINK IT'D MAKE THINGS REALLY EASY FOR ME.
YOU THINK ABOUT STUFF THAT WOULD NEVER EVEN CROSS MY MIND.

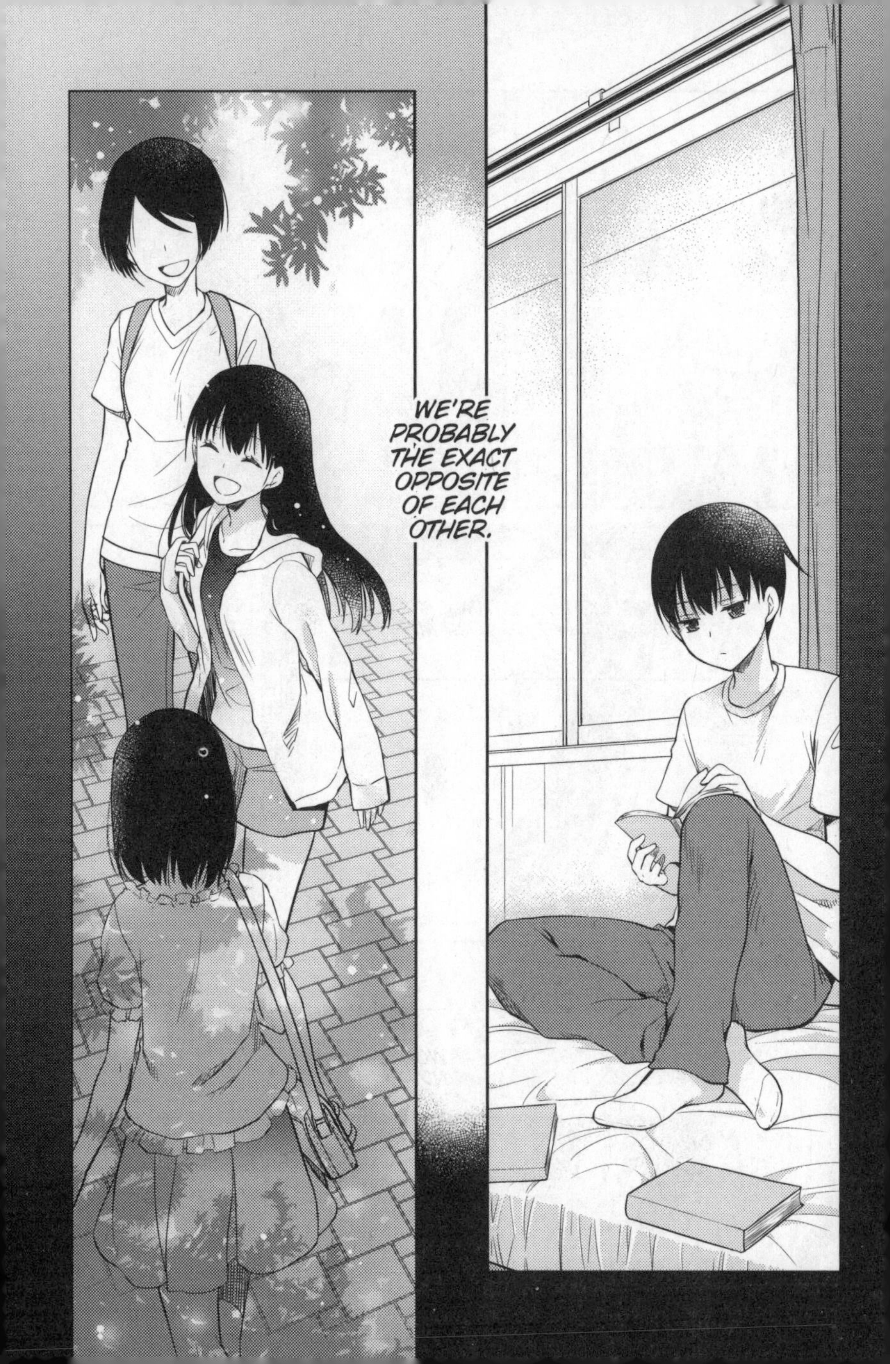
WE'RE PROBABLY THE EXACT OPPOSITE OF EACH OTHER.

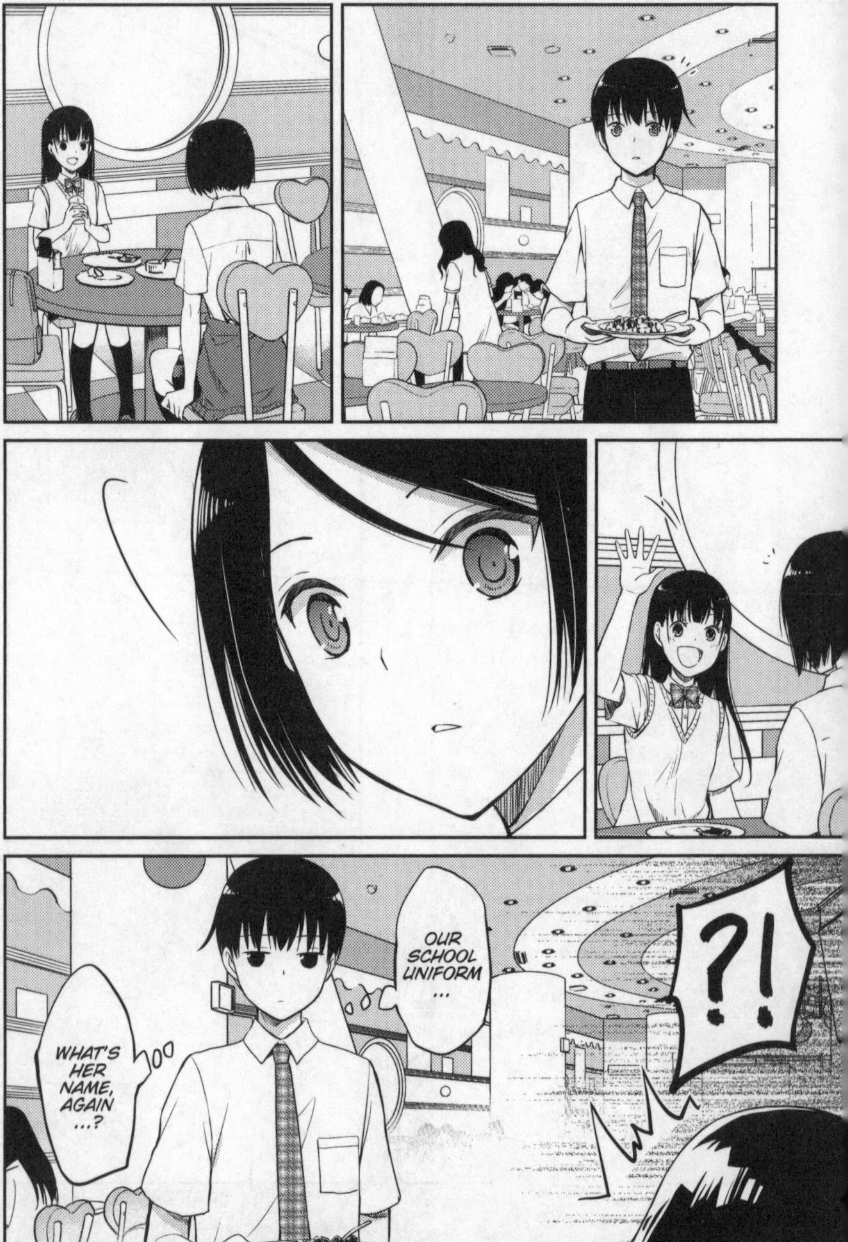

?!
OUR SCHOOL UNIFORM ...
WHAT'S HER NAME, AGAIN ...?

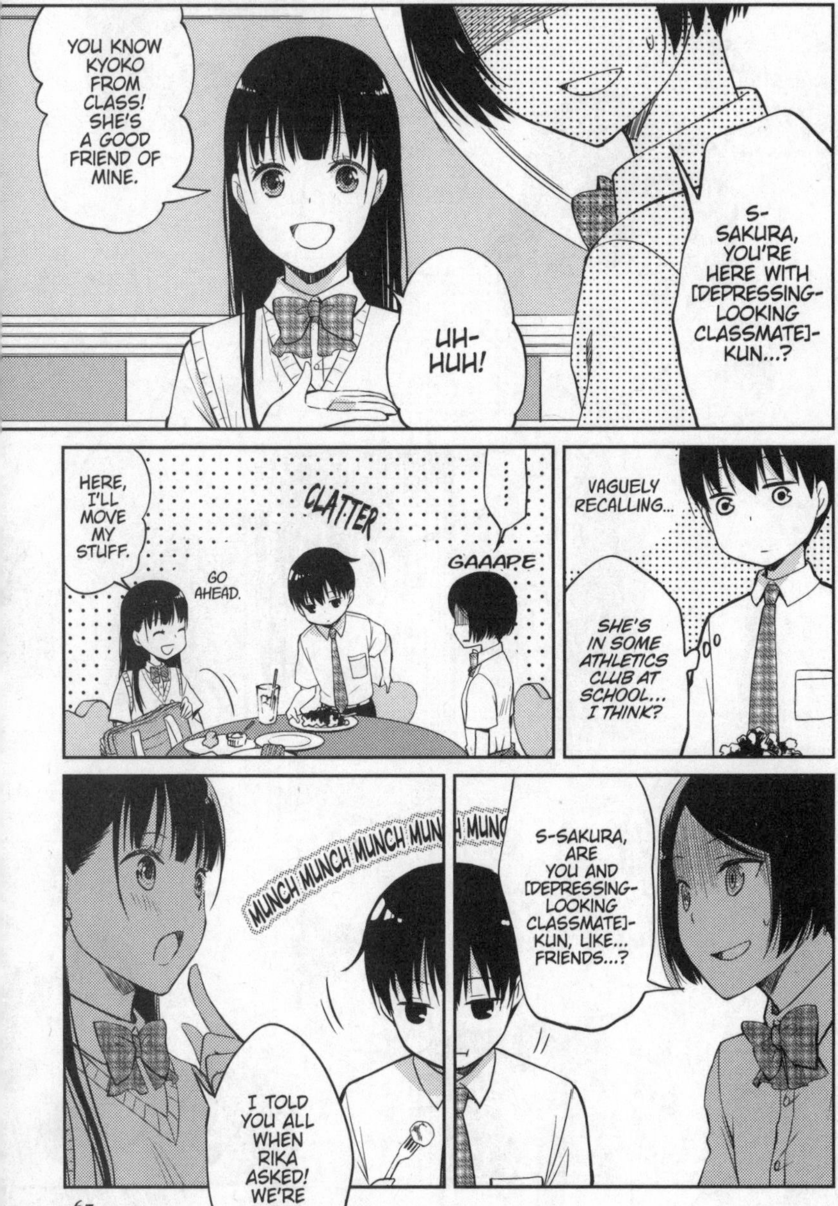

S-SAKURA, YOU'RE HERE WITH [DEPRESSING-LOOKING CLASSMATE]-KUN...?
UH-HUH!
YOU KNOW KYOKO FROM CLASS! SHE'S A GOOD FRIEND OF MINE.
VAGUELY RECALLING...
SHE'S IN SOME ATHLETICS CLUB AT SCHOOL... I THINK?
......
GAAAPE
CLATTER
HERE, I'LL MOVE MY STUFF.
GO AHEAD.
S-SAKURA, ARE YOU AND [DEPRESSING-LOOKING CLASSMATE]-KUN, LIKE... FRIENDS...?
MUNCH MUNCH MUNCH MUN H MUNC
I TOLD YOU ALL WHEN RIKA ASKED! WE'RE CLOSE.

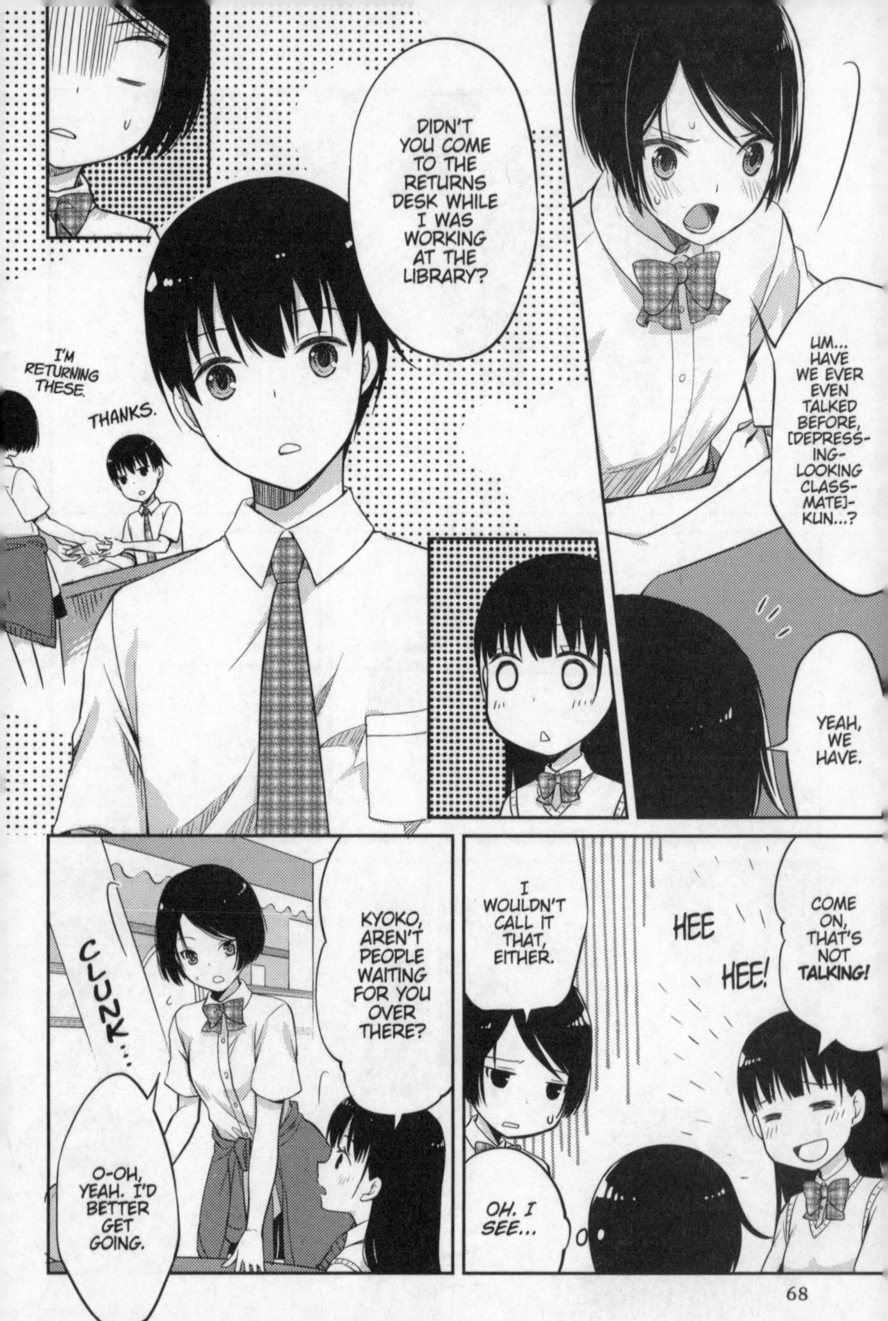
UM... HAVE WE EVER EVEN TALKED BEFORE, [DEPRESSING-LOOKING CLASSMATE]-KUN...?
YEAH, WE HAVE.
DIDN'T YOU COME TO THE RETURNS DESK WHILE I WAS WORKING AT THE LIBRARY?
I'M RETURNING THESE.
THANKS.
COME ON, THAT'S NOT TALKING!
HEE HEE!
I WOULDN'T CALL IT THAT, EITHER.
OH. I SEE...
KYOKO, AREN'T PEOPLE WAITING FOR YOU OVER THERE?
CLUNK...
O-OH, YEAH. I'D BETTER GET GOING.

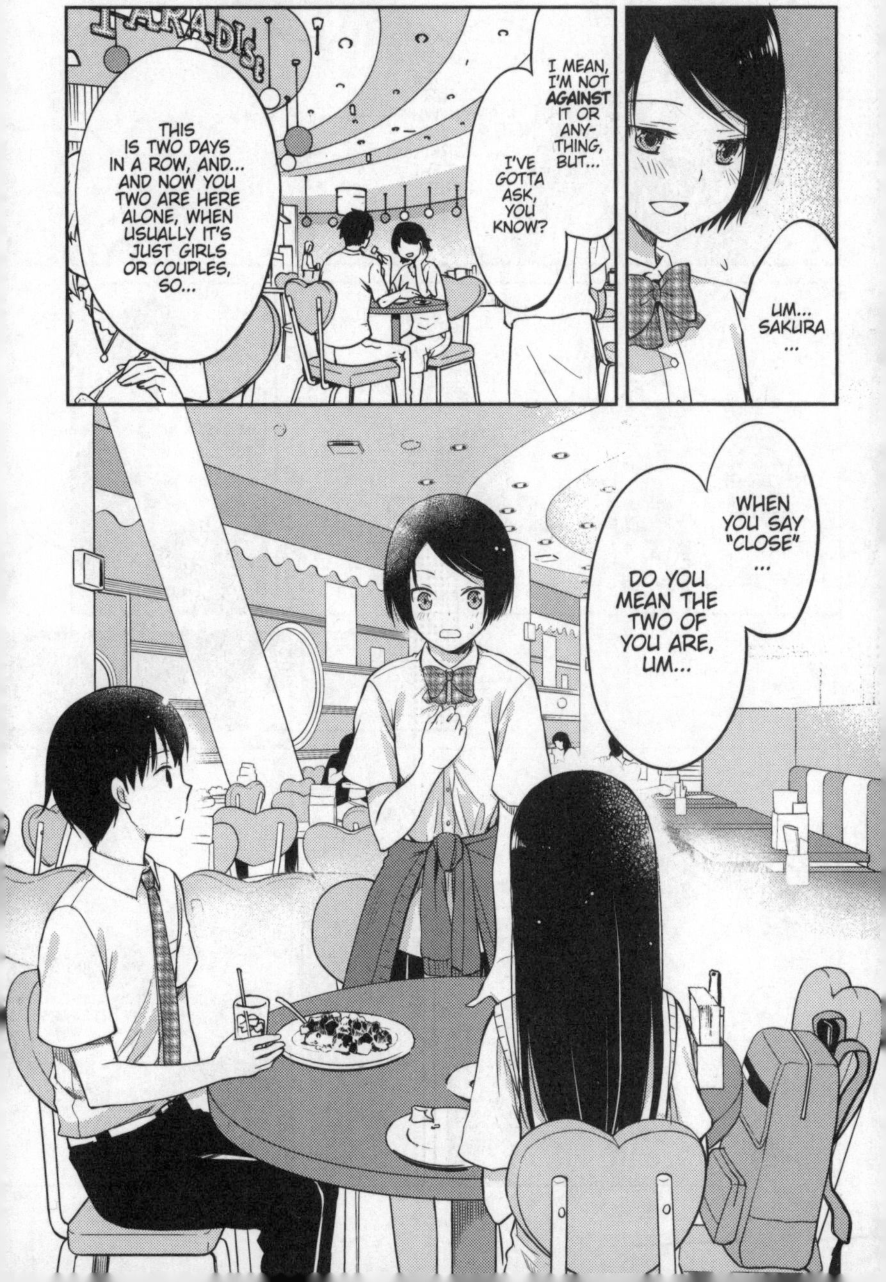
UM... SAKURA ...
I MEAN, I'M NOT **AGAINST** IT OR ANY-THING, BUT...
I'VE GOTTA ASK, YOU KNOW?
THIS IS TWO DAYS IN A ROW, AND... AND NOW YOU TWO ARE HERE ALONE, WHEN USUALLY IT'S JUST GIRLS OR COUPLES, SO...
WHEN YOU SAY "CLOSE" ...
DO YOU MEAN THE TWO OF YOU ARE, UM...

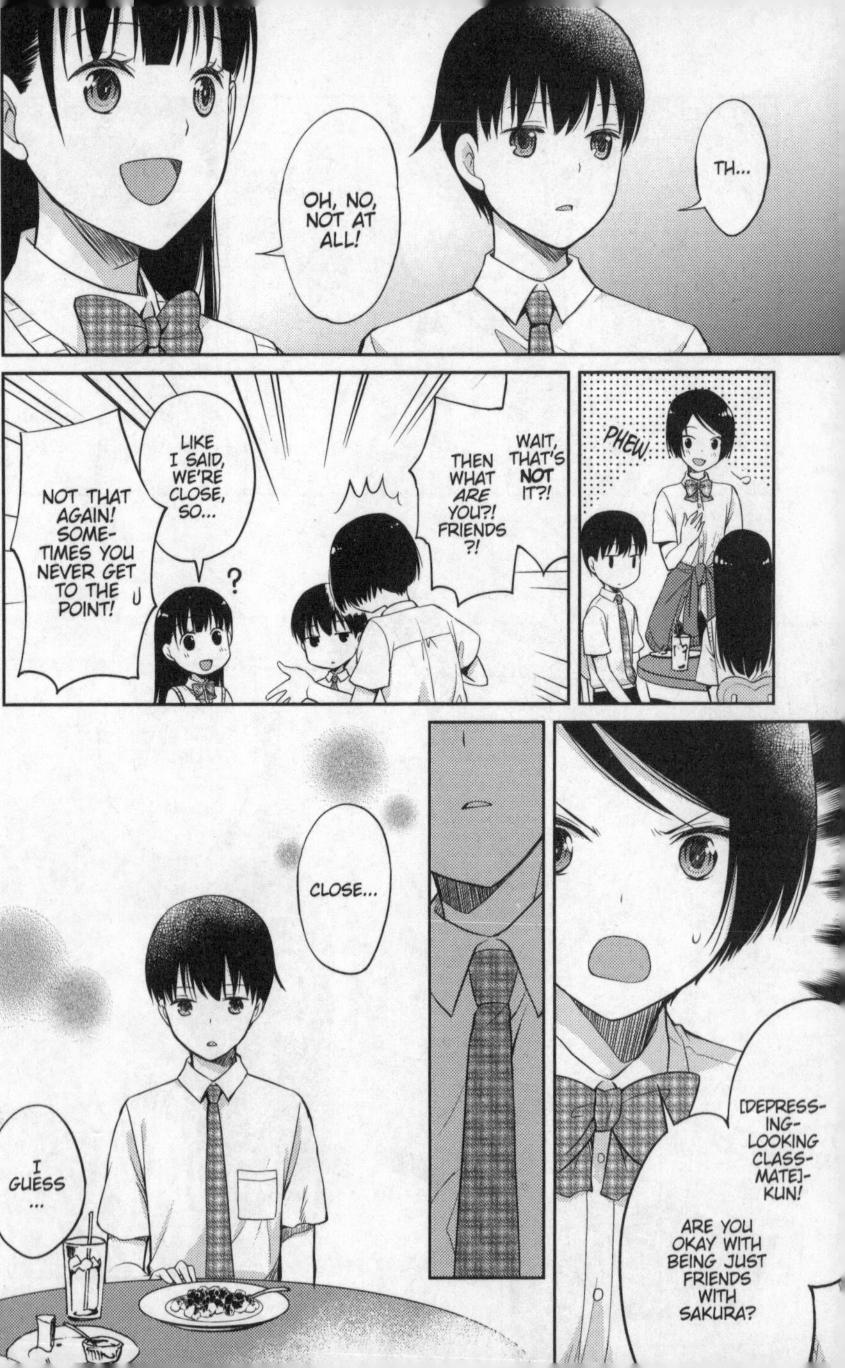
TH...
OH, NO, NOT AT ALL!
PHEW.
WAIT, THAT'S NOT IT?!
THEN WHAT ARE YOU?! FRIENDS?!
LIKE I SAID, WE'RE CLOSE, SO...
NOT THAT AGAIN! SOMETIMES YOU NEVER GET TO THE POINT!
[DEPRESSING-LOOKING CLASSMATE]-KUN!
ARE YOU OKAY WITH BEING JUST FRIENDS WITH SAKURA?
CLOSE...
I GUESS...

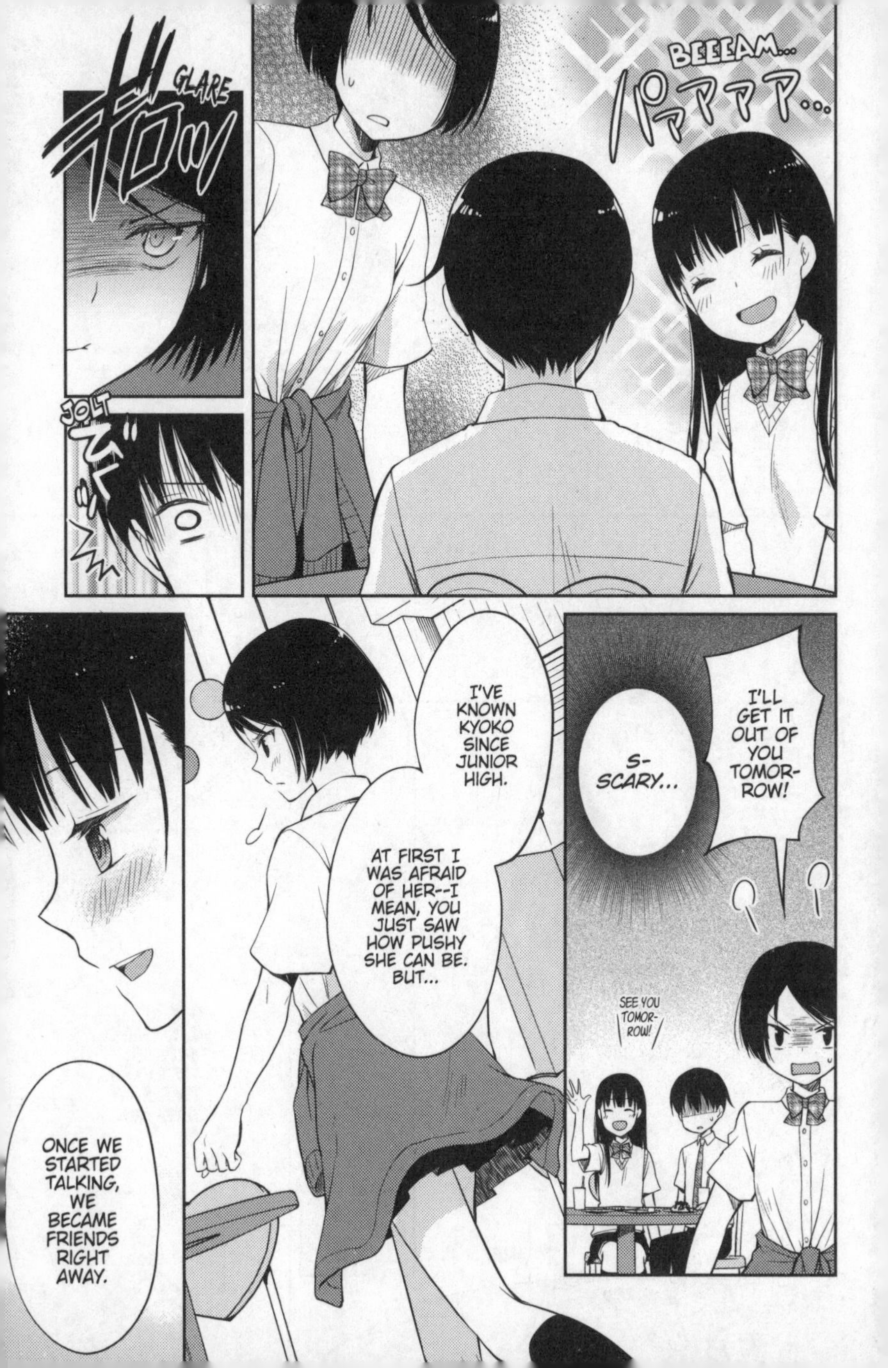
BEEEAM...
パァァァア…
GLARE
ギロッ
JOLT
I'LL GET IT OUT OF YOU TOMORROW!
S-SCARY...
SEE YOU TOMORROW!
I'VE KNOWN KYOKO SINCE JUNIOR HIGH.
AT FIRST I WAS AFRAID OF HER--I MEAN, YOU JUST SAW HOW PUSHY SHE CAN BE. BUT...
ONCE WE STARTED TALKING, WE BECAME FRIENDS RIGHT AWAY.

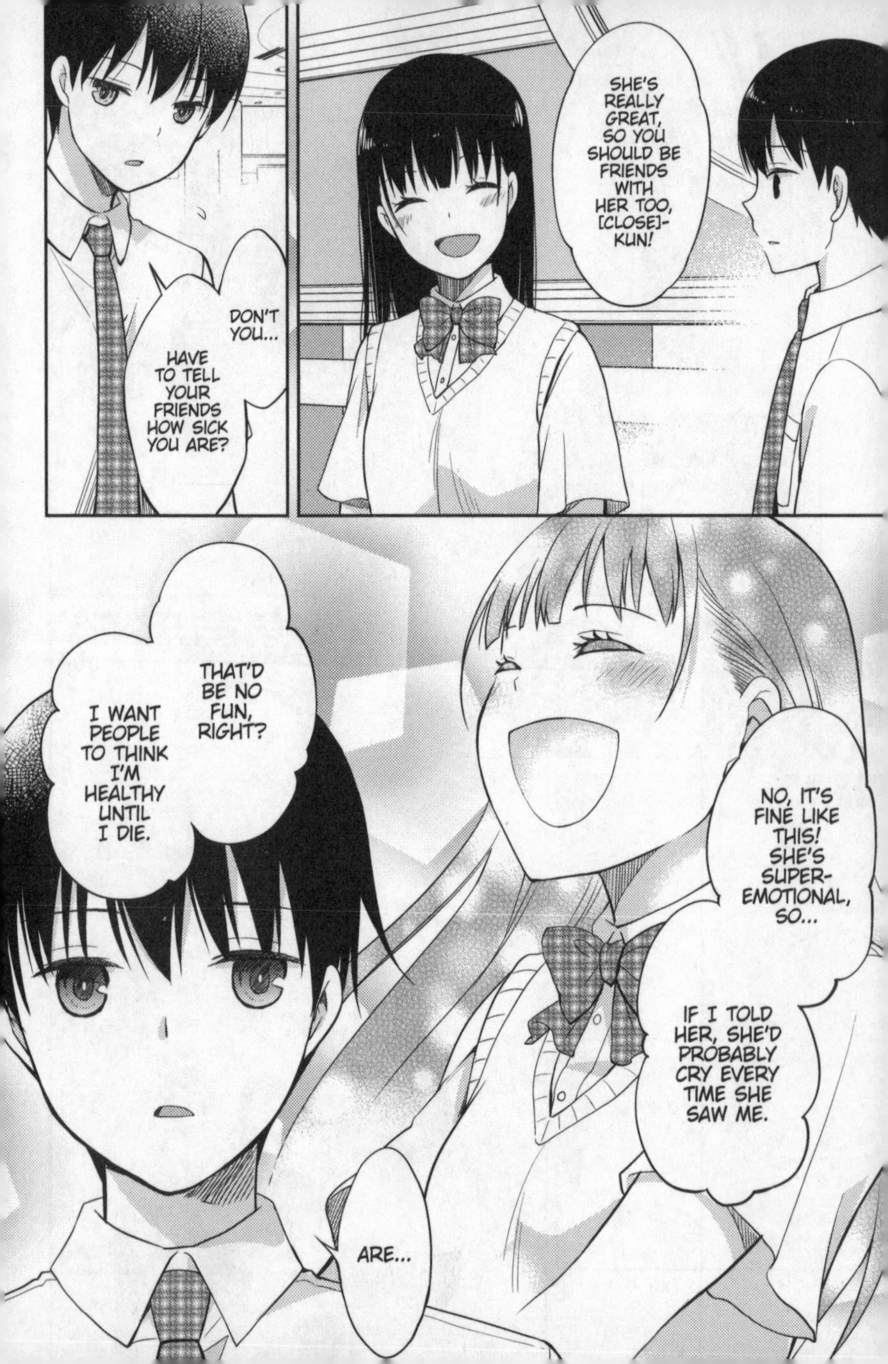
SHE'S REALLY GREAT, SO YOU SHOULD BE FRIENDS WITH HER TOO, [CLOSE]-KUN!
DON'T YOU...
HAVE TO TELL YOUR FRIENDS HOW SICK YOU ARE?
NO, IT'S FINE LIKE THIS! SHE'S SUPER-EMOTIONAL, SO...
IF I TOLD HER, SHE'D PROBABLY CRY EVERY TIME SHE SAW ME.
THAT'D BE NO FUN, RIGHT?
I WANT PEOPLE TO THINK I'M HEALTHY UNTIL I DIE.
ARE...

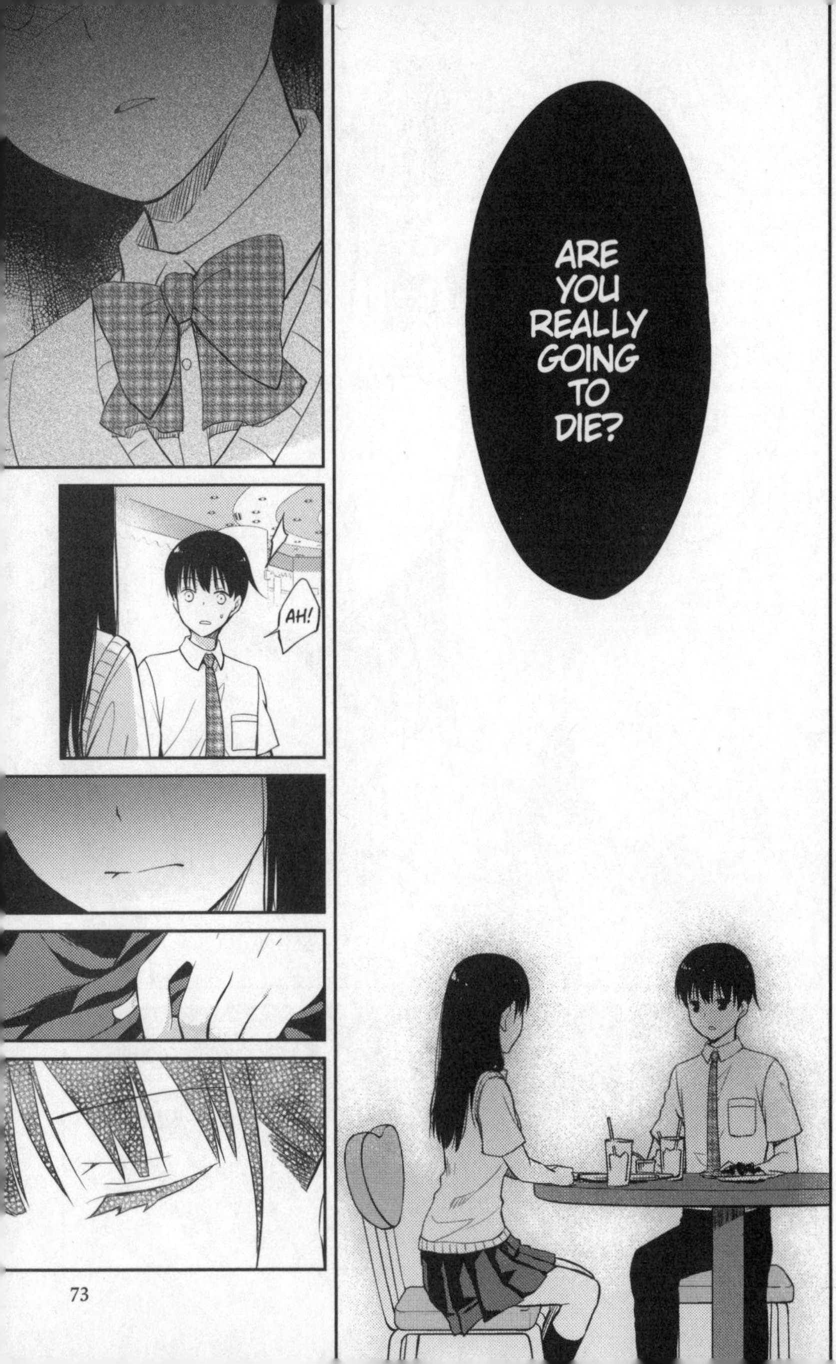
ARE YOU REALLY GOING TO DIE?
AH!

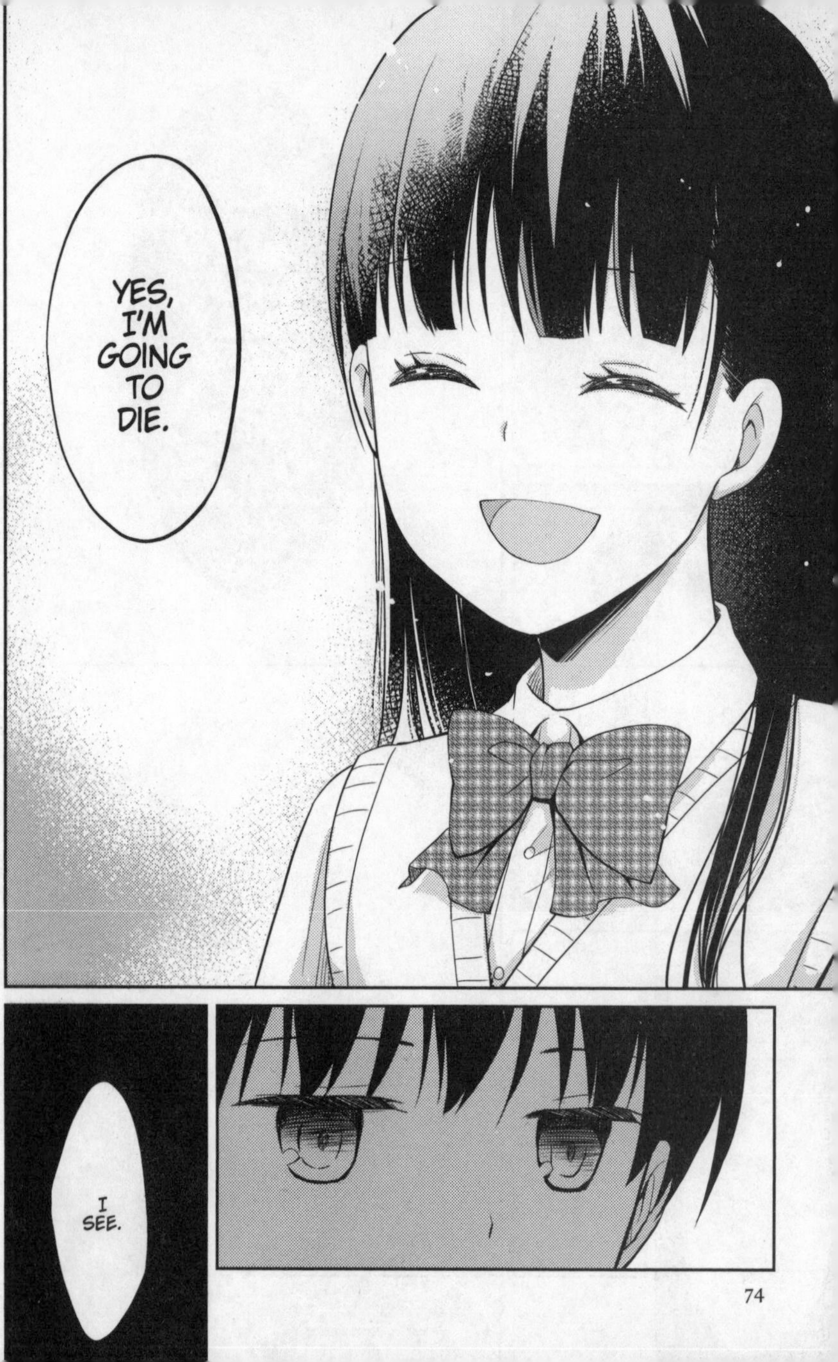
YES, I'M GOING TO DIE.
I SEE.

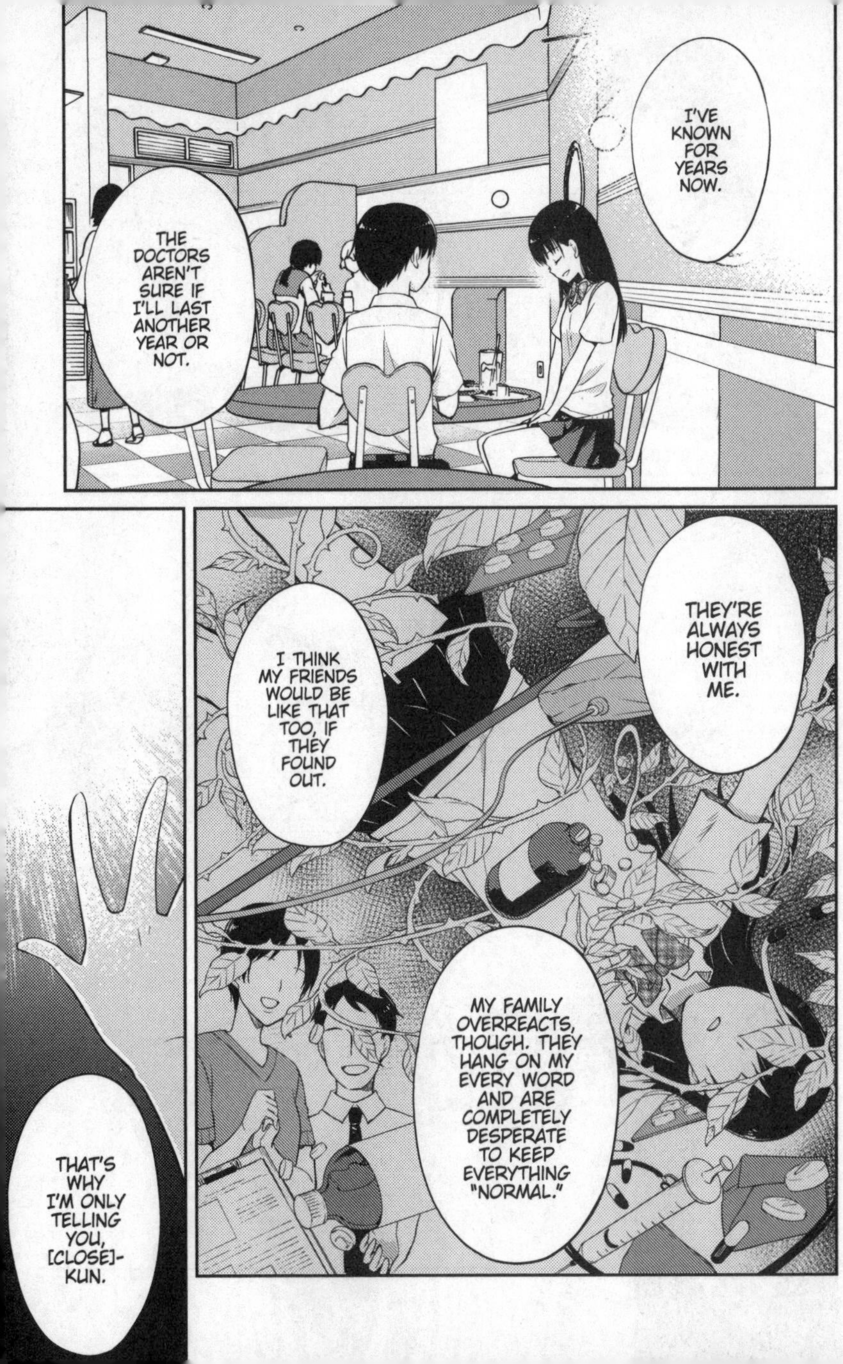
I'VE KNOWN FOR YEARS NOW.
THE DOCTORS AREN'T SURE IF I'LL LAST ANOTHER YEAR OR NOT.
THEY'RE ALWAYS HONEST WITH ME.
I THINK MY FRIENDS WOULD BE LIKE THAT TOO, IF THEY FOUND OUT.
MY FAMILY OVERREACTS, THOUGH. THEY HANG ON MY EVERY WORD AND ARE COMPLETELY DESPERATE TO KEEP EVERYTHING "NORMAL."
THAT'S WHY I'M ONLY TELLING YOU, [CLOSE]-KUN.

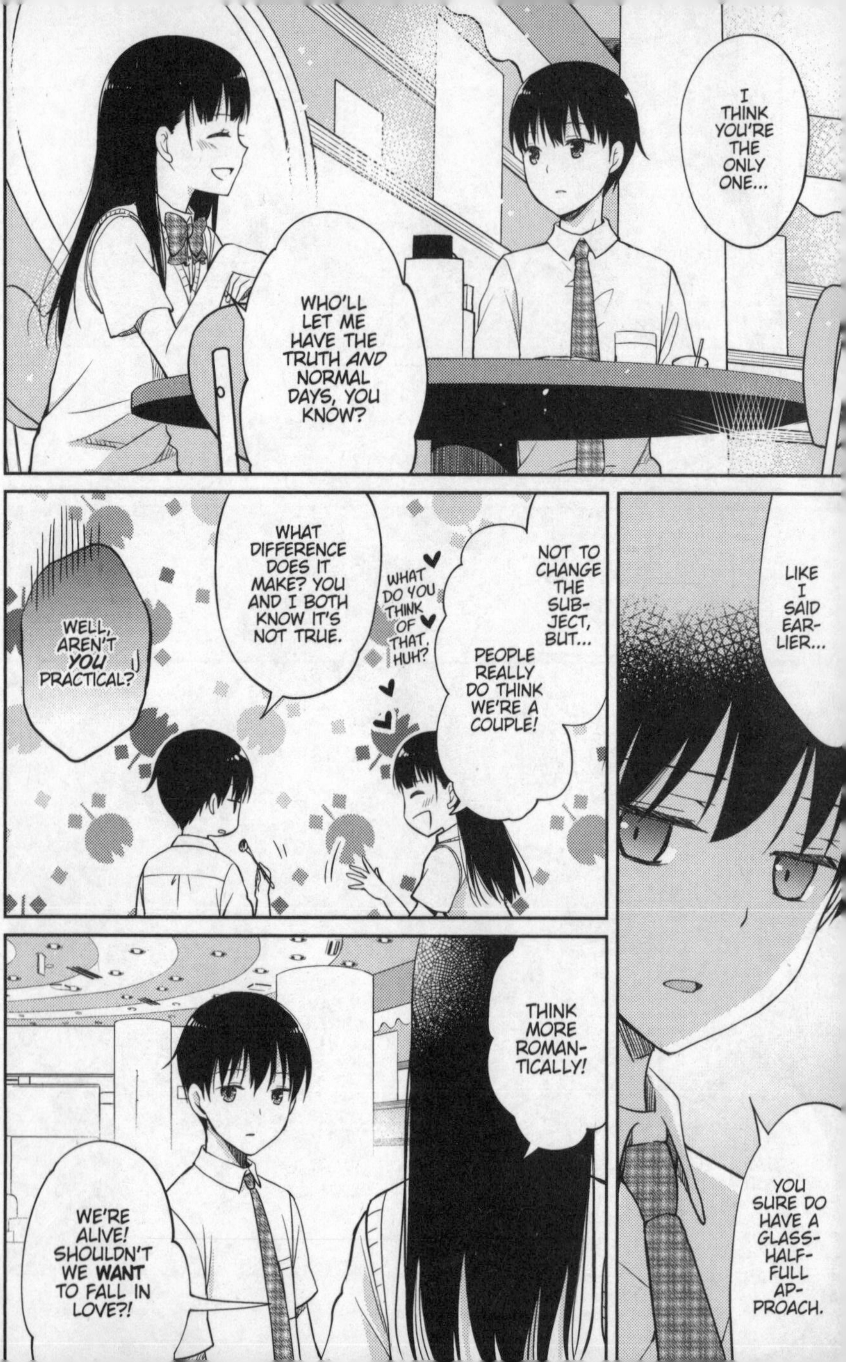
I THINK YOU'RE THE ONLY ONE...
WHO'LL LET ME HAVE THE TRUTH *AND* NORMAL DAYS, YOU KNOW?
LIKE I SAID EARLIER...
YOU SURE DO HAVE A GLASS-HALF-FULL APPROACH.
NOT TO CHANGE THE SUBJECT, BUT...
PEOPLE REALLY DO THINK WE'RE A COUPLE!
WHAT DO YOU THINK OF THAT, HUH?
WHAT DIFFERENCE DOES IT MAKE? YOU AND I BOTH KNOW IT'S NOT TRUE.
WELL, AREN'T ***YOU*** PRACTICAL?
THINK MORE ROMANTICALLY!
WE'RE ALIVE! SHOULDN'T WE **WANT** TO FALL IN LOVE?!

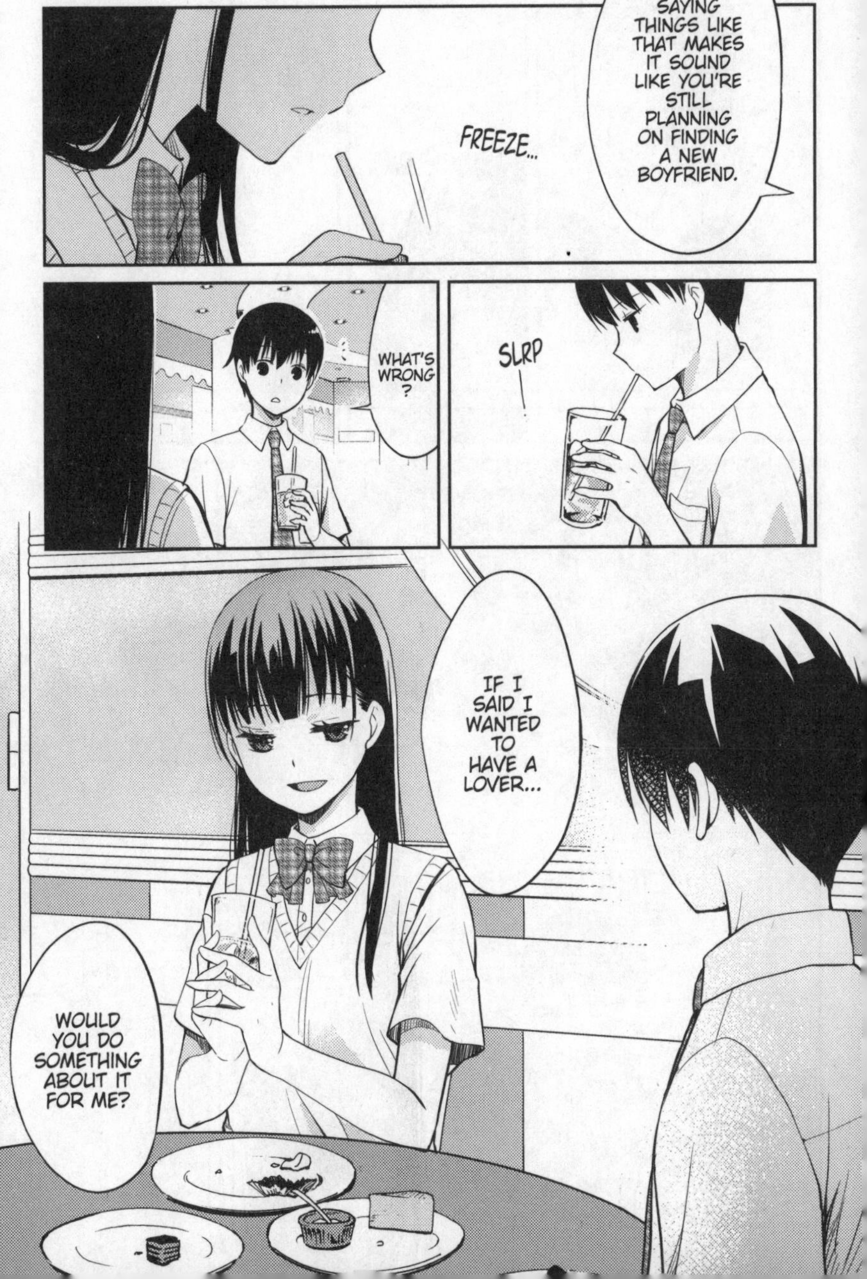
SAYING THINGS LIKE THAT MAKES IT SOUND LIKE YOU'RE STILL PLANNING ON FINDING A NEW BOYFRIEND.
FREEZE...
SLRP
WHAT'S WRONG?
IF I SAID I WANTED TO HAVE A LOVER...
WOULD YOU DO SOMETHING ABOUT IT FOR ME?

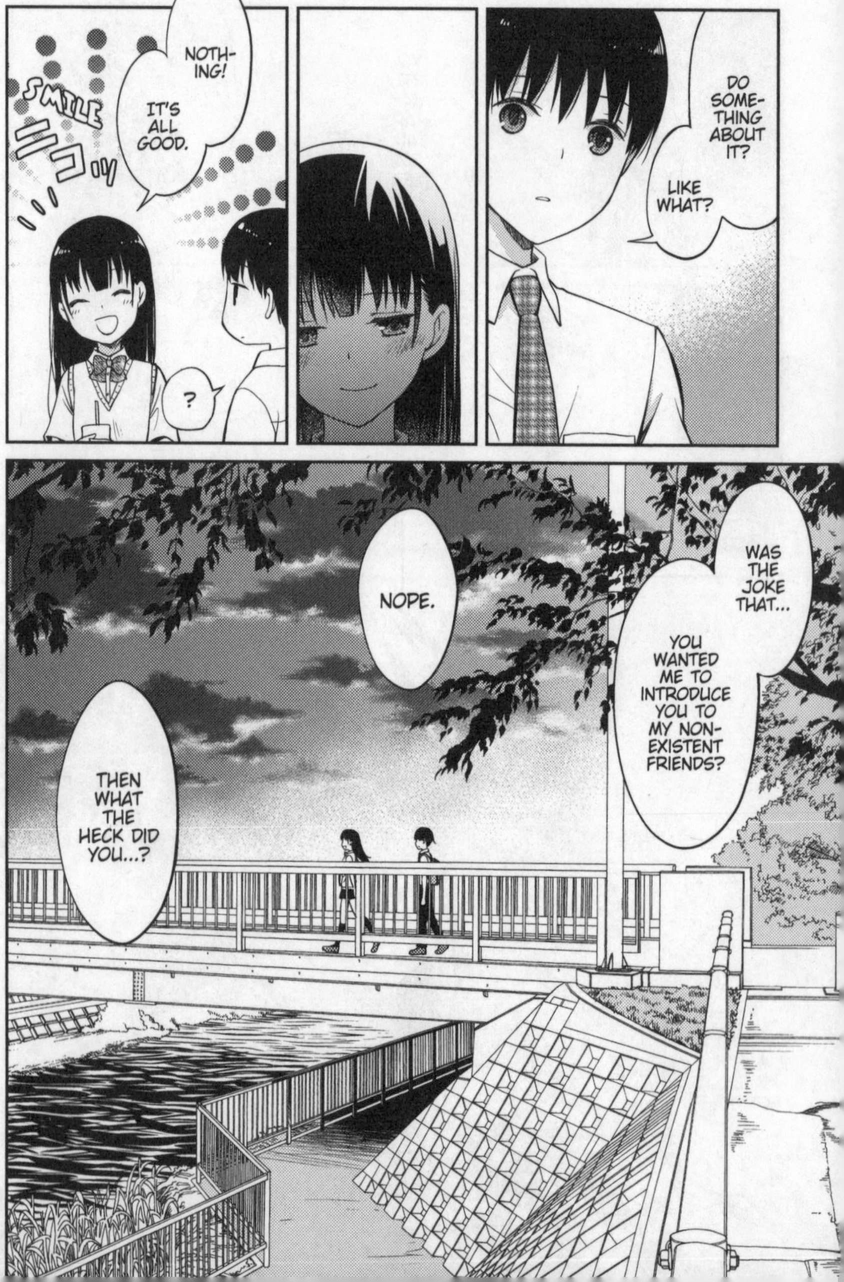
DO SOMETHING ABOUT IT?
LIKE WHAT?
NOTHING! IT'S ALL GOOD.
SMILE
ニコッ
?
WAS THE JOKE THAT...
YOU WANTED ME TO INTRODUCE YOU TO MY NON-EXISTENT FRIENDS?
NOPE.
THEN WHAT THE HECK DID YOU...?

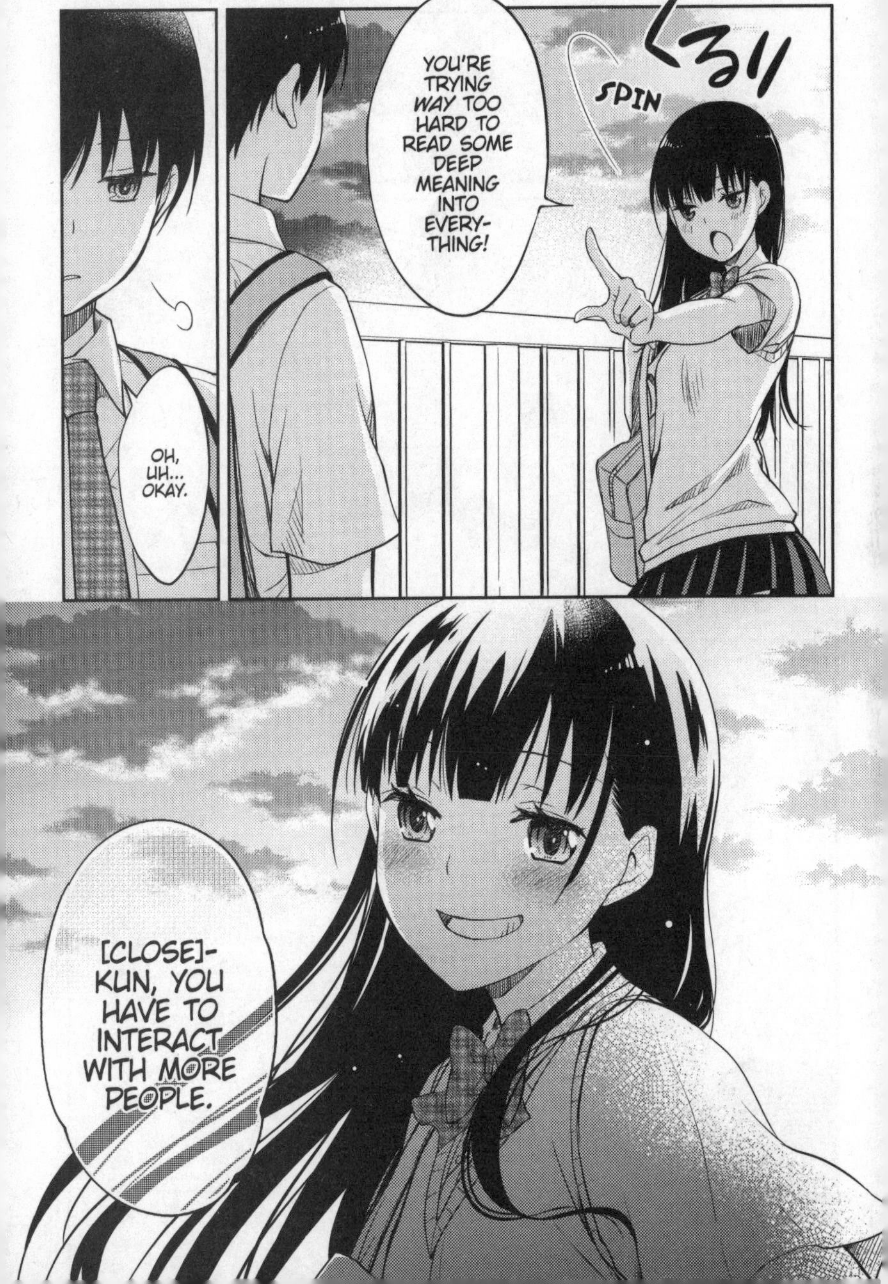
くるり
SPIN
YOU'RE TRYING WAY TOO HARD TO READ SOME DEEP MEANING INTO EVERY-THING!
OH, UH... OKAY.
[CLOSE]-KUN, YOU HAVE TO INTERACT WITH MORE PEOPLE.

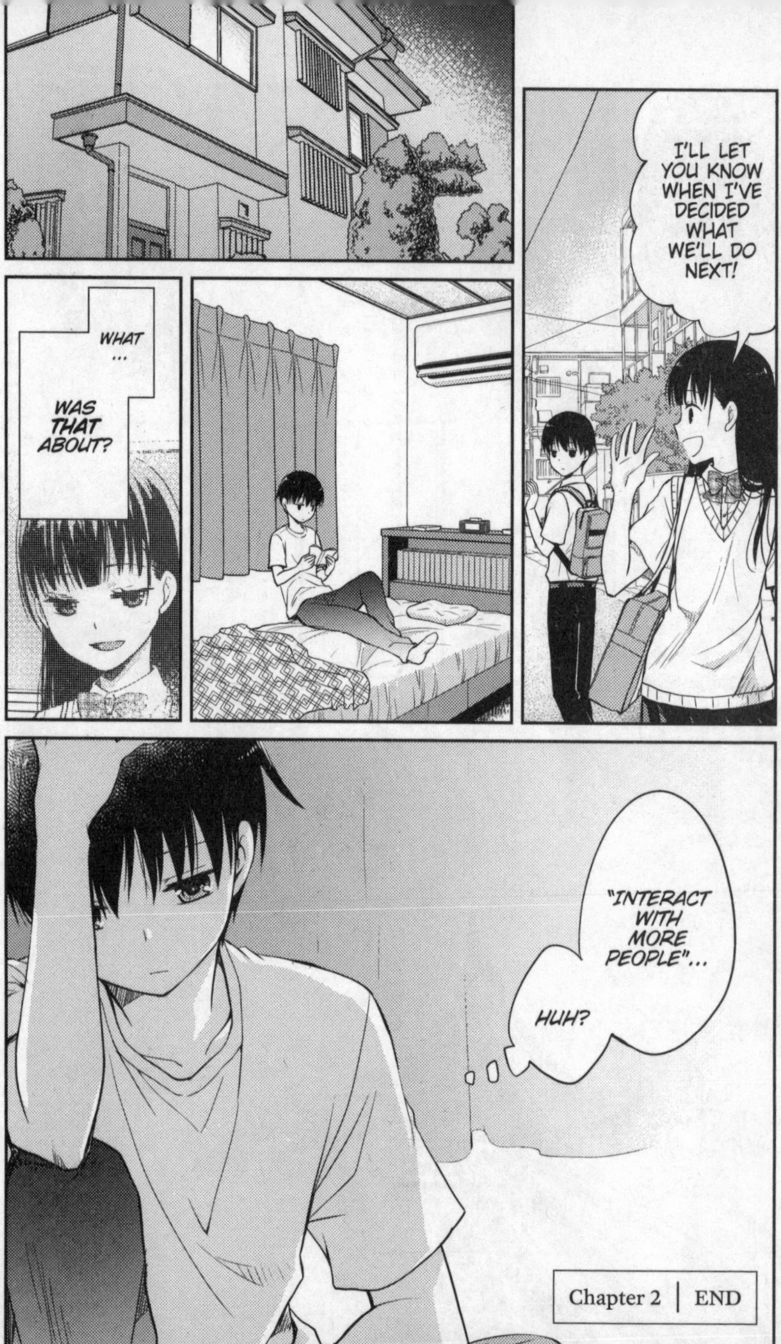
I'LL LET YOU KNOW WHEN I'VE DECIDED WHAT WE'LL DO NEXT!
WHAT ...
WAS THAT ABOUT?
"INTERACT WITH MORE PEOPLE"...
HUH?

Chapter 2 | END

Chapter 3 | Places I Want To Go Before I Die

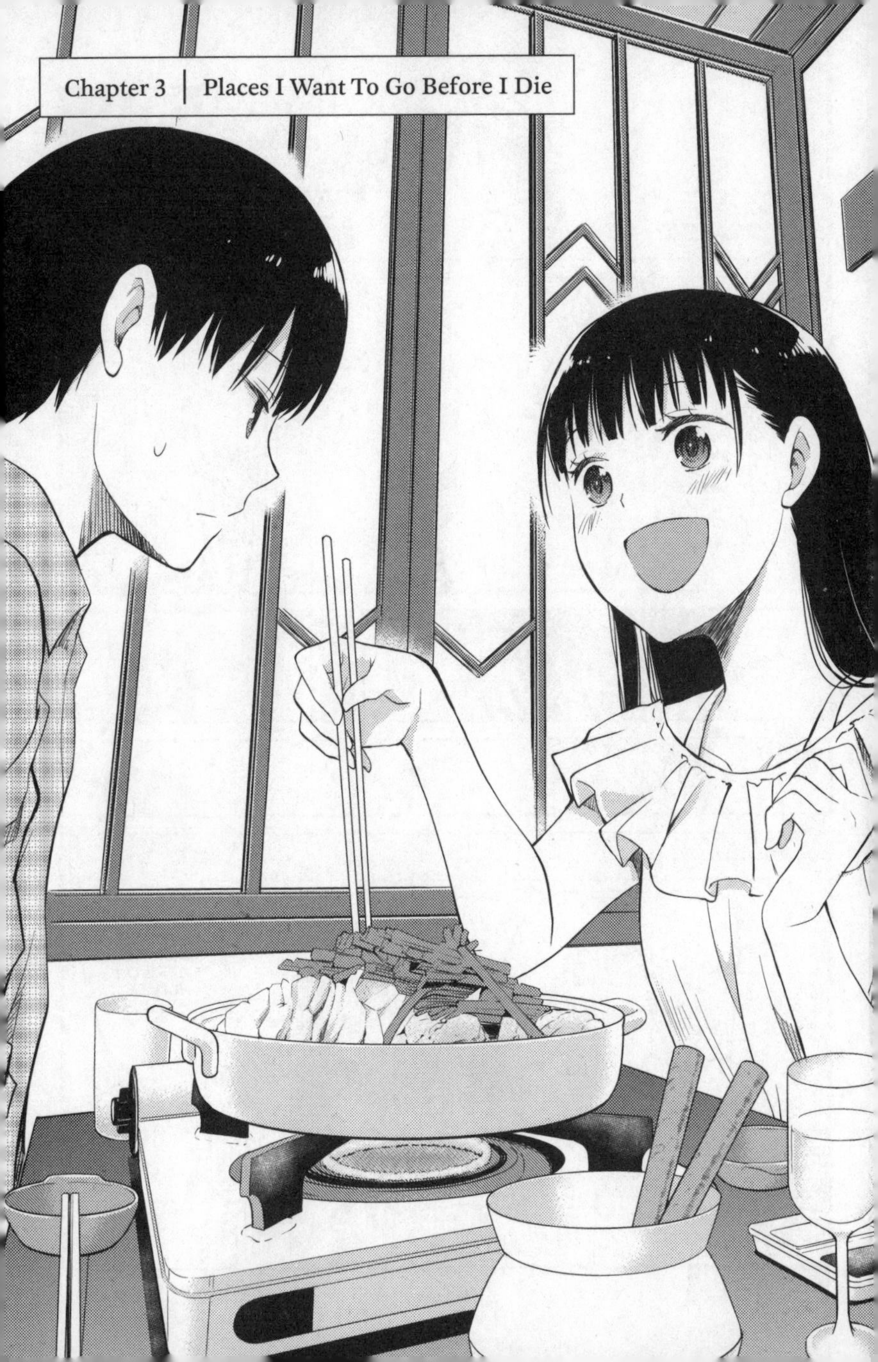

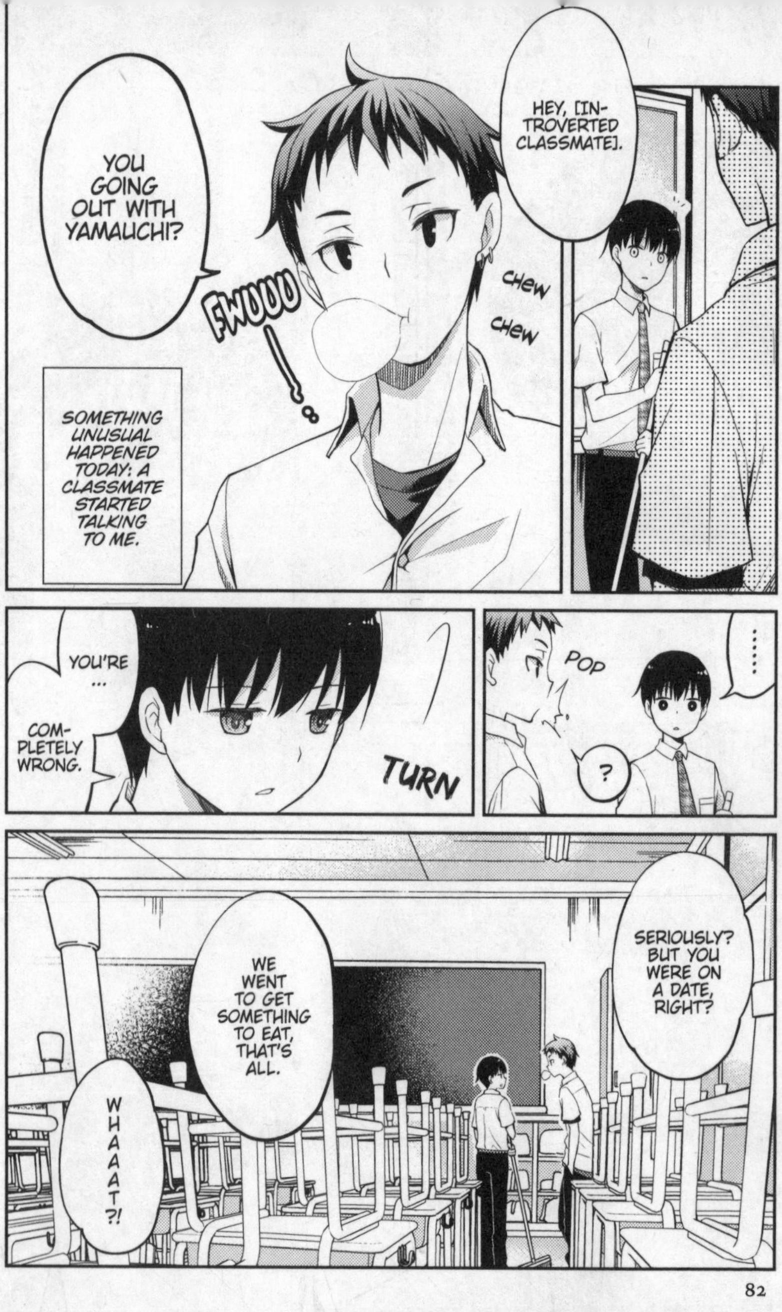
HEY, [IN-TROVERTED CLASSMATE].
YOU GOING OUT WITH YAMAUCHI?
CHEW CHEW
FWOOO
SOMETHING UNUSUAL HAPPENED TODAY: A CLASSMATE STARTED TALKING TO ME.
......
POP
?
TURN
YOU'RE ...
COM-PLETELY WRONG.
SERIOUSLY? BUT YOU WERE ON A DATE, RIGHT?
WE WENT TO GET SOMETHING TO EAT, THAT'S ALL.
WHAAAAT?!

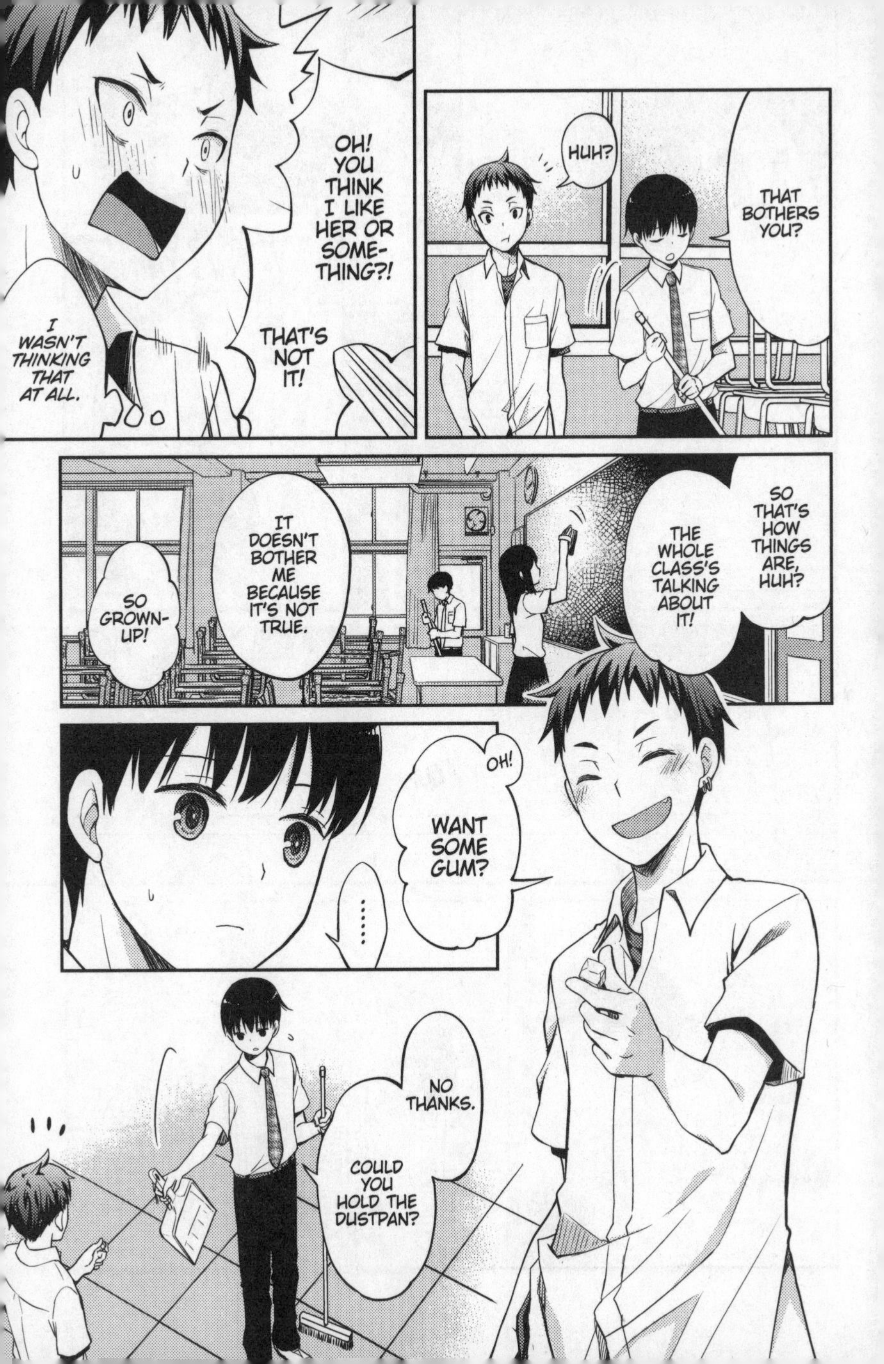
THAT BOTHERS YOU?
HUH?
OH! YOU THINK I LIKE HER OR SOME-THING?!
THAT'S NOT IT!
I WASN'T THINKING THAT AT ALL.
SO THAT'S HOW THINGS ARE, HUH?
THE WHOLE CLASS'S TALKING ABOUT IT!
IT DOESN'T BOTHER ME BECAUSE IT'S NOT TRUE.
SO GROWN-UP!
OH!
WANT SOME GUM?
......
NO THANKS.
COULD YOU HOLD THE DUSTPAN?

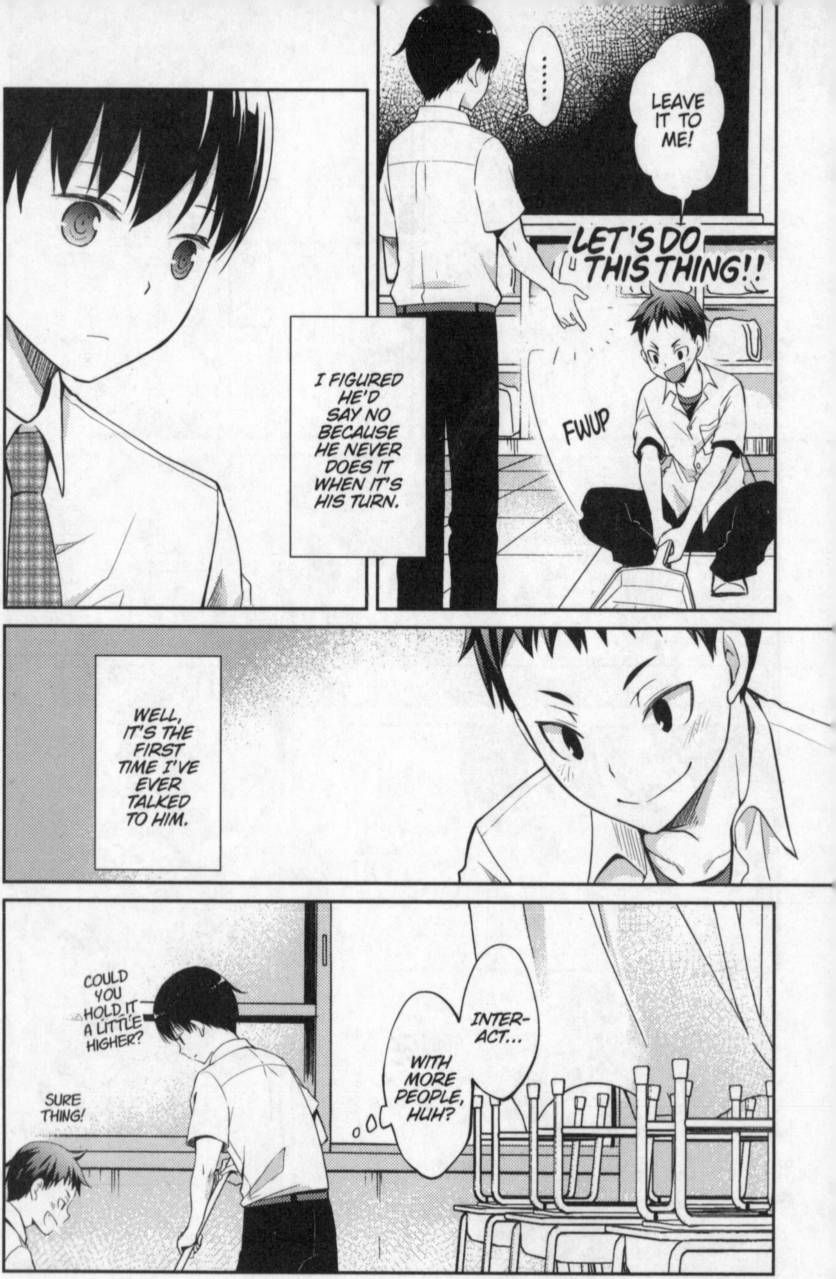
LEAVE IT TO ME!
LET'S DO THIS THING!!
......
FWUP
I FIGURED HE'D SAY NO BECAUSE HE NEVER DOES IT WHEN IT'S HIS TURN.
WELL, IT'S THE FIRST TIME I'VE EVER TALKED TO HIM.
INTER-ACT...
WITH MORE PEOPLE, HUH?
COULD YOU HOLD IT A LITTLE HIGHER?
SURE THING!

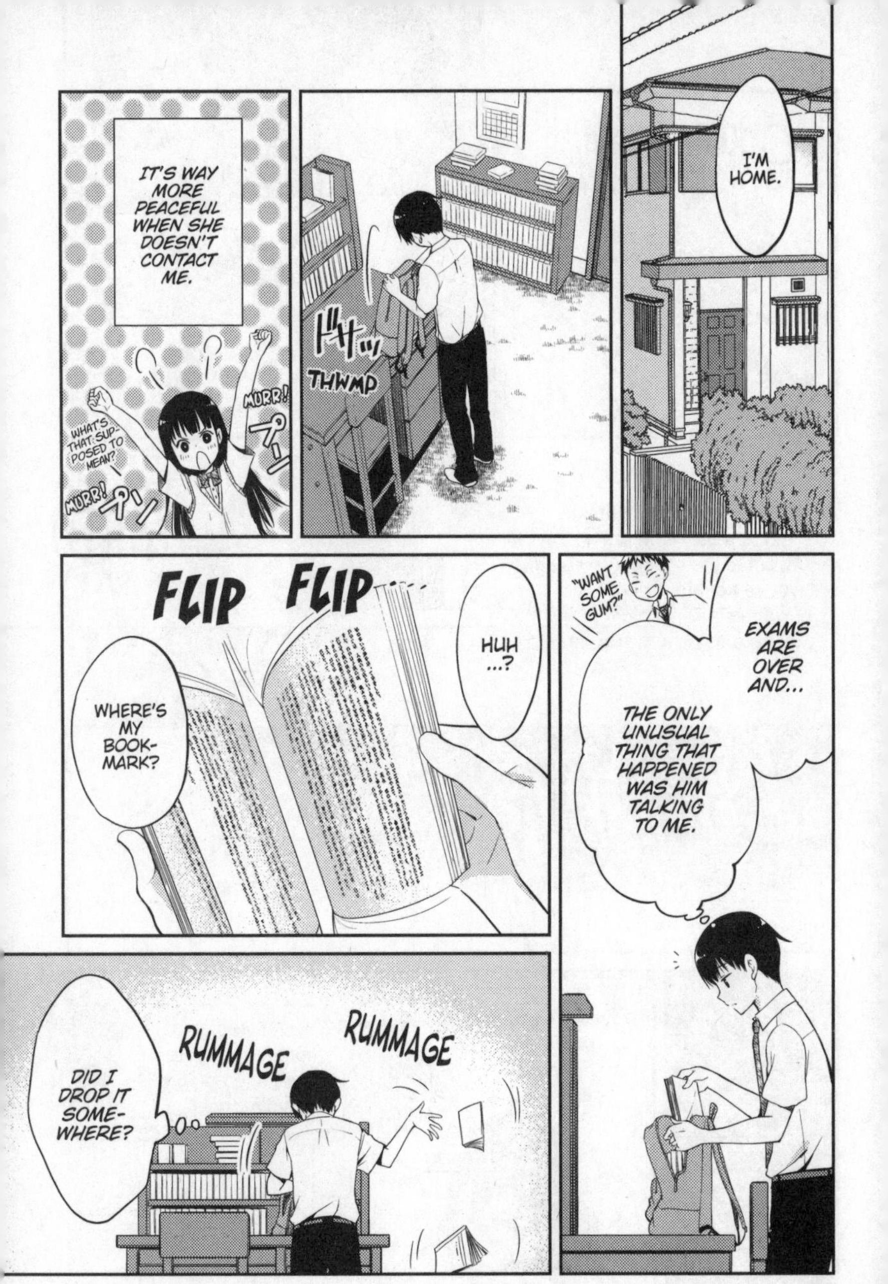
I'M HOME.
ドサッ
THWMP
IT'S WAY MORE PEACEFUL WHEN SHE DOESN'T CONTACT ME.
MURR!
MURR!
WHAT'S THAT SUPPOSED TO MEAN?
"WANT SOME GUM?"
EXAMS ARE OVER AND...
THE ONLY UNUSUAL THING THAT HAPPENED WAS HIM TALKING TO ME.
HUH ...?
FLIP FLIP
WHERE'S MY BOOKMARK?
RUMMAGE RUMMAGE
DID I DROP IT SOMEWHERE?

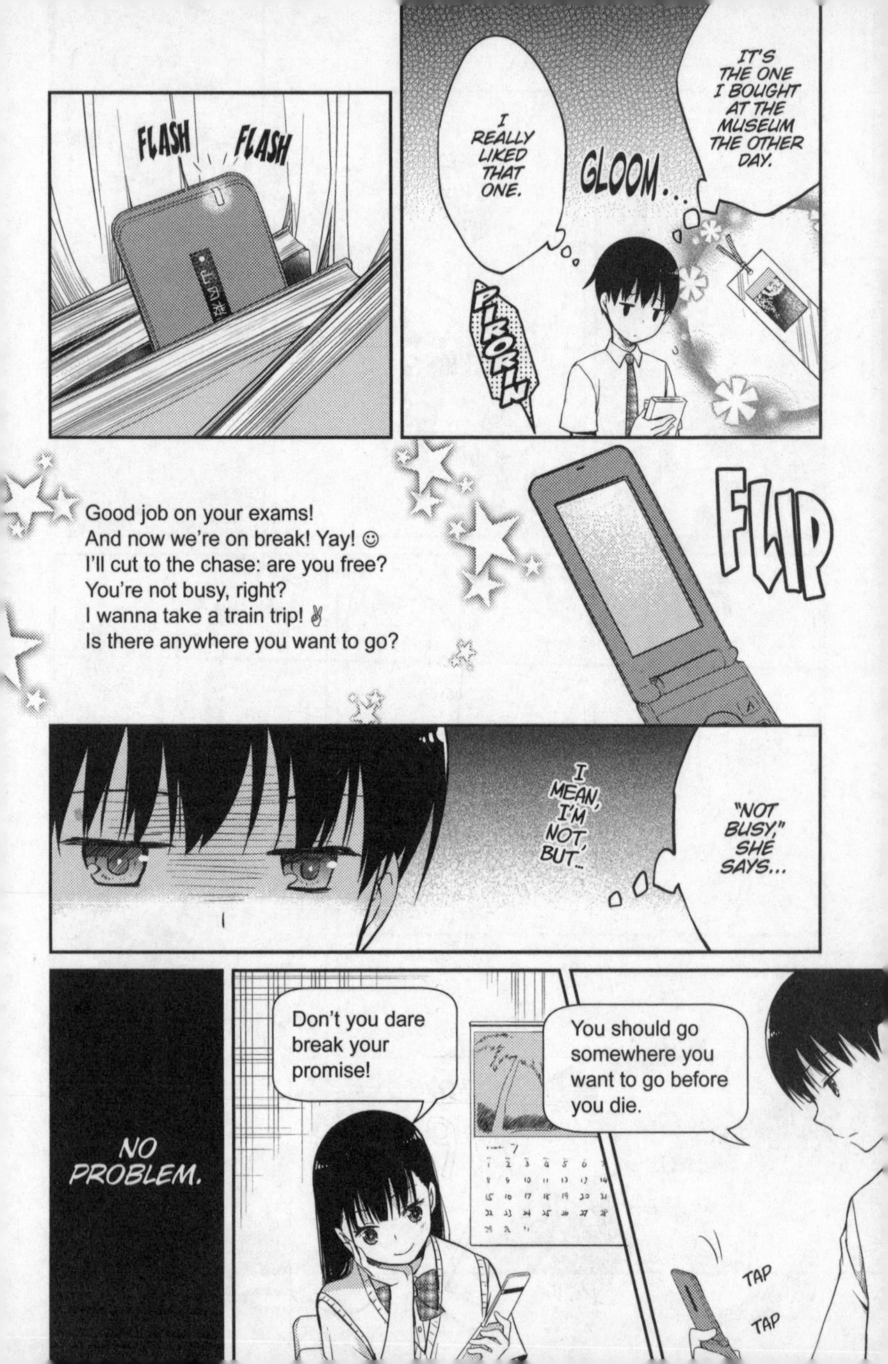
IT'S THE ONE I BOUGHT AT THE MUSEUM THE OTHER DAY.
GLOOM...
I REALLY LIKED THAT ONE.
PIRORIN
FLASH
FLASH
FLIP
Good job on your exams!
And now we're on break! Yay! ☺
I'll cut to the chase: are you free?
You're not busy, right?
I wanna take a train trip! ✌
Is there anywhere you want to go?
"NOT BUSY," SHE SAYS...
I MEAN, I'M NOT, BUT...
You should go somewhere you want to go before you die.
Don't you dare break your promise!
TAP
TAP
NO PROBLEM.

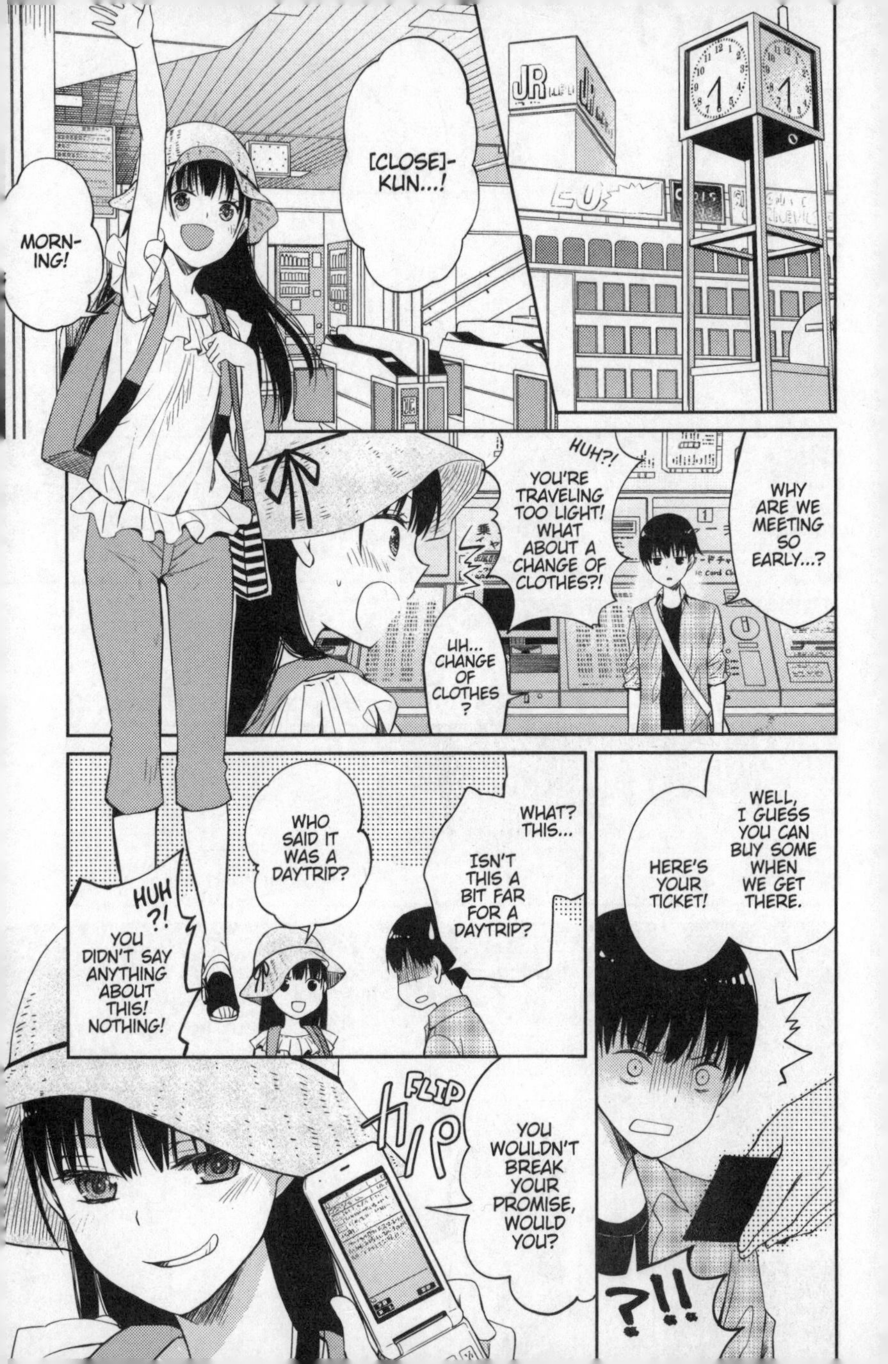
[CLOSE]-KUN...!
MORNING!
WHY ARE WE MEETING SO EARLY...?
HUH?!
YOU'RE TRAVELING TOO LIGHT! WHAT ABOUT A CHANGE OF CLOTHES?!
UH... CHANGE OF CLOTHES?
WELL, I GUESS YOU CAN BUY SOME WHEN WE GET THERE.
HERE'S YOUR TICKET!
WHAT? THIS...
ISN'T THIS A BIT FAR FOR A DAYTRIP?
WHO SAID IT WAS A DAYTRIP?
HUH?!
YOU DIDN'T SAY ANYTHING ABOUT THIS! NOTHING!
?!!
YOU WOULDN'T BREAK YOUR PROMISE, WOULD YOU?
FLIP

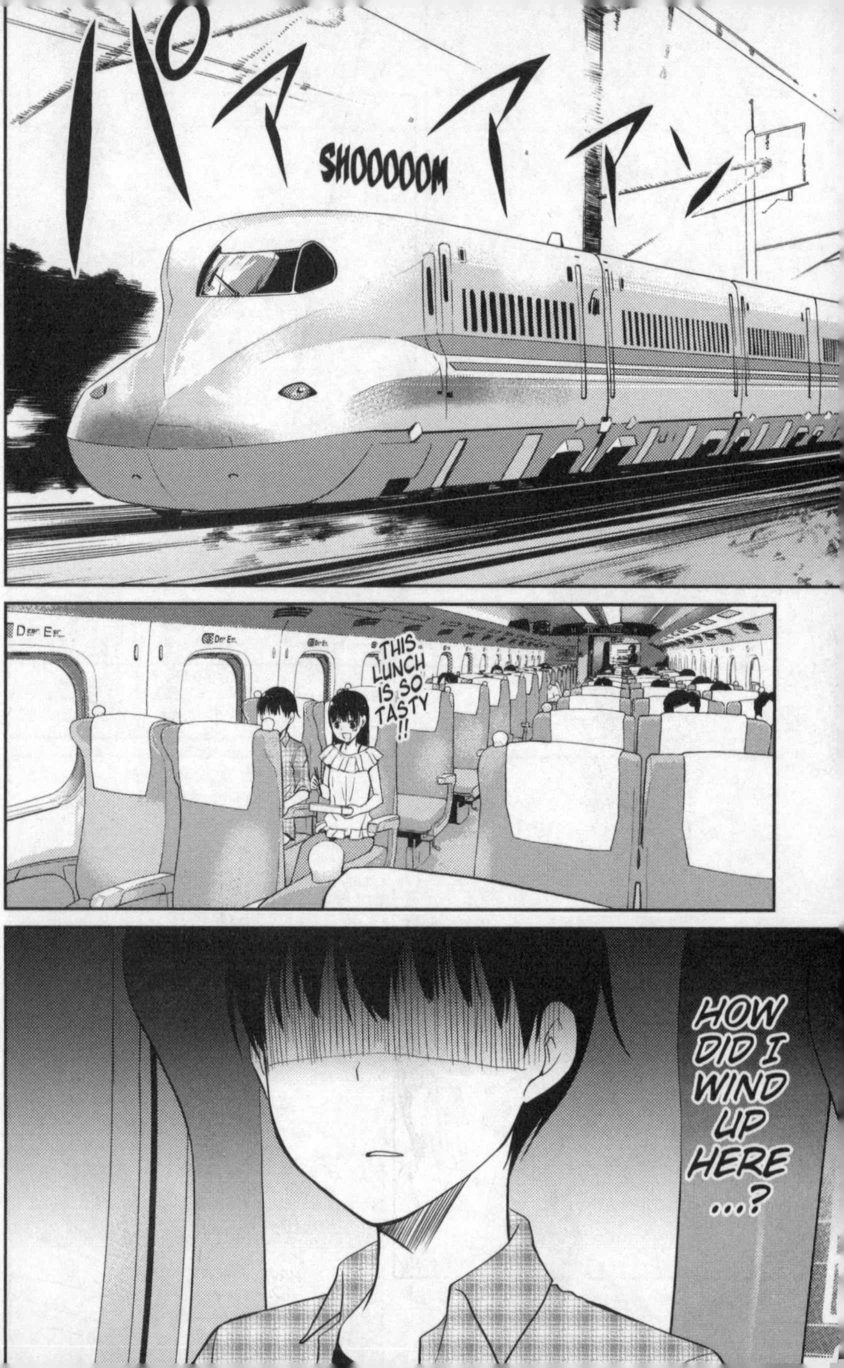
パァアァン
SHOOOOOM
THIS LUNCH IS SO TASTY!!
HOW DID I WIND UP HERE...?

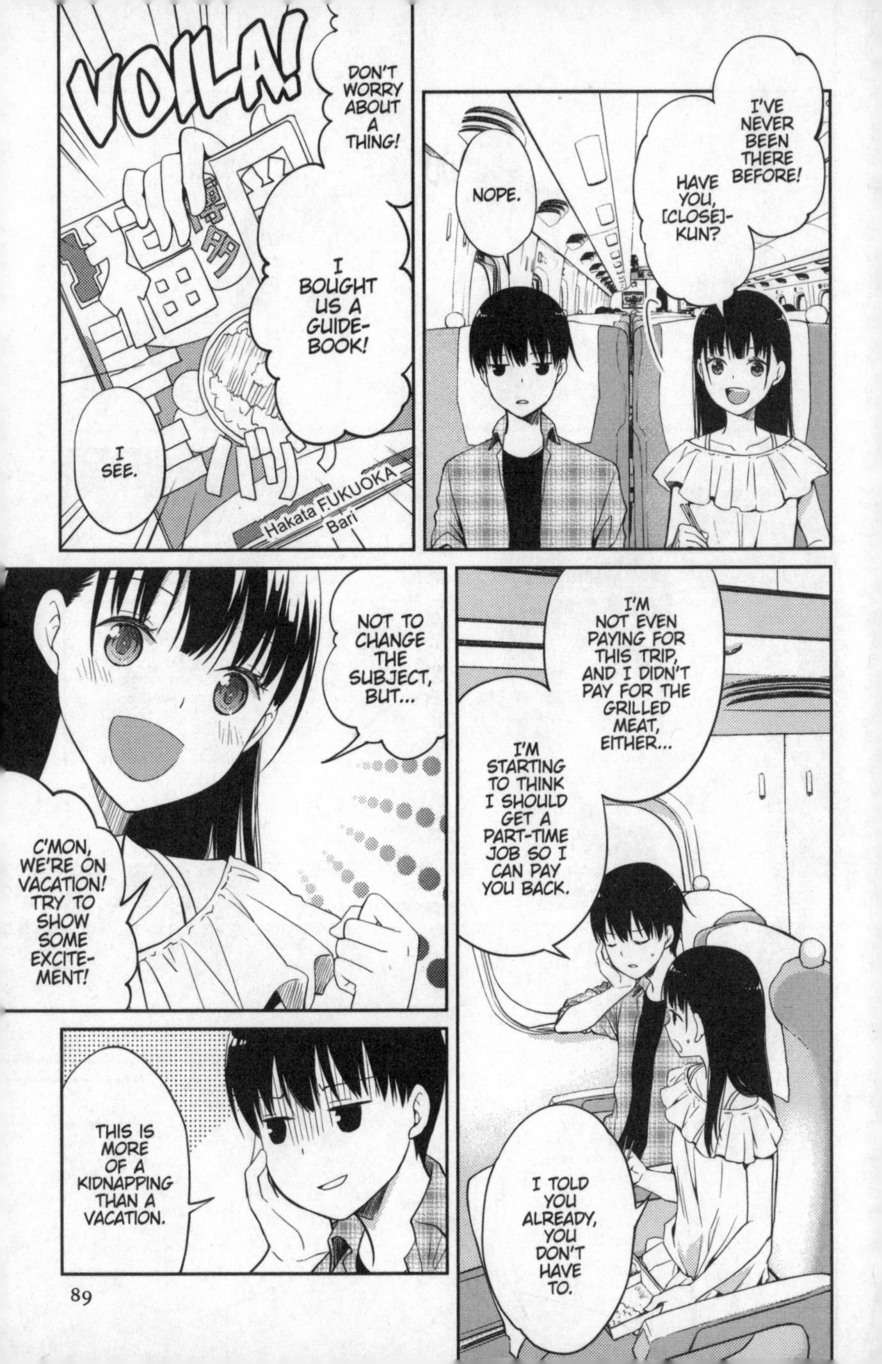
I'VE NEVER BEEN THERE BEFORE!
HAVE YOU, [CLOSE]-KUN?
NOPE.
DON'T WORRY ABOUT A THING!
VOILA!
I BOUGHT US A GUIDE-BOOK!
I SEE.
Hakata FUKUOKA
Bari
I'M NOT EVEN PAYING FOR THIS TRIP, AND I DIDN'T PAY FOR THE GRILLED MEAT, EITHER...
I'M STARTING TO THINK I SHOULD GET A PART-TIME JOB SO I CAN PAY YOU BACK.
I TOLD YOU ALREADY, YOU DON'T HAVE TO.
NOT TO CHANGE THE SUBJECT, BUT...
C'MON, WE'RE ON VACATION! TRY TO SHOW SOME EXCITE-MENT!
THIS IS MORE OF A KIDNAPPING THAN A VACATION.

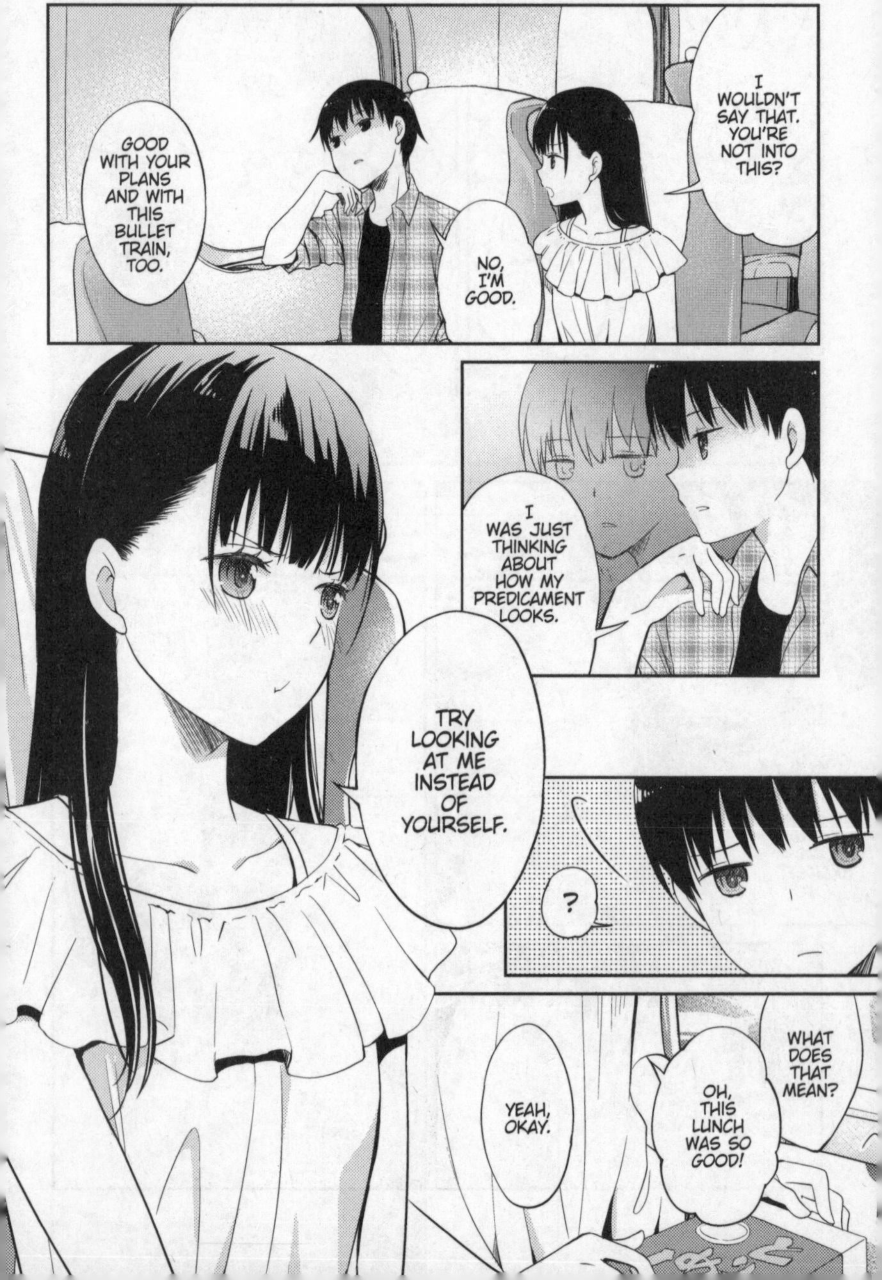
I WOULDN'T SAY THAT. YOU'RE NOT INTO THIS?
NO, I'M GOOD.
GOOD WITH YOUR PLANS AND WITH THIS BULLET TRAIN, TOO.
I WAS JUST THINKING ABOUT HOW MY PREDICAMENT LOOKS.
TRY LOOKING AT ME INSTEAD OF YOURSELF.
?
WHAT DOES THAT MEAN?
OH, THIS LUNCH WAS SO GOOD!
YEAH, OKAY.

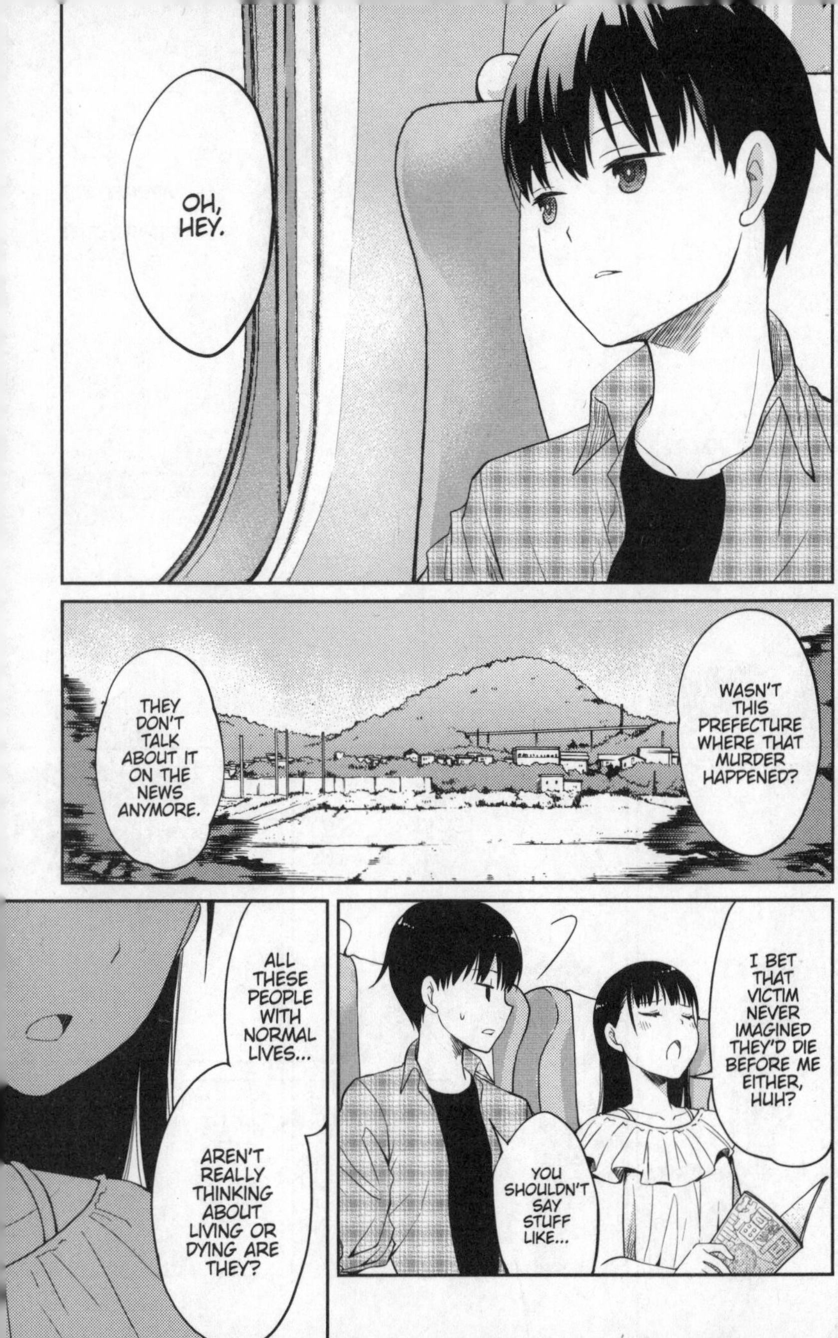
OH, HEY.
WASN'T THIS PREFECTURE WHERE THAT MURDER HAPPENED?
THEY DON'T TALK ABOUT IT ON THE NEWS ANYMORE.
I BET THAT VICTIM NEVER IMAGINED THEY'D DIE BEFORE ME EITHER, HUH?
YOU SHOULDN'T SAY STUFF LIKE...
ALL THESE PEOPLE WITH NORMAL LIVES...
AREN'T REALLY THINKING ABOUT LIVING OR DYING ARE THEY?

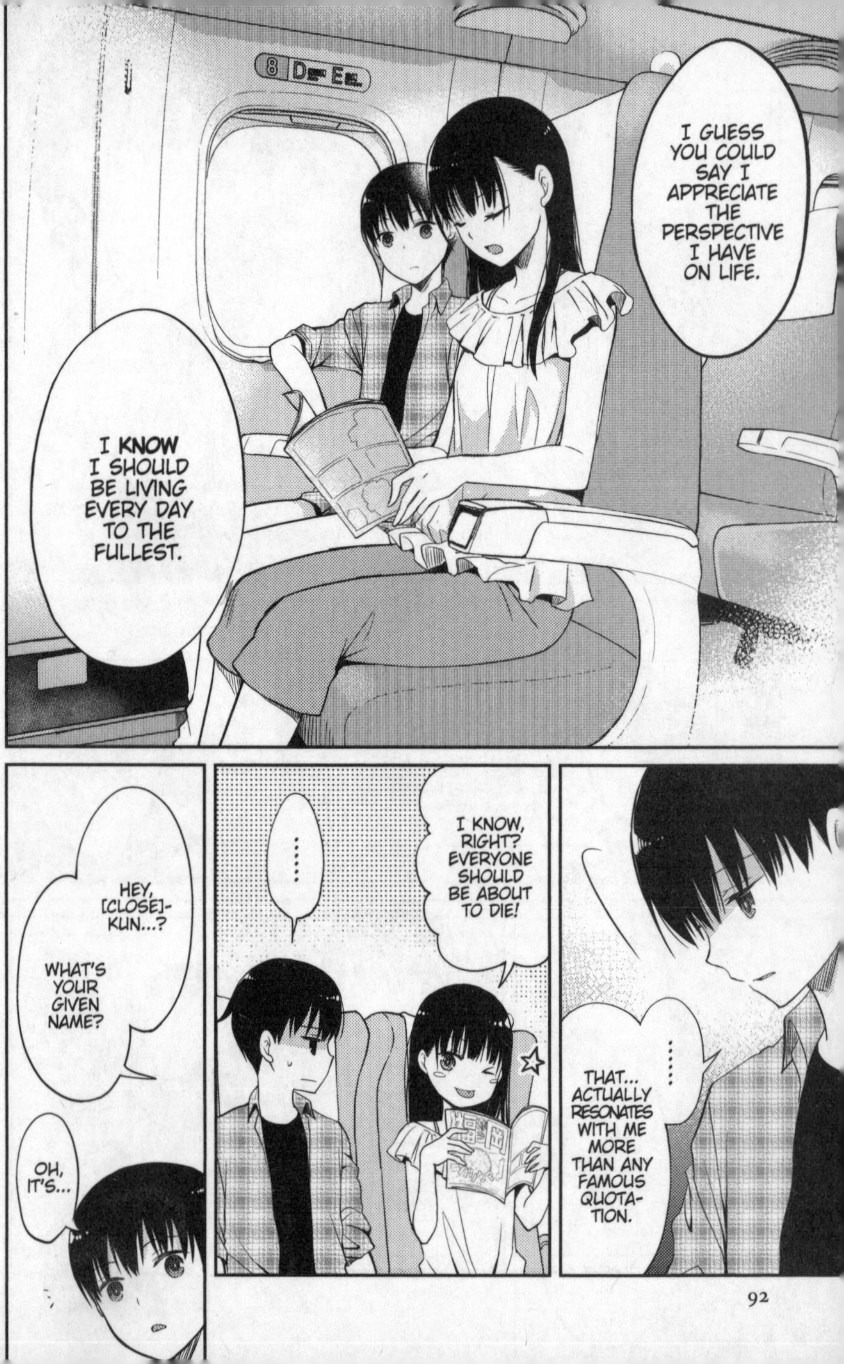
I GUESS YOU COULD SAY I APPRECIATE THE PERSPECTIVE I HAVE ON LIFE.
I KNOW I SHOULD BE LIVING EVERY DAY TO THE FULLEST.
......
THAT... ACTUALLY RESONATES WITH ME MORE THAN ANY FAMOUS QUOTATION.
I KNOW, RIGHT? EVERYONE SHOULD BE ABOUT TO DIE!
......
HEY, [CLOSE]-KUN...?
WHAT'S YOUR GIVEN NAME?
OH, IT'S...

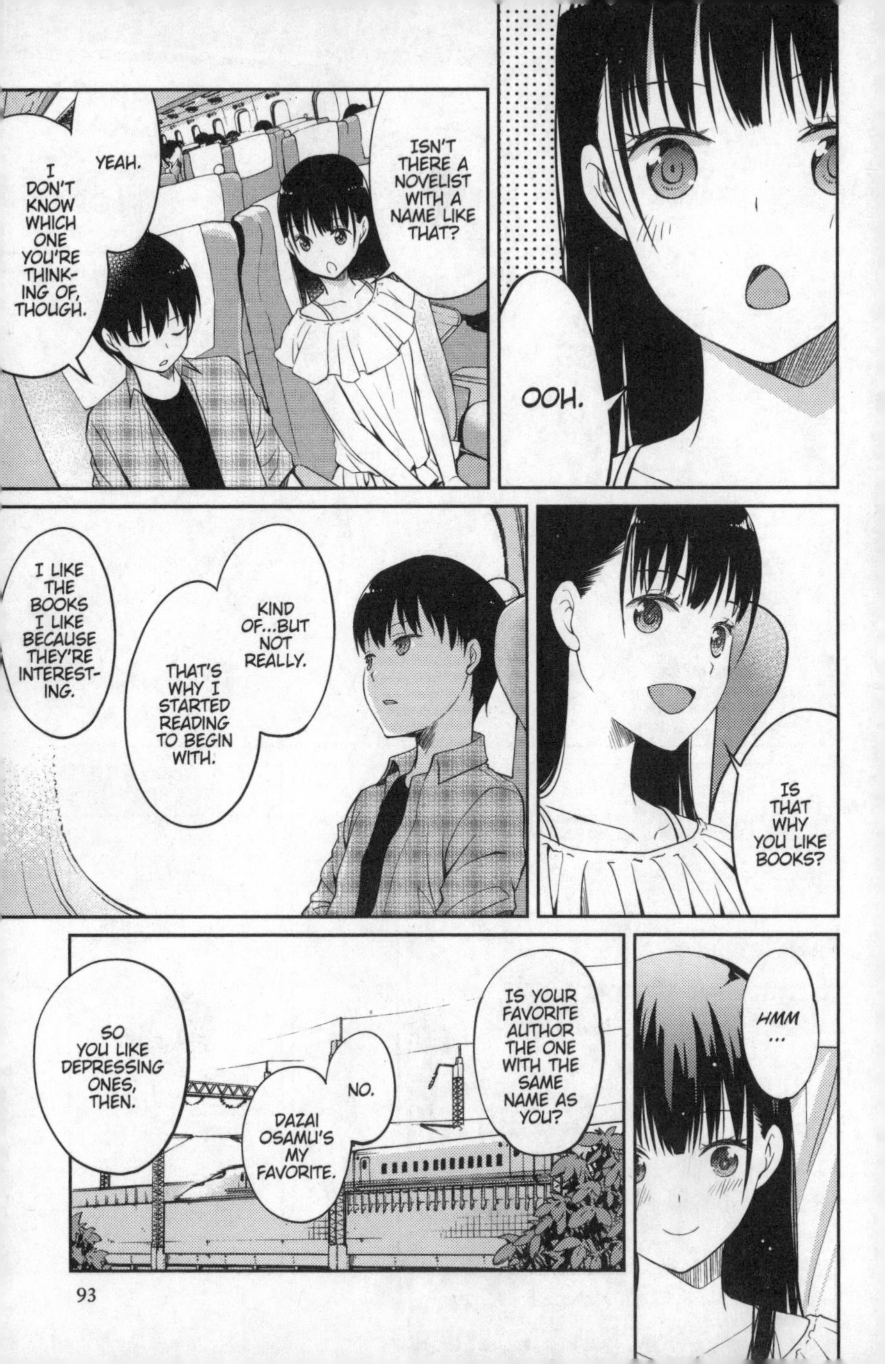
OOH.
ISN'T THERE A NOVELIST WITH A NAME LIKE THAT?
YEAH.
I DON'T KNOW WHICH ONE YOU'RE THINKING OF, THOUGH.
IS THAT WHY YOU LIKE BOOKS?
KIND OF...BUT NOT REALLY.
THAT'S WHY I STARTED READING TO BEGIN WITH.
I LIKE THE BOOKS I LIKE BECAUSE THEY'RE INTERESTING.
HMM ...
IS YOUR FAVORITE AUTHOR THE ONE WITH THE SAME NAME AS YOU?
NO.
DAZAI OSAMU'S MY FAVORITE.
SO YOU LIKE DEPRESSING ONES, THEN.

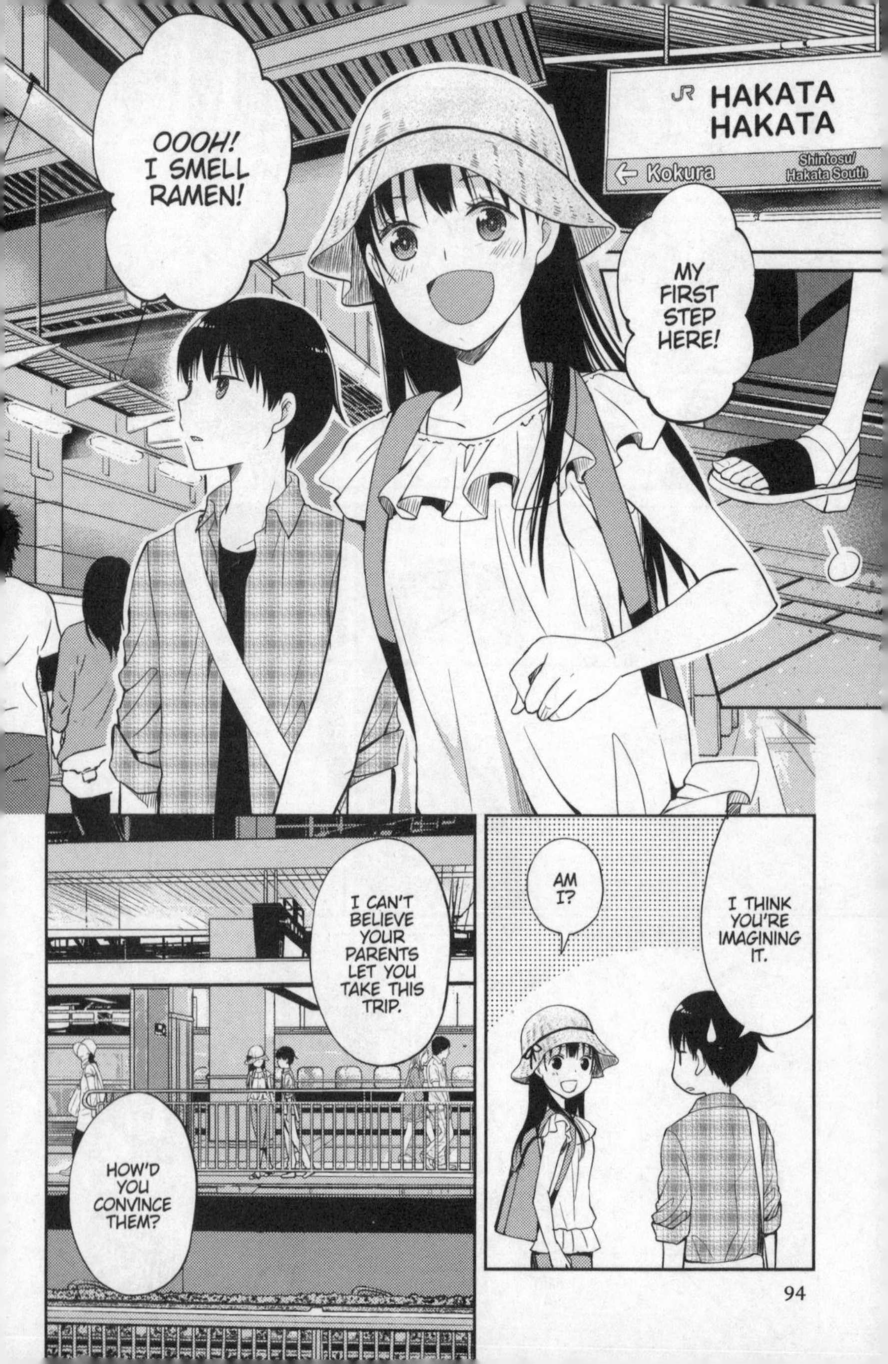
HAKATA
HAKATA
Kokura
Shintosu/
Hakata South
MY FIRST STEP HERE!
OOOH! I SMELL RAMEN!
I THINK YOU'RE IMAGINING IT.
AM I?
I CAN'T BELIEVE YOUR PARENTS LET YOU TAKE THIS TRIP.
HOW'D YOU CONVINCE THEM?

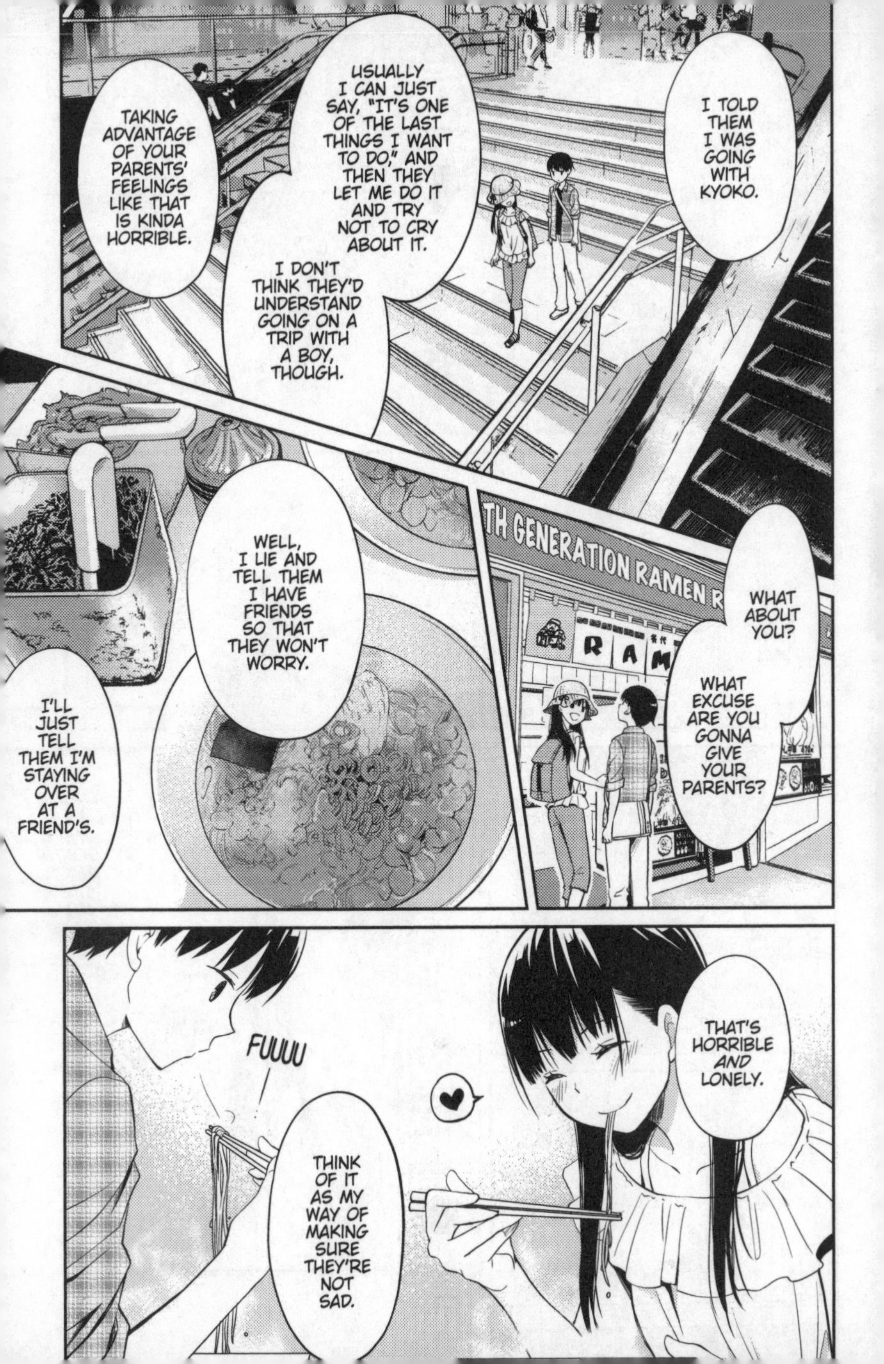
I TOLD THEM I WAS GOING WITH KYOKO.
USUALLY I CAN JUST SAY, "IT'S ONE OF THE LAST THINGS I WANT TO DO," AND THEN THEY LET ME DO IT AND TRY NOT TO CRY ABOUT IT.
I DON'T THINK THEY'D UNDERSTAND GOING ON A TRIP WITH A BOY, THOUGH.
TAKING ADVANTAGE OF YOUR PARENTS' FEELINGS LIKE THAT IS KINDA HORRIBLE.
TH GENERATION RAMEN R
RAM
WHAT ABOUT YOU?
WHAT EXCUSE ARE YOU GONNA GIVE YOUR PARENTS?
WELL, I LIE AND TELL THEM I HAVE FRIENDS SO THAT THEY WON'T WORRY.
I'LL JUST TELL THEM I'M STAYING OVER AT A FRIEND'S.
THAT'S HORRIBLE *AND* LONELY.
FUUUU
THINK OF IT AS MY WAY OF MAKING SURE THEY'RE NOT SAD.

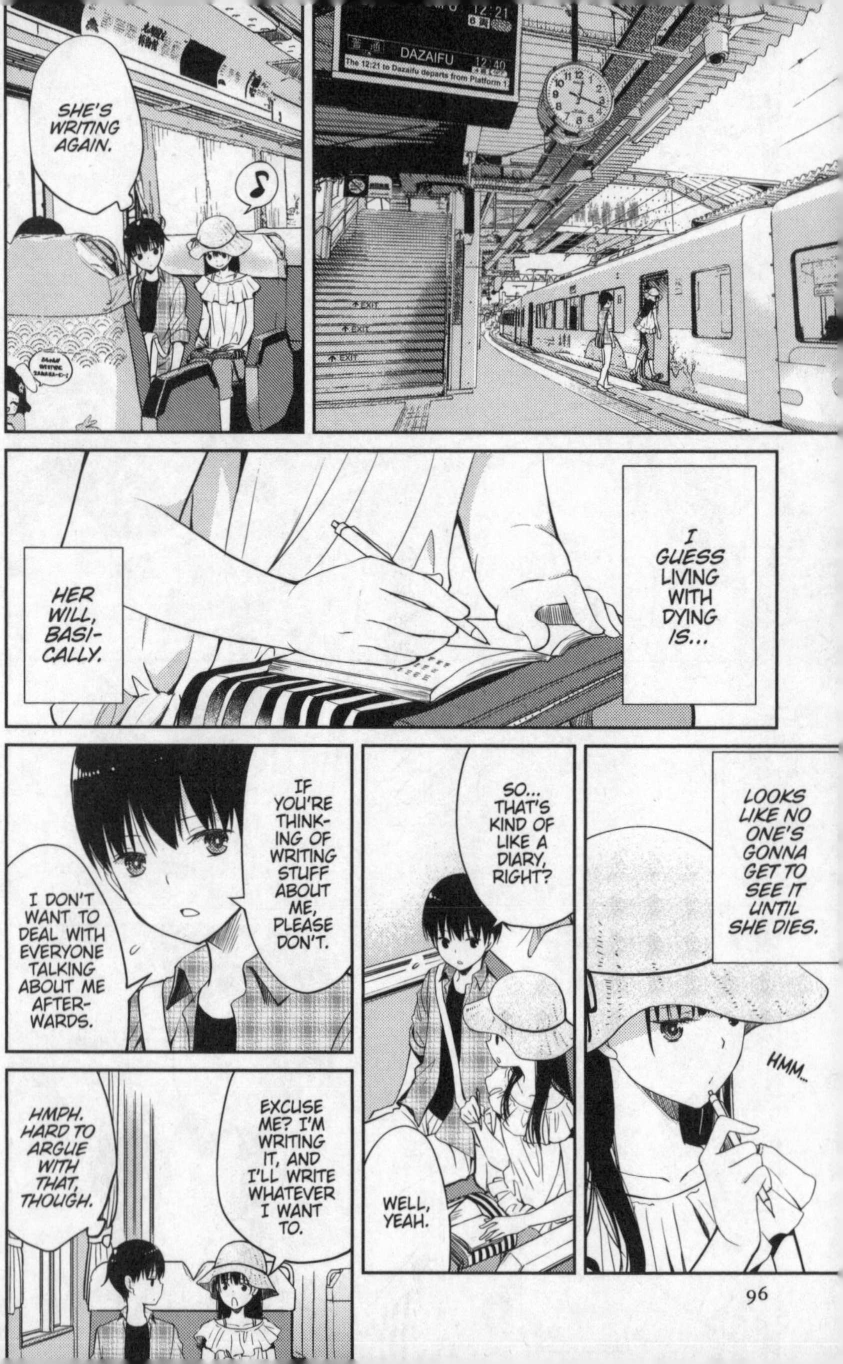

DAZAIFU 12:40
The 12:21 to Dazaifu departs from Platform 1
EXIT
EXIT
EXIT
♪
SHE'S WRITING AGAIN.
I GUESS LIVING WITH DYING IS...
HER WILL, BASI-CALLY.
LOOKS LIKE NO ONE'S GONNA GET TO SEE IT UNTIL SHE DIES.
HMM...
SO... THAT'S KIND OF LIKE A DIARY, RIGHT?
WELL, YEAH.
IF YOU'RE THINKING OF WRITING STUFF ABOUT ME, PLEASE DON'T.
I DON'T WANT TO DEAL WITH EVERYONE TALKING ABOUT ME AFTER-WARDS.
EXCUSE ME? I'M WRITING IT, AND I'LL WRITE WHATEVER I WANT TO.
HMPH. HARD TO ARGUE WITH THAT, THOUGH.

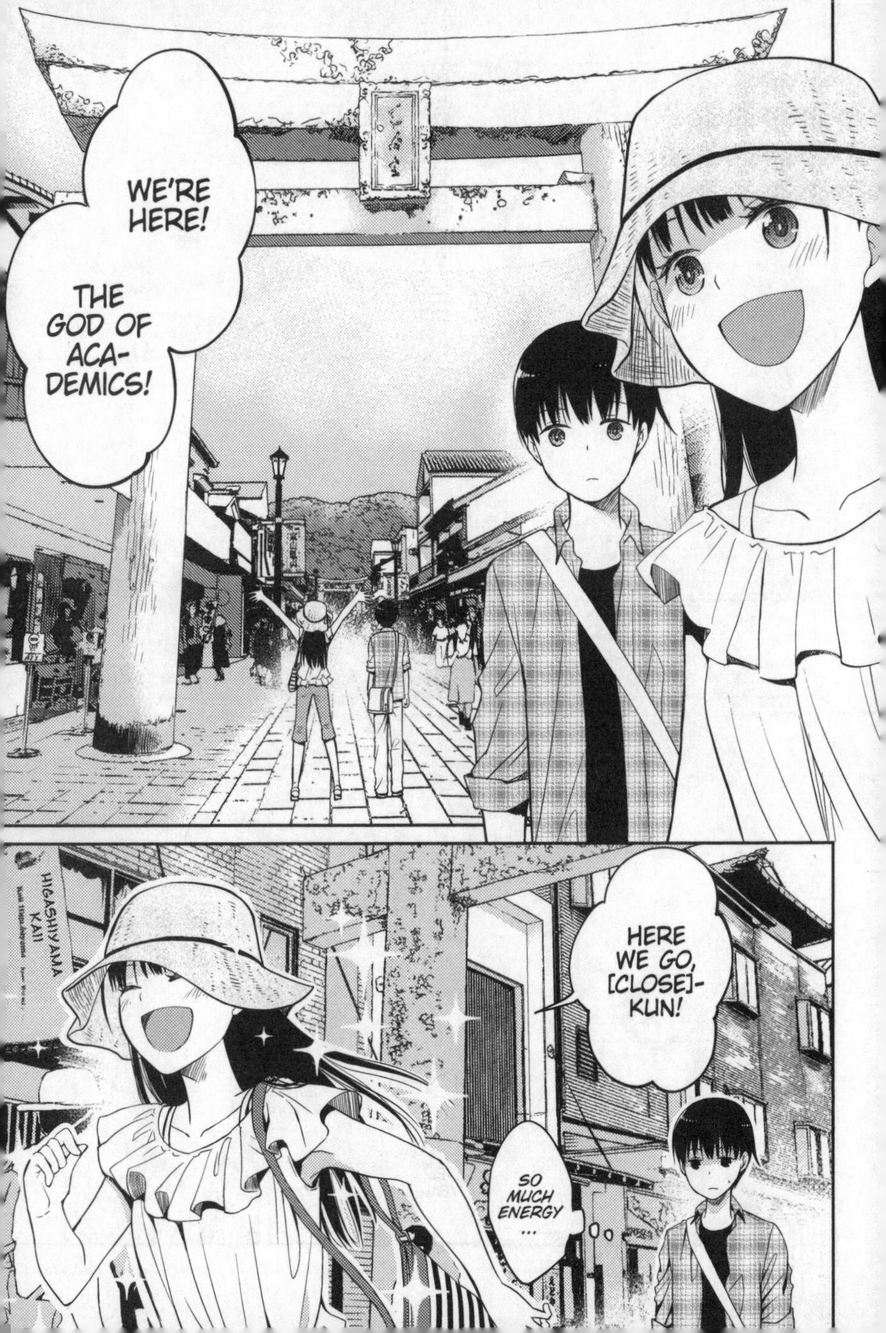
WE'RE HERE!
THE GOD OF ACA-DEMICS!
HERE WE GO, [CLOSE]-KUN!
SO MUCH ENERGY ...
HIGASHIYAMA KAII

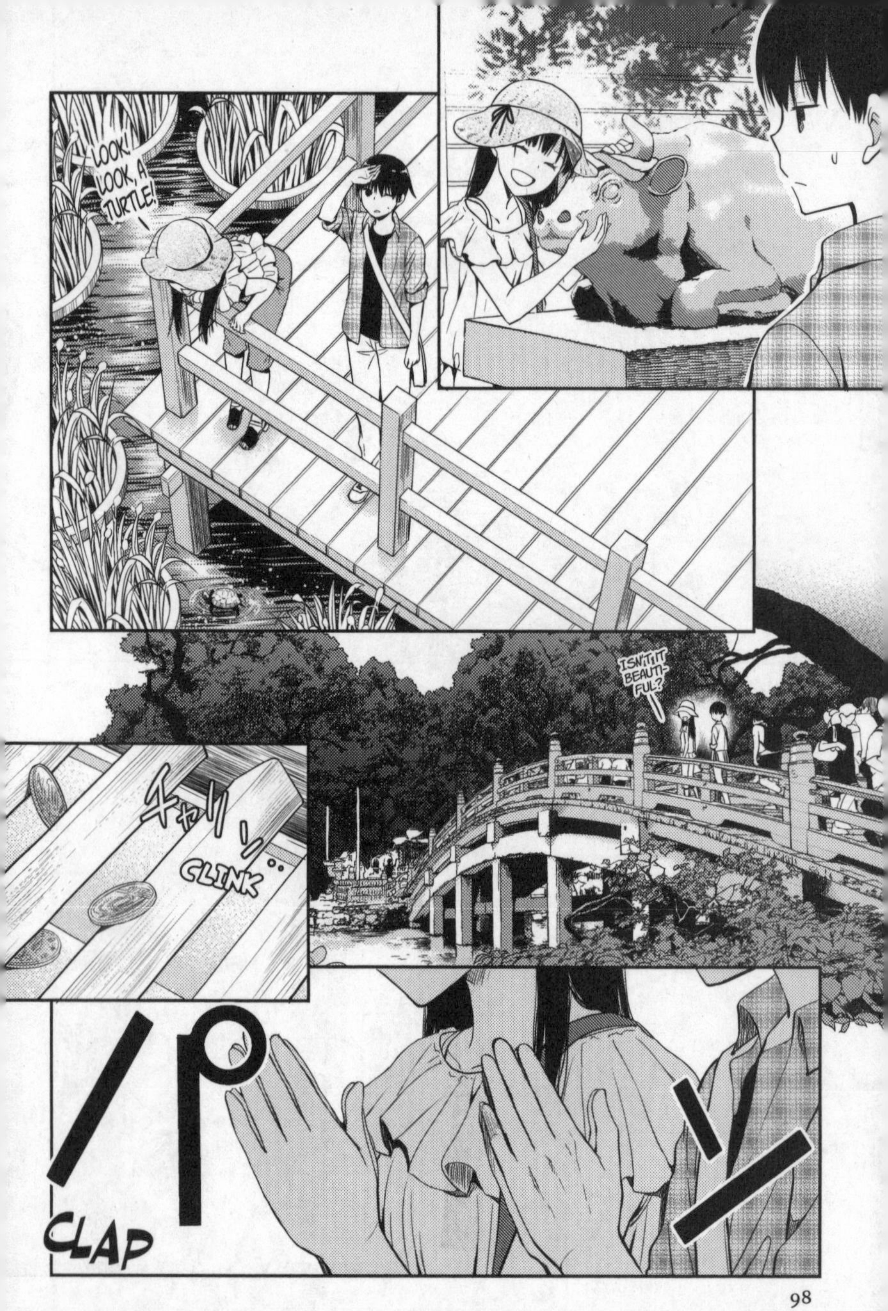
LOOK! LOOK, A TURTLE!
ISN'T IT BEAUTIFUL?
CLINK
CLAP

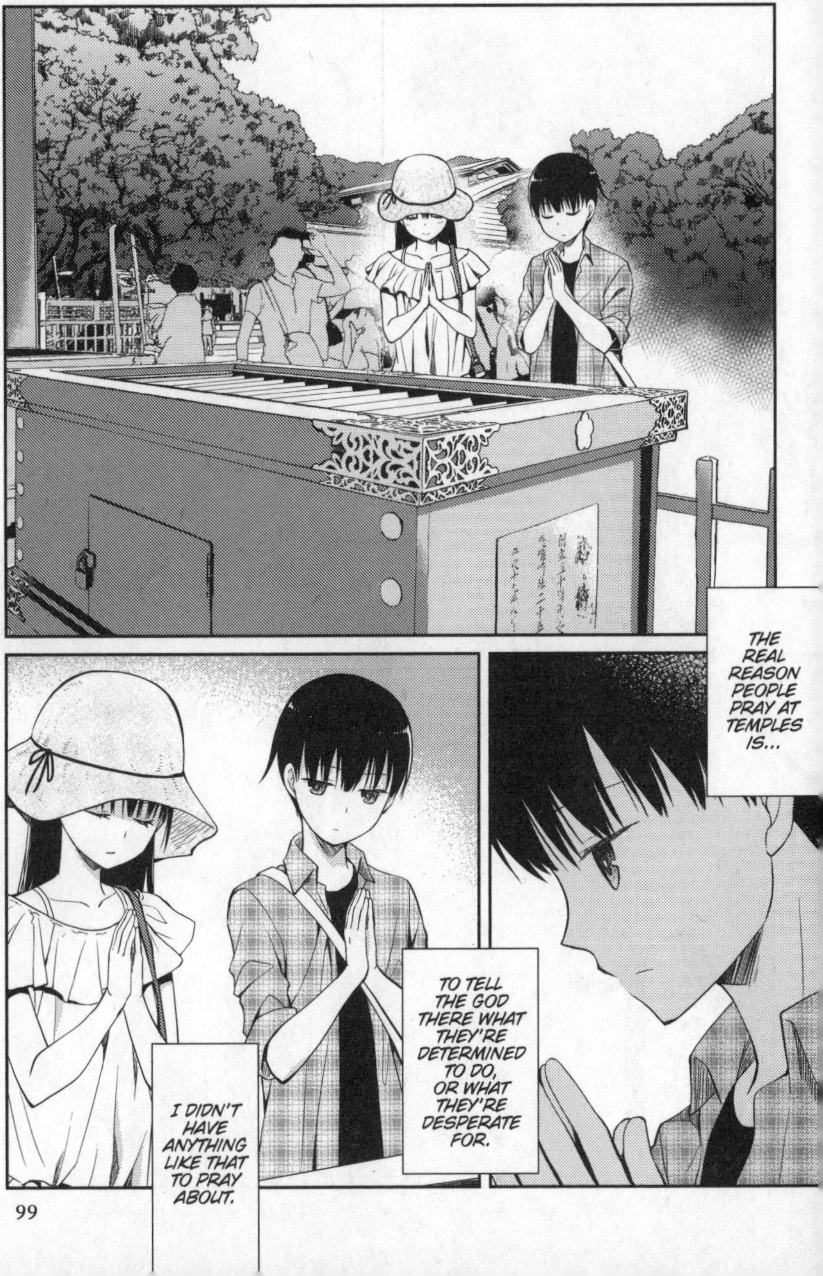
THE REAL REASON PEOPLE PRAY AT TEMPLES IS...
TO TELL THE GOD THERE WHAT THEY'RE DETERMINED TO DO, OR WHAT THEY'RE DESPERATE FOR.
I DIDN'T HAVE ANYTHING LIKE THAT TO PRAY ABOUT.

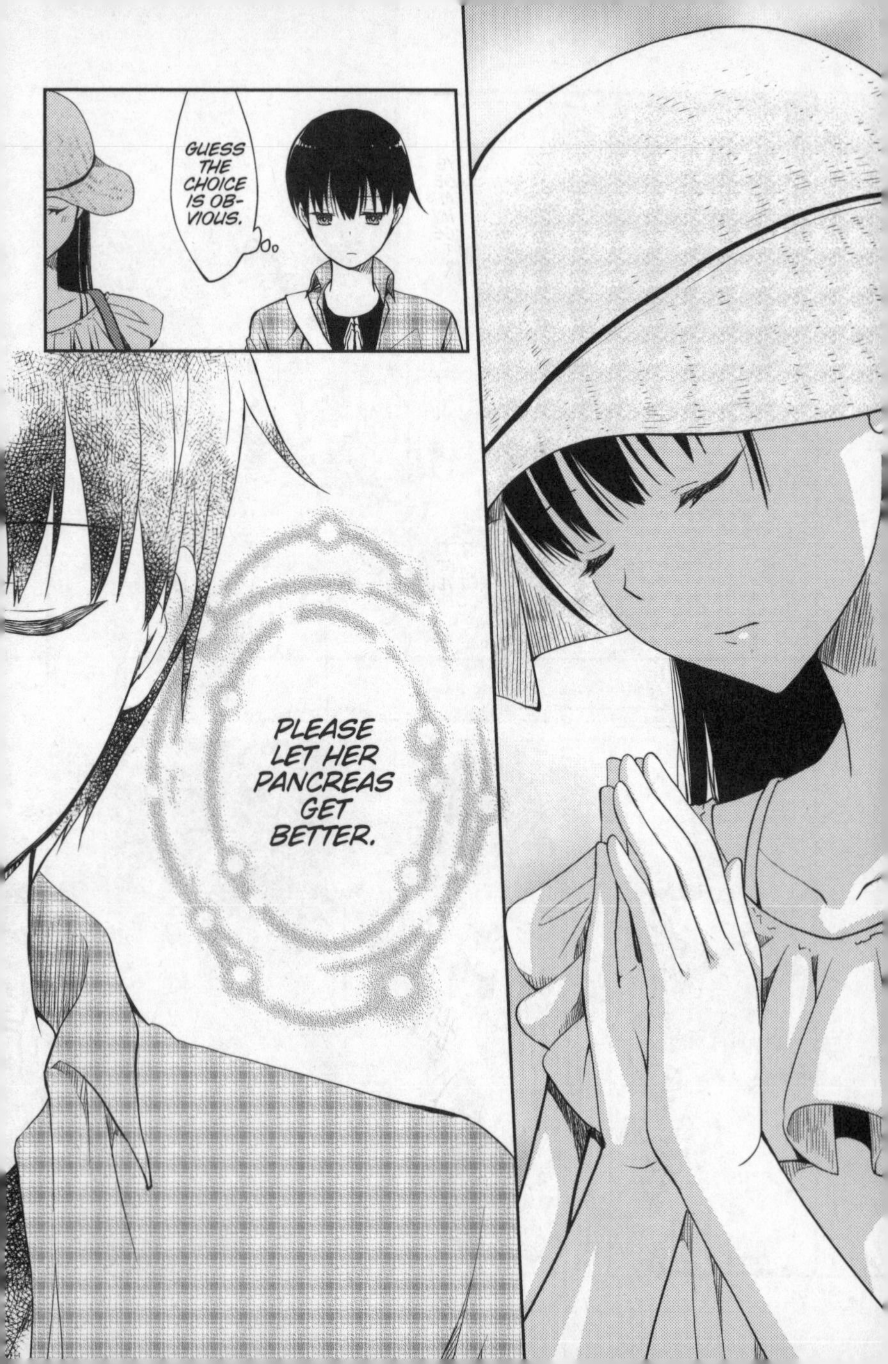
GUESS THE CHOICE IS OB-VIOUS.
PLEASE LET HER PANCREAS GET BETTER.

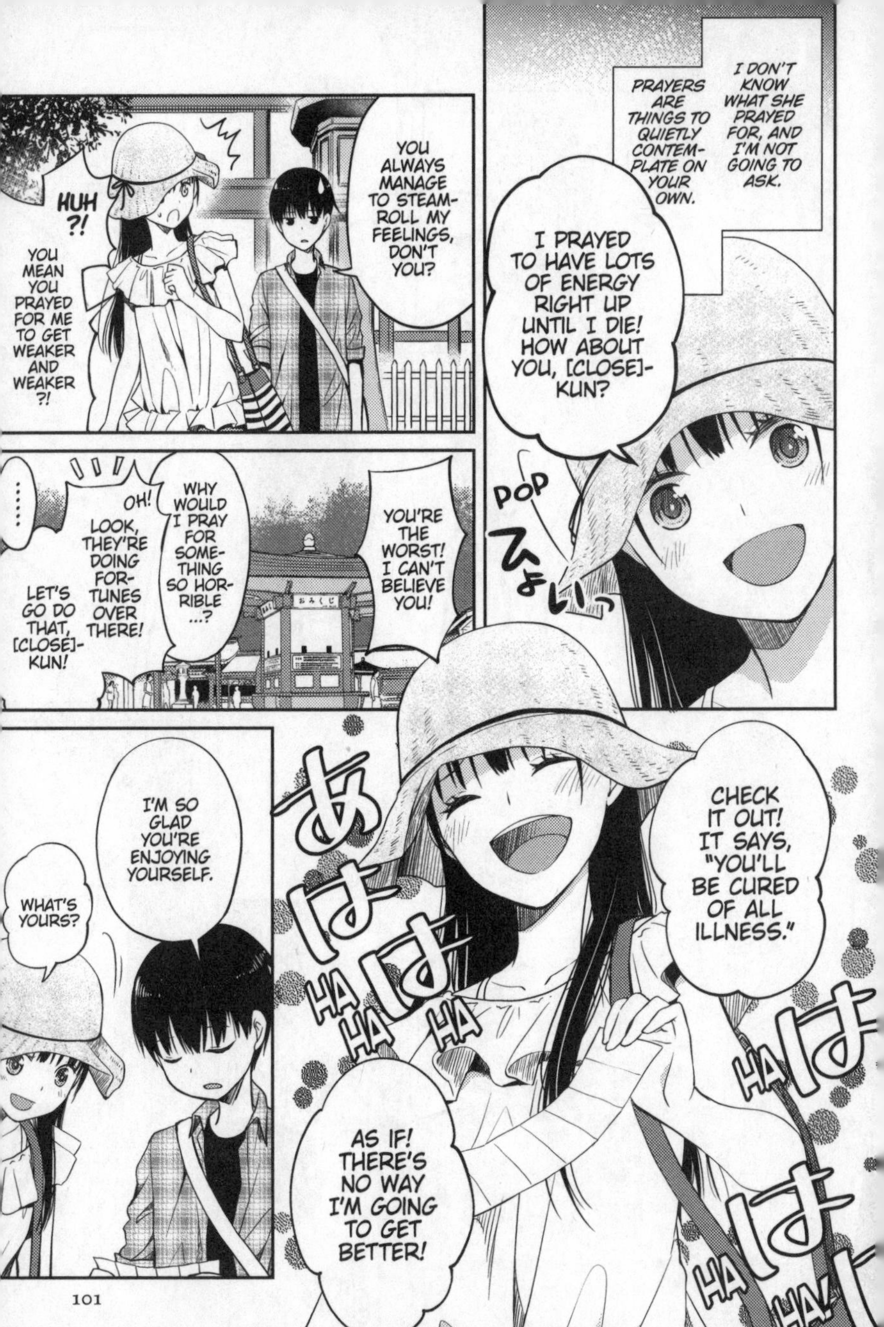
I DON'T KNOW WHAT SHE PRAYED FOR, AND I'M NOT GOING TO ASK.
PRAYERS ARE THINGS TO QUIETLY CONTEM-PLATE ON YOUR OWN.
I PRAYED TO HAVE LOTS OF ENERGY RIGHT UP UNTIL I DIE! HOW ABOUT YOU, [CLOSE]-KUN?
POP
ひょいっ
YOU ALWAYS MANAGE TO STEAM-ROLL MY FEELINGS, DON'T YOU?
HUH ?!
YOU MEAN YOU PRAYED FOR ME TO GET WEAKER AND WEAKER ?!
YOU'RE THE WORST! I CAN'T BELIEVE YOU!
おみくじ
WHY WOULD I PRAY FOR SOME-THING SO HOR-RIBLE ...?
OH!
LOOK, THEY'RE DOING FOR-TUNES OVER THERE!
......
LET'S GO DO THAT, [CLOSE]-KUN!
CHECK IT OUT! IT SAYS, "YOU'LL BE CURED OF ALL ILLNESS."
あははははは
HA HA HA HA HA HA HA
AS IF! THERE'S NO WAY I'M GOING TO GET BETTER!
I'M SO GLAD YOU'RE ENJOYING YOURSELF.
WHAT'S YOURS?

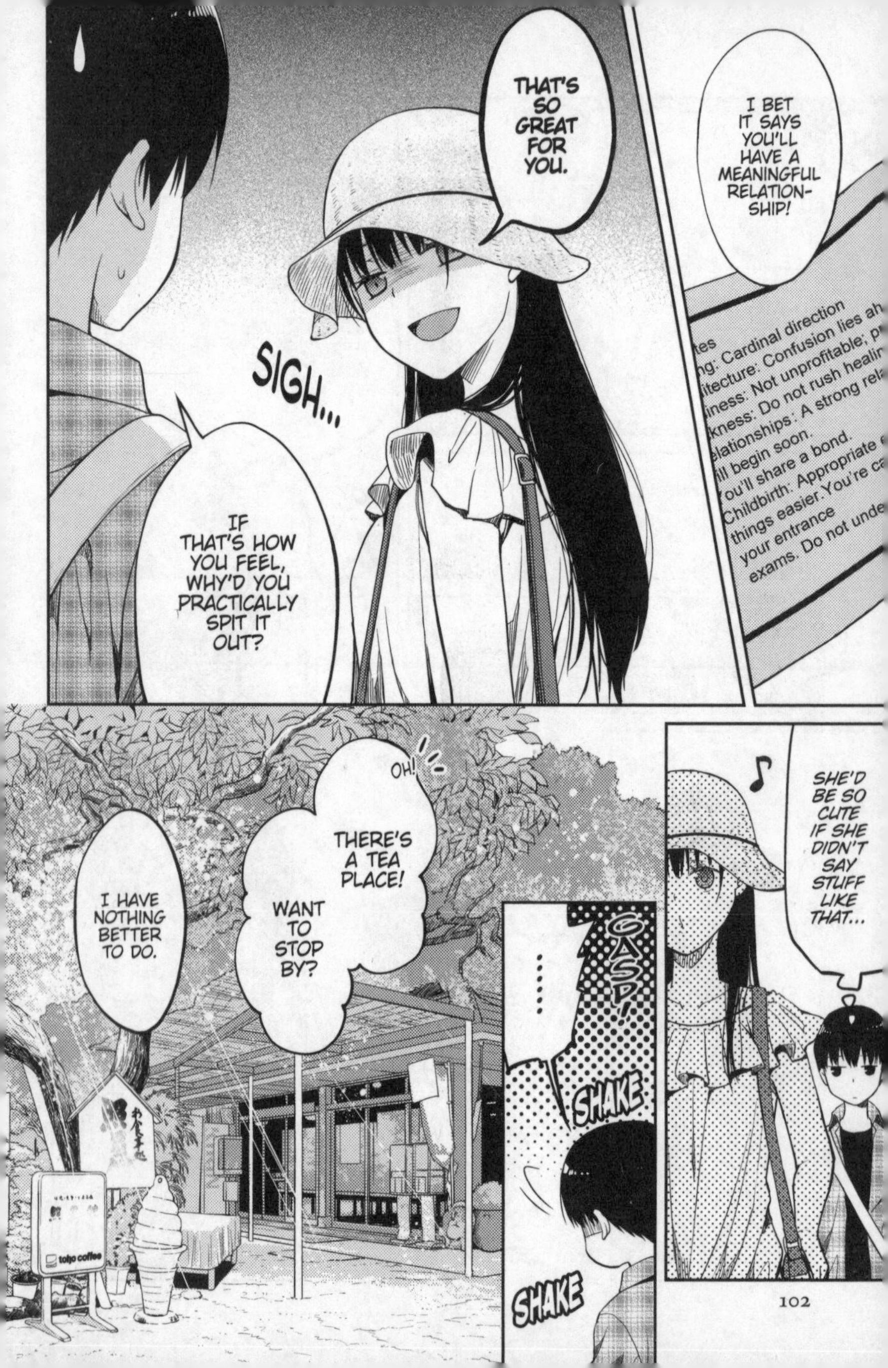
I BET IT SAYS YOU'LL HAVE A MEANINGFUL RELATIONSHIP!
tes
ng: Cardinal direction
itecture: Confusion lies ah
iness: Not unprofitable; p
kness: Do not rush healin
elationships: A strong rela
ill begin soon.
You'll share a bond.
Childbirth: Appropriate e
things easier. You're ca
your entrance
exams. Do not unde
THAT'S SO GREAT FOR YOU.
SIGH...
IF THAT'S HOW YOU FEEL, WHY'D YOU PRACTICALLY SPIT IT OUT?
SHE'D BE SO CUTE IF SHE DIDN'T SAY STUFF LIKE THAT...
GASP!
......
SHAKE
SHAKE
OH!
THERE'S A TEA PLACE!
WANT TO STOP BY?
I HAVE NOTHING BETTER TO DO.

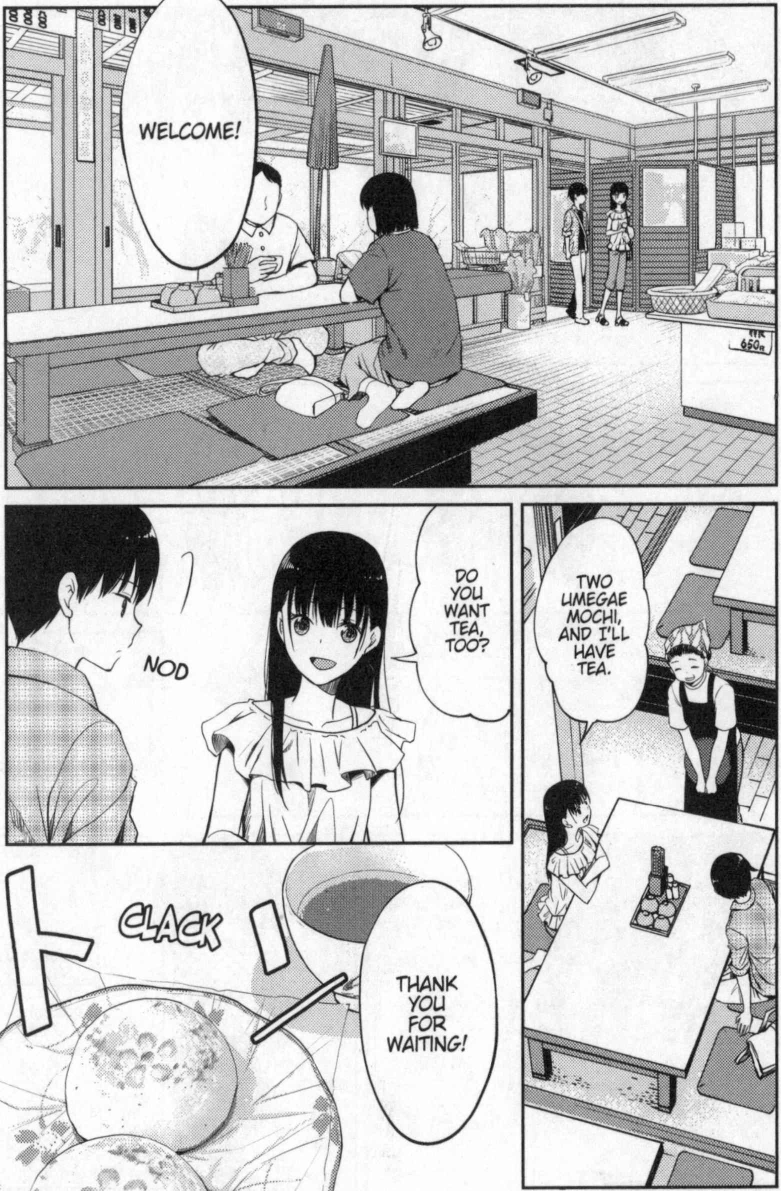
WELCOME!
TWO UMEGAE MOCHI, AND I'LL HAVE TEA.
DO YOU WANT TEA, TOO?
NOD
CLACK
THANK YOU FOR WAITING!

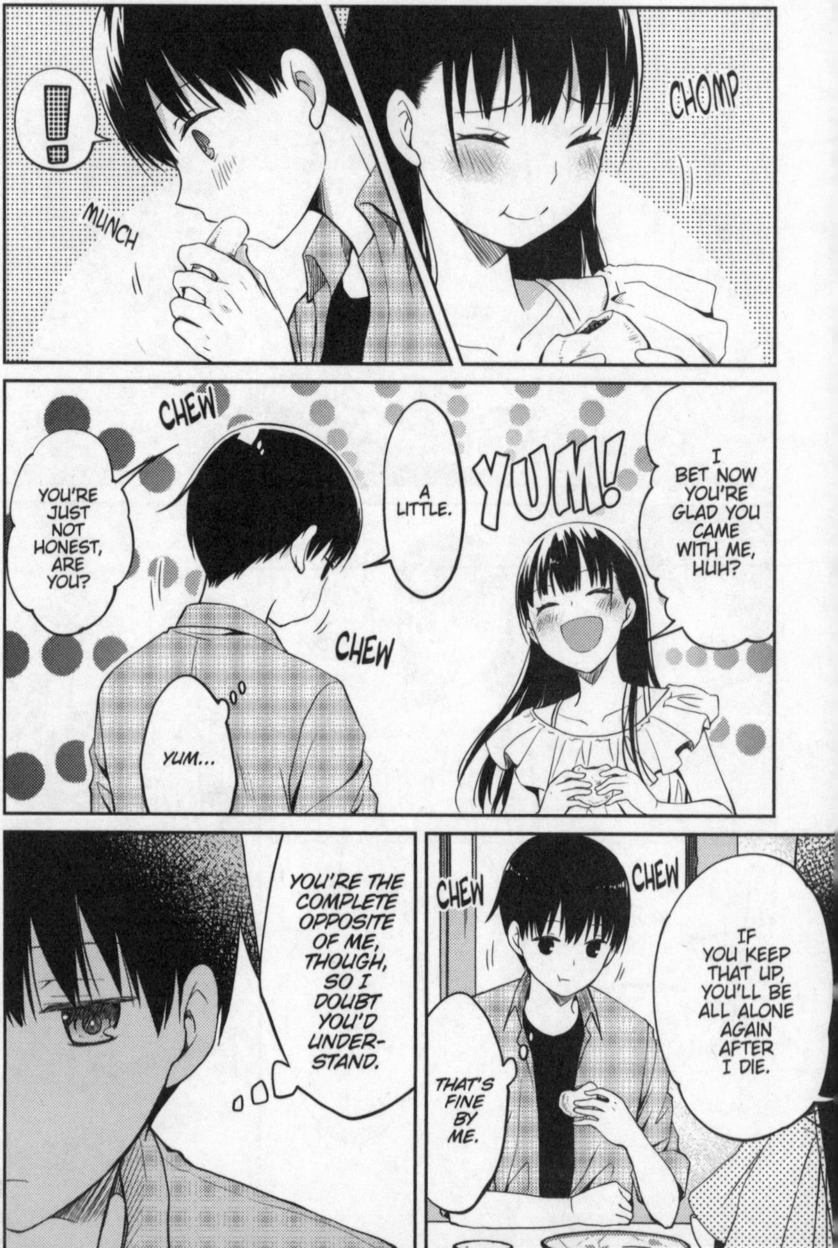
CHOMP
!
MUNCH
I BET NOW YOU'RE GLAD YOU CAME WITH ME, HUH?
YUM!
A LITTLE.
CHEW
YOU'RE JUST NOT HONEST, ARE YOU?
CHEW
YUM...
IF YOU KEEP THAT UP, YOU'LL BE ALL ALONE AGAIN AFTER I DIE.
CHEW
CHEW
THAT'S FINE BY ME.
YOU'RE THE COMPLETE OPPOSITE OF ME, THOUGH, SO I DOUBT YOU'D UNDER-STAND.

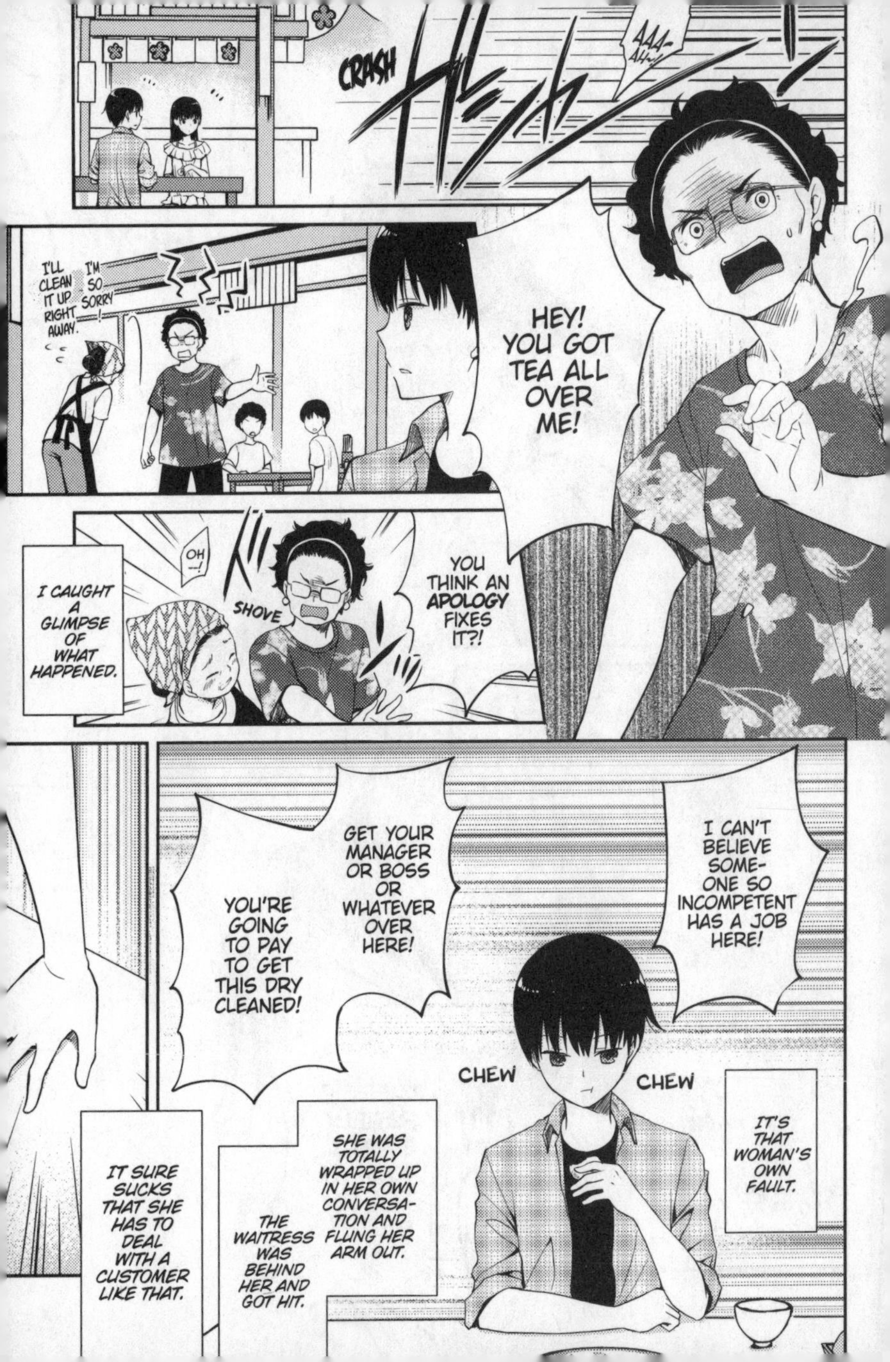
AAA-AHH-!
CRASH
HEY! YOU GOT TEA ALL OVER ME!
I'M SO SORRY!
I'LL CLEAN IT UP RIGHT AWAY.
YOU THINK AN APOLOGY FIXES IT?!
SHOVE
OH—!
I CAUGHT A GLIMPSE OF WHAT HAPPENED.
I CAN'T BELIEVE SOME-ONE SO INCOMPETENT HAS A JOB HERE!
GET YOUR MANAGER OR BOSS OR WHATEVER OVER HERE!
YOU'RE GOING TO PAY TO GET THIS DRY CLEANED!
CHEW
CHEW
IT'S THAT WOMAN'S OWN FAULT.
SHE WAS TOTALLY WRAPPED UP IN HER OWN CONVERSA-TION AND FLUNG HER ARM OUT.
THE WAITRESS WAS BEHIND HER AND GOT HIT.
IT SURE SUCKS THAT SHE HAS TO DEAL WITH A CUSTOMER LIKE THAT.

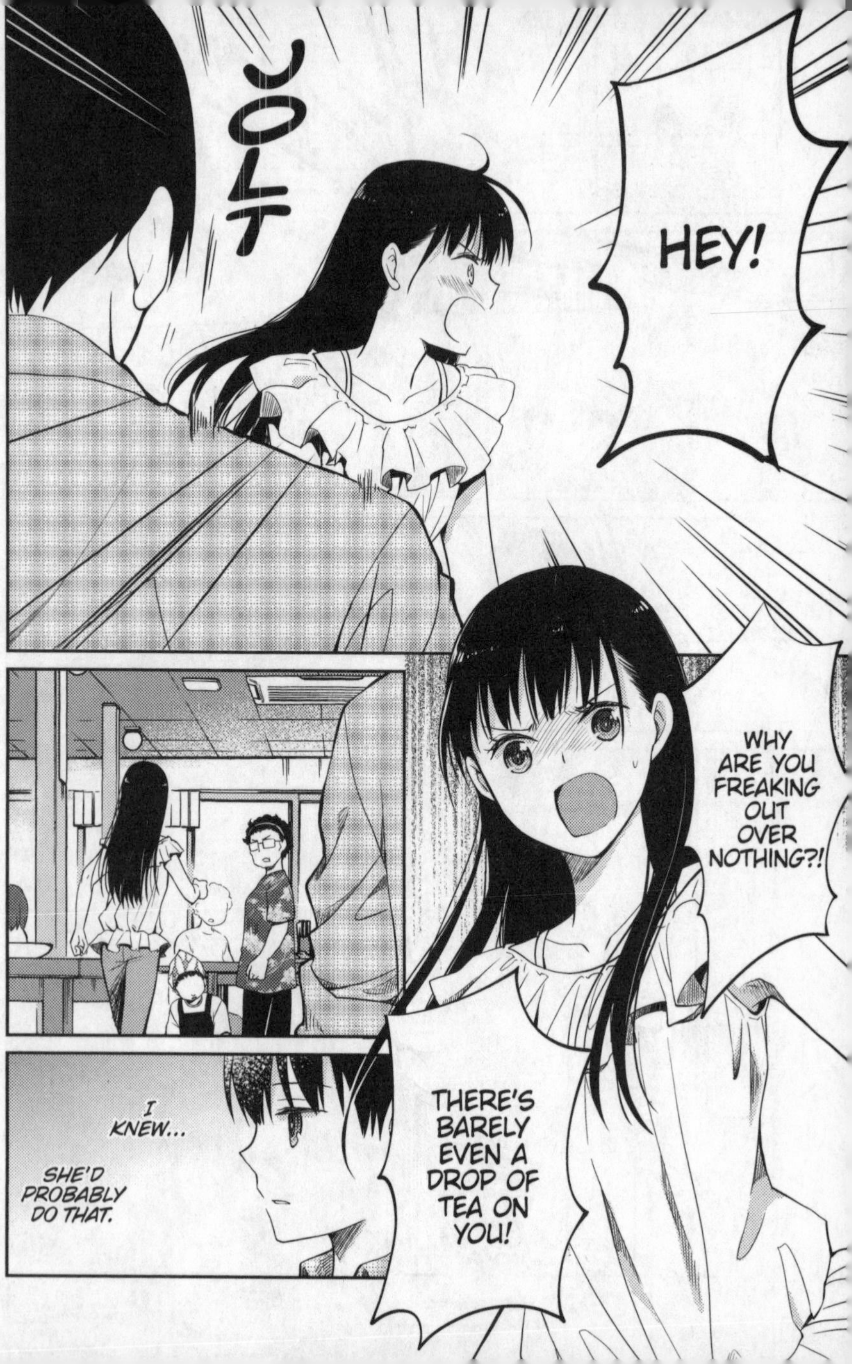
HEY!
JOLT
WHY ARE YOU FREAKING OUT OVER NOTHING?!
THERE'S BARELY EVEN A DROP OF TEA ON YOU!
I KNEW...
SHE'D PROBABLY DO THAT.

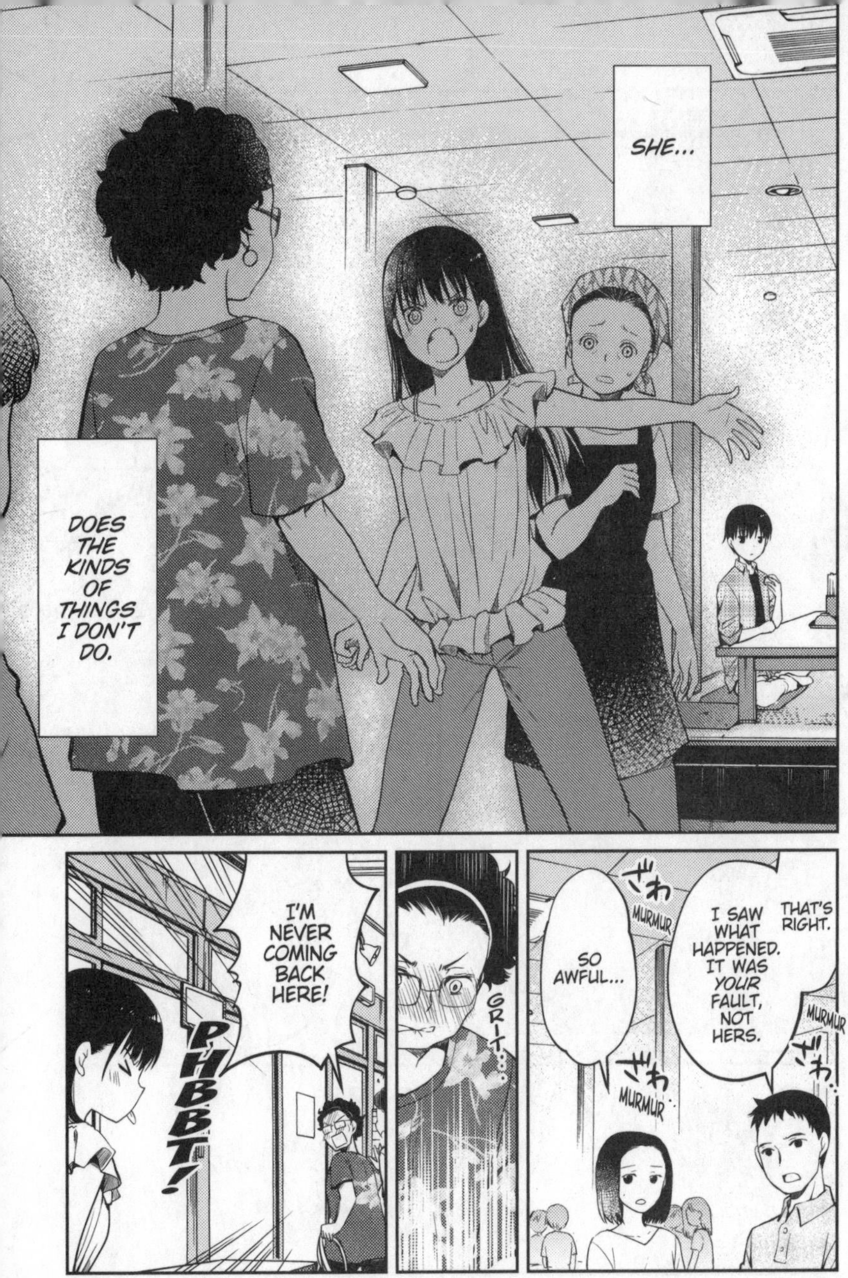
SHE...
DOES THE KINDS OF THINGS I DON'T DO.
ざわ
MURMUR
THAT'S RIGHT.
I SAW WHAT HAPPENED. IT WAS *YOUR* FAULT, NOT HERS.
ざわ
MURMUR
SO AWFUL...
ざわ
MURMUR
I'M NEVER COMING BACK HERE!
GRIT...
PHBBT!

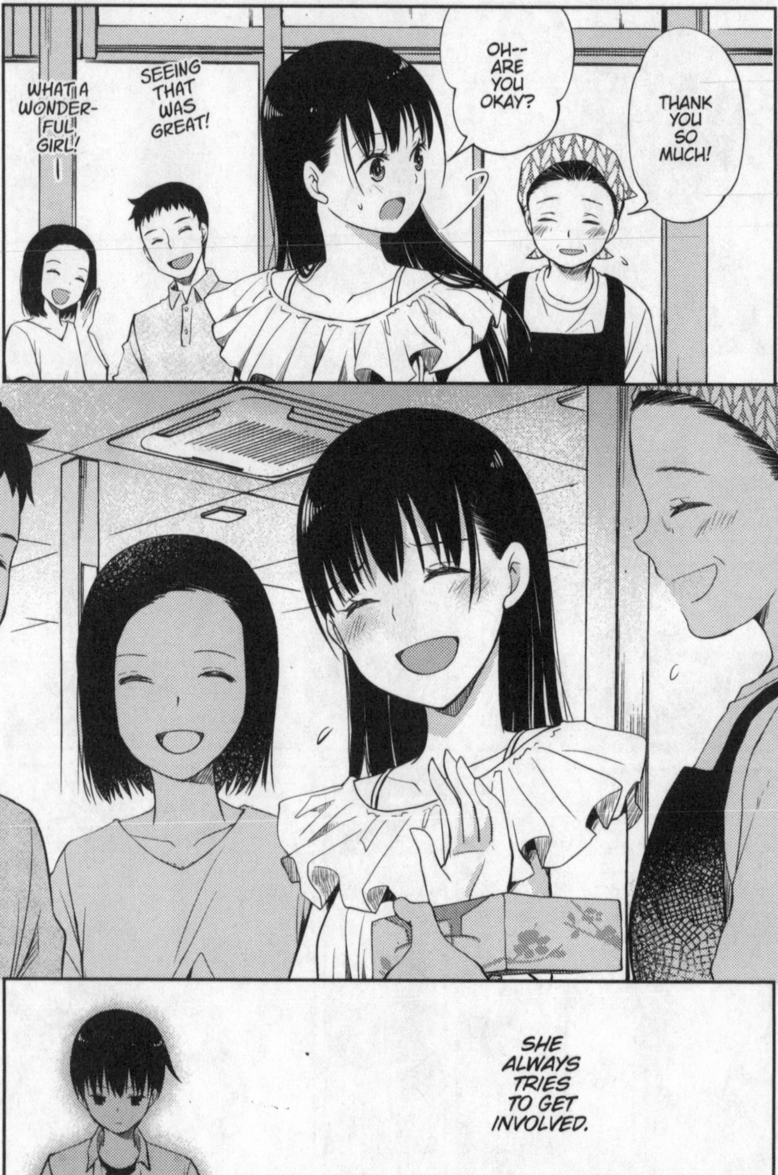
THANK YOU SO MUCH!
OH-- ARE YOU OKAY?
SEEING THAT WAS GREAT!
WHAT A WONDERFUL GIRL!
SHE ALWAYS TRIES TO GET INVOLVED.

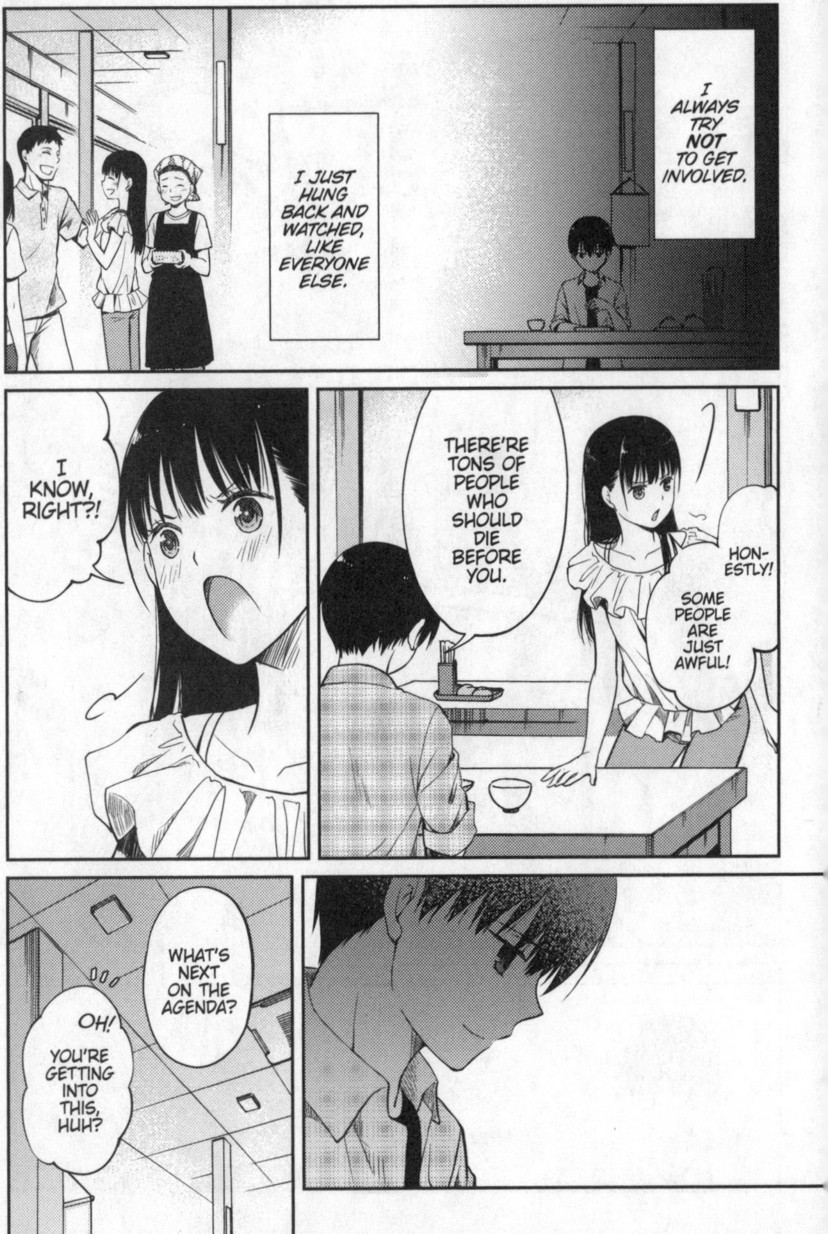
I ALWAYS TRY NOT TO GET INVOLVED.
I JUST HUNG BACK AND WATCHED, LIKE EVERYONE ELSE.
HON-ESTLY!
SOME PEOPLE ARE JUST AWFUL!
THERE'RE TONS OF PEOPLE WHO SHOULD DIE BEFORE YOU.
I KNOW, RIGHT?!
WHAT'S NEXT ON THE AGENDA?
OH!
YOU'RE GETTING INTO THIS, HUH?

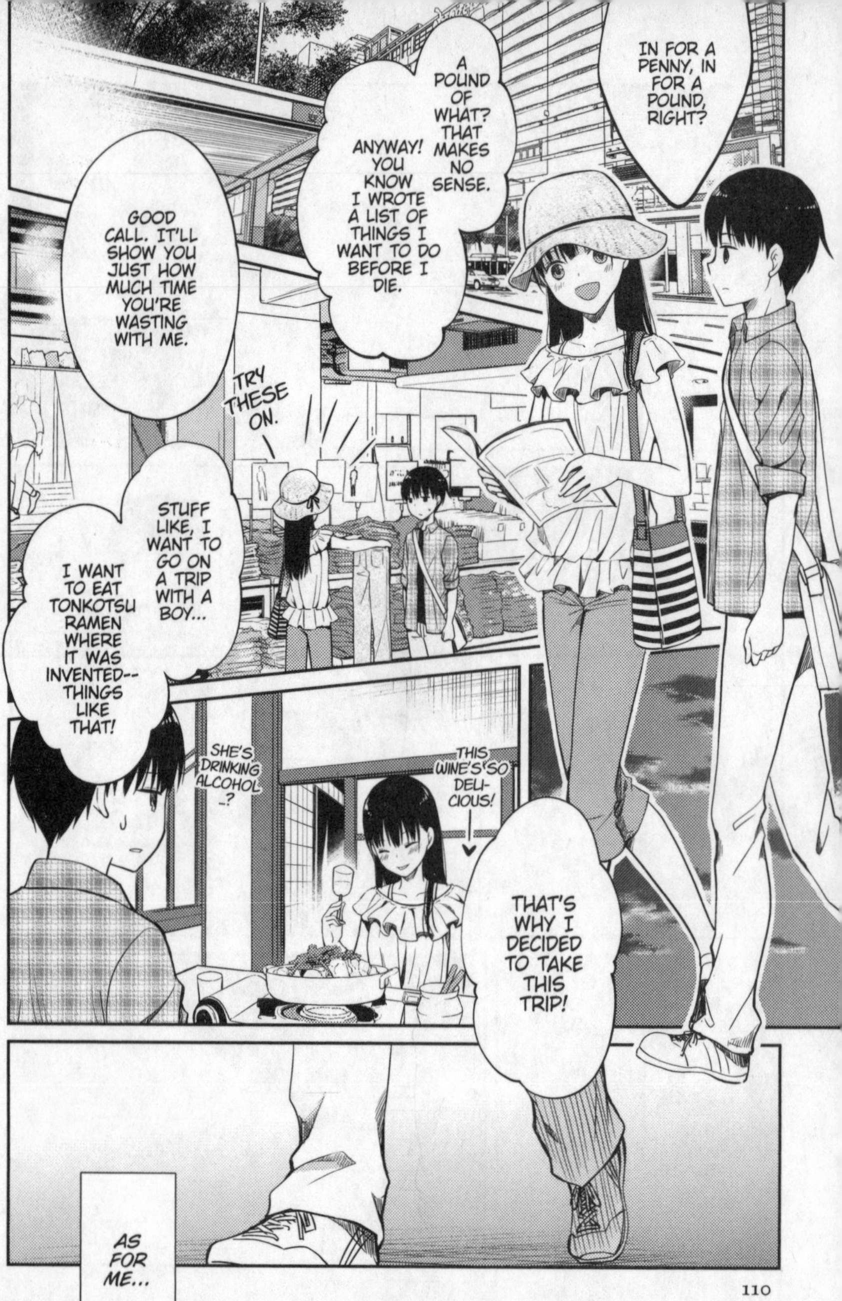
IN FOR A PENNY, IN FOR A POUND, RIGHT?
A POUND OF WHAT? THAT MAKES NO SENSE.
ANYWAY! YOU KNOW I WROTE A LIST OF THINGS I WANT TO DO BEFORE I DIE.
GOOD CALL. IT'LL SHOW YOU JUST HOW MUCH TIME YOU'RE WASTING WITH ME.
TRY THESE ON.
STUFF LIKE, I WANT TO GO ON A TRIP WITH A BOY...
I WANT TO EAT TONKOTSU RAMEN WHERE IT WAS INVENTED-- THINGS LIKE THAT!
THIS WINE'S SO DELICIOUS!
SHE'S DRINKING ALCOHOL ..?
THAT'S WHY I DECIDED TO TAKE THIS TRIP!
AS FOR ME...

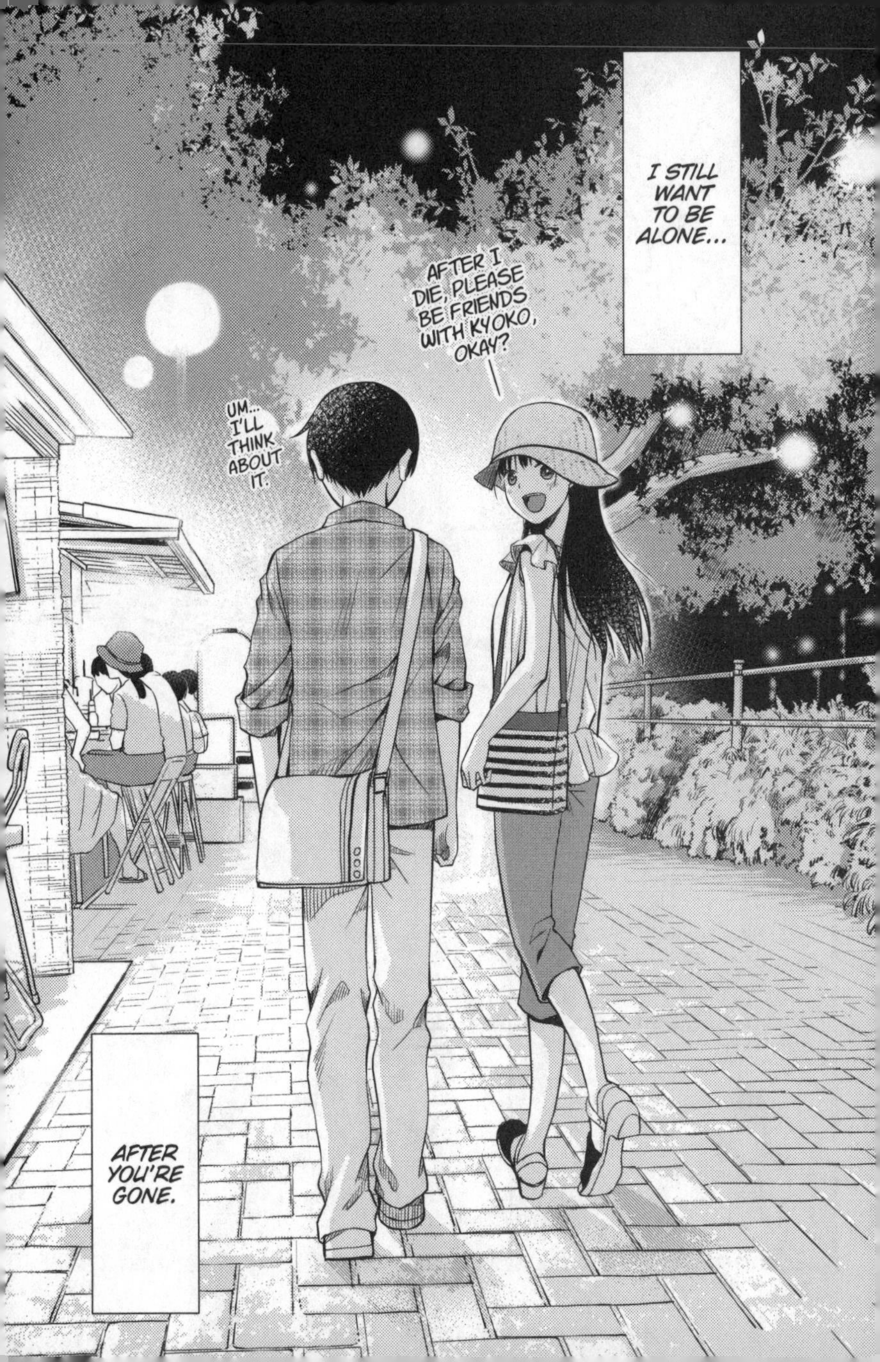
I STILL WANT TO BE ALONE...
AFTER I DIE, PLEASE BE FRIENDS WITH KYOKO, OKAY?
UM... I'LL THINK ABOUT IT.
AFTER YOU'RE GONE.

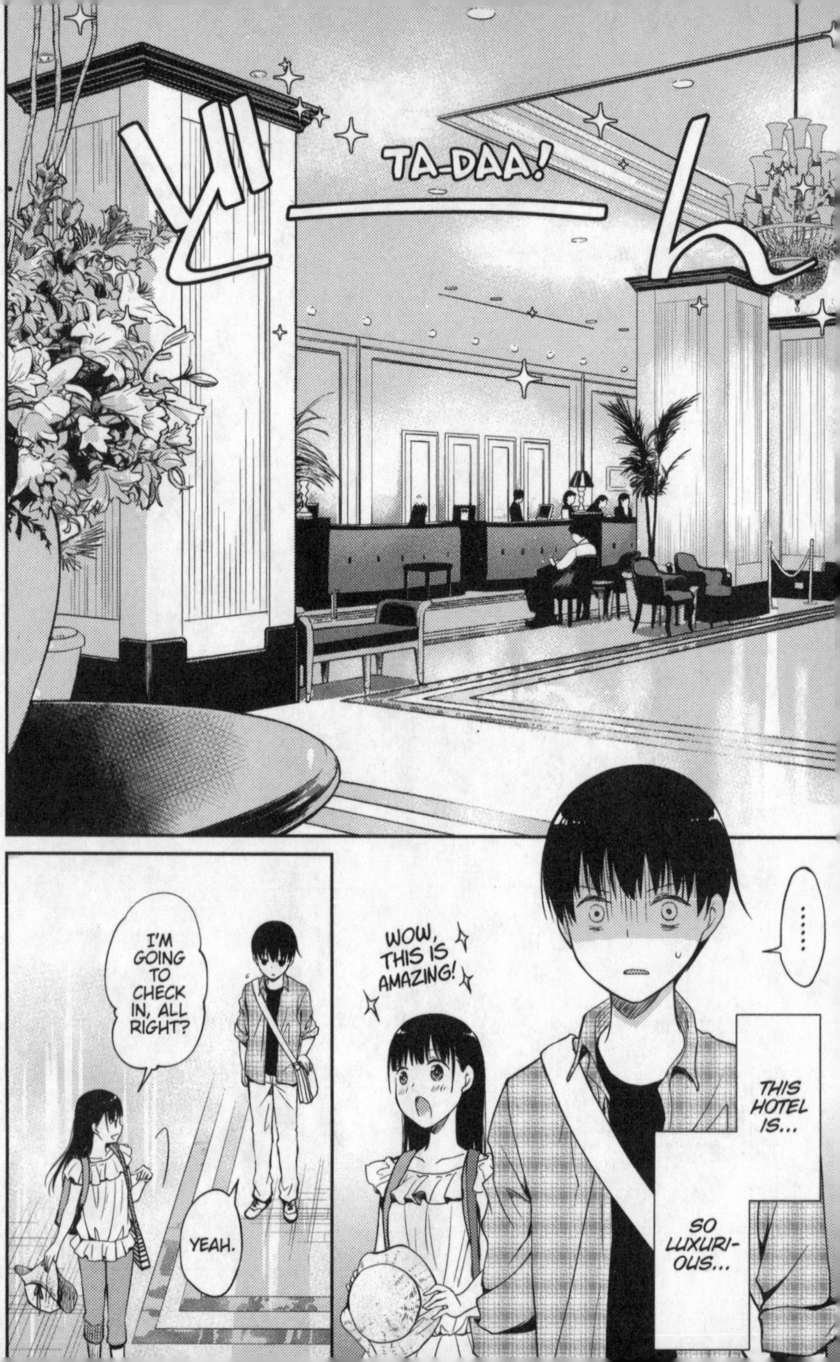
TA-DAA!
......
WOW, THIS IS AMAZING!
I'M GOING TO CHECK IN, ALL RIGHT?
YEAH.
THIS HOTEL IS...
SO LUXURI-OUS...

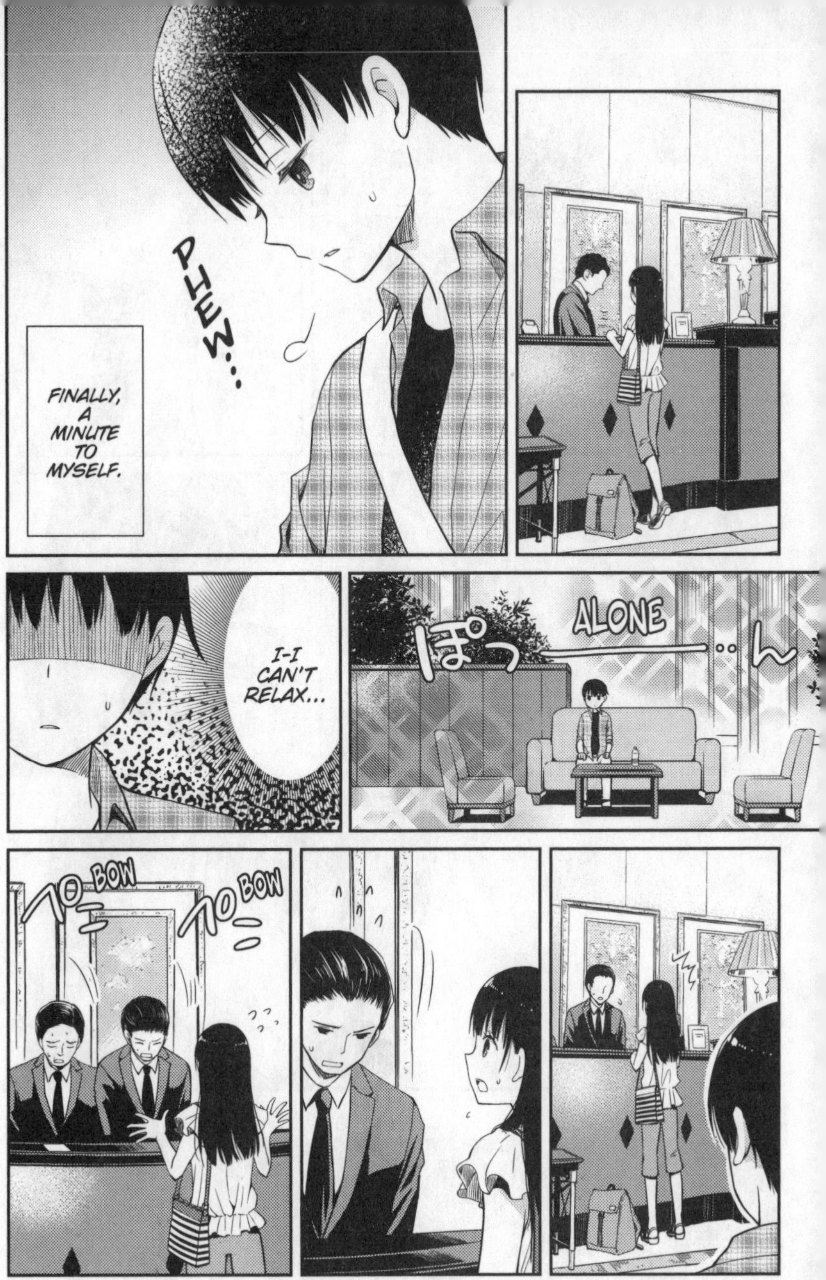
PHEW...
FINALLY, A MINUTE TO MYSELF.
ALONE
ぽっ——————…ん
I-I CAN'T RELAX...
ヘコ BOW
ヘコ BOW

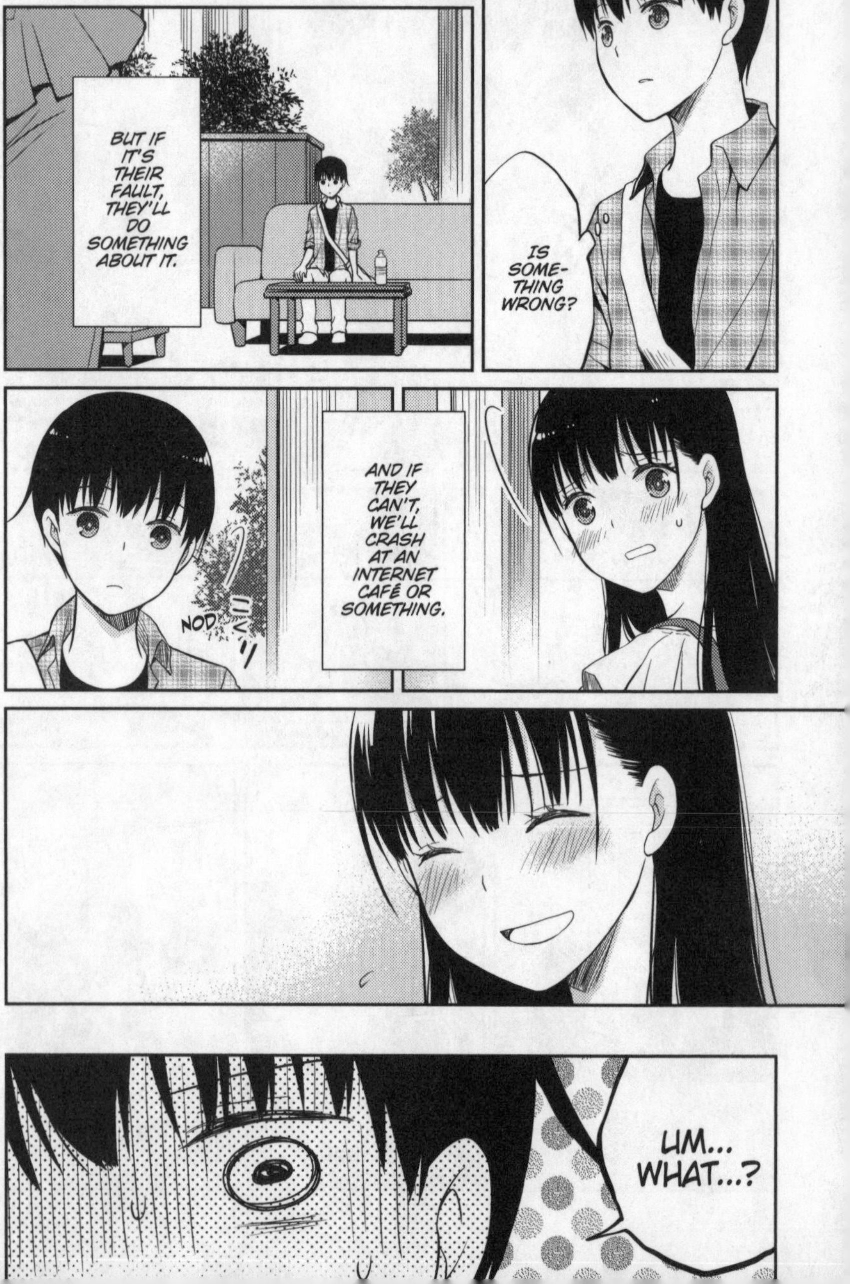
IS SOMETHING WRONG?
BUT IF IT'S THEIR FAULT, THEY'LL DO SOMETHING ABOUT IT.
AND IF THEY CAN'T, WE'LL CRASH AT AN INTERNET CAFÉ OR SOMETHING.
NOD
UM... WHAT...?

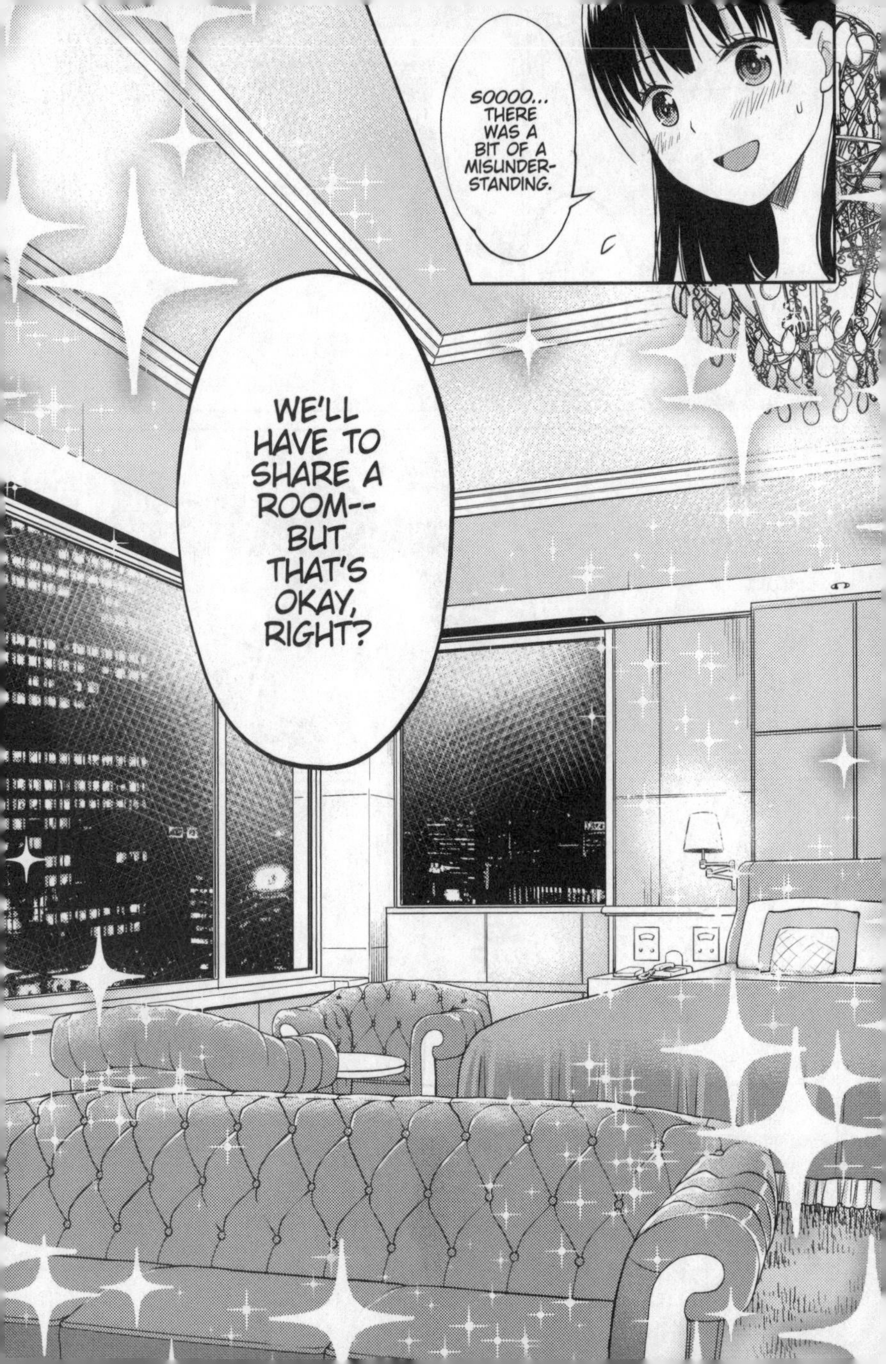
SOOOO... THERE WAS A BIT OF A MISUNDER-STANDING.
WE'LL HAVE TO SHARE A ROOM-- BUT THAT'S OKAY, RIGHT?

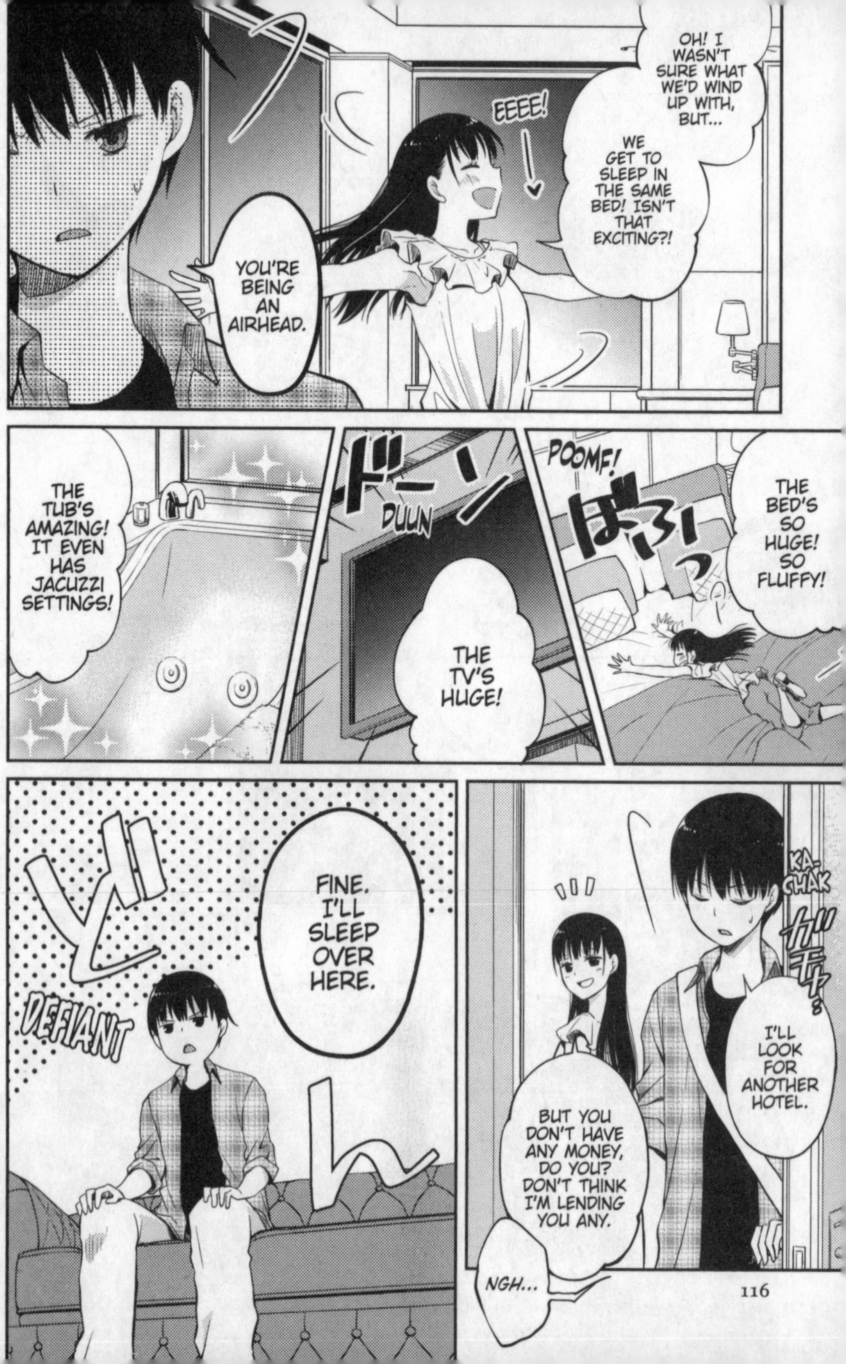

OH! I WASN'T SURE WHAT WE'D WIND UP WITH, BUT...
EEEE!
WE GET TO SLEEP IN THE SAME BED! ISN'T THAT EXCITING?!
YOU'RE BEING AN AIRHEAD.
POOMF!
ぼふっ
THE BED'S SO HUGE! SO FLUFFY!
ドーン
DUUN
THE TV'S HUGE!
THE TUB'S AMAZING! IT EVEN HAS JACUZZI SETTINGS!
KA-CHAK
ガチャ
I'LL LOOK FOR ANOTHER HOTEL.
BUT YOU DON'T HAVE ANY MONEY, DO YOU? DON'T THINK I'M LENDING YOU ANY.
NGH...
FINE. I'LL SLEEP OVER HERE.
DEFIANT

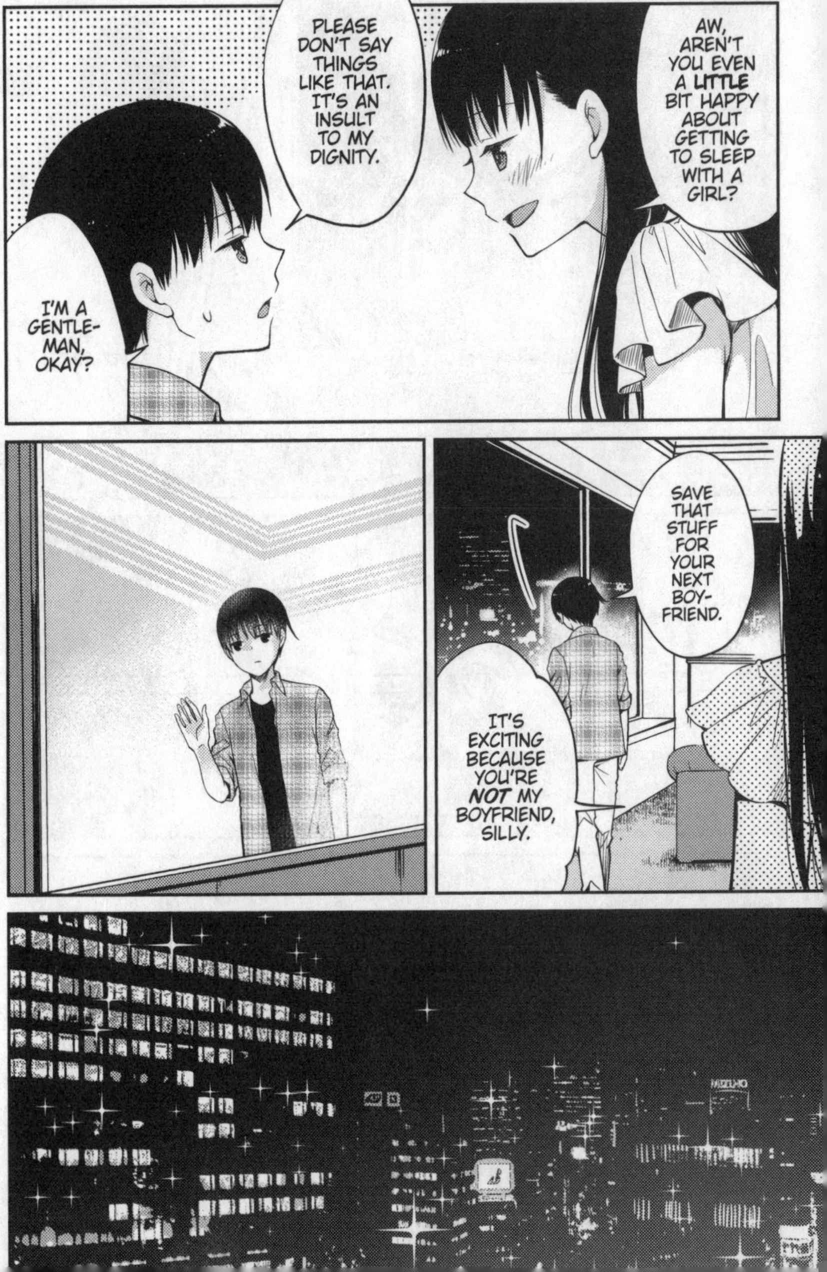
AW, AREN'T YOU EVEN A **LITTLE** BIT HAPPY ABOUT GETTING TO SLEEP WITH A GIRL?
PLEASE DON'T SAY THINGS LIKE THAT. IT'S AN INSULT TO MY DIGNITY.
I'M A GENTLE-MAN, OKAY?
SAVE THAT STUFF FOR YOUR NEXT BOY-FRIEND.
IT'S EXCITING BECAUSE YOU'RE ***NOT*** MY BOYFRIEND, SILLY.

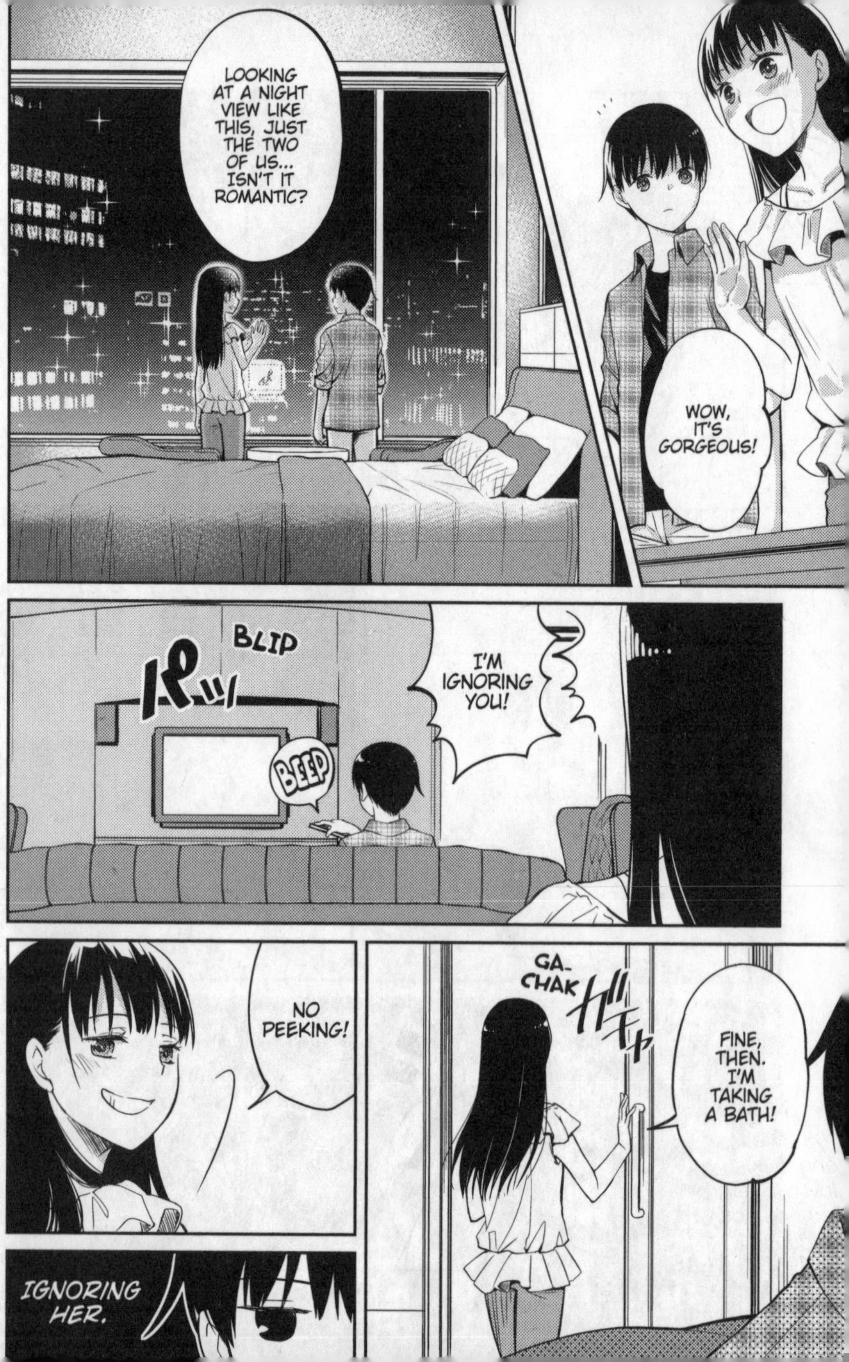
WOW, IT'S GORGEOUS!
LOOKING AT A NIGHT VIEW LIKE THIS, JUST THE TWO OF US... ISN'T IT ROMANTIC?
I'M IGNORING YOU!
BLIP
パッ
BEEP
GA-CHAK
ガチャ
FINE, THEN. I'M TAKING A BATH!
NO PEEKING!
IGNORING HER.

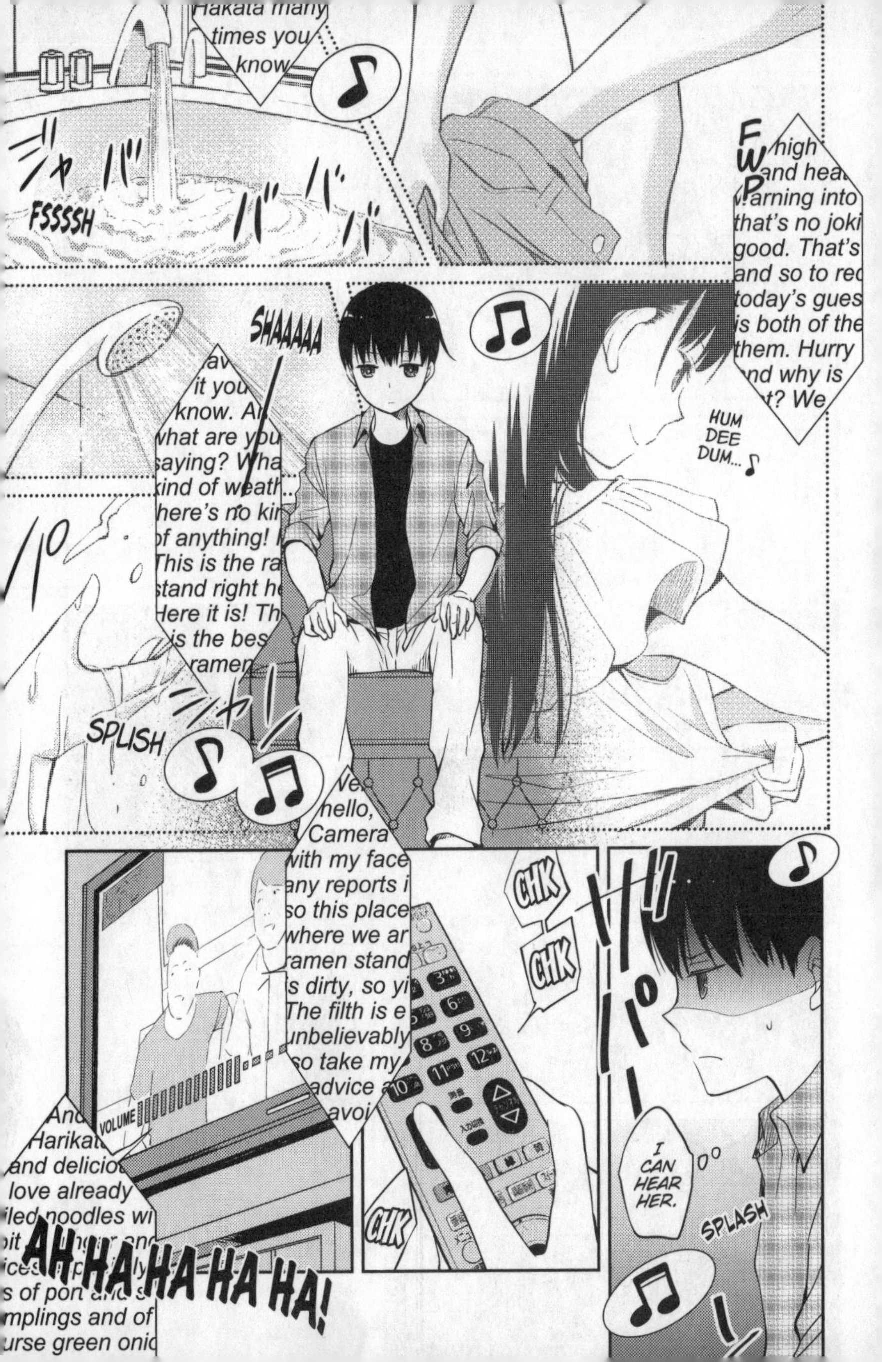

Hakata many times you know
FSSSSH
ジャババババ
high and hea warning into that's no joki good. That's and so to rec today's gues is both of the them. Hurry nd why is t? We
FWP
HUM DEE DUM...
SHAAAAA
it you know. A what are you saying? Wha kind of weath here's no kin of anything! This is the ra stand right he Here it is! Th is the bes ramen
パ
SPLISH
シャー
I CAN HEAR HER.
SPLASH
CHK
CHK
CHK
We hello, Camera with my face any reports i so this place where we ar ramen stand is dirty, so yo The filth is e unbelievably so take my advice a avoi
VOLUME
And Harikat and delicio love already filed noodles wi ices s of por mplings and of urse green onic
AH HA HA HA HA HA!

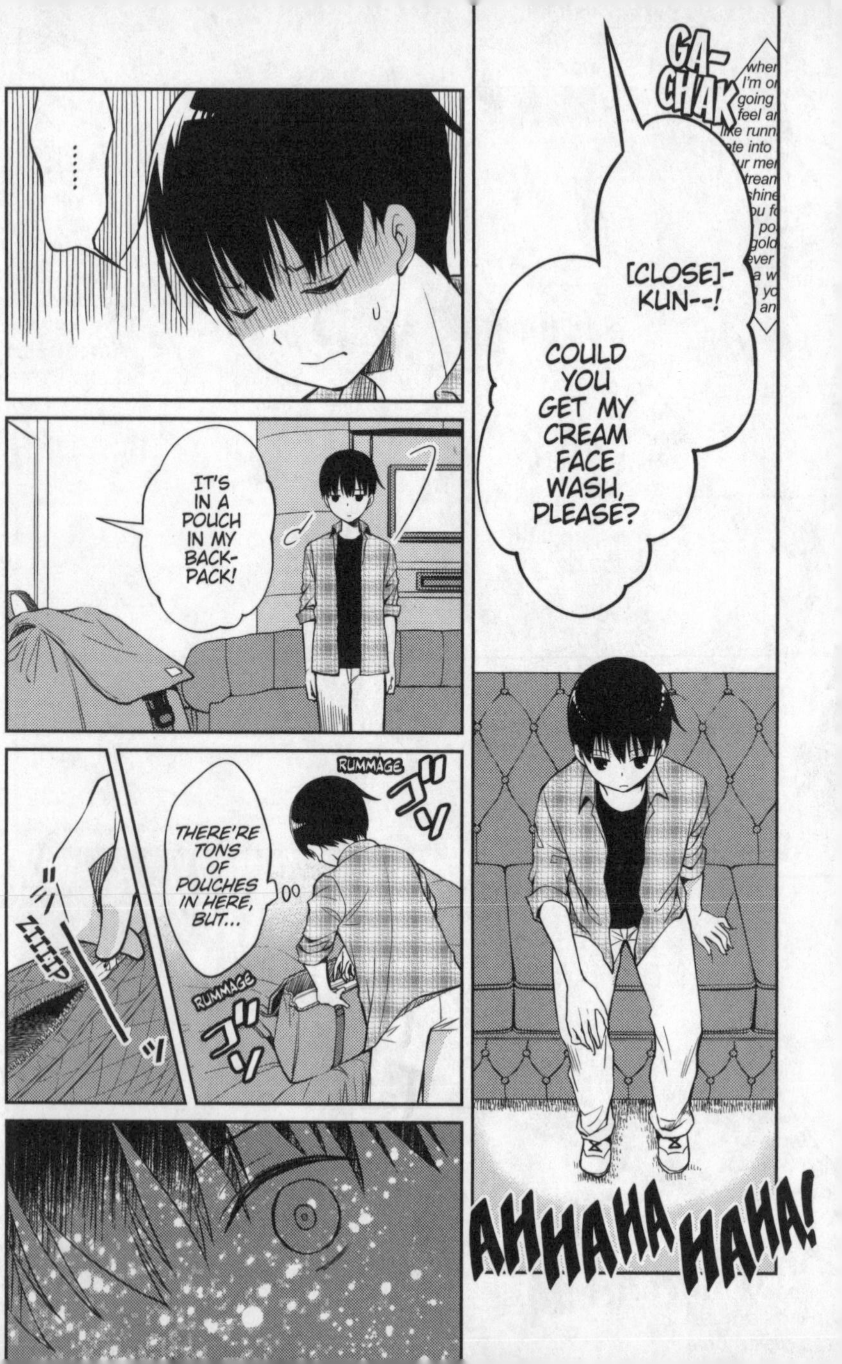
GA-CHAK
[CLOSE]-KUN--!
COULD YOU GET MY CREAM FACE WASH, PLEASE?
AHHAHA HAHA!
......
IT'S IN A POUCH IN MY BACK-PACK!
RUMMAGE
THERE'RE TONS OF POUCHES IN HERE, BUT...
ZIIIP
RUMMAGE

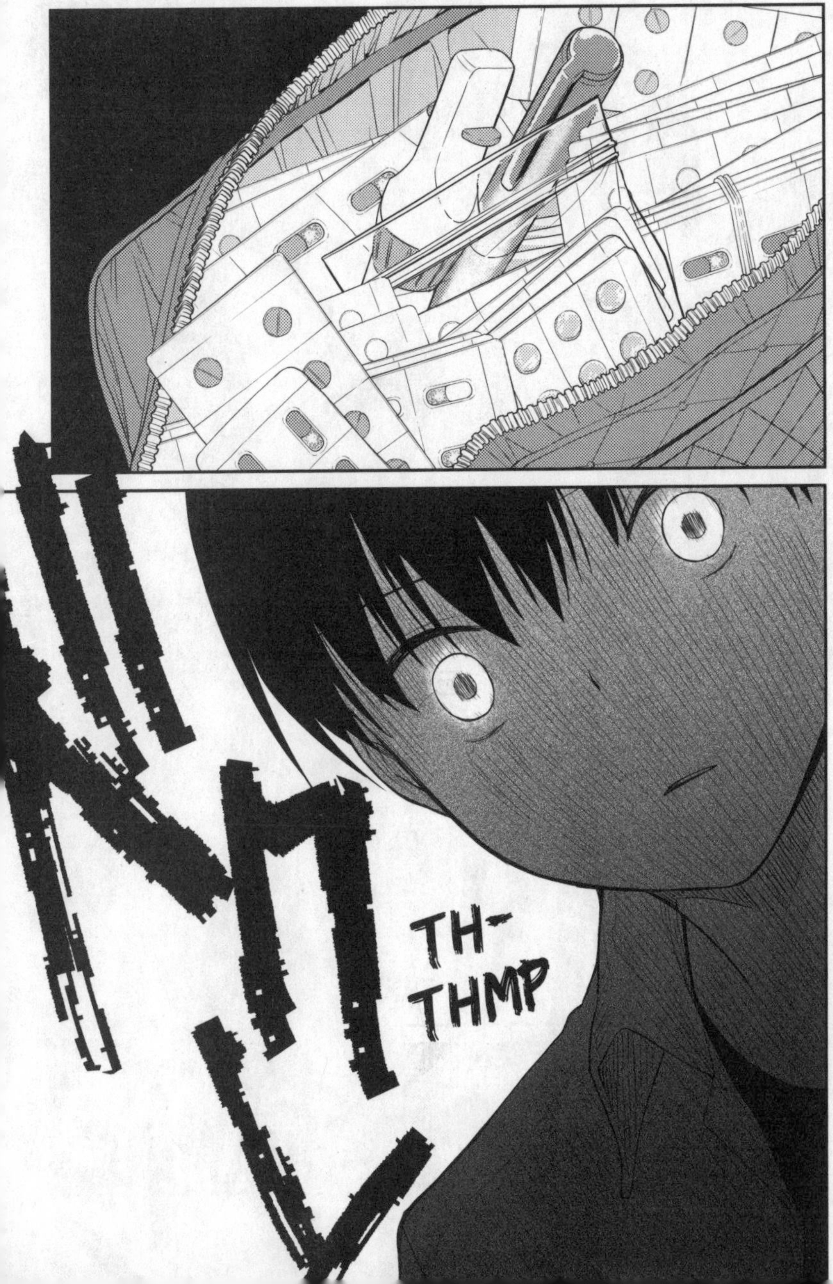
TH-
THMP

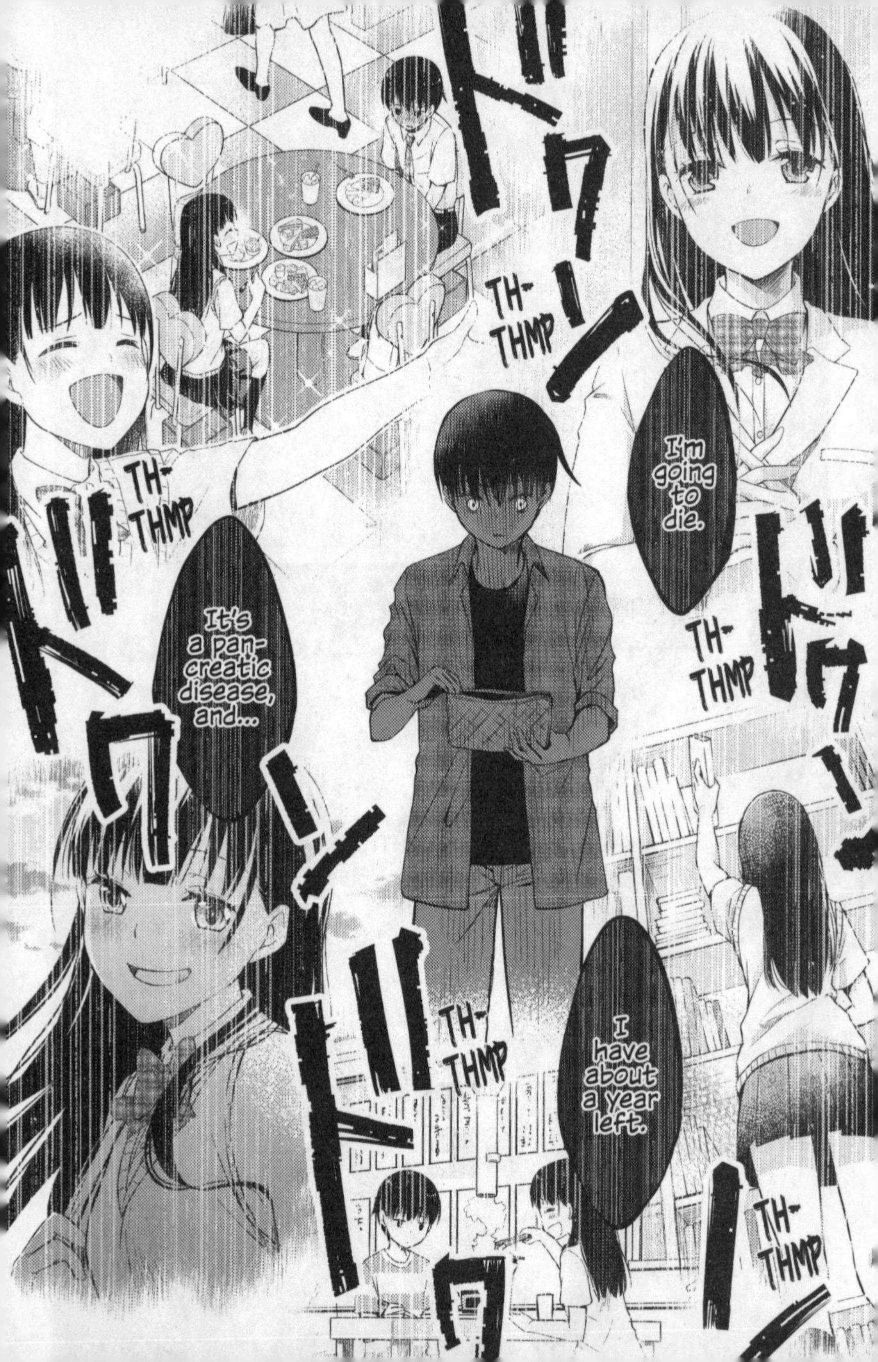
TH-THMP
I'm going to die.
TH-THMP
TH-THMP
It's a pan-creatic disease, and...
TH-THMP
I have about a year left.
TH-THMP
TH-THMP

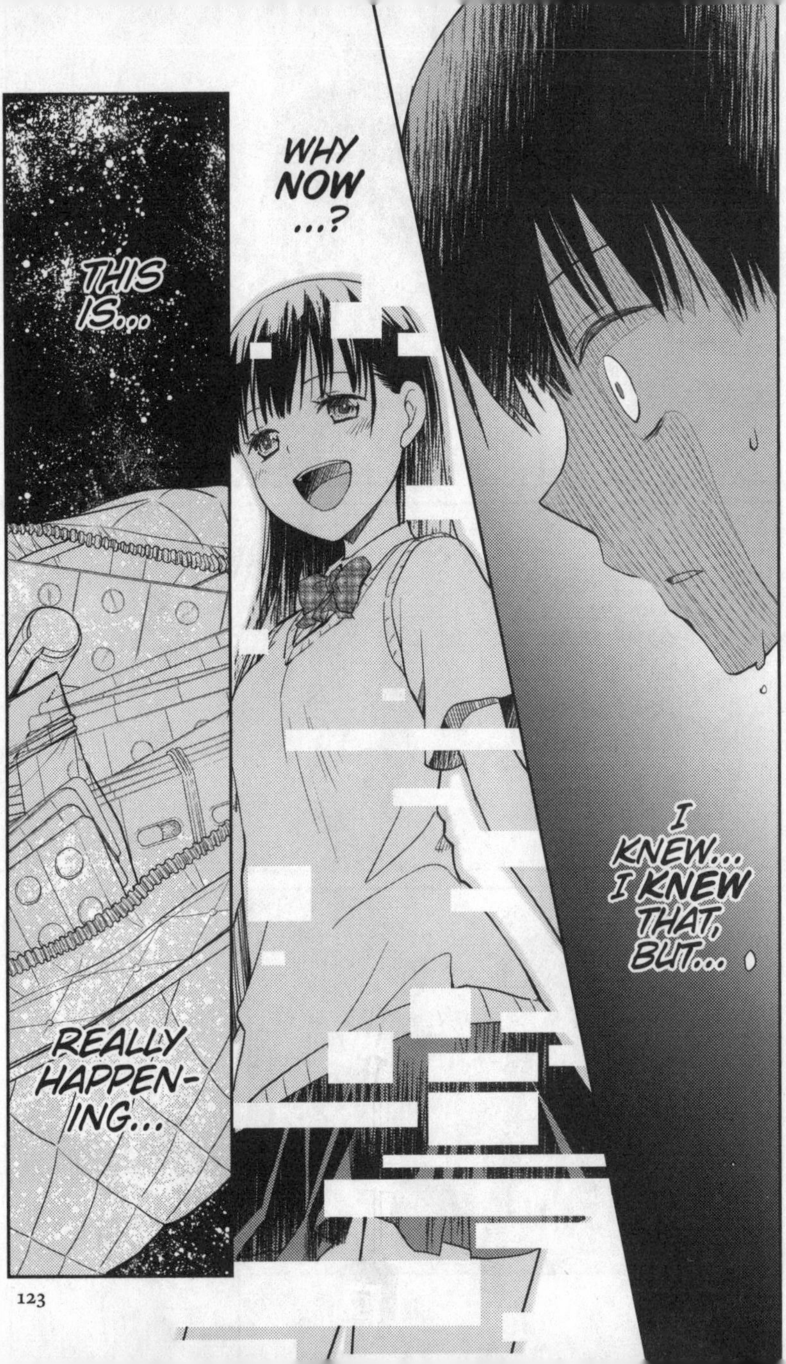
I KNEW... I KNEW THAT, BUT...
WHY NOW ...?
THIS IS...
REALLY HAPPEN-ING...

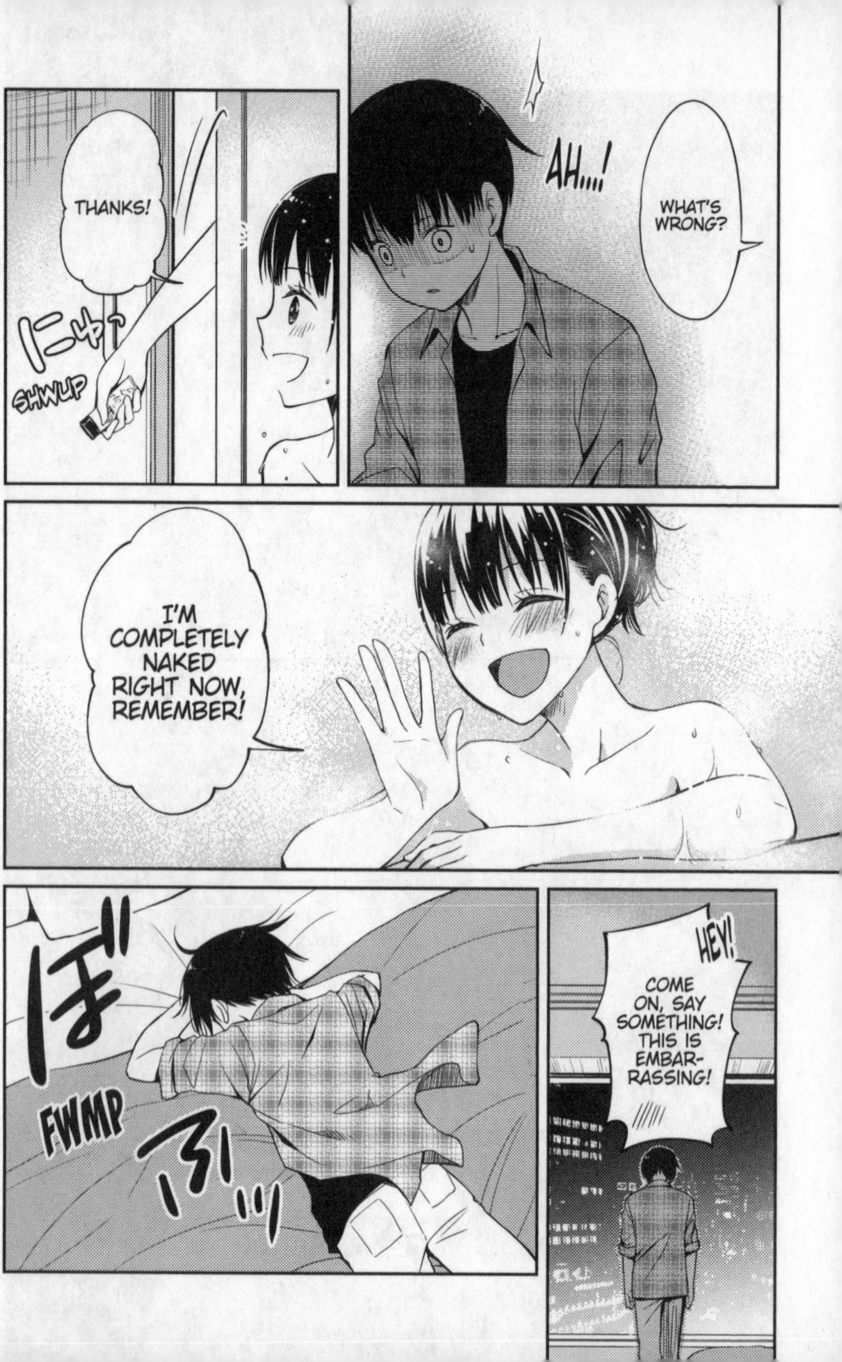
WHAT'S WRONG?
AH...!
THANKS!
にゅっ
SHWUP
I'M COMPLETELY NAKED RIGHT NOW, REMEMBER!
HEY!
COME ON, SAY SOMETHING! THIS IS EMBARRASSING!
ぼ
ふ
FWMP

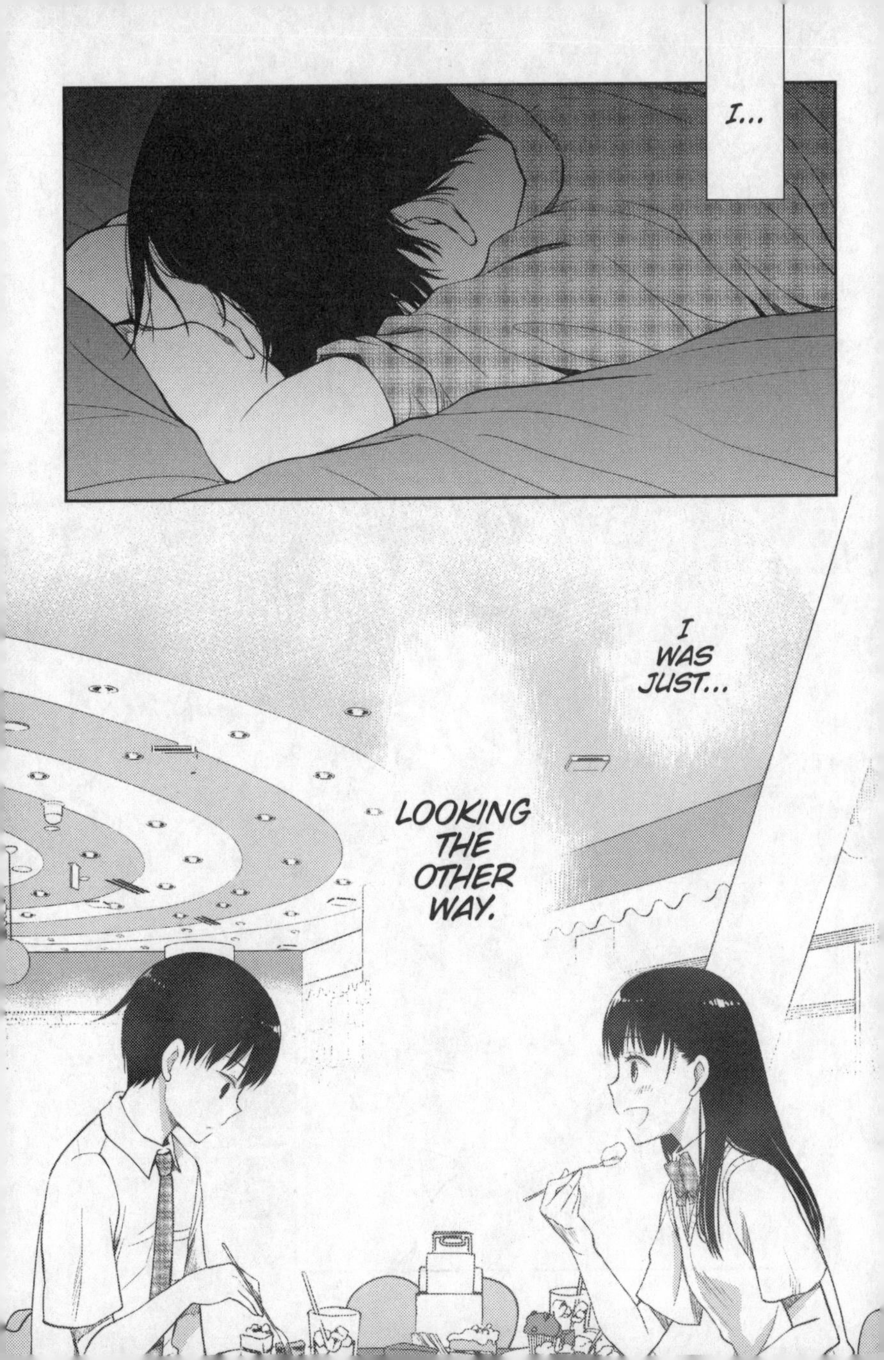
I...
I WAS JUST...
LOOKING THE OTHER WAY.

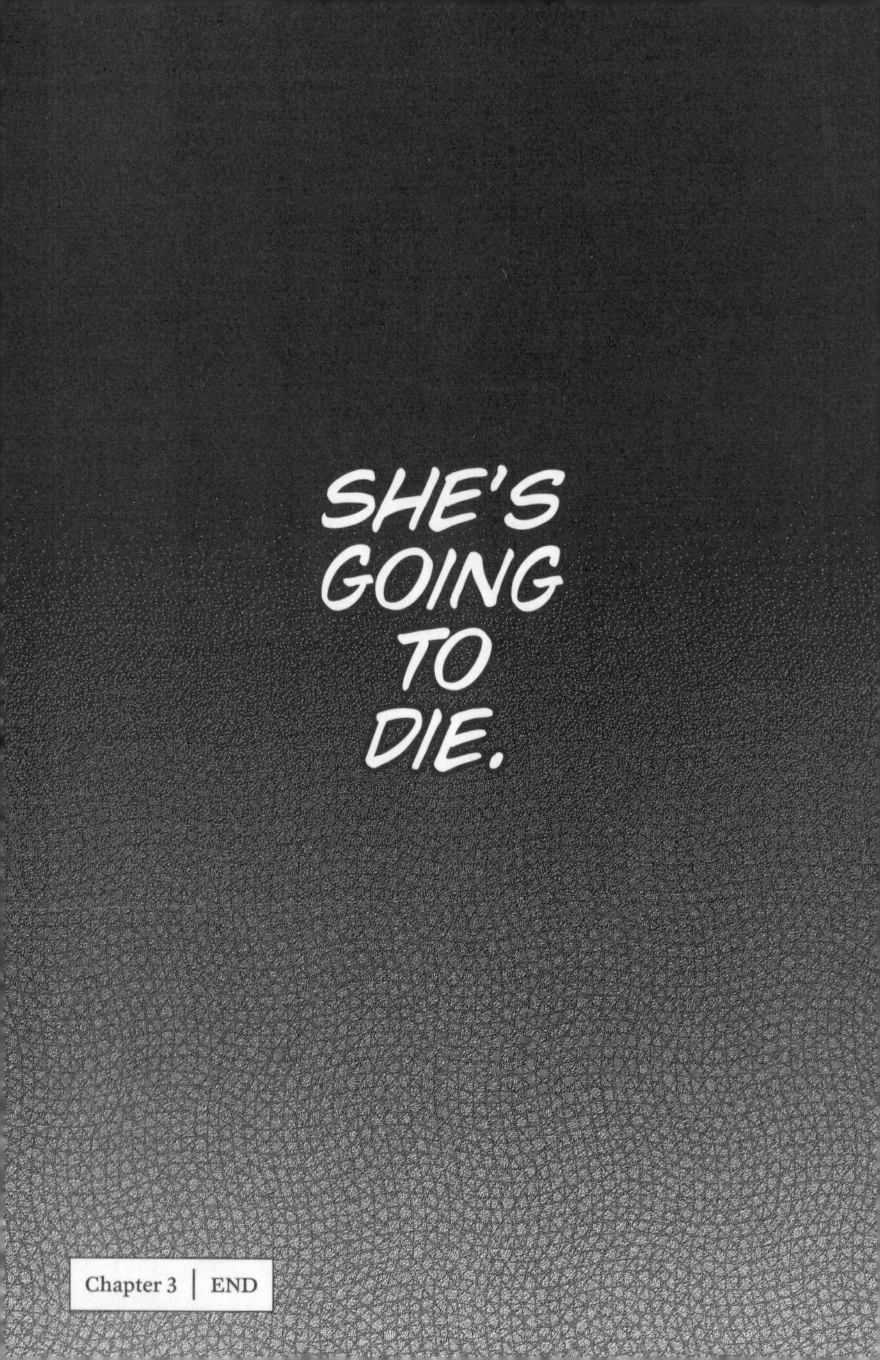
SHE'S GOING TO DIE.
Chapter 3 | END

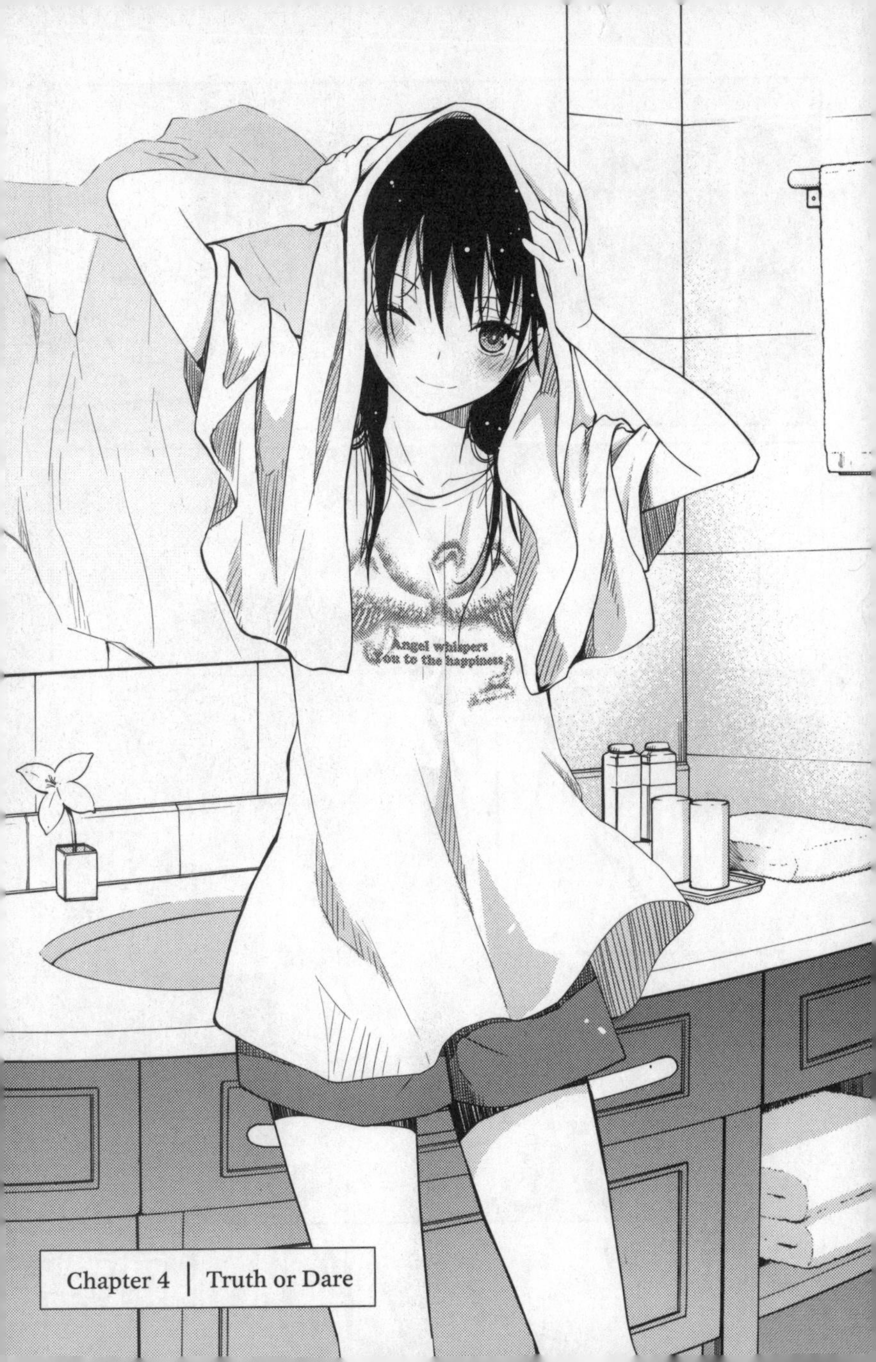
Angel whispers
You to the happiness

Chapter 4 | Truth or Dare

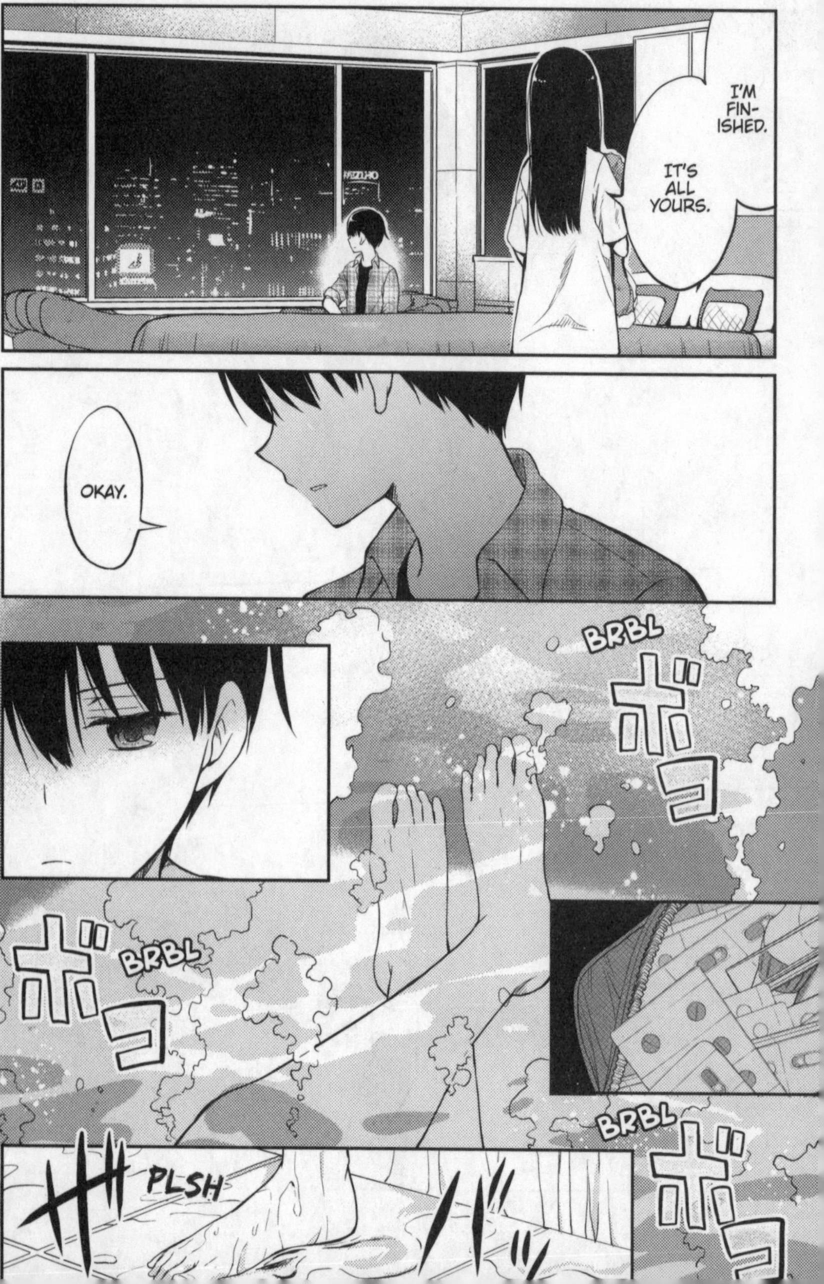
I'M FIN-ISHED.
IT'S ALL YOURS.
OKAY.
BRBL
ボコ
BRBL
ボコ
BRBL
ボコ
PLSH

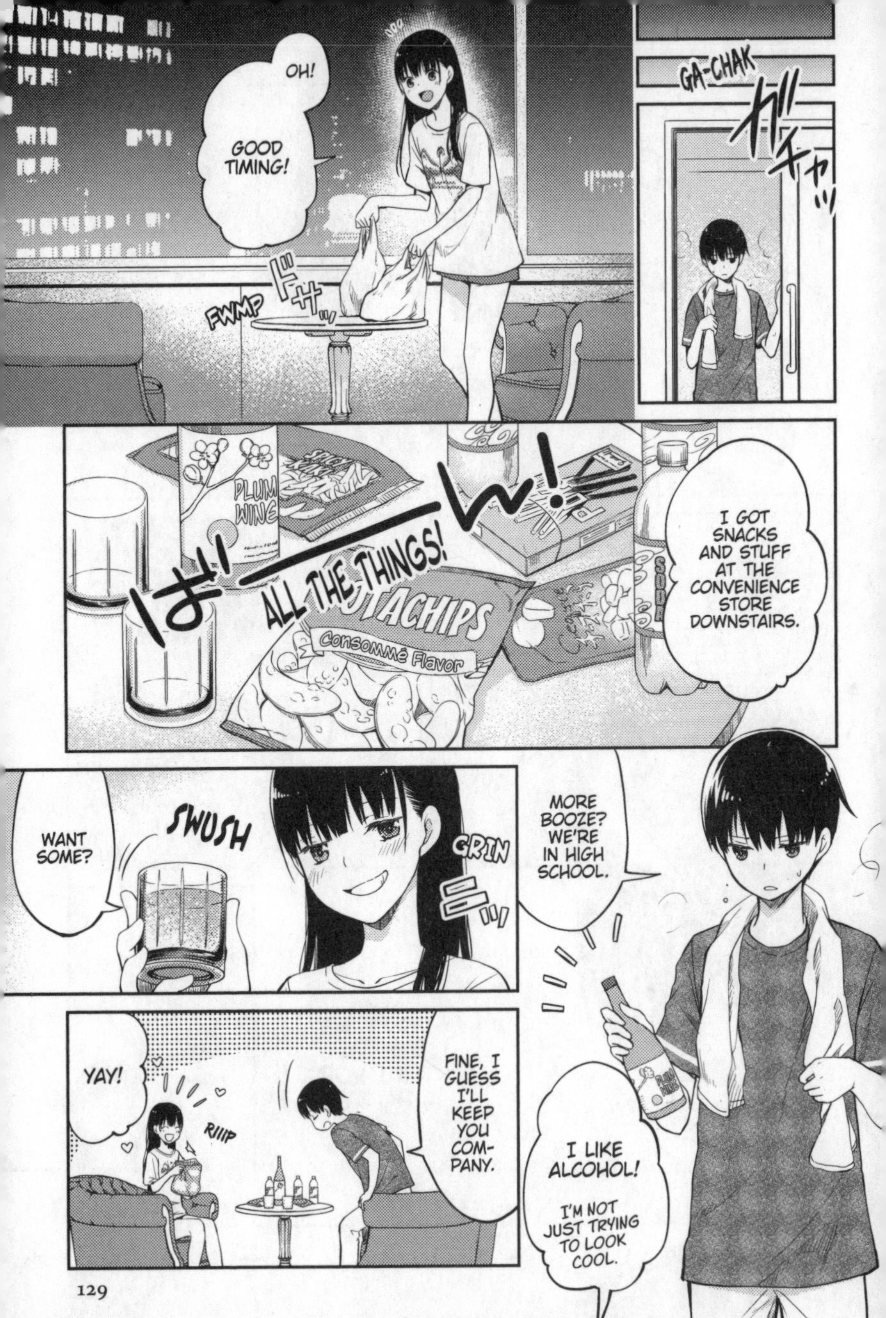
GA-CHAK
ガチャッ
OH!
GOOD TIMING!
FWMP
ドサッ
I GOT SNACKS AND STUFF AT THE CONVENIENCE STORE DOWNSTAIRS.
ALL THE THINGS!
PLUM WINE
TACHIPS
Consommé Flavor
SODA
MORE BOOZE? WE'RE IN HIGH SCHOOL.
GRIN
SWUSH
WANT SOME?
I LIKE ALCOHOL!
I'M NOT JUST TRYING TO LOOK COOL.
FINE, I GUESS I'LL KEEP YOU COM-PANY.
RIIIP
YAY!

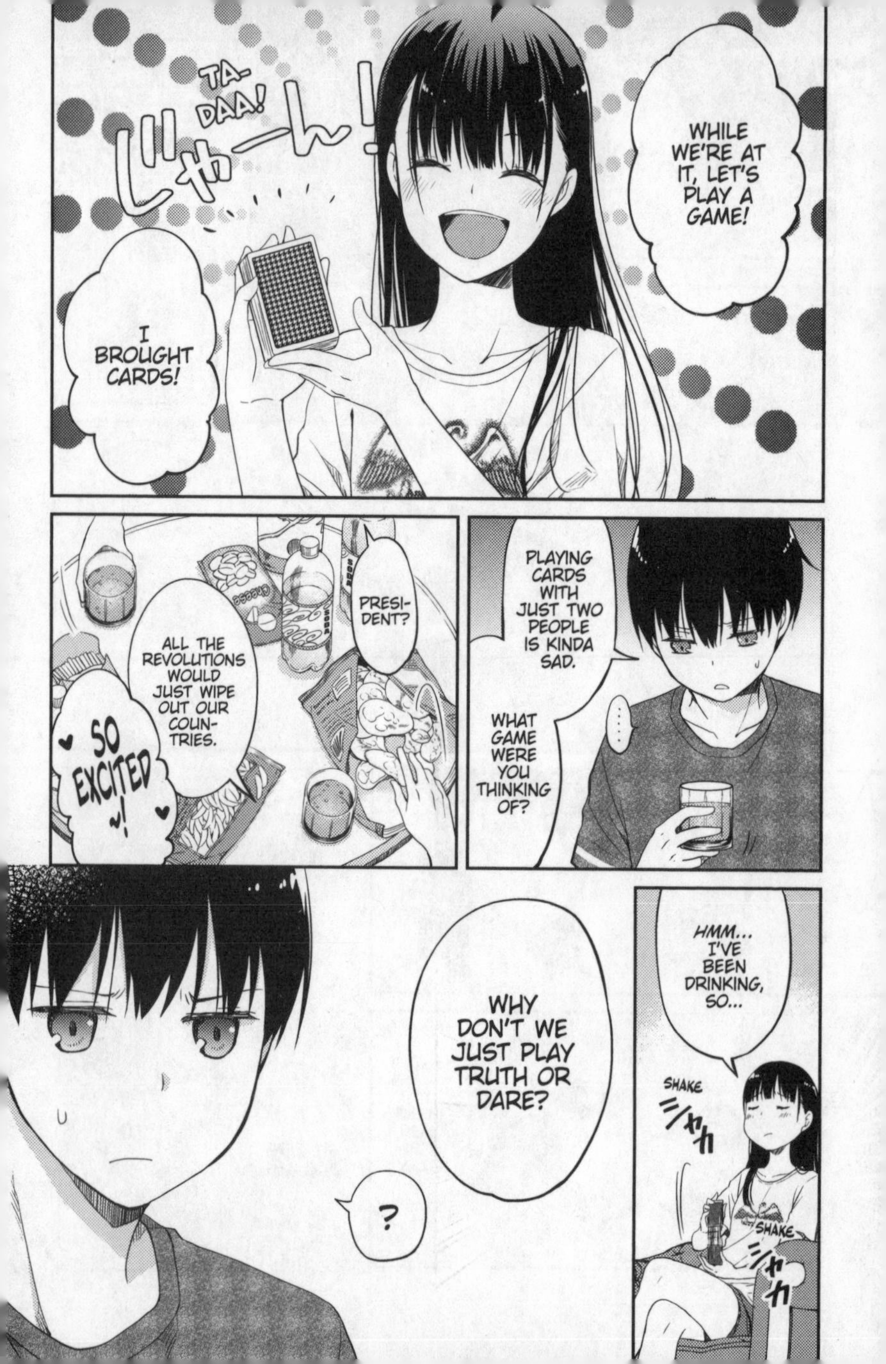
WHILE WE'RE AT IT, LET'S PLAY A GAME!
TA-DAA!
I BROUGHT CARDS!
PLAYING CARDS WITH JUST TWO PEOPLE IS KINDA SAD.
...
WHAT GAME WERE YOU THINKING OF?
PRESI-DENT?
ALL THE REVOLUTIONS WOULD JUST WIPE OUT OUR COUN-TRIES.
SO EXCITED ~!
HMM... I'VE BEEN DRINKING, SO...
SHAKE
SHAKE
WHY DON'T WE JUST PLAY TRUTH OR DARE?
?

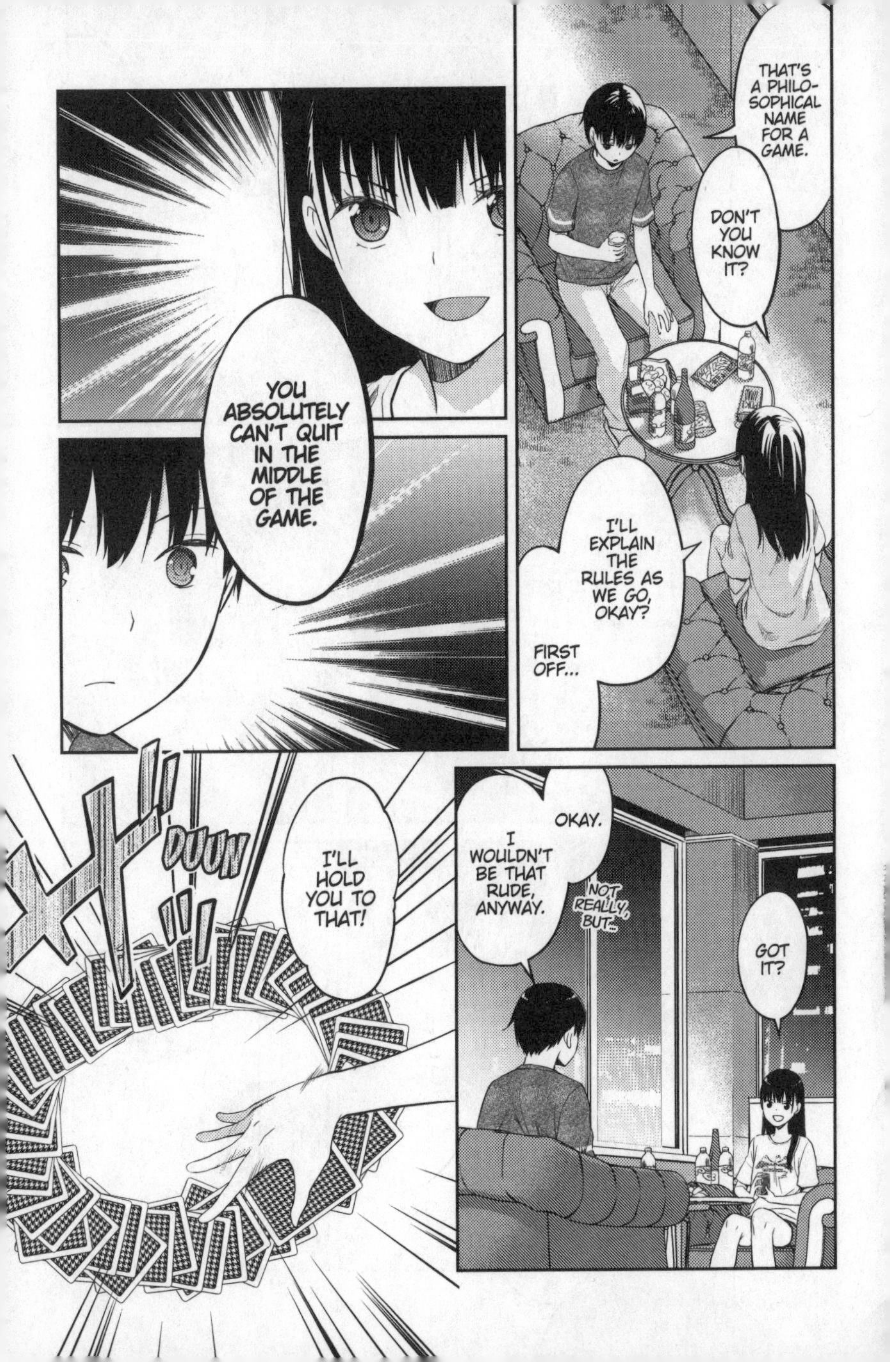
THAT'S A PHILOSOPHICAL NAME FOR A GAME.
DON'T YOU KNOW IT?
I'LL EXPLAIN THE RULES AS WE GO, OKAY?
FIRST OFF...
YOU ABSOLUTELY CAN'T QUIT IN THE MIDDLE OF THE GAME.
GOT IT?
NOT REALLY, BUT...
OKAY.
I WOULDN'T BE THAT RUDE, ANYWAY.
I'LL HOLD YOU TO THAT!
DUUN

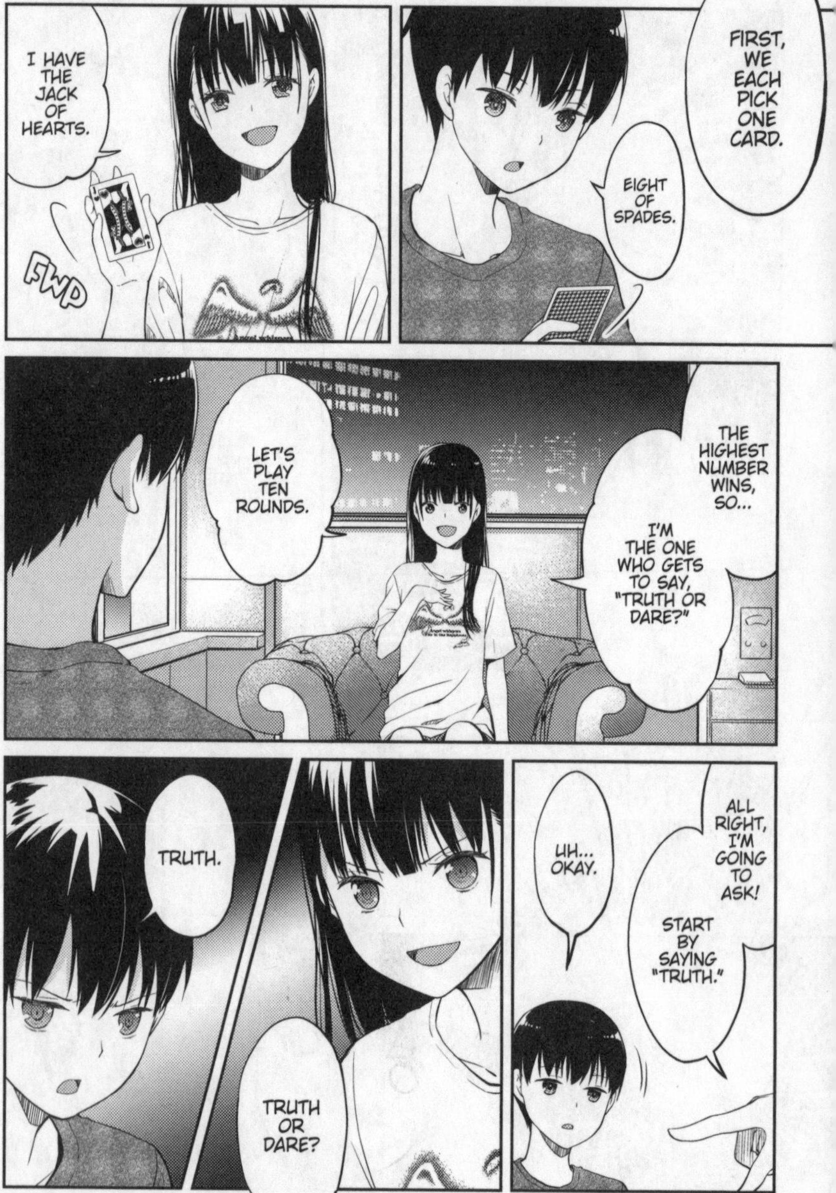
FIRST, WE EACH PICK ONE CARD.
EIGHT OF SPADES.
I HAVE THE JACK OF HEARTS.
FWP
THE HIGHEST NUMBER WINS, SO...
I'M THE ONE WHO GETS TO SAY, "TRUTH OR DARE?"
LET'S PLAY TEN ROUNDS.
ALL RIGHT, I'M GOING TO ASK!
START BY SAYING "TRUTH."
UH... OKAY.
TRUTH OR DARE?
TRUTH.

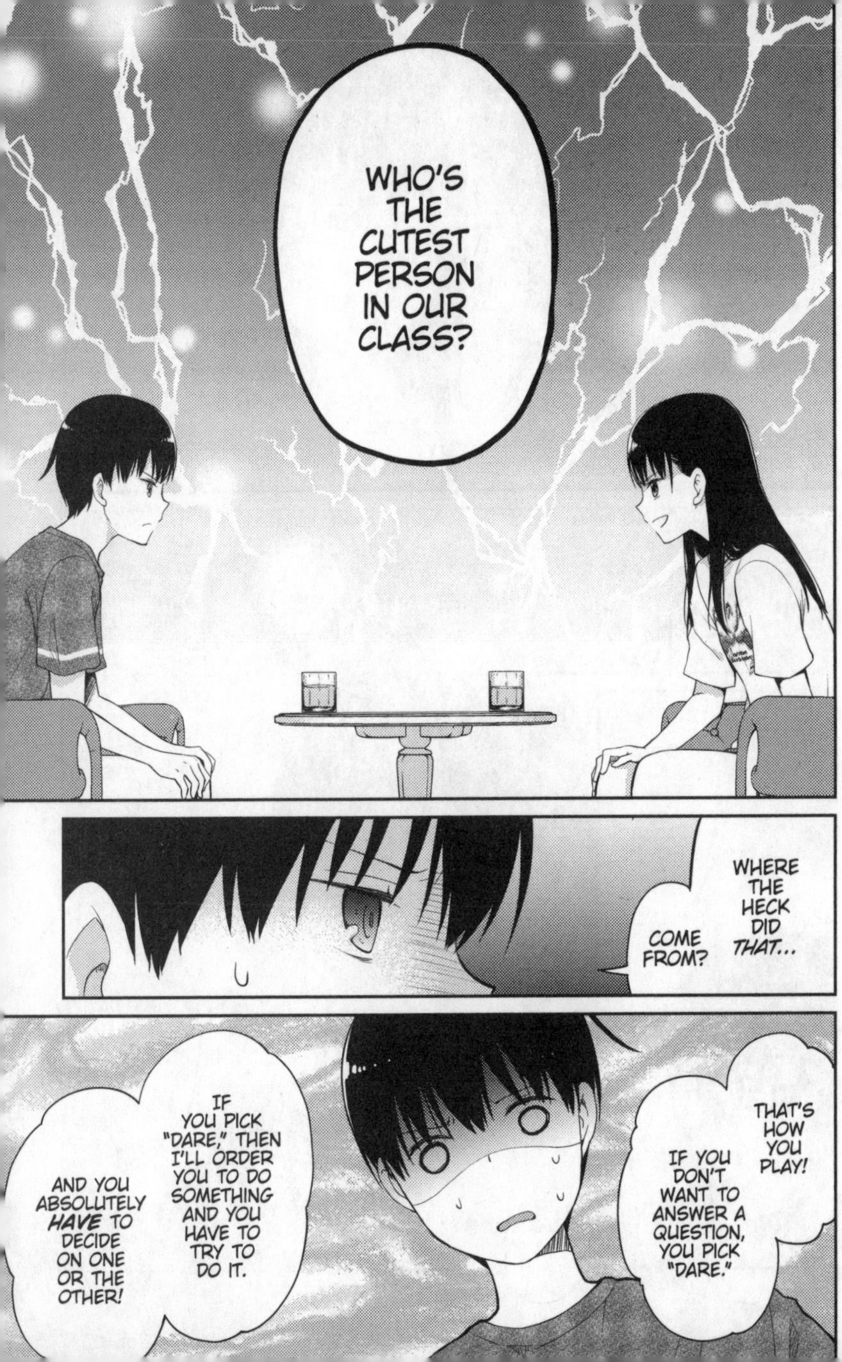
WHO'S THE CUTEST PERSON IN OUR CLASS?
WHERE THE HECK DID *THAT*...
COME FROM?
THAT'S HOW YOU PLAY!
IF YOU DON'T WANT TO ANSWER A QUESTION, YOU PICK "DARE."
IF YOU PICK "DARE," THEN I'LL ORDER YOU TO DO SOMETHING AND YOU HAVE TO TRY TO DO IT.
AND YOU ABSOLUTELY ***HAVE*** TO DECIDE ON ONE OR THE OTHER!

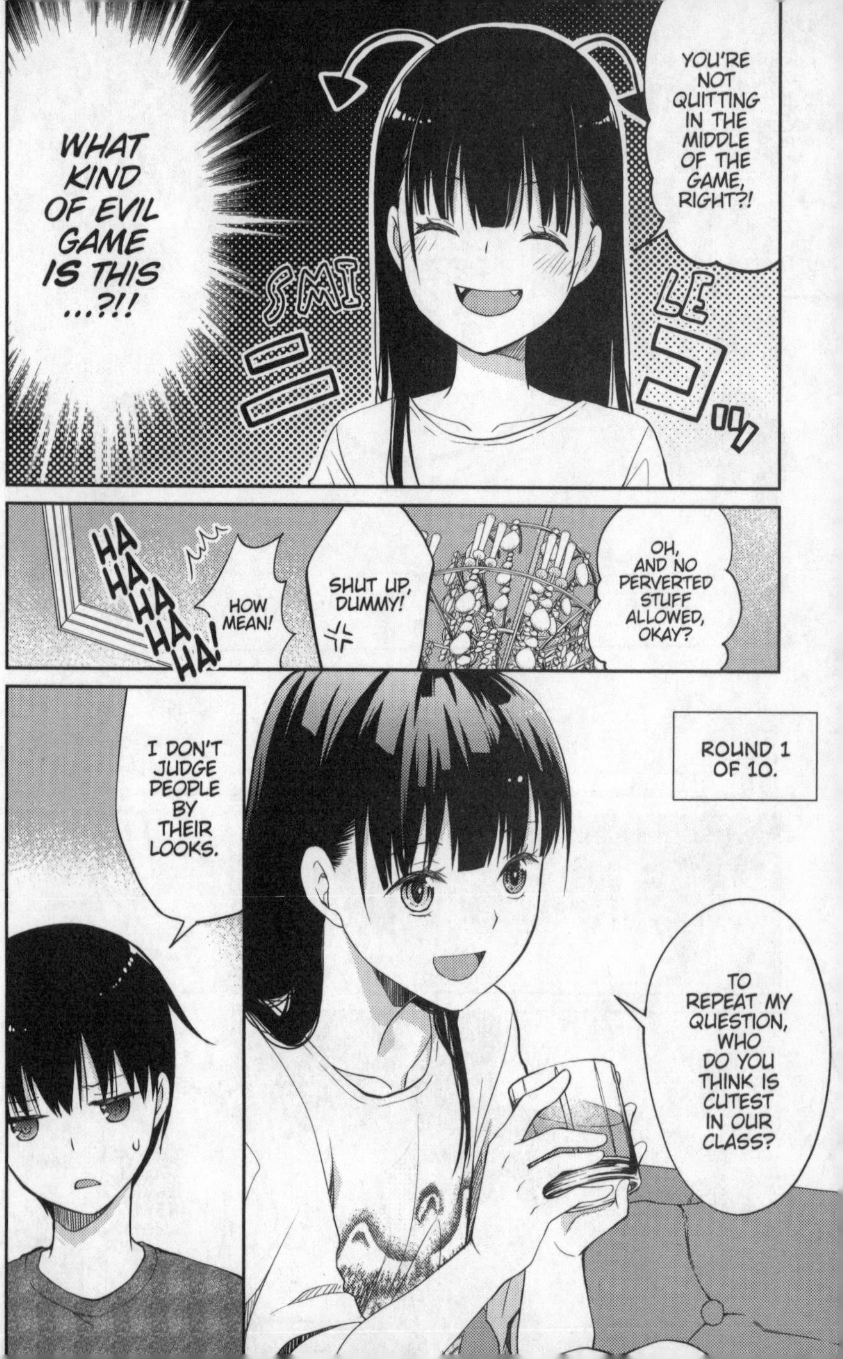
YOU'RE NOT QUITTING IN THE MIDDLE OF THE GAME, RIGHT?!
SMI LE
WHAT KIND OF EVIL GAME IS THIS ...?!!
OH, AND NO PERVERTED STUFF ALLOWED, OKAY?
SHUT UP, DUMMY!
HOW MEAN!
HA HA HA HA HA!
ROUND 1 OF 10.
TO REPEAT MY QUESTION, WHO DO YOU THINK IS CUTEST IN OUR CLASS?
I DON'T JUDGE PEOPLE BY THEIR LOOKS.

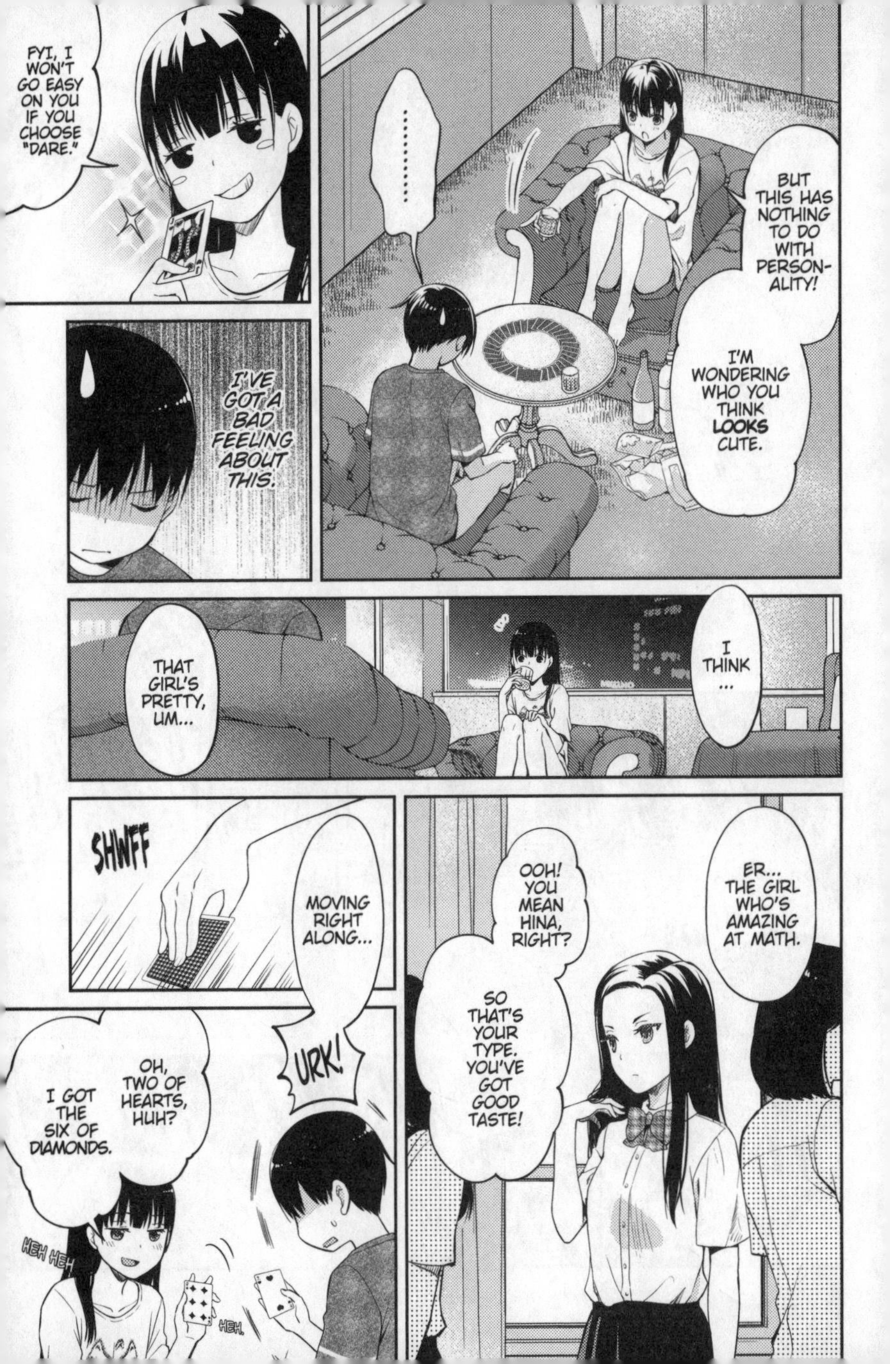
BUT THIS HAS NOTHING TO DO WITH PERSONALITY!
I'M WONDERING WHO YOU THINK LOOKS CUTE.
......
FYI, I WON'T GO EASY ON YOU IF YOU CHOOSE "DARE."
I'VE GOT A BAD FEELING ABOUT THIS.
I THINK ...
THAT GIRL'S PRETTY, UM...
ER... THE GIRL WHO'S AMAZING AT MATH.
OOH! YOU MEAN HINA, RIGHT?
SO THAT'S YOUR TYPE. YOU'VE GOT GOOD TASTE!
MOVING RIGHT ALONG...
SHWFF
URK!
OH, TWO OF HEARTS, HUH?
I GOT THE SIX OF DIAMONDS.
HEH HEH
HEH.

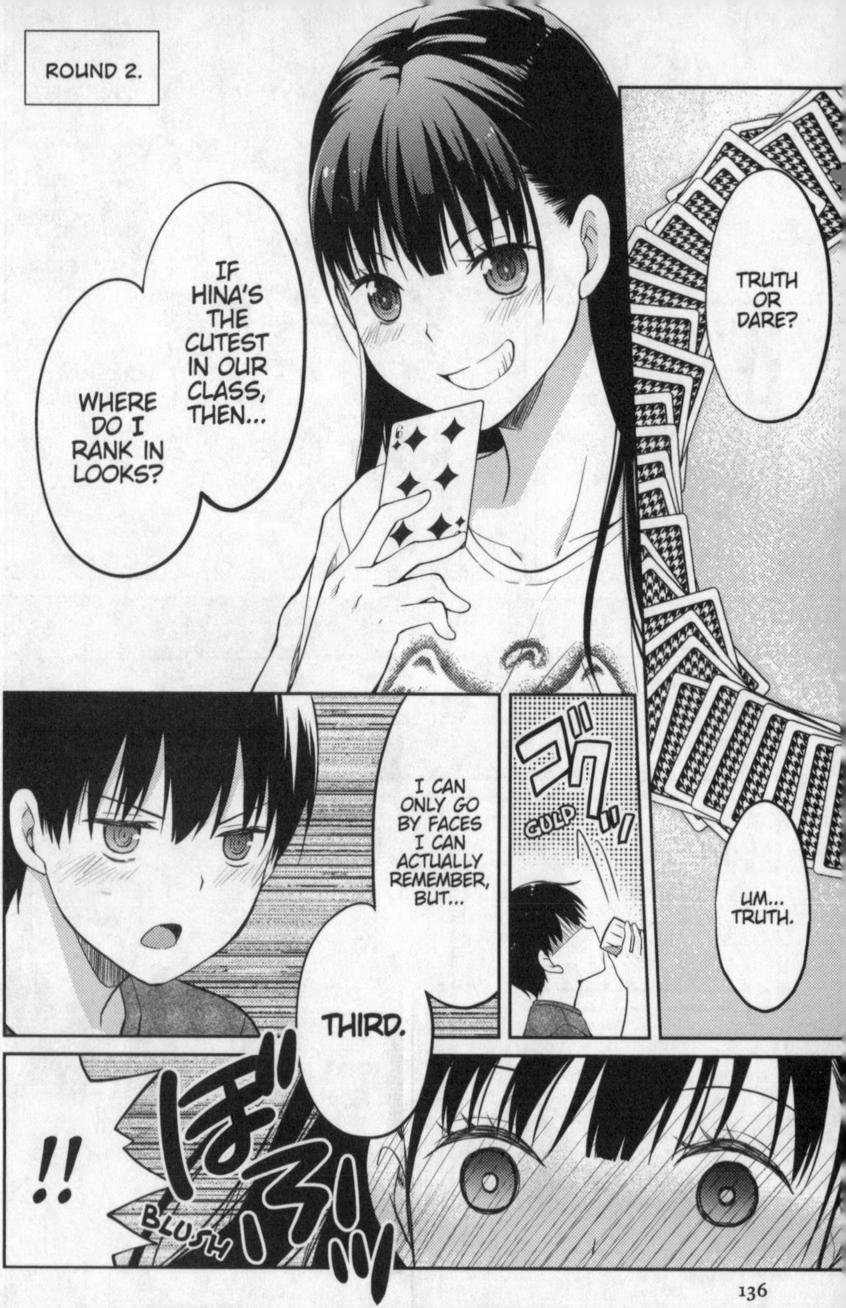
ROUND 2.
TRUTH OR DARE?
IF HINA'S THE CUTEST IN OUR CLASS, THEN...
WHERE DO I RANK IN LOOKS?
UM... TRUTH.
GULP
I CAN ONLY GO BY FACES I CAN ACTUALLY REMEMBER, BUT...
THIRD.
!!
BLUSH

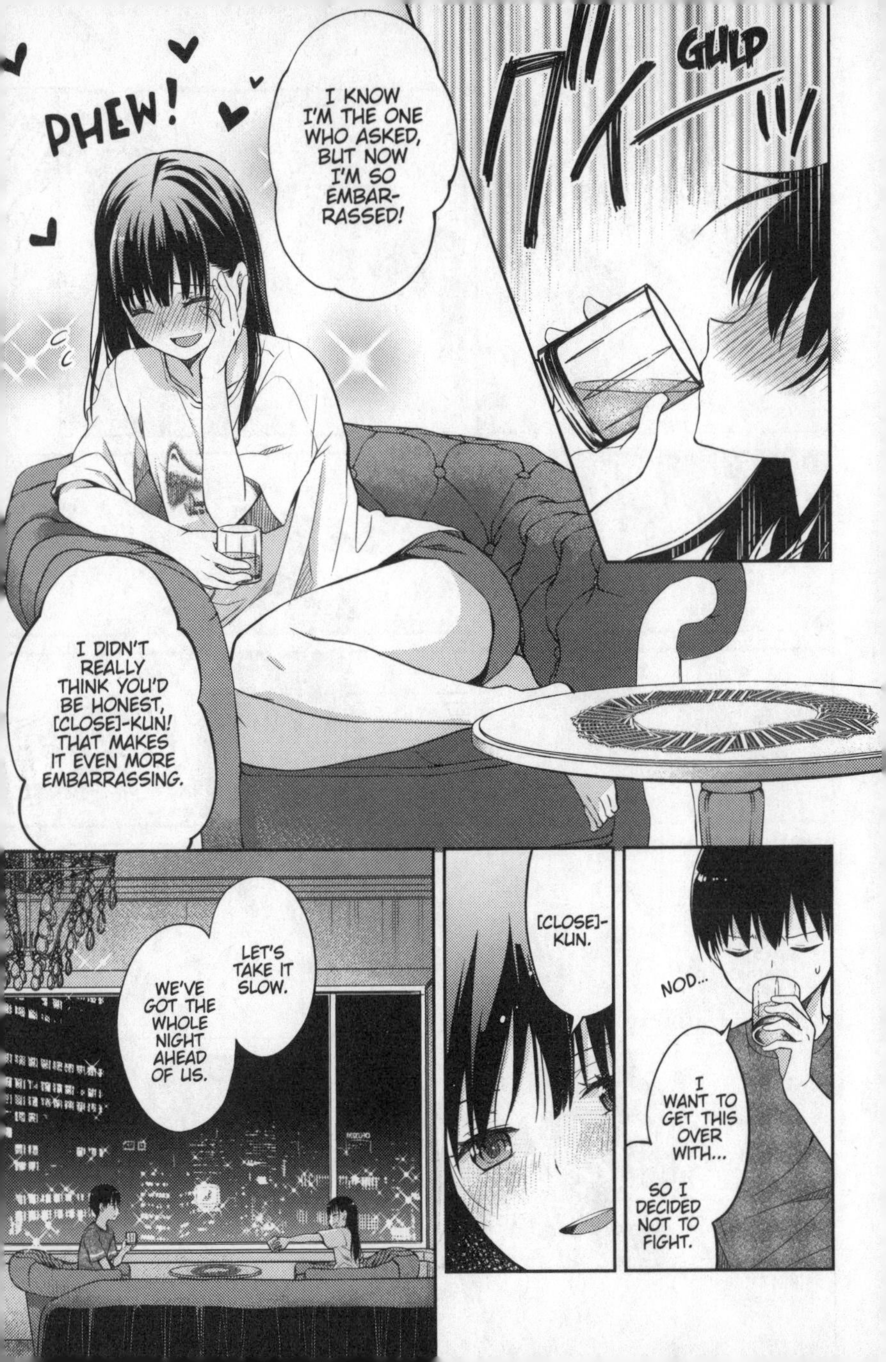
GULP
PHEW!
I KNOW I'M THE ONE WHO ASKED, BUT NOW I'M SO EMBAR-RASSED!
I DIDN'T REALLY THINK YOU'D BE HONEST, [CLOSE]-KUN! THAT MAKES IT EVEN MORE EMBARRASSING.
NOD...
I WANT TO GET THIS OVER WITH...
SO I DECIDED NOT TO FIGHT.
[CLOSE]-KUN.
LET'S TAKE IT SLOW.
WE'VE GOT THE WHOLE NIGHT AHEAD OF US.

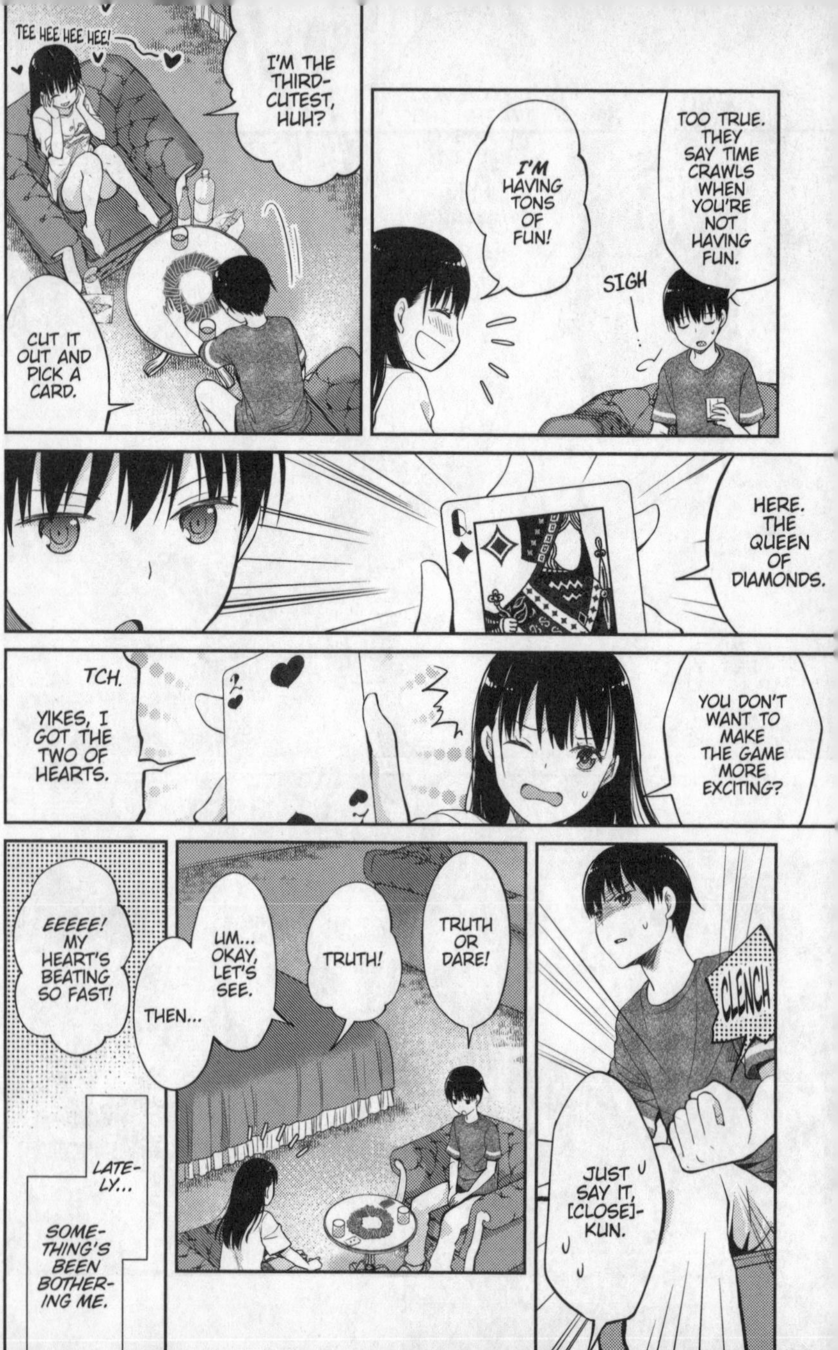
TEE HEE HEE HEE!
I'M THE THIRD-CUTEST, HUH?
CUT IT OUT AND PICK A CARD.
TOO TRUE. THEY SAY TIME CRAWLS WHEN YOU'RE NOT HAVING FUN.
SIGH
I'M HAVING TONS OF FUN!
HERE. THE QUEEN OF DIAMONDS.
YOU DON'T WANT TO MAKE THE GAME MORE EXCITING?
TCH.
YIKES, I GOT THE TWO OF HEARTS.
CLENCH
JUST SAY IT, [CLOSE]-KUN.
TRUTH OR DARE!
TRUTH!
UM... OKAY, LET'S SEE.
THEN...
EEEEE! MY HEART'S BEATING SO FAST!
LATELY...
SOMETHING'S BEEN BOTHERING ME.

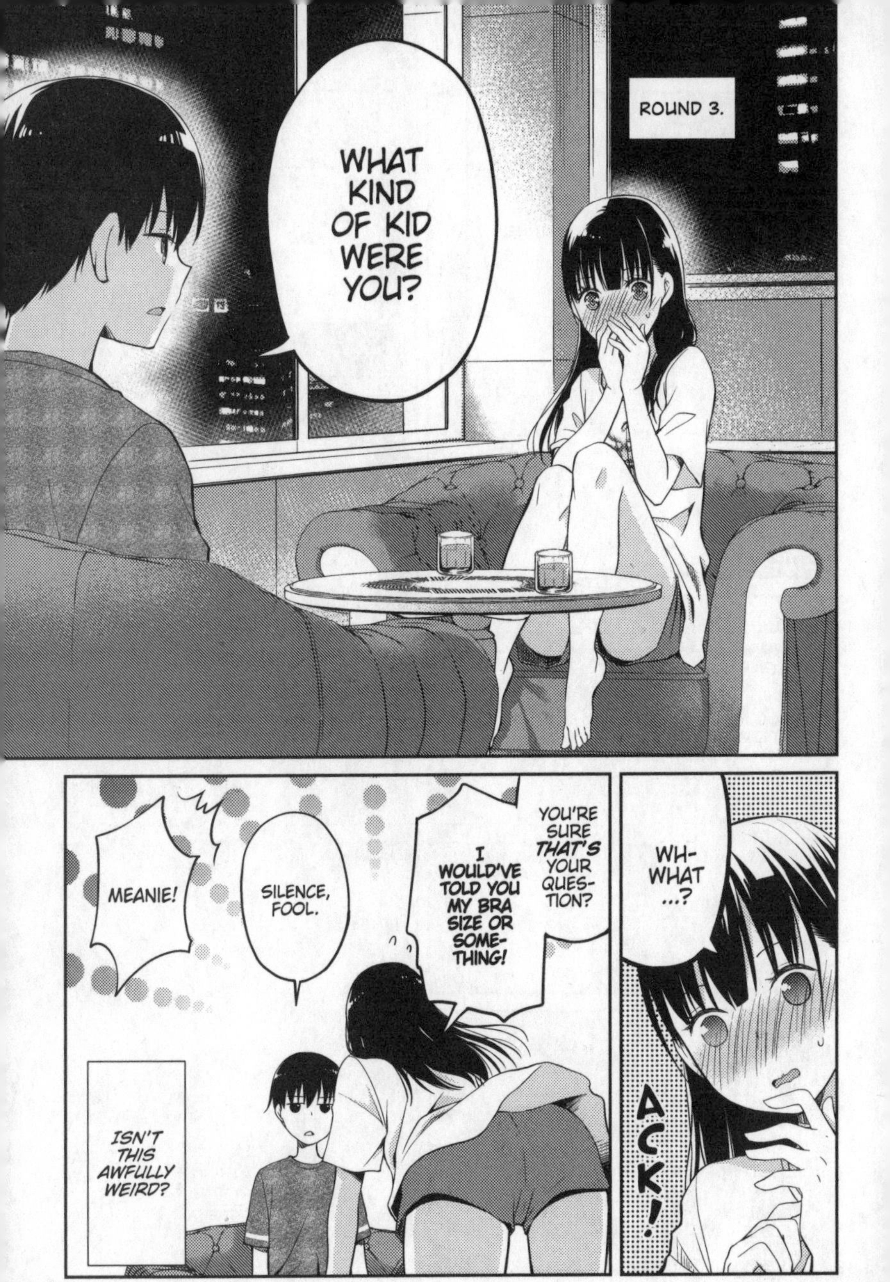
ROUND 3.
WHAT KIND OF KID WERE YOU?
WH-WHAT ...?
ACK!
YOU'RE SURE *THAT'S* YOUR QUES-TION?
I WOULD'VE TOLD YOU MY BRA SIZE OR SOME-THING!
SILENCE, FOOL.
MEANIE!
ISN'T THIS AWFULLY WEIRD?

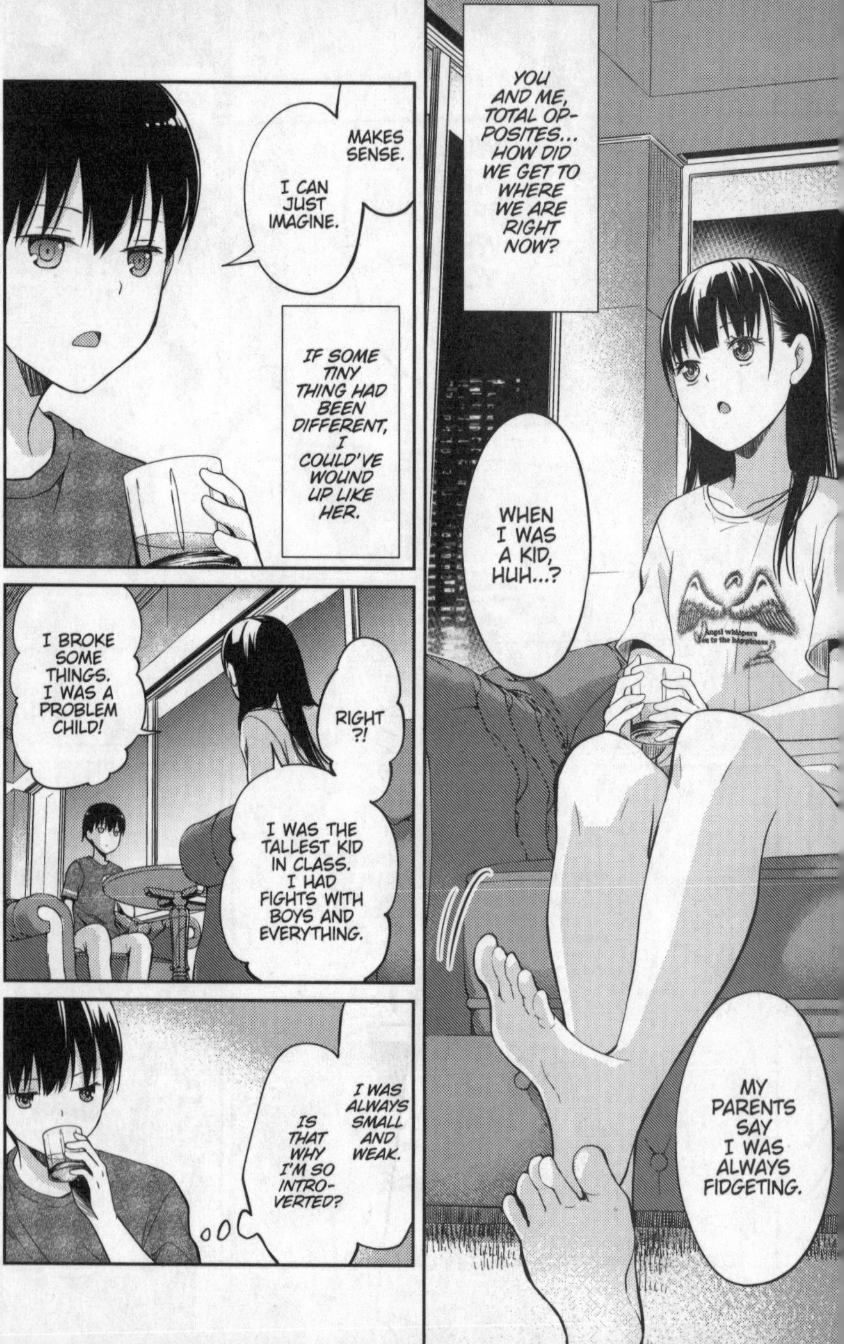
YOU AND ME, TOTAL OP-POSITES... HOW DID WE GET TO WHERE WE ARE RIGHT NOW?
WHEN I WAS A KID, HUH...?
MY PARENTS SAY I WAS ALWAYS FIDGETING.
MAKES SENSE.
I CAN JUST IMAGINE.
IF SOME TINY THING HAD BEEN DIFFERENT, I COULD'VE WOUND UP LIKE HER.
RIGHT ?!
I BROKE SOME THINGS. I WAS A PROBLEM CHILD!
I WAS THE TALLEST KID IN CLASS. I HAD FIGHTS WITH BOYS AND EVERYTHING.
I WAS ALWAYS SMALL AND WEAK.
IS THAT WHY I'M SO INTRO-VERTED?

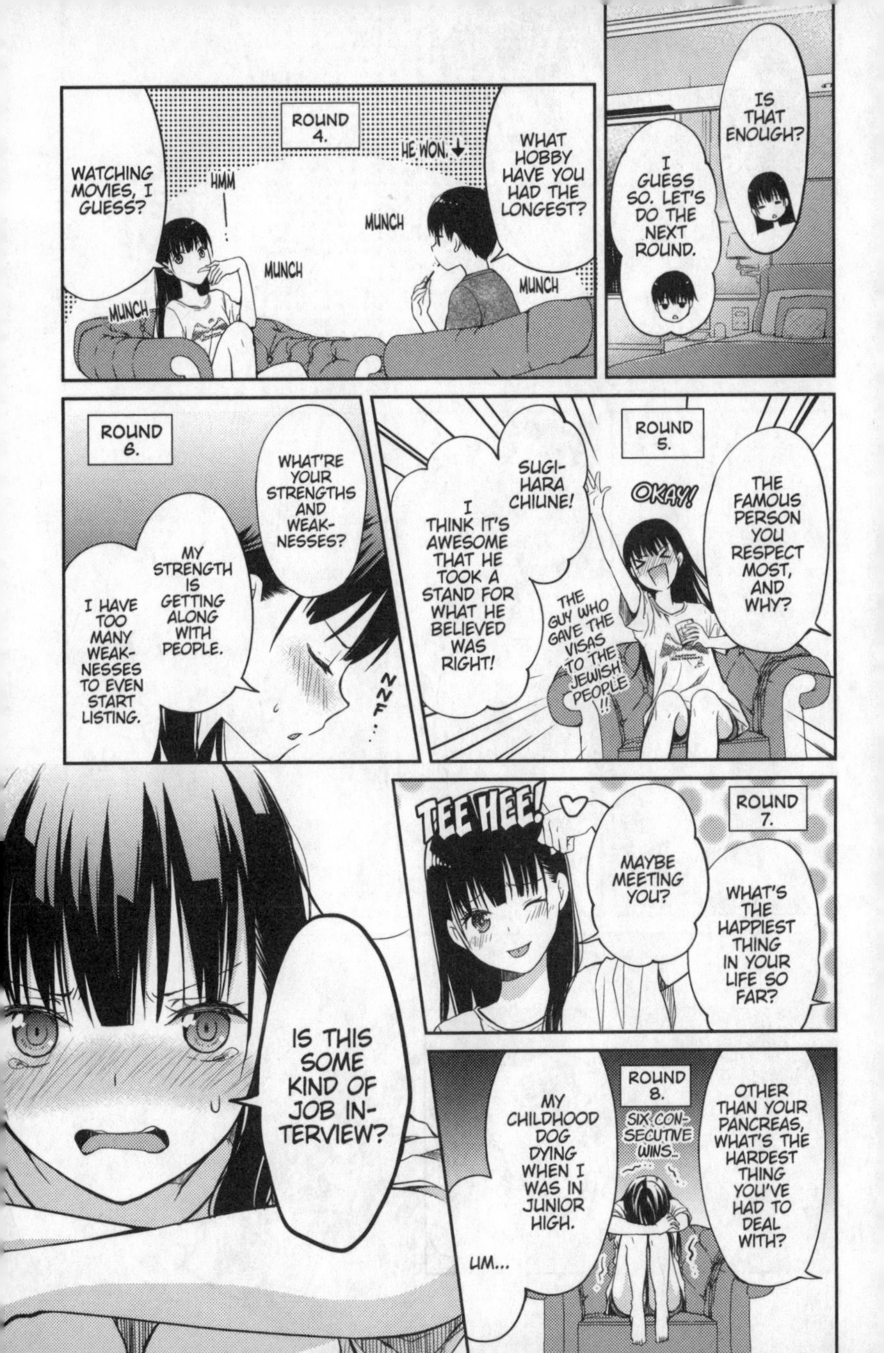
IS THAT ENOUGH?
I GUESS SO. LET'S DO THE NEXT ROUND.
ROUND 4.
WHAT HOBBY HAVE YOU HAD THE LONGEST?
HE WON.↓
MUNCH
MUNCH
HMM
WATCHING MOVIES, I GUESS?
MUNCH
MUNCH
ROUND 5.
THE FAMOUS PERSON YOU RESPECT MOST, AND WHY?
OKAY!
SUGIHARA CHIUNE!
I THINK IT'S AWESOME THAT HE TOOK A STAND FOR WHAT HE BELIEVED WAS RIGHT!
THE GUY WHO GAVE THE VISAS TO THE JEWISH PEOPLE!!
ROUND 6.
WHAT'RE YOUR STRENGTHS AND WEAKNESSES?
NNF...
MY STRENGTH IS GETTING ALONG WITH PEOPLE.
I HAVE TOO MANY WEAKNESSES TO EVEN START LISTING.
ROUND 7.
WHAT'S THE HAPPIEST THING IN YOUR LIFE SO FAR?
MAYBE MEETING YOU?
TEE HEE!
ROUND 8.
OTHER THAN YOUR PANCREAS, WHAT'S THE HARDEST THING YOU'VE HAD TO DEAL WITH?
SIX CONSECUTIVE WINS...
MY CHILDHOOD DOG DYING WHEN I WAS IN JUNIOR HIGH.
UM...
IS THIS SOME KIND OF JOB INTERVIEW?

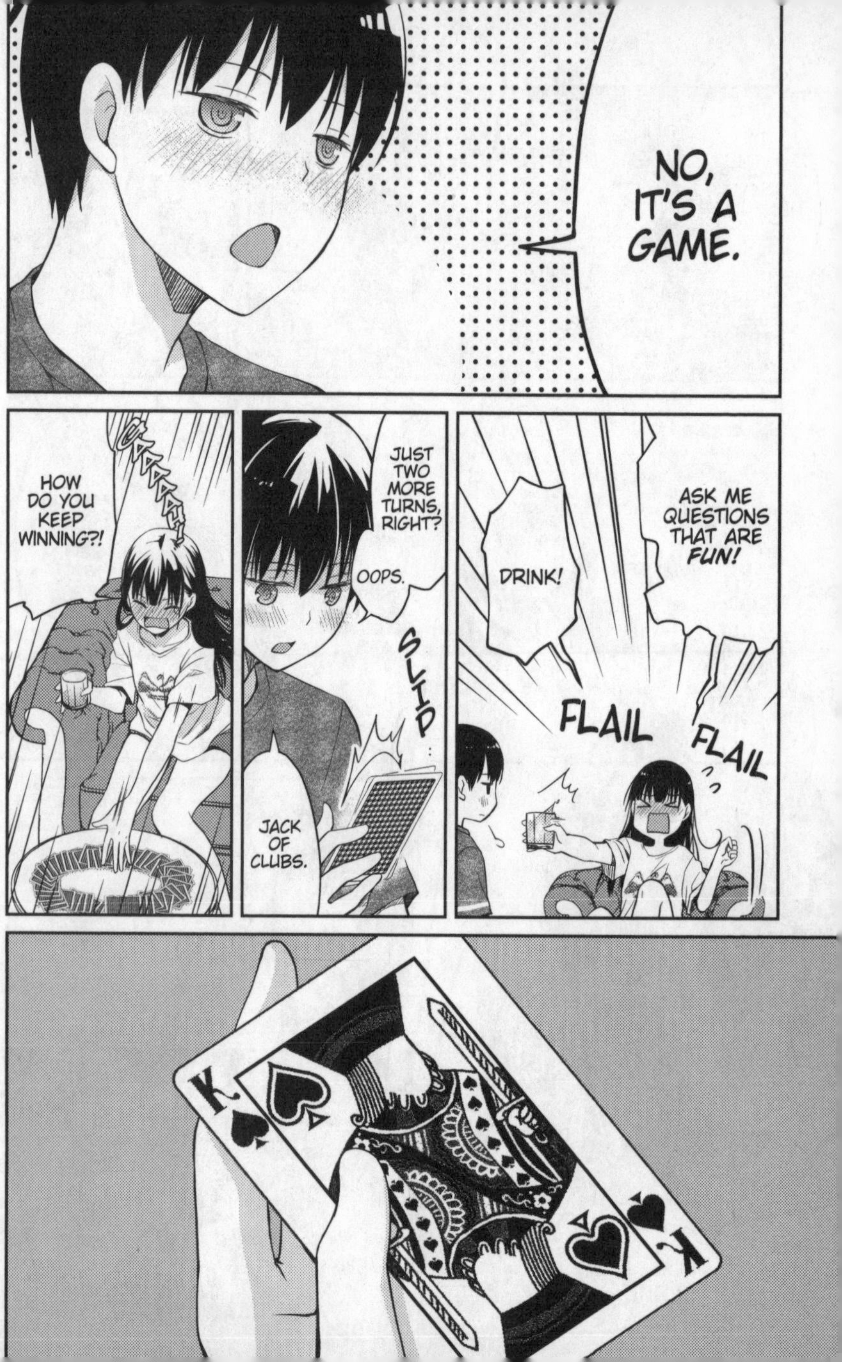
NO, IT'S A GAME.
ASK ME QUESTIONS THAT ARE FUN!
DRINK!
FLAIL
FLAIL
JUST TWO MORE TURNS, RIGHT?
OOPS.
SLIP
JACK OF CLUBS.
HOW DO YOU KEEP WINNING?!

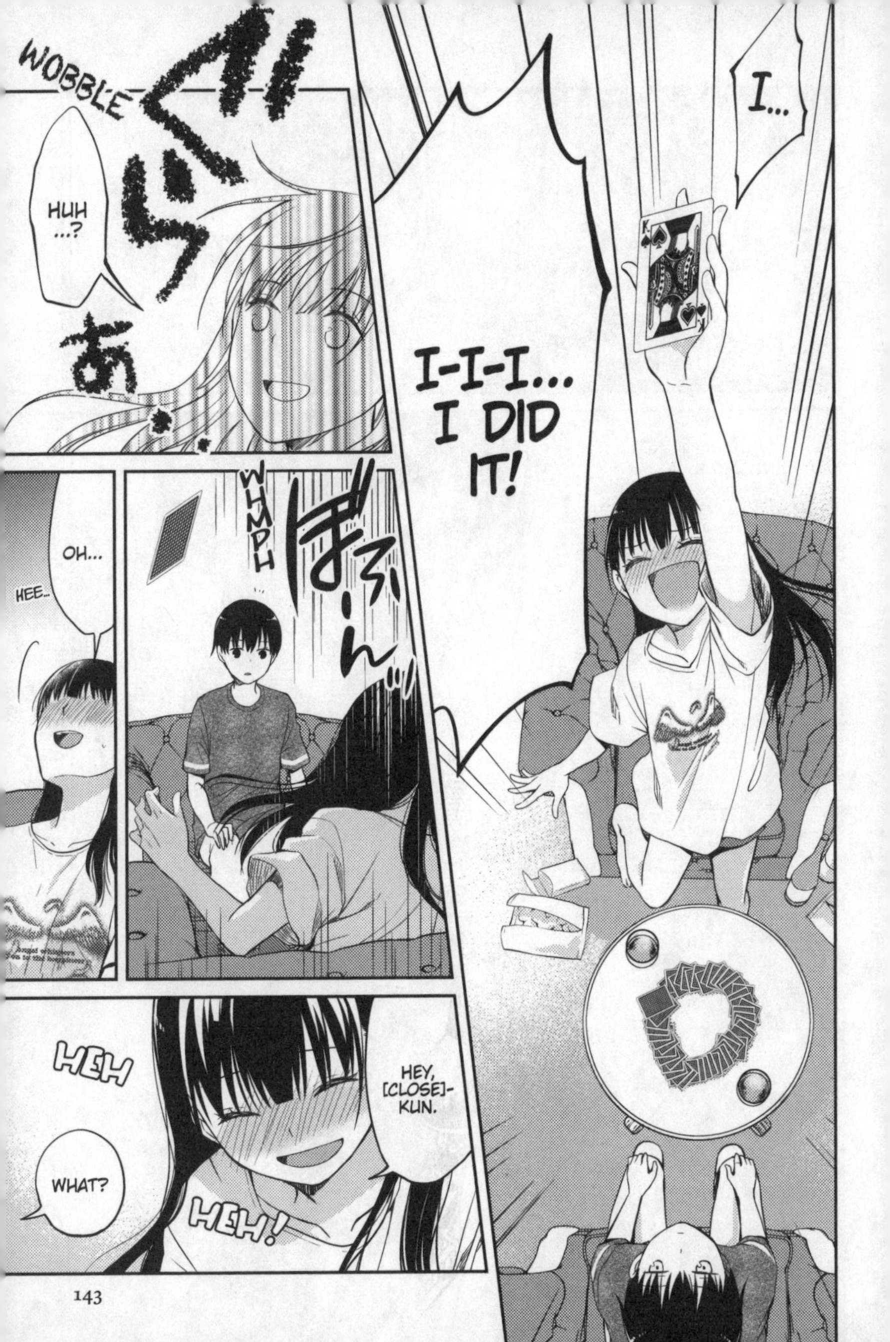
I...
I-I-I... I DID IT!
WOBBLE
HUH ...?
WHMPH
OH...
HEE...
HEY, [CLOSE]-KUN.
HEH
HEH!
WHAT?

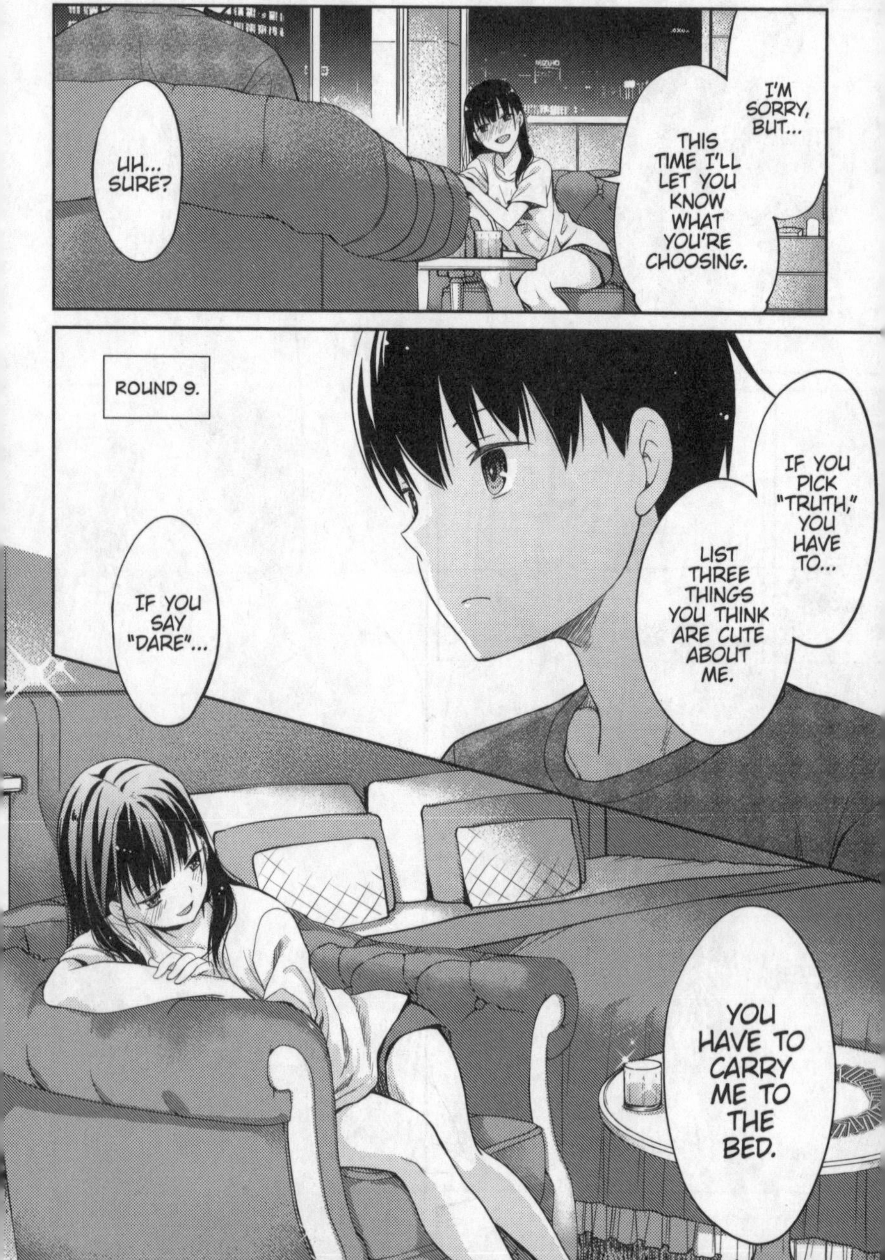
I'M SORRY, BUT...
THIS TIME I'LL LET YOU KNOW WHAT YOU'RE CHOOSING.
UH... SURE?
ROUND 9.
IF YOU PICK "TRUTH," YOU HAVE TO...
LIST THREE THINGS YOU THINK ARE CUTE ABOUT ME.
IF YOU SAY "DARE"...
YOU HAVE TO CARRY ME TO THE BED.

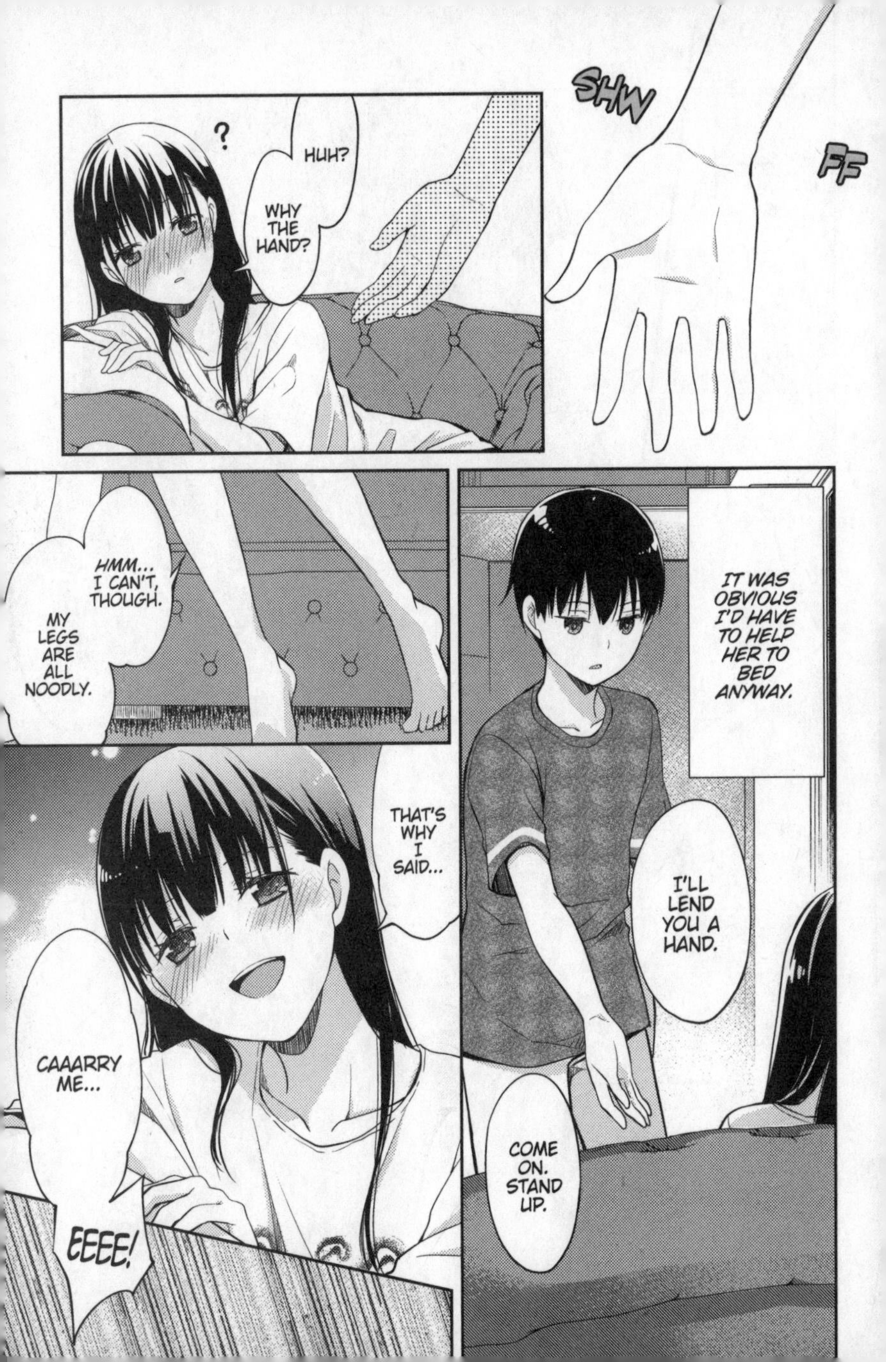
SHW
FF
?
HUH?
WHY THE HAND?
IT WAS OBVIOUS I'D HAVE TO HELP HER TO BED ANYWAY.
I'LL LEND YOU A HAND.
COME ON. STAND UP.
HMM... I CAN'T, THOUGH.
MY LEGS ARE ALL NOODLY.
THAT'S WHY I SAID...
CAAARRY ME...
EEEE!

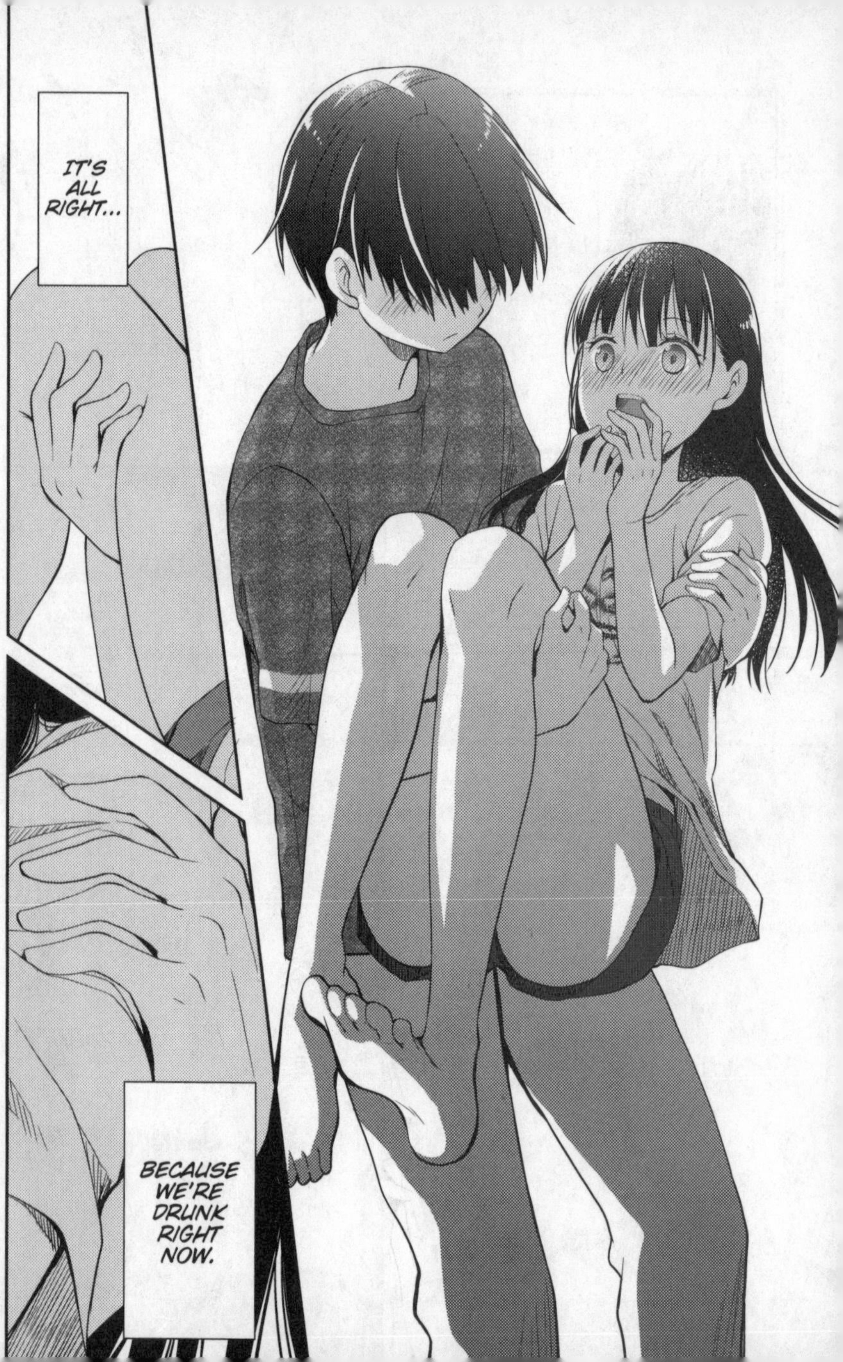
IT'S ALL RIGHT...
BECAUSE WE'RE DRUNK RIGHT NOW.

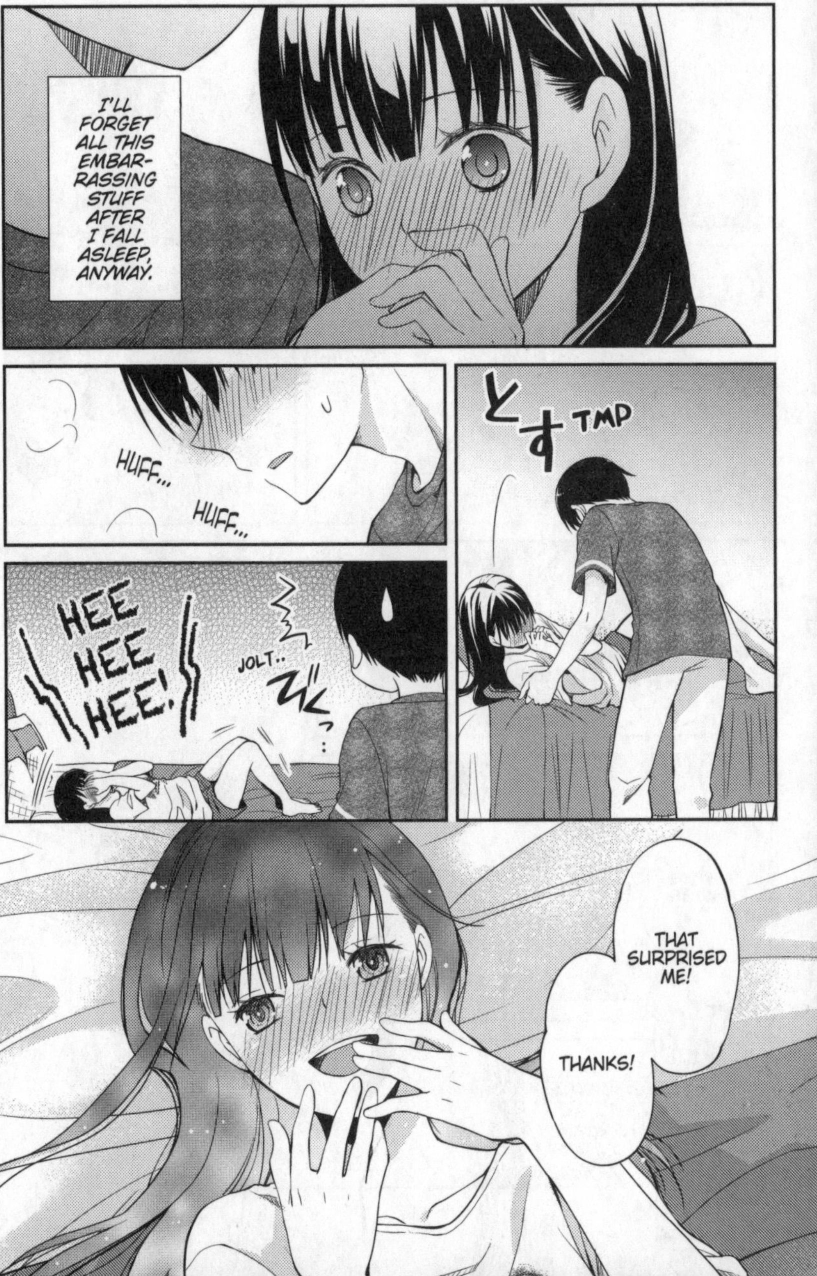
I'LL FORGET ALL THIS EMBARRASSING STUFF AFTER I FALL ASLEEP, ANYWAY.
とす TMP
HUFF...
HUFF...
HEE HEE HEE!
ビくっ JOLT..
THAT SURPRISED ME!
THANKS!

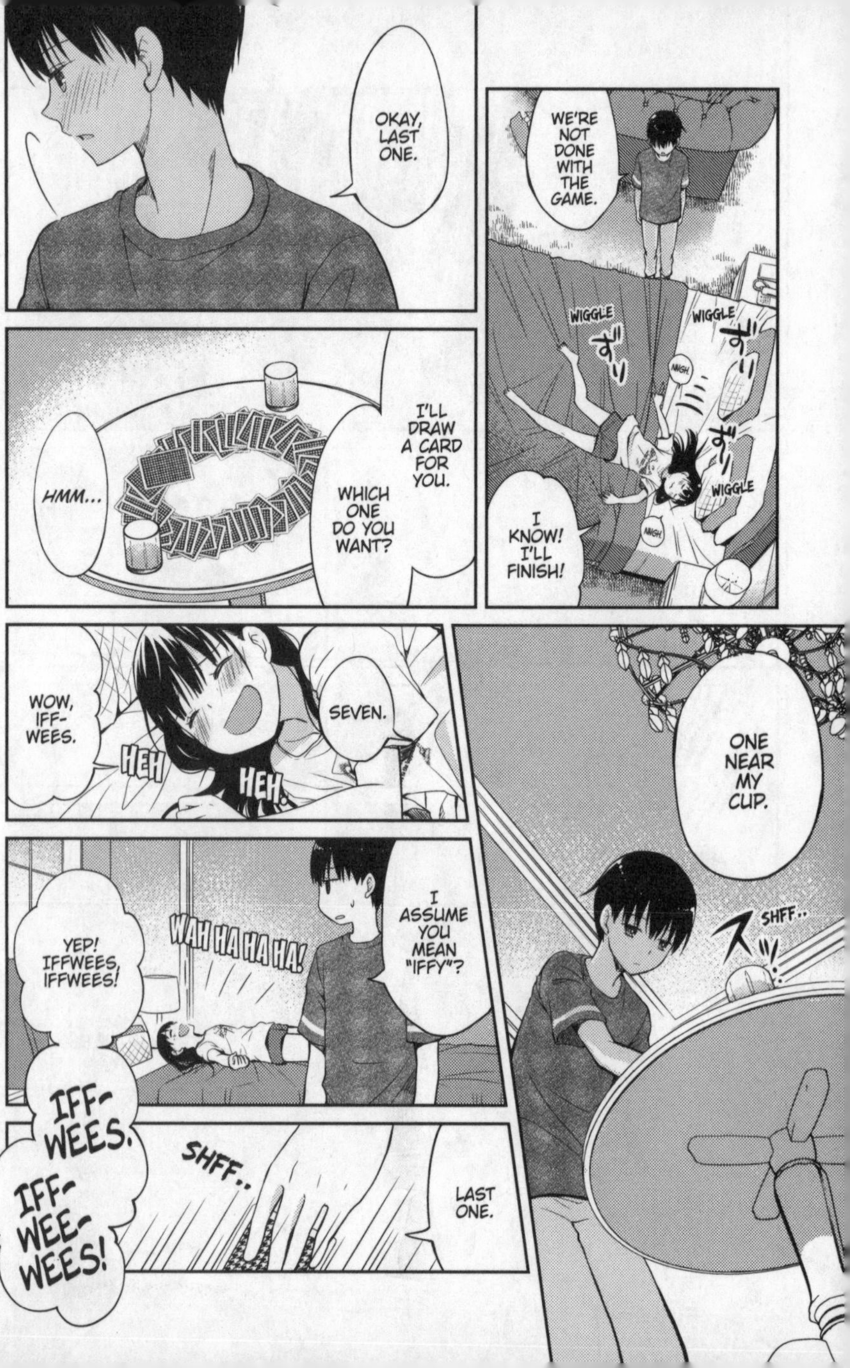

WE'RE NOT DONE WITH THE GAME.
WIGGLE
ずり
WIGGLE
ずり
NNGH.
NNGH.
WIGGLE
I KNOW! I'LL FINISH!
OKAY, LAST ONE.
I'LL DRAW A CARD FOR YOU.
WHICH ONE DO YOU WANT?
HMM...
ONE NEAR MY CUP.
SHFF..
SEVEN.
WOW, IFF-WEES.
HEH
HEH.
I ASSUME YOU MEAN "IFFY"?
WAH HA HA HA!
YEP! IFFWEES, IFFWEES!
LAST ONE.
SHFF..
IFF-WEES.
IFF-WEE-WEES!

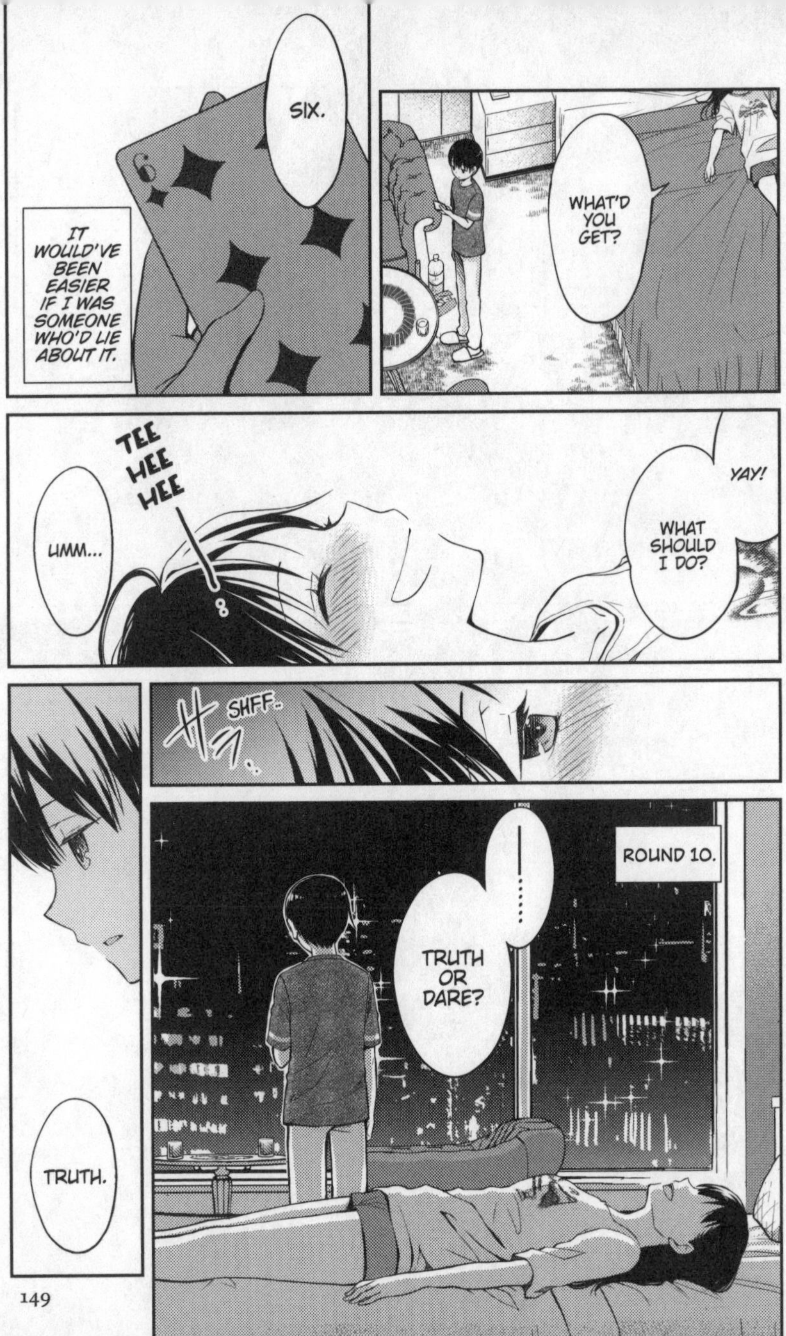
WHAT'D YOU GET?
SIX.
IT WOULD'VE BEEN EASIER IF I WAS SOMEONE WHO'D LIE ABOUT IT.
YAY!
WHAT SHOULD I DO?
TEE HEE HEE
UMM...
SHFF..
ROUND 10.
......
TRUTH OR DARE?
TRUTH.

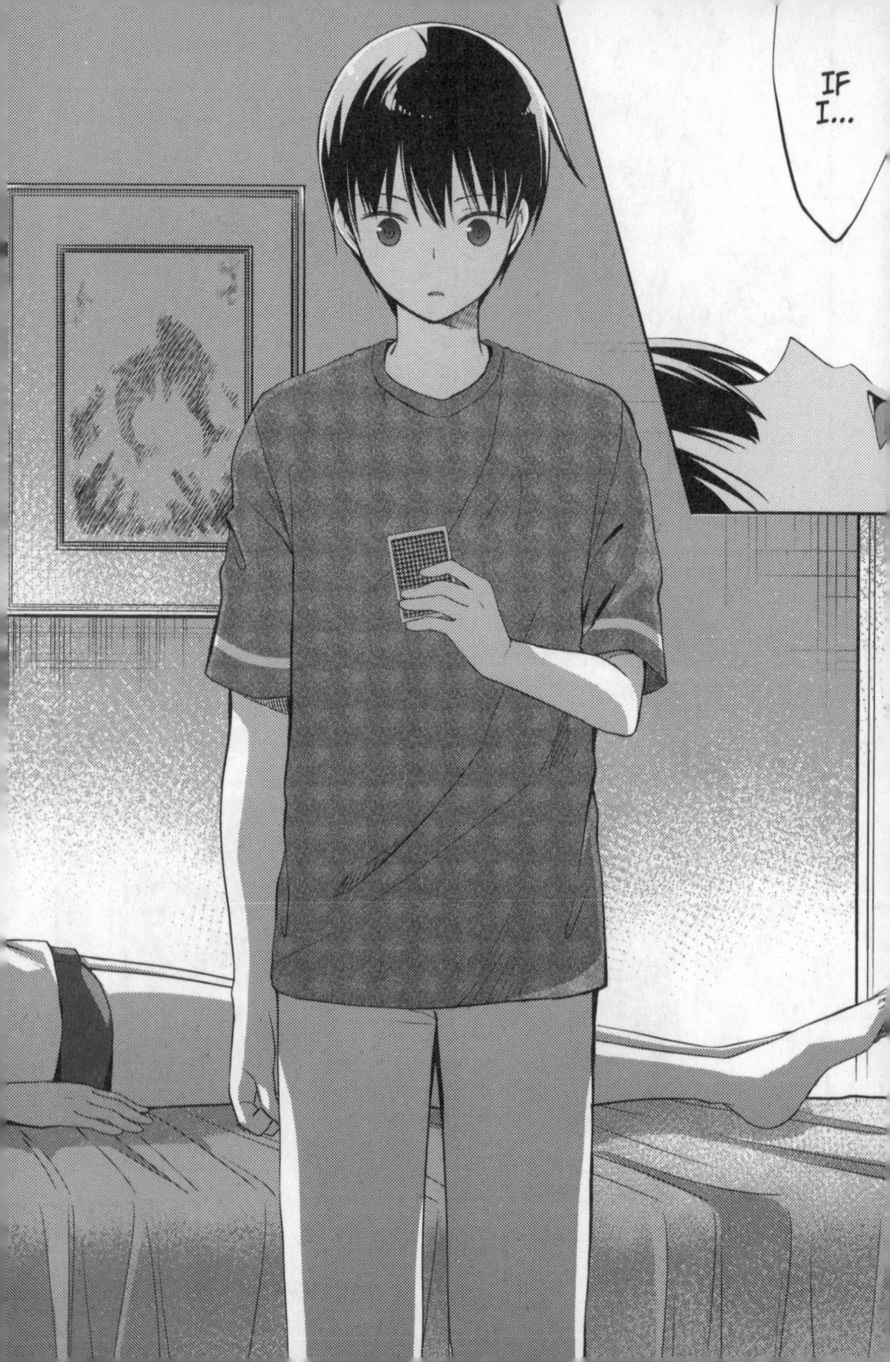
IF I...

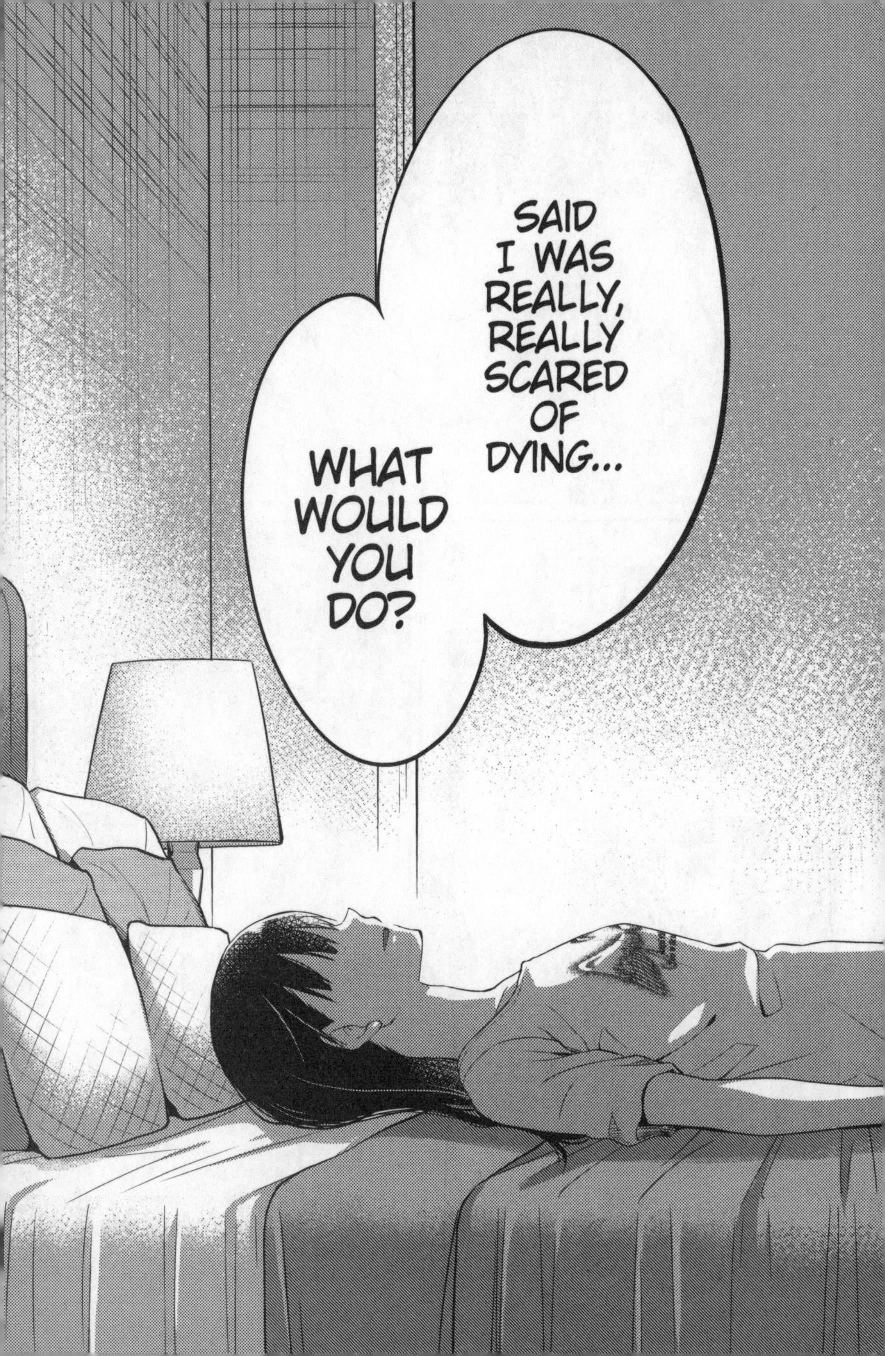
SAID I WAS REALLY, REALLY SCARED OF DYING...
WHAT WOULD YOU DO?

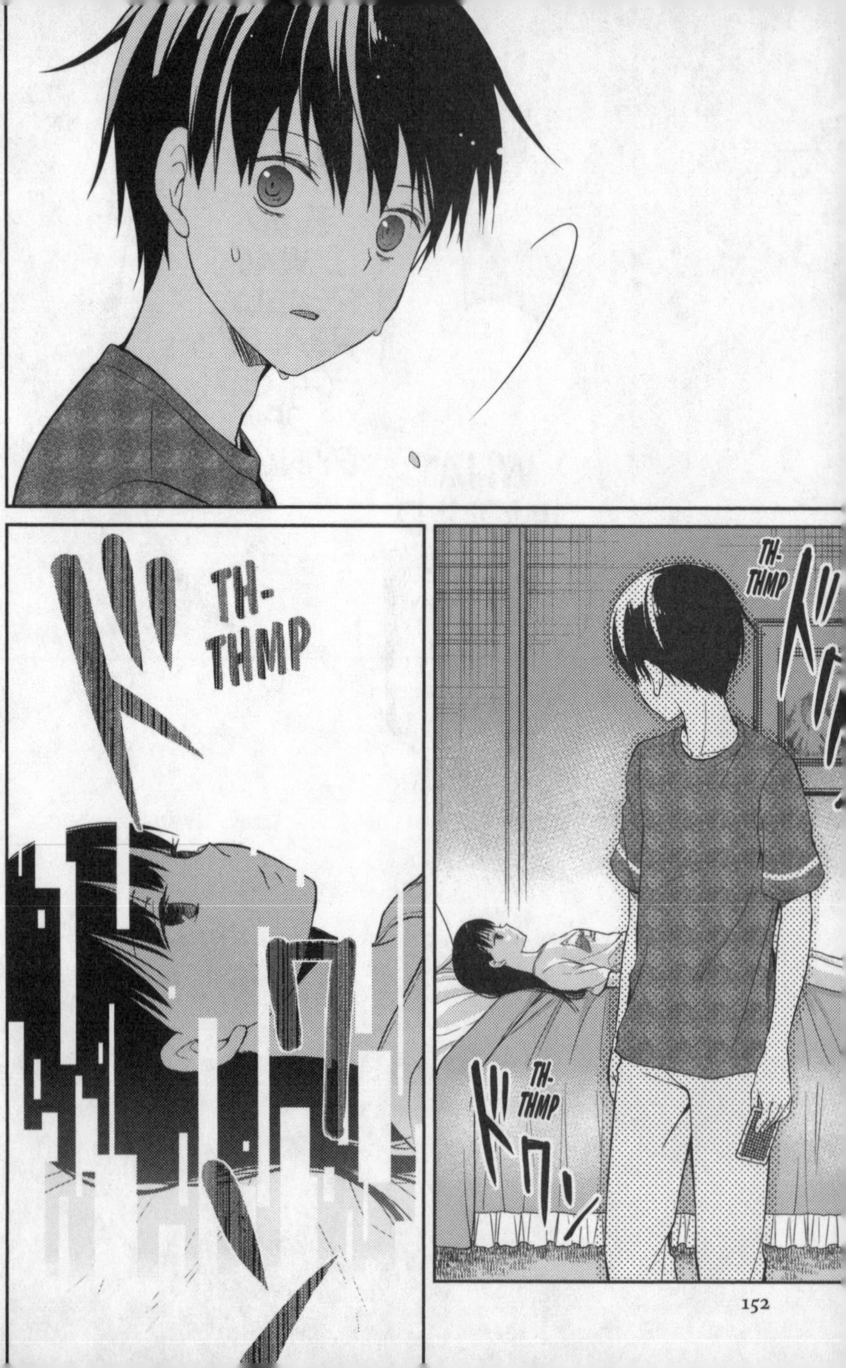
TH-
THMP
TH-
THMP
TH-
THMP

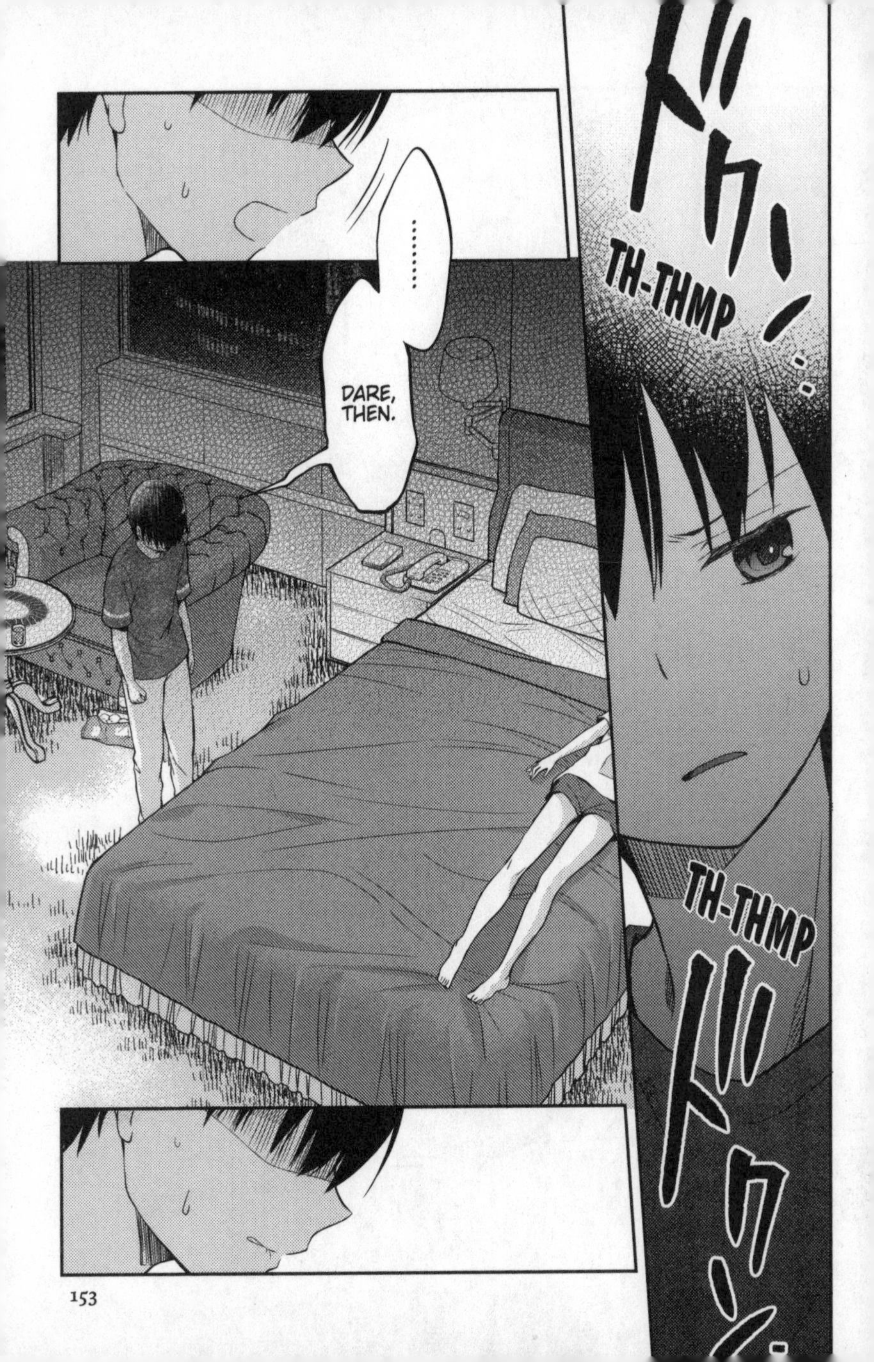

TH-THMP
......
DARE, THEN.
TH-THMP

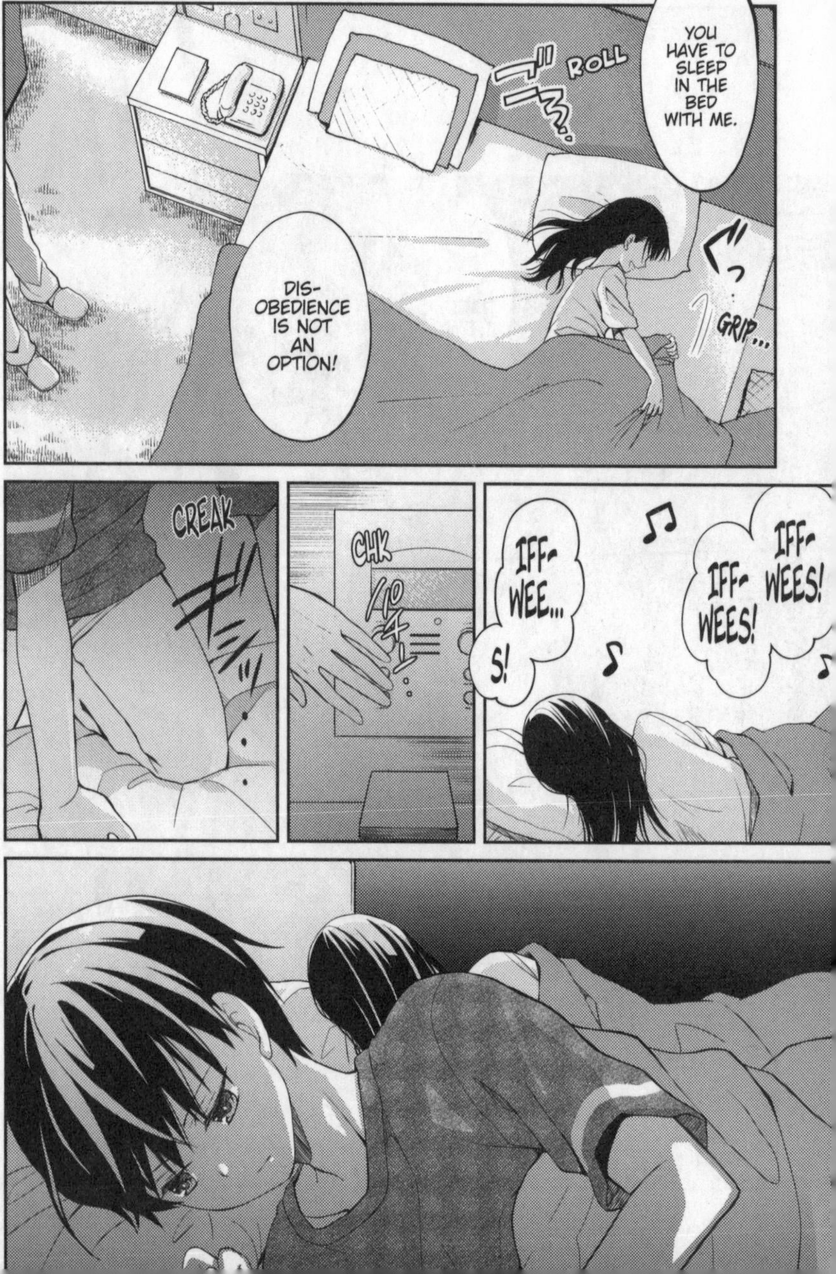
YOU HAVE TO SLEEP IN THE BED WITH ME.
ROLL
DIS-OBEDIENCE IS NOT AN OPTION!
GRIP...
CREAK
CHK
IFF-WEE...S!
IFF-WEES!
IFF-WEES!

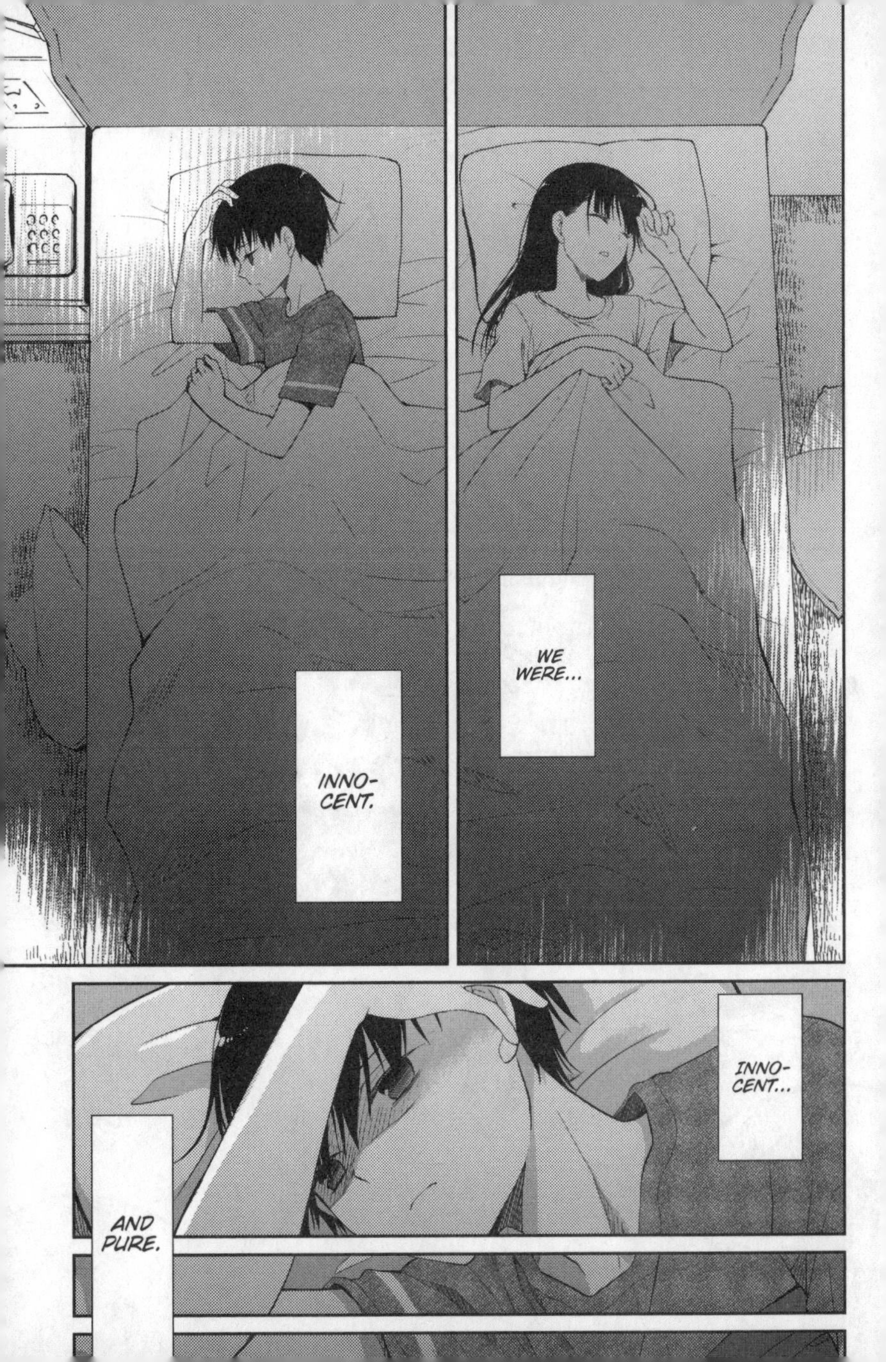
WE WERE...
INNO-CENT.
INNO-CENT...
AND PURE.

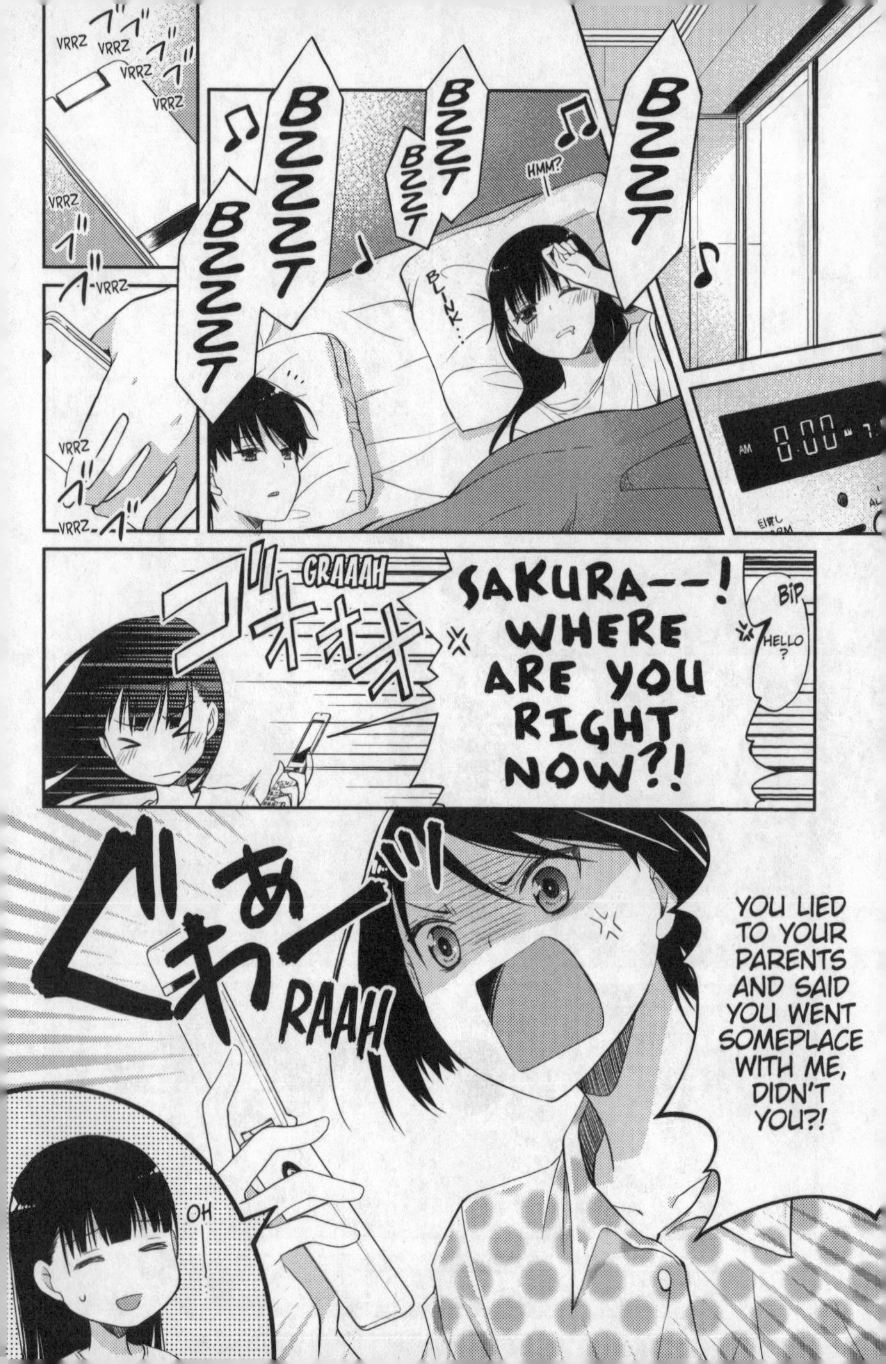
BZZZT
HMM?
BZZZT
BZZZT
BZZZT
BZZZZT
BLINK...
AM 0:00
VRRZ
VRRZ
VRRZ
VRRZ
VRRZ
VRRZ
VRRZ
VRRZ
BIP
HELLO?
SAKURA--! WHERE ARE YOU RIGHT NOW?!
GRAAAH
YOU LIED TO YOUR PARENTS AND SAID YOU WENT SOMEPLACE WITH ME, DIDN'T YOU?!
RAAH
OH —

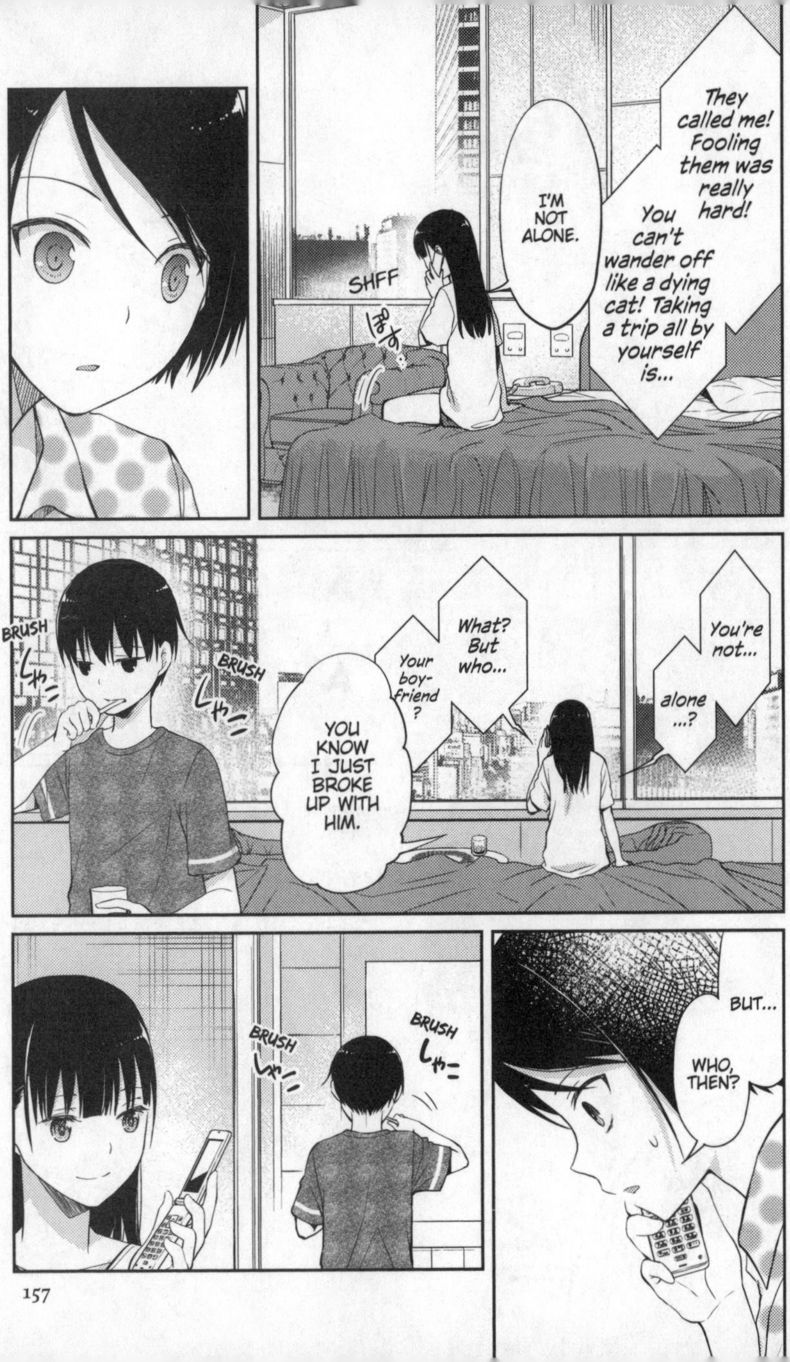
They called me! Fooling them was really hard!
You can't wander off like a dying cat! Taking a trip all by yourself is...
I'M NOT ALONE.
SHFF
ぽす
You're not...
alone ...?
What? But who...
Your boy-friend ?
YOU KNOW I JUST BROKE UP WITH HIM.
BRUSH
しゃこ
BRUSH
しゃー
BUT...
WHO, THEN?
BRUSH
しゃこ
BRUSH
しゃこ

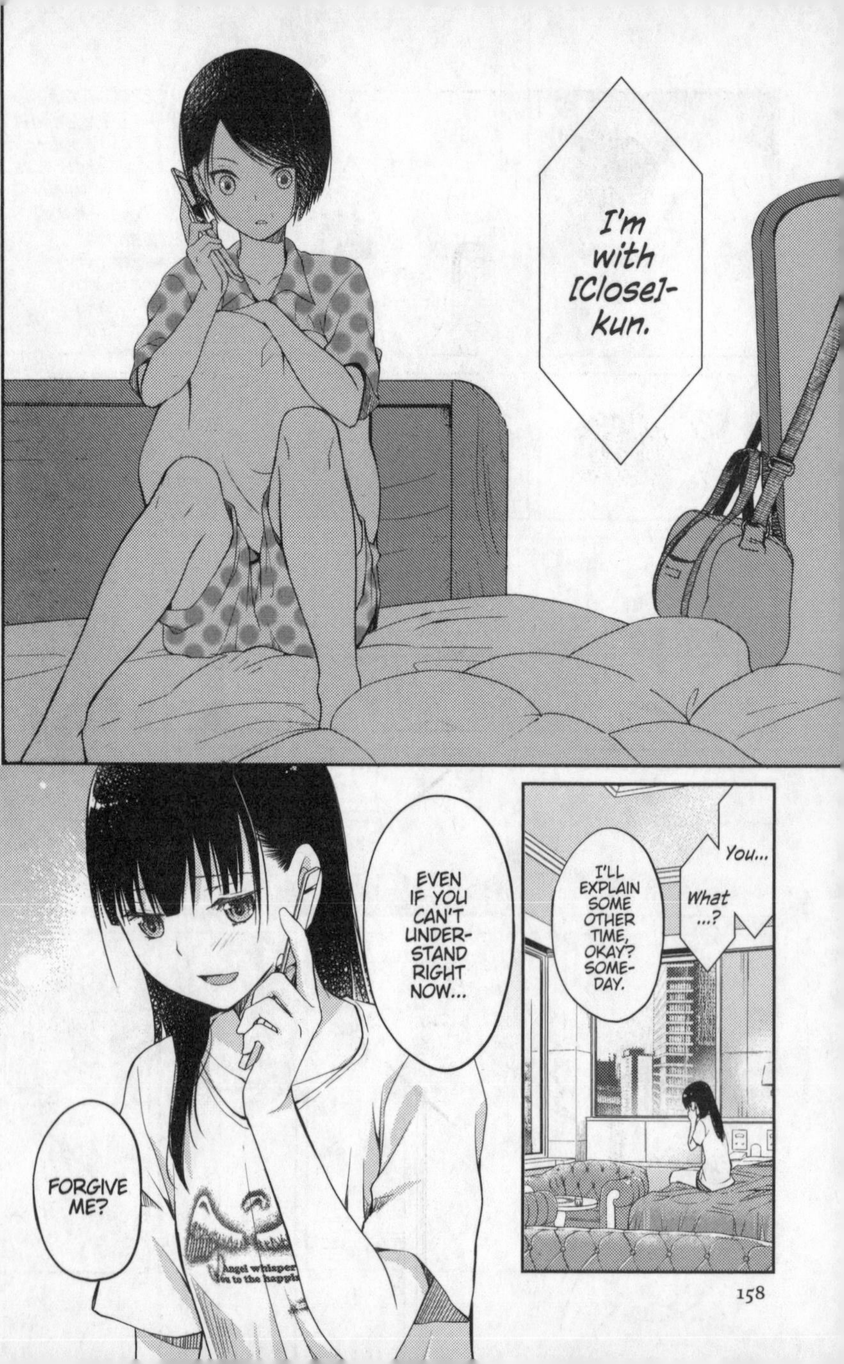
I'm with [Close]-kun.
You...
What ...?
I'LL EXPLAIN SOME OTHER TIME, OKAY? SOME-DAY.
EVEN IF YOU CAN'T UNDER-STAND RIGHT NOW...
FORGIVE ME?

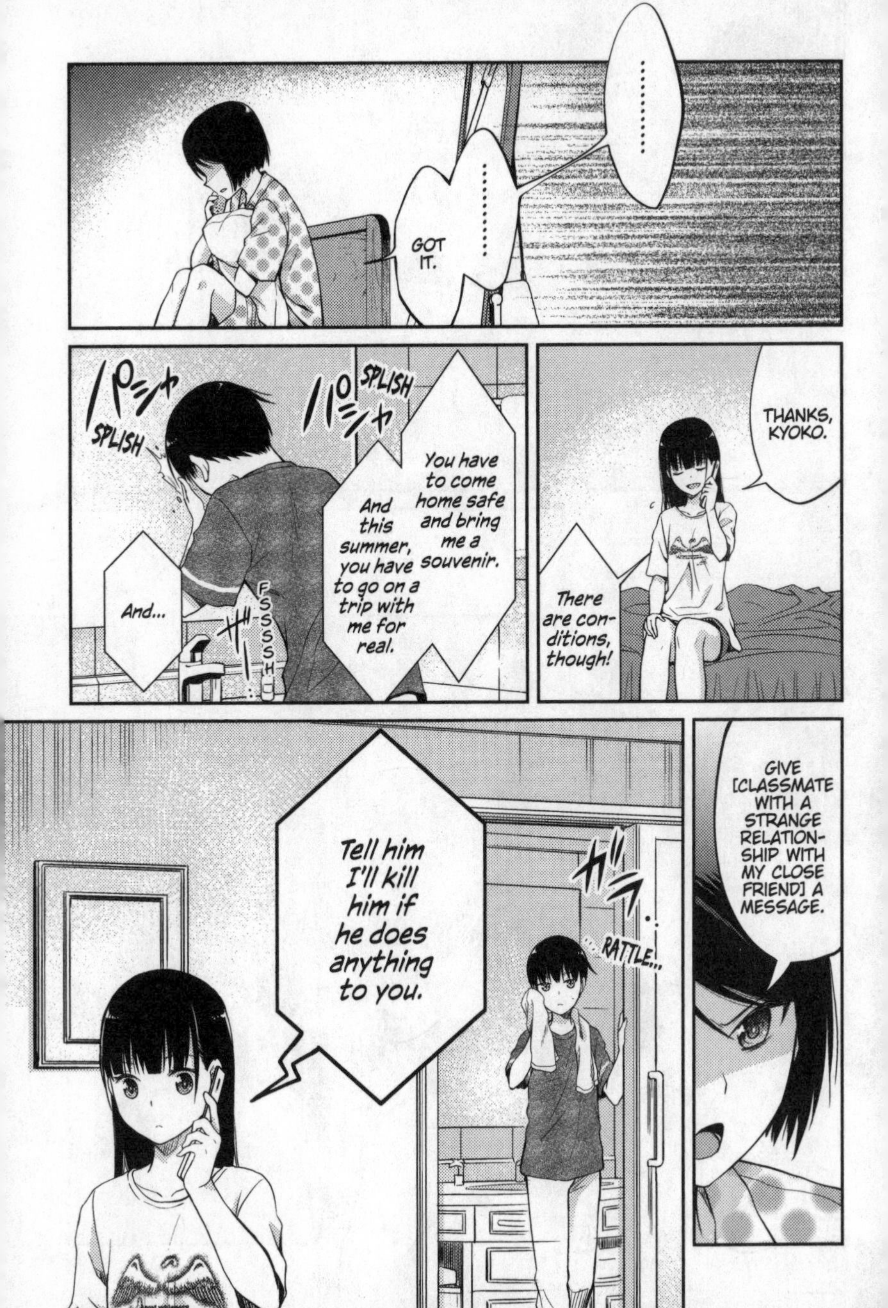
......
......
GOT IT.
THANKS, KYOKO.
There are conditions, though!
SPLISH
SPLISH
You have to come home safe and bring me a souvenir.
And this summer, you have to go on a trip with me for real.
And...
FSSSSH
GIVE [CLASSMATE WITH A STRANGE RELATIONSHIP WITH MY CLOSE FRIEND] A MESSAGE.
RATTLE...
Tell him I'll kill him if he does anything to you.

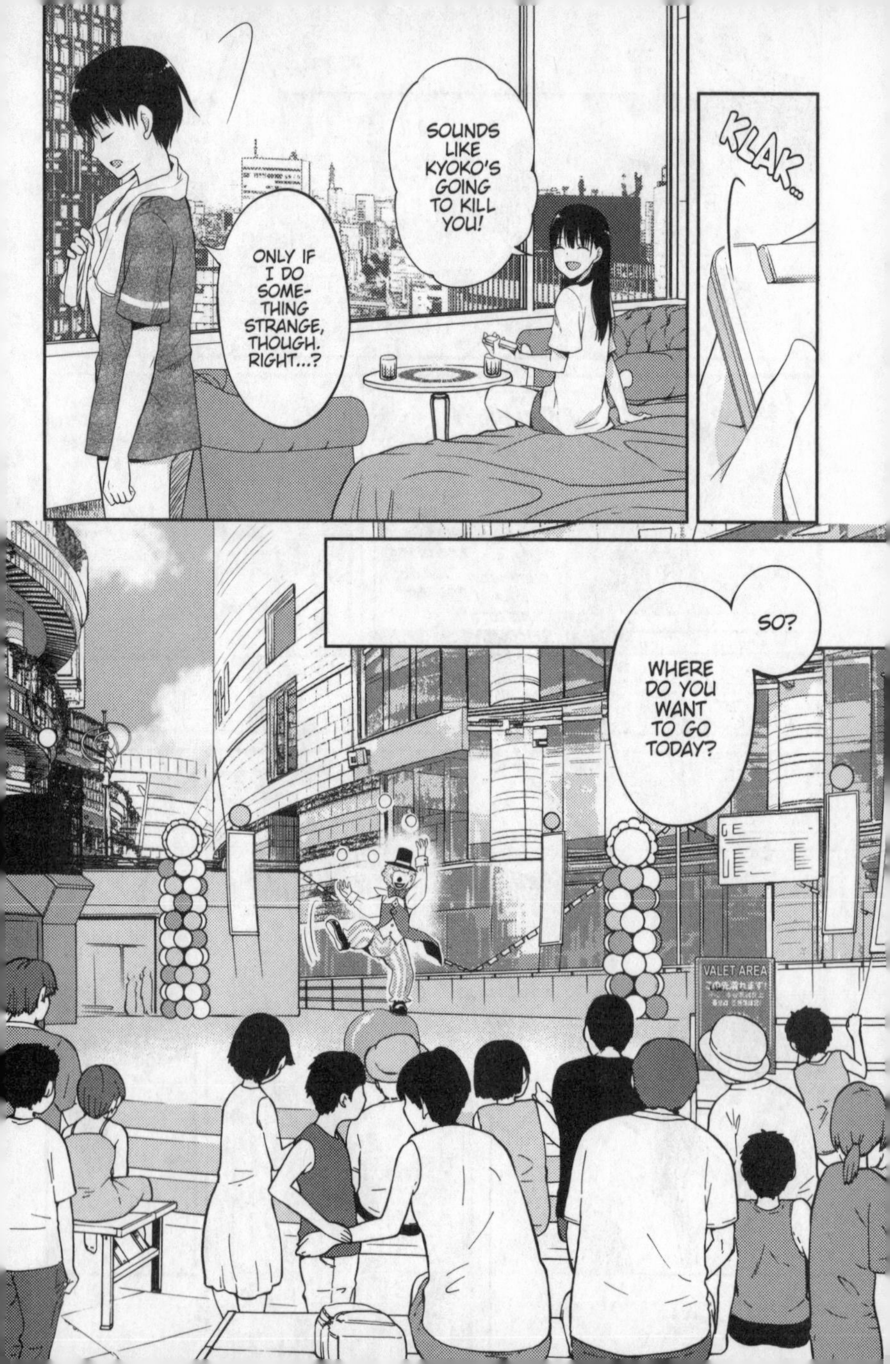

KLAK...
SOUNDS LIKE KYOKO'S GOING TO KILL YOU!
ONLY IF I DO SOME-THING STRANGE, THOUGH. RIGHT...?
SO?
WHERE DO YOU WANT TO GO TODAY?
VALET AREA

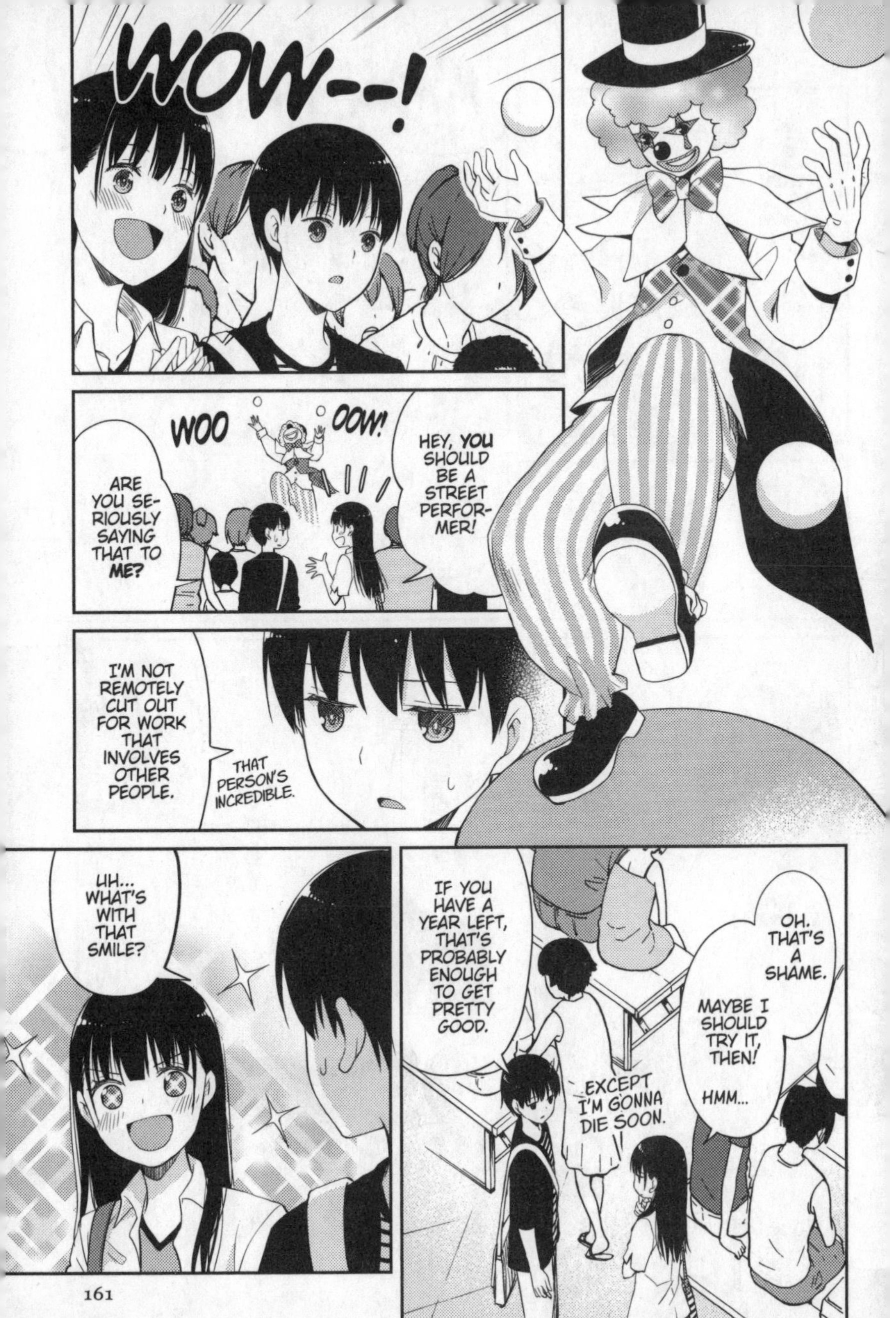
WOW--!
WOO OOW!
HEY, YOU SHOULD BE A STREET PERFORMER!
ARE YOU SERIOUSLY SAYING THAT TO ME?
THAT PERSON'S INCREDIBLE.
I'M NOT REMOTELY CUT OUT FOR WORK THAT INVOLVES OTHER PEOPLE.
OH. THAT'S A SHAME.
MAYBE I SHOULD TRY IT, THEN!
HMM...
EXCEPT I'M GONNA DIE SOON.
IF YOU HAVE A YEAR LEFT, THAT'S PROBABLY ENOUGH TO GET PRETTY GOOD.
UH... WHAT'S WITH THAT SMILE?

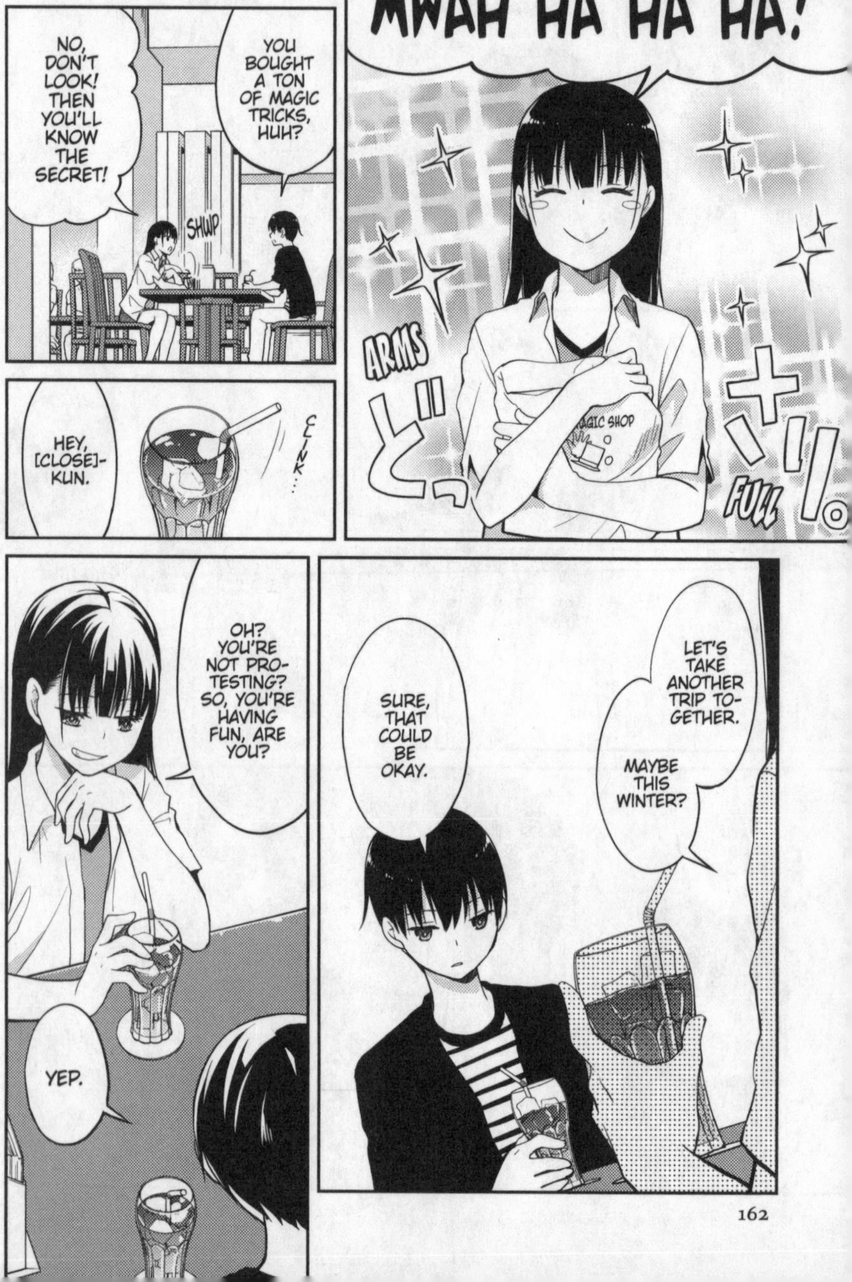
MWAH HA HA HA!
ARMS
FULL
YOU BOUGHT A TON OF MAGIC TRICKS, HUH?
NO, DON'T LOOK! THEN YOU'LL KNOW THE SECRET!
SHWP
CLINK...
HEY, [CLOSE]-KUN.
LET'S TAKE ANOTHER TRIP TOGETHER.
MAYBE THIS WINTER?
SURE, THAT COULD BE OKAY.
OH? YOU'RE NOT PRO-TESTING? SO, YOU'RE HAVING FUN, ARE YOU?
YEP.

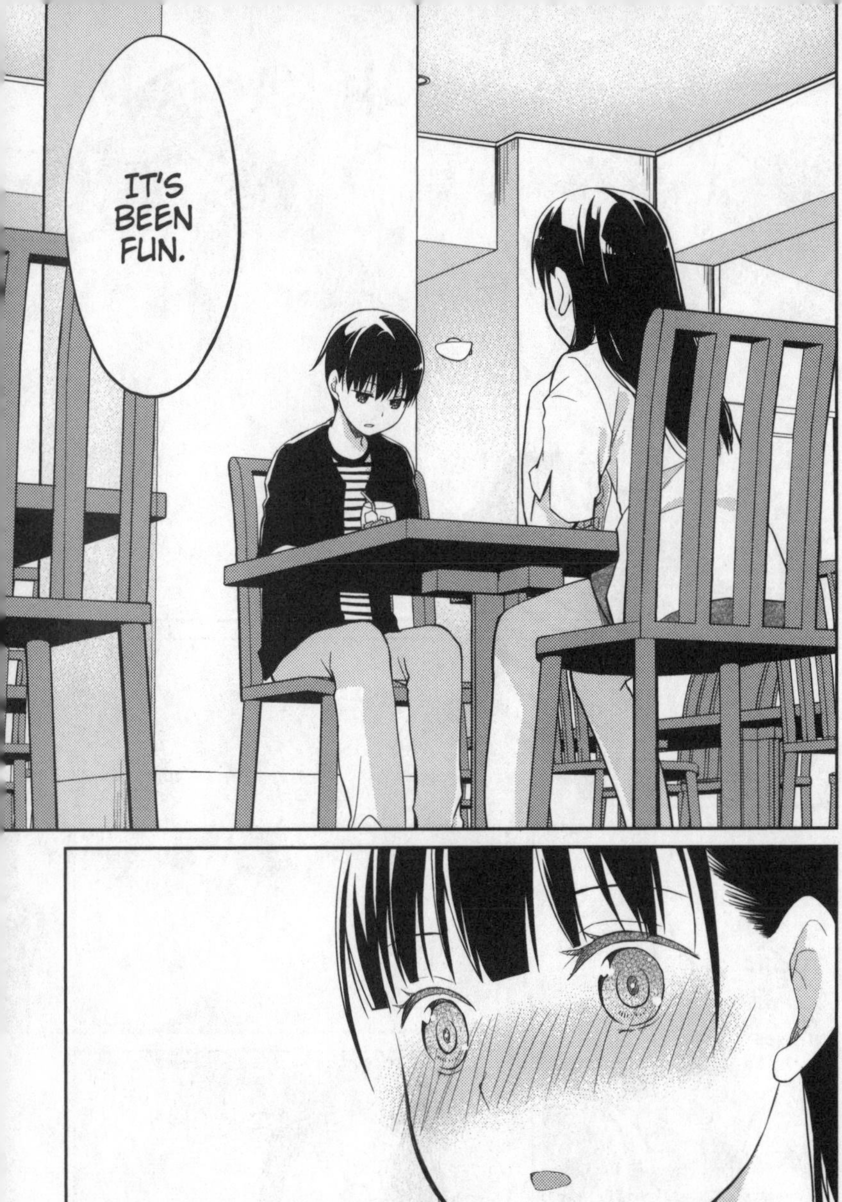
IT'S BEEN FUN.

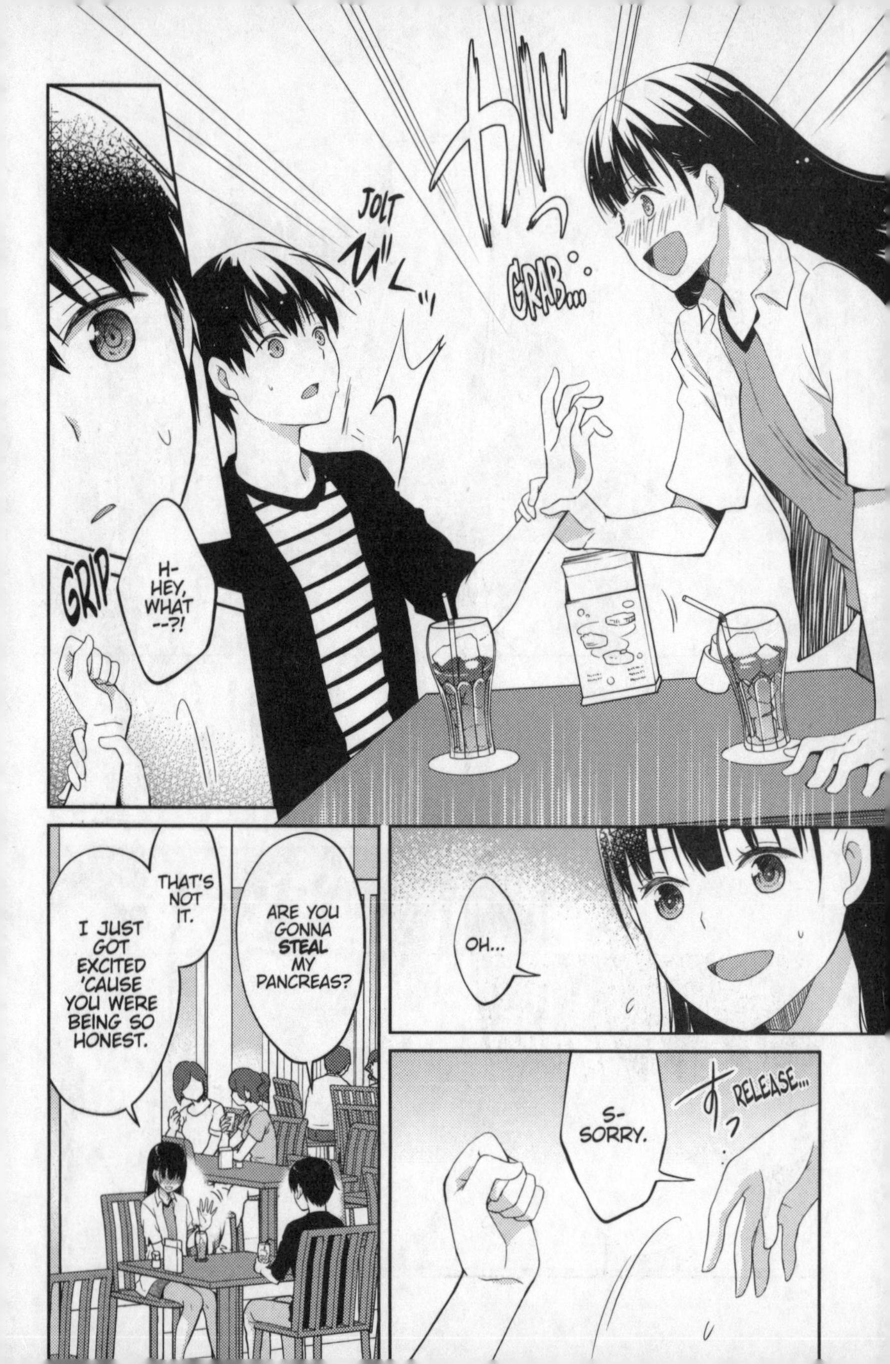
GRAB...
JOLT
H-HEY, WHAT--?!
GRIP
OH...
S-SORRY.
RELEASE...
ARE YOU GONNA STEAL MY PANCREAS?
THAT'S NOT IT.
I JUST GOT EXCITED 'CAUSE YOU WERE BEING SO HONEST.

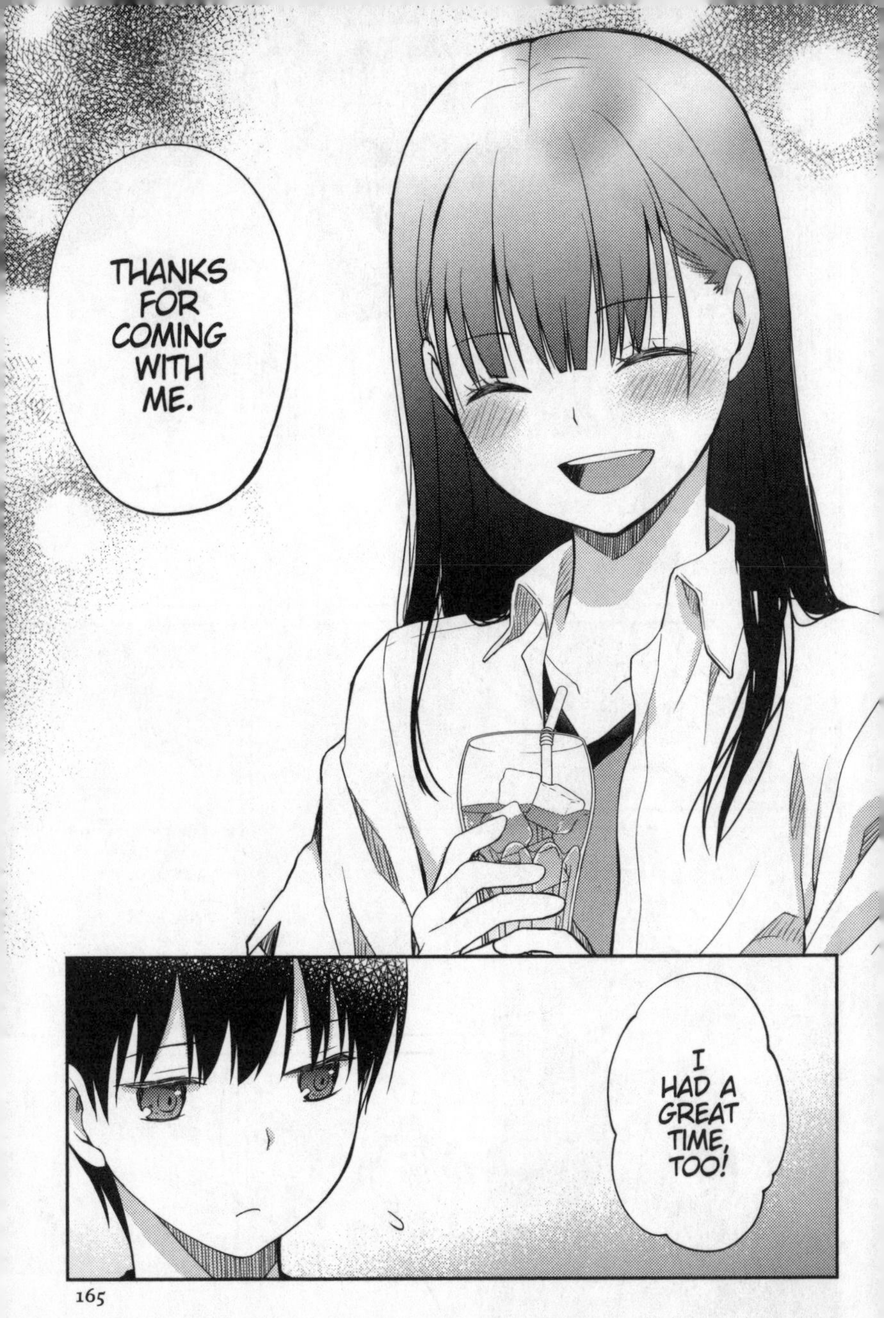
THANKS FOR COMING WITH ME.
I HAD A GREAT TIME, TOO!

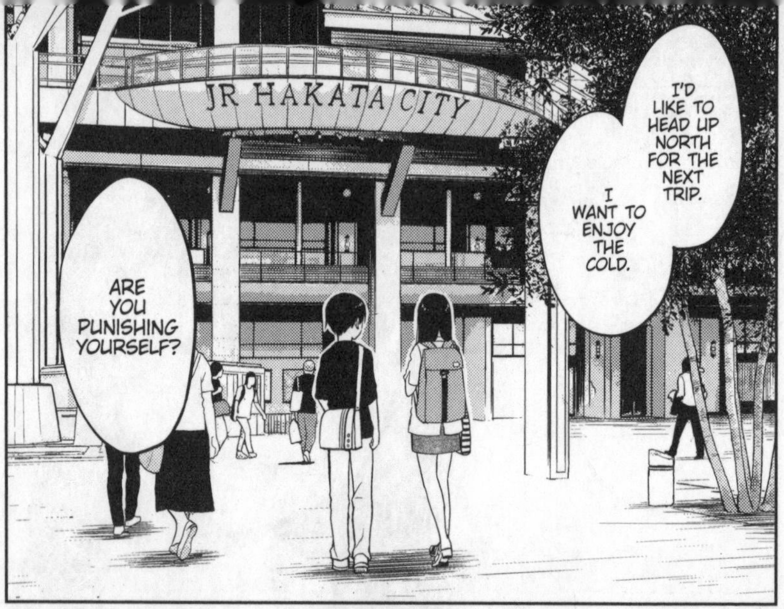
JR HAKATA CITY
I'D LIKE TO HEAD UP NORTH FOR THE NEXT TRIP.
I WANT TO ENJOY THE COLD.
ARE YOU PUNISHING YOURSELF?

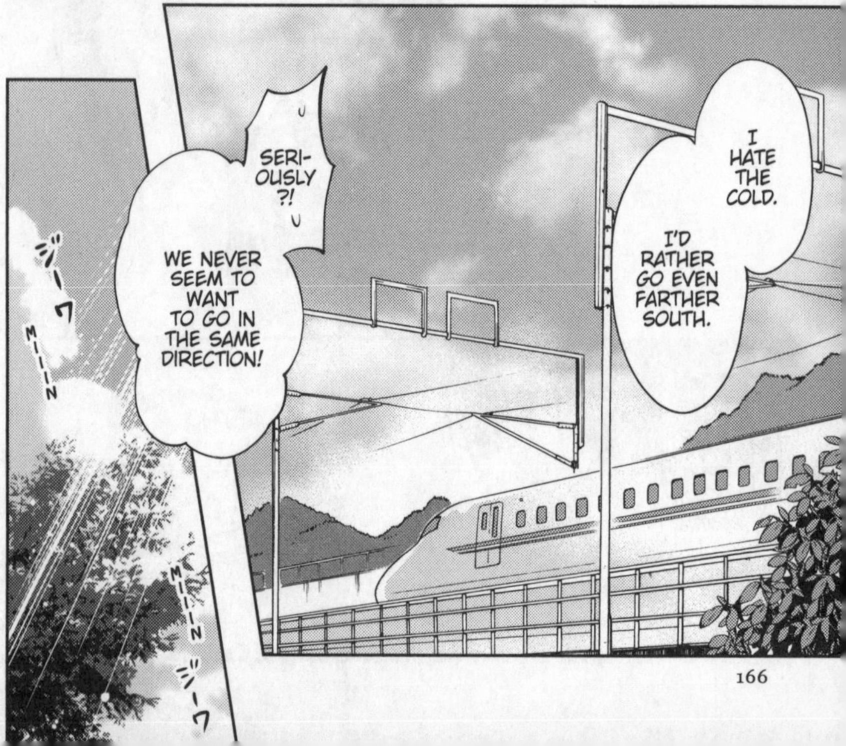
I HATE THE COLD.
I'D RATHER GO EVEN FARTHER SOUTH.
SERIOUSLY?!
WE NEVER SEEM TO WANT TO GO IN THE SAME DIRECTION!
ジーワ
MIIIN
MIIIN
ジーワ

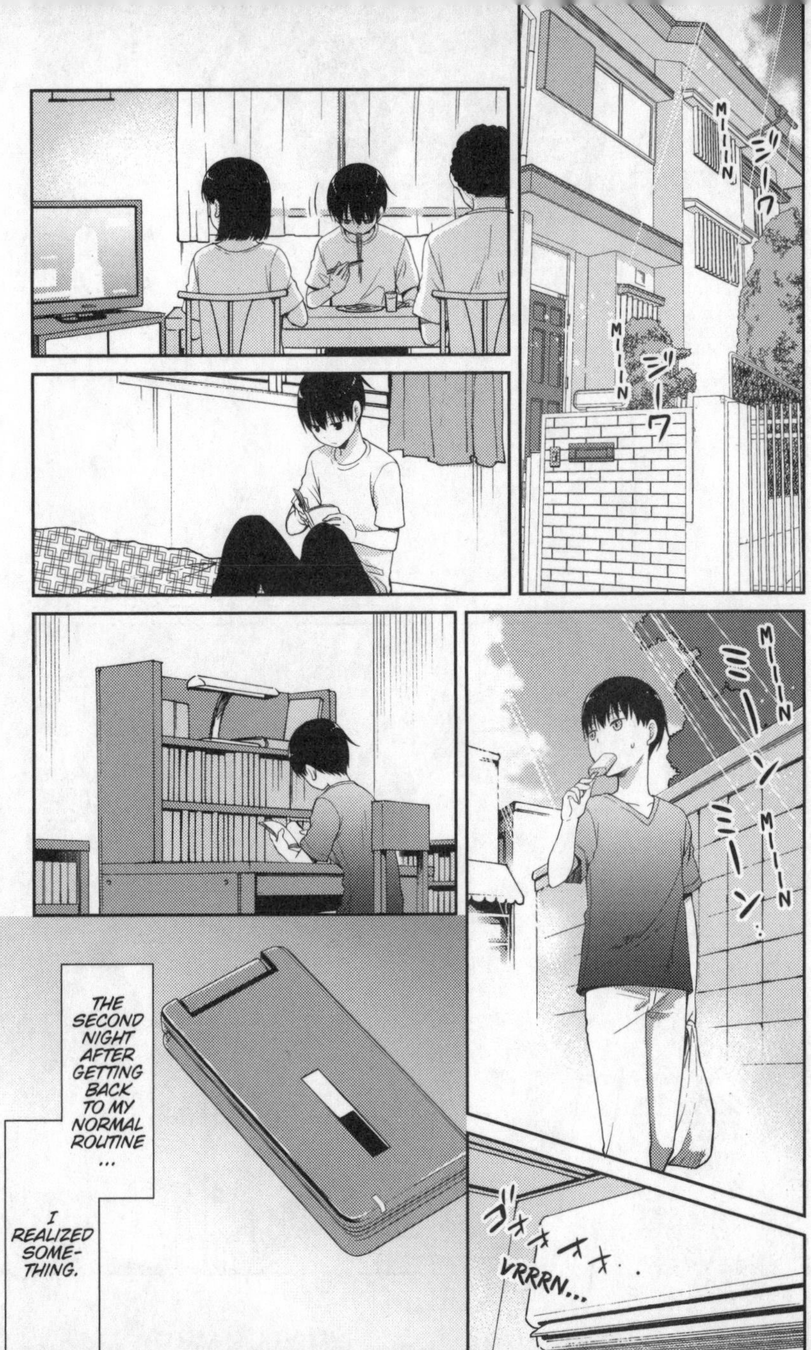
MIIIN
ジーワ
MIIIN
ジーワ
MIIIN
ミーン
MIIIN
ミーン.
THE SECOND NIGHT AFTER GETTING BACK TO MY NORMAL ROUTINE...
I REALIZED SOME-THING.
VRRRN...

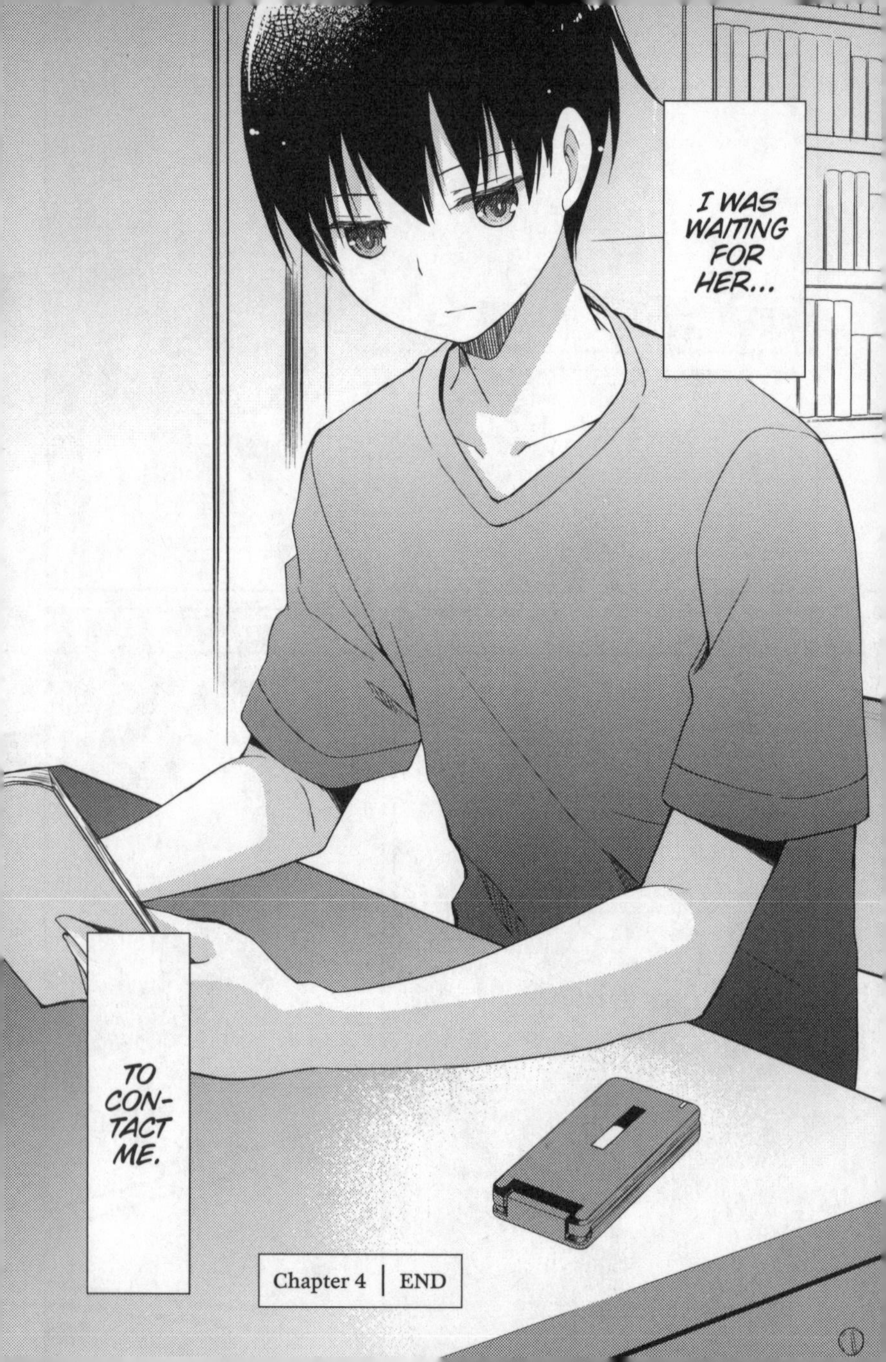

I WAS WAITING FOR HER...
TO CON-TACT ME.
Chapter 4 | END

Chapter 5 | Things One Shouldn't Do

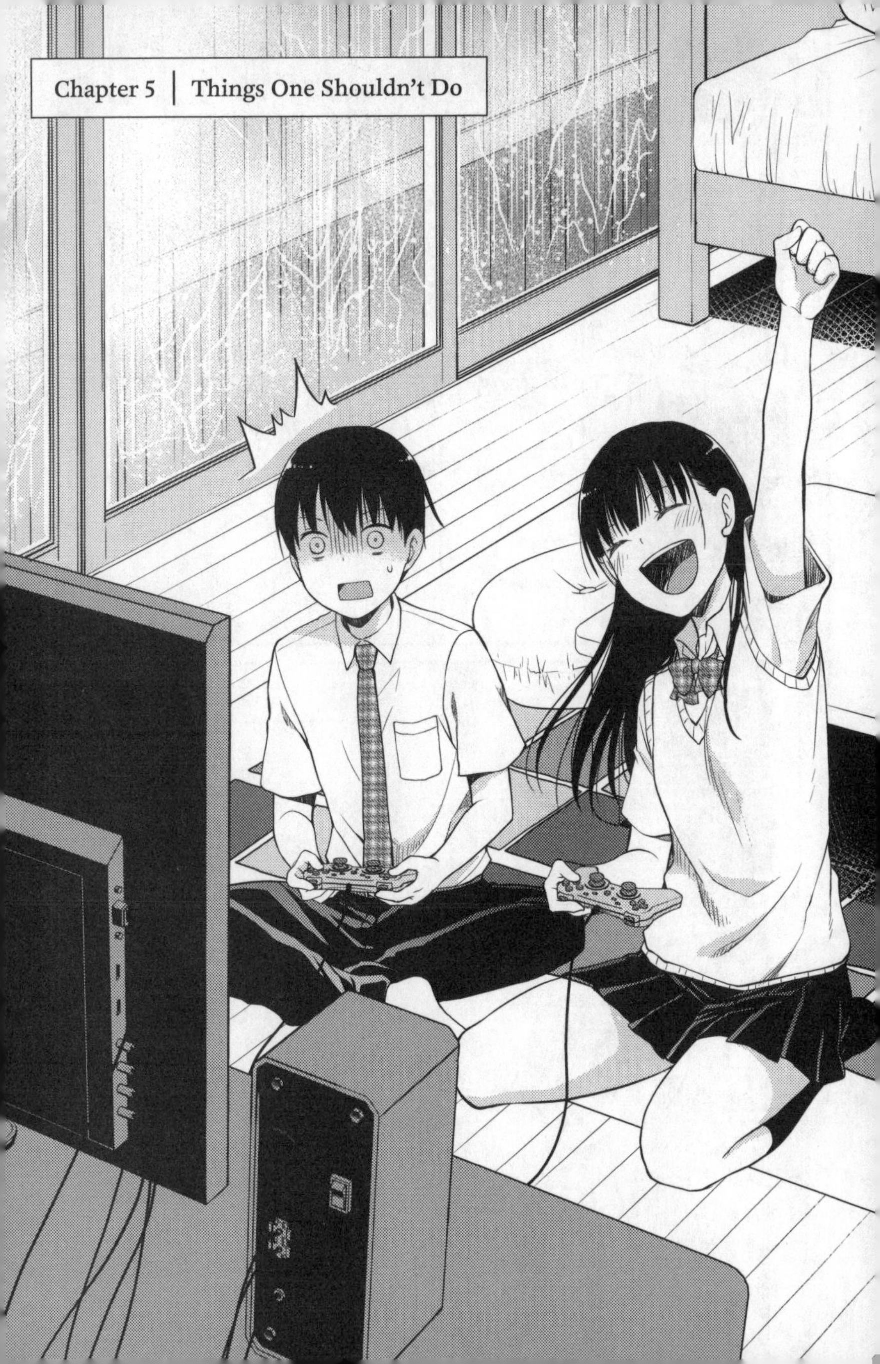

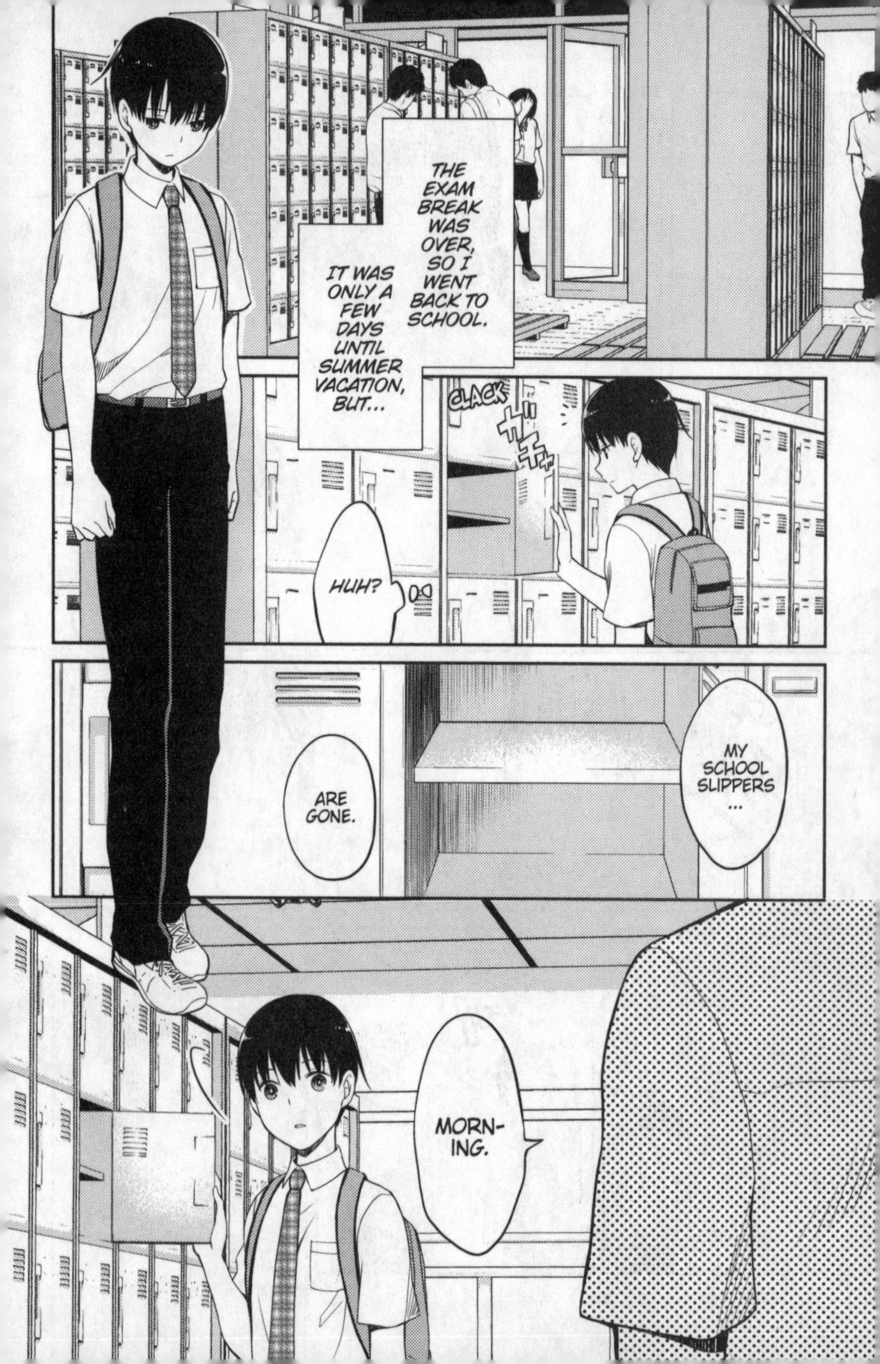
THE EXAM BREAK WAS OVER, SO I WENT BACK TO SCHOOL.
IT WAS ONLY A FEW DAYS UNTIL SUMMER VACATION, BUT...
CLACK
HUH?
MY SCHOOL SLIPPERS ...
ARE GONE.
MORN-ING.

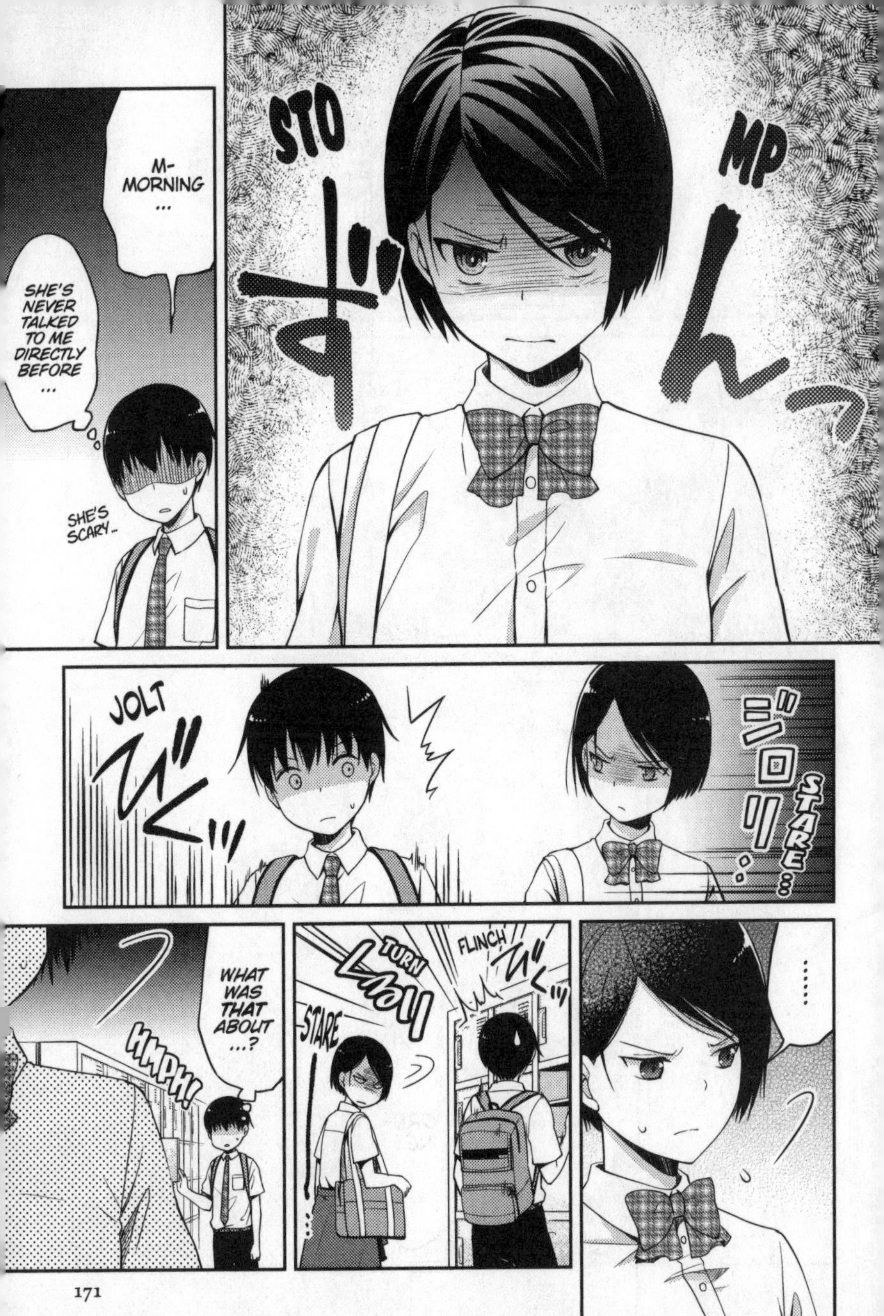
STOMP
M-MORNING...
SHE'S NEVER TALKED TO ME DIRECTLY BEFORE...
SHE'S SCARY...
STARE...
JOLT
......
FLINCH
TURN
STARE
WHAT WAS THAT ABOUT...?
HMPH!

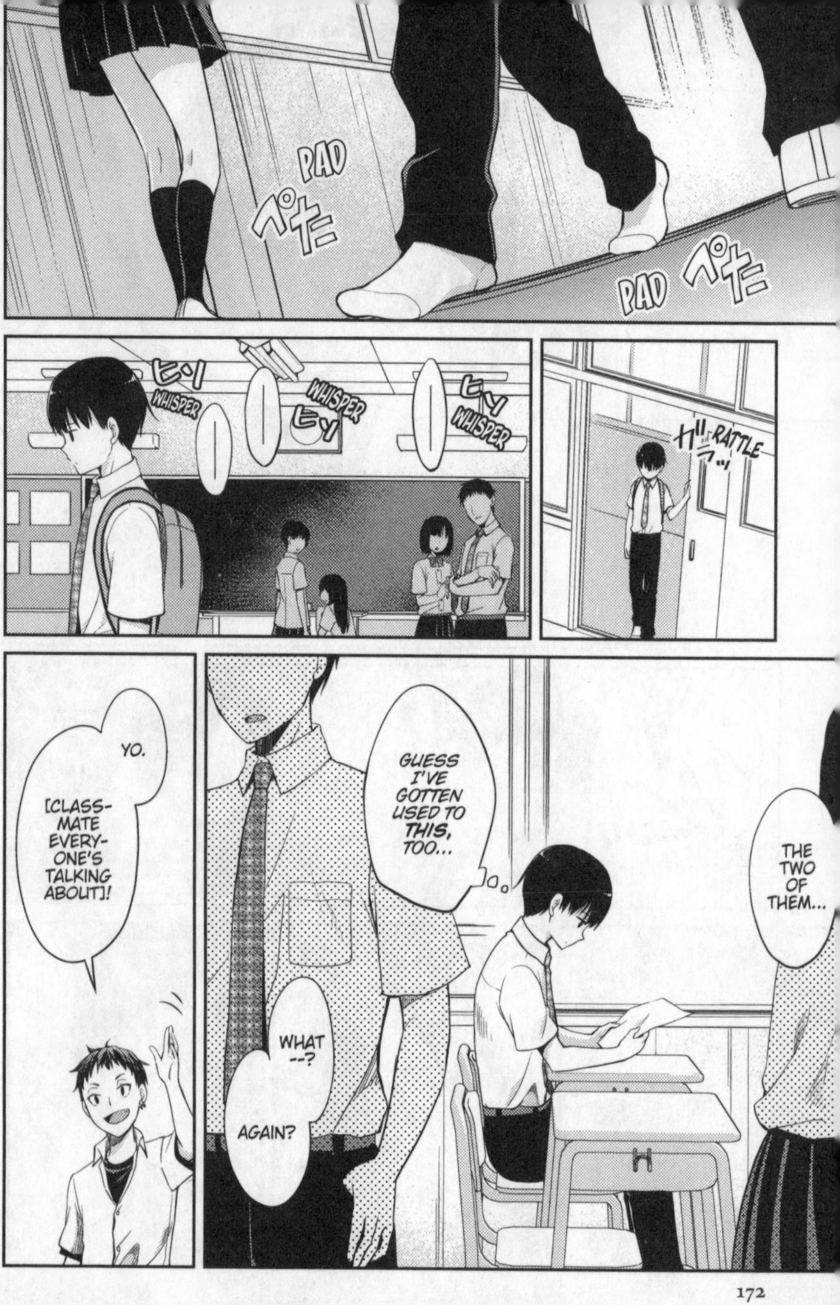
PAD ぺた
PAD ぺた
ガラッ RATTLE
ヒソ WHISPER
ヒソ WHISPER
ヒソ WHISPER
THE TWO OF THEM...
GUESS I'VE GOTTEN USED TO THIS, TOO...
WHAT--?
AGAIN?
YO.
[CLASSMATE EVERYONE'S TALKING ABOUT]!

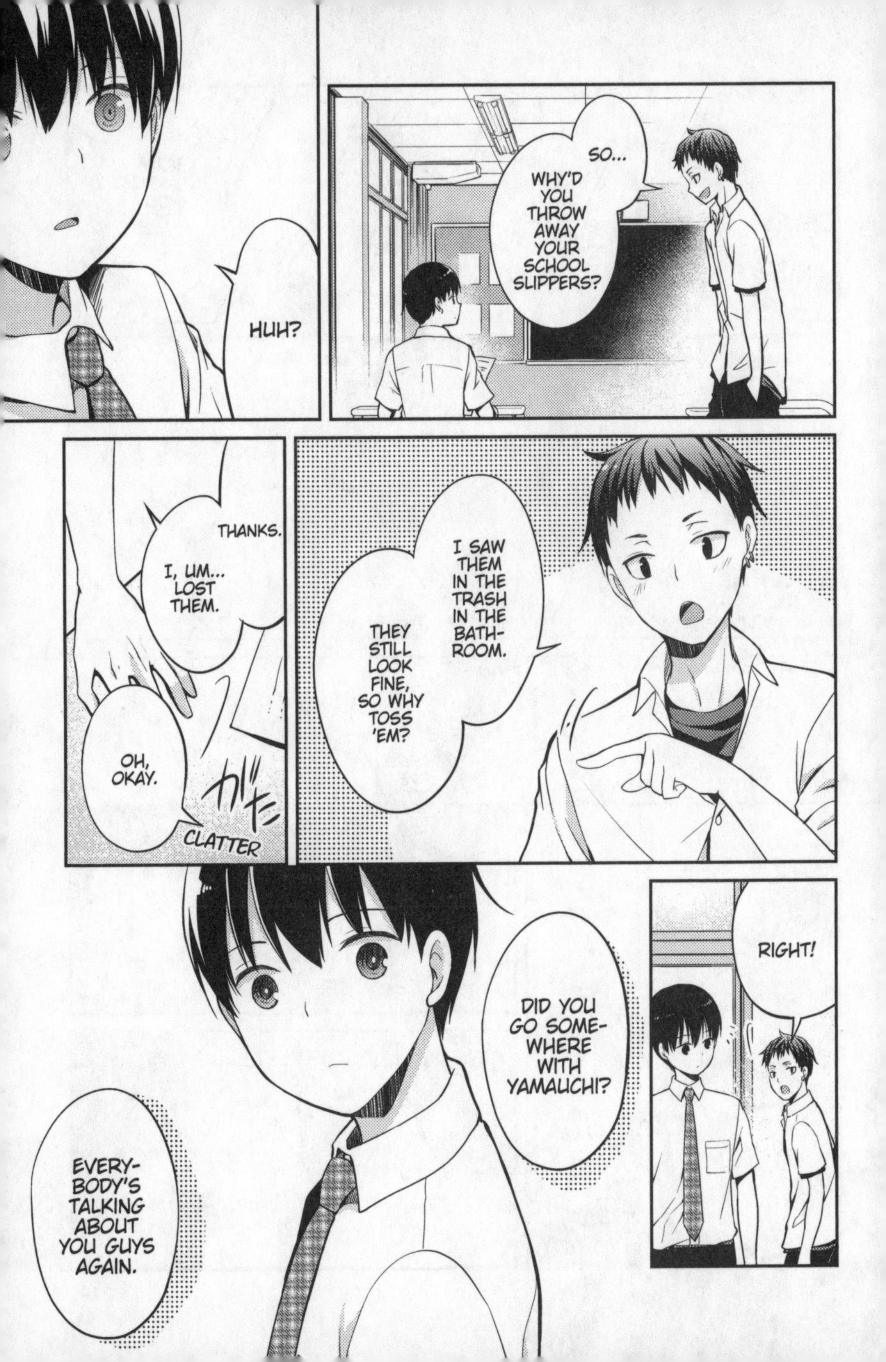
SO... WHY'D YOU THROW AWAY YOUR SCHOOL SLIPPERS?
HUH?
I SAW THEM IN THE TRASH IN THE BATH-ROOM.
THEY STILL LOOK FINE, SO WHY TOSS 'EM?
THANKS.
I, UM... LOST THEM.
OH, OKAY.
CLATTER
RIGHT!
DID YOU GO SOME-WHERE WITH YAMAUCHI?
EVERY-BODY'S TALKING ABOUT YOU GUYS AGAIN.

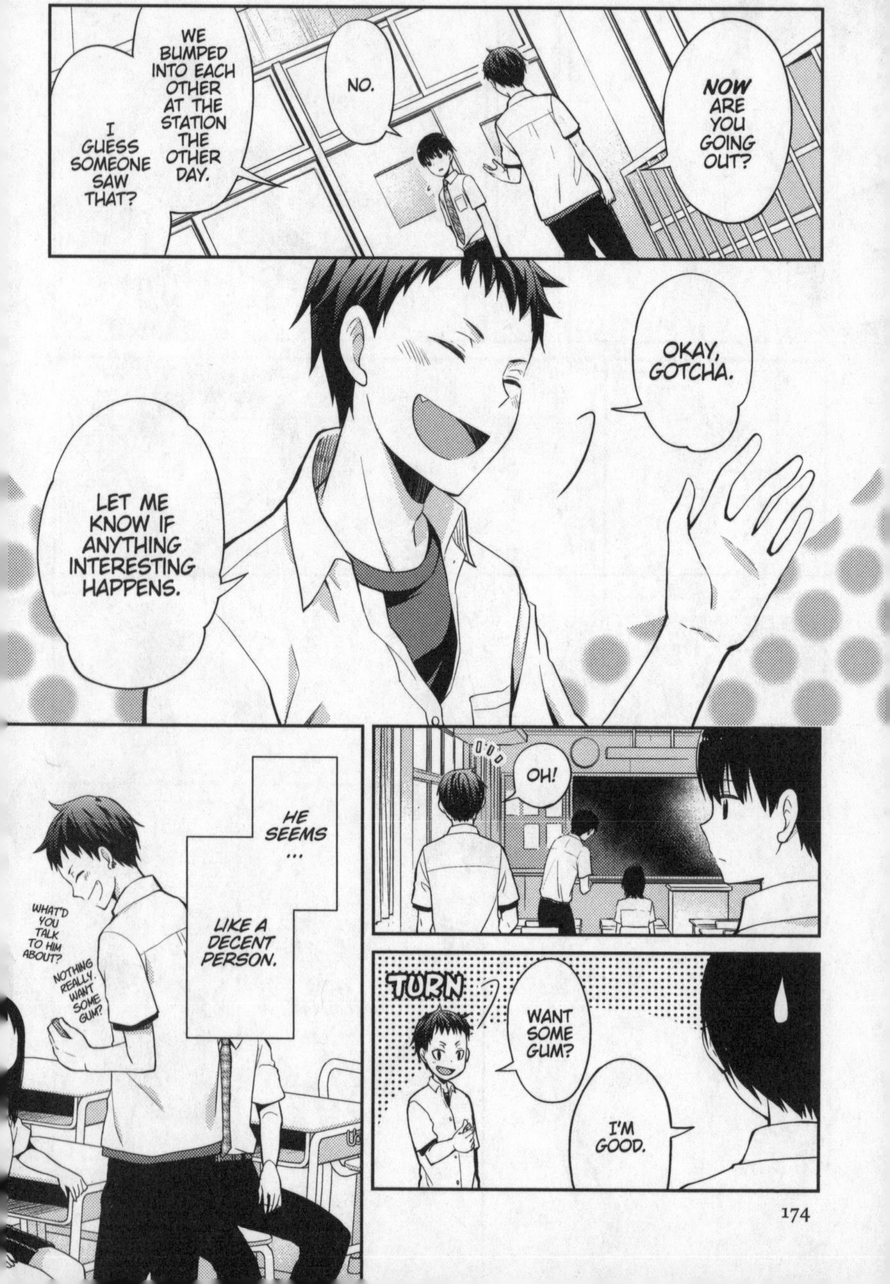
NOW ARE YOU GOING OUT?
NO.
WE BUMPED INTO EACH OTHER AT THE STATION THE OTHER DAY.
I GUESS SOMEONE SAW THAT?
OKAY, GOTCHA.
LET ME KNOW IF ANYTHING INTERESTING HAPPENS.
OH!
HE SEEMS ...
LIKE A DECENT PERSON.
WHAT'D YOU TALK TO HIM ABOUT?
NOTHING REALLY. WANT SOME GUM?
TURN
WANT SOME GUM?
I'M GOOD.

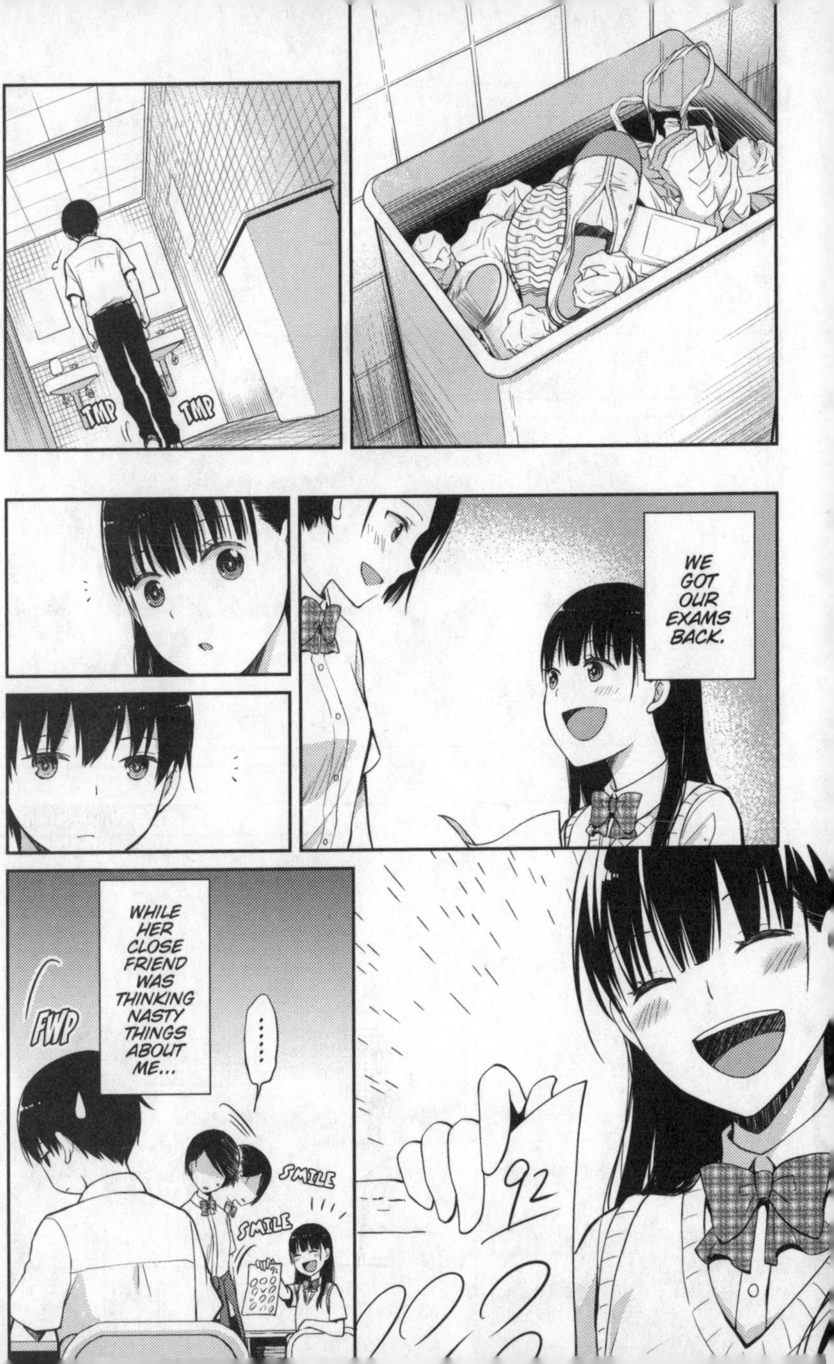
TMP
TMP
WE GOT OUR EXAMS BACK.
WHILE HER CLOSE FRIEND WAS THINKING NASTY THINGS ABOUT ME...
92
FWP
......
SMILE
SMILE

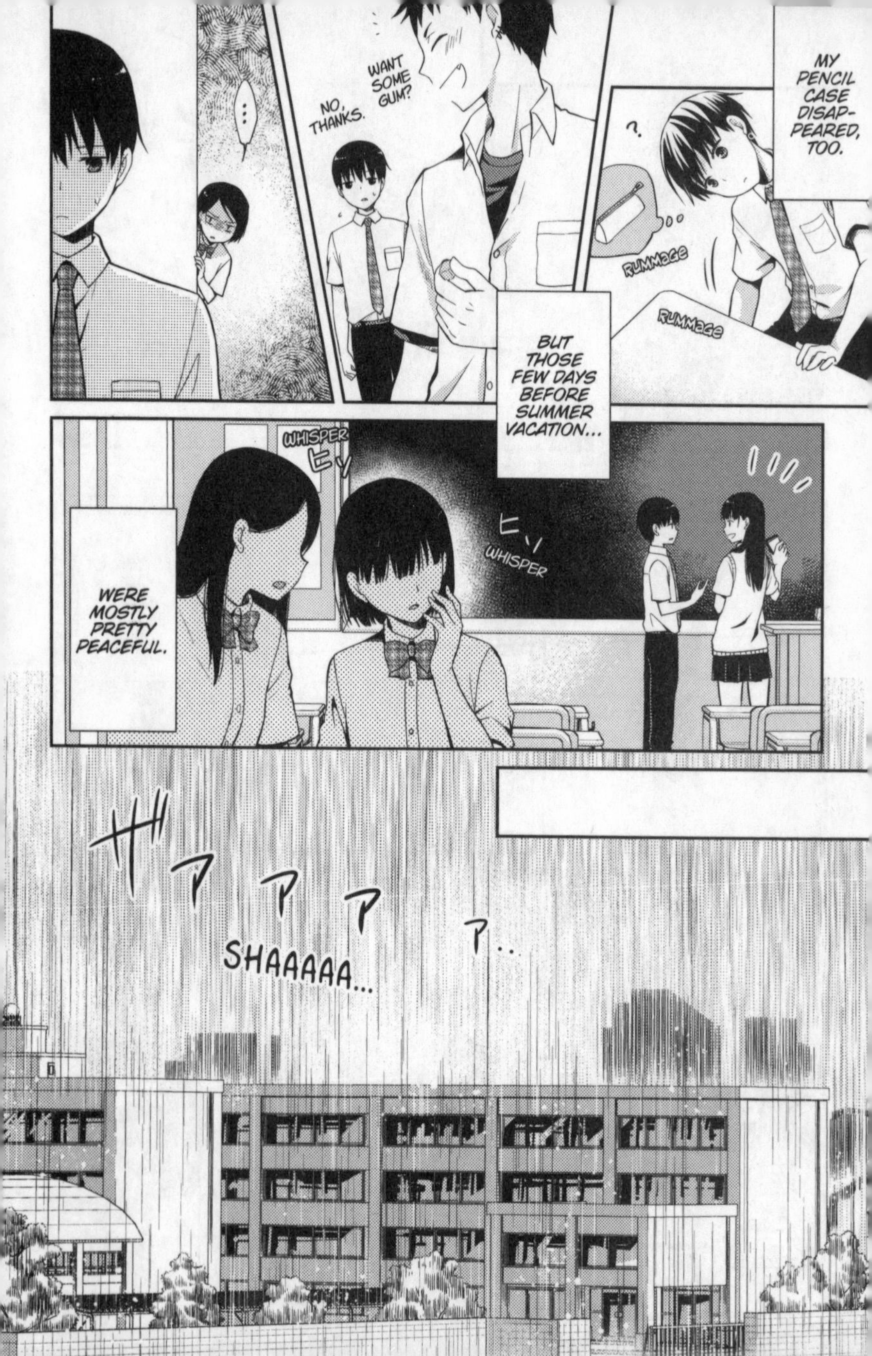
MY PENCIL CASE DISAP-PEARED, TOO.
?
RUMMAGE
RUMMAGE
WANT SOME GUM?
NO, THANKS.
...
BUT THOSE FEW DAYS BEFORE SUMMER VACATION...
WHISPER
WHISPER
WERE MOSTLY PRETTY PEACEFUL.
SHAAAAA...

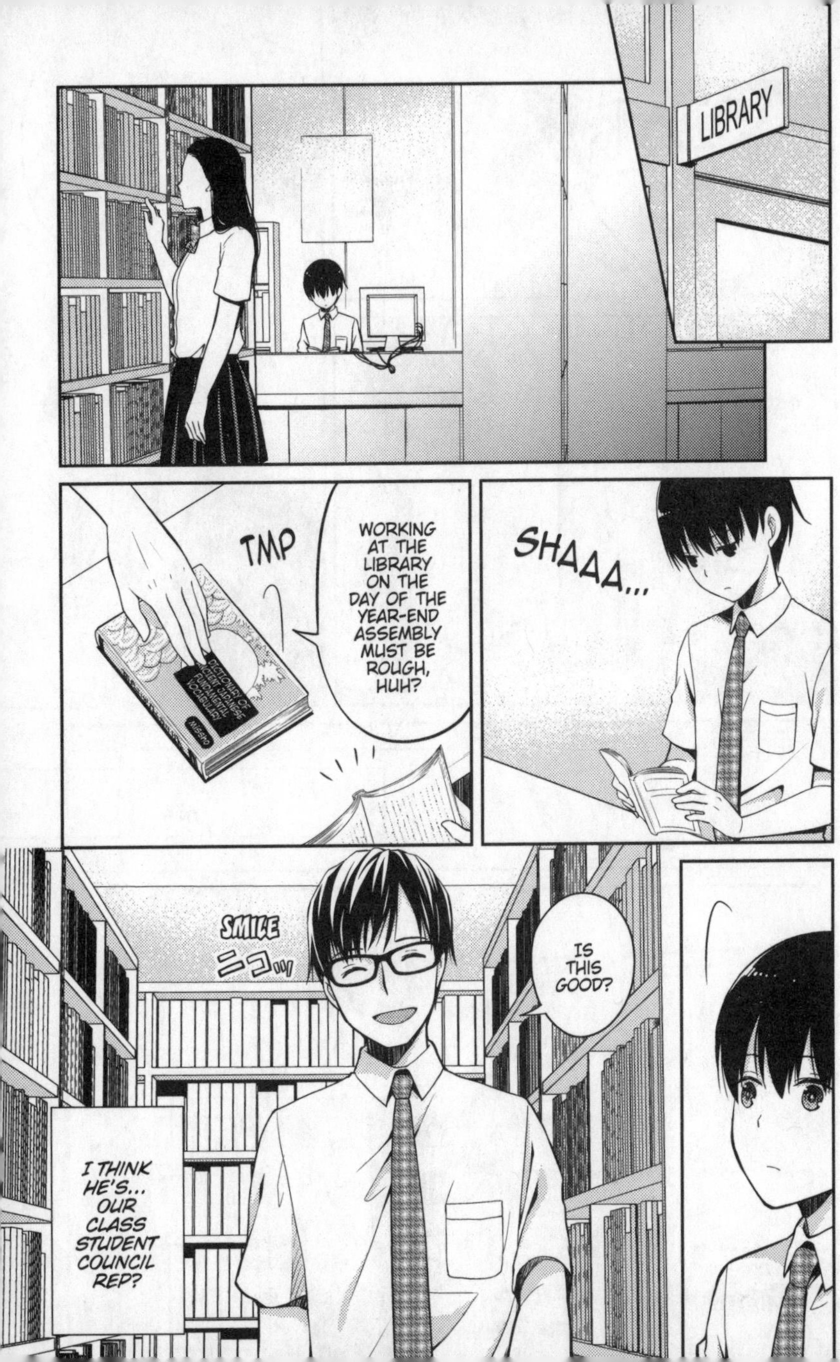

LIBRARY
SHAAA...
TMP
WORKING AT THE LIBRARY ON THE DAY OF THE YEAR-END ASSEMBLY MUST BE ROUGH, HUH?
IS THIS GOOD?
SMILE
ニコッ
I THINK HE'S... OUR CLASS STUDENT COUNCIL REP?

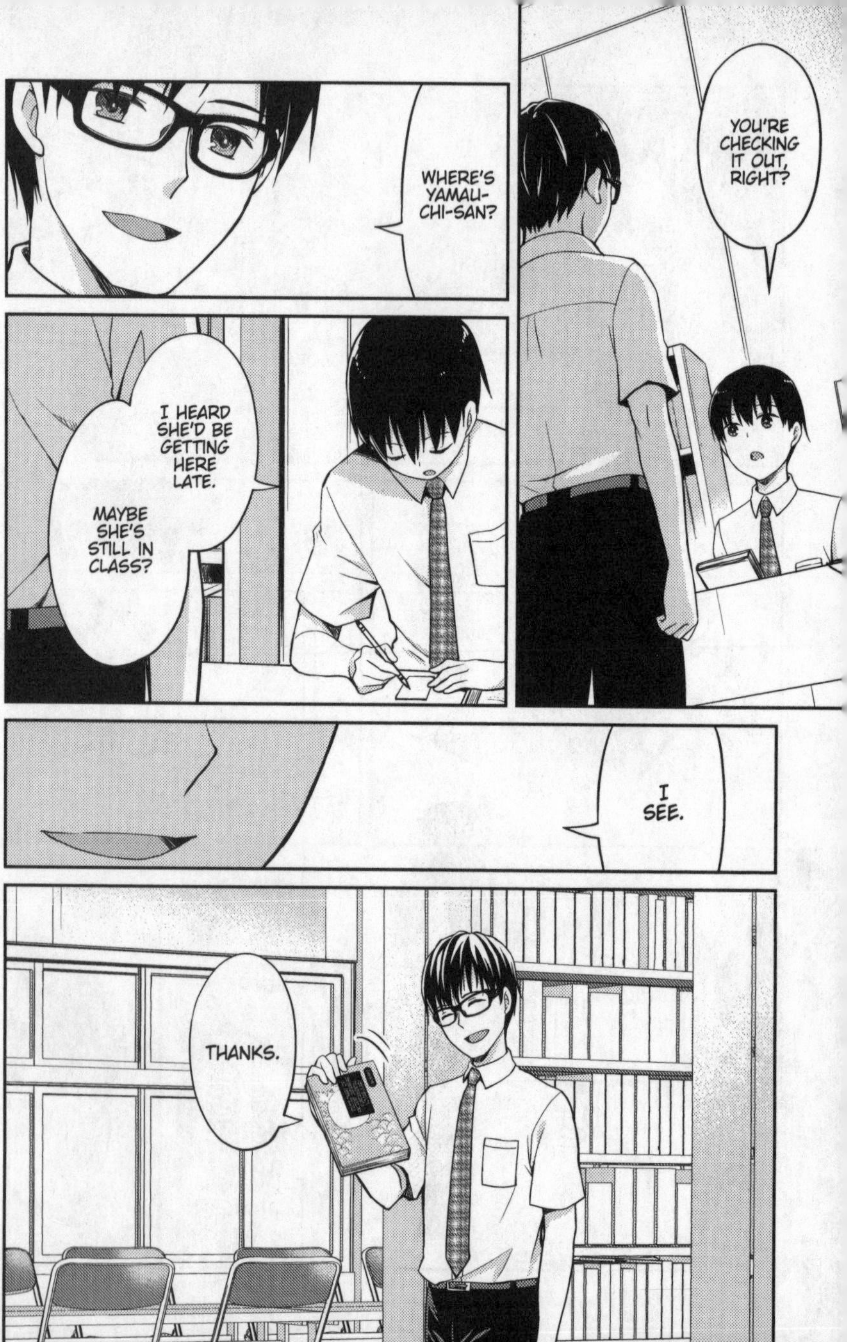
YOU'RE CHECKING IT OUT, RIGHT?
WHERE'S YAMAU-CHI-SAN?
I HEARD SHE'D BE GETTING HERE LATE.
MAYBE SHE'S STILL IN CLASS?
I SEE.
THANKS.

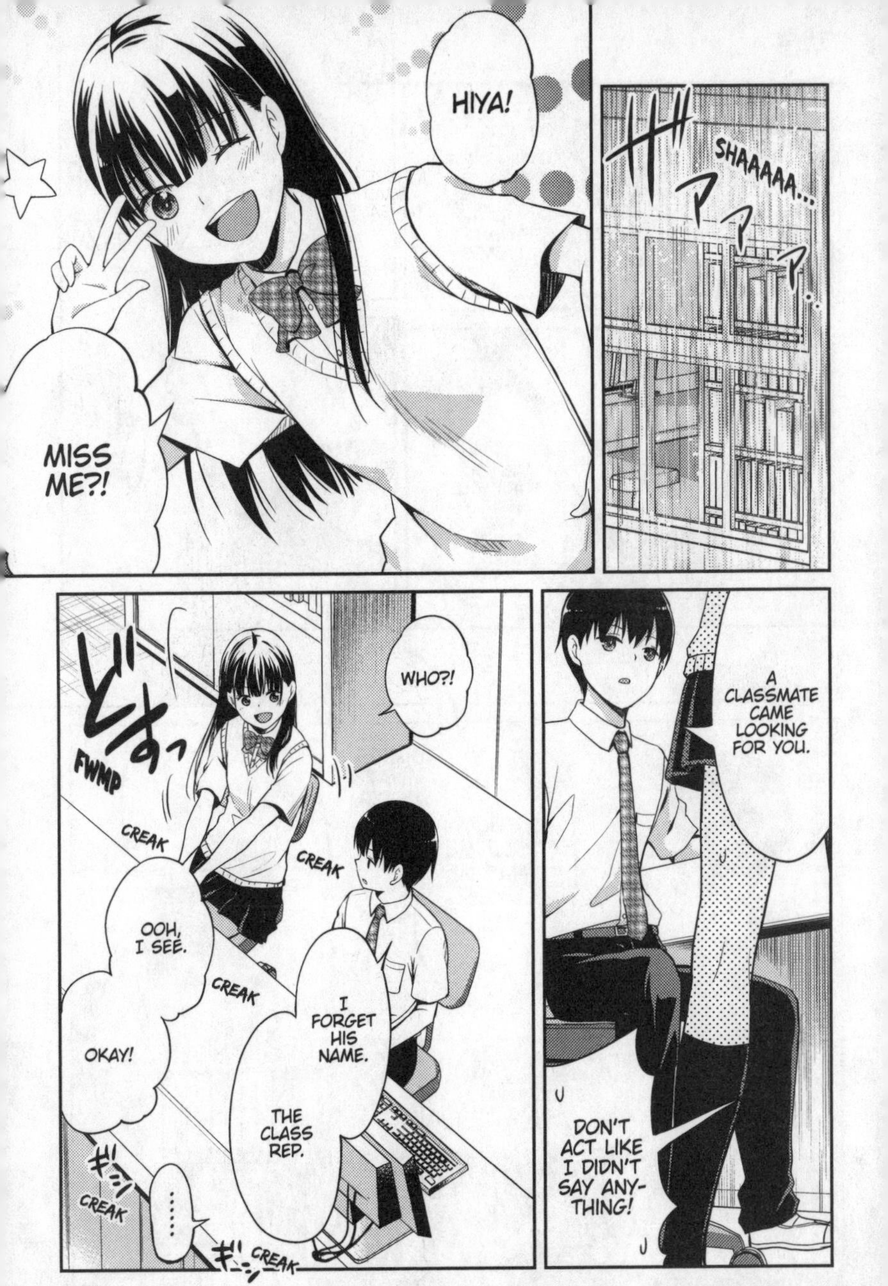

ザァァァ
SHAAAAA...
HIYA!
MISS ME?!
A CLASSMATE CAME LOOKING FOR YOU.
DON'T ACT LIKE I DIDN'T SAY ANY-THING!
WHO?!
どすっ
FWMP
CREAK
CREAK
OOH, I SEE.
CREAK
OKAY!
I FORGET HIS NAME.
THE CLASS REP.
......
ギシ
CREAK
ギシ
CREAK

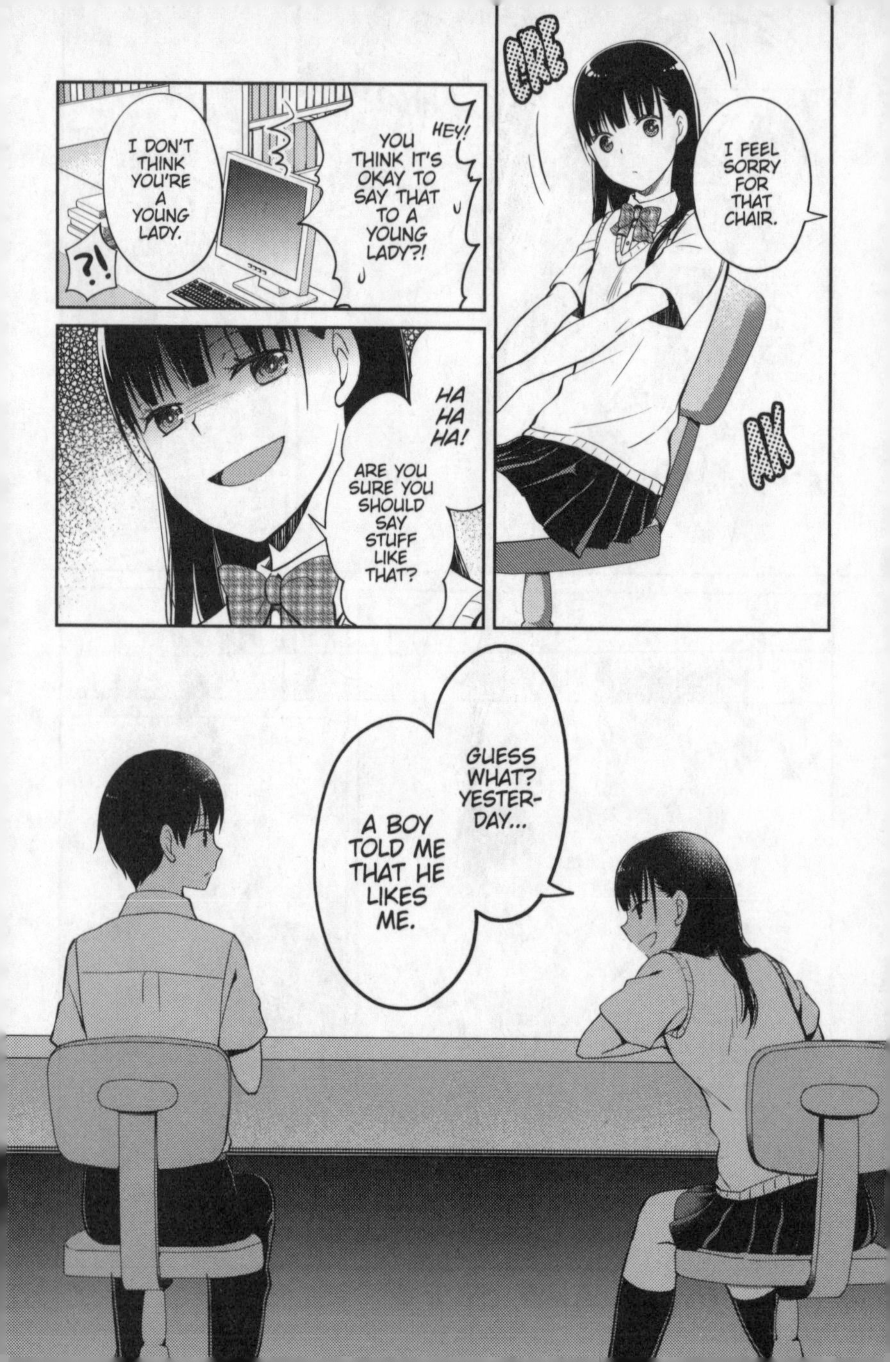
I FEEL SORRY FOR THAT CHAIR.
HEY!
YOU THINK IT'S OKAY TO SAY THAT TO A YOUNG LADY?!
I DON'T THINK YOU'RE A YOUNG LADY.
?!
HA HA HA!
ARE YOU SURE YOU SHOULD SAY STUFF LIKE THAT?
GUESS WHAT? YESTER-DAY...
A BOY TOLD ME THAT HE LIKES ME.

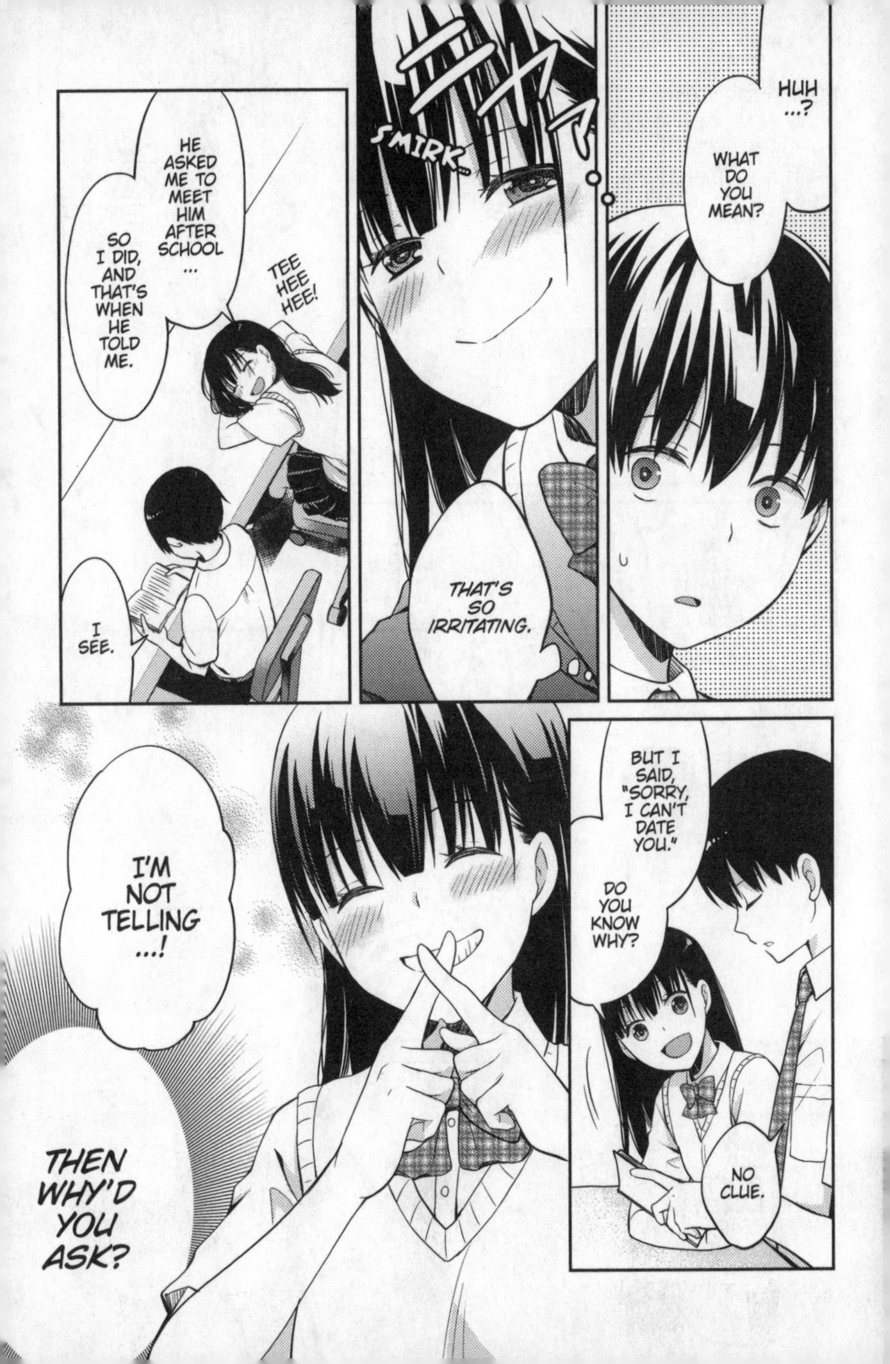

HUH ...?
WHAT DO YOU MEAN?
SMIRK...
THAT'S SO IRRITATING.
HE ASKED ME TO MEET HIM AFTER SCHOOL ...
SO I DID, AND THAT'S WHEN HE TOLD ME.
TEE HEE HEE!
I SEE.
BUT I SAID, "SORRY, I CAN'T DATE YOU."
DO YOU KNOW WHY?
NO CLUE.
I'M NOT TELLING ...!
THEN WHY'D YOU ASK?

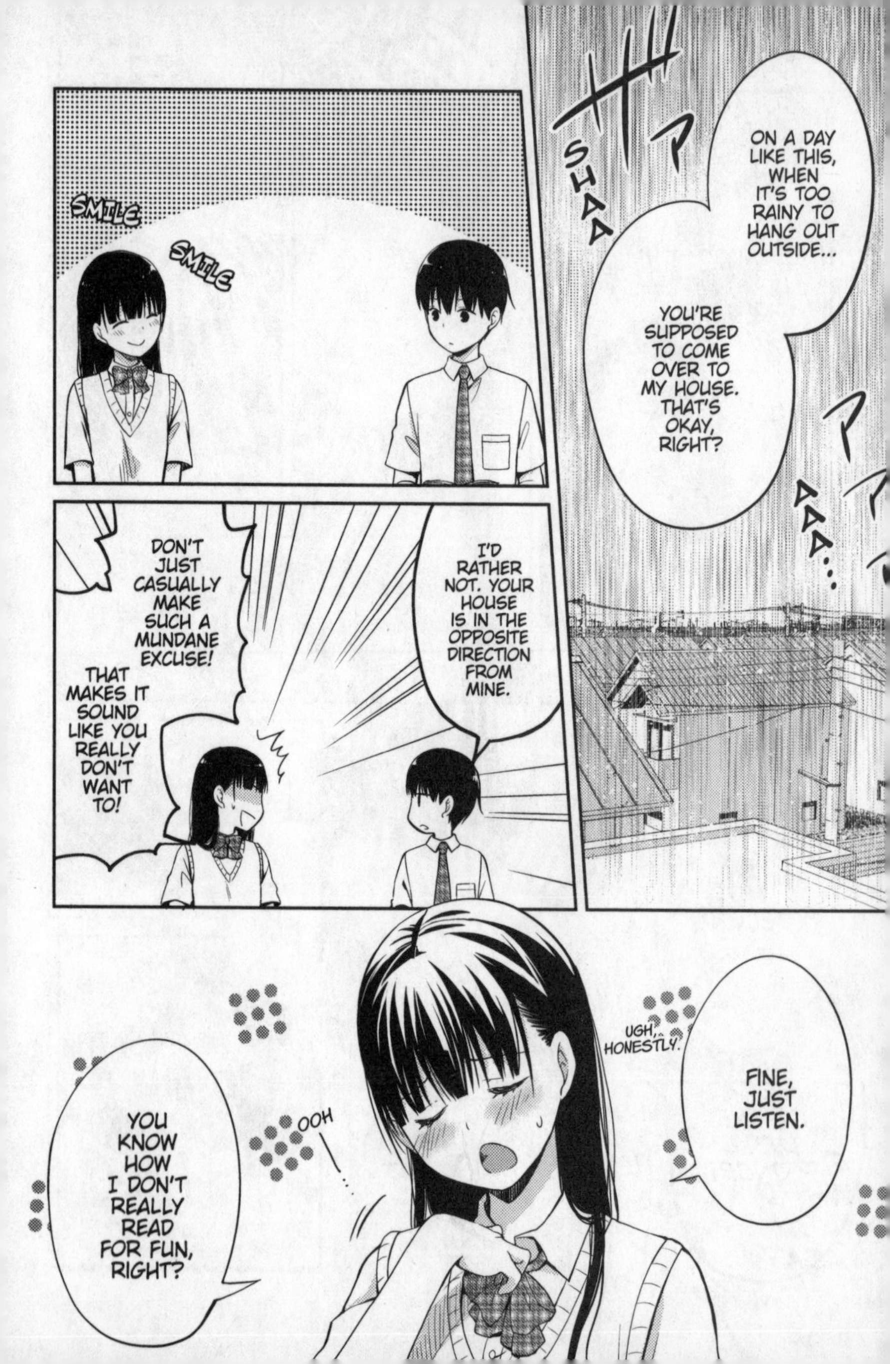
SHAA
ON A DAY LIKE THIS, WHEN IT'S TOO RAINY TO HANG OUT OUTSIDE...
YOU'RE SUPPOSED TO COME OVER TO MY HOUSE. THAT'S OKAY, RIGHT?
AAA...
SMILE
SMILE
I'D RATHER NOT. YOUR HOUSE IS IN THE OPPOSITE DIRECTION FROM MINE.
DON'T JUST CASUALLY MAKE SUCH A MUNDANE EXCUSE!
THAT MAKES IT SOUND LIKE YOU REALLY DON'T WANT TO!
UGH, HONESTLY.
FINE, JUST LISTEN.
OOH
YOU KNOW HOW I DON'T REALLY READ FOR FUN, RIGHT?

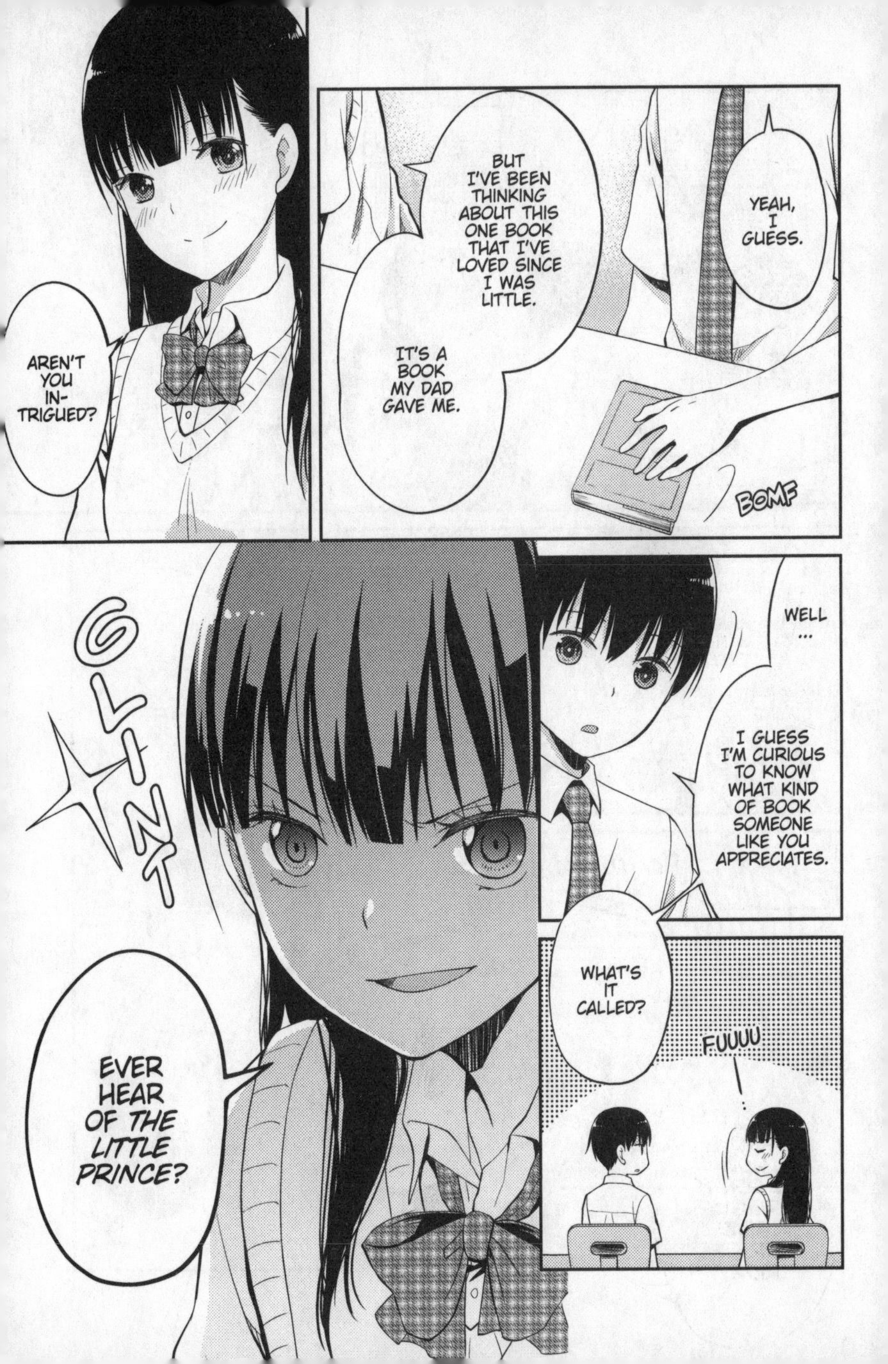
YEAH, I GUESS.
BUT I'VE BEEN THINKING ABOUT THIS ONE BOOK THAT I'VE LOVED SINCE I WAS LITTLE.
IT'S A BOOK MY DAD GAVE ME.
BOMF
AREN'T YOU IN-TRIGUED?
WELL ...
I GUESS I'M CURIOUS TO KNOW WHAT KIND OF BOOK SOMEONE LIKE YOU APPRECIATES.
WHAT'S IT CALLED?
FUUUU
GLINT
EVER HEAR OF THE LITTLE PRINCE?

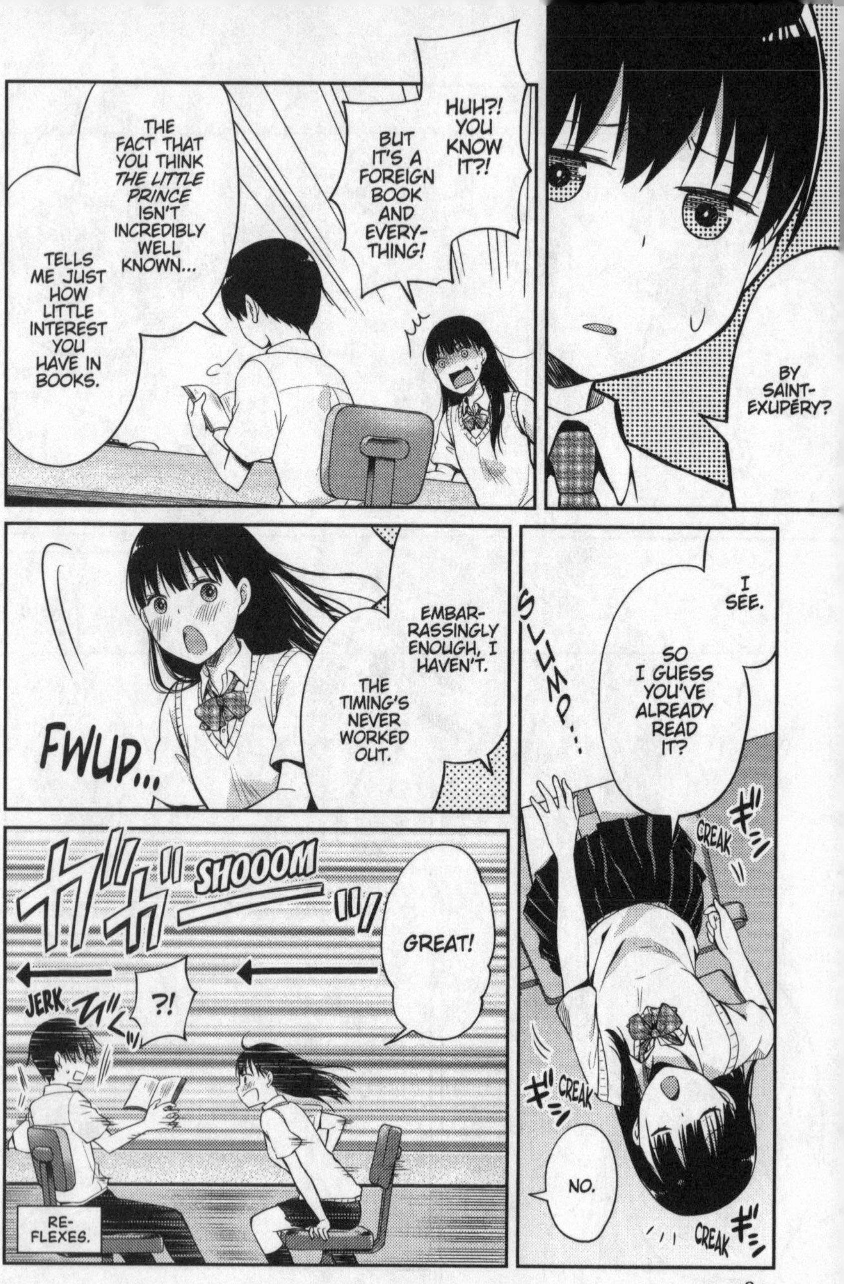
BY SAINT-EXUPÉRY?
HUH?! YOU KNOW IT?!
BUT IT'S A FOREIGN BOOK AND EVERY-THING!
THE FACT THAT YOU THINK *THE LITTLE PRINCE* ISN'T INCREDIBLY WELL KNOWN...
TELLS ME JUST HOW LITTLE INTEREST YOU HAVE IN BOOKS.
I SEE.
SO I GUESS YOU'VE ALREADY READ IT?
SLUMP...
CREAK
CREAK
NO.
CREAK
EMBAR-RASSINGLY ENOUGH, I HAVEN'T.
THE TIMING'S NEVER WORKED OUT.
FWUP...
GREAT!
SHOOOM
?!
JERK
RE-FLEXES.

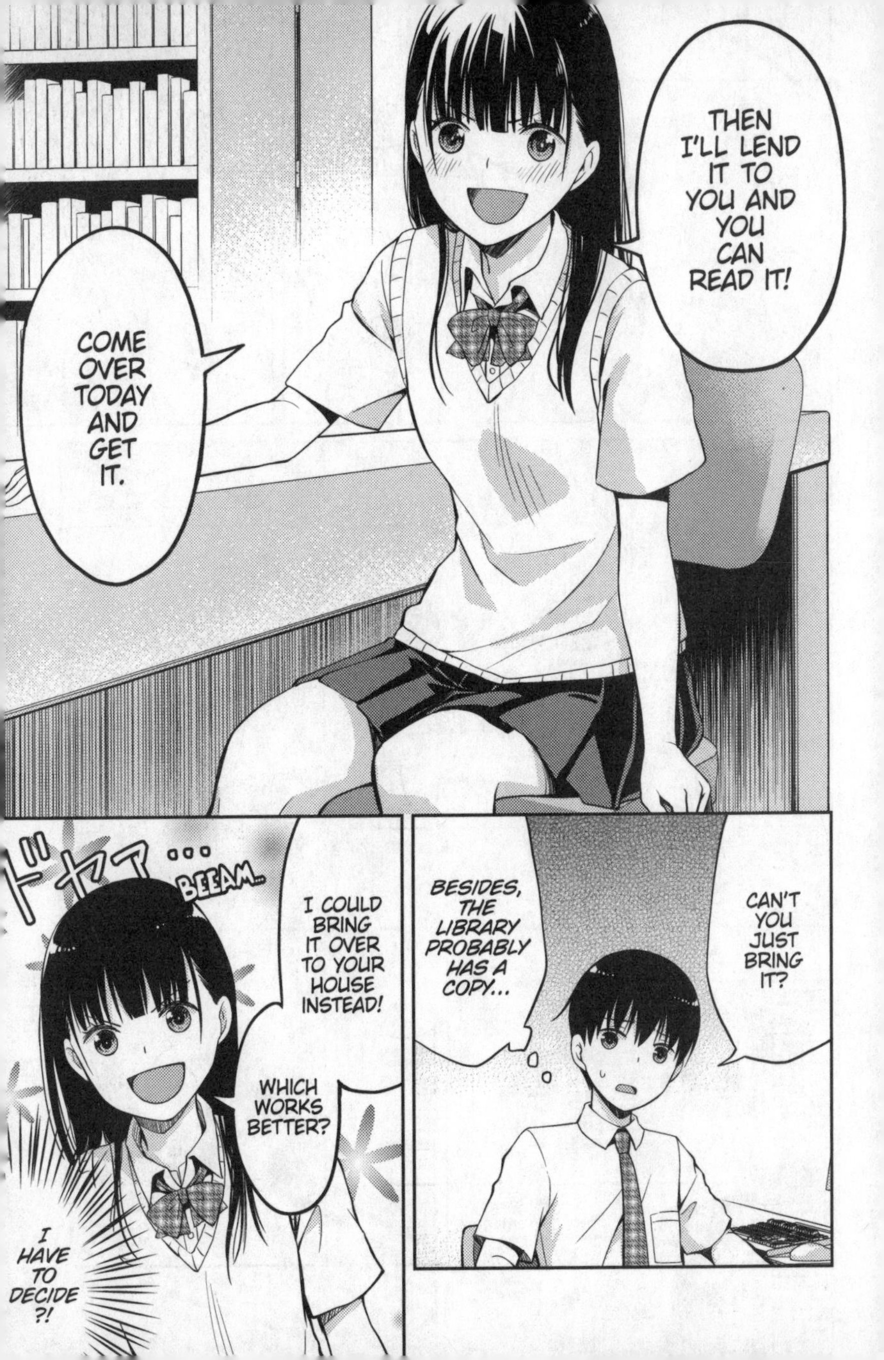
THEN I'LL LEND IT TO YOU AND YOU CAN READ IT!
COME OVER TODAY AND GET IT.
CAN'T YOU JUST BRING IT?
BESIDES, THE LIBRARY PROBABLY HAS A COPY...
ドヤア...
BEEAM...
I COULD BRING IT OVER TO YOUR HOUSE INSTEAD!
WHICH WORKS BETTER?
I HAVE TO DECIDE ?!

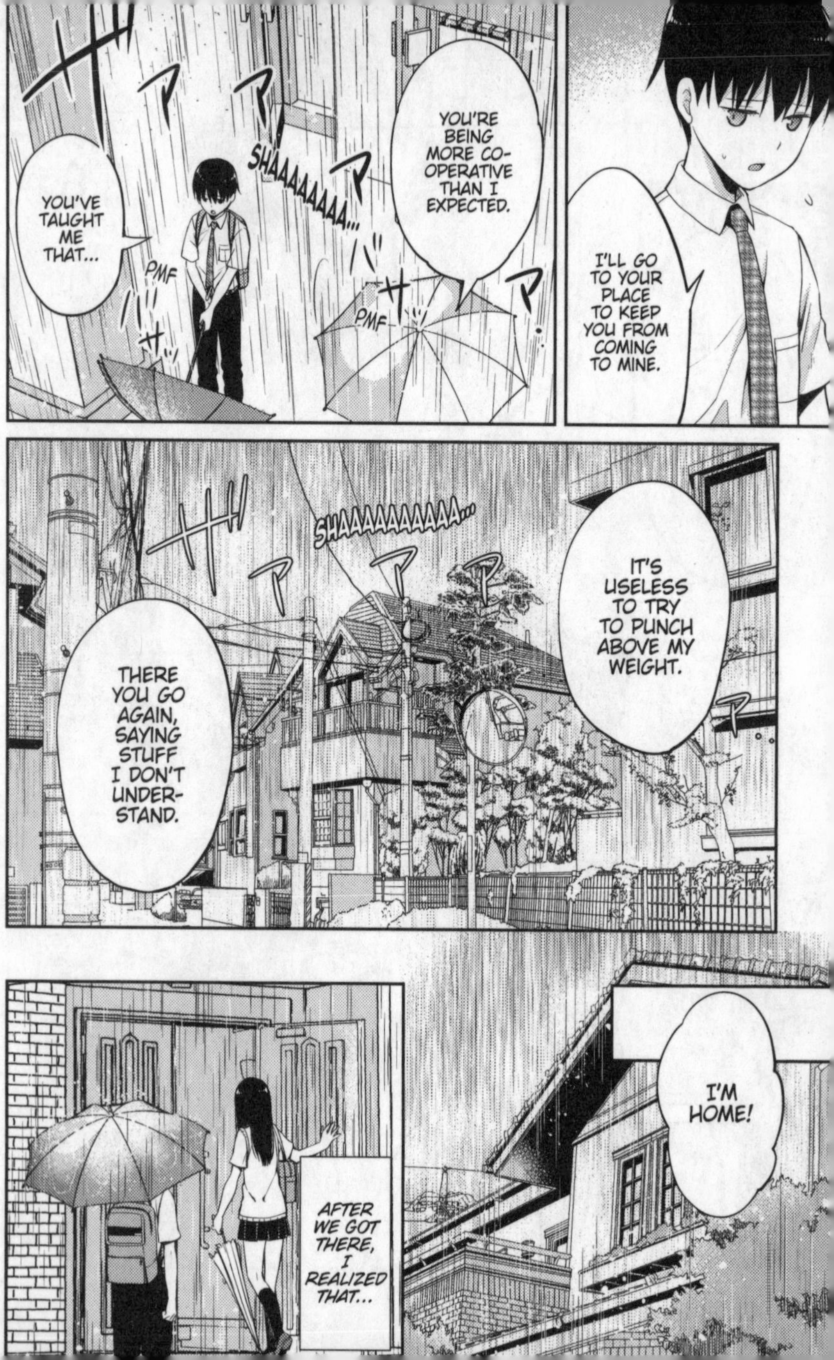
I'LL GO TO YOUR PLACE TO KEEP YOU FROM COMING TO MINE.
YOU'RE BEING MORE CO-OPERATIVE THAN I EXPECTED.
SHAAAAAAAA...
PMF
PMF
YOU'VE TAUGHT ME THAT...
IT'S USELESS TO TRY TO PUNCH ABOVE MY WEIGHT.
SHAAAAAAAAAA...
THERE YOU GO AGAIN, SAYING STUFF I DON'T UNDER-STAND.
I'M HOME!
AFTER WE GOT THERE, I REALIZED THAT...

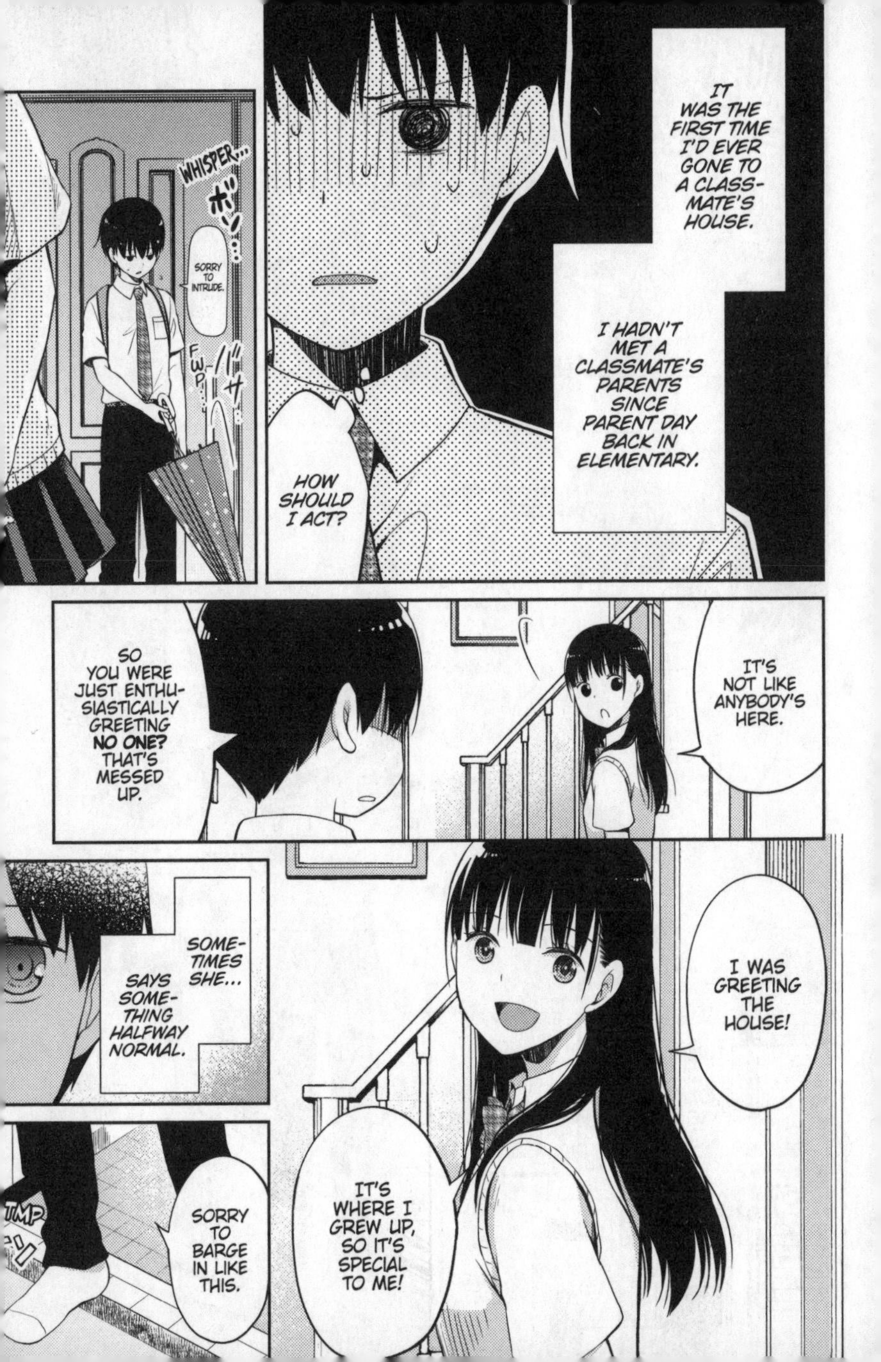
IT WAS THE FIRST TIME I'D EVER GONE TO A CLASS-MATE'S HOUSE.
I HADN'T MET A CLASSMATE'S PARENTS SINCE PARENT DAY BACK IN ELEMENTARY.
HOW SHOULD I ACT?
WHISPER...
ボソ…
SORRY TO INTRUDE.
FWP...
バサ
IT'S NOT LIKE ANYBODY'S HERE.
SO YOU WERE JUST ENTHU-SIASTICALLY GREETING NO ONE? THAT'S MESSED UP.
I WAS GREETING THE HOUSE!
SOME-TIMES SHE... SAYS SOME-THING HALFWAY NORMAL.
IT'S WHERE I GREW UP, SO IT'S SPECIAL TO ME!
SORRY TO BARGE IN LIKE THIS.
TMP

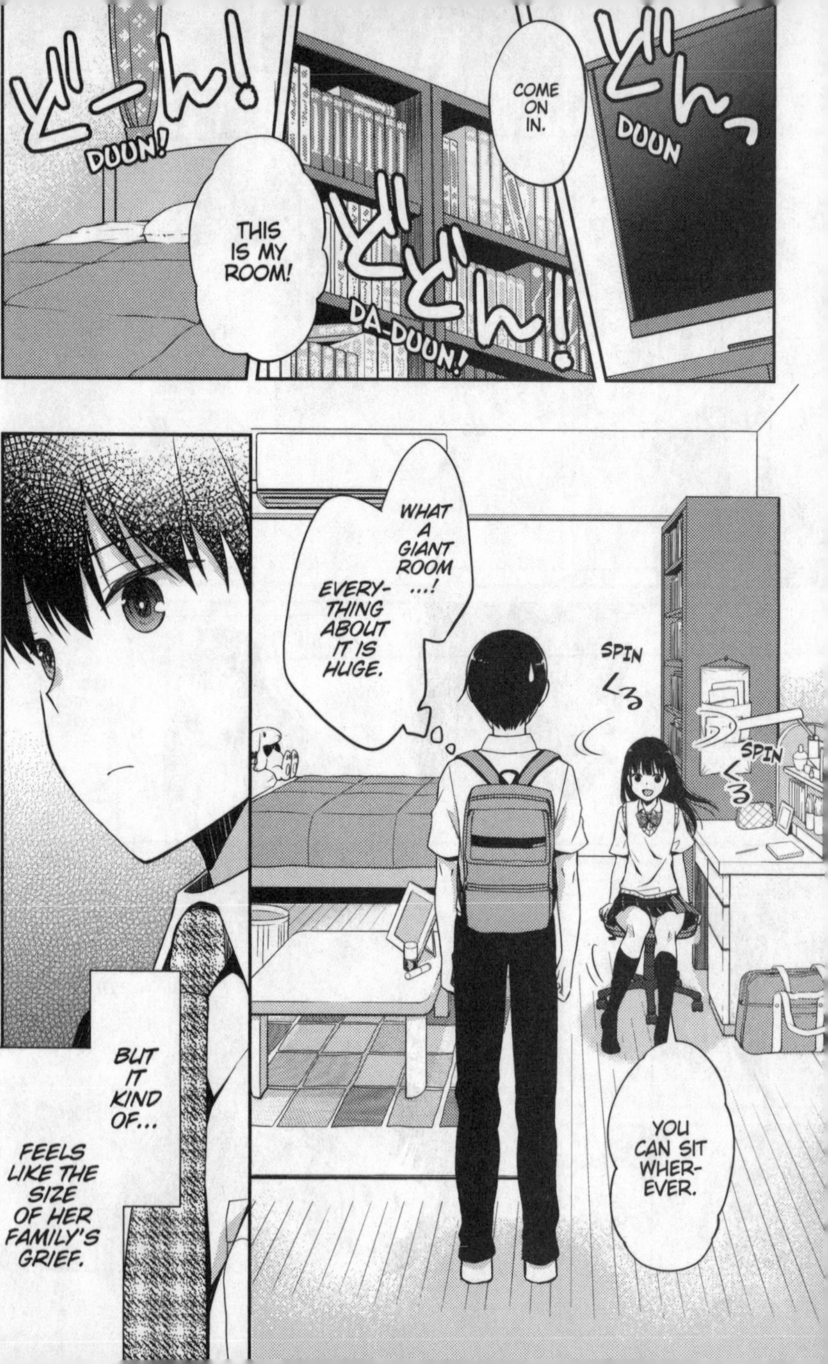
COME ON IN.
どんっ
DUUN
THIS IS MY ROOM!
どどん!
DA-DUUN!
どーん!
DUUN!
WHAT A GIANT ROOM...!
EVERY-THING ABOUT IT IS HUGE.
SPIN
くる
SPIN
くる
YOU CAN SIT WHER-EVER.
BUT IT KIND OF...
FEELS LIKE THE SIZE OF HER FAMILY'S GRIEF.

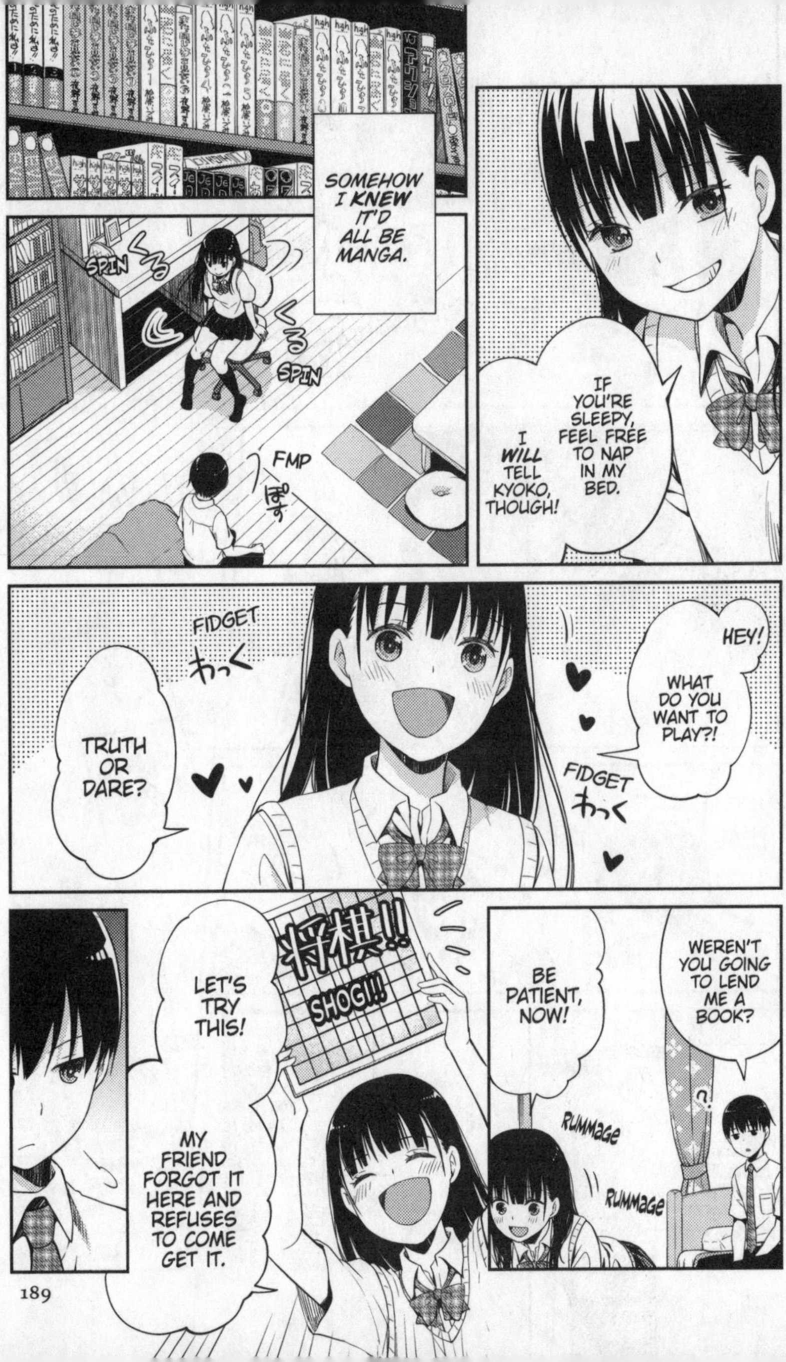
SOMEHOW I KNEW IT'D ALL BE MANGA.
IF YOU'RE SLEEPY, FEEL FREE TO NAP IN MY BED.
I WILL TELL KYOKO, THOUGH!
SPIN くる
くる SPIN
FMP ぽす
HEY!
WHAT DO YOU WANT TO PLAY?!
FIDGET わっく
FIDGET わっく
TRUTH OR DARE?
WEREN'T YOU GOING TO LEND ME A BOOK?
BE PATIENT, NOW!
RUMMAGE
RUMMAGE
将棋!!
SHOGI!!
LET'S TRY THIS!
MY FRIEND FORGOT IT HERE AND REFUSES TO COME GET IT.

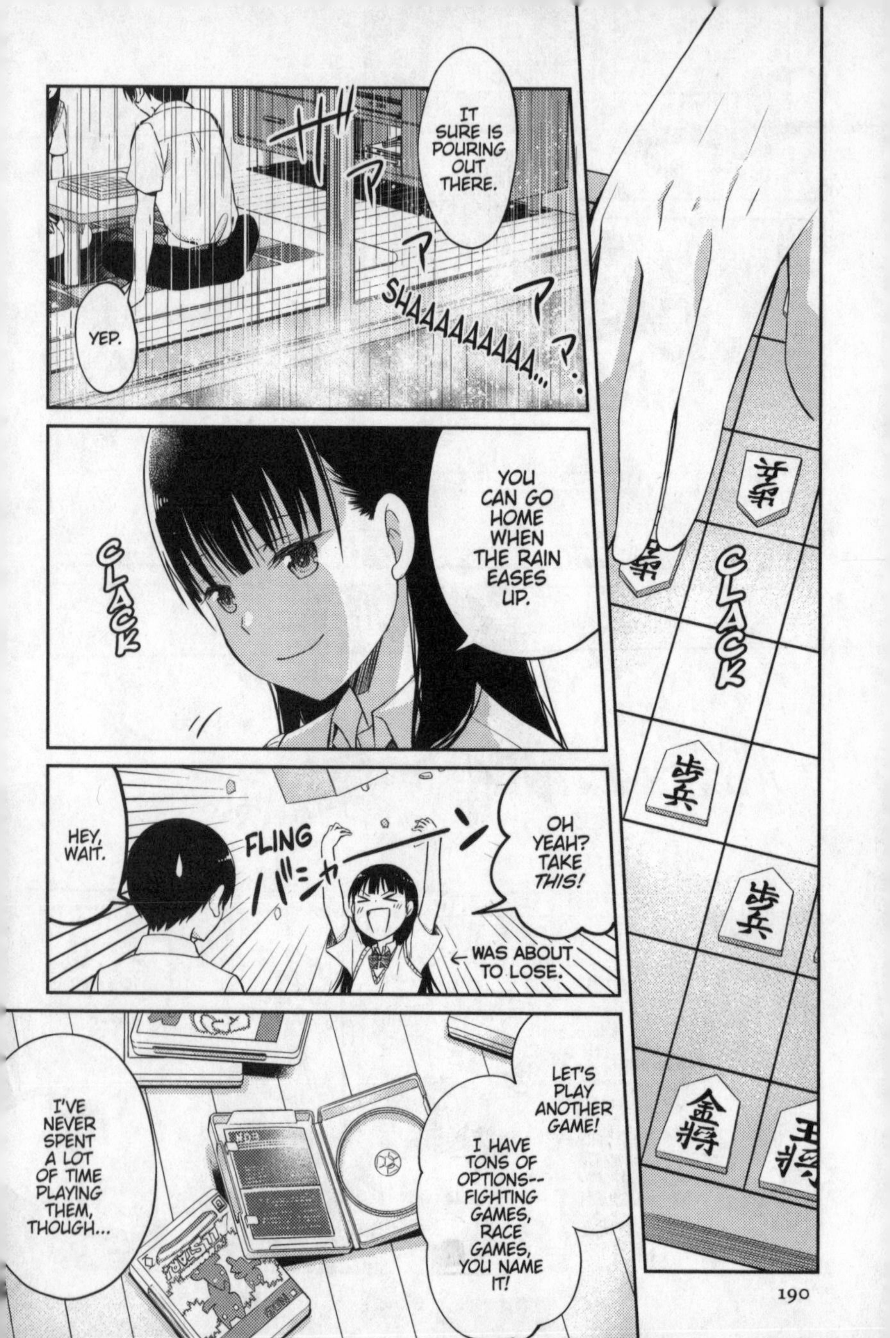

IT SURE IS POURING OUT THERE.
ザァァァァ
SHAAAAAAAAA...
YEP.
CLACK
YOU CAN GO HOME WHEN THE RAIN EASES UP.
CLACK
OH YEAH? TAKE THIS!
FLING
バシャーン
HEY, WAIT.
← WAS ABOUT TO LOSE.
LET'S PLAY ANOTHER GAME!
I HAVE TONS OF OPTIONS-- FIGHTING GAMES, RACE GAMES, YOU NAME IT!
I'VE NEVER SPENT A LOT OF TIME PLAYING THEM, THOUGH...

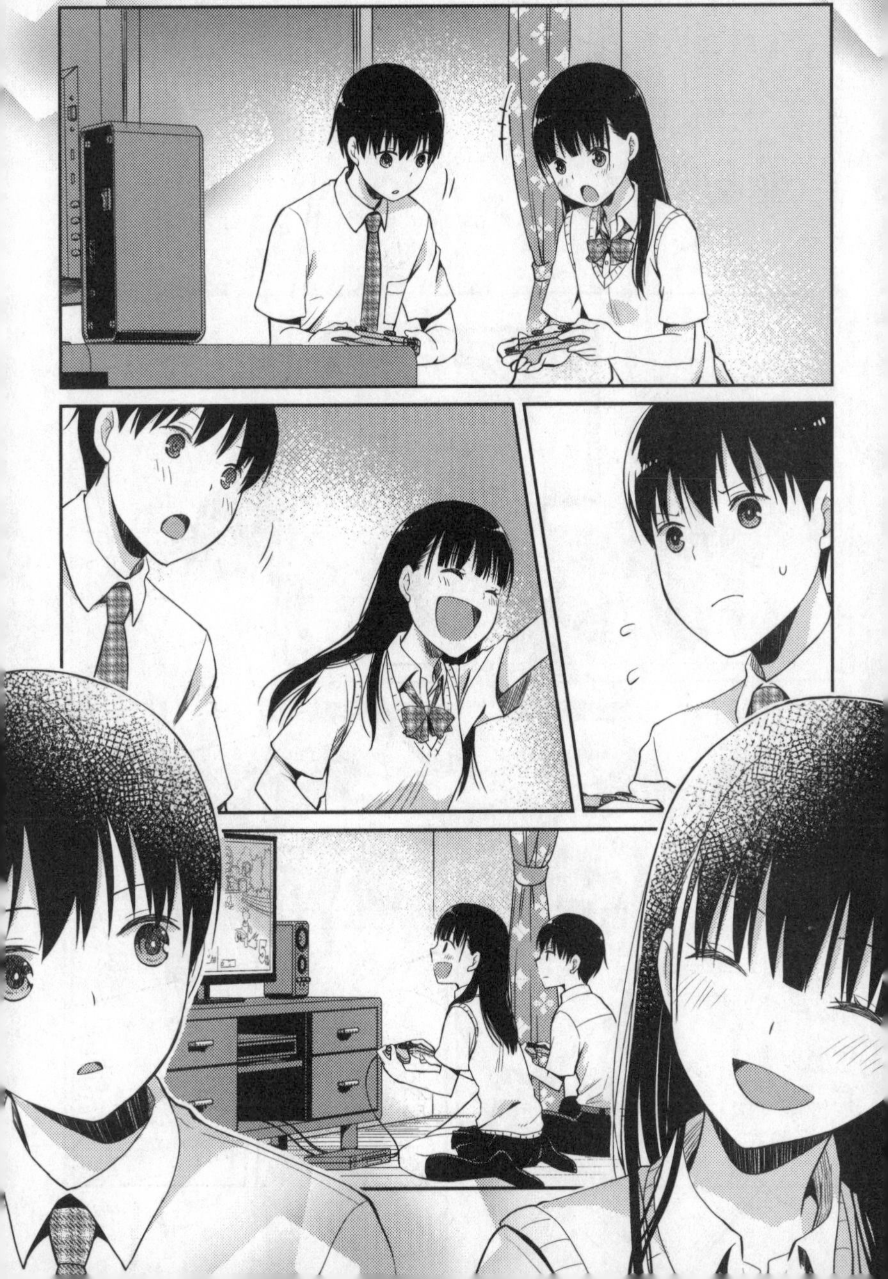

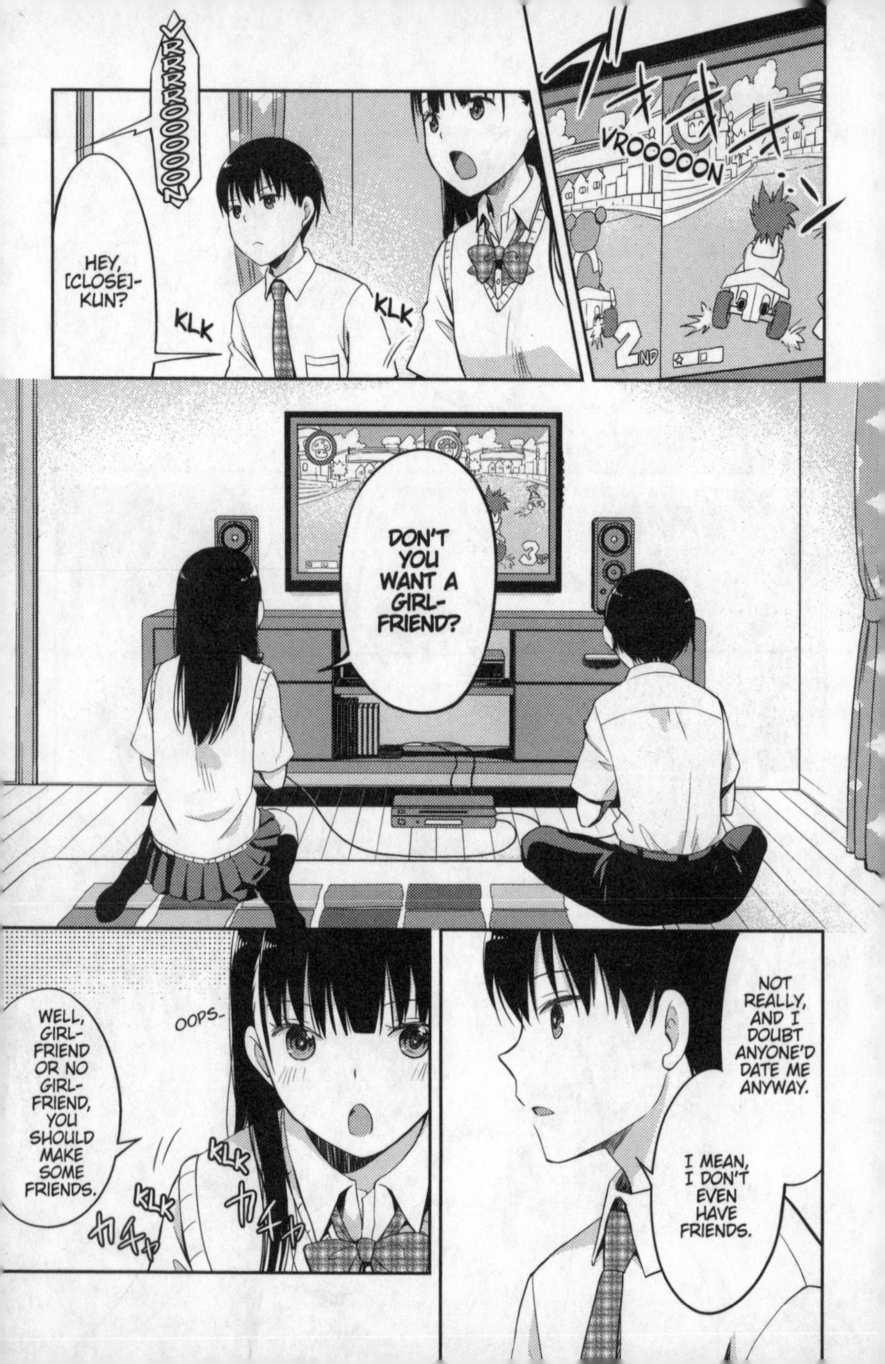
VROOOOON
VRRRROOOOOON
HEY, [CLOSE]-KUN?
KLK
KLK
DON'T YOU WANT A GIRL-FRIEND?
NOT REALLY, AND I DOUBT ANYONE'D DATE ME ANYWAY.
I MEAN, I DON'T EVEN HAVE FRIENDS.
OOPS..
WELL, GIRL-FRIEND OR NO GIRL-FRIEND, YOU SHOULD MAKE SOME FRIENDS.
KLK
KLK

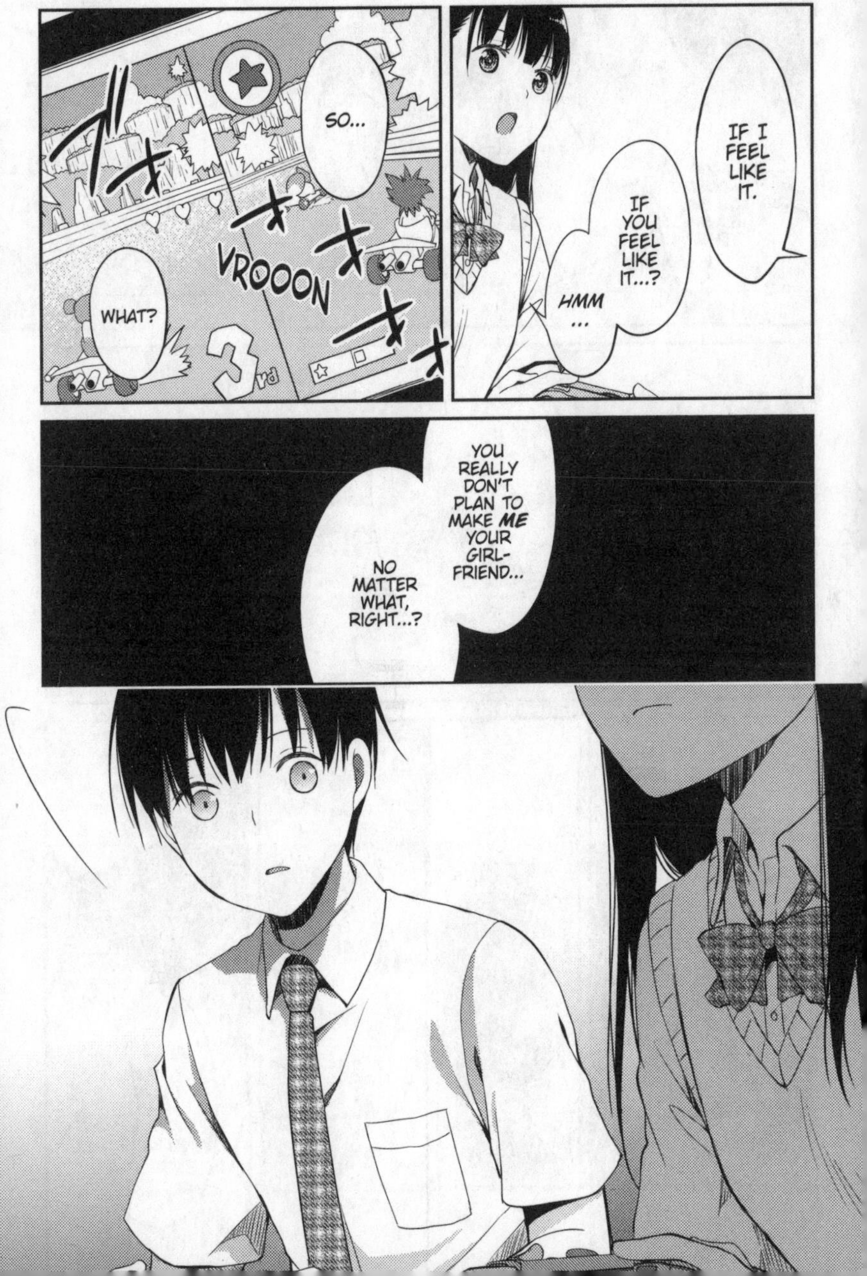
IF I FEEL LIKE IT.
IF YOU FEEL LIKE IT...?
HMM...
SO...
VROOON
WHAT?
3rd
YOU REALLY DON'T PLAN TO MAKE *ME* YOUR GIRL-FRIEND...
NO MATTER WHAT, RIGHT...?

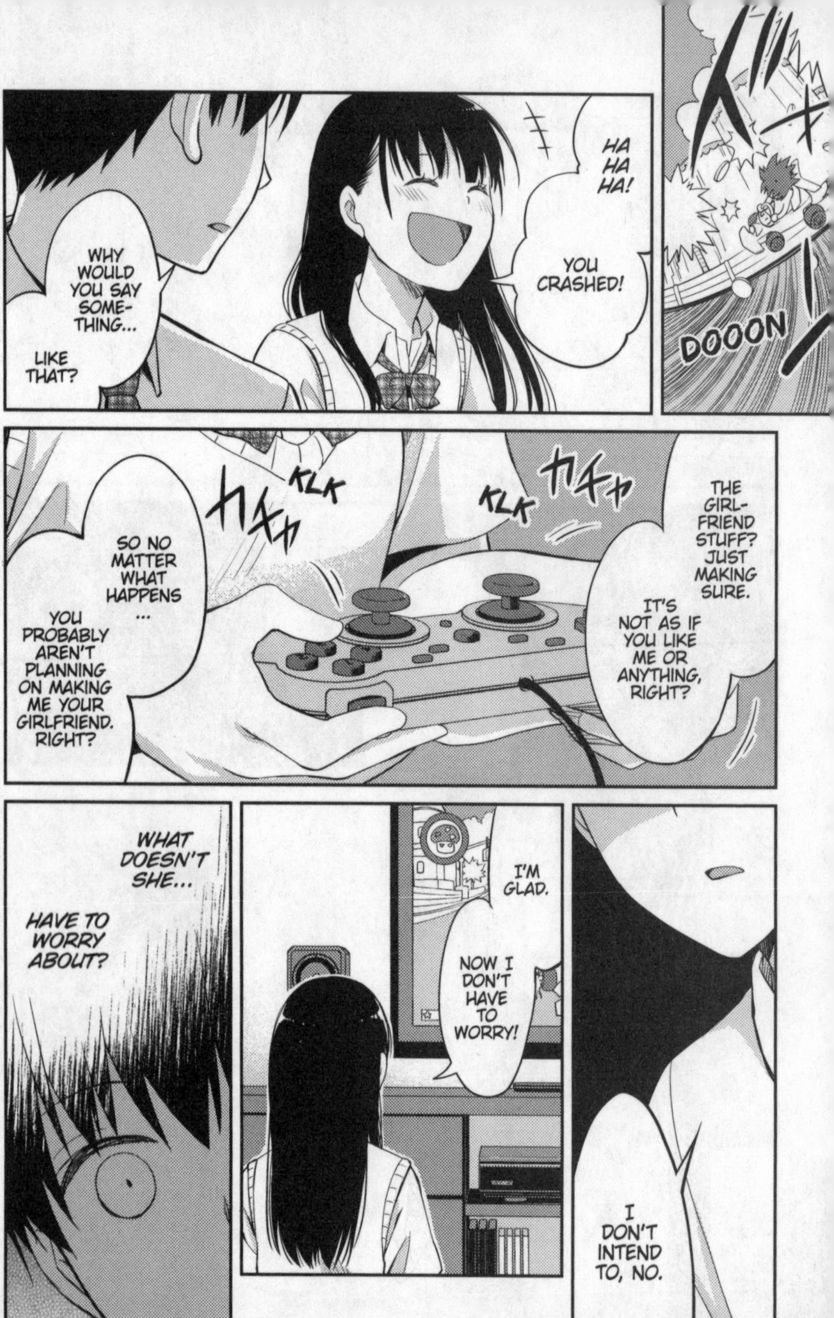

DOOON
HA HA HA!
YOU CRASHED!
WHY WOULD YOU SAY SOME-THING...
LIKE THAT?
THE GIRL-FRIEND STUFF? JUST MAKING SURE.
IT'S NOT AS IF YOU LIKE ME OR ANYTHING, RIGHT?
KLK
カチャ
KLK
カチャ
SO NO MATTER WHAT HAPPENS ...
YOU PROBABLY AREN'T PLANNING ON MAKING ME YOUR GIRLFRIEND. RIGHT?
I DON'T INTEND TO, NO.
I'M GLAD.
NOW I DON'T HAVE TO WORRY!
WHAT DOESN'T SHE...
HAVE TO WORRY ABOUT?

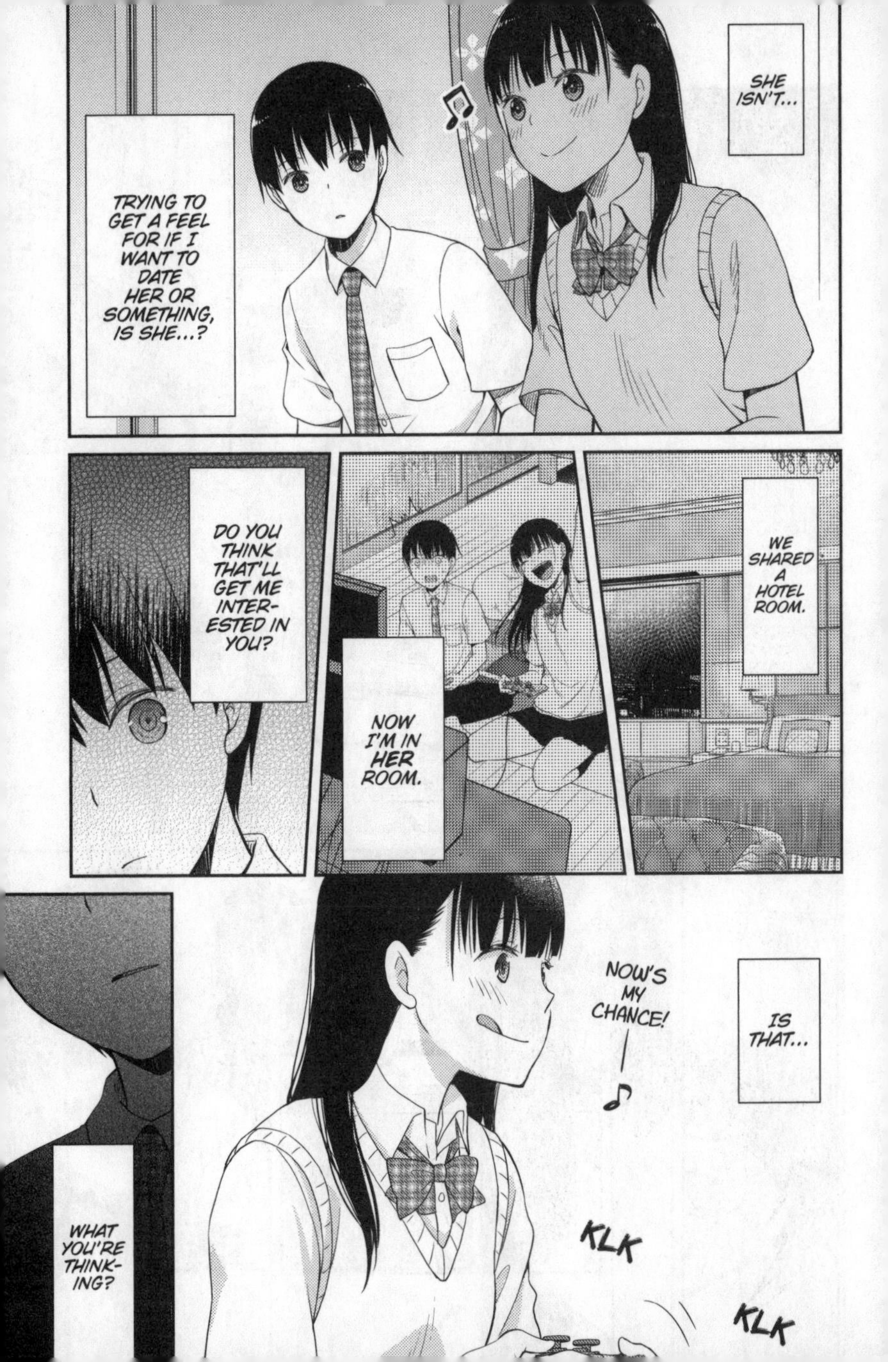
SHE ISN'T...
TRYING TO GET A FEEL FOR IF I WANT TO DATE HER OR SOMETHING, IS SHE...?
WE SHARED A HOTEL ROOM.
NOW I'M IN HER ROOM.
DO YOU THINK THAT'LL GET ME INTER-ESTED IN YOU?
IS THAT...
NOW'S MY CHANCE!
KLK
KLK
WHAT YOU'RE THINK-ING?

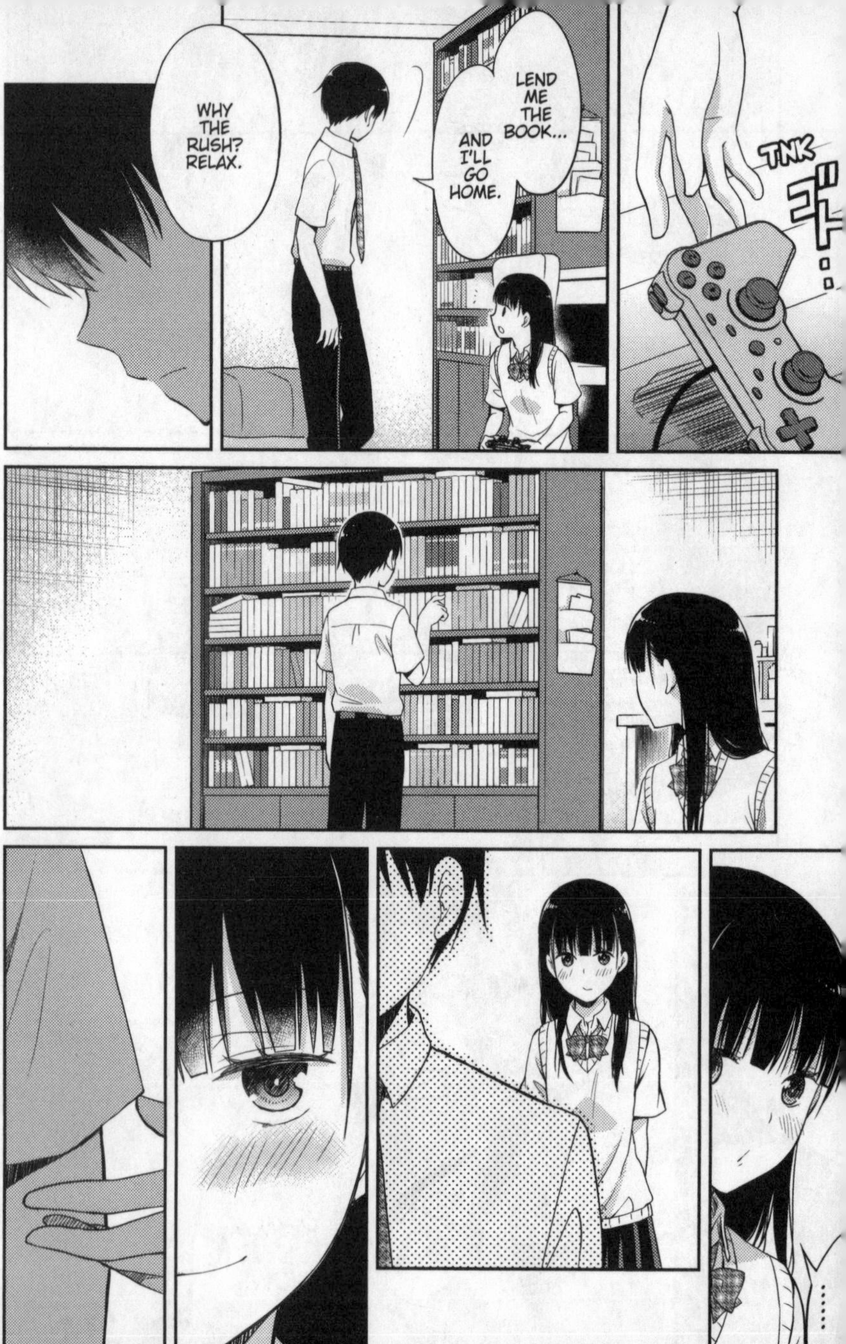
TNK
ゴト…
LEND ME THE BOOK...
AND I'LL GO HOME.
WHY THE RUSH? RELAX.
......

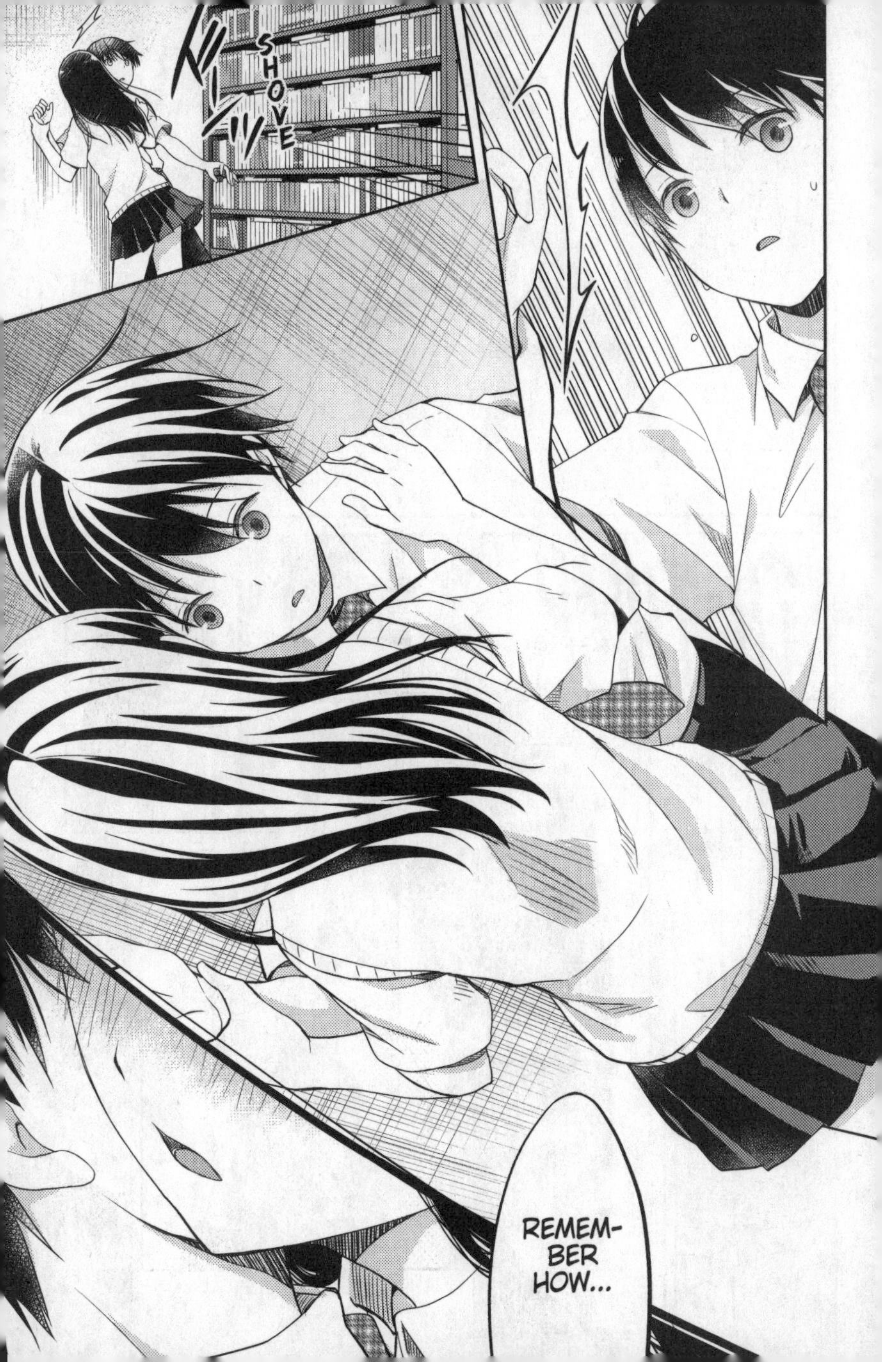
SHOVE
REMEM-
BER
HOW...

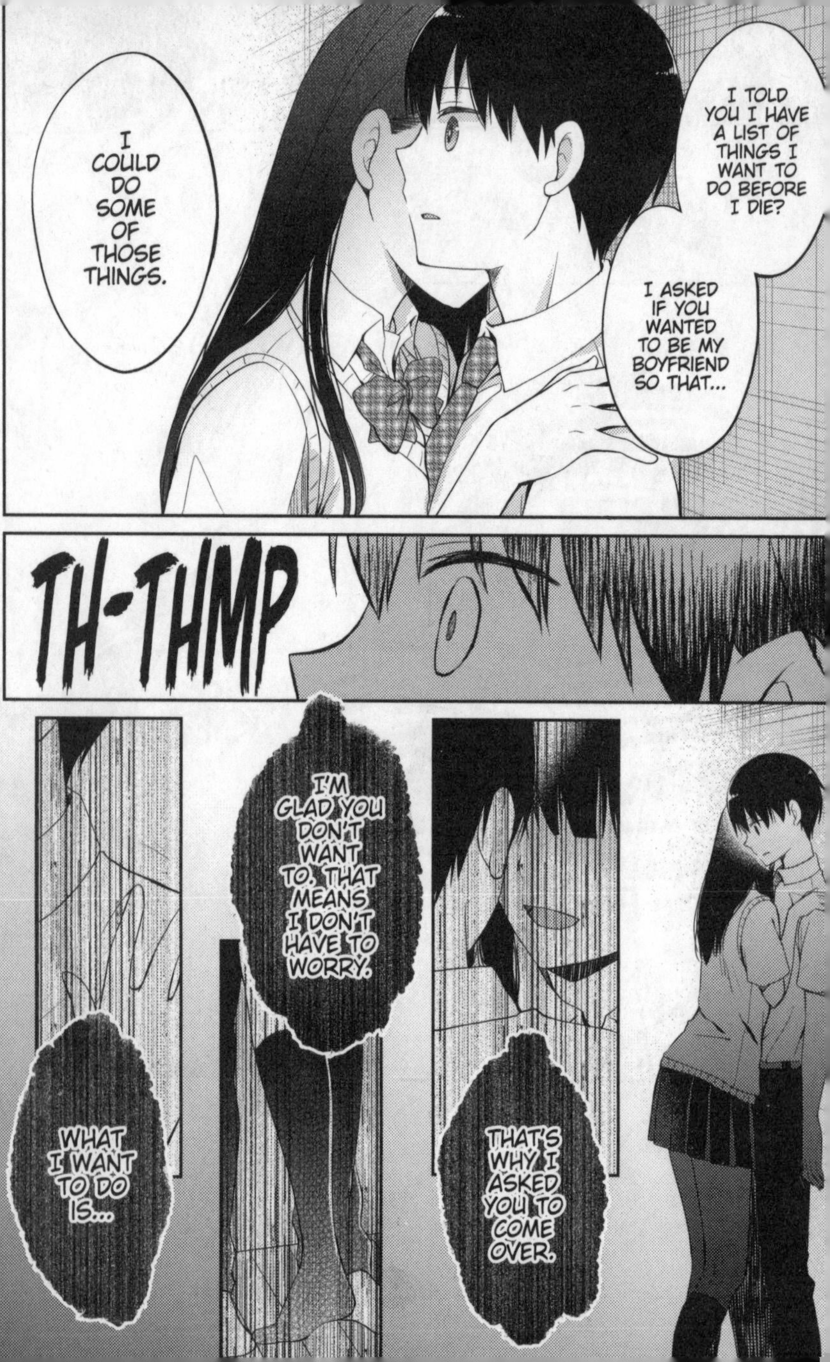
I TOLD YOU I HAVE A LIST OF THINGS I WANT TO DO BEFORE I DIE?
I ASKED IF YOU WANTED TO BE MY BOYFRIEND SO THAT...
I COULD DO SOME OF THOSE THINGS.
TH-THMP
I'M GLAD YOU DON'T WANT TO. THAT MEANS I DON'T HAVE TO WORRY.
THAT'S WHY I ASKED YOU TO COME OVER.
WHAT I WANT TO DO IS...

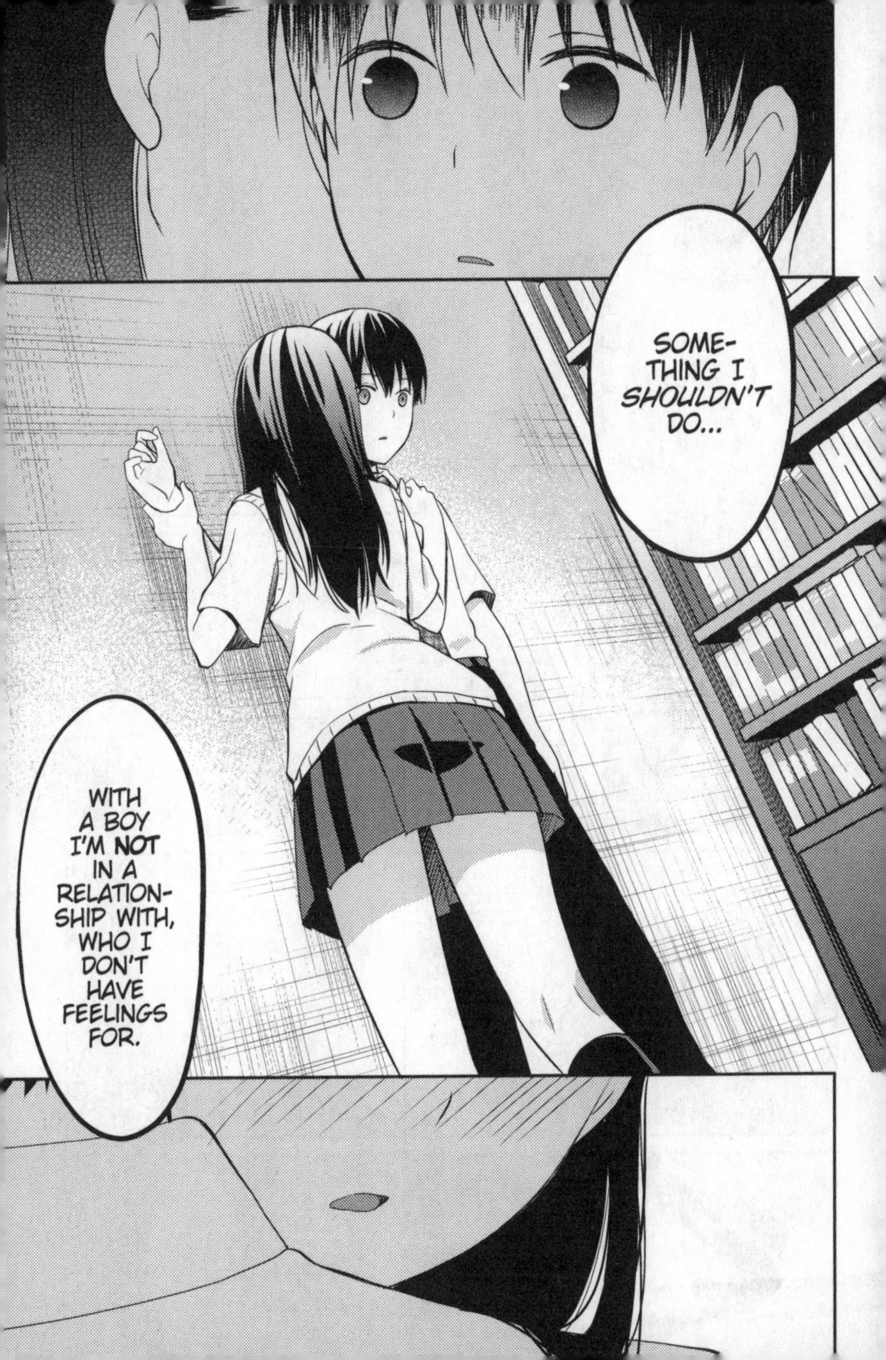
SOME-THING I SHOULDN'T DO...
WITH A BOY I'M NOT IN A RELATION-SHIP WITH, WHO I DON'T HAVE FEELINGS FOR.

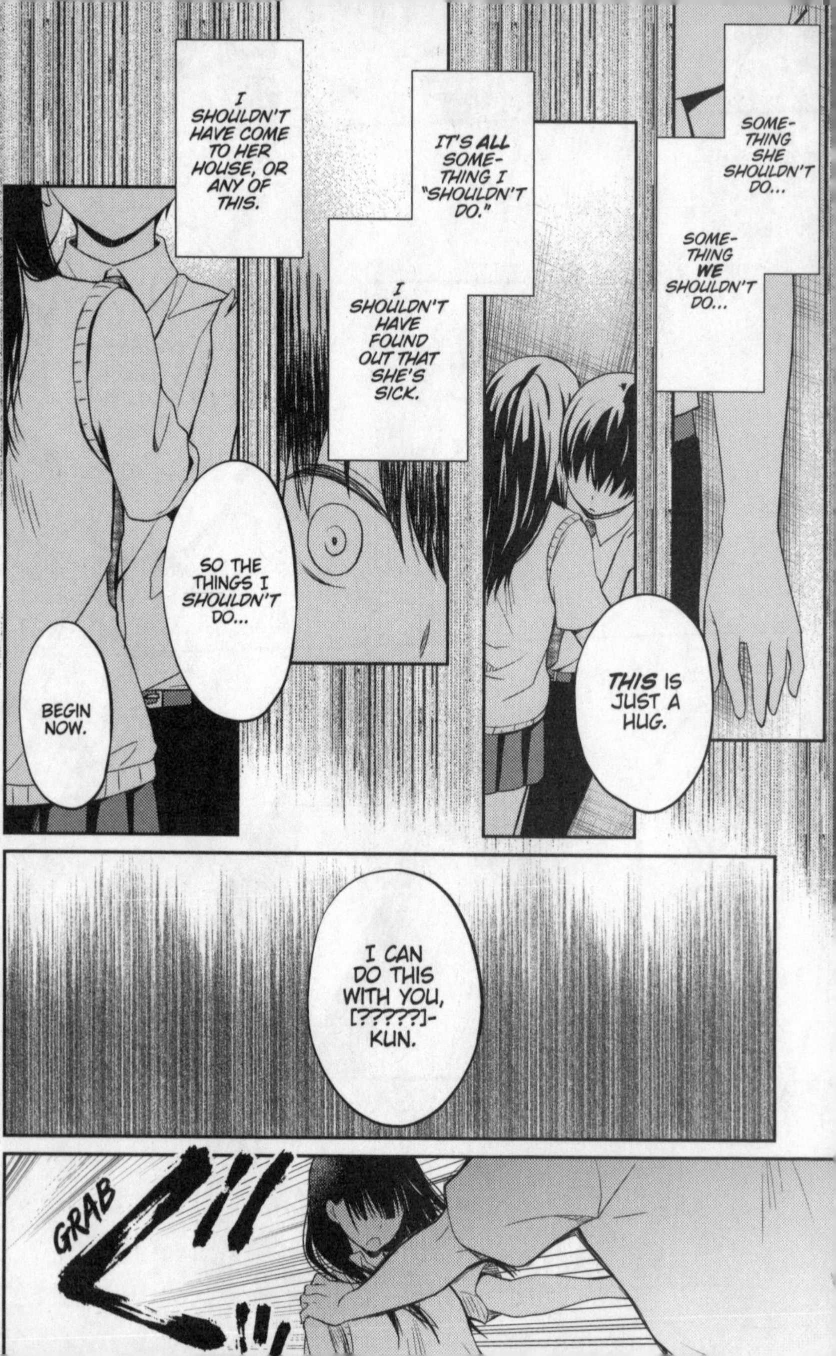
I SHOULDN'T HAVE COME TO HER HOUSE, OR ANY OF THIS.
IT'S ALL SOMETHING I "SHOULDN'T DO."
I SHOULDN'T HAVE FOUND OUT THAT SHE'S SICK.
SOMETHING SHE SHOULDN'T DO...
SOMETHING WE SHOULDN'T DO...
THIS IS JUST A HUG.
SO THE THINGS I SHOULDN'T DO...
BEGIN NOW.
I CAN DO THIS WITH YOU, [?????]-KUN.
GRAB

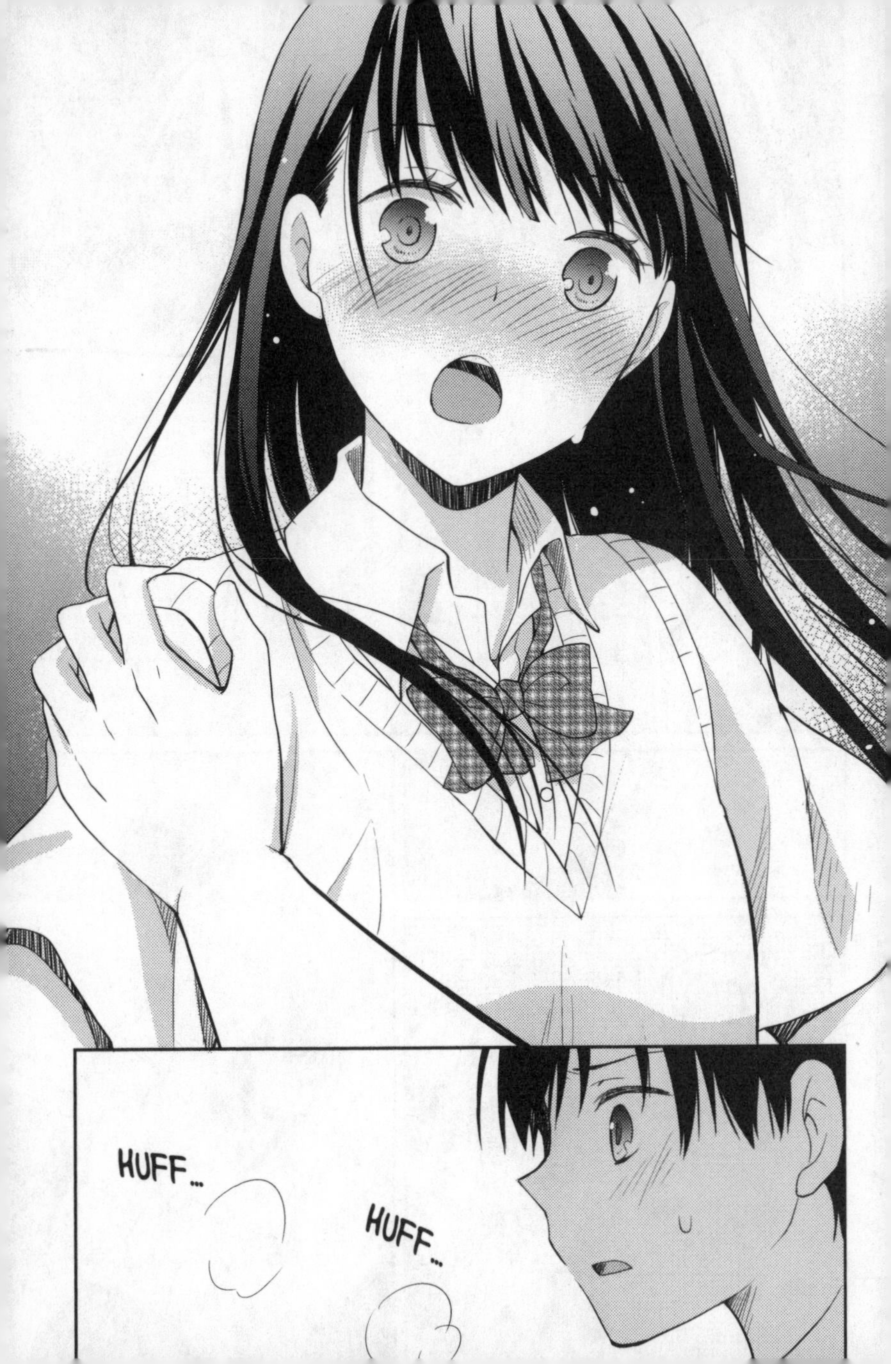
HUFF...
HUFF...

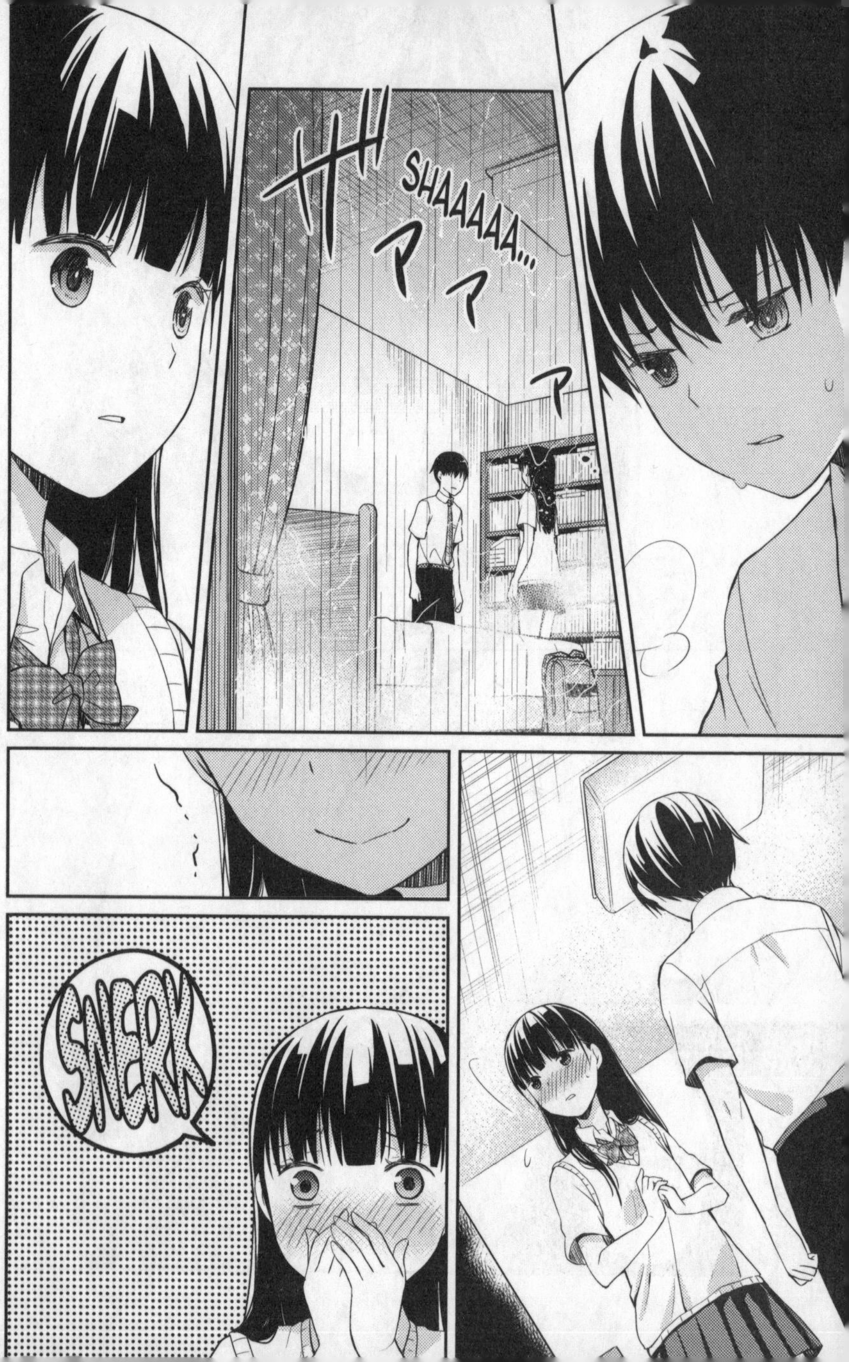
SHAAAAAA...
SNERK

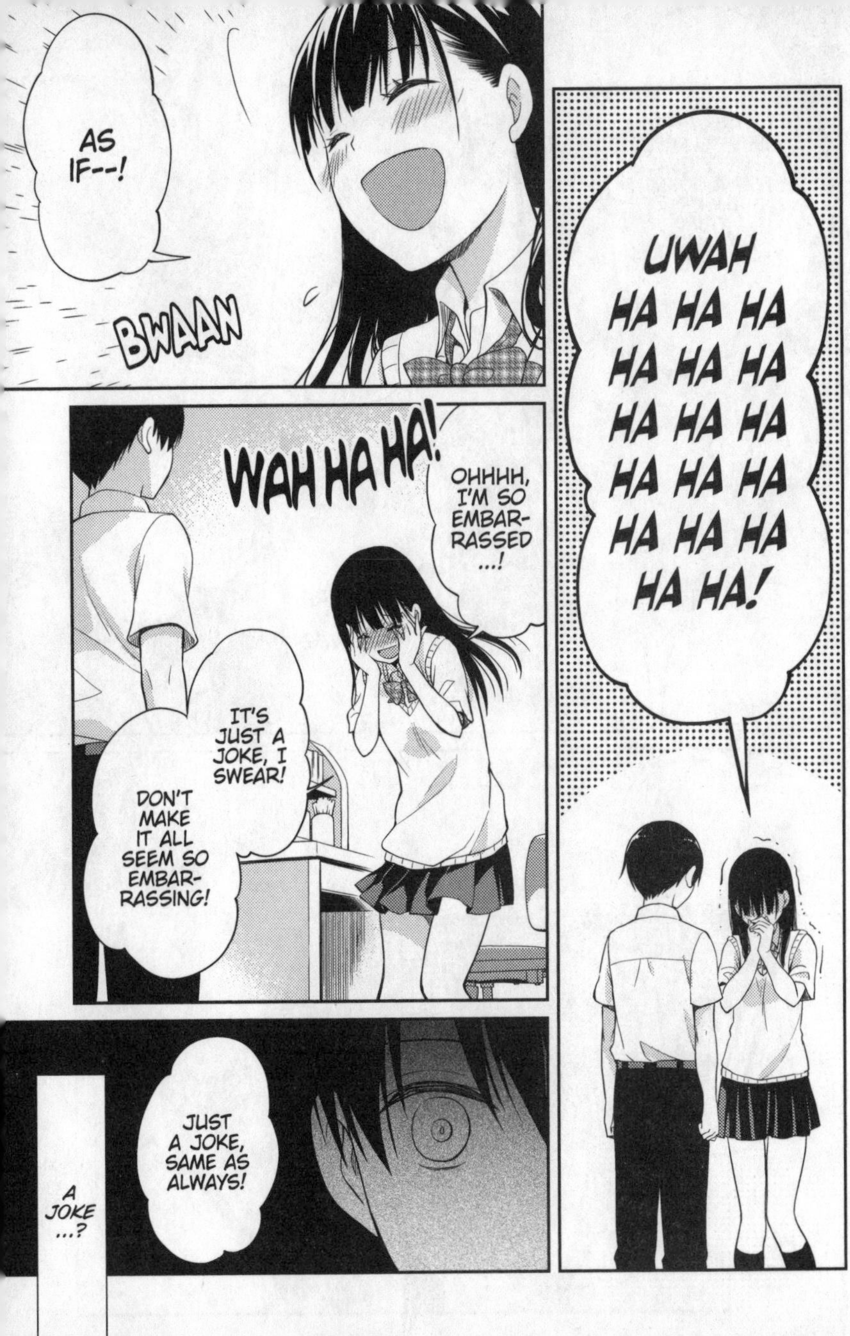

AS IF--!
BWAAN
UWAH HA HA HA HA HA HA HA HA HA HA HA HA HA HA HA HA HA HA!
WAH HA HA!
OHHHH, I'M SO EMBAR-RASSED ...!
IT'S JUST A JOKE, I SWEAR!
DON'T MAKE IT ALL SEEM SO EMBAR-RASSING!
JUST A JOKE, SAME AS ALWAYS!
A JOKE ...?

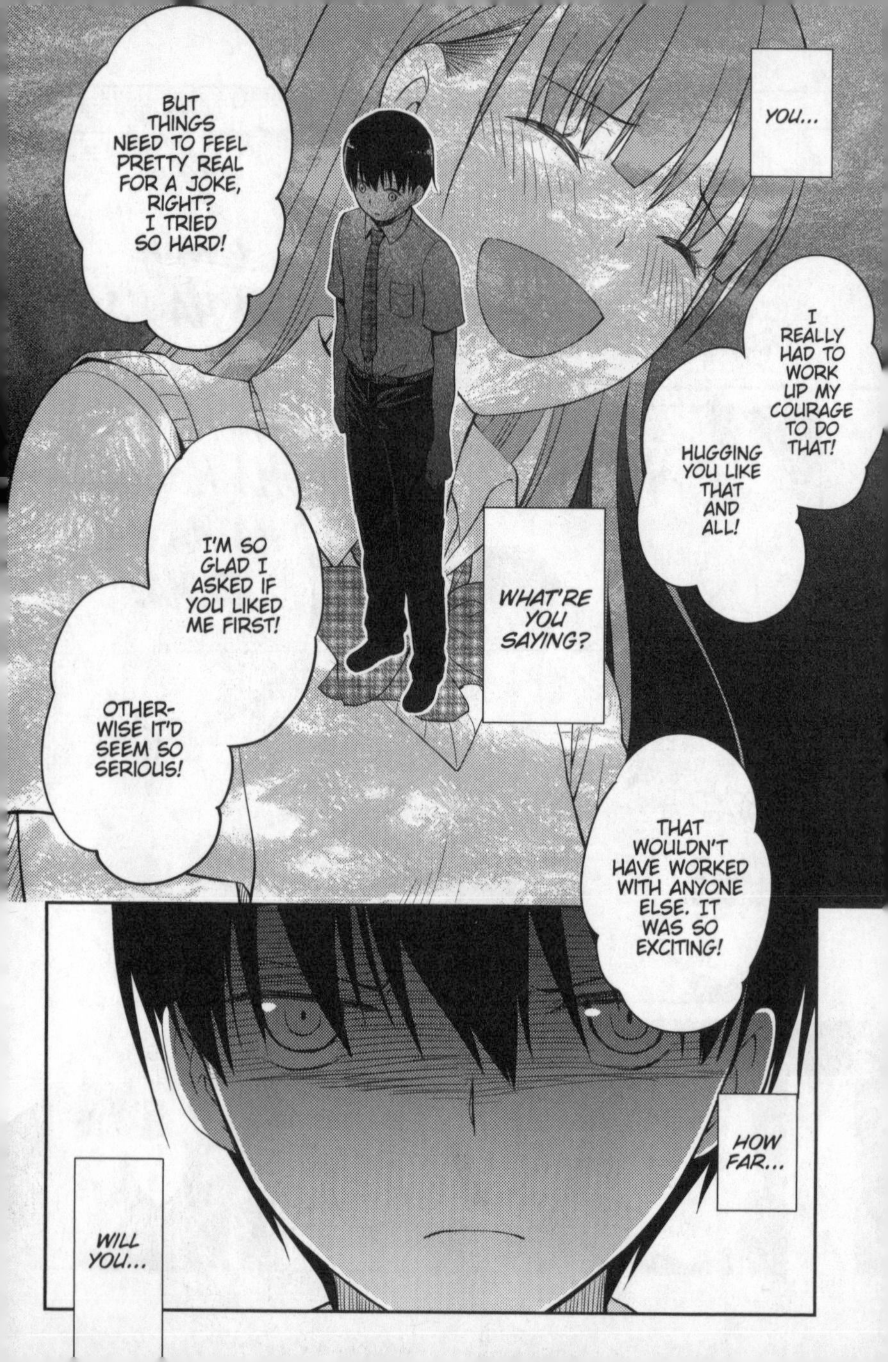
YOU...
BUT THINGS NEED TO FEEL PRETTY REAL FOR A JOKE, RIGHT? I TRIED SO HARD!
I REALLY HAD TO WORK UP MY COURAGE TO DO THAT!
HUGGING YOU LIKE THAT AND ALL!
WHAT'RE YOU SAYING?
I'M SO GLAD I ASKED IF YOU LIKED ME FIRST!
OTHER-WISE IT'D SEEM SO SERIOUS!
THAT WOULDN'T HAVE WORKED WITH ANYONE ELSE. IT WAS SO EXCITING!
HOW FAR...
WILL YOU...

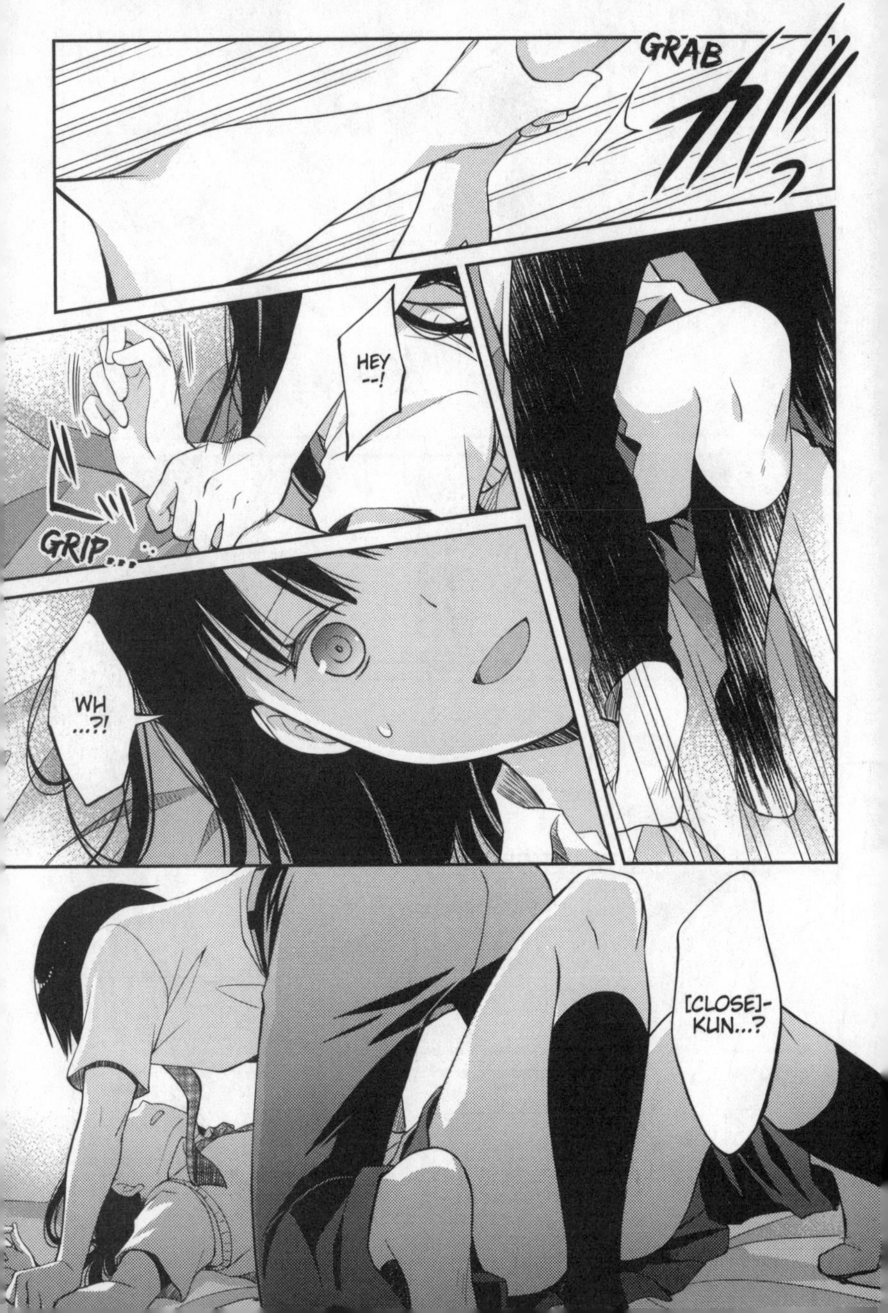
GRAB
HEY
--!
GRIP...
WH
...?!
[CLOSE]-
KUN...?

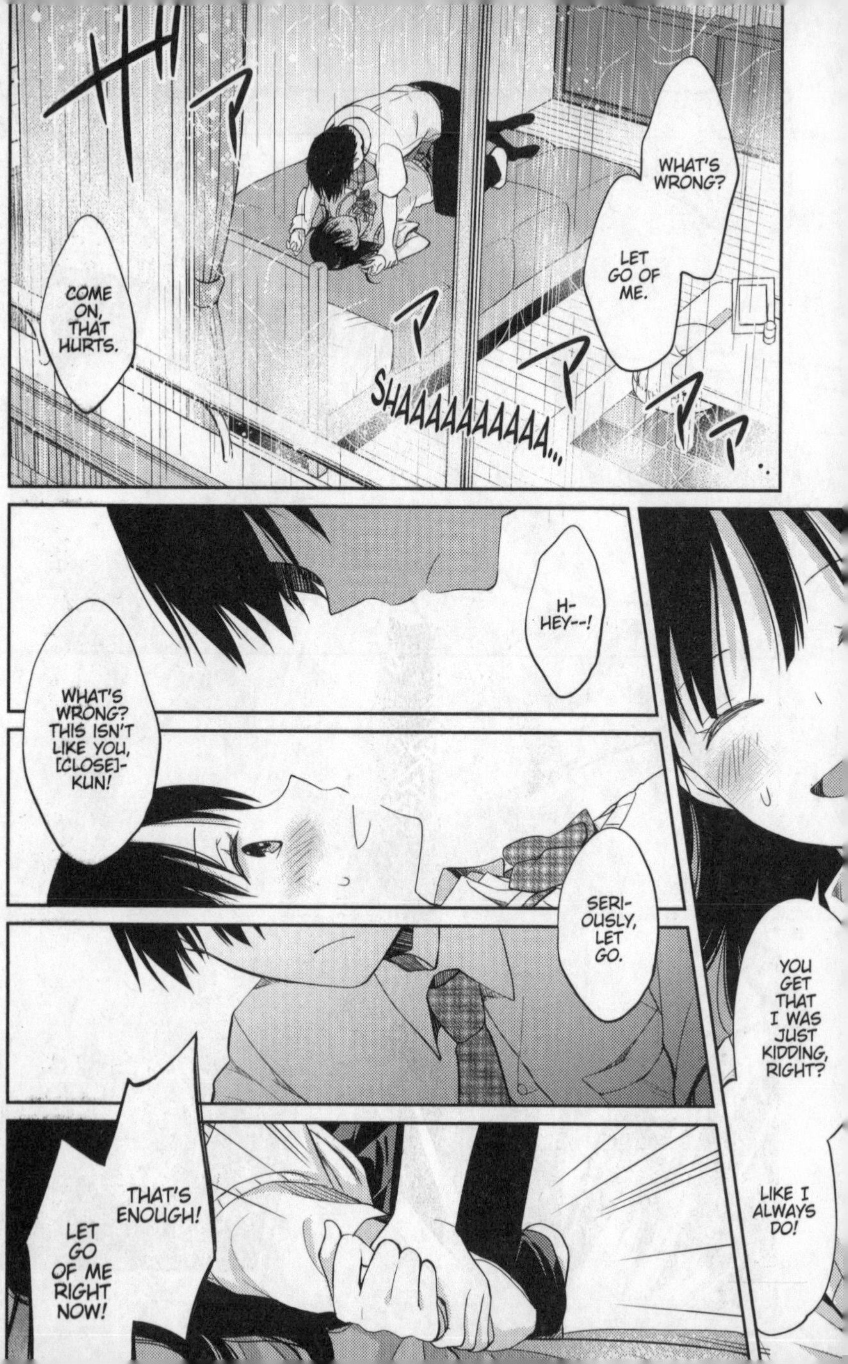

WHAT'S WRONG?
LET GO OF ME.
COME ON, THAT HURTS.
SHAAAAAAAAAA...
H-HEY--!
WHAT'S WRONG? THIS ISN'T LIKE YOU, [CLOSE]-KUN!
SERI-OUSLY, LET GO.
YOU GET THAT I WAS JUST KIDDING, RIGHT?
LIKE I ALWAYS DO!
THAT'S ENOUGH!
LET GO OF ME RIGHT NOW!

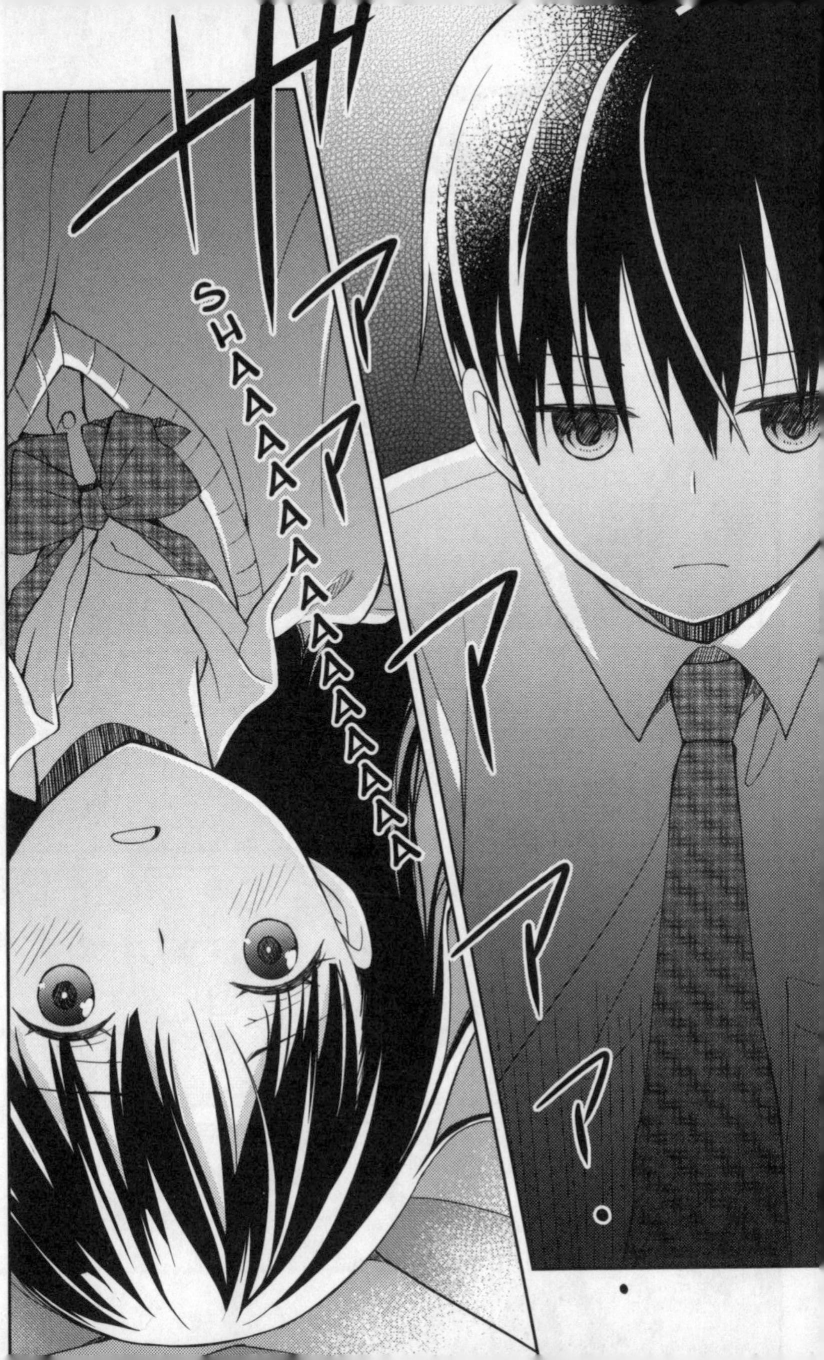
SHAAAAAAAAAAAAAA

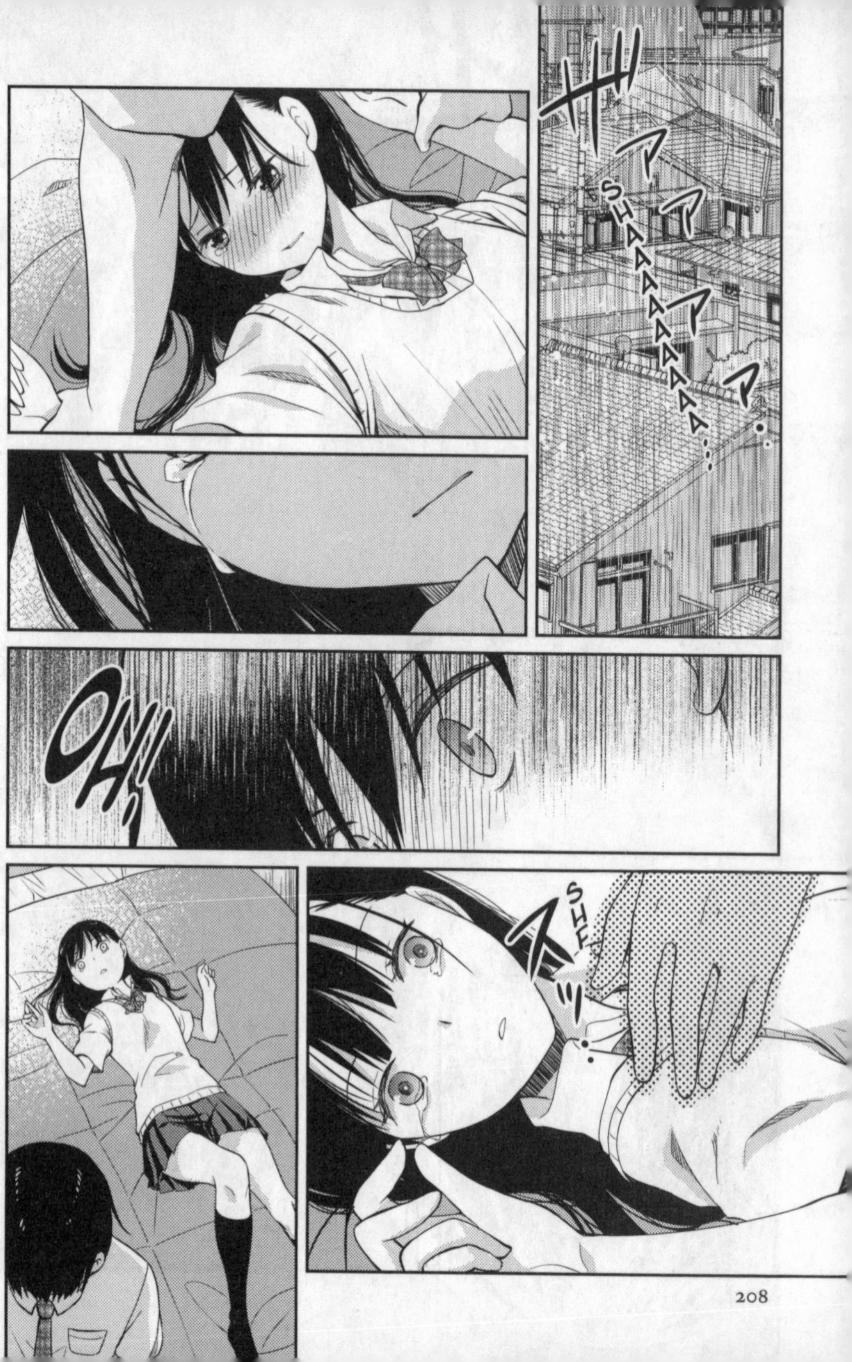
ザァァァア…
SHAAAAAAAAA…
OH!!
SHF
スッ…

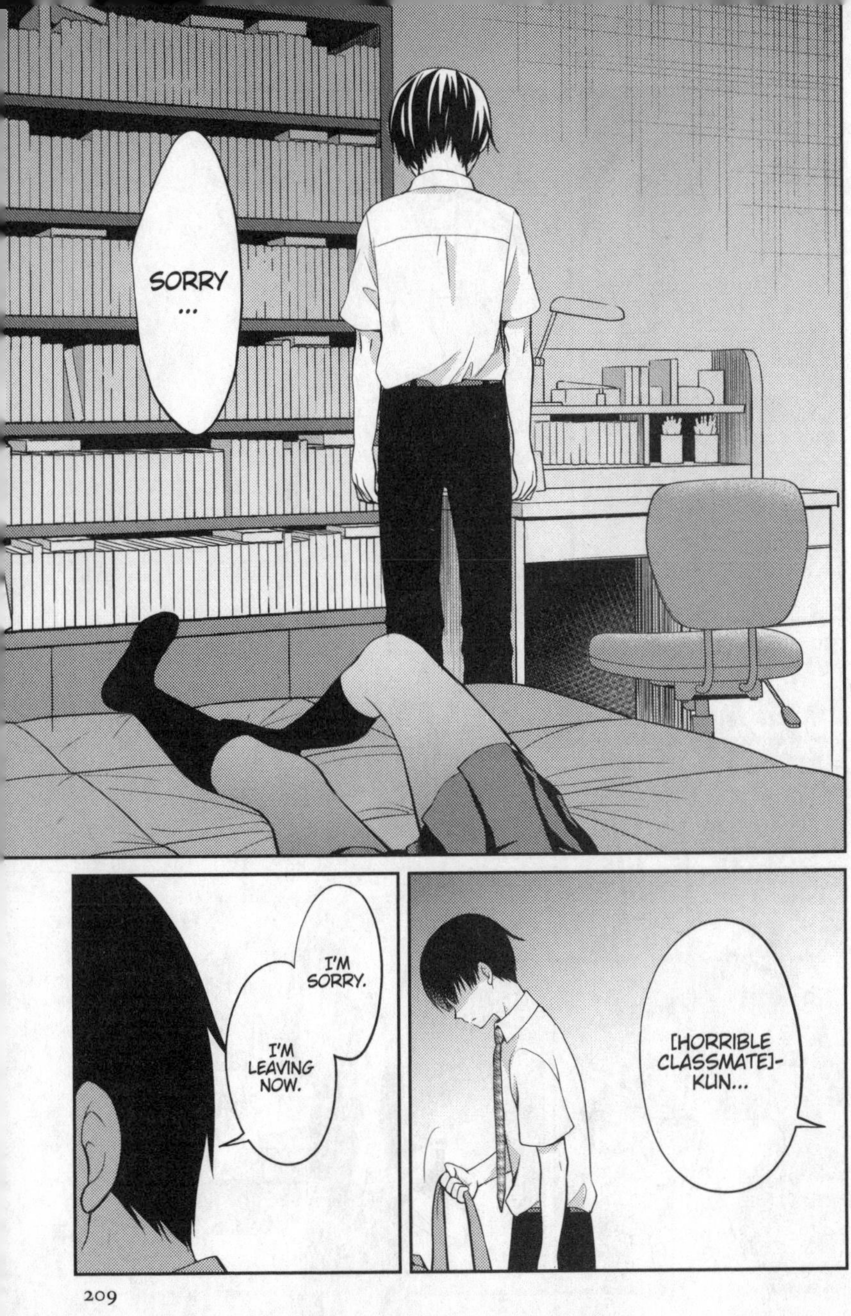
SORRY
...
[HORRIBLE CLASSMATE]-KUN...
I'M SORRY.
I'M LEAVING NOW.

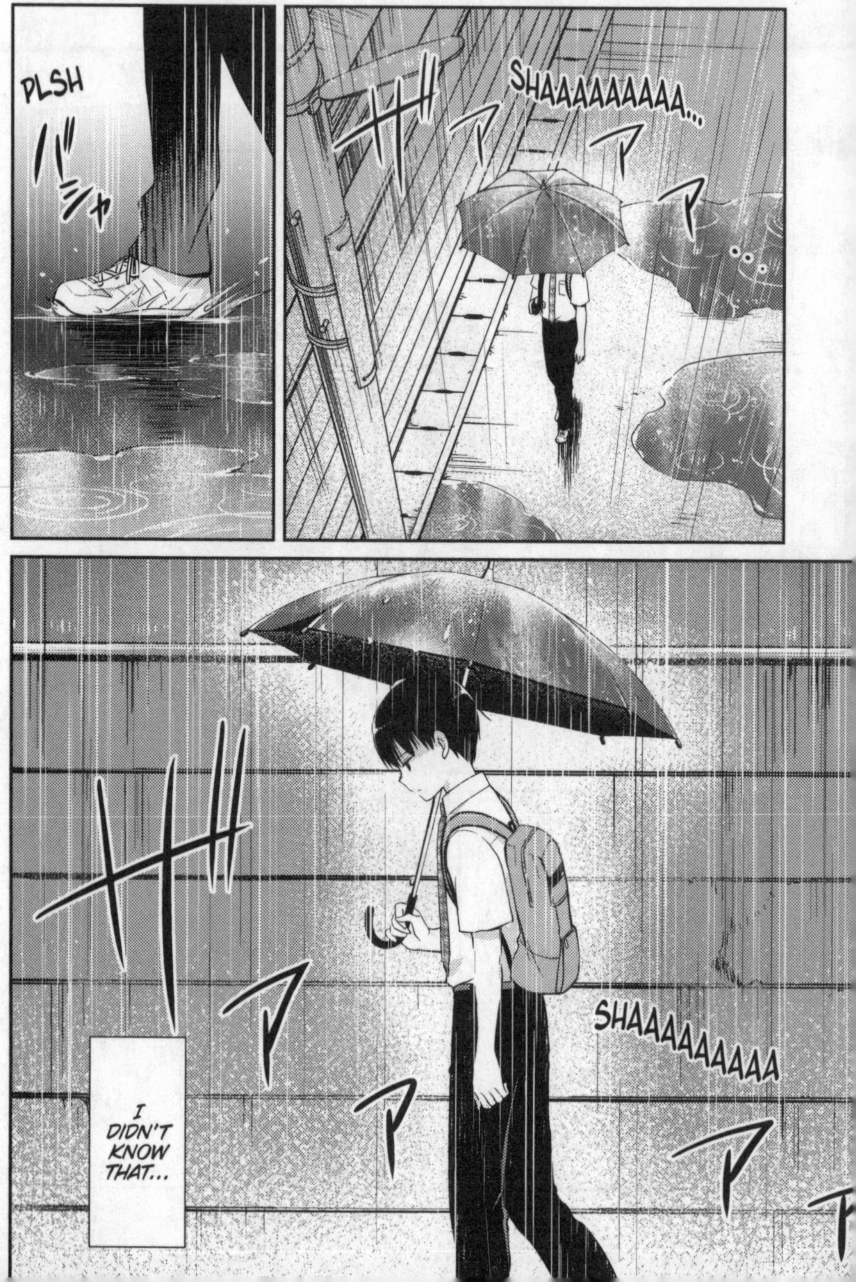
SHAAAAAAAAA...
ザァァァ
...
PLSH
バシャ
SHAAAAAAAAAA
ザァァァ
I DIDN'T KNOW THAT...

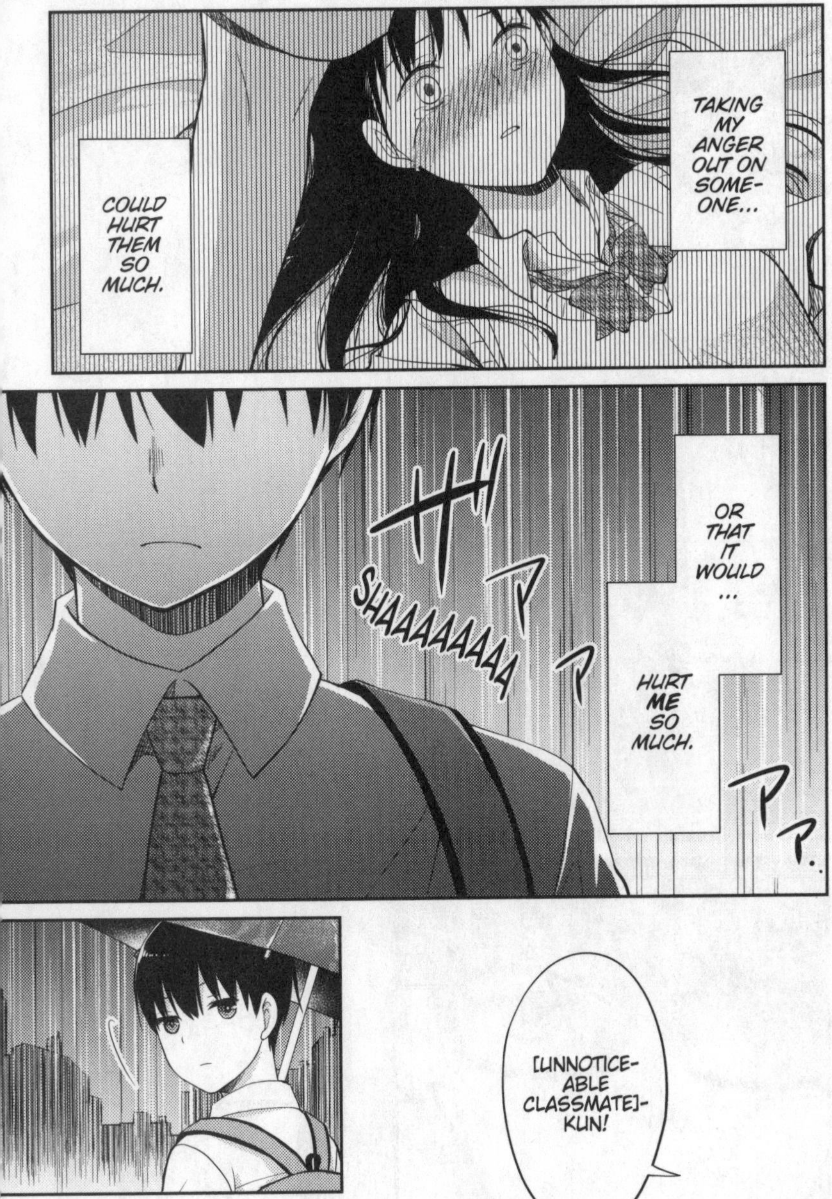

TAKING MY ANGER OUT ON SOME-ONE...
COULD HURT THEM SO MUCH.
OR THAT IT WOULD ...
HURT ME SO MUCH.
SHAAAAAAAAA
[UNNOTICE-ABLE CLASSMATE]-KUN!

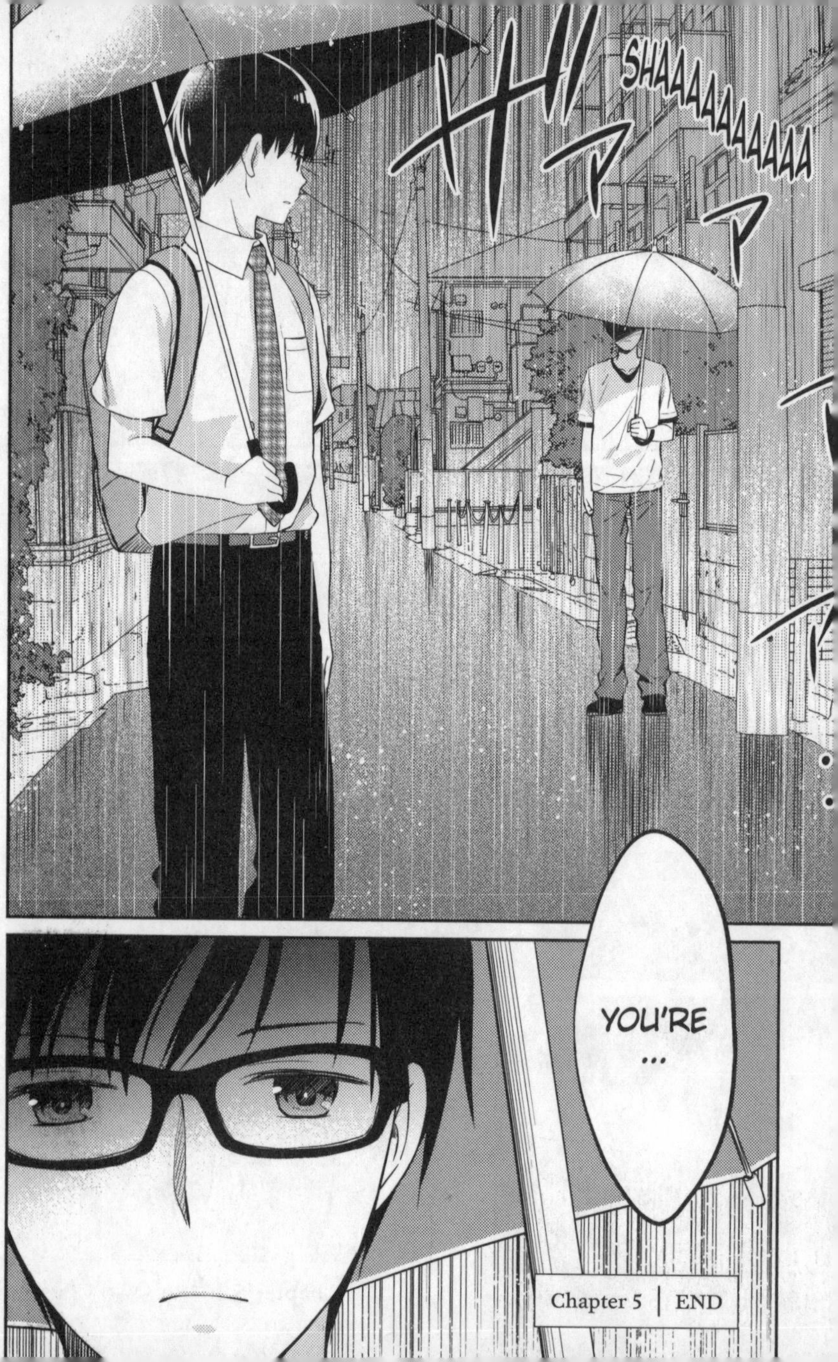
SHAAAAAAAAAA
YOU'RE ...
Chapter 5 | END

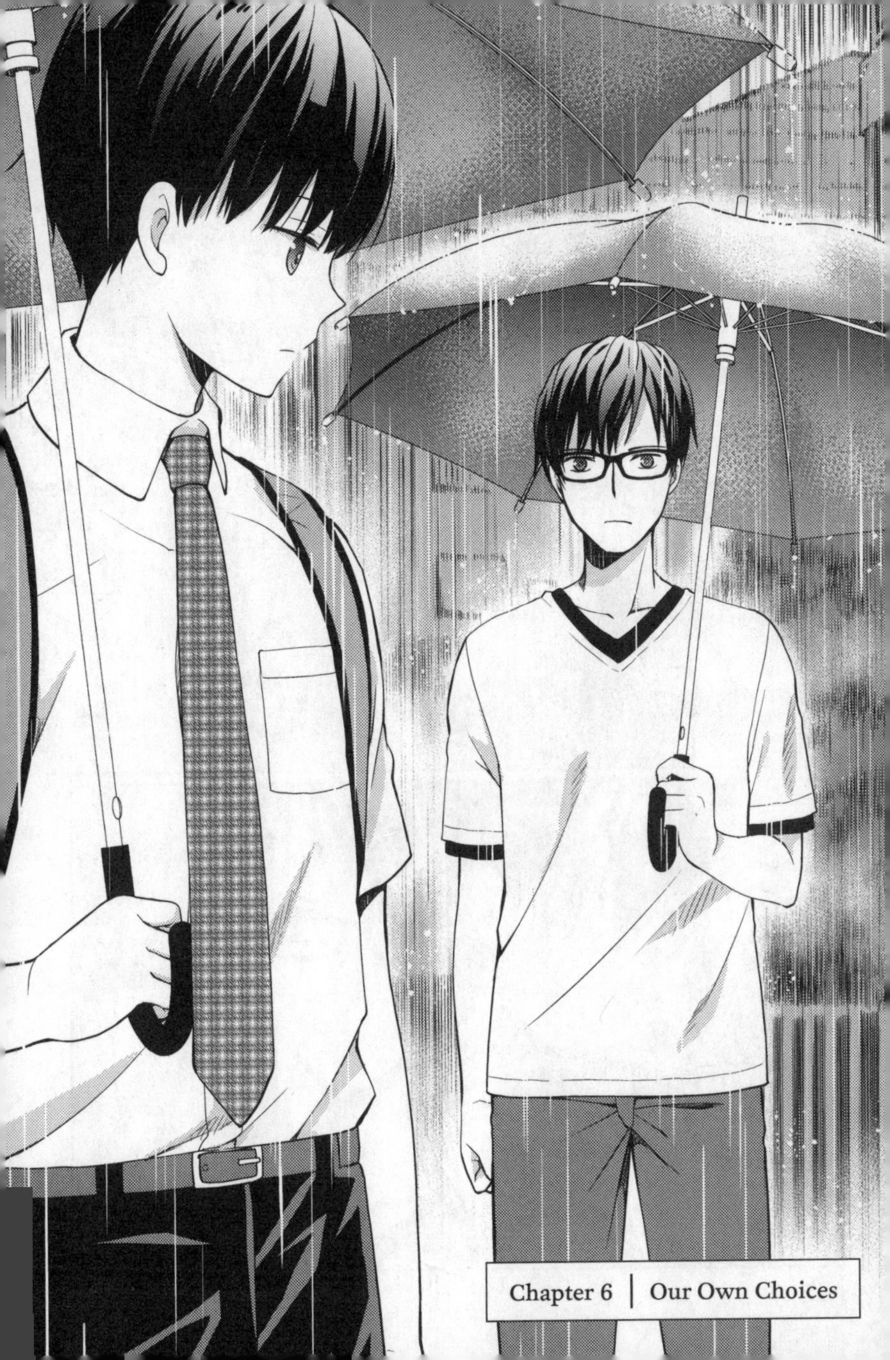

Chapter 6 | Our Own Choices

SHAAAAAA...

SOMETHING ABOUT HIM SEEMS... WEIRD.

HEY.

IT'S THE STUDENT COUNCIL REPRESENTATIVE.

BUT...

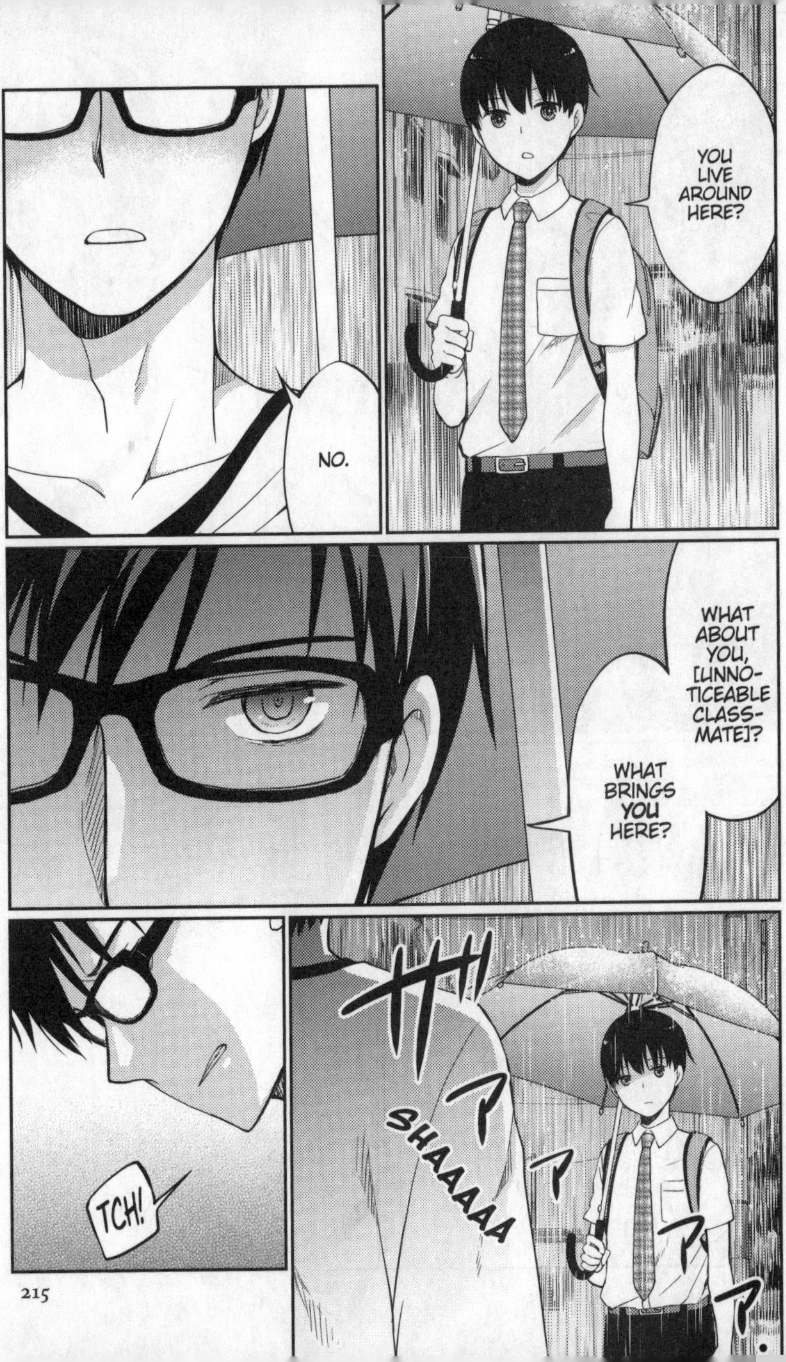
YOU LIVE AROUND HERE?
NO.
WHAT ABOUT YOU, [UNNOTICEABLE CLASSMATE]?
WHAT BRINGS YOU HERE?
SHAAAAAA
TCH!

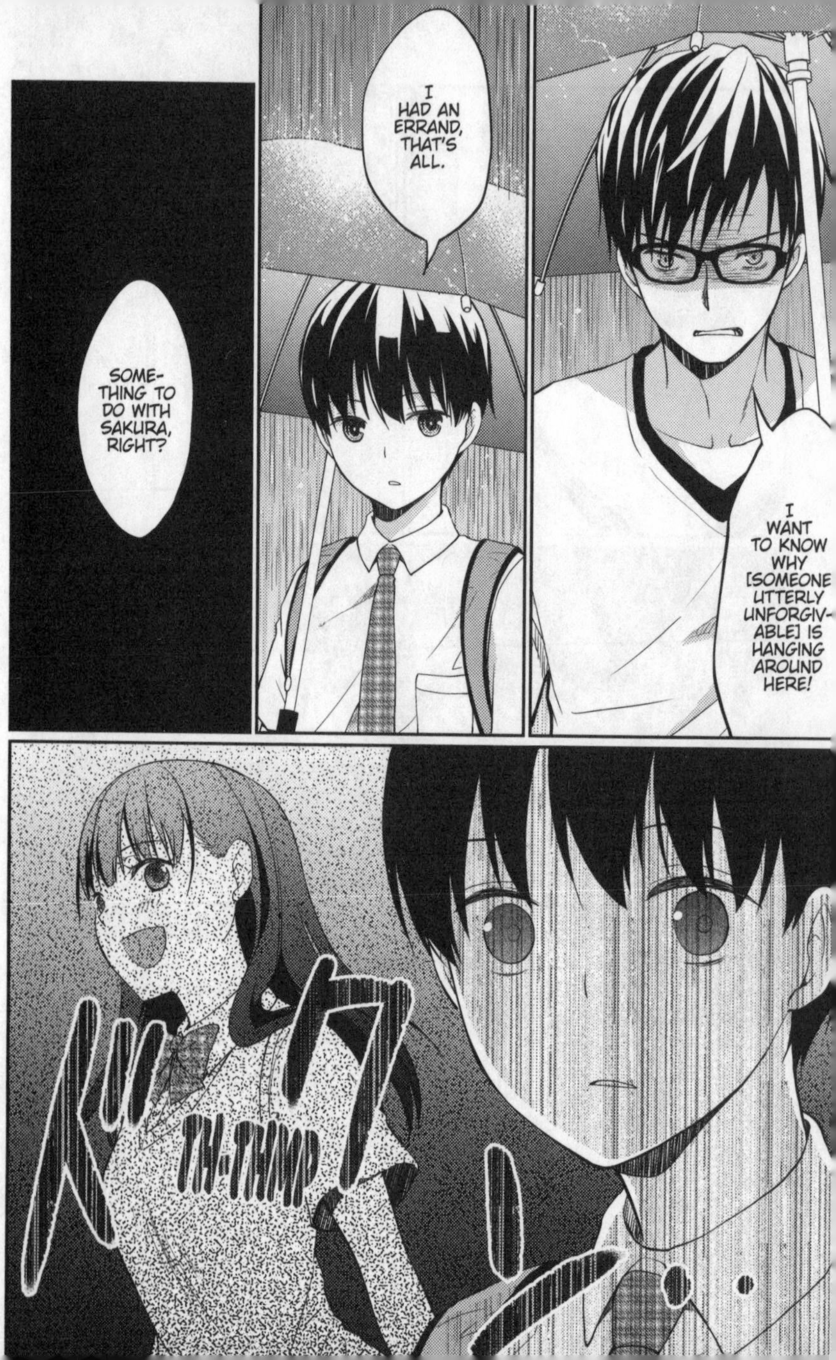
I WANT TO KNOW WHY [SOMEONE UTTERLY UNFORGIVABLE] IS HANGING AROUND HERE!
I HAD AN ERRAND, THAT'S ALL.
SOMETHING TO DO WITH SAKURA, RIGHT?
TH-THMP

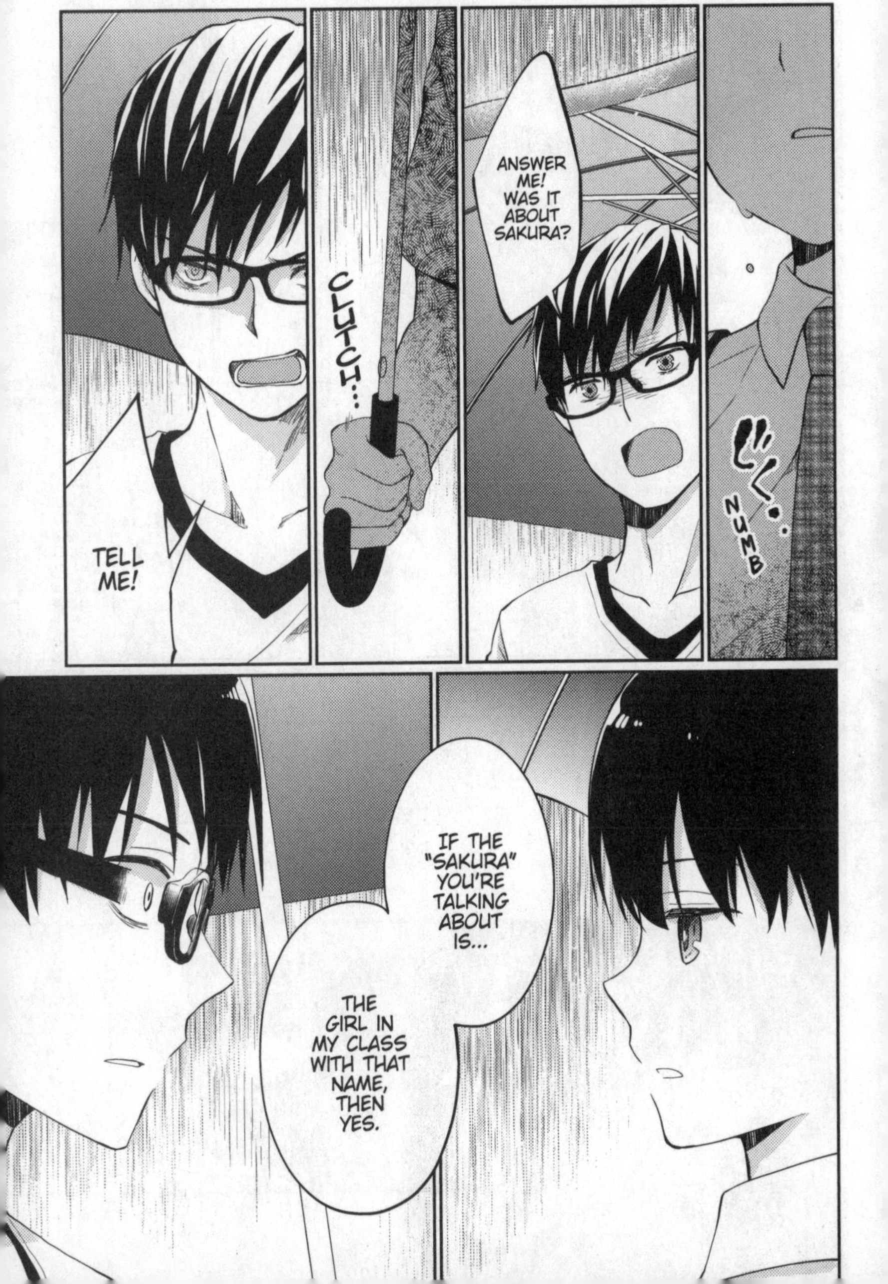
NUMB
ANSWER ME! WAS IT ABOUT SAKURA?
CLUTCH...
TELL ME!
IF THE "SAKURA" YOU'RE TALKING ABOUT IS...
THE GIRL IN MY CLASS WITH THAT NAME, THEN YES.

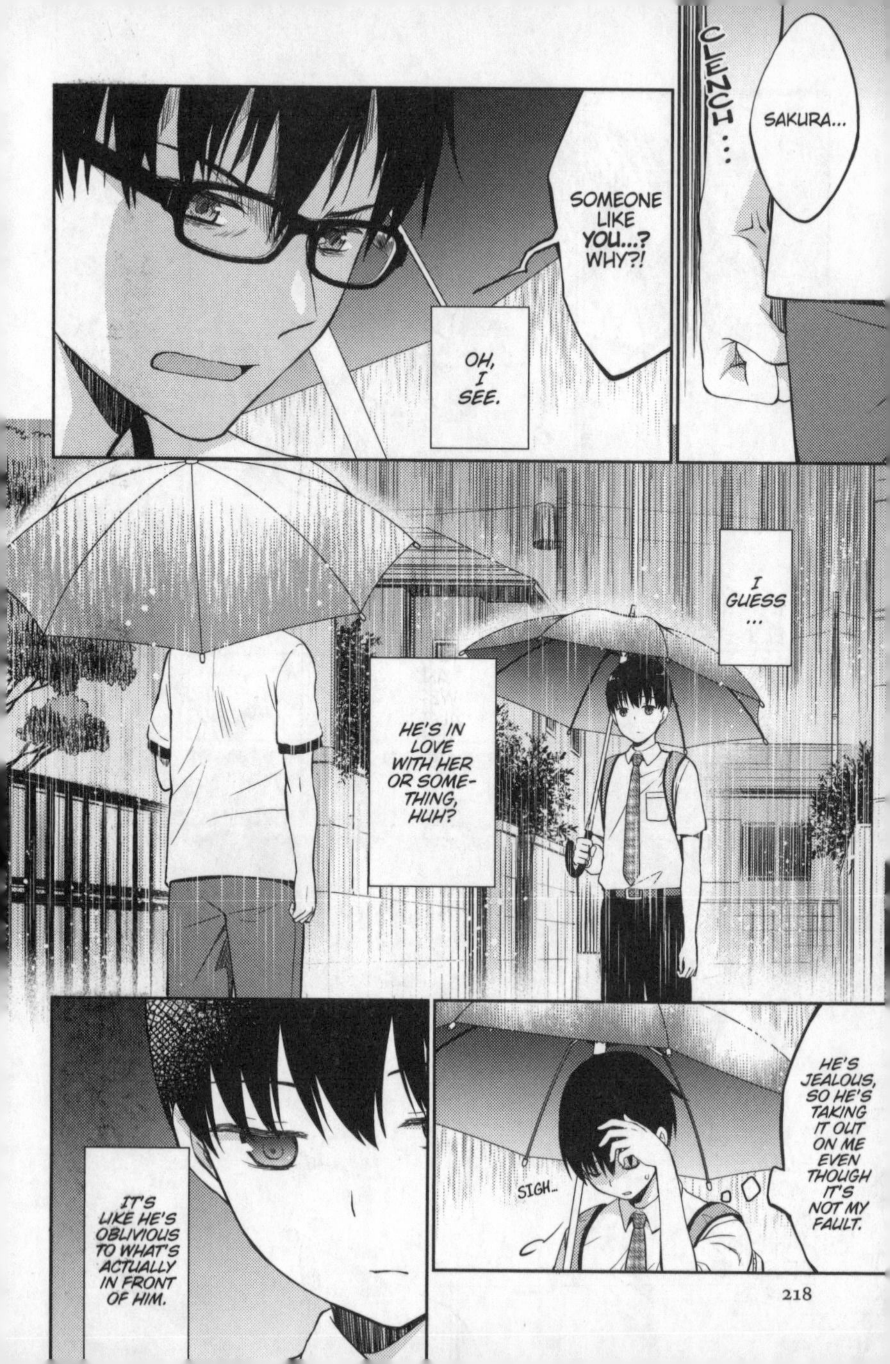
SAKURA...
CLENCH...
SOMEONE LIKE YOU...? WHY?!
OH, I SEE.
I GUESS...
HE'S IN LOVE WITH HER OR SOME-THING, HUH?
HE'S JEALOUS, SO HE'S TAKING IT OUT ON ME EVEN THOUGH IT'S NOT MY FAULT.
SIGH..
IT'S LIKE HE'S OBLIVIOUS TO WHAT'S ACTUALLY IN FRONT OF HIM.

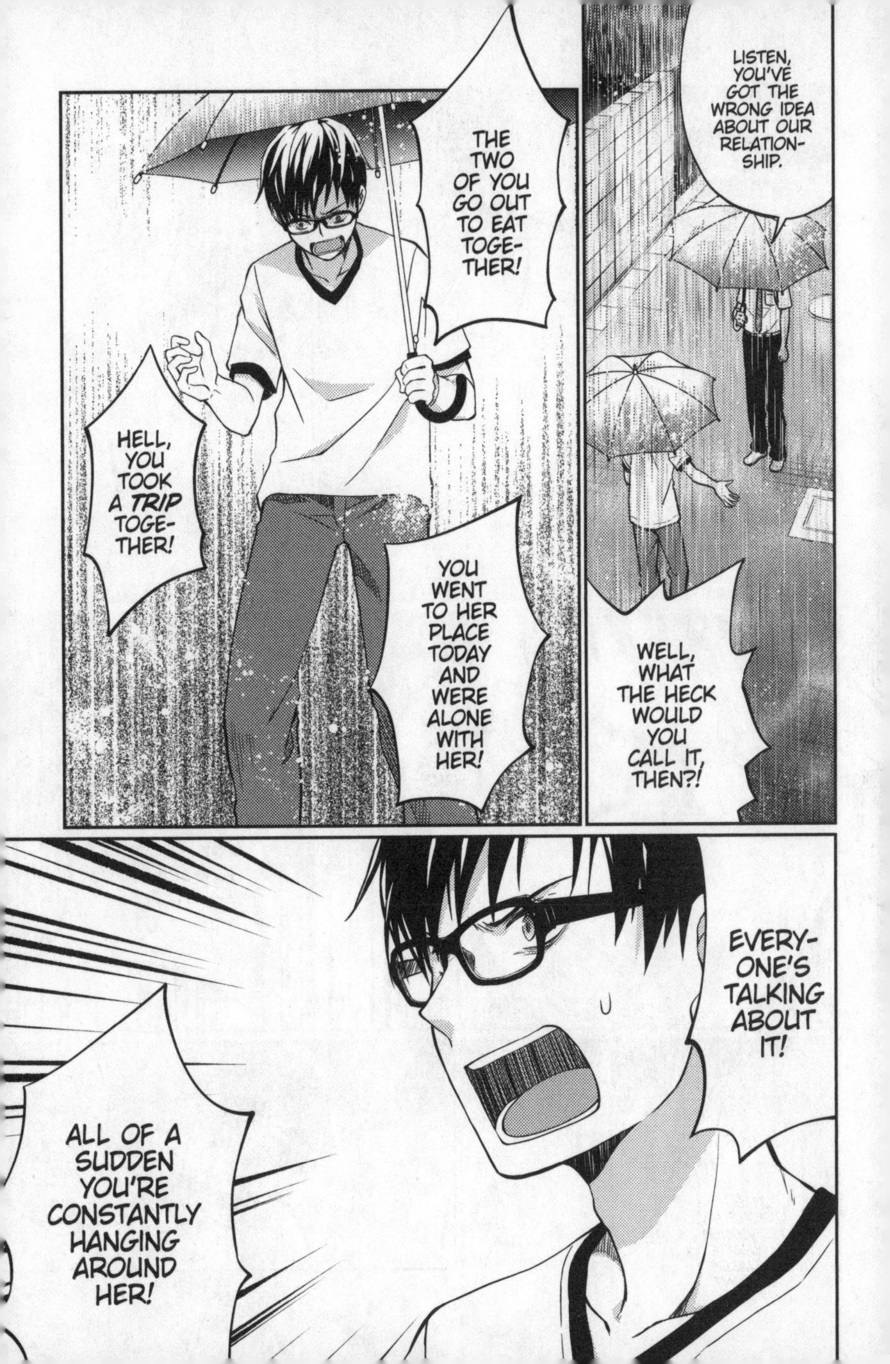
LISTEN, YOU'VE GOT THE WRONG IDEA ABOUT OUR RELATIONSHIP.
THE TWO OF YOU GO OUT TO EAT TOGETHER!
WELL, WHAT THE HECK WOULD YOU CALL IT, THEN?!
YOU WENT TO HER PLACE TODAY AND WERE ALONE WITH HER!
HELL, YOU TOOK A *TRIP* TOGETHER!
EVERYONE'S TALKING ABOUT IT!
ALL OF A SUDDEN YOU'RE CONSTANTLY HANGING AROUND HER!

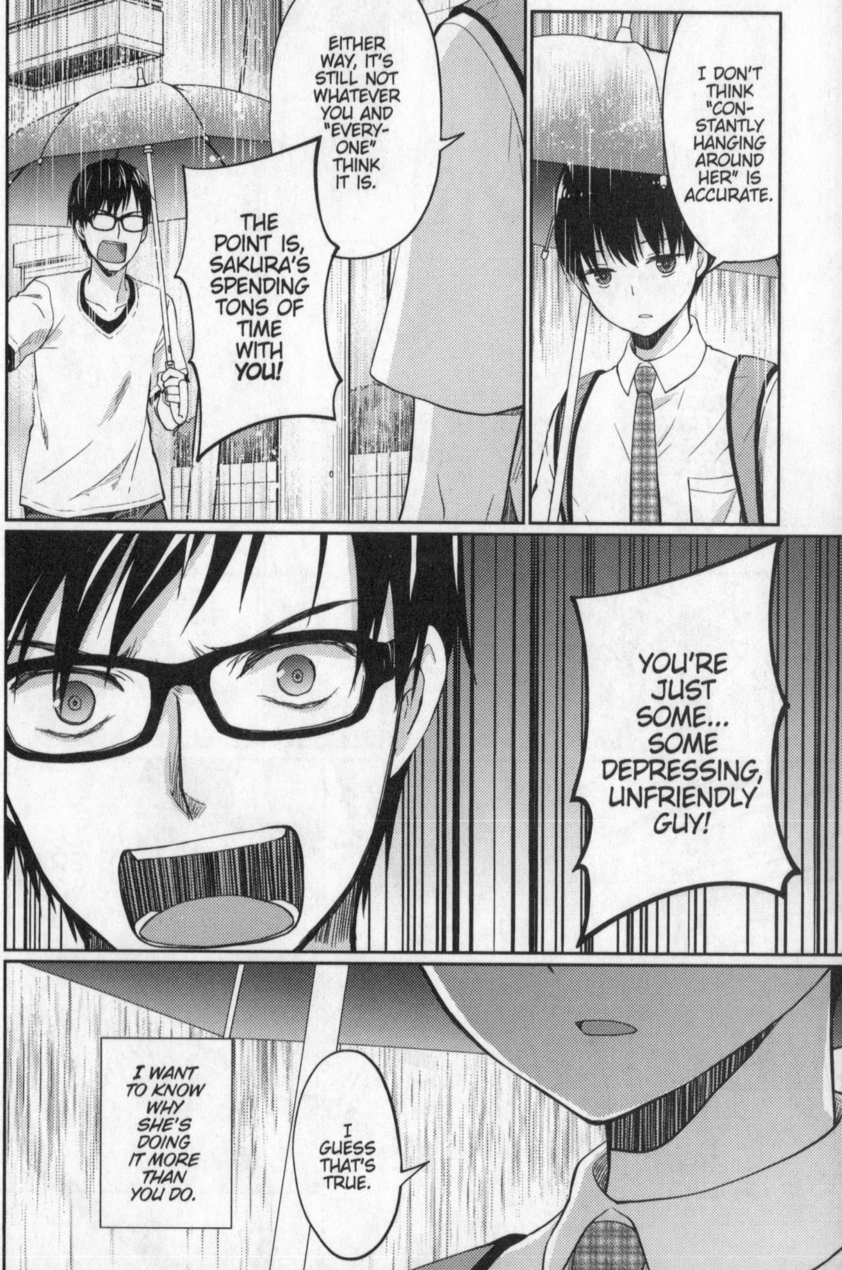
I DON'T THINK "CON-STANTLY HANGING AROUND HER" IS ACCURATE.
EITHER WAY, IT'S STILL NOT WHATEVER YOU AND "EVERY-ONE" THINK IT IS.
THE POINT IS, SAKURA'S SPENDING TONS OF TIME WITH YOU!
YOU'RE JUST SOME... SOME DEPRESSING, UNFRIENDLY GUY!
I GUESS THAT'S TRUE.
I WANT TO KNOW WHY SHE'S DOING IT MORE THAN YOU DO.

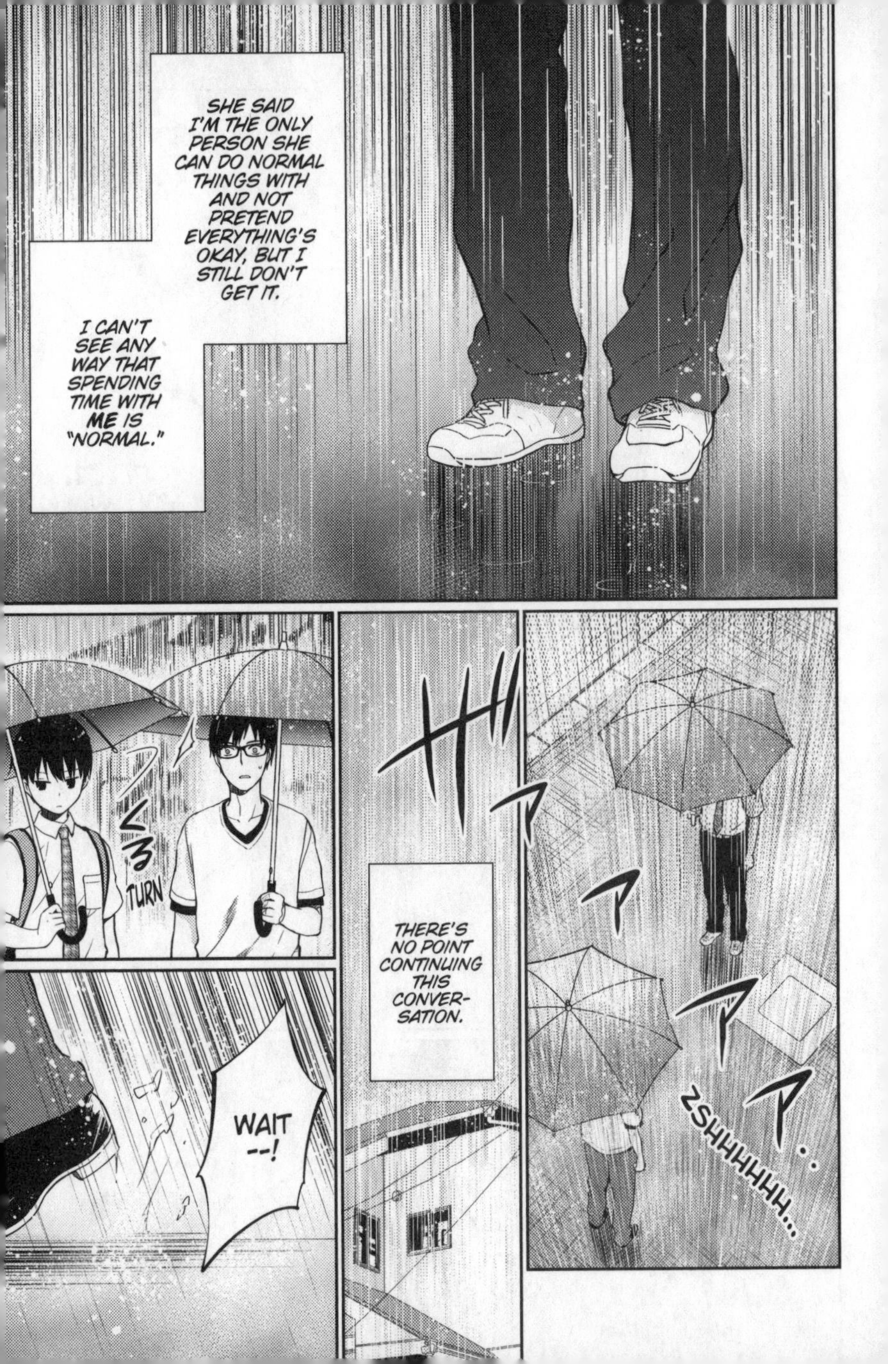
SHE SAID I'M THE ONLY PERSON SHE CAN DO NORMAL THINGS WITH AND NOT PRETEND EVERYTHING'S OKAY, BUT I STILL DON'T GET IT.
I CAN'T SEE ANY WAY THAT SPENDING TIME WITH ME IS "NORMAL."
ZSHHHHHH...
THERE'S NO POINT CONTINUING THIS CONVER-SATION.
くる
TURN
WAIT --!

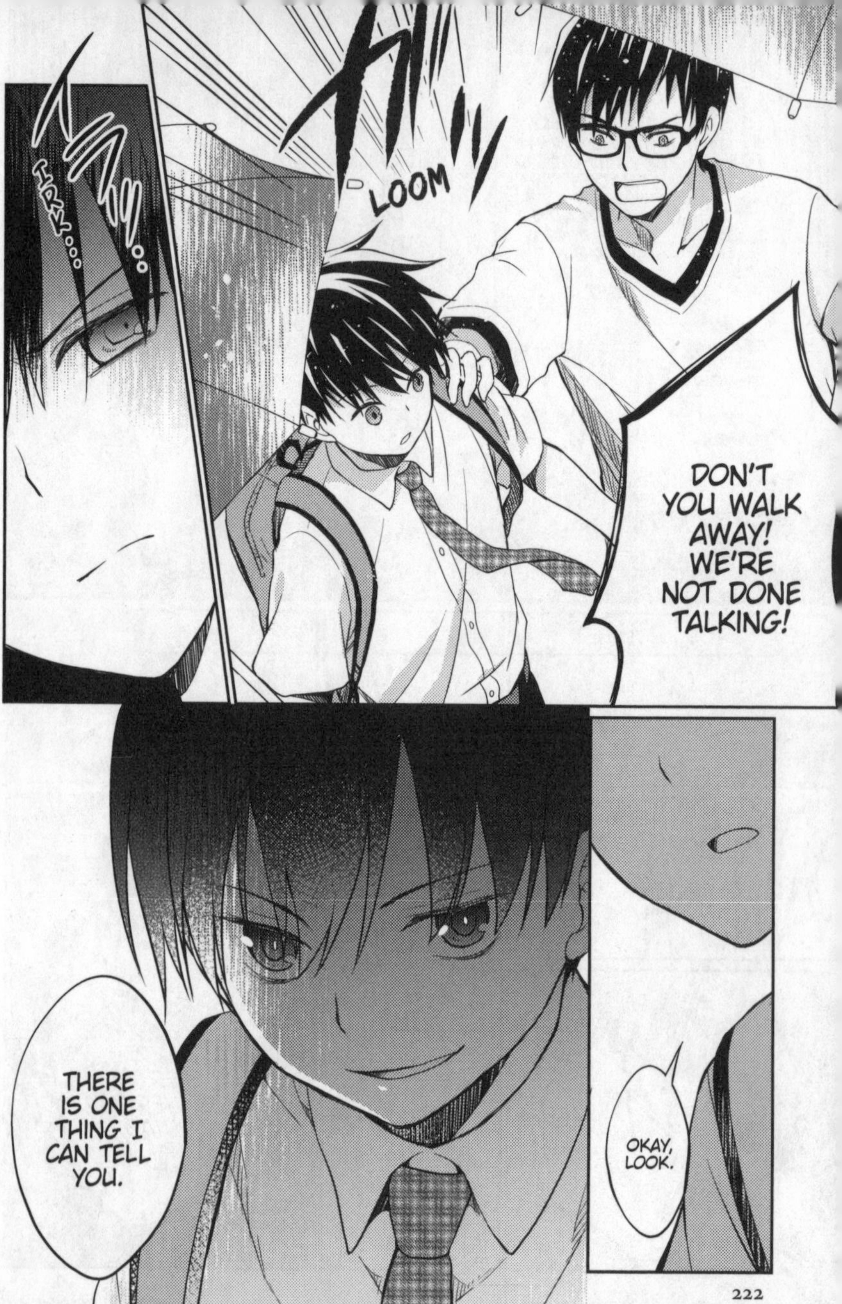
DON'T YOU WALK AWAY! WE'RE NOT DONE TALKING!
LOOM
IRK...
OKAY, LOOK.
THERE IS ONE THING I CAN TELL YOU.

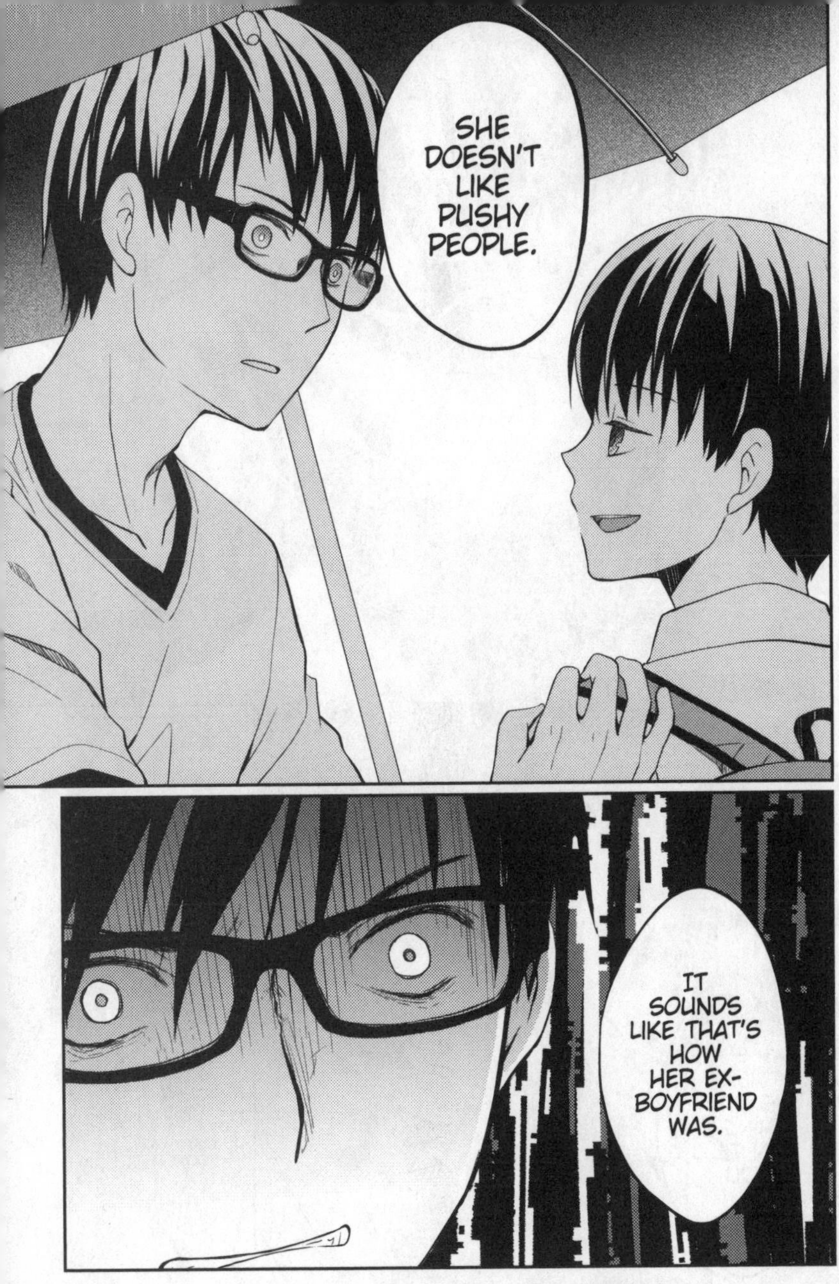
SHE DOESN'T LIKE PUSHY PEOPLE.
IT SOUNDS LIKE THAT'S HOW HER EX-BOYFRIEND WAS.

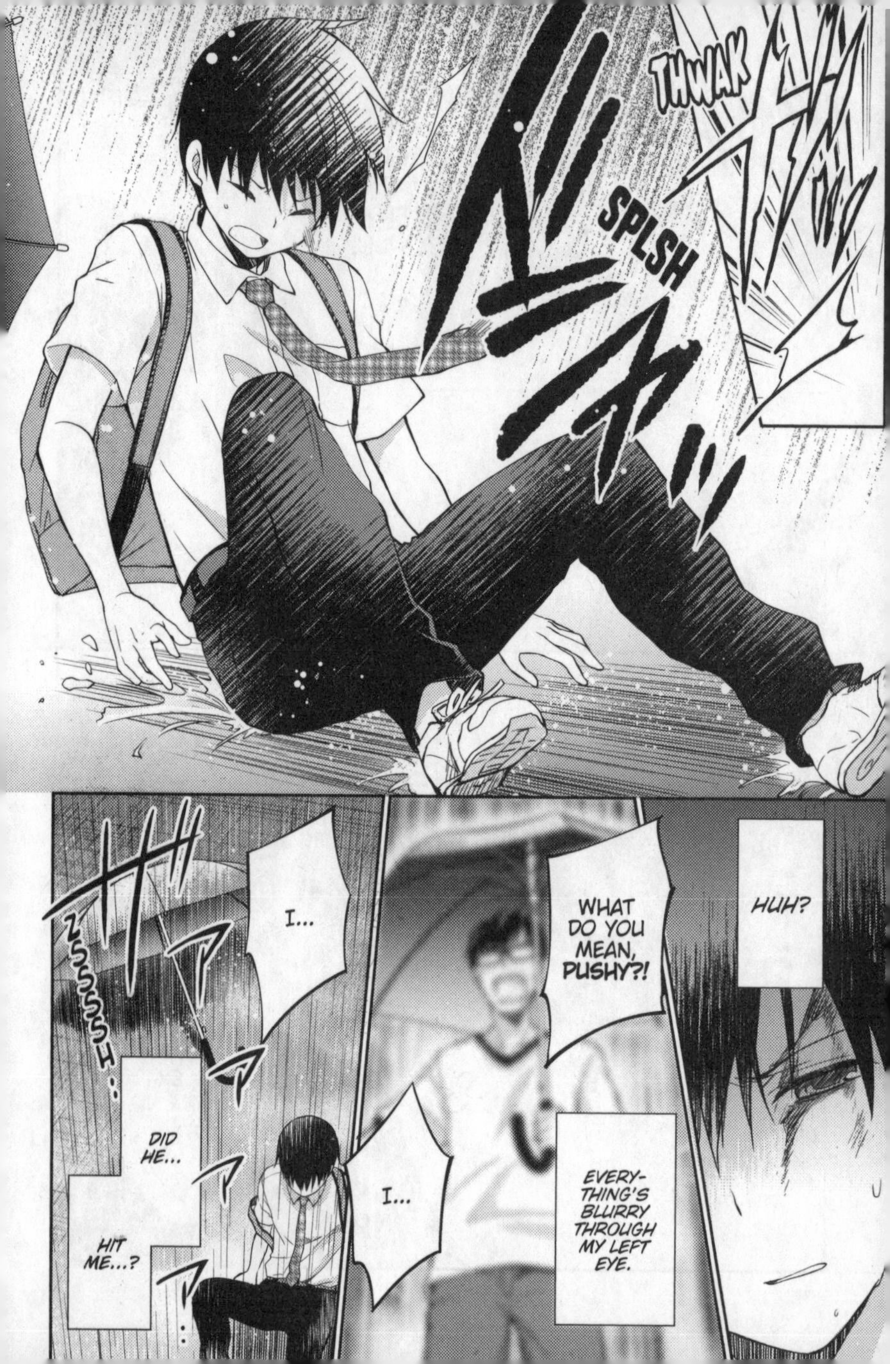
THWAK
SPLSH
HUH?
WHAT DO YOU MEAN, PUSHY?!
I...
EVERY-THING'S BLURRY THROUGH MY LEFT EYE.
I...
DID HE...
HIT ME...?
ZSSSSH...

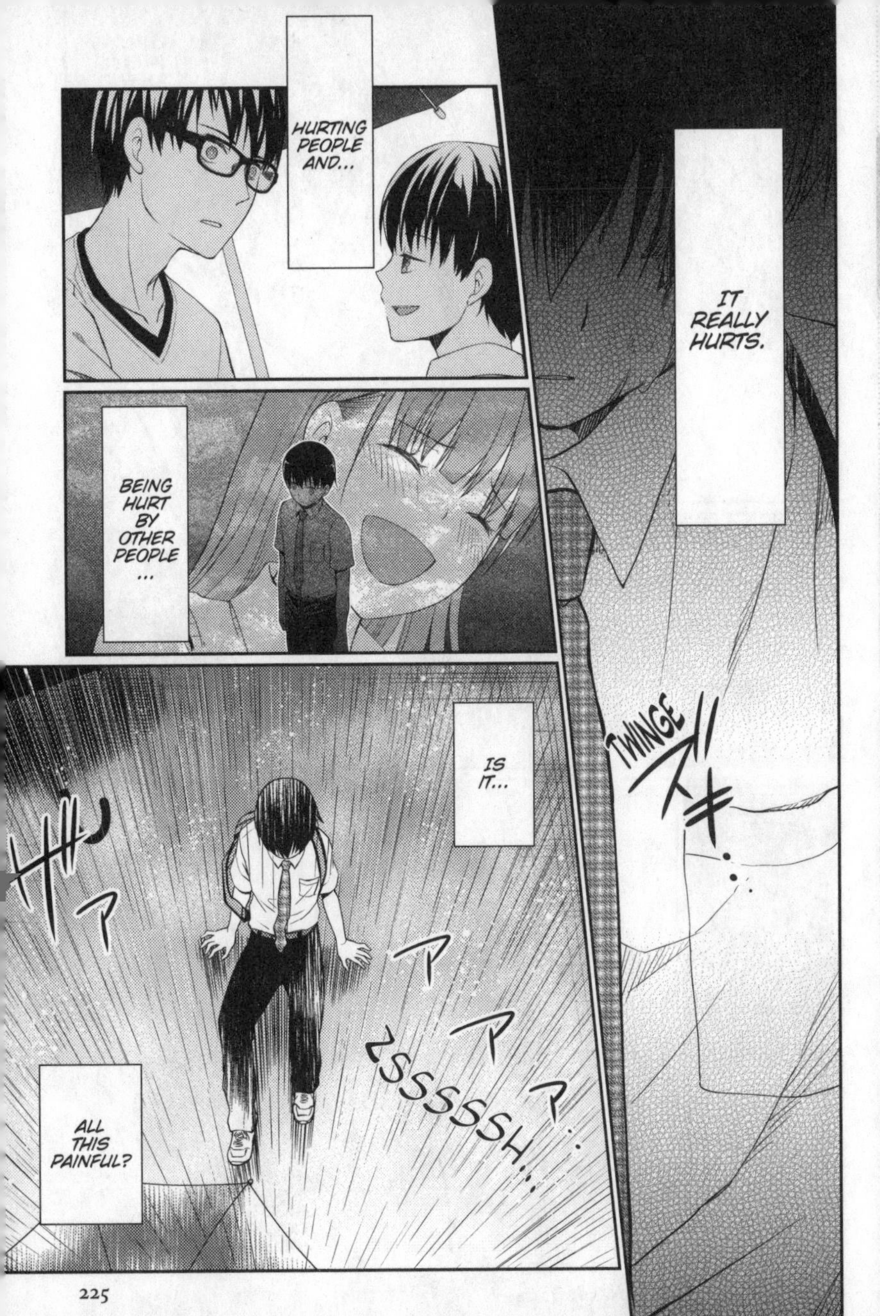
HURTING PEOPLE AND...
IT REALLY HURTS.
BEING HURT BY OTHER PEOPLE ...
TWINGE
ズキ
IS IT...
ALL THIS PAINFUL?
ZSSSSSH...
ザァ
アアア

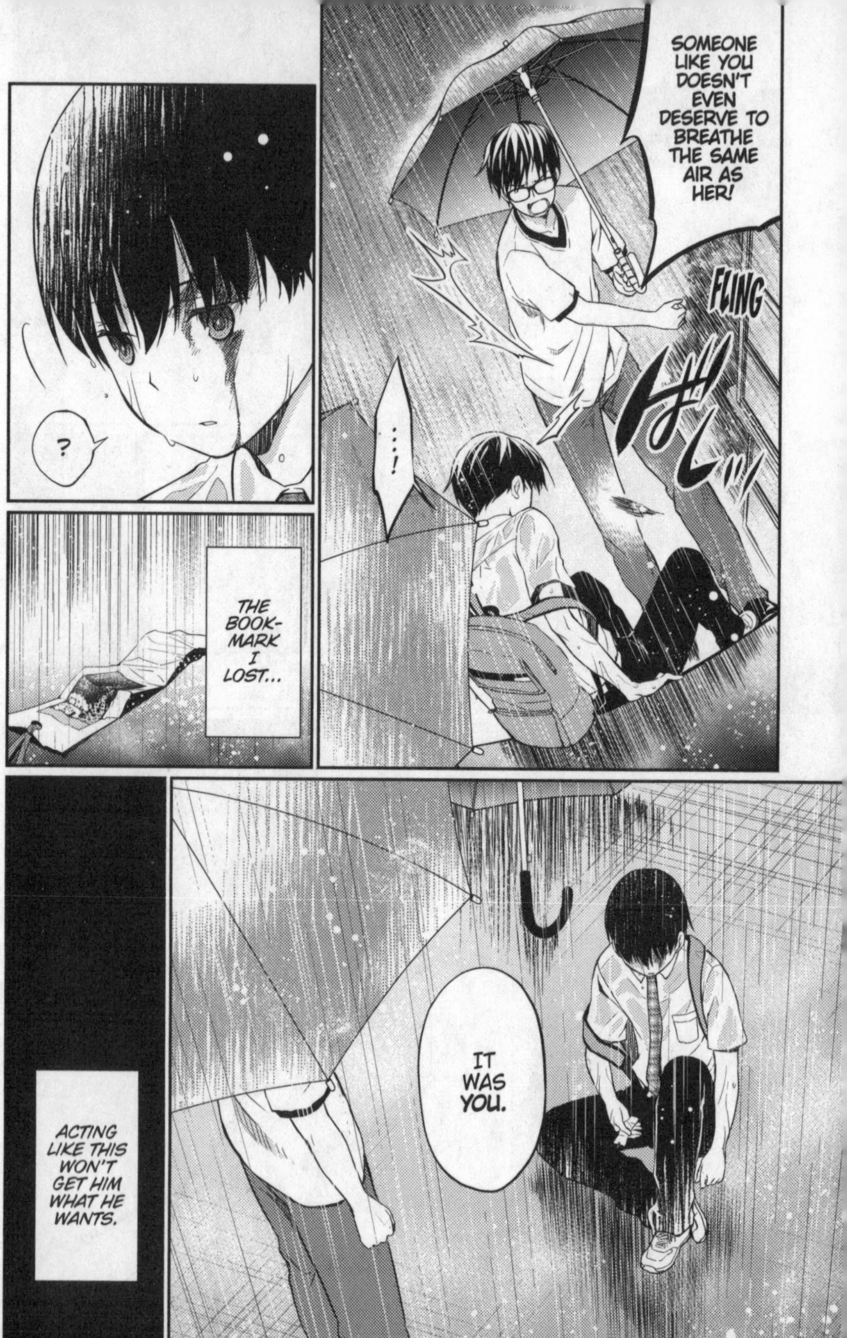
SOMEONE LIKE YOU DOESN'T EVEN DESERVE TO BREATHE THE SAME AIR AS HER!
FLING
ばしッ
...!
?
THE BOOK-MARK I LOST...
IT WAS YOU.
ACTING LIKE THIS WON'T GET HIM WHAT HE WANTS.

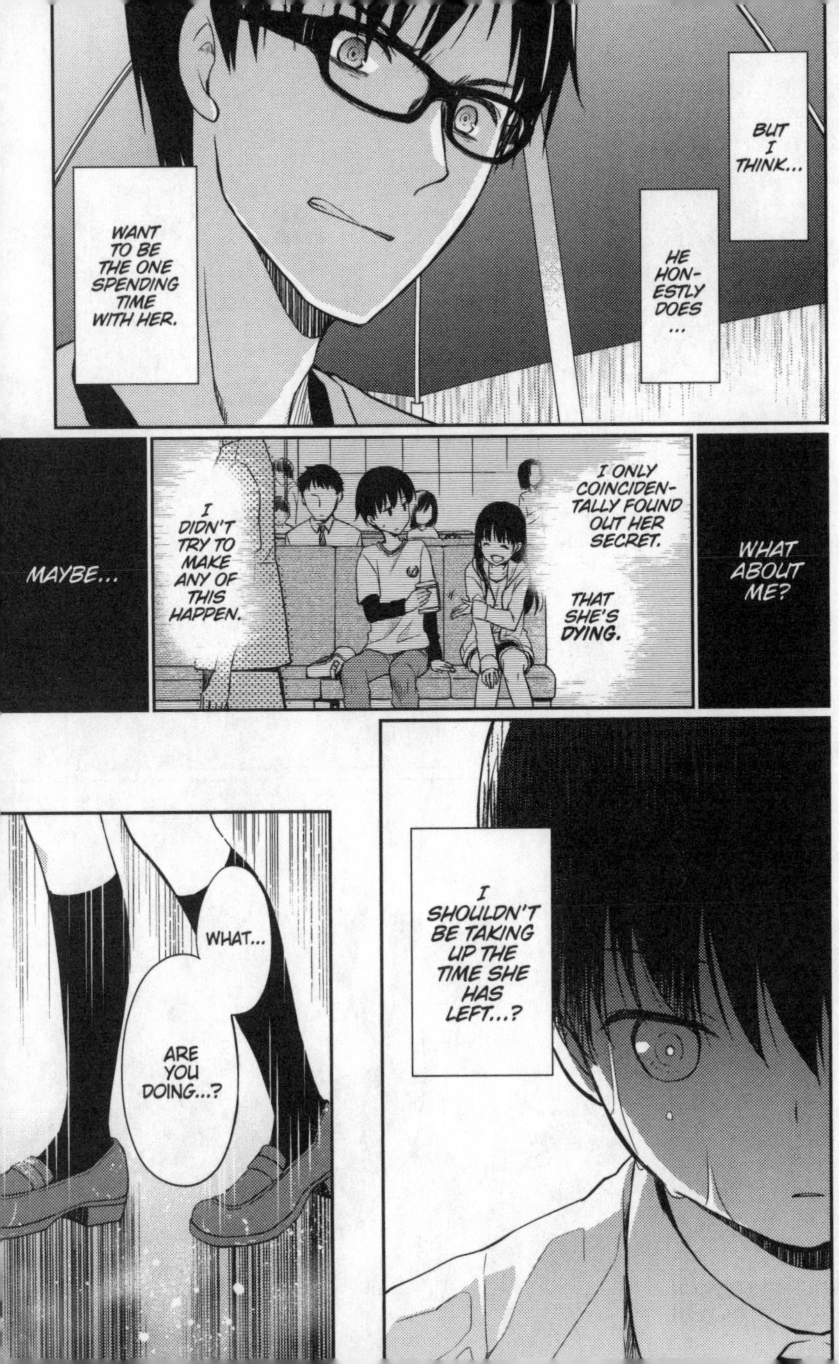
BUT I THINK...
HE HONESTLY DOES...
WANT TO BE THE ONE SPENDING TIME WITH HER.
WHAT ABOUT ME?
I ONLY COINCIDENTALLY FOUND OUT HER SECRET.
THAT SHE'S DYING.
I DIDN'T TRY TO MAKE ANY OF THIS HAPPEN.
MAYBE...
I SHOULDN'T BE TAKING UP THE TIME SHE HAS LEFT...?
WHAT...
ARE YOU DOING...?

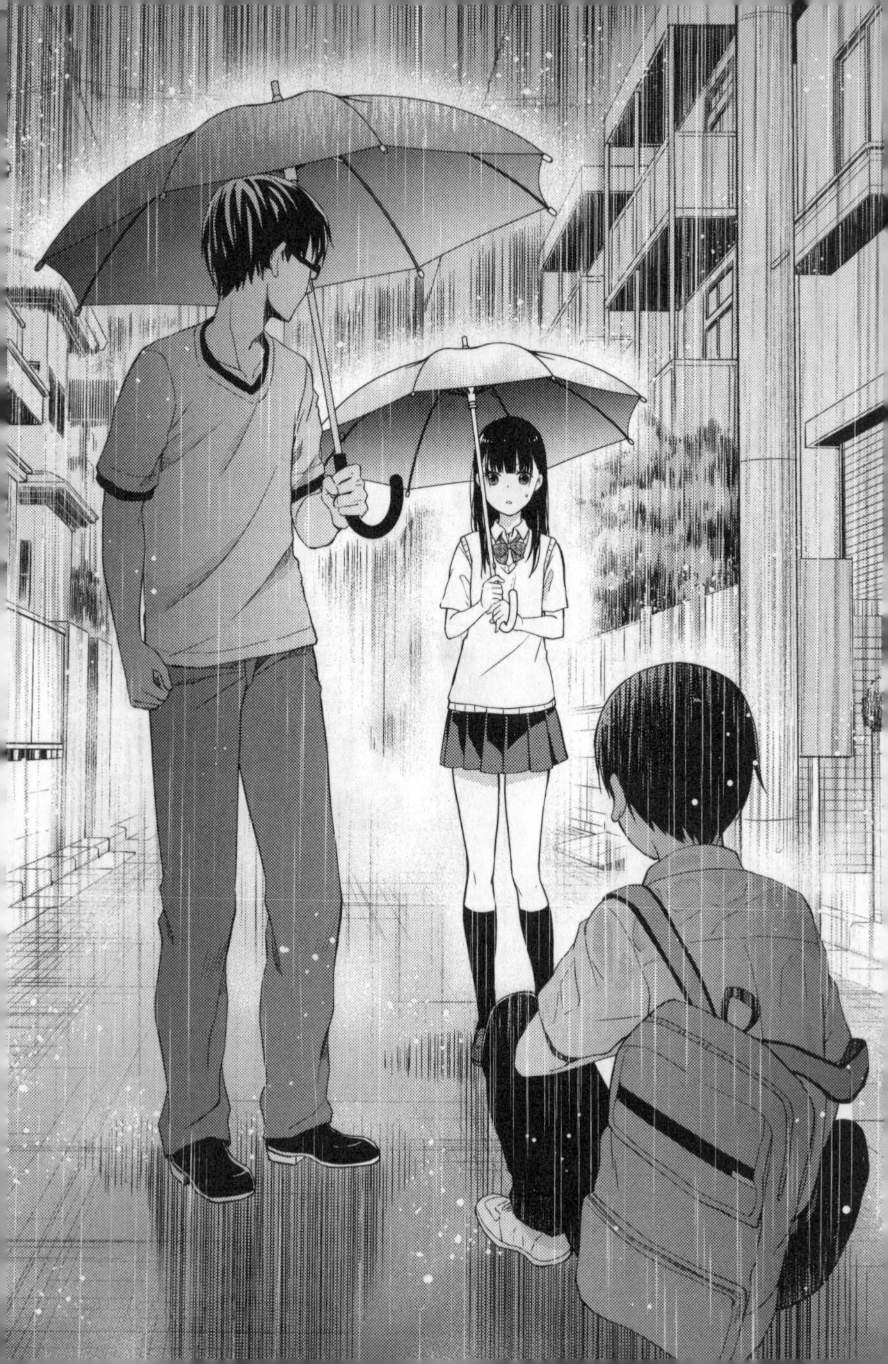

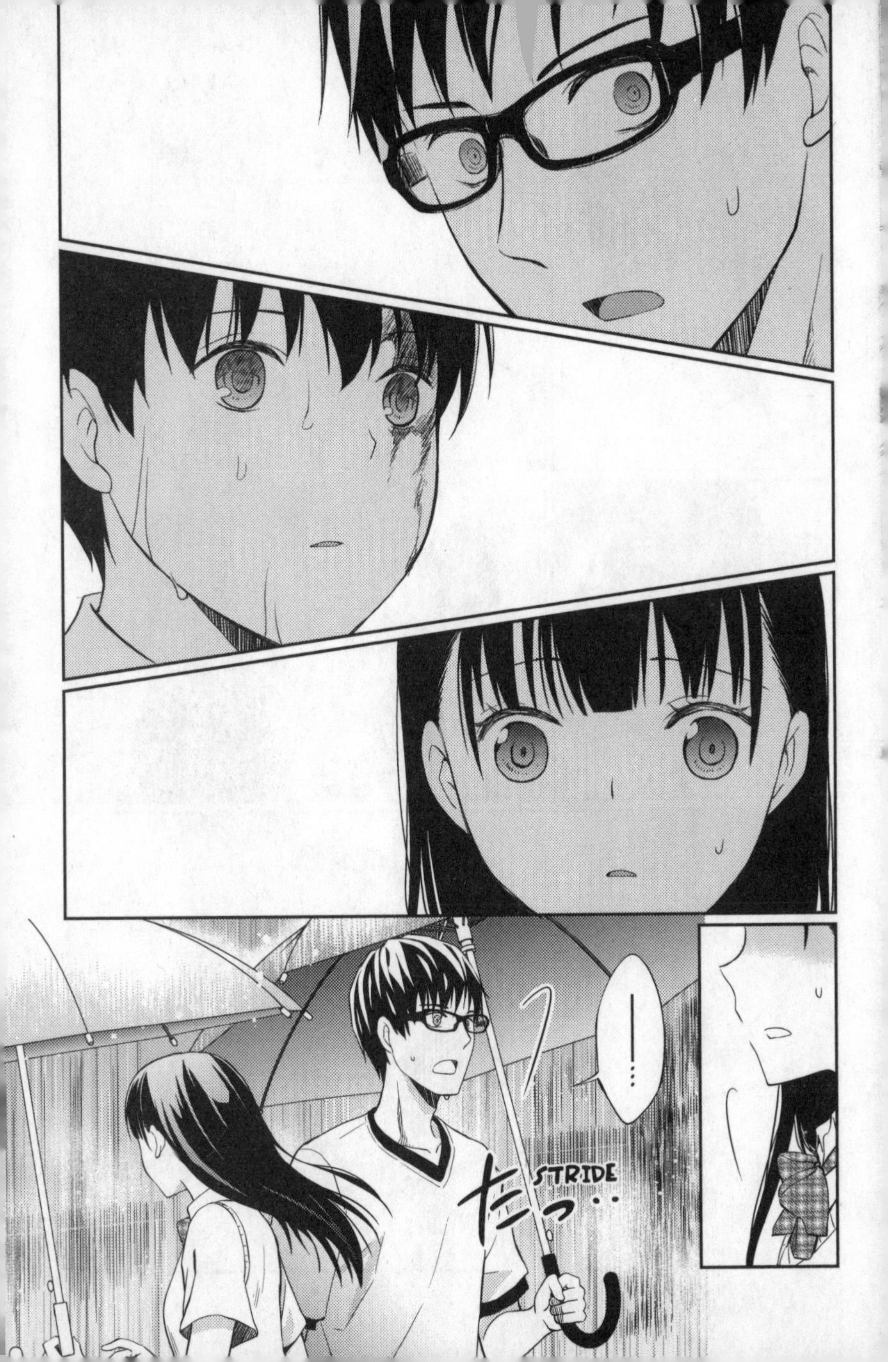

—...
STRIDE

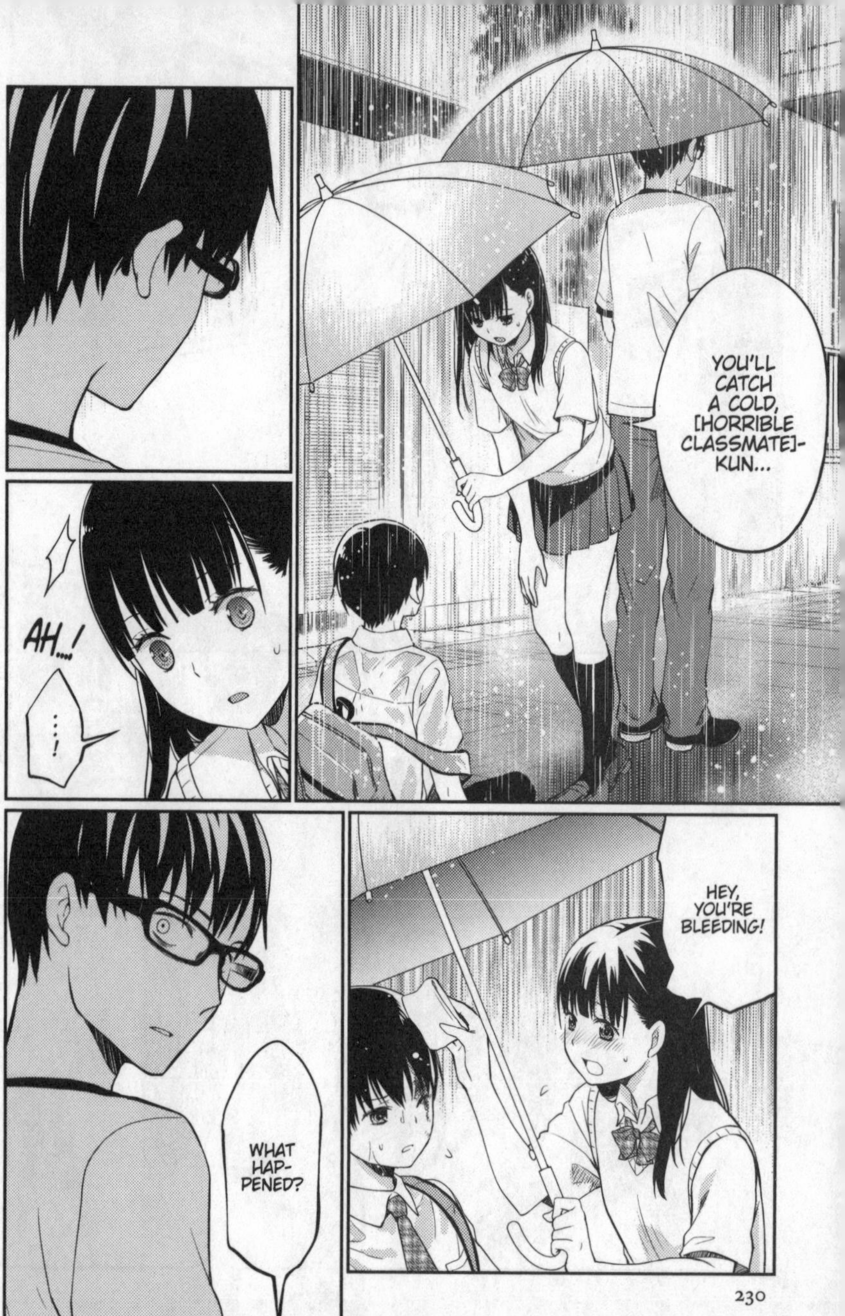
YOU'LL CATCH A COLD, [HORRIBLE CLASSMATE]-KUN...
AH...!
...!
HEY, YOU'RE BLEEDING!
WHAT HAP-PENED?

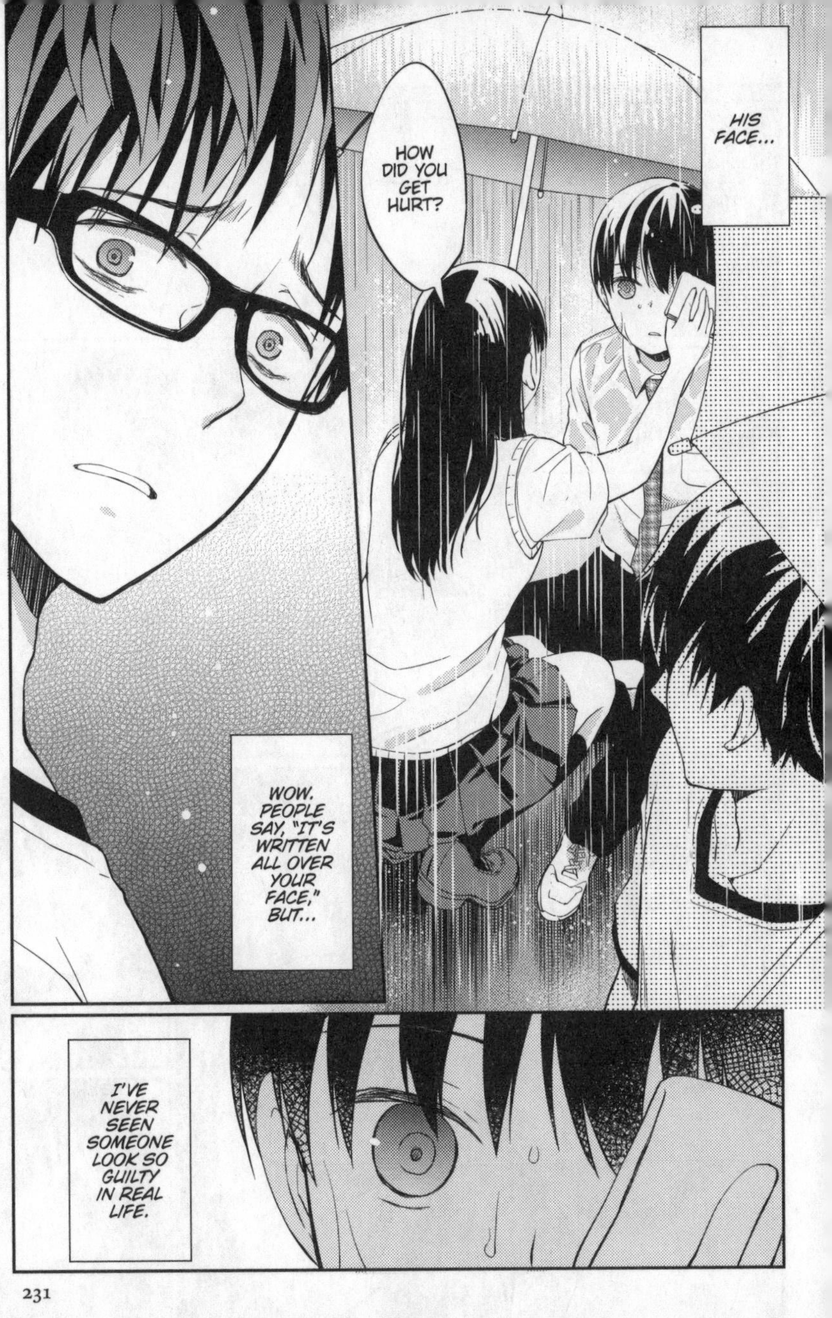
HIS FACE...
HOW DID YOU GET HURT?
WOW. PEOPLE SAY, "IT'S WRITTEN ALL OVER YOUR FACE," BUT...
I'VE NEVER SEEN SOMEONE LOOK SO GUILTY IN REAL LIFE.

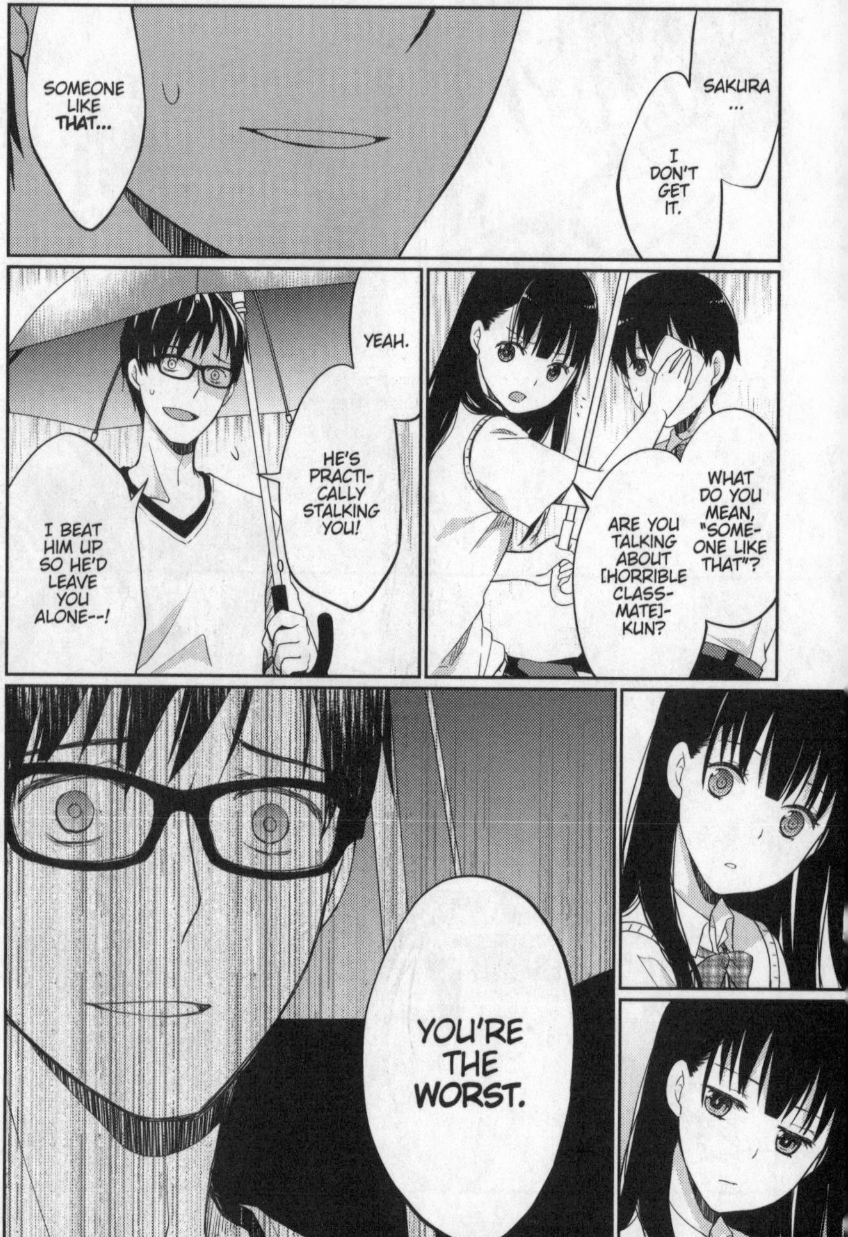
SAKURA ... I DON'T GET IT.
SOMEONE LIKE THAT...
WHAT DO YOU MEAN, "SOME-ONE LIKE THAT"?
ARE YOU TALKING ABOUT [HORRIBLE CLASS-MATE]-KUN?
YEAH.
HE'S PRACTI-CALLY STALKING YOU!
I BEAT HIM UP SO HE'D LEAVE YOU ALONE--!
YOU'RE THE WORST.

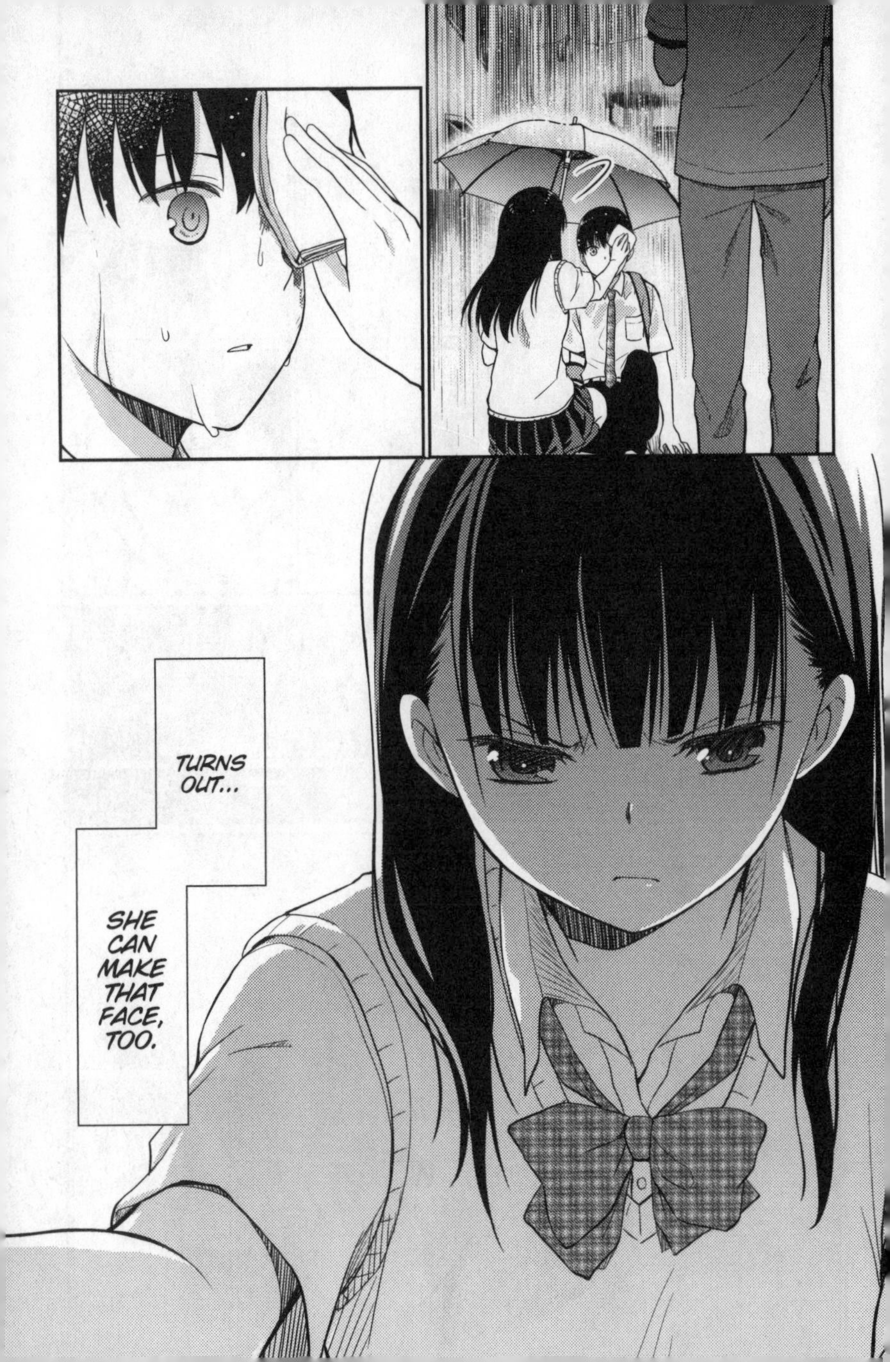
TURNS OUT...
SHE CAN MAKE THAT FACE, TOO.

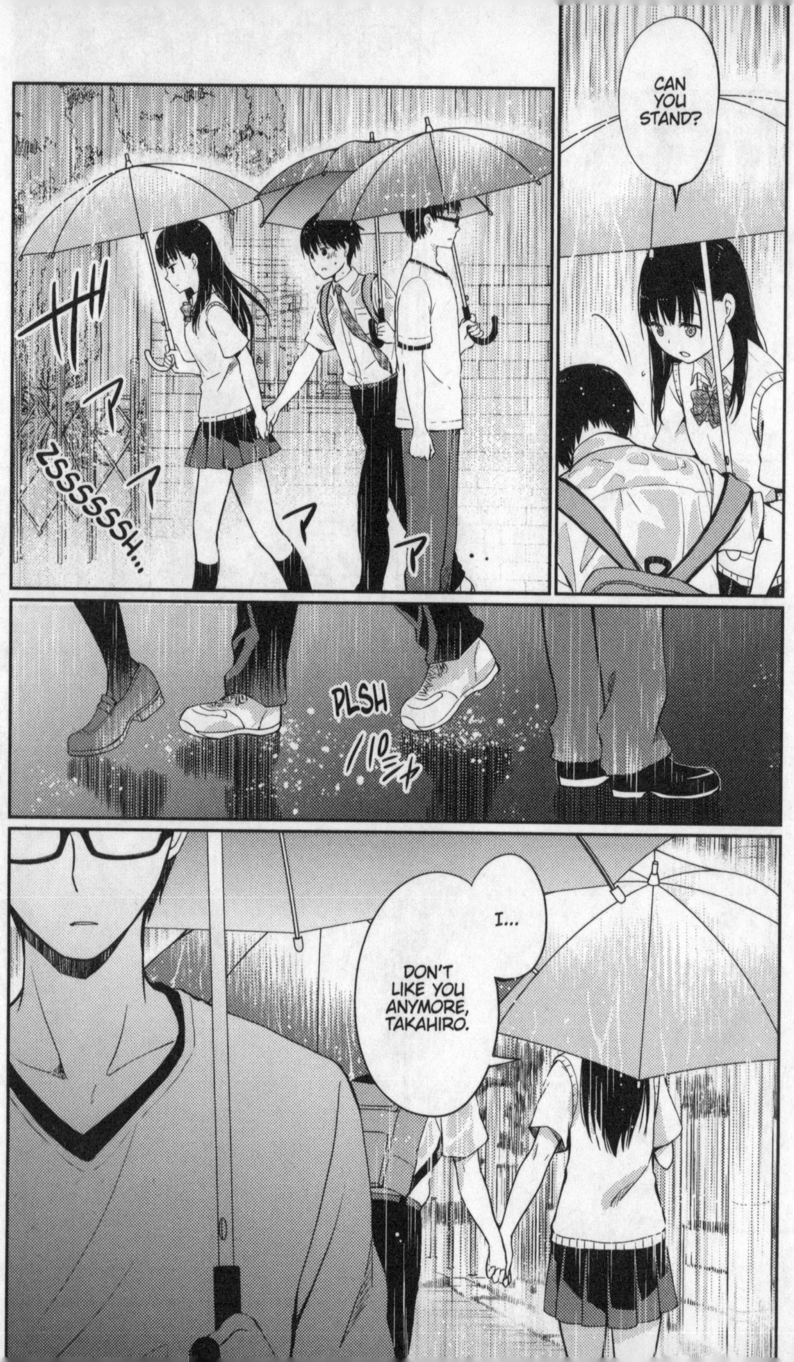
CAN YOU STAND?
ザァァァ
ZSSSSSSH...
PLSH
パシャ
I...
DON'T LIKE YOU ANYMORE, TAKAHIRO.

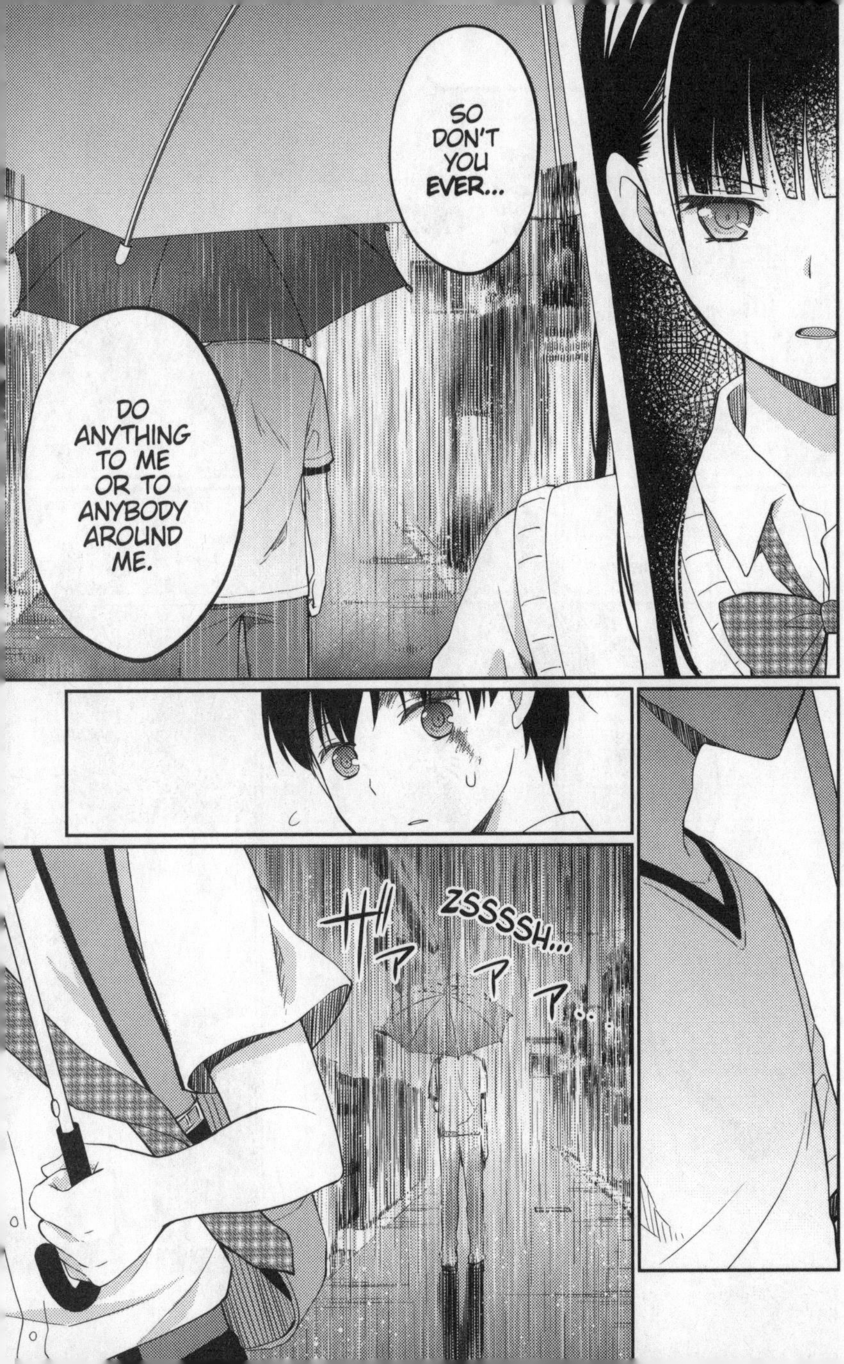
SO DON'T YOU EVER...
DO ANYTHING TO ME OR TO ANYBODY AROUND ME.
ザァァァ...
ZSSSSH...

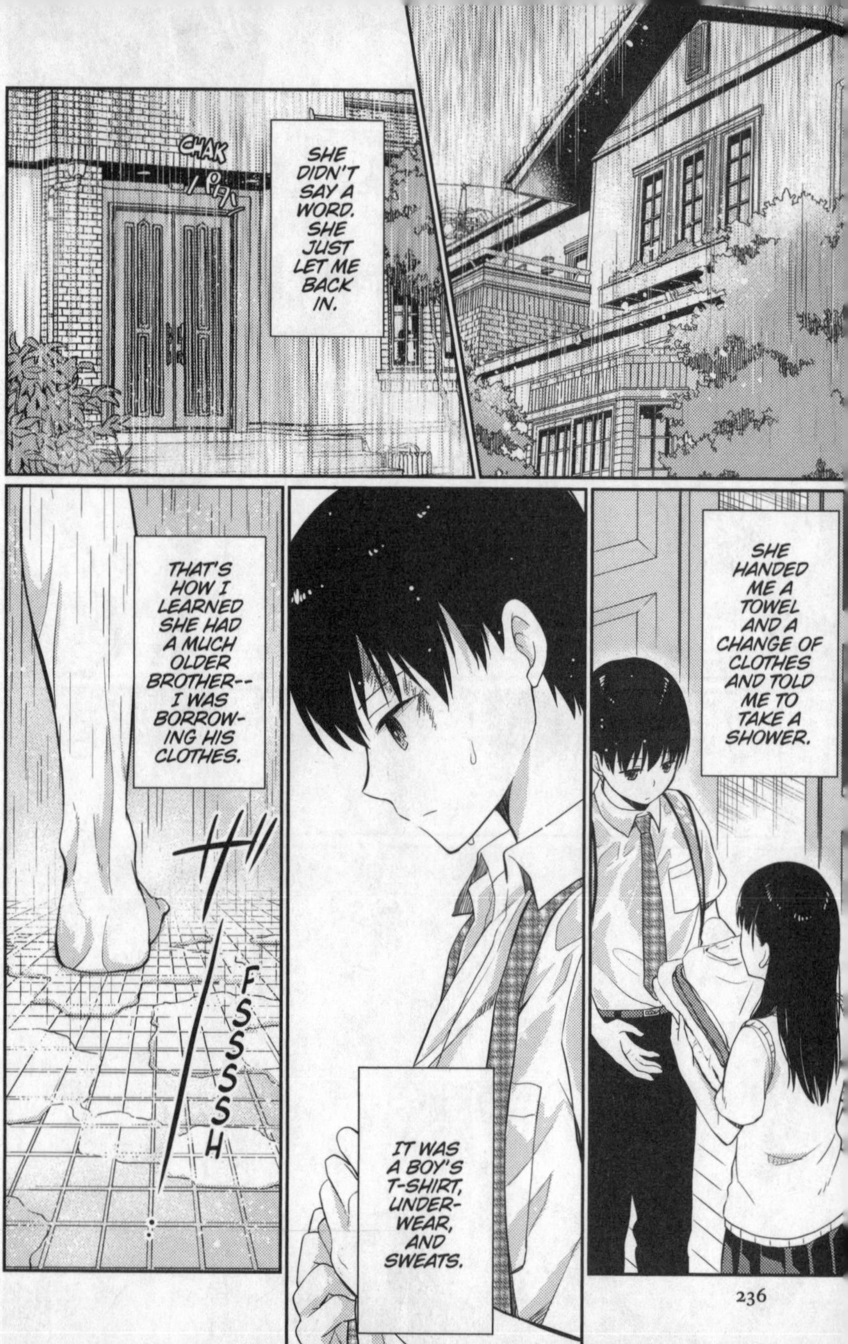
CHAK
SHE DIDN'T SAY A WORD. SHE JUST LET ME BACK IN.
SHE HANDED ME A TOWEL AND A CHANGE OF CLOTHES AND TOLD ME TO TAKE A SHOWER.
IT WAS A BOY'S T-SHIRT, UNDER-WEAR, AND SWEATS.
THAT'S HOW I LEARNED SHE HAD A MUCH OLDER BROTHER-- I WAS BORROW-ING HIS CLOTHES.
FSSSSH

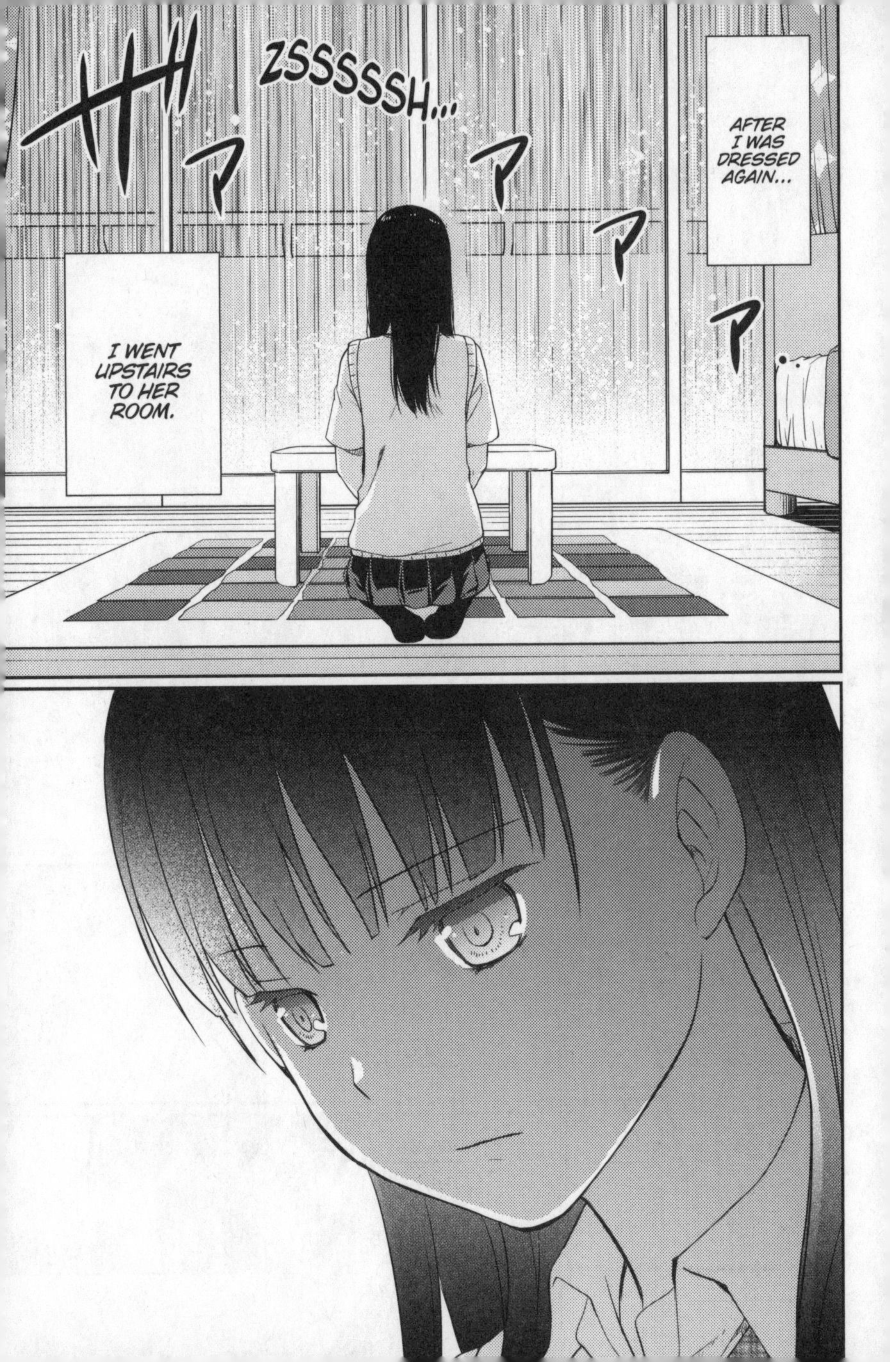
AFTER I WAS DRESSED AGAIN...
ZSSSSSSH...
I WENT UPSTAIRS TO HER ROOM.

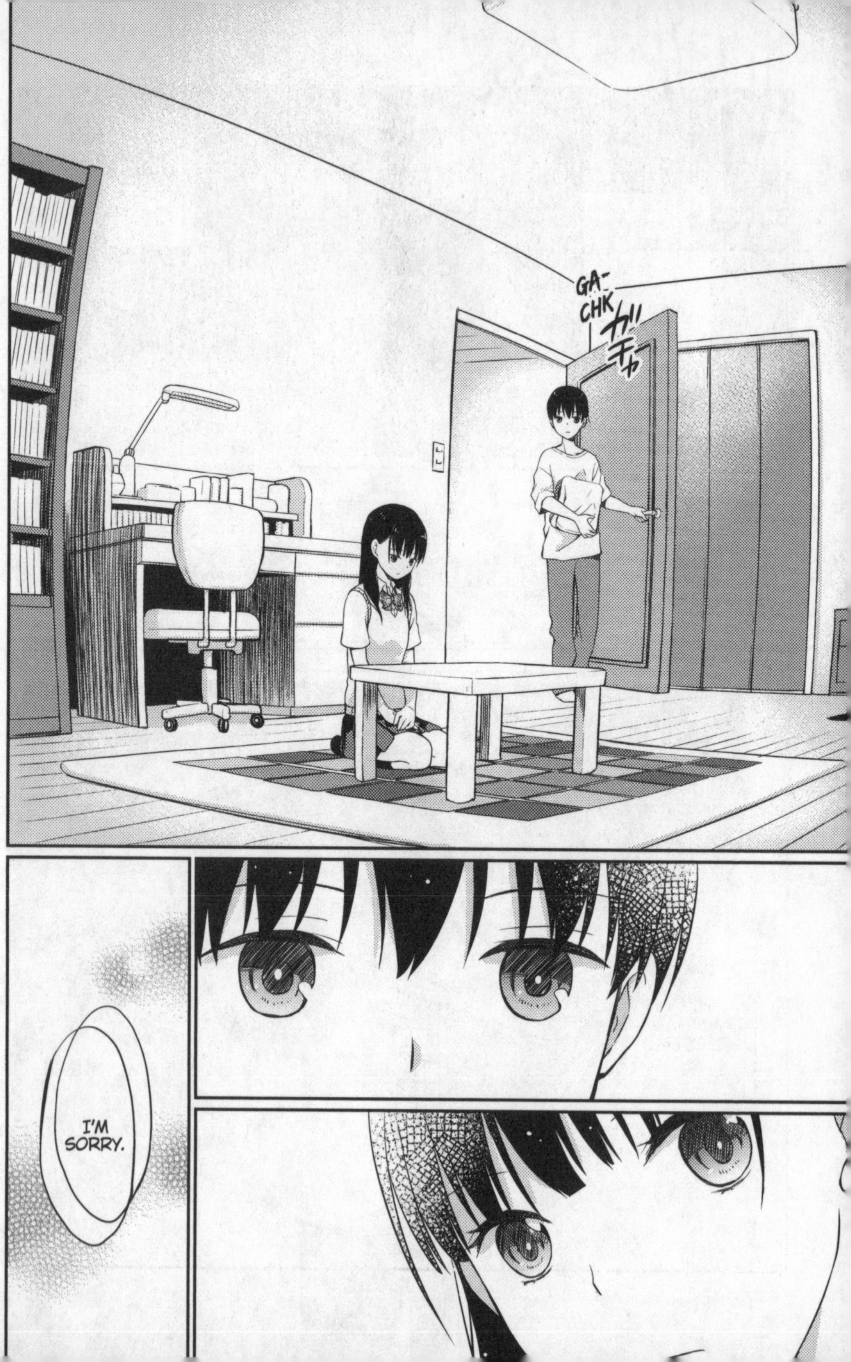
GA-CHK ガチャ
I'M SORRY.

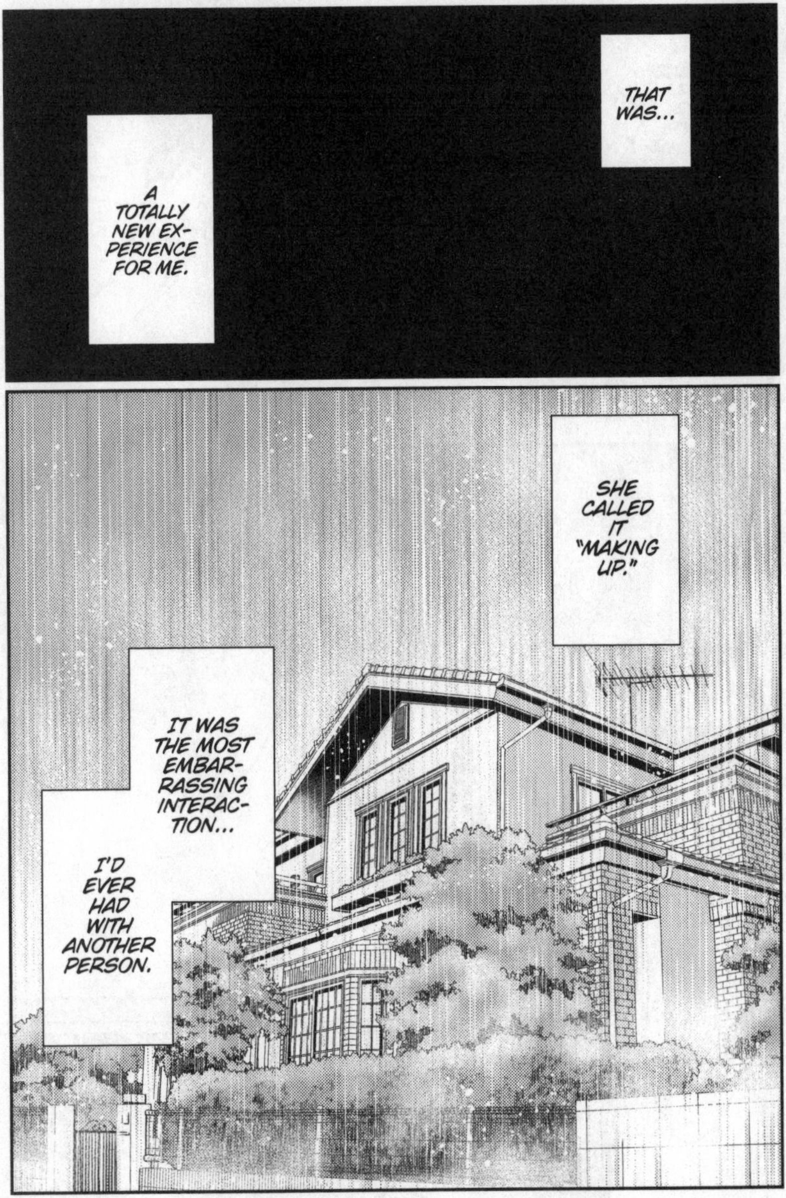
THAT WAS...
A TOTALLY NEW EX-PERIENCE FOR ME.
SHE CALLED IT "MAKING UP."
IT WAS THE MOST EMBAR-RASSING INTERAC-TION...
I'D EVER HAD WITH ANOTHER PERSON.

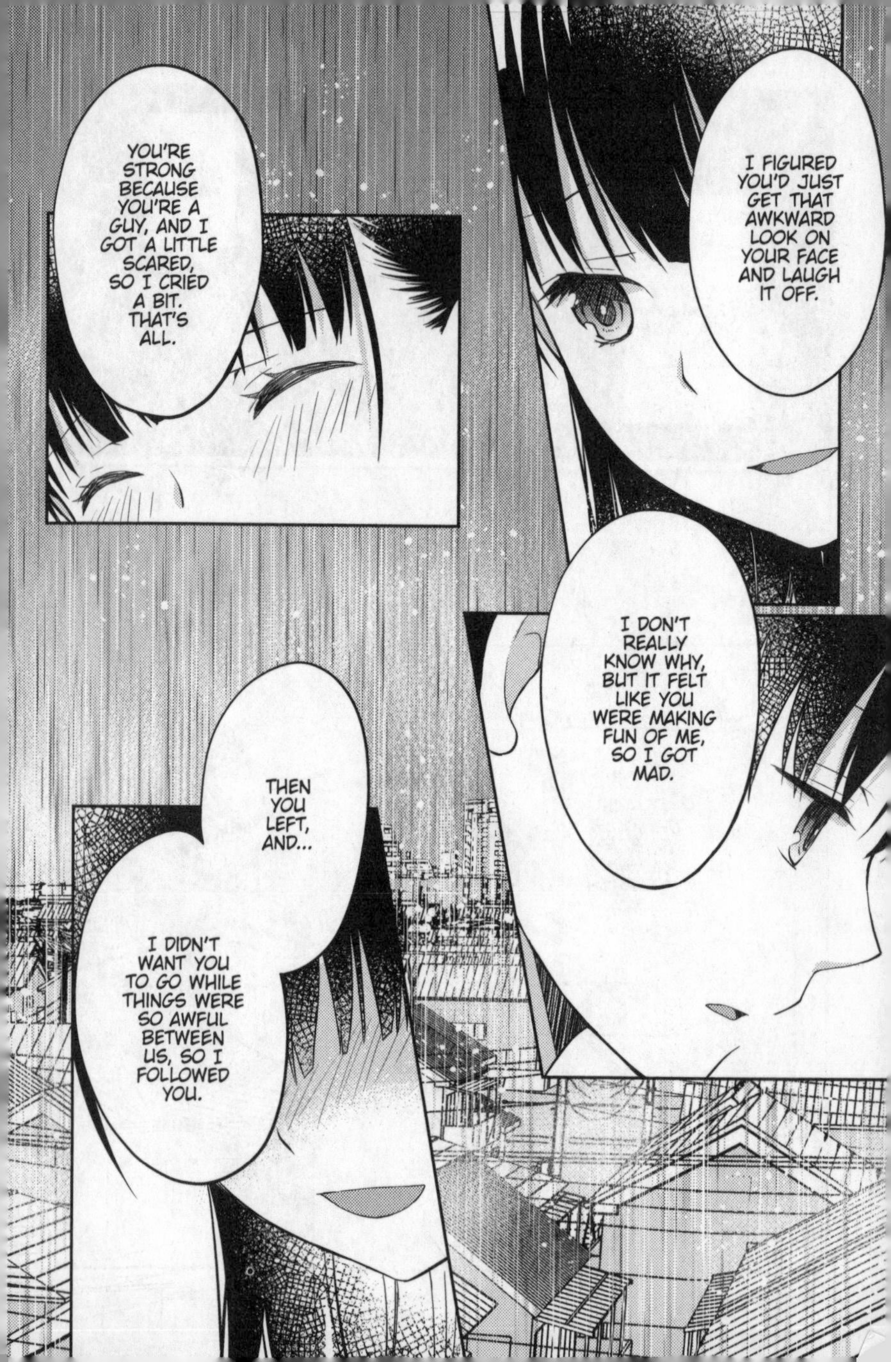
I FIGURED YOU'D JUST GET THAT AWKWARD LOOK ON YOUR FACE AND LAUGH IT OFF.
YOU'RE STRONG BECAUSE YOU'RE A GUY, AND I GOT A LITTLE SCARED, SO I CRIED A BIT. THAT'S ALL.
I DON'T REALLY KNOW WHY, BUT IT FELT LIKE YOU WERE MAKING FUN OF ME, SO I GOT MAD.
THEN YOU LEFT, AND...
I DIDN'T WANT YOU TO GO WHILE THINGS WERE SO AWFUL BETWEEN US, SO I FOLLOWED YOU.

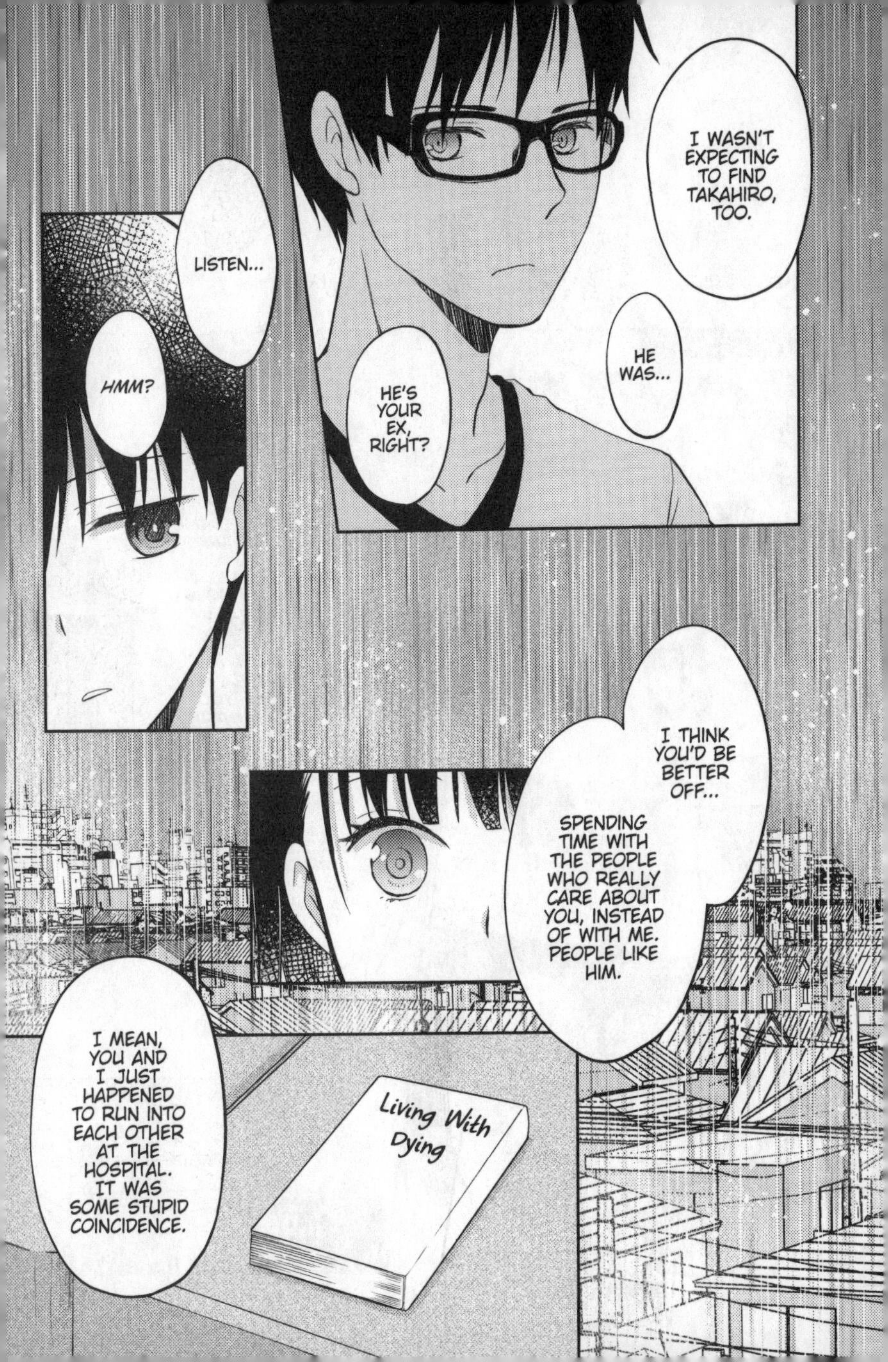
I WASN'T EXPECTING TO FIND TAKAHIRO, TOO.
HE WAS...
HE'S YOUR EX, RIGHT?
LISTEN...
HMM?
I THINK YOU'D BE BETTER OFF...
SPENDING TIME WITH THE PEOPLE WHO REALLY CARE ABOUT YOU, INSTEAD OF WITH ME. PEOPLE LIKE HIM.
Living With Dying
I MEAN, YOU AND I JUST HAPPENED TO RUN INTO EACH OTHER AT THE HOSPITAL. IT WAS SOME STUPID COINCIDENCE.

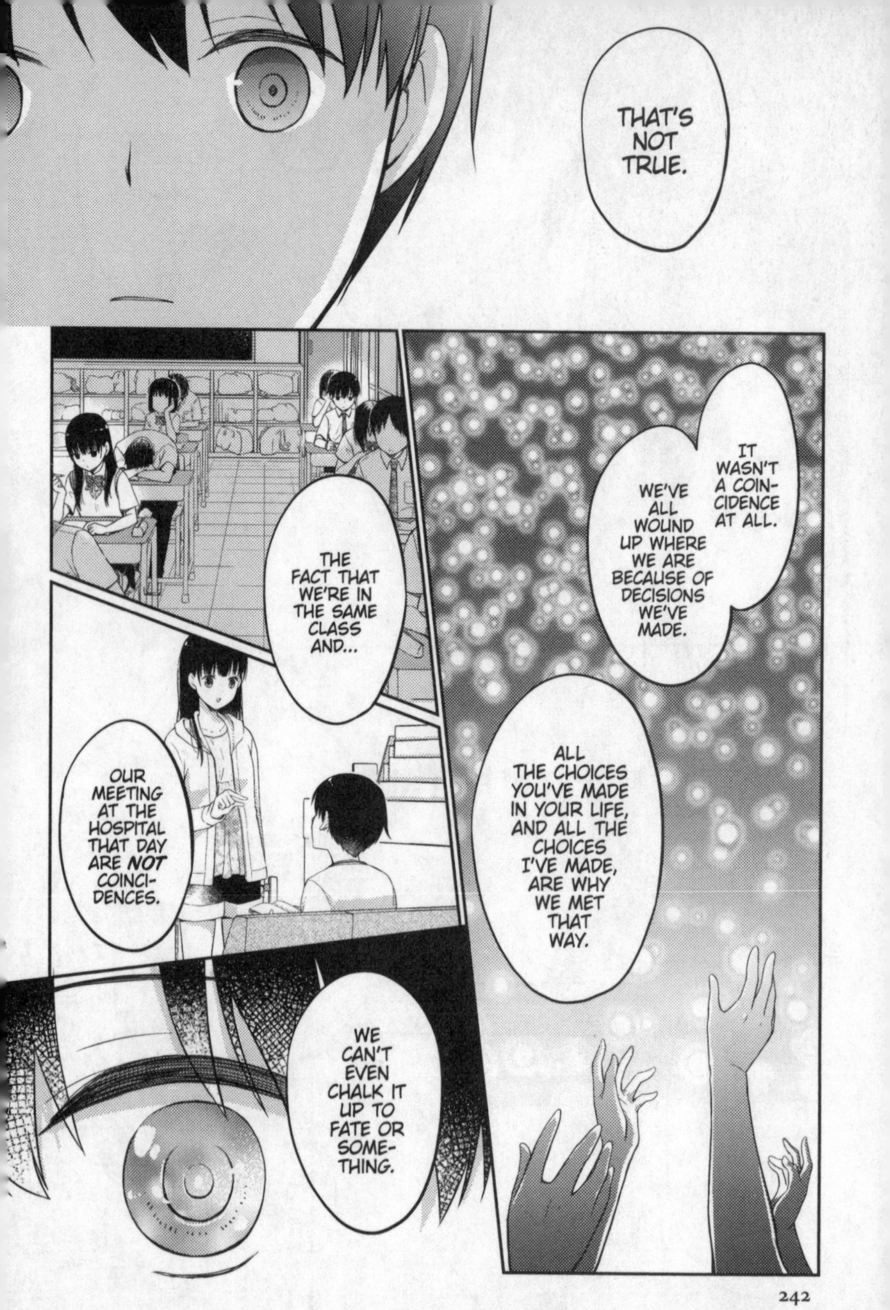
THAT'S NOT TRUE.
IT WASN'T A COINCIDENCE AT ALL.
WE'VE ALL WOUND UP WHERE WE ARE BECAUSE OF DECISIONS WE'VE MADE.
THE FACT THAT WE'RE IN THE SAME CLASS AND...
OUR MEETING AT THE HOSPITAL THAT DAY ARE *NOT* COINCIDENCES.
ALL THE CHOICES YOU'VE MADE IN YOUR LIFE, AND ALL THE CHOICES I'VE MADE, ARE WHY WE MET THAT WAY.
WE CAN'T EVEN CHALK IT UP TO FATE OR SOMETHING.

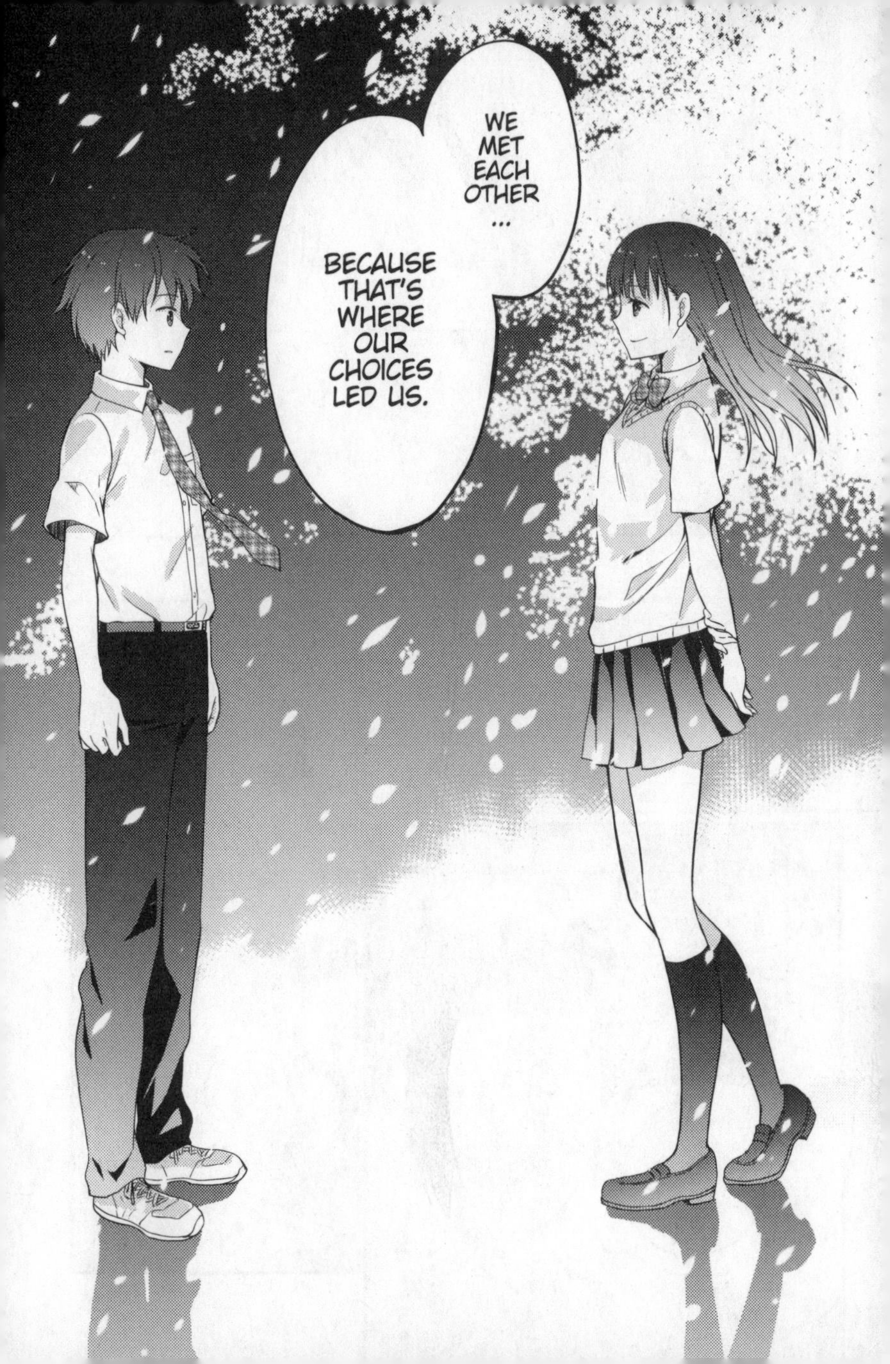
WE MET EACH OTHER ...
BECAUSE THAT'S WHERE OUR CHOICES LED US.

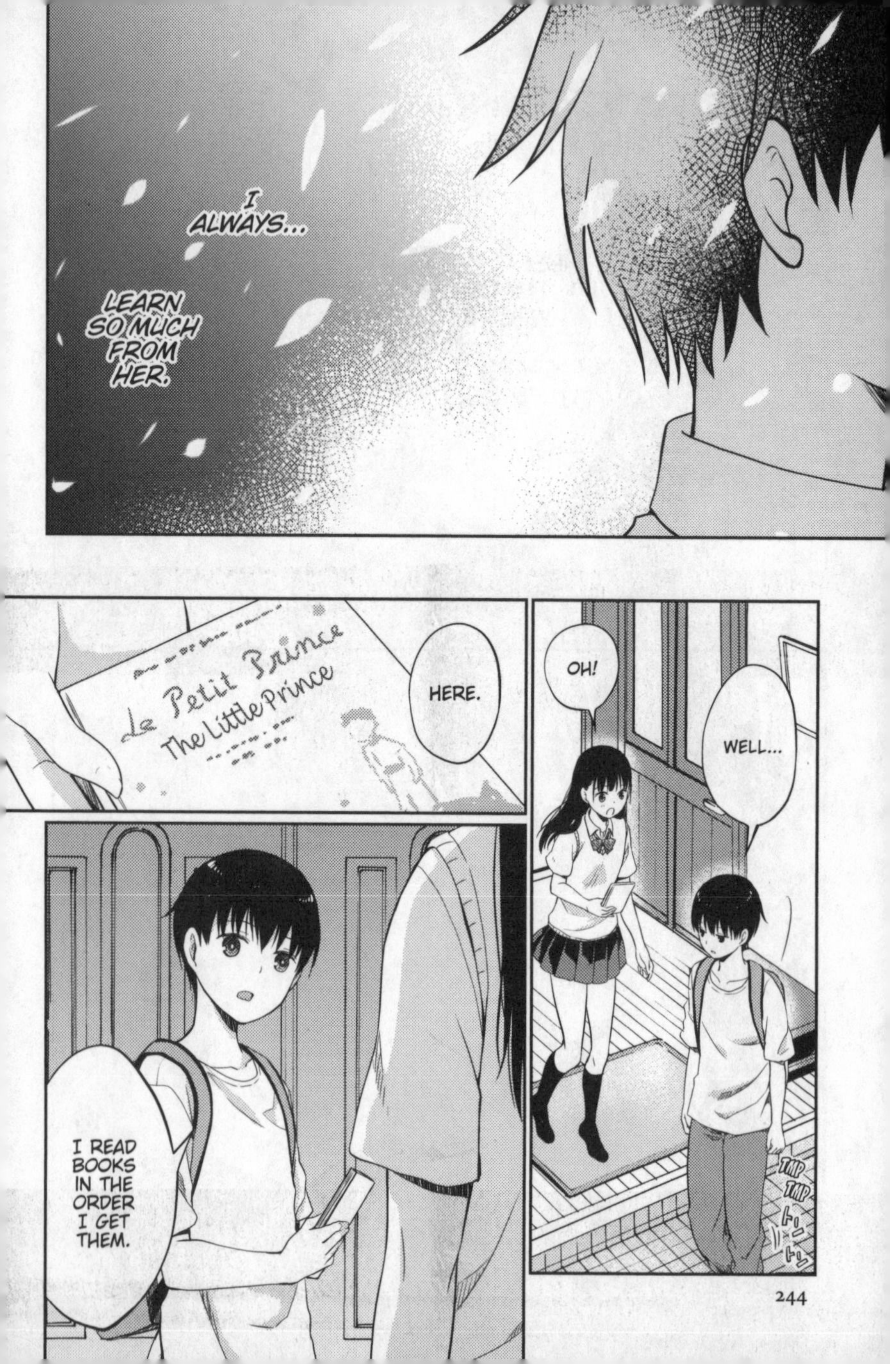
I ALWAYS...
LEARN SO MUCH FROM HER.
OH!
WELL...
TMP TMP
トン トン
Le Petit Prince
The Little Prince
HERE.
I READ BOOKS IN THE ORDER I GET THEM.

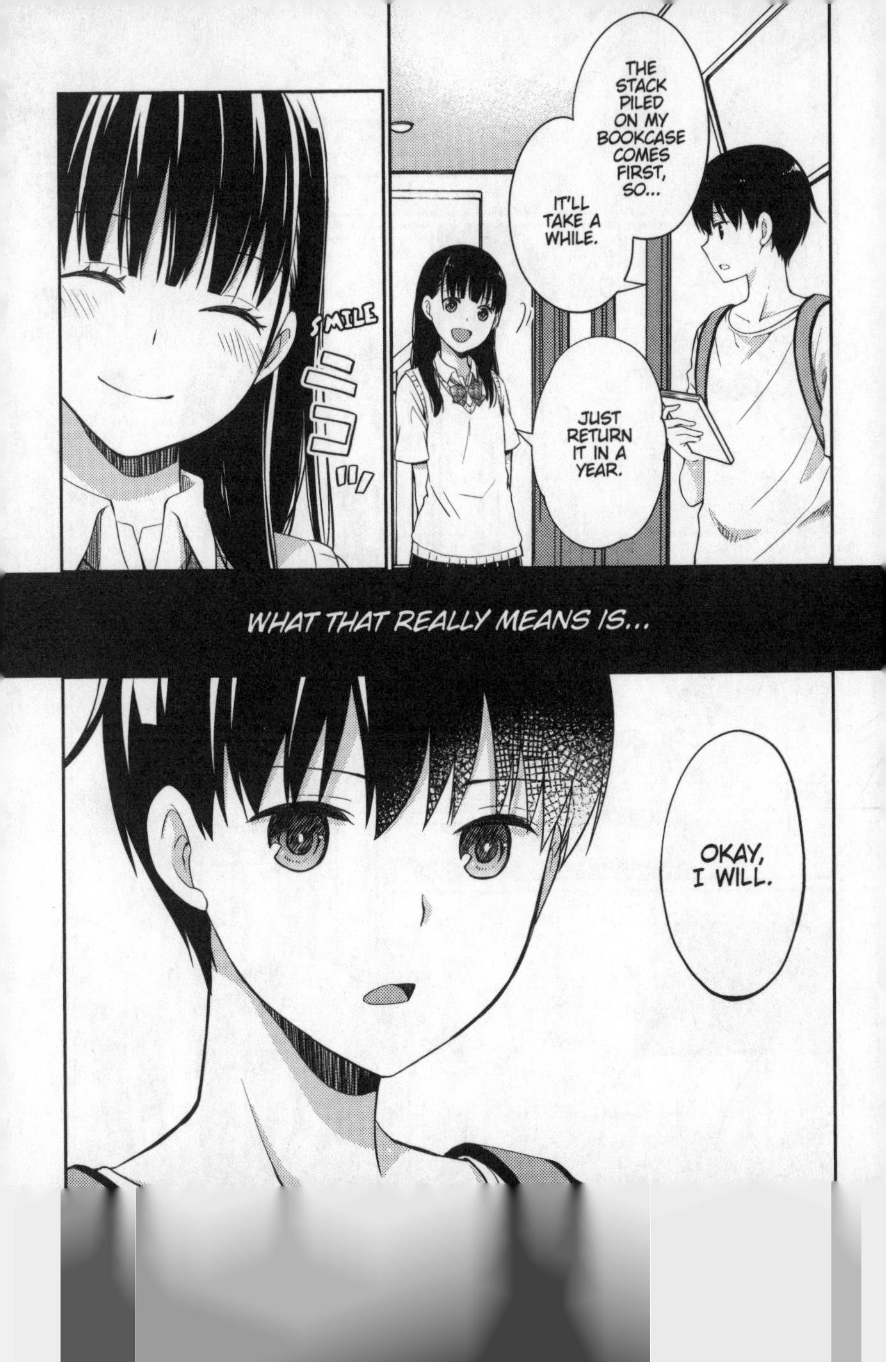
THE STACK PILED ON MY BOOKCASE COMES FIRST, SO...
IT'LL TAKE A WHILE.
JUST RETURN IT IN A YEAR.
SMILE
WHAT THAT REALLY MEANS IS...
OKAY, I WILL.

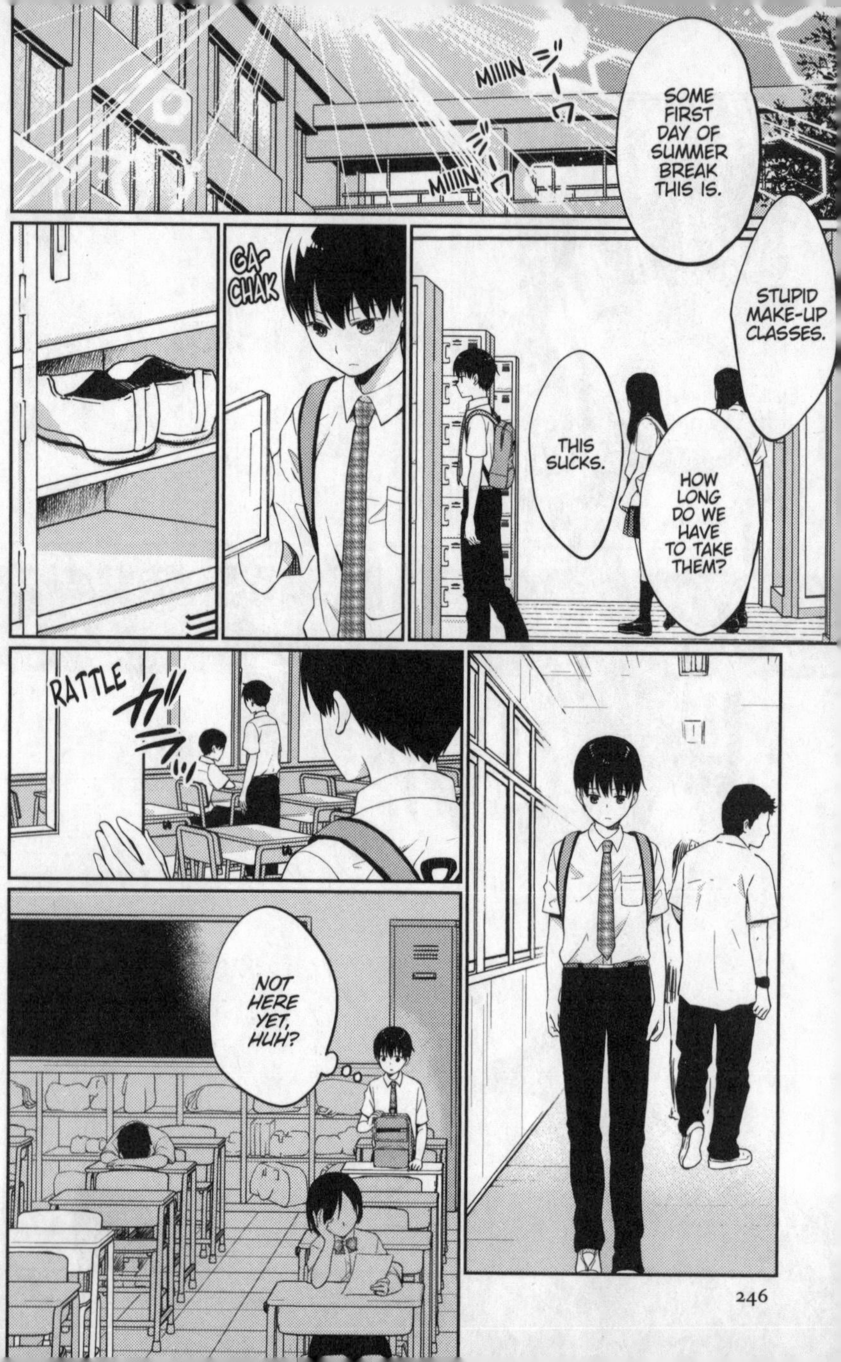
MIIIN
MIIIN
SOME FIRST DAY OF SUMMER BREAK THIS IS.
STUPID MAKE-UP CLASSES.
HOW LONG DO WE HAVE TO TAKE THEM?
THIS SUCKS.
GA-CHAK
RATTLE
NOT HERE YET, HUH?

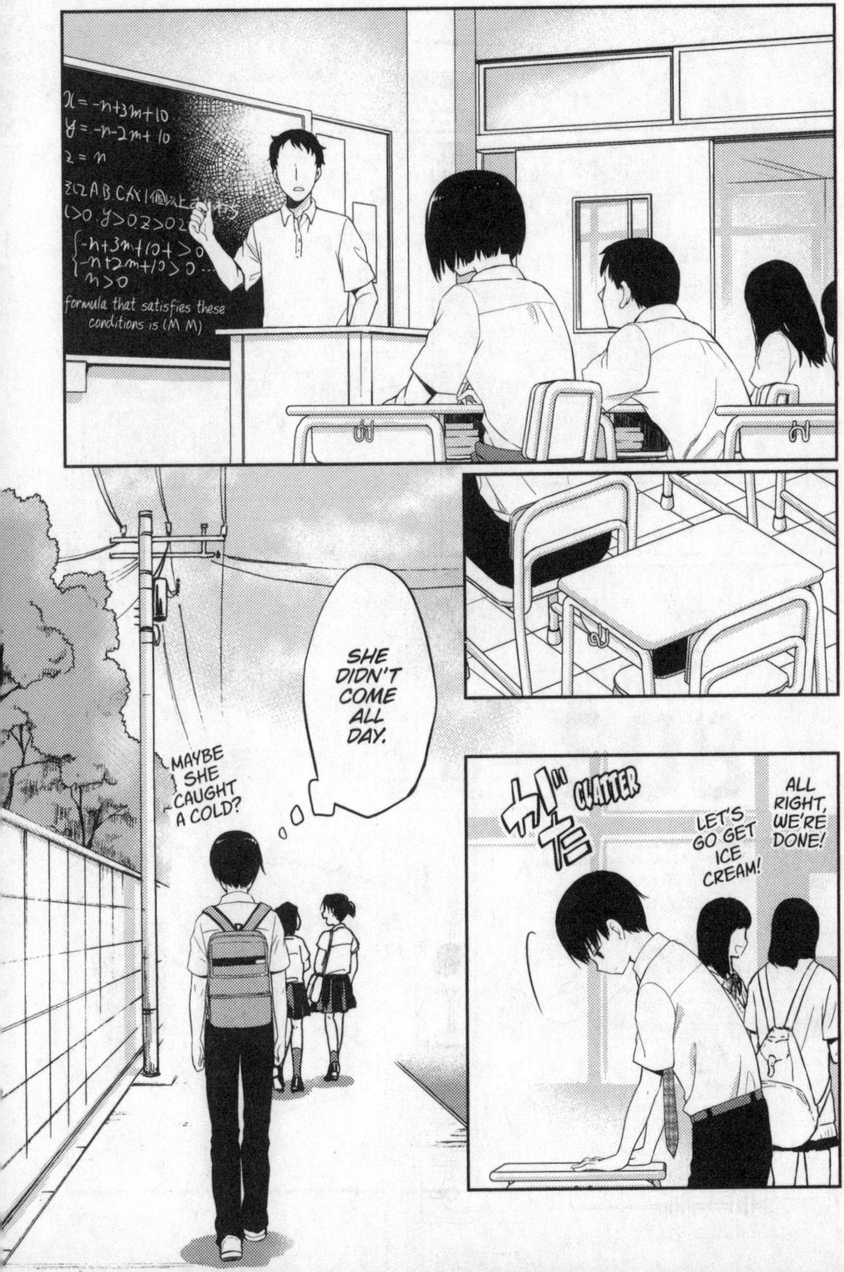
x = -n+3m+10
y = -n-2m+10
z = n
formula that satisfies these conditions is (M M)
ALL RIGHT, WE'RE DONE!
LET'S GO GET ICE CREAM!
CLATTER
SHE DIDN'T COME ALL DAY.
MAYBE SHE CAUGHT A COLD?

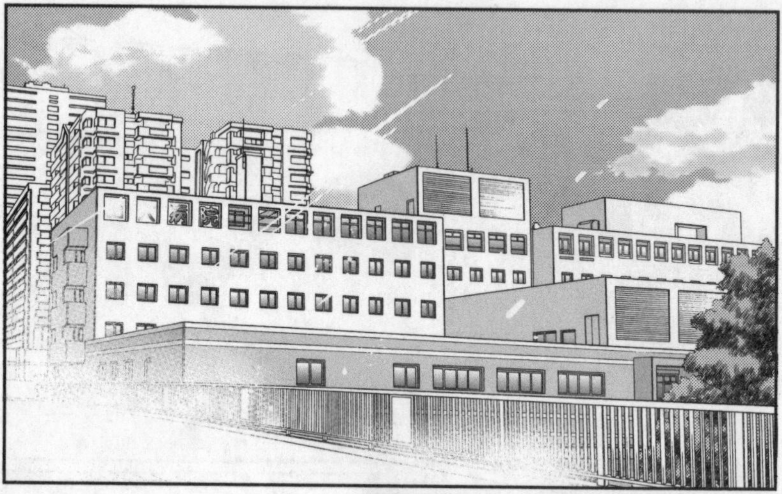
病院

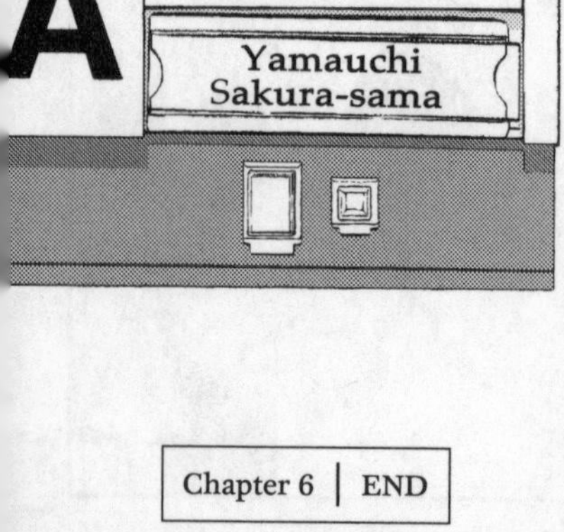
A 803
Yamauchi
Sakura-sama

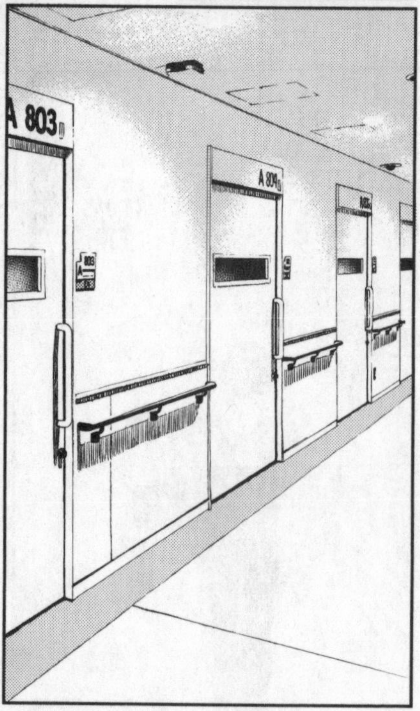
A 803

Chapter 6 | END

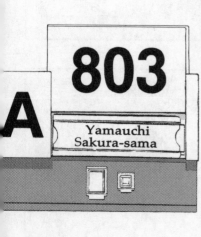

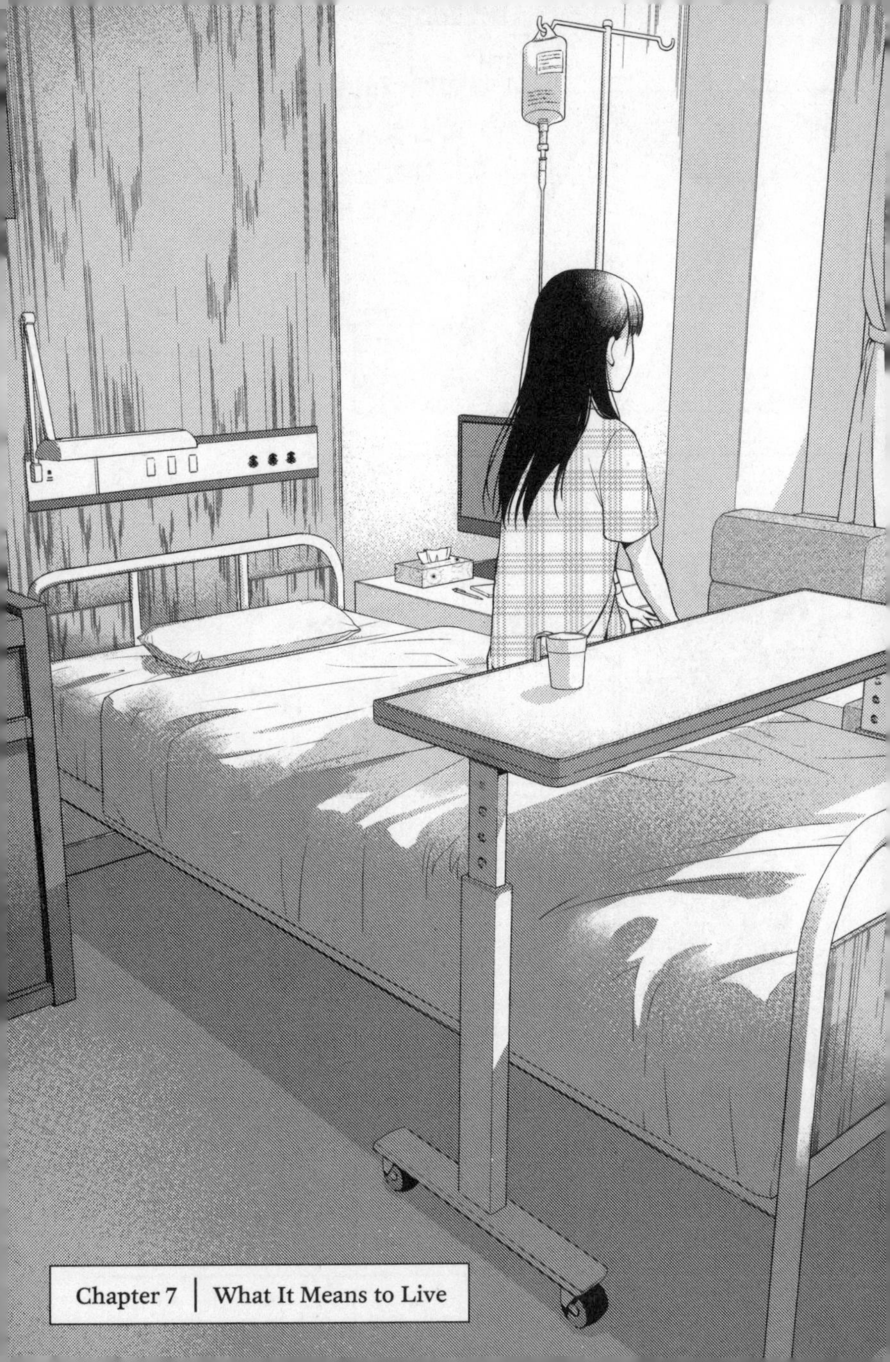

Chapter 7 | What It Means to Live

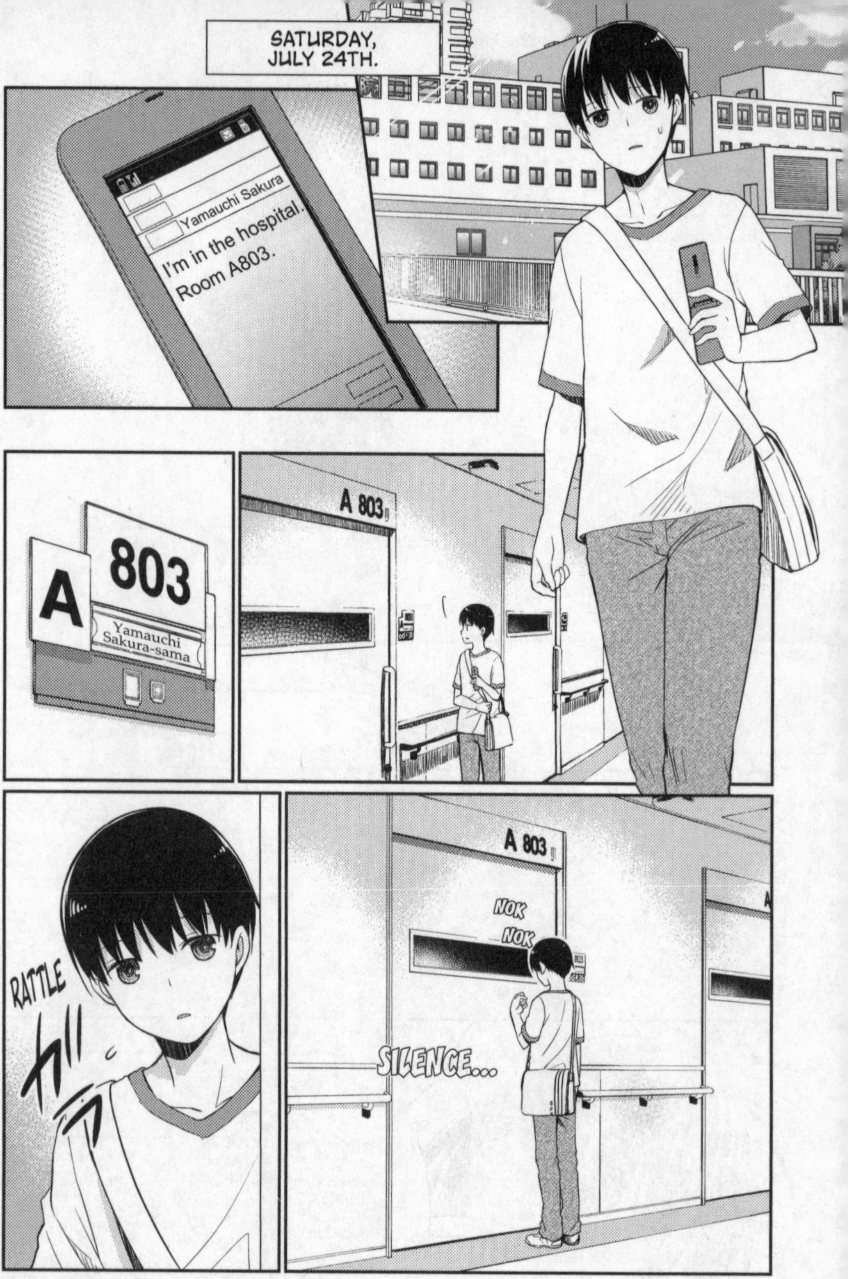
SATURDAY, JULY 24TH.
Yamauchi Sakura
I'm in the hospital. Room A803.
A 803
Yamauchi Sakura-sama
A 803
A 803
NOK NOK
SILENCE...
RATTLE

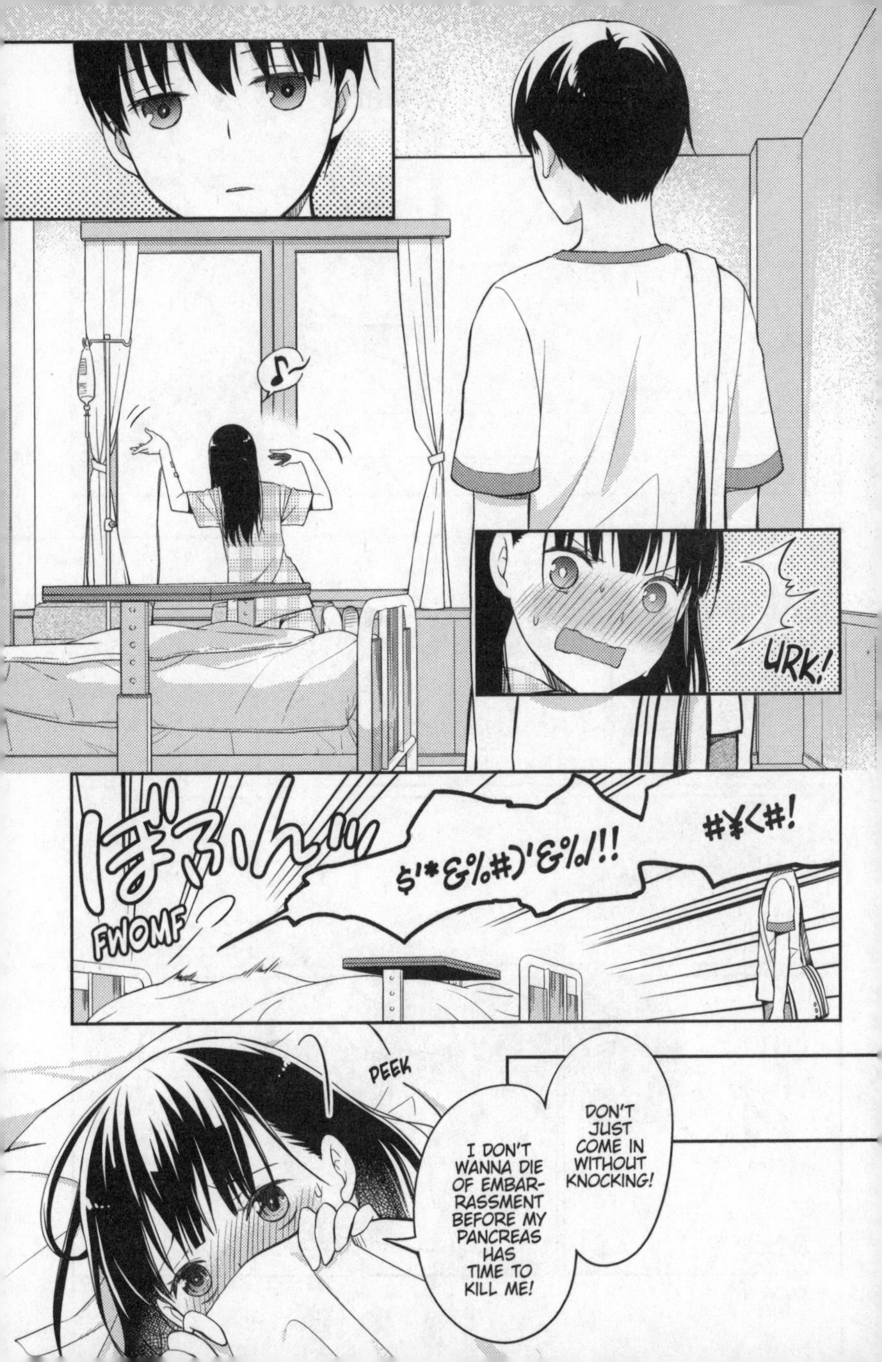
URK!
ぼふん…
FWOMF
$'*&%#)'&%!!
#¥<#!
PEEK
DON'T JUST COME IN WITHOUT KNOCKING!
I DON'T WANNA DIE OF EMBARRASSMENT BEFORE MY PANCREAS HAS TIME TO KILL ME!

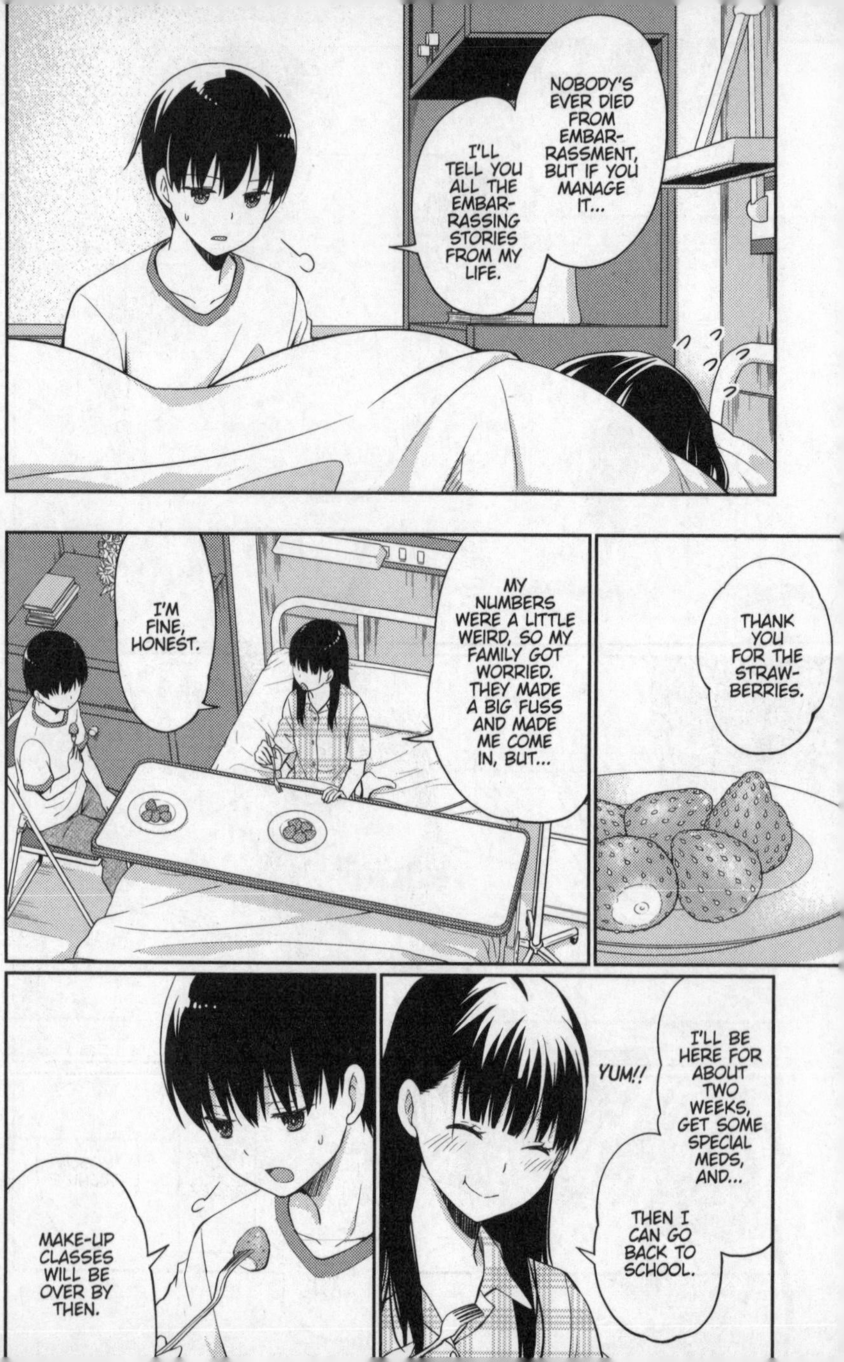
NOBODY'S EVER DIED FROM EMBARRASSMENT, BUT IF YOU MANAGE IT...
I'LL TELL YOU ALL THE EMBARRASSING STORIES FROM MY LIFE.
THANK YOU FOR THE STRAWBERRIES.
MY NUMBERS WERE A LITTLE WEIRD, SO MY FAMILY GOT WORRIED. THEY MADE A BIG FUSS AND MADE ME COME IN, BUT...
I'M FINE, HONEST.
YUM!!
I'LL BE HERE FOR ABOUT TWO WEEKS, GET SOME SPECIAL MEDS, AND...
THEN I CAN GO BACK TO SCHOOL.
MAKE-UP CLASSES WILL BE OVER BY THEN.

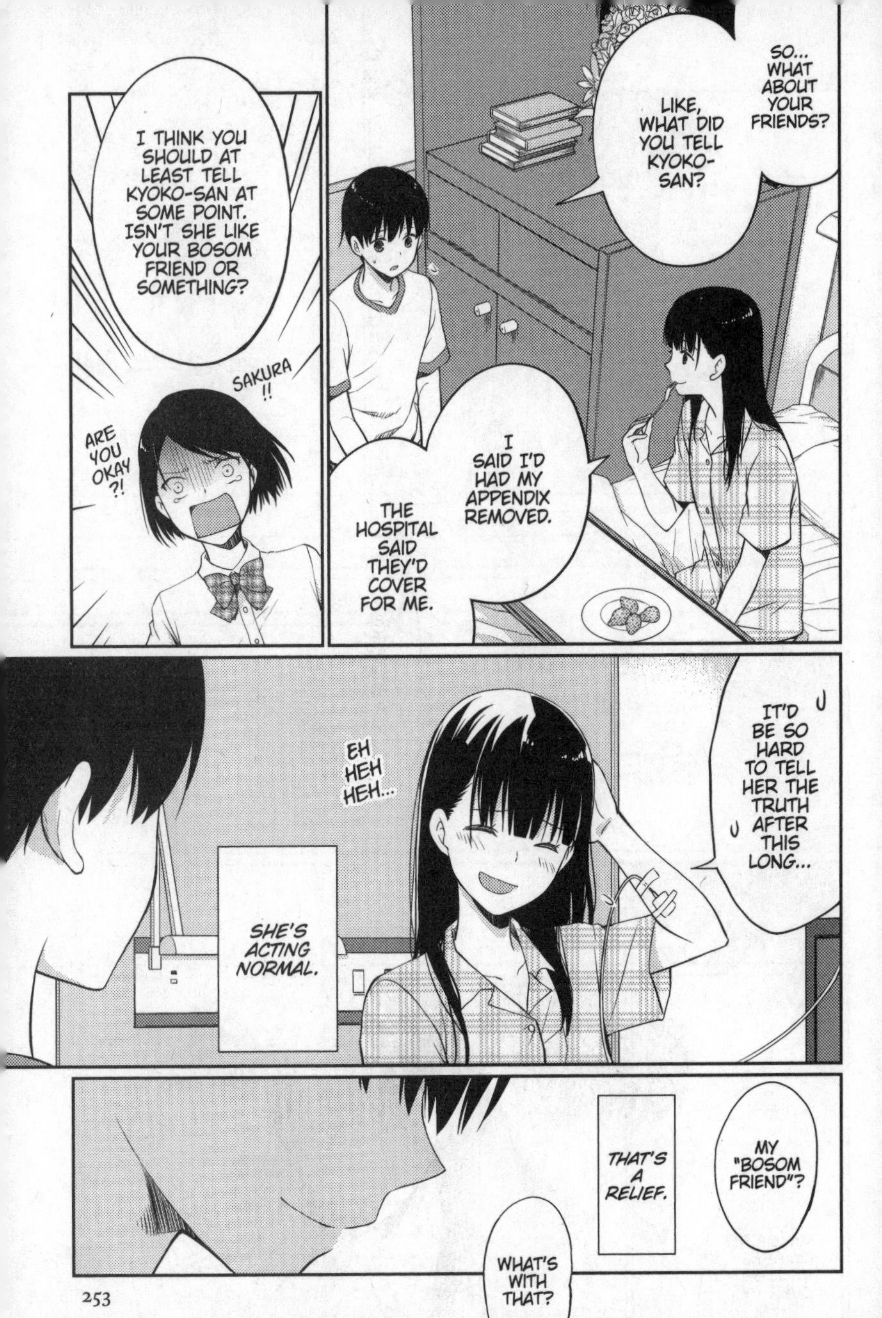
SO... WHAT ABOUT YOUR FRIENDS?
LIKE, WHAT DID YOU TELL KYOKO-SAN?
I SAID I'D HAD MY APPENDIX REMOVED.
THE HOSPITAL SAID THEY'D COVER FOR ME.
I THINK YOU SHOULD AT LEAST TELL KYOKO-SAN AT SOME POINT. ISN'T SHE LIKE YOUR BOSOM FRIEND OR SOMETHING?
SAKURA!!
ARE YOU OKAY?!
IT'D BE SO HARD TO TELL HER THE TRUTH AFTER THIS LONG...
EH HEH HEH...
SHE'S ACTING NORMAL.
MY "BOSOM FRIEND"?
THAT'S A RELIEF.
WHAT'S WITH THAT?

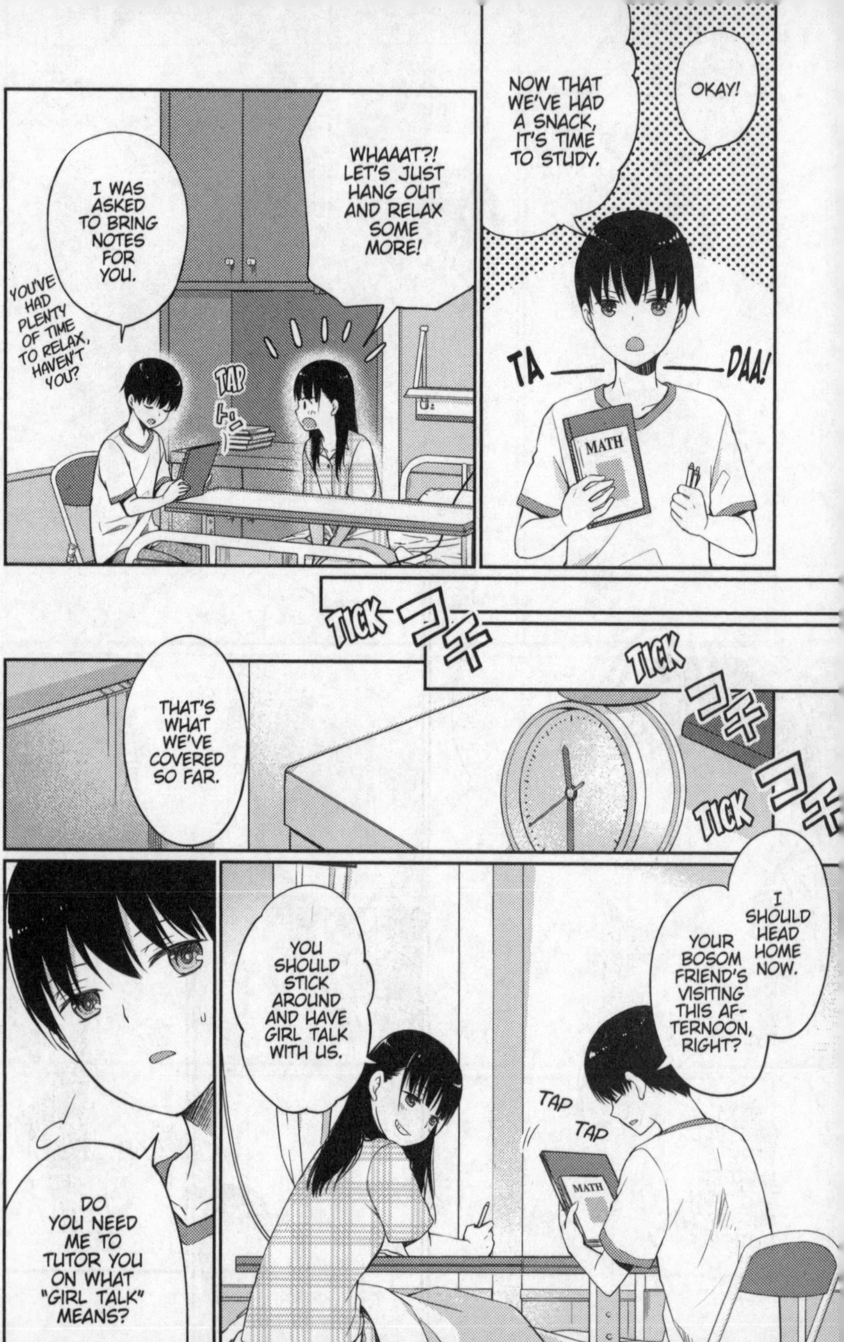
OKAY!
NOW THAT WE'VE HAD A SNACK, IT'S TIME TO STUDY.
TA—— ——DAA!
MATH
WHAAAT?! LET'S JUST HANG OUT AND RELAX SOME MORE!
I WAS ASKED TO BRING NOTES FOR YOU.
YOU'VE HAD PLENTY OF TIME TO RELAX, HAVEN'T YOU?
TAP
TICK コチ
TICK コチ
TICK コチ
THAT'S WHAT WE'VE COVERED SO FAR.
I SHOULD HEAD HOME NOW.
YOUR BOSOM FRIEND'S VISITING THIS AFTERNOON, RIGHT?
TAP
TAP
MATH
YOU SHOULD STICK AROUND AND HAVE GIRL TALK WITH US.
DO YOU NEED ME TO TUTOR YOU ON WHAT "GIRL TALK" MEANS?

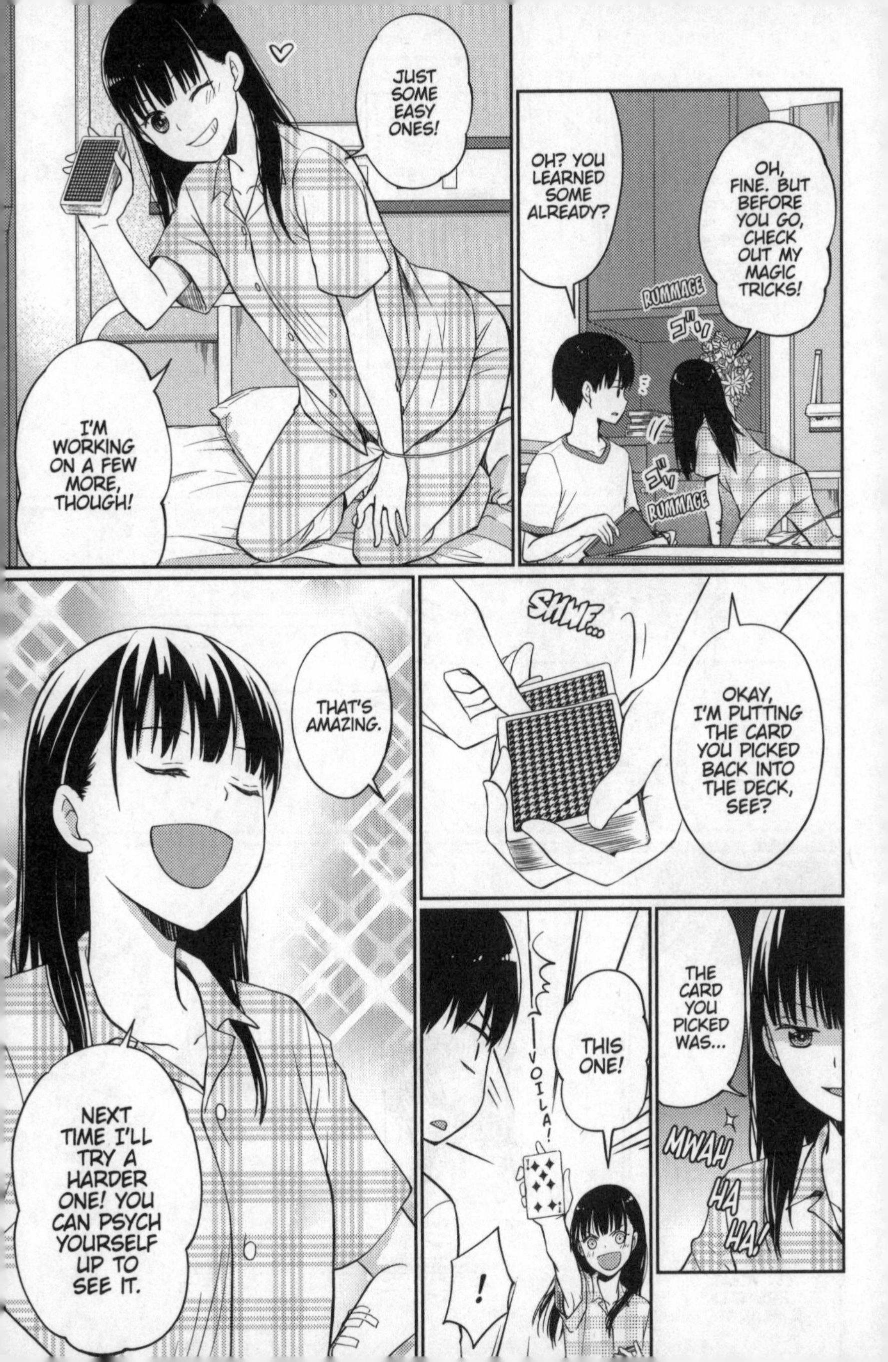
OH, FINE. BUT BEFORE YOU GO, CHECK OUT MY MAGIC TRICKS!
RUMMAGE
RUMMAGE
OH? YOU LEARNED SOME ALREADY?
JUST SOME EASY ONES!
I'M WORKING ON A FEW MORE, THOUGH!
SHWF...
OKAY, I'M PUTTING THE CARD YOU PICKED BACK INTO THE DECK, SEE?
THE CARD YOU PICKED WAS...
MWAH HA HA!
THIS ONE!
VOILA!
!
THAT'S AMAZING.
NEXT TIME I'LL TRY A HARDER ONE! YOU CAN PSYCH YOURSELF UP TO SEE IT.

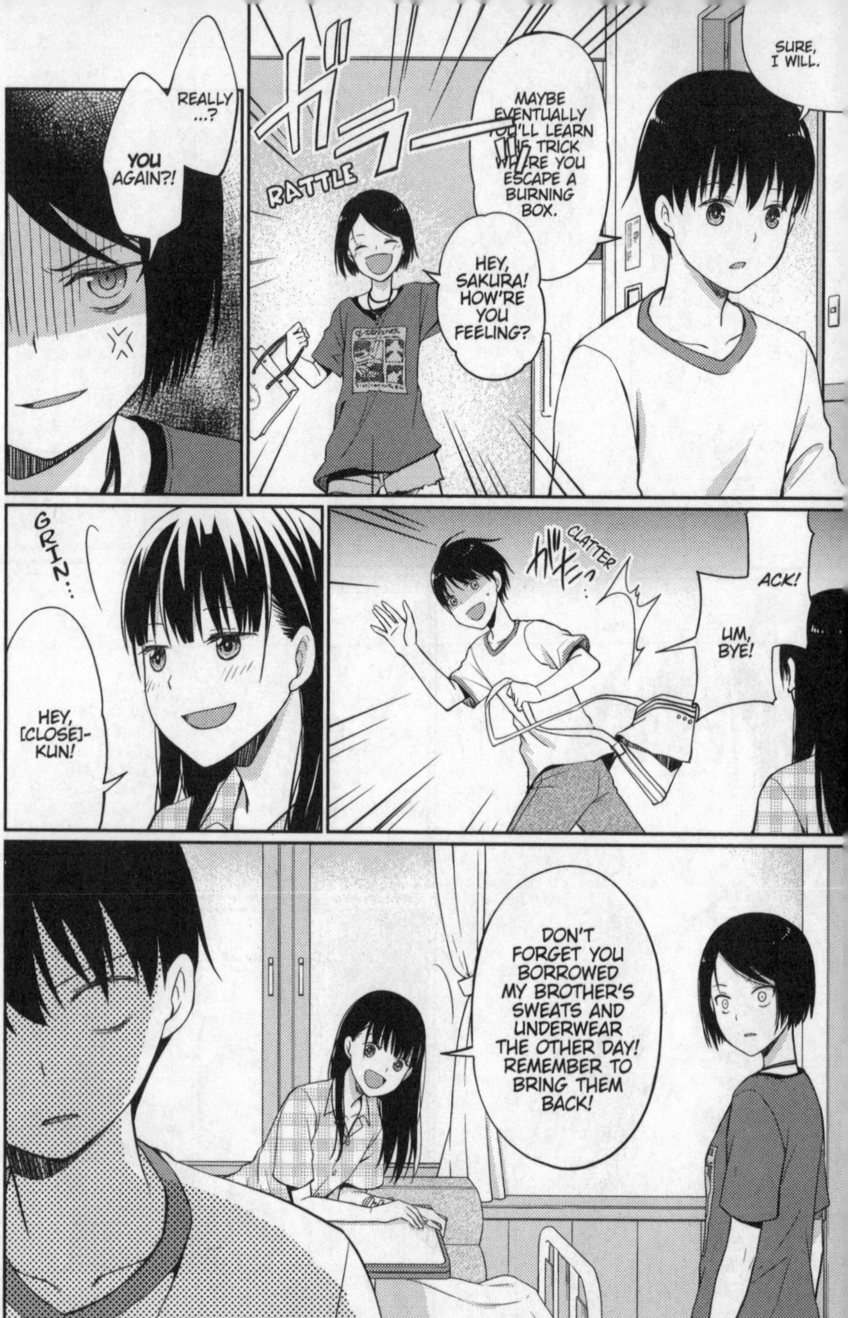
SURE, I WILL.
MAYBE EVENTUALLY YOU'LL LEARN THE TRICK WHERE YOU ESCAPE A BURNING BOX.
RATTLE
HEY, SAKURA! HOW'RE YOU FEELING?
REALLY ...?
YOU AGAIN?!
ACK!
UM, BYE!
CLATTER
GRIN...
HEY, [CLOSE]-KUN!
DON'T FORGET YOU BORROWED MY BROTHER'S SWEATS AND UNDERWEAR THE OTHER DAY! REMEMBER TO BRING THEM BACK!

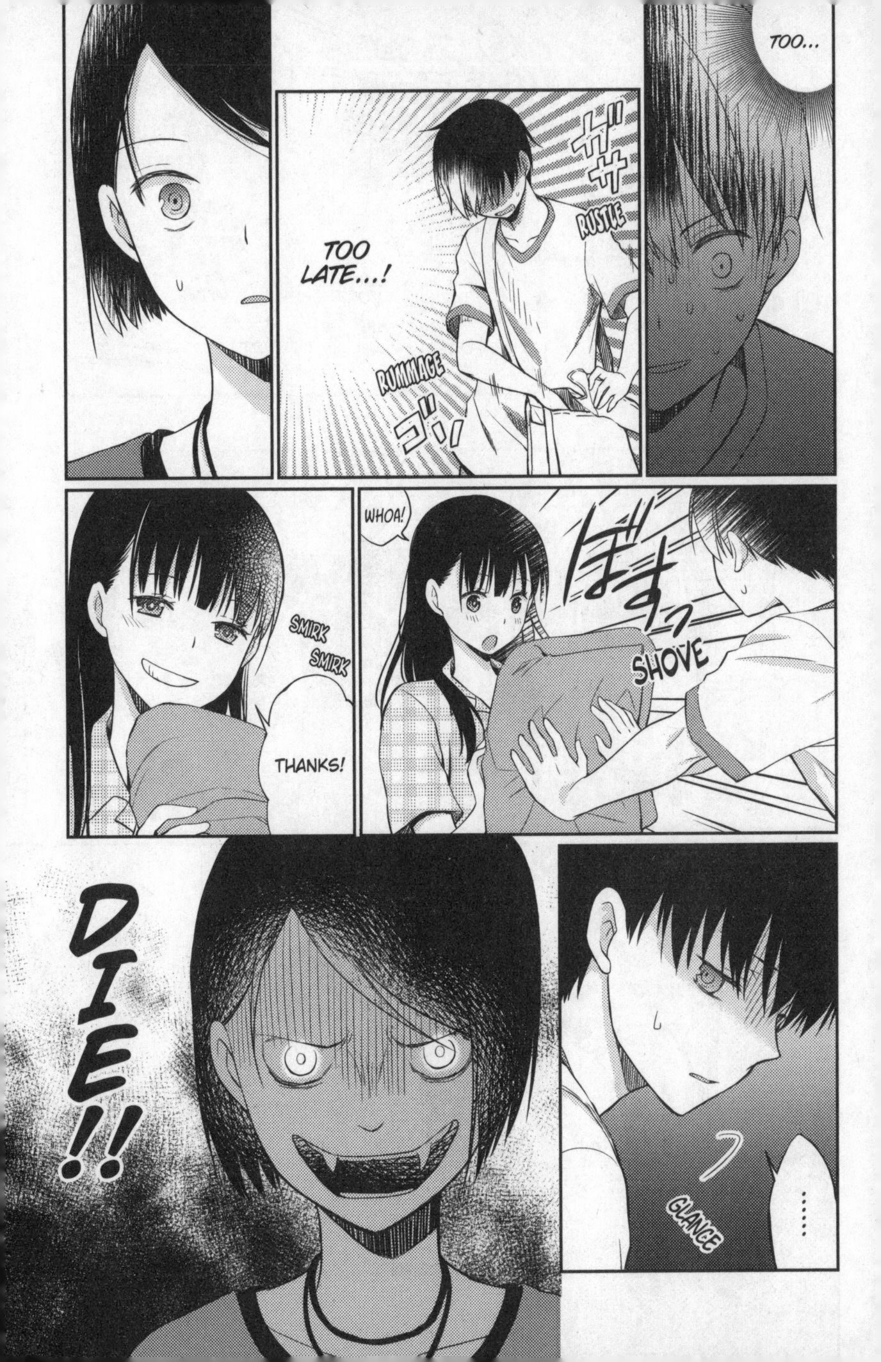
TOO...
ガサ
RUSTLE
TOO LATE...!
RUMMAGE
ゴソ
ぼすっ
SHOVE
WHOA!
SMIRK
SMIRK
THANKS!
GLANCE
......
DIE!!

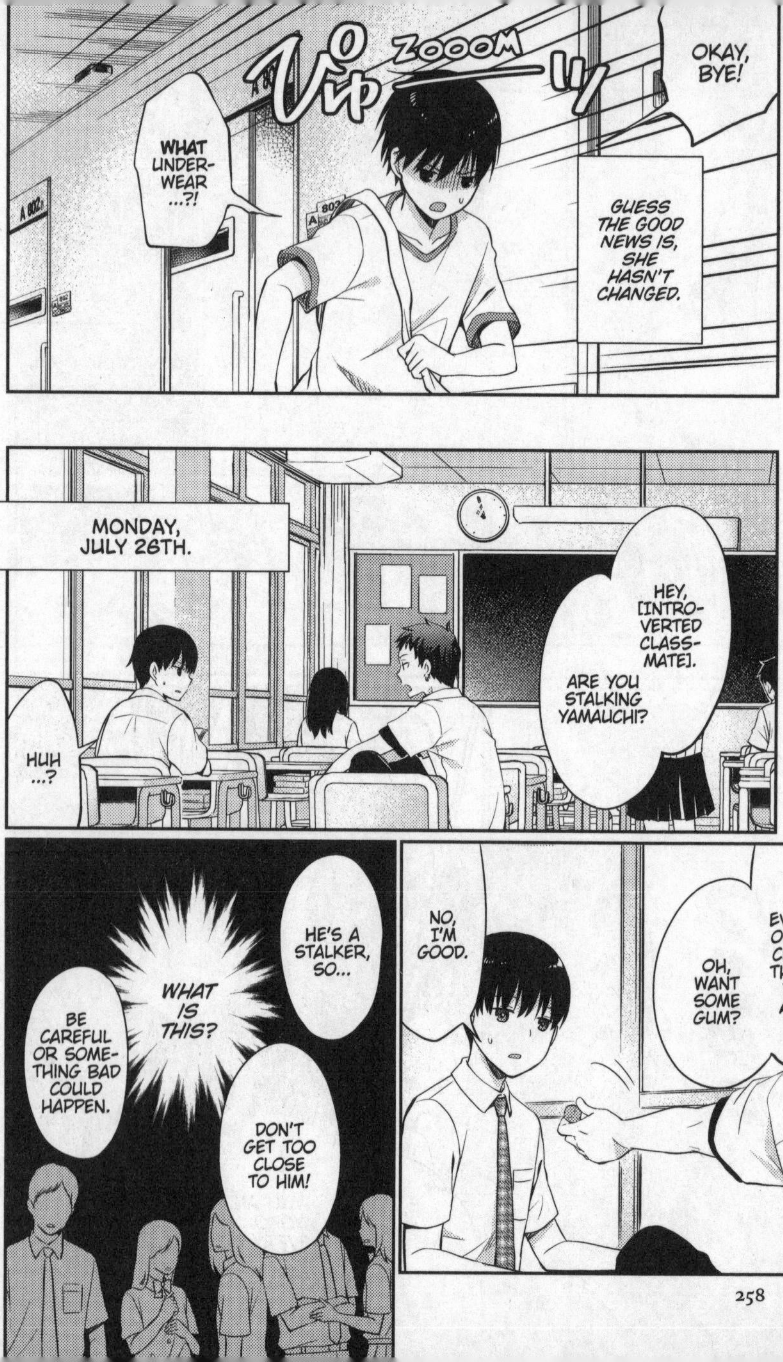
OKAY, BYE!
ZOOOM
WHAT UNDER-WEAR ...?!
GUESS THE GOOD NEWS IS, SHE HASN'T CHANGED.
MONDAY, JULY 26TH.
HEY, [INTRO-VERTED CLASS-MATE].
ARE YOU STALKING YAMAUCHI?
HUH ...?
EVERY-ONE IN CLASS THINKS YOU ARE.
OH, WANT SOME GUM?
NO, I'M GOOD.
HE'S A STALKER, SO...
WHAT IS THIS?
BE CAREFUL OR SOME-THING BAD COULD HAPPEN.
DON'T GET TOO CLOSE TO HIM!

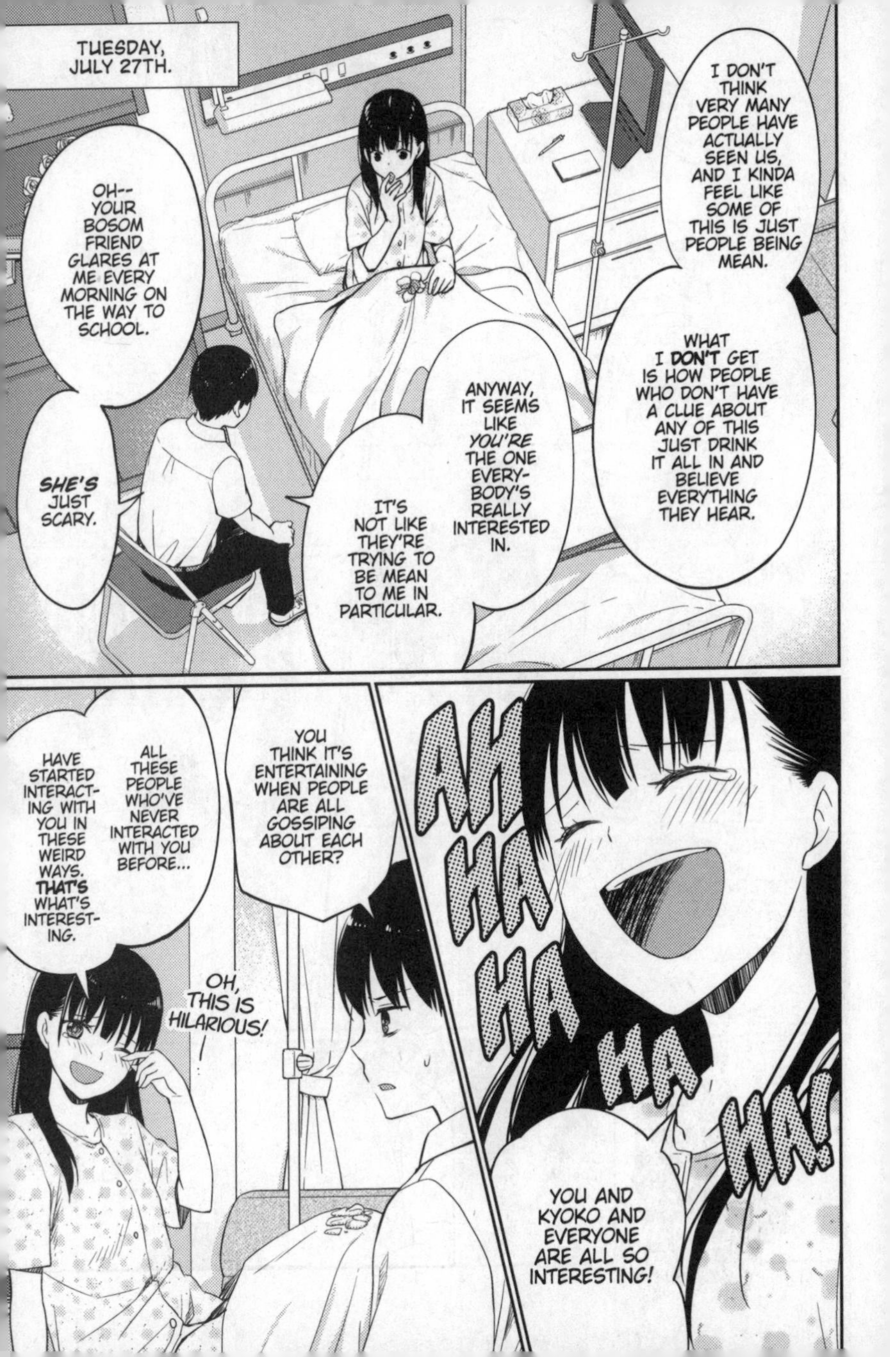
TUESDAY, JULY 27TH.
I DON'T THINK VERY MANY PEOPLE HAVE ACTUALLY SEEN US, AND I KINDA FEEL LIKE SOME OF THIS IS JUST PEOPLE BEING MEAN.
WHAT I **DON'T** GET IS HOW PEOPLE WHO DON'T HAVE A CLUE ABOUT ANY OF THIS JUST DRINK IT ALL IN AND BELIEVE EVERYTHING THEY HEAR.
ANYWAY, IT SEEMS LIKE *YOU'RE* THE ONE EVERYBODY'S REALLY INTERESTED IN.
IT'S NOT LIKE THEY'RE TRYING TO BE MEAN TO ME IN PARTICULAR.
OH-- YOUR BOSOM FRIEND GLARES AT ME EVERY MORNING ON THE WAY TO SCHOOL.
SHE'S JUST SCARY.
AH HA HA HA HA!
YOU AND KYOKO AND EVERYONE ARE ALL SO INTERESTING!
YOU THINK IT'S ENTERTAINING WHEN PEOPLE ARE ALL GOSSIPING ABOUT EACH OTHER?
ALL THESE PEOPLE WHO'VE NEVER INTERACTED WITH YOU BEFORE...
HAVE STARTED INTERACTING WITH YOU IN THESE WEIRD WAYS. **THAT'S** WHAT'S INTERESTING.
OH, THIS IS HILARIOUS!

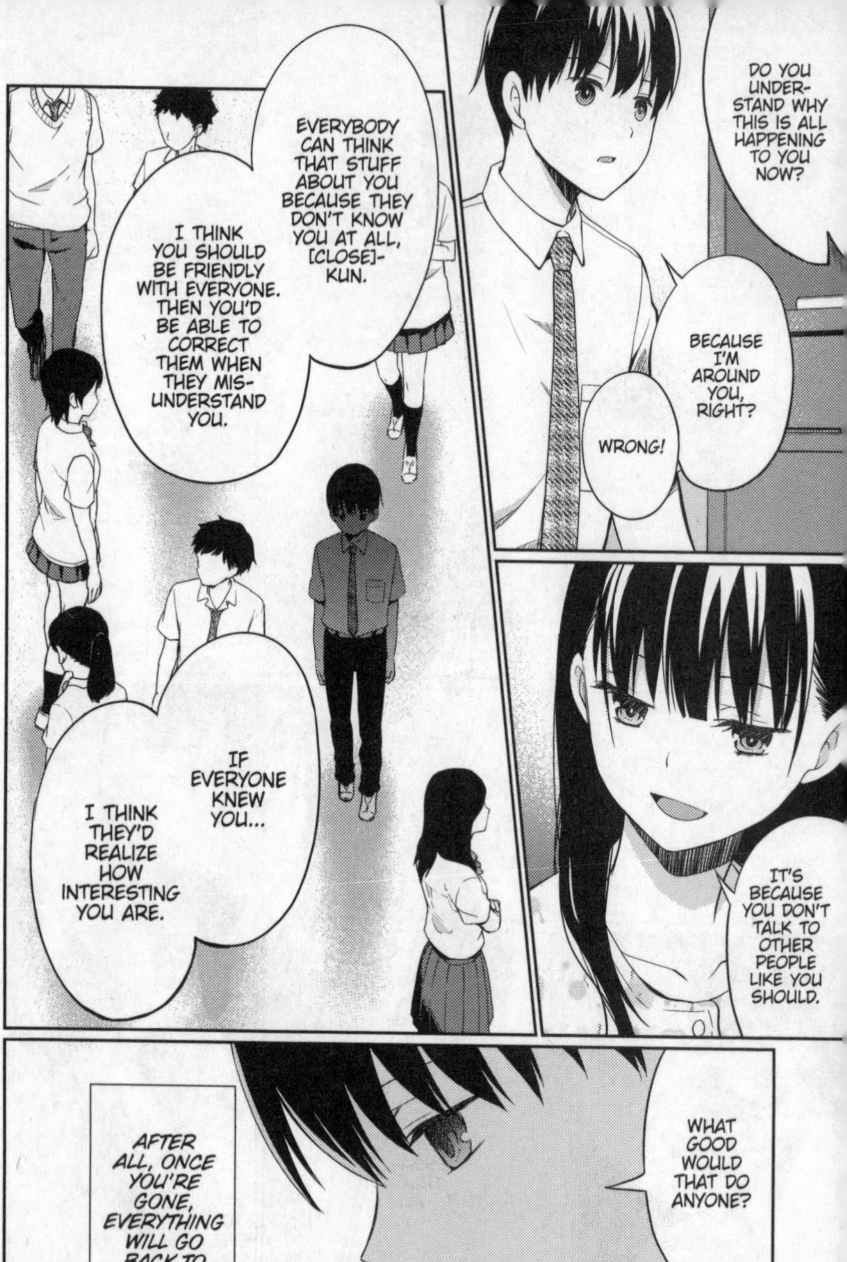
DO YOU UNDERSTAND WHY THIS IS ALL HAPPENING TO YOU NOW?
BECAUSE I'M AROUND YOU, RIGHT?
WRONG!
IT'S BECAUSE YOU DON'T TALK TO OTHER PEOPLE LIKE YOU SHOULD.
EVERYBODY CAN THINK THAT STUFF ABOUT YOU BECAUSE THEY DON'T KNOW YOU AT ALL, [CLOSE]-KUN.
I THINK YOU SHOULD BE FRIENDLY WITH EVERYONE. THEN YOU'D BE ABLE TO CORRECT THEM WHEN THEY MIS-UNDERSTAND YOU.
IF EVERYONE KNEW YOU...
I THINK THEY'D REALIZE HOW INTERESTING YOU ARE.
WHAT GOOD WOULD THAT DO ANYONE?
AFTER ALL, ONCE YOU'RE GONE, EVERYTHING WILL GO BACK TO NORMAL.

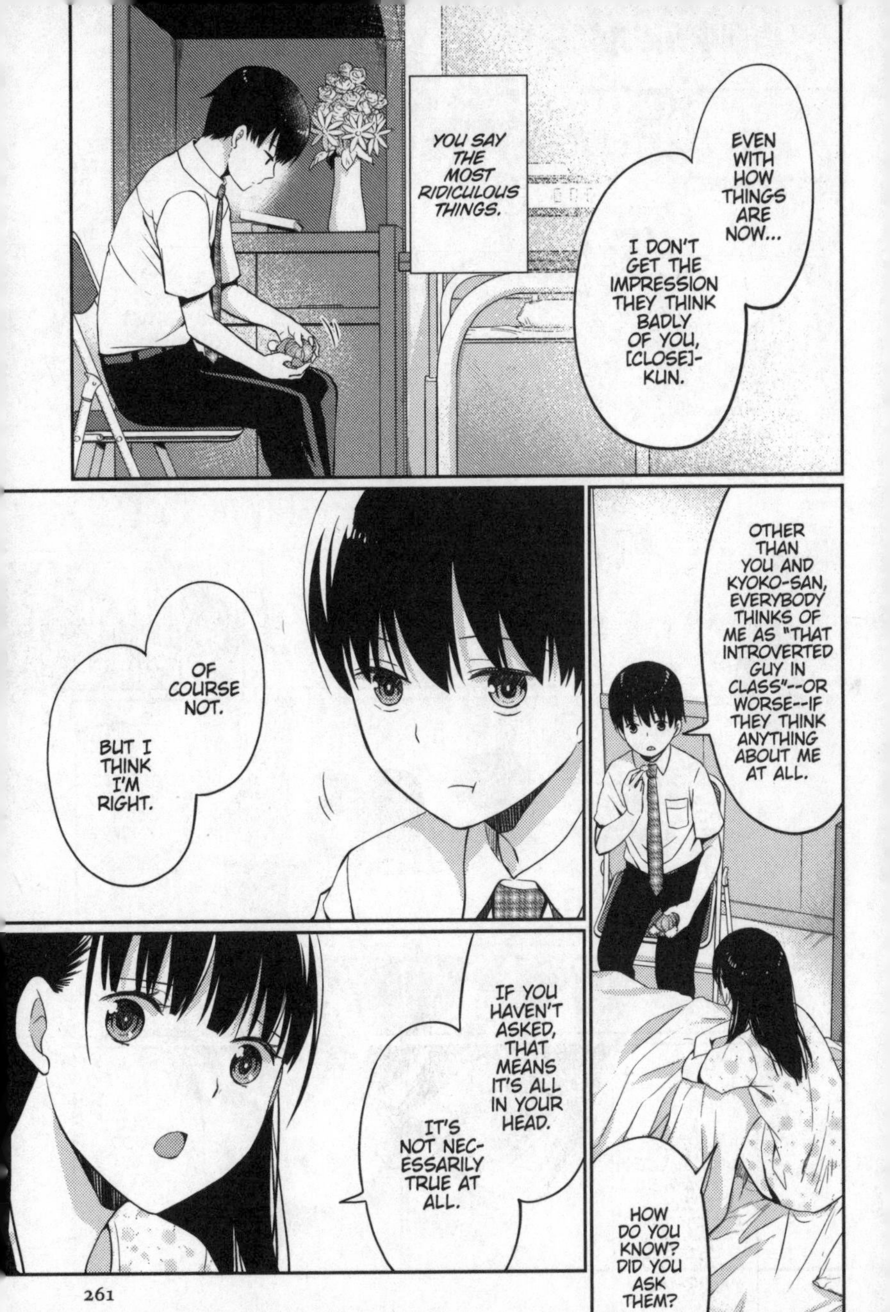
EVEN WITH HOW THINGS ARE NOW...
I DON'T GET THE IMPRESSION THEY THINK BADLY OF YOU, [CLOSE]-KUN.
YOU SAY THE MOST RIDICULOUS THINGS.
OTHER THAN YOU AND KYOKO-SAN, EVERYBODY THINKS OF ME AS "THAT INTROVERTED GUY IN CLASS"--OR WORSE--IF THEY THINK ANYTHING ABOUT ME AT ALL.
OF COURSE NOT.
BUT I THINK I'M RIGHT.
HOW DO YOU KNOW? DID YOU ASK THEM?
IF YOU HAVEN'T ASKED, THAT MEANS IT'S ALL IN YOUR HEAD.
IT'S NOT NEC-ESSARILY TRUE AT ALL.

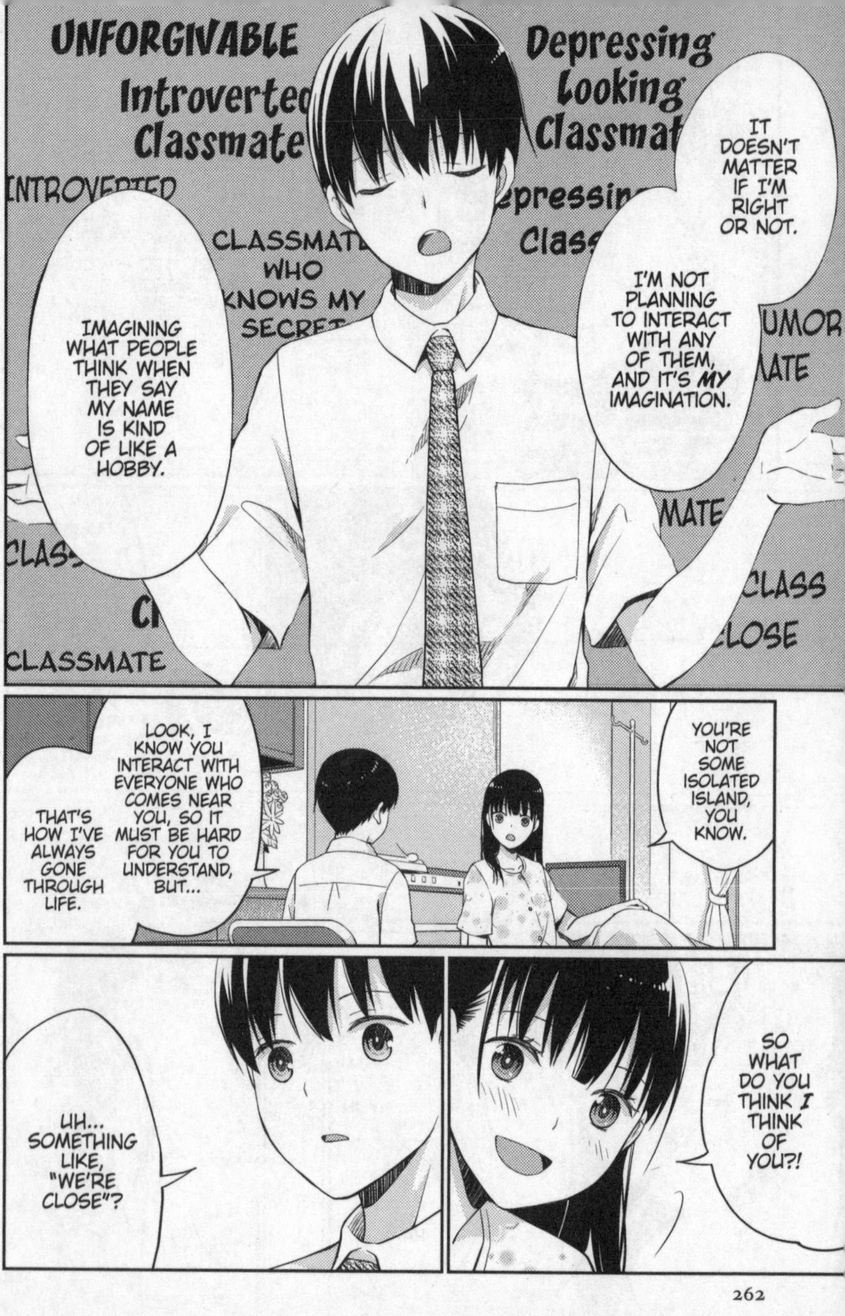
UNFORGIVABLE
Depressing Looking
Classmate
CLASSMATE
IT DOESN'T MATTER IF I'M RIGHT OR NOT.
I'M NOT PLANNING TO INTERACT WITH ANY OF THEM, AND IT'S *MY* IMAGINATION.
IMAGINING WHAT PEOPLE THINK WHEN THEY SAY MY NAME IS KIND OF LIKE A HOBBY.
YOU'RE NOT SOME ISOLATED ISLAND, YOU KNOW.
LOOK, I KNOW YOU INTERACT WITH EVERYONE WHO COMES NEAR YOU, SO IT MUST BE HARD FOR YOU TO UNDERSTAND, BUT...
THAT'S HOW I'VE ALWAYS GONE THROUGH LIFE.
SO WHAT DO YOU THINK *I* THINK OF YOU?!
UH... SOMETHING LIKE, "WE'RE CLOSE"?

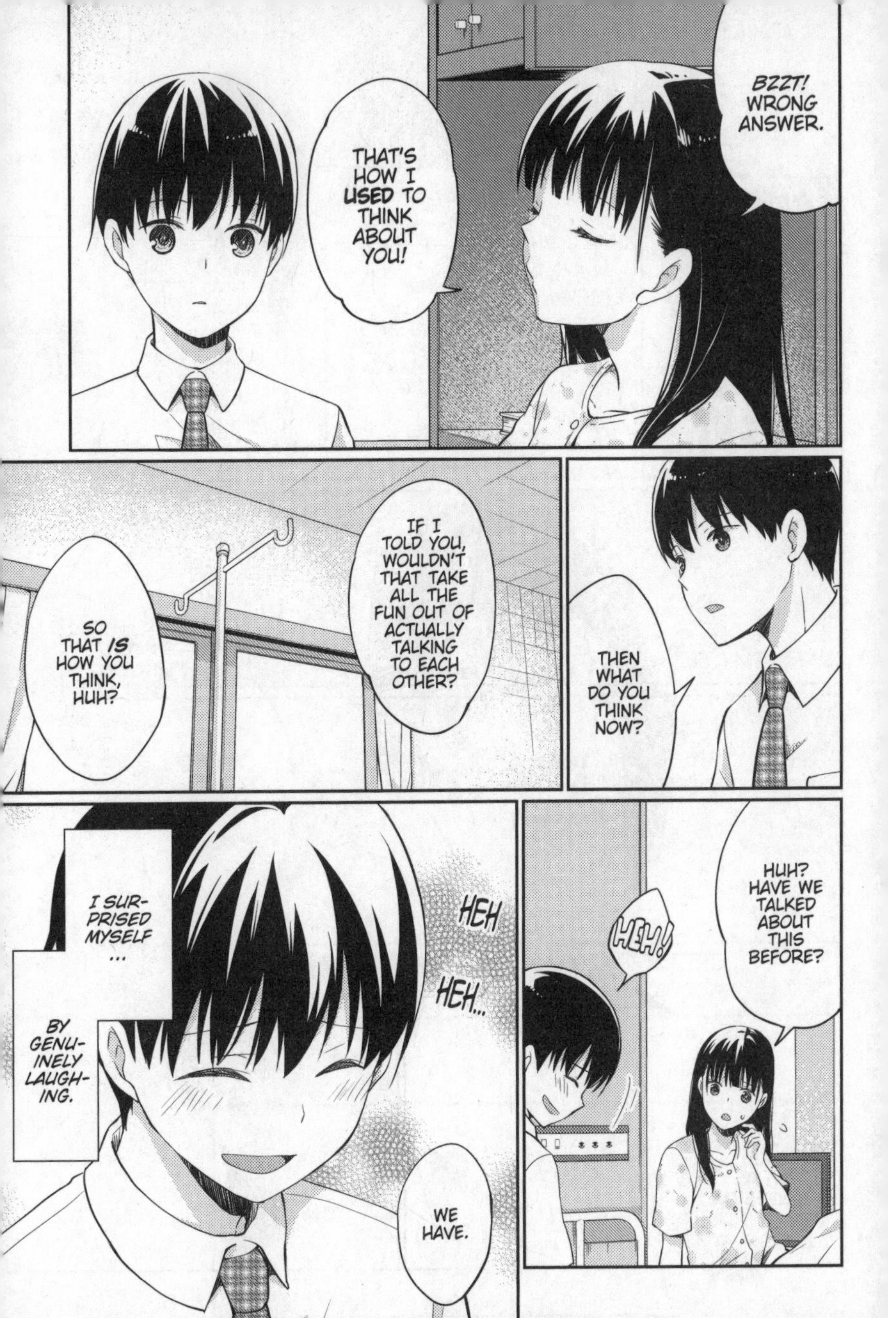

BZZT! WRONG ANSWER.
THAT'S HOW I USED TO THINK ABOUT YOU!
THEN WHAT DO YOU THINK NOW?
IF I TOLD YOU, WOULDN'T THAT TAKE ALL THE FUN OUT OF ACTUALLY TALKING TO EACH OTHER?
SO THAT IS HOW YOU THINK, HUH?
HUH? HAVE WE TALKED ABOUT THIS BEFORE?
HEH!
WE HAVE.
HEH
HEH...
I SUR-PRISED MYSELF ...
BY GENU-INELY LAUGH-ING.

BEFORE I HAD ANY IDEA IT WAS HAPPENING...

SHE'D ALREADY CHANGED ME SO MUCH.

TEE HEE!...

I WANT TO TELL EVERYONE THAT...

[?????]-KUN IS A GENUINELY GOOD PERSON.

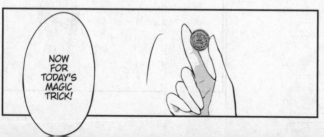

NOW FOR TODAY'S MAGIC TRICK!

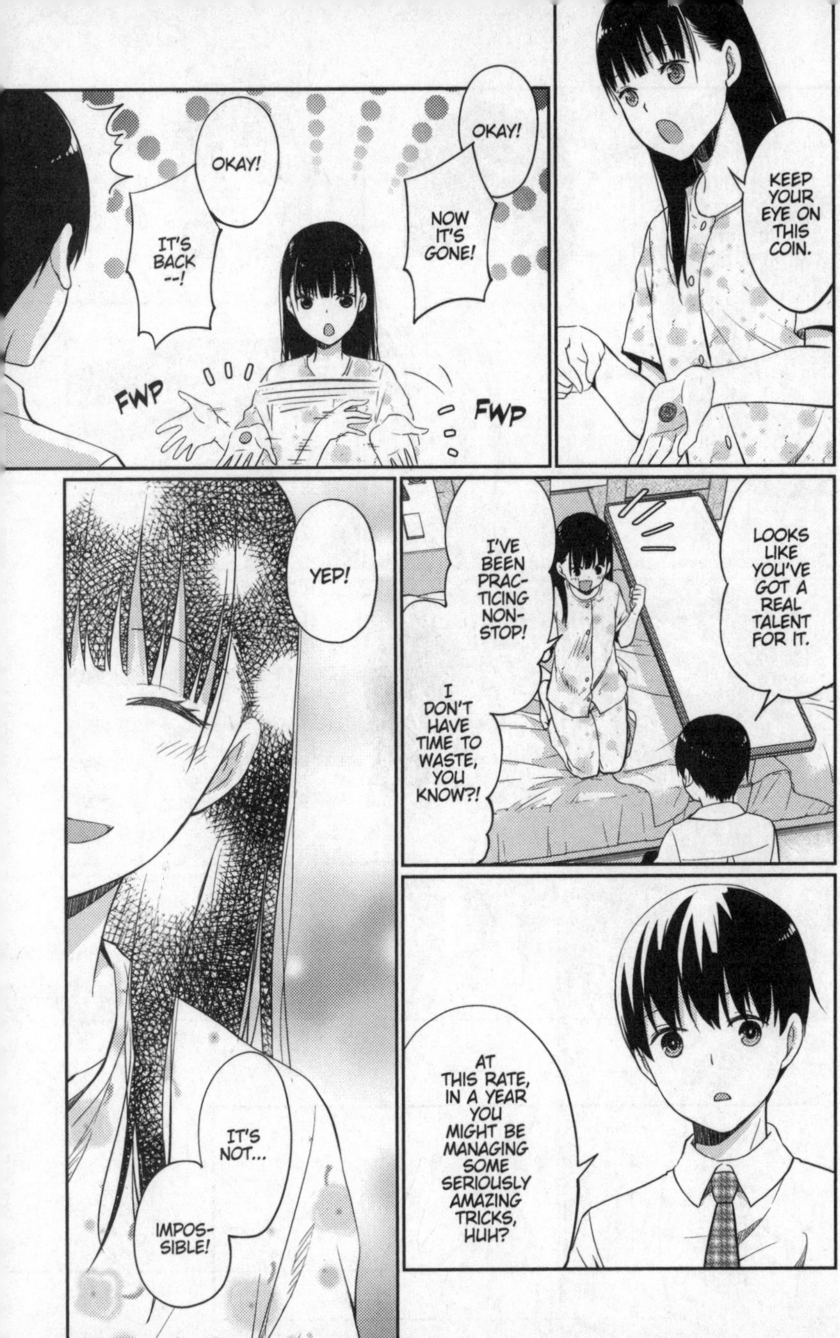
KEEP YOUR EYE ON THIS COIN.
OKAY!
NOW IT'S GONE!
OKAY!
IT'S BACK --!
FWP
FWP
LOOKS LIKE YOU'VE GOT A REAL TALENT FOR IT.
I'VE BEEN PRACTICING NON-STOP!
I DON'T HAVE TIME TO WASTE, YOU KNOW?!
YEP!
AT THIS RATE, IN A YEAR YOU MIGHT BE MANAGING SOME SERIOUSLY AMAZING TRICKS, HUH?
IT'S NOT...
IMPOSSIBLE!

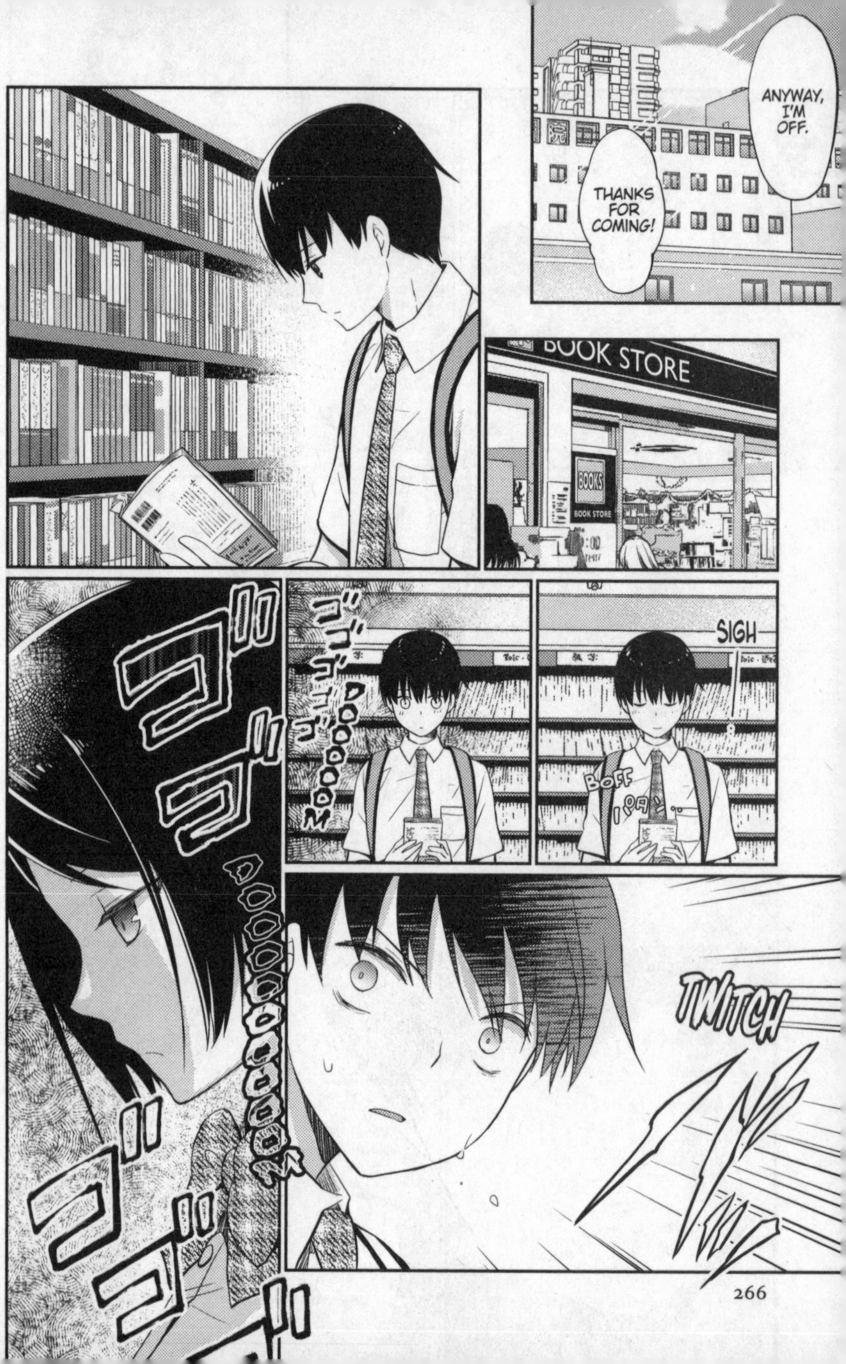
ANYWAY, I'M OFF.
THANKS FOR COMING!
BOOK STORE
BOOKS
BOOK STORE
SIGH
BOFF
DOOOOOOOOM
TWITCH

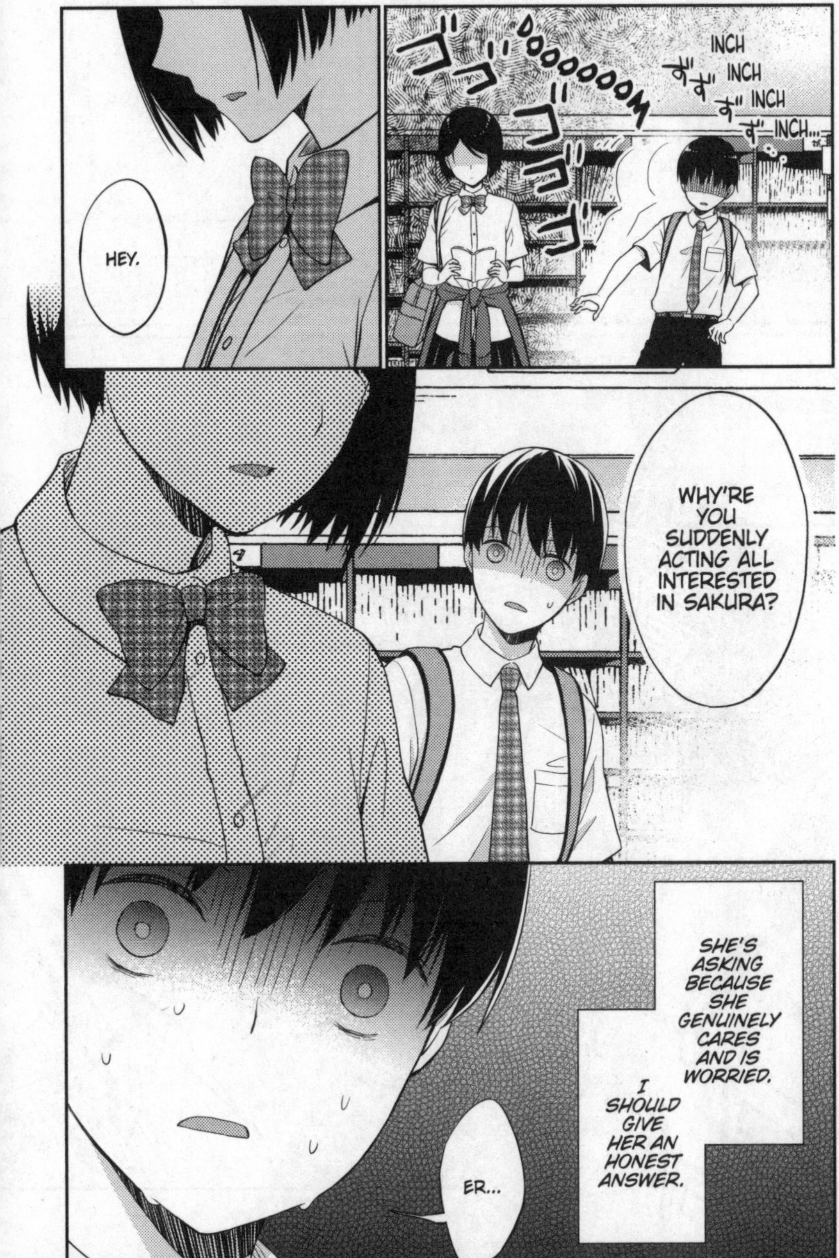
DOOOOOOOM
INCH INCH INCH INCH...
HEY.
WHY'RE YOU SUDDENLY ACTING ALL INTERESTED IN SAKURA?
SHE'S ASKING BECAUSE SHE GENUINELY CARES AND IS WORRIED.
I SHOULD GIVE HER AN HONEST ANSWER.
ER...

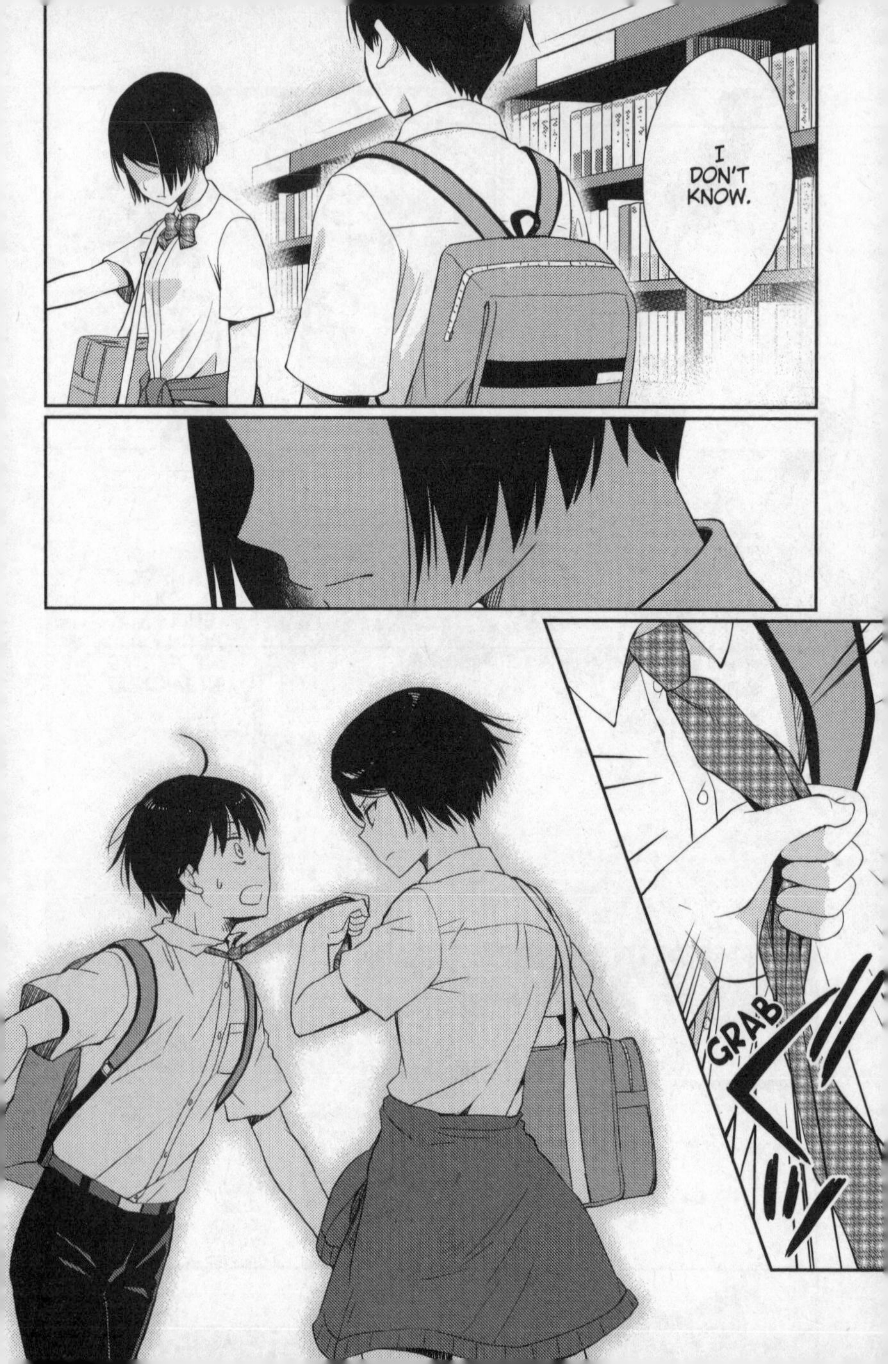
I DON'T KNOW.
GRAB

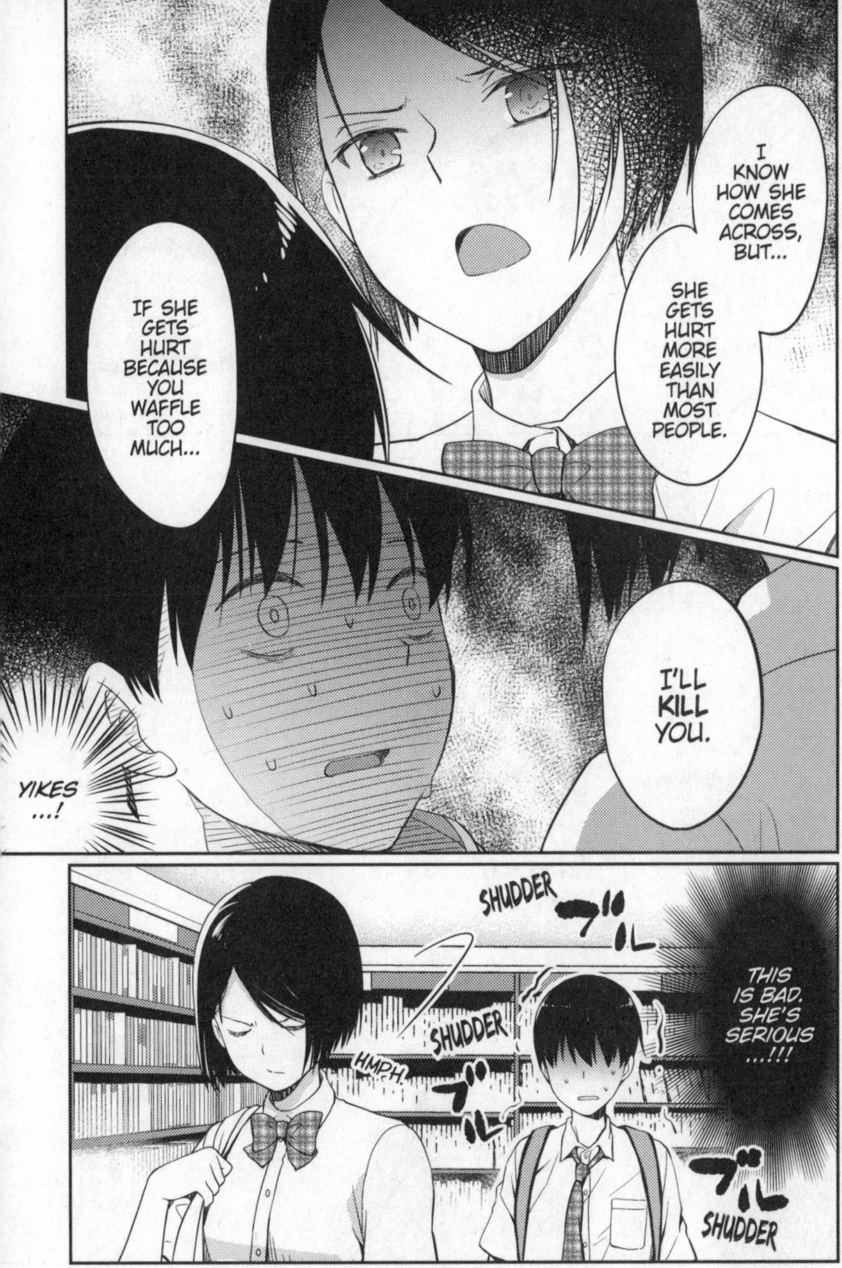
I KNOW HOW SHE COMES ACROSS, BUT...
SHE GETS HURT MORE EASILY THAN MOST PEOPLE.
IF SHE GETS HURT BECAUSE YOU WAFFLE TOO MUCH...
I'LL **KILL** YOU.
YIKES ...!
SHUDDER
ブル
THIS IS BAD. SHE'S SERIOUS ...!!!
SHUDDER
ブル
HMPH
ブル
SHUDDER

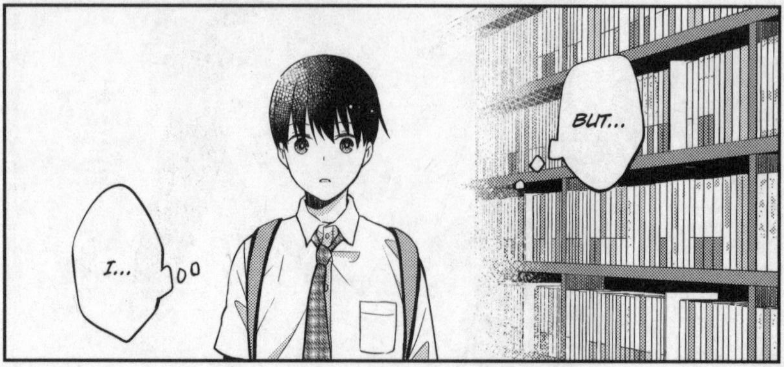
BUT...
I...

REALLY DON'T KNOW...

EXACTLY HOW I FEEL OR THINK ABOUT HER.

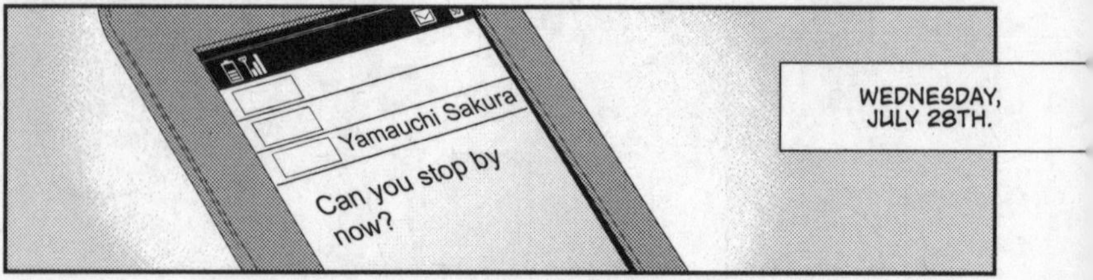
WEDNESDAY, JULY 28TH.
Yamauchi Sakura
Can you stop by now?

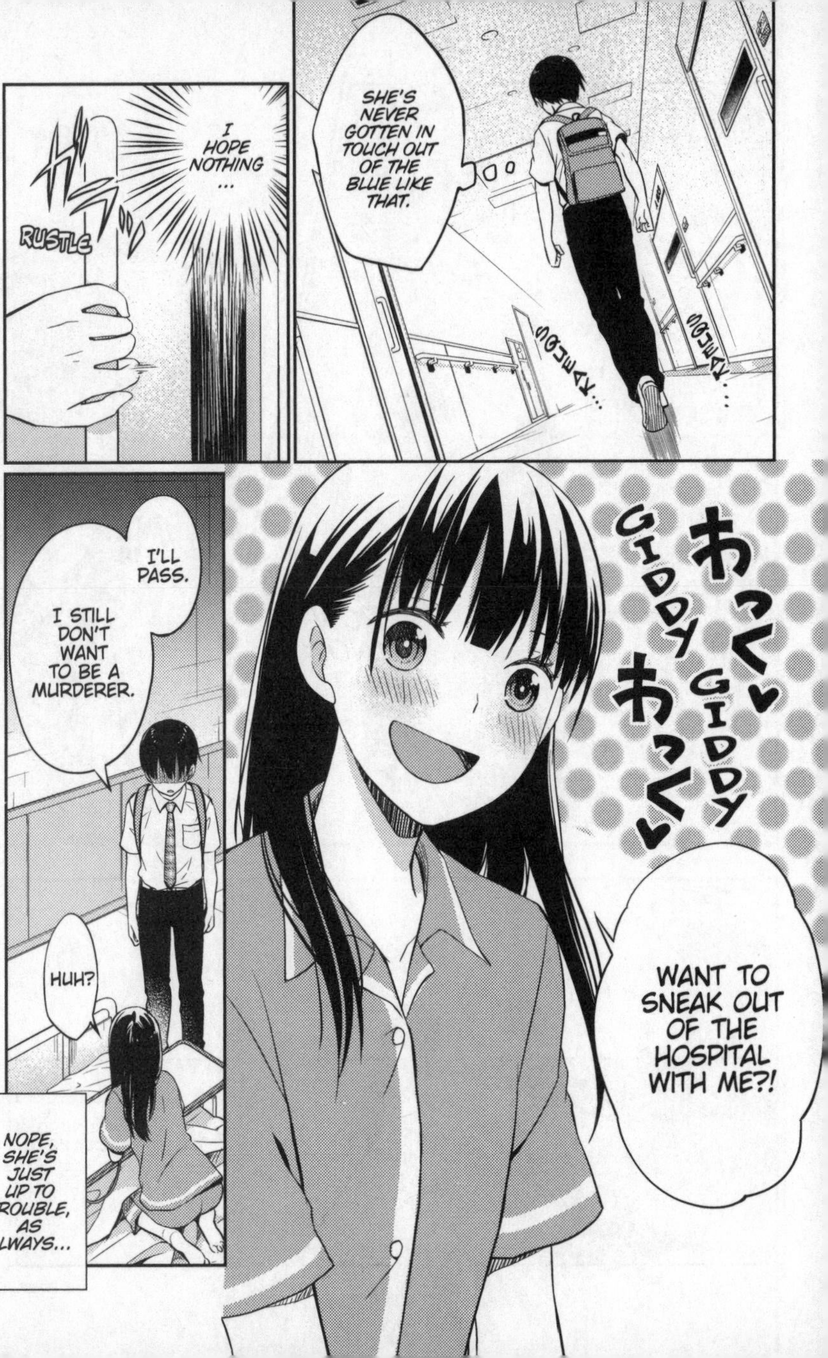

SHE'S NEVER GOTTEN IN TOUCH OUT OF THE BLUE LIKE THAT.
SQUEAK...
SQUEAK...
I HOPE NOTHING ...
RUSTLE
わっくわっく
GIDDY GIDDY
WANT TO SNEAK OUT OF THE HOSPITAL WITH ME?!
I'LL PASS.
I STILL DON'T WANT TO BE A MURDERER.
HUH?
NOPE, SHE'S JUST UP TO TROUBLE, AS ALWAYS...

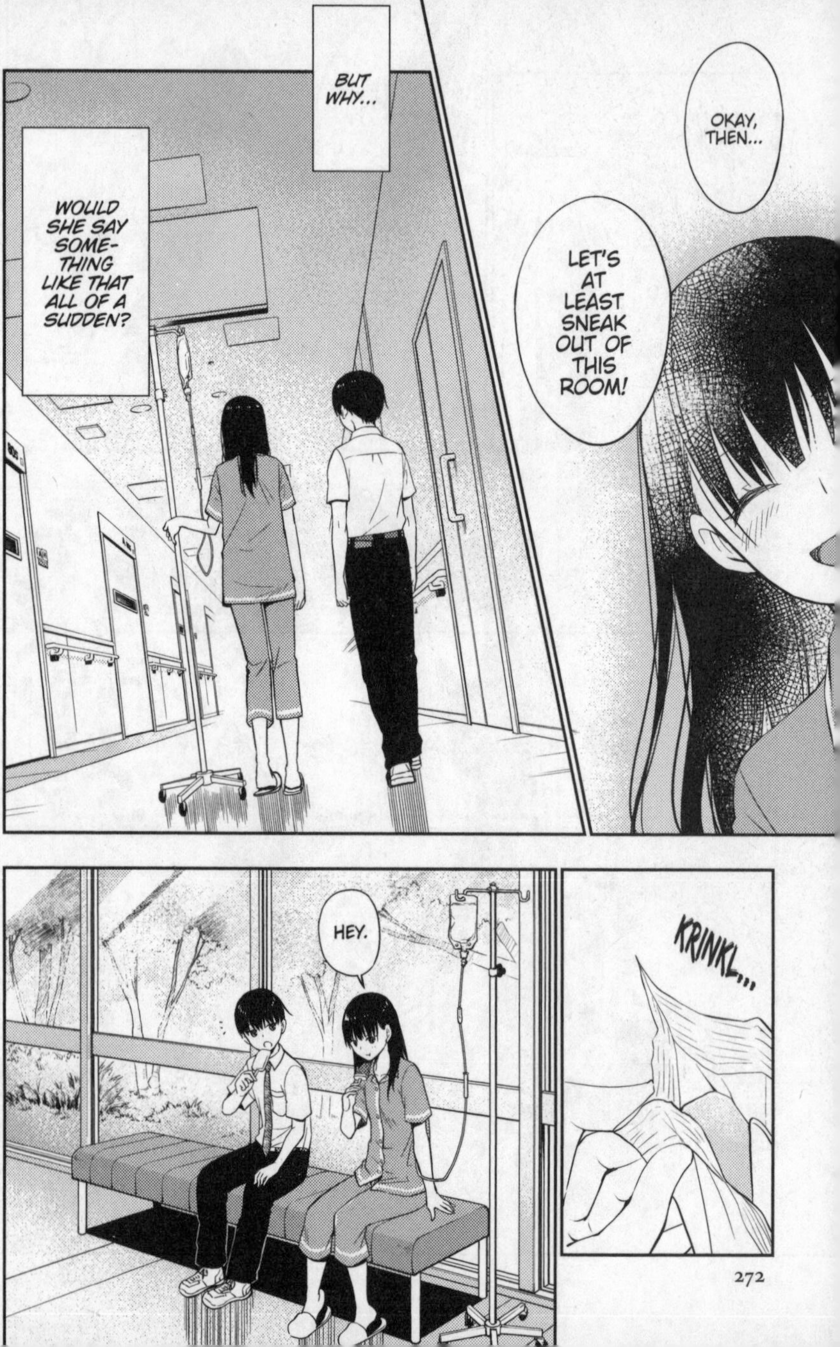
OKAY, THEN...
LET'S AT LEAST SNEAK OUT OF THIS ROOM!
BUT WHY...
WOULD SHE SAY SOME-THING LIKE THAT ALL OF A SUDDEN?
KRINKL...
HEY.

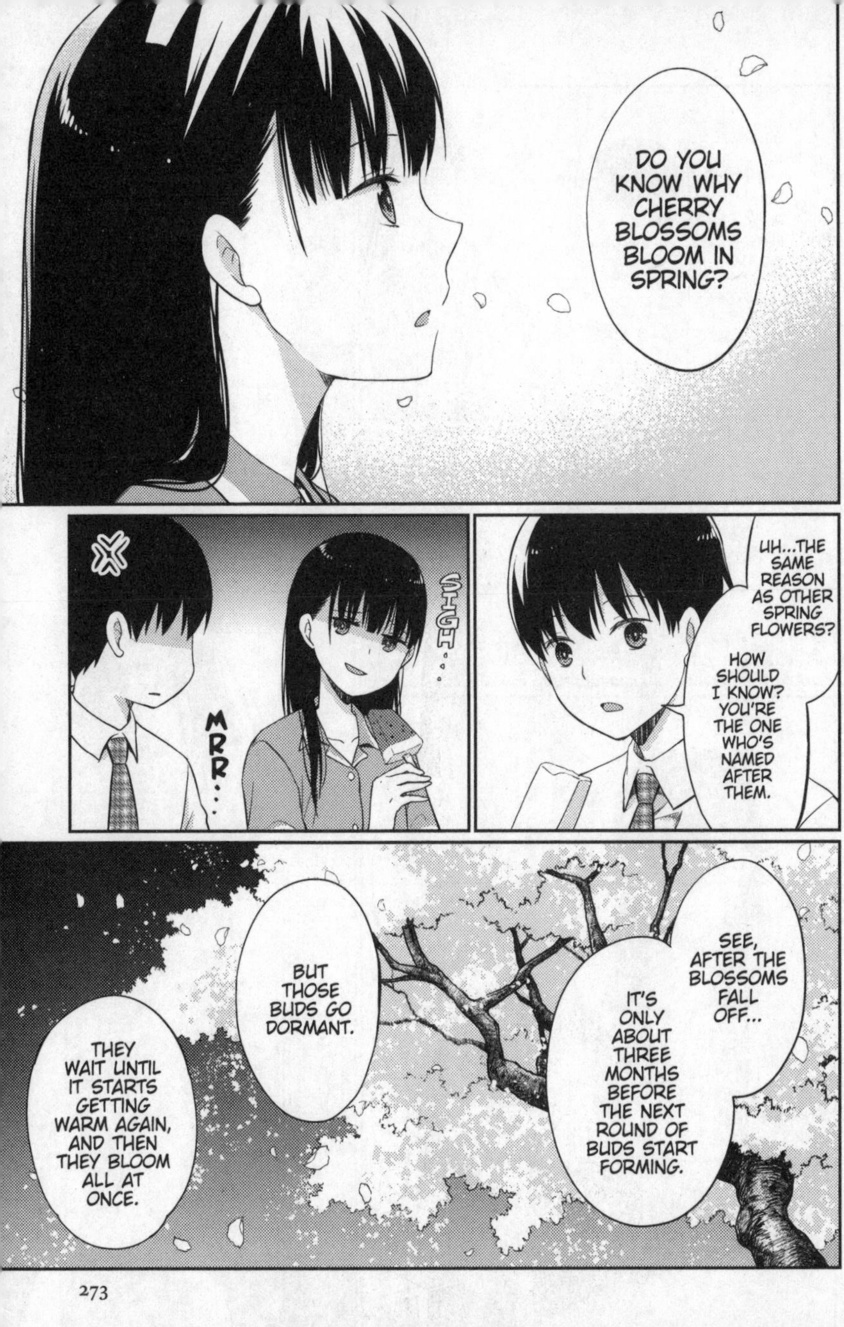
DO YOU KNOW WHY CHERRY BLOSSOMS BLOOM IN SPRING?
UH...THE SAME REASON AS OTHER SPRING FLOWERS?
HOW SHOULD I KNOW? YOU'RE THE ONE WHO'S NAMED AFTER THEM.
SIGH...
MRR...
SEE, AFTER THE BLOSSOMS FALL OFF...
IT'S ONLY ABOUT THREE MONTHS BEFORE THE NEXT ROUND OF BUDS START FORMING.
BUT THOSE BUDS GO DORMANT.
THEY WAIT UNTIL IT STARTS GETTING WARM AGAIN, AND THEN THEY BLOOM ALL AT ONCE.

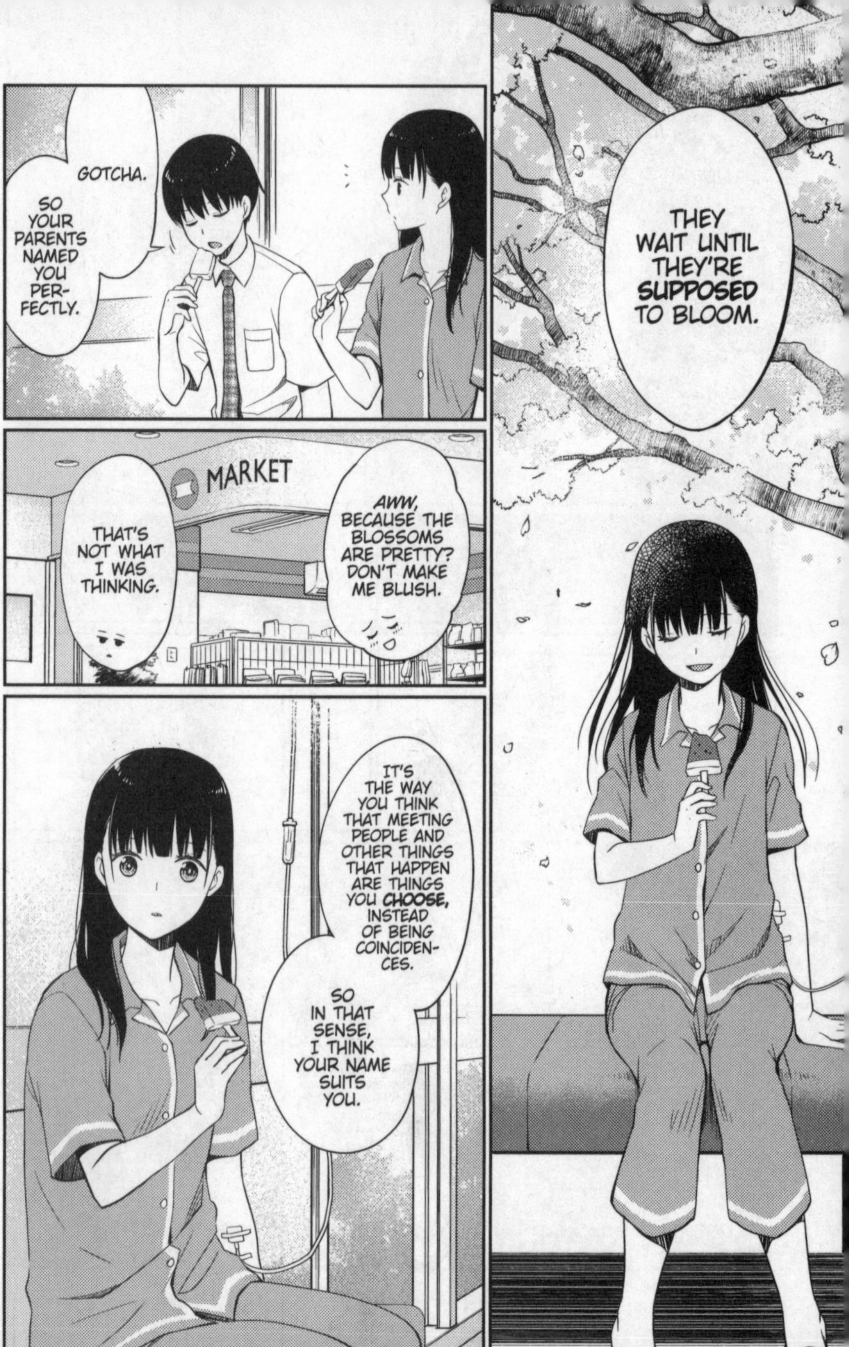
THEY WAIT UNTIL THEY'RE **SUPPOSED** TO BLOOM.
GOTCHA.
SO YOUR PARENTS NAMED YOU PER-FECTLY.
AWW, BECAUSE THE BLOSSOMS ARE PRETTY? DON'T MAKE ME BLUSH.
MARKET
THAT'S NOT WHAT I WAS THINKING.
IT'S THE WAY YOU THINK THAT MEETING PEOPLE AND OTHER THINGS THAT HAPPEN ARE THINGS YOU **CHOOSE,** INSTEAD OF BEING COINCIDEN-CES.
SO IN THAT SENSE, I THINK YOUR NAME SUITS YOU.

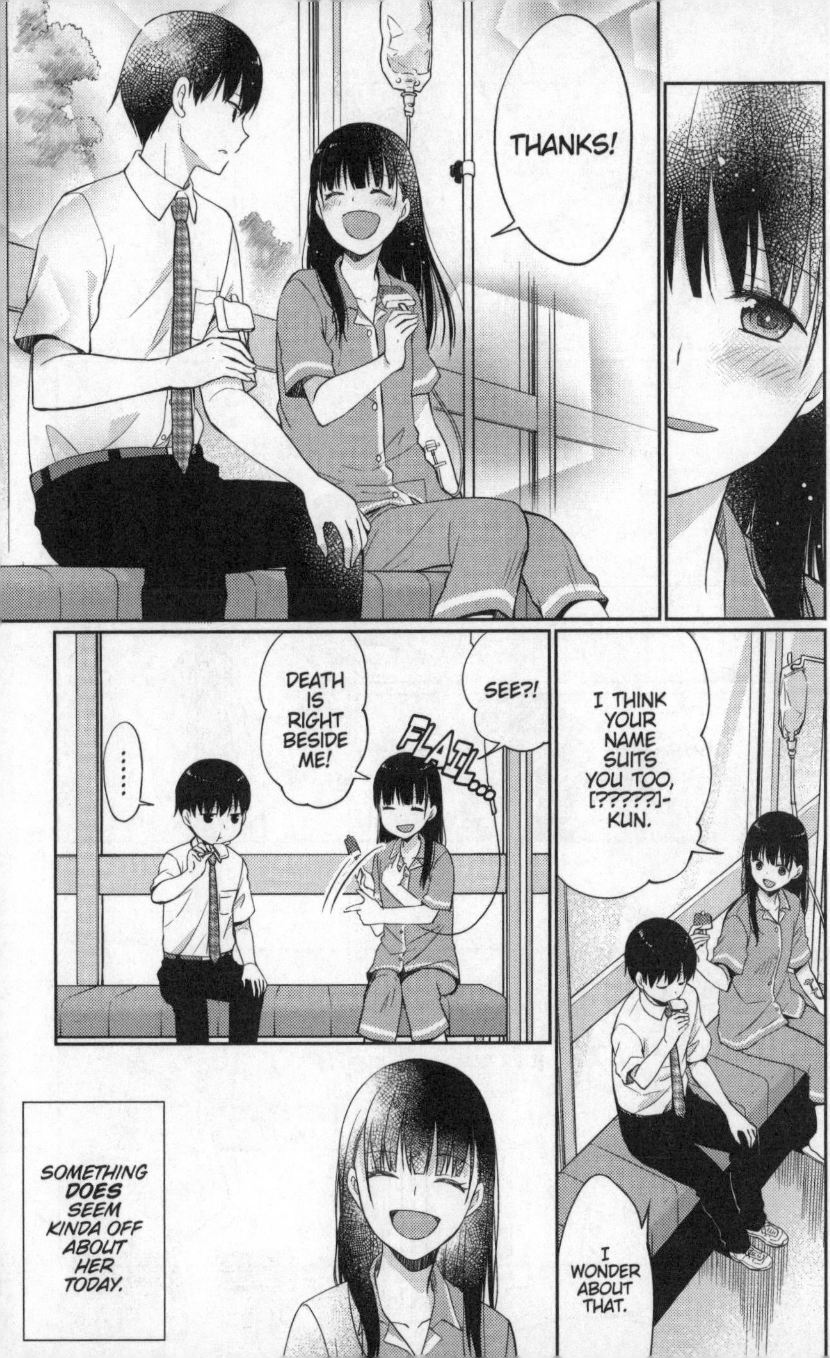
THANKS!
I THINK YOUR NAME SUITS YOU TOO, [?????]-KUN.
SEE?!
DEATH IS RIGHT BESIDE ME!
FLAIL...
......
I WONDER ABOUT THAT.
SOMETHING **DOES** SEEM KINDA OFF ABOUT HER TODAY.

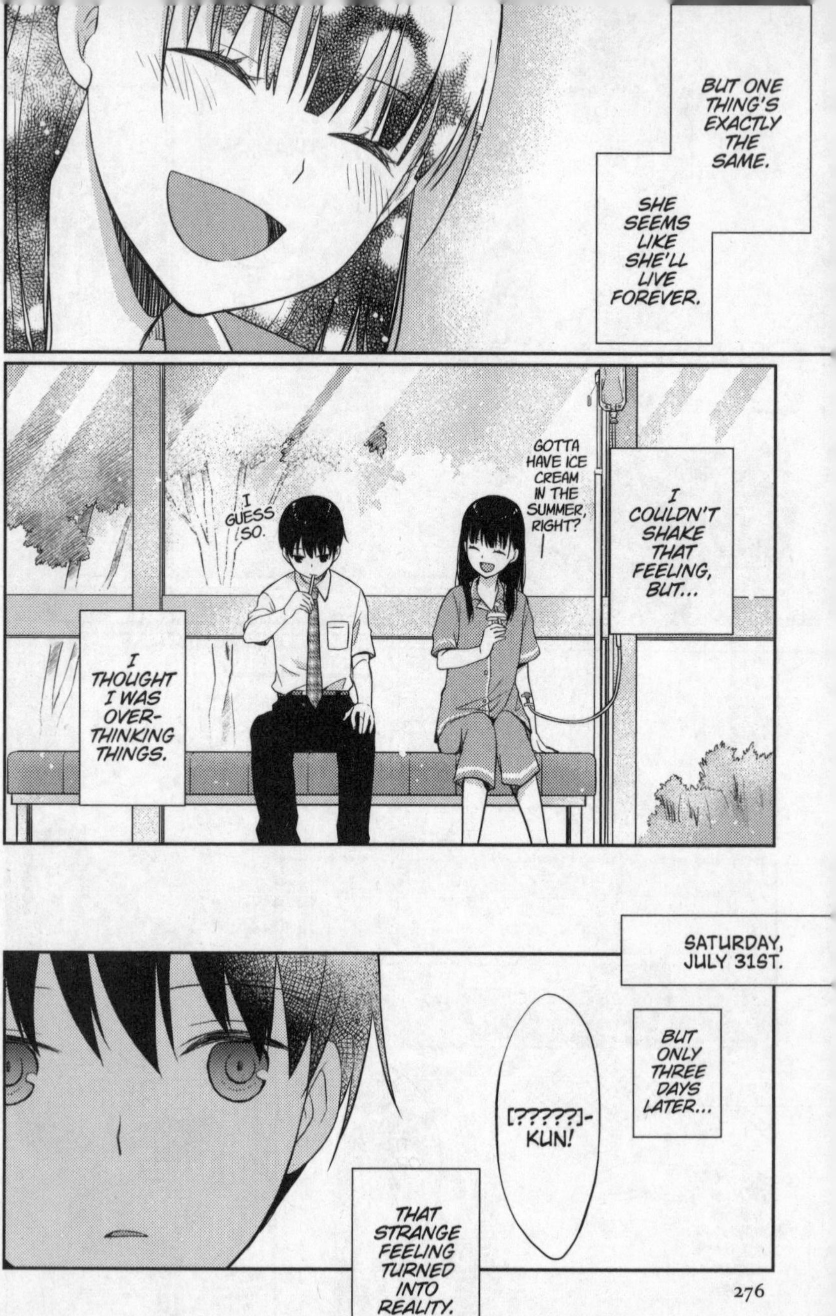
BUT ONE THING'S EXACTLY THE SAME.
SHE SEEMS LIKE SHE'LL LIVE FOREVER.
I COULDN'T SHAKE THAT FEELING, BUT...
GOTTA HAVE ICE CREAM IN THE SUMMER, RIGHT?
I GUESS SO.
I THOUGHT I WAS OVER-THINKING THINGS.
SATURDAY, JULY 31ST.
BUT ONLY THREE DAYS LATER...
[?????]-KUN!
THAT STRANGE FEELING TURNED INTO REALITY.

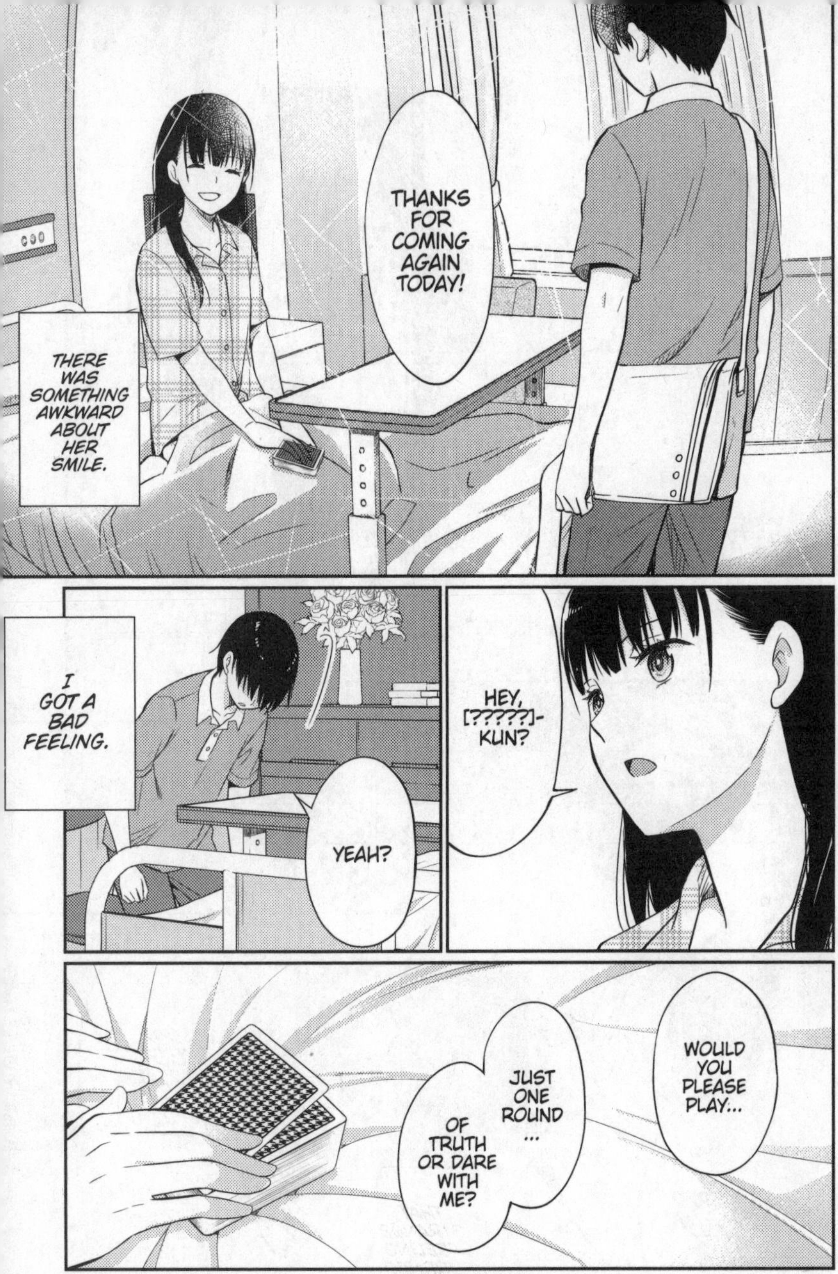
THANKS FOR COMING AGAIN TODAY!
THERE WAS SOMETHING AWKWARD ABOUT HER SMILE.
HEY, [?????]-KUN?
I GOT A BAD FEELING.
YEAH?
WOULD YOU PLEASE PLAY...
JUST ONE ROUND...
OF TRUTH OR DARE WITH ME?

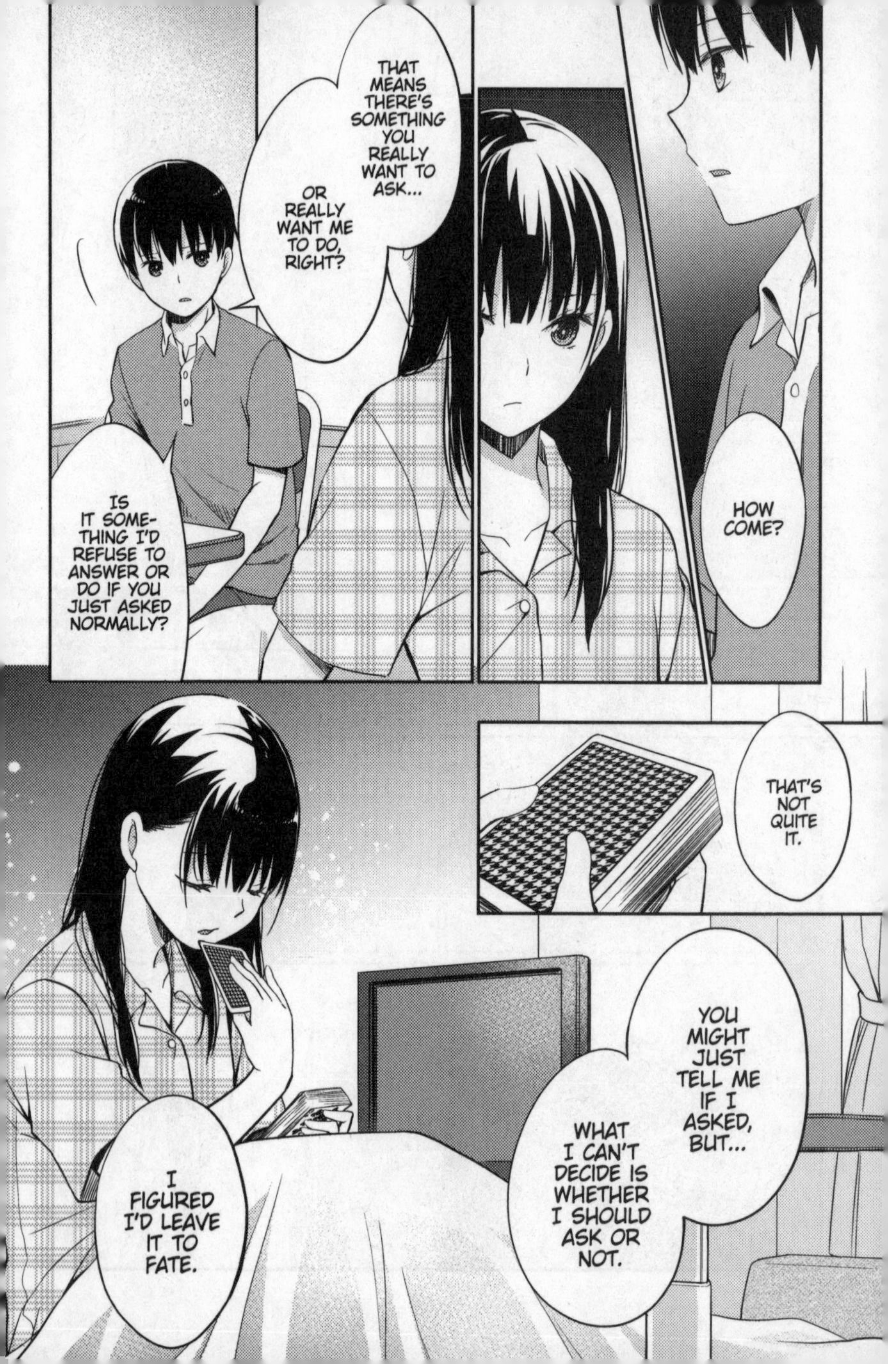
HOW COME?
THAT MEANS THERE'S SOMETHING YOU REALLY WANT TO ASK...
OR REALLY WANT ME TO DO, RIGHT?
IS IT SOME-THING I'D REFUSE TO ANSWER OR DO IF YOU JUST ASKED NORMALLY?
THAT'S NOT QUITE IT.
YOU MIGHT JUST TELL ME IF I ASKED, BUT...
WHAT I CAN'T DECIDE IS WHETHER I SHOULD ASK OR NOT.
I FIGURED I'D LEAVE IT TO FATE.

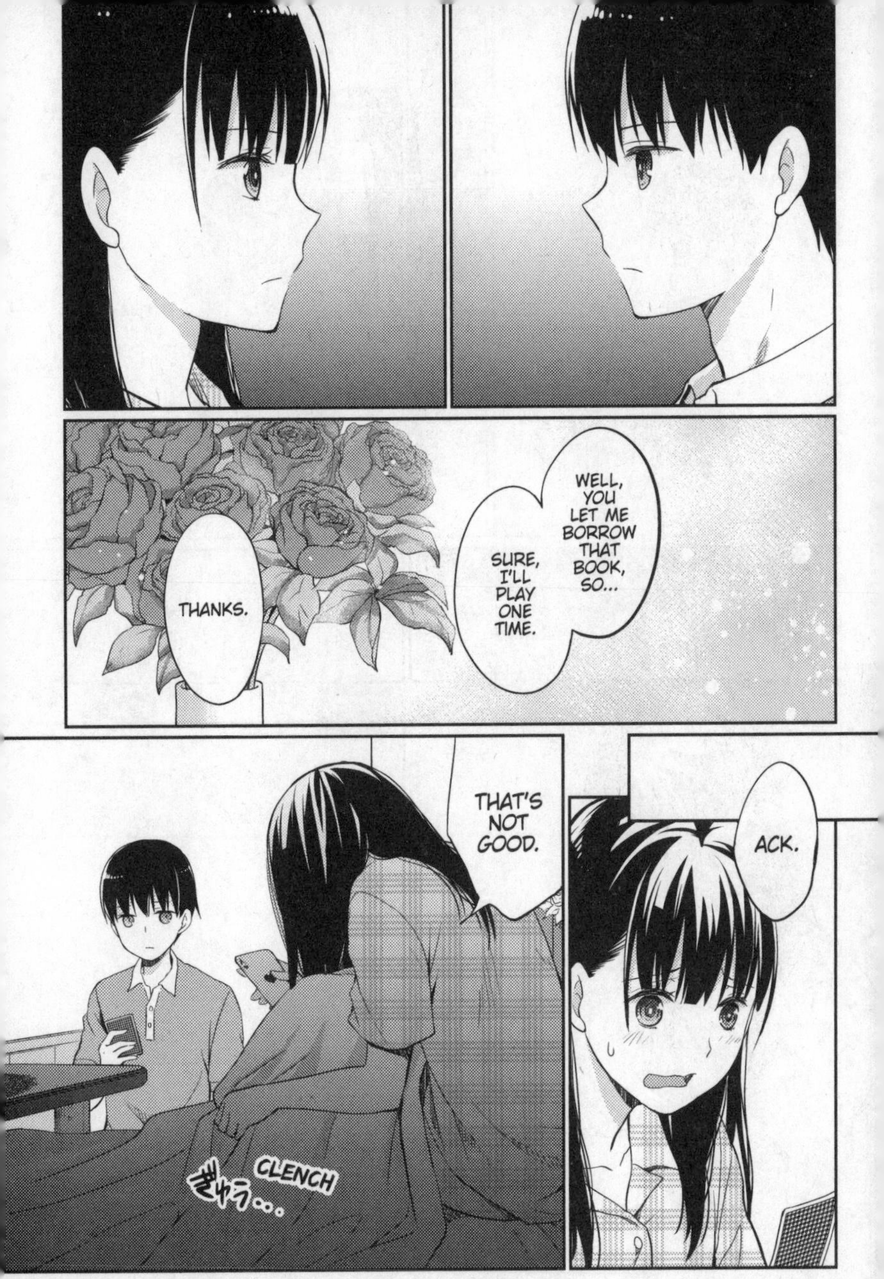
WELL, YOU LET ME BORROW THAT BOOK, SO...
SURE, I'LL PLAY ONE TIME.
THANKS.
ACK.
THAT'S NOT GOOD.
CLENCH
ぎゅう…

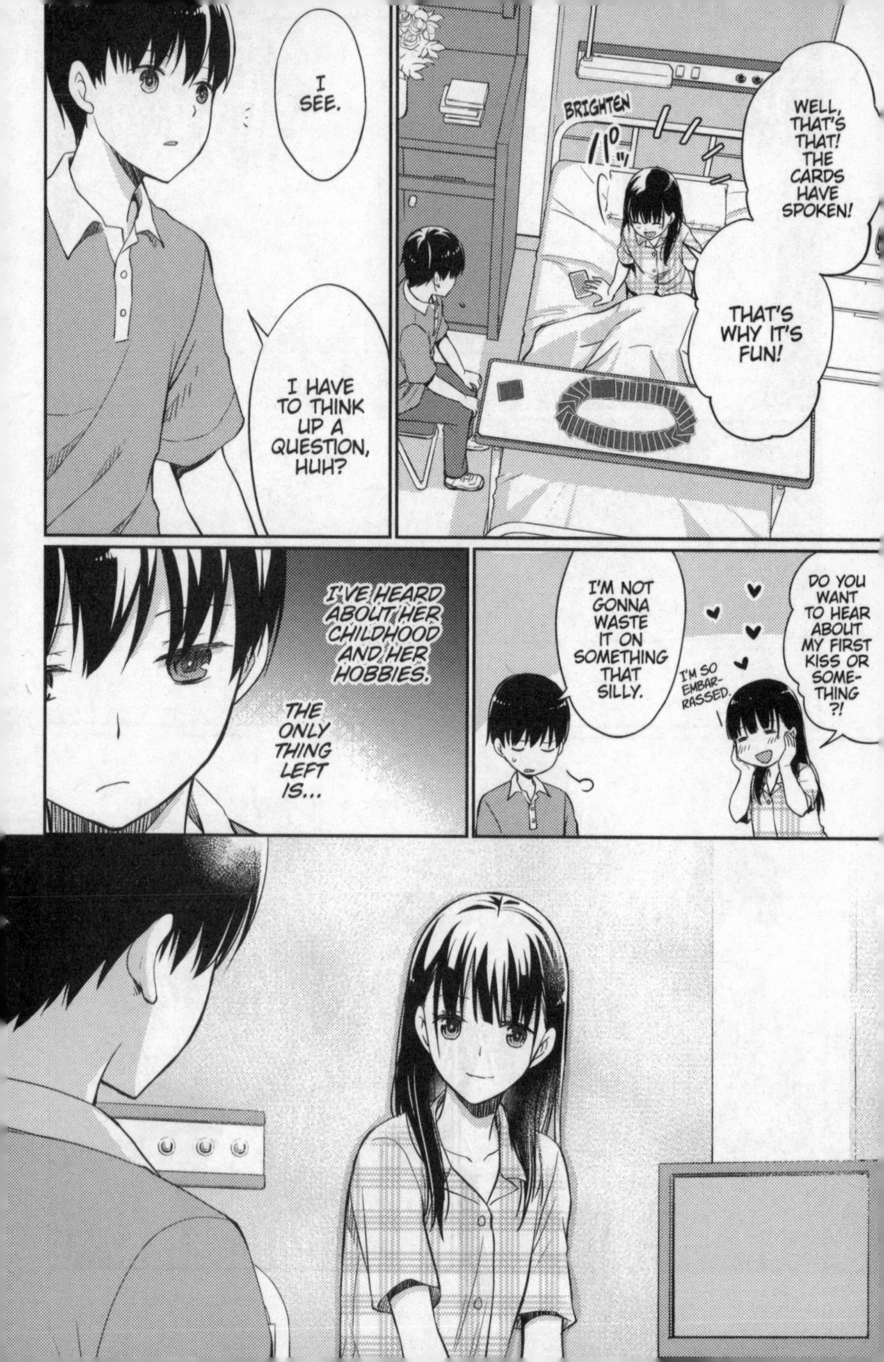
WELL, THAT'S THAT! THE CARDS HAVE SPOKEN!
BRIGHTEN
THAT'S WHY IT'S FUN!
I SEE.
I HAVE TO THINK UP A QUESTION, HUH?
DO YOU WANT TO HEAR ABOUT MY FIRST KISS OR SOME-THING?!
I'M SO EMBAR-RASSED.
I'M NOT GONNA WASTE IT ON SOMETHING THAT SILLY.
I'VE HEARD ABOUT HER CHILDHOOD AND HER HOBBIES.
THE ONLY THING LEFT IS...

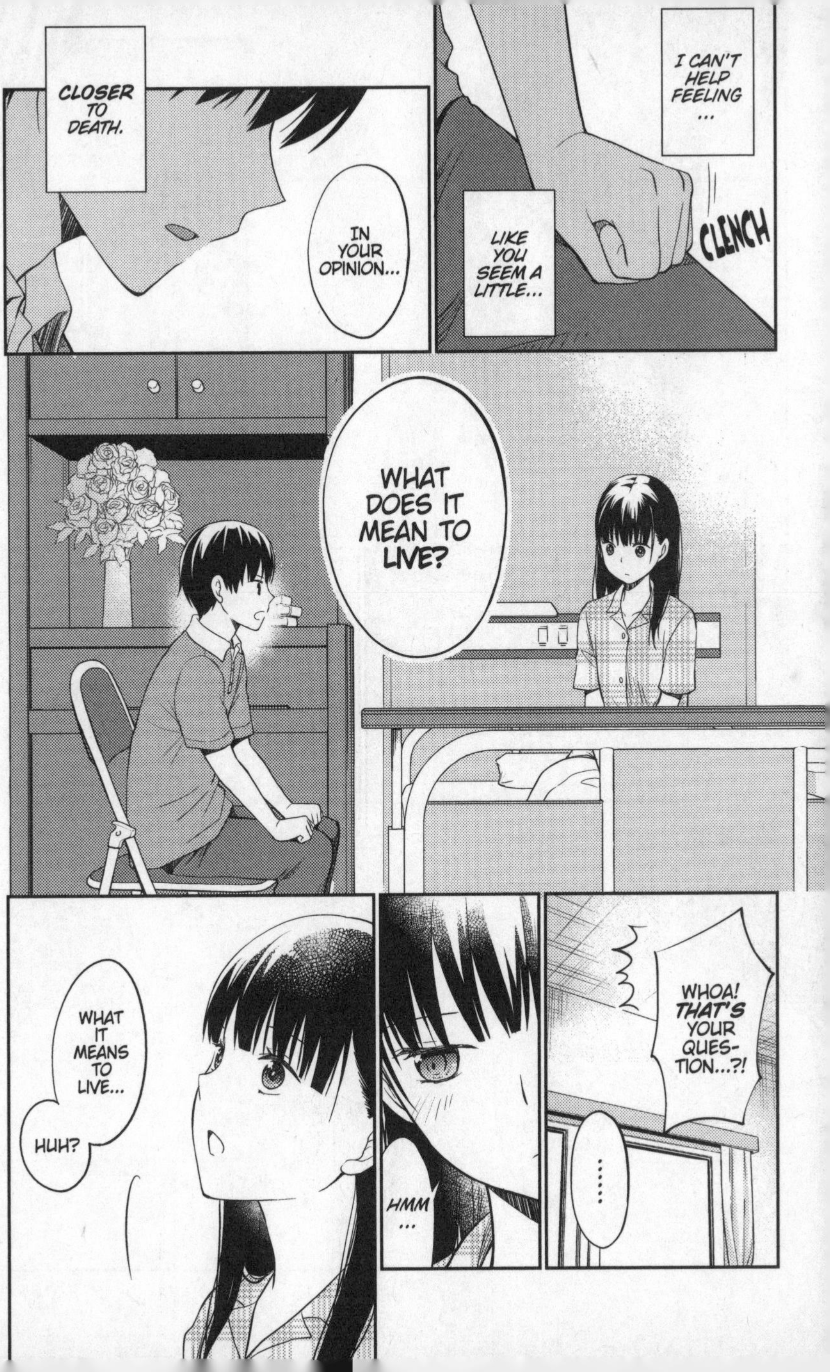
I CAN'T HELP FEELING...
LIKE YOU SEEM A LITTLE...
CLENCH
CLOSER TO DEATH.
IN YOUR OPINION...
WHAT DOES IT MEAN TO LIVE?
WHOA! THAT'S YOUR QUES-TION...?!
......
HMM...
WHAT IT MEANS TO LIVE...
HUH?

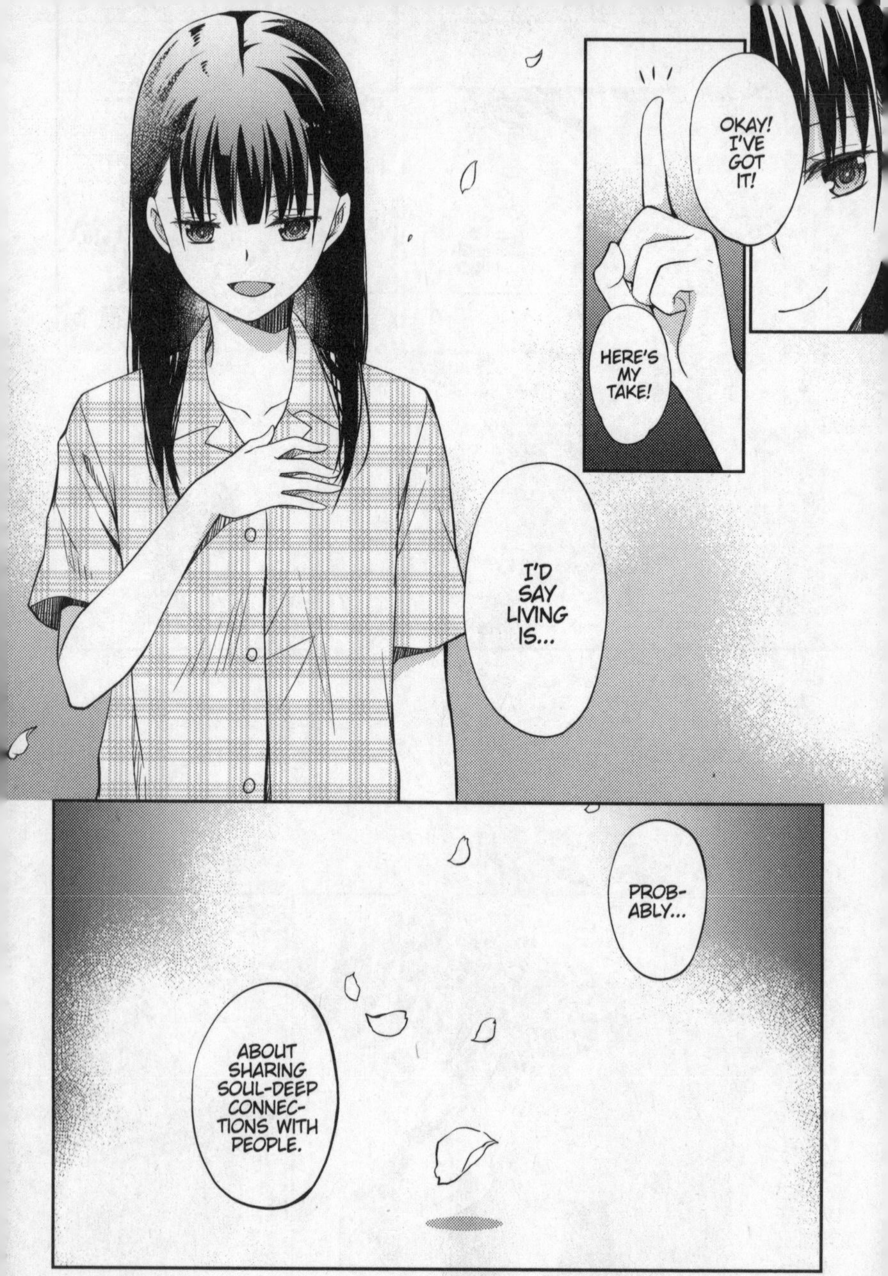
OKAY! I'VE GOT IT!
HERE'S MY TAKE!
I'D SAY LIVING IS...
PROB-ABLY...
ABOUT SHARING SOUL-DEEP CONNEC-TIONS WITH PEOPLE.

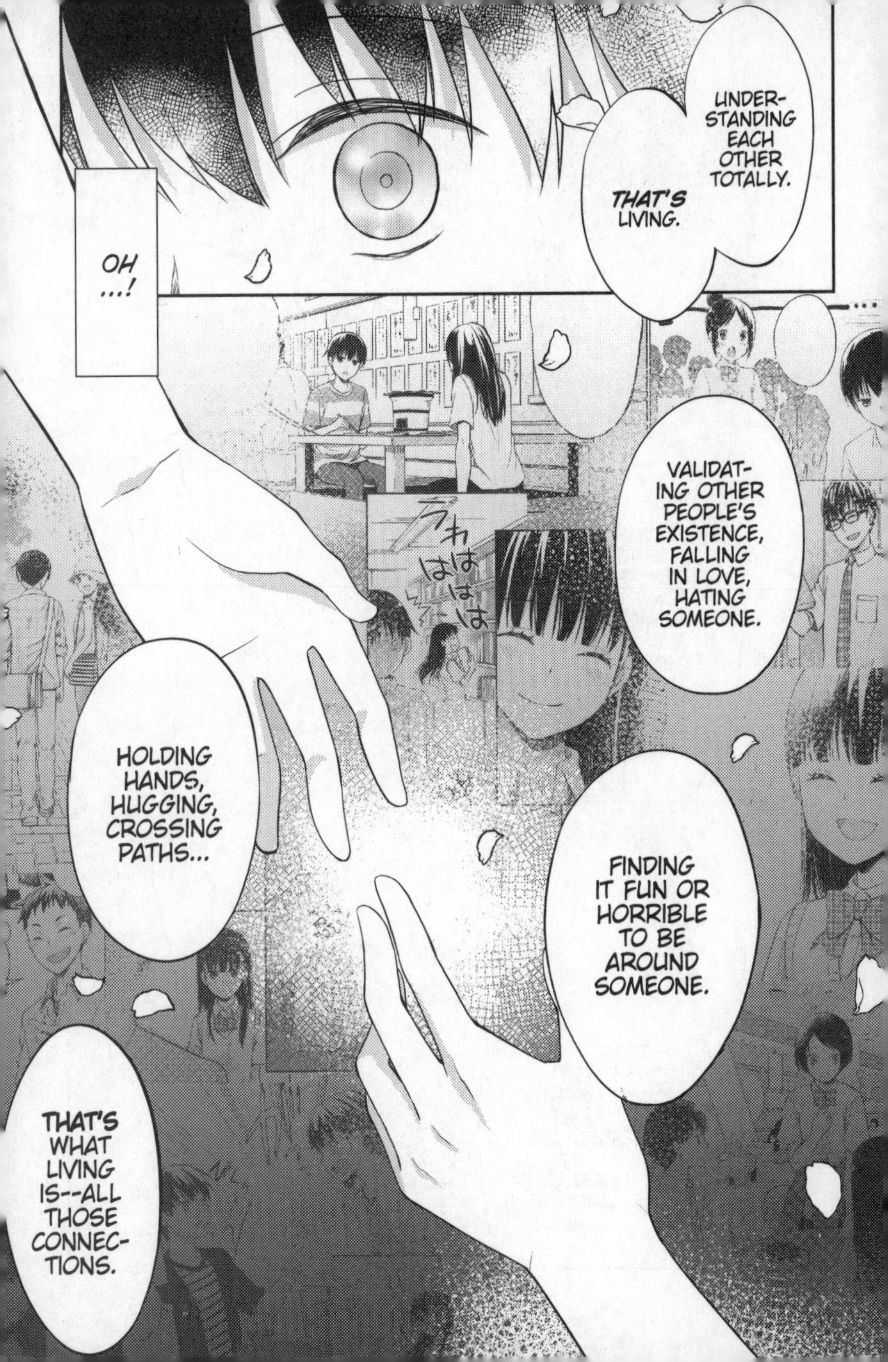
UNDER-STANDING EACH OTHER TOTALLY.
THAT'S LIVING.
OH ...!
VALIDATING OTHER PEOPLE'S EXISTENCE, FALLING IN LOVE, HATING SOMEONE.
FINDING IT FUN OR HORRIBLE TO BE AROUND SOMEONE.
HOLDING HANDS, HUGGING, CROSSING PATHS...
THAT'S WHAT LIVING IS--ALL THOSE CONNEC-TIONS.

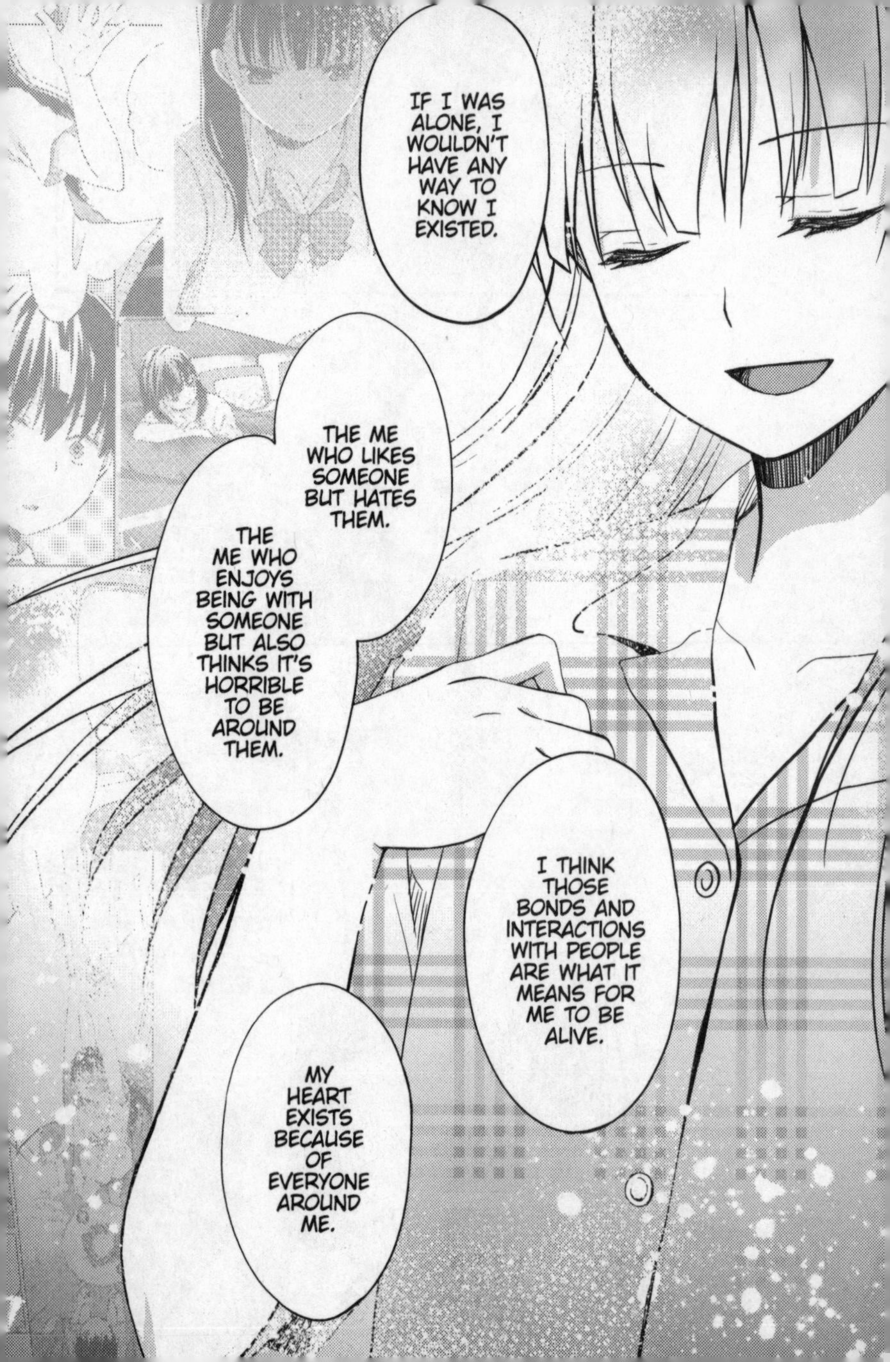
IF I WAS ALONE, I WOULDN'T HAVE ANY WAY TO KNOW I EXISTED.
THE ME WHO LIKES SOMEONE BUT HATES THEM.
THE ME WHO ENJOYS BEING WITH SOMEONE BUT ALSO THINKS IT'S HORRIBLE TO BE AROUND THEM.
I THINK THOSE BONDS AND INTERACTIONS WITH PEOPLE ARE WHAT IT MEANS FOR ME TO BE ALIVE.
MY HEART EXISTS BECAUSE OF EVERYONE AROUND ME.

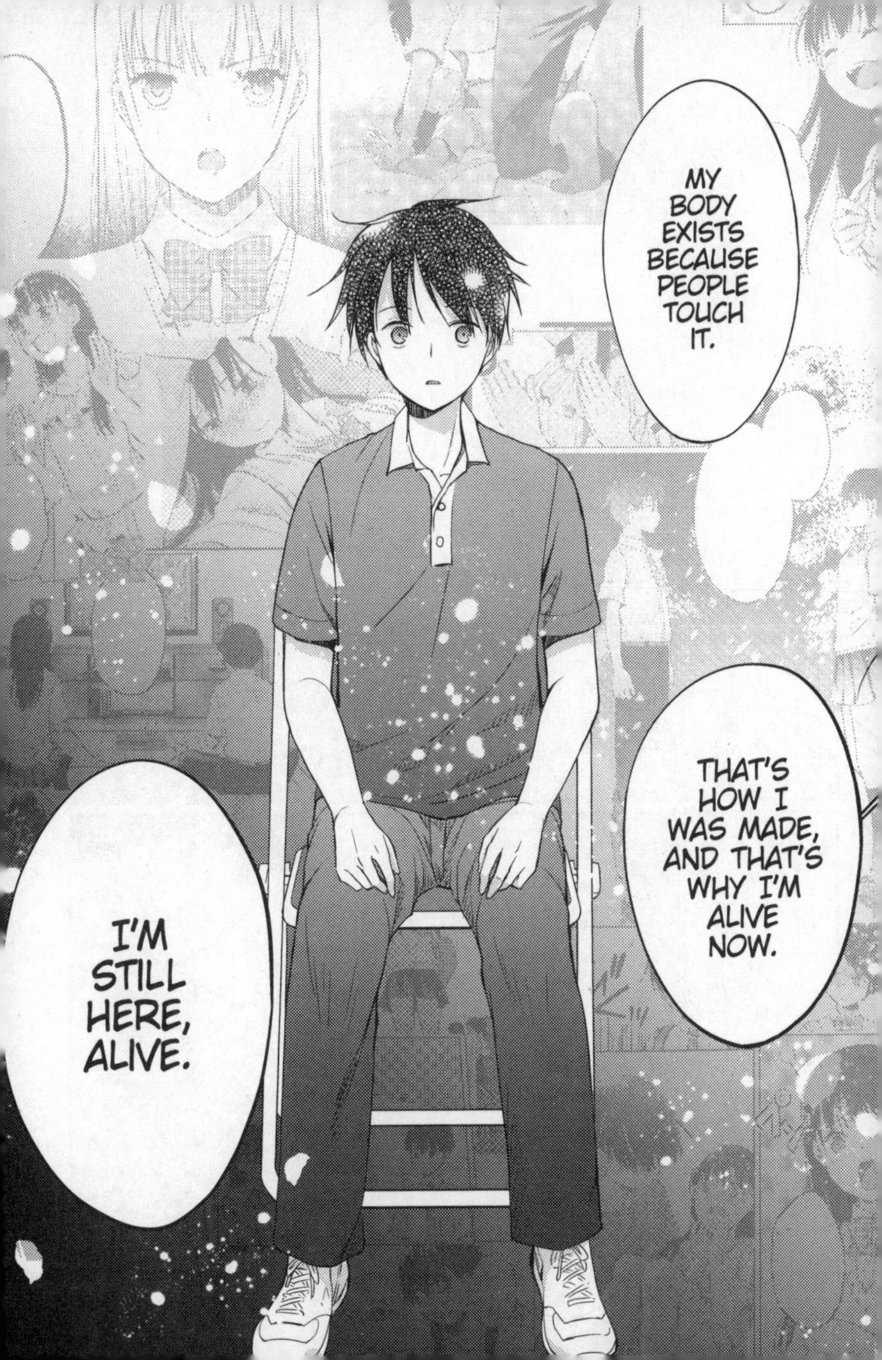
MY BODY EXISTS BECAUSE PEOPLE TOUCH IT.
THAT'S HOW I WAS MADE, AND THAT'S WHY I'M ALIVE NOW.
I'M STILL HERE, ALIVE.

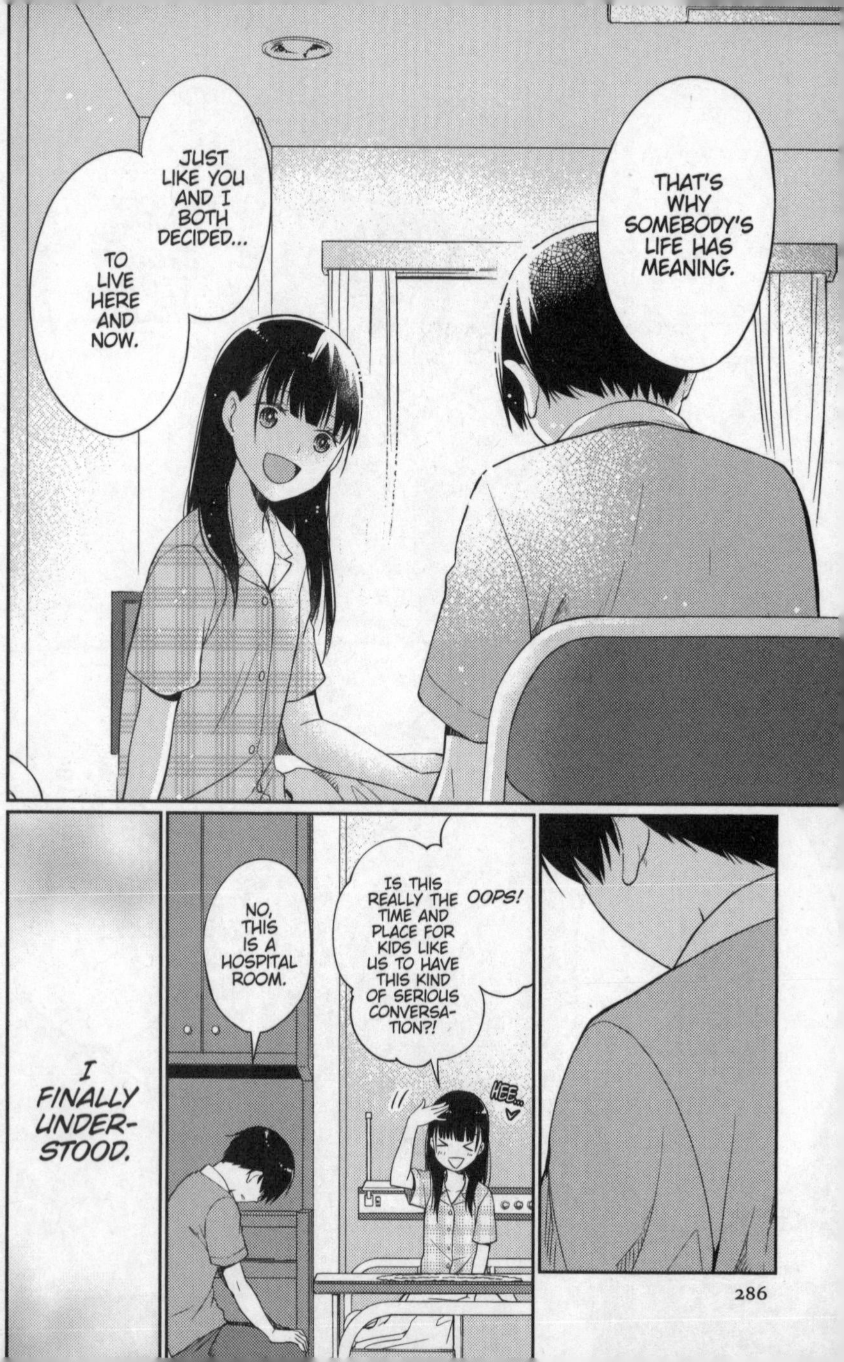
THAT'S WHY SOMEBODY'S LIFE HAS MEANING.
JUST LIKE YOU AND I BOTH DECIDED...
TO LIVE HERE AND NOW.
IS THIS REALLY THE TIME AND PLACE FOR KIDS LIKE US TO HAVE THIS KIND OF SERIOUS CONVERSA-TION?!
OOPS!
HEE...
NO, THIS IS A HOSPITAL ROOM.
I FINALLY UNDER-STOOD.

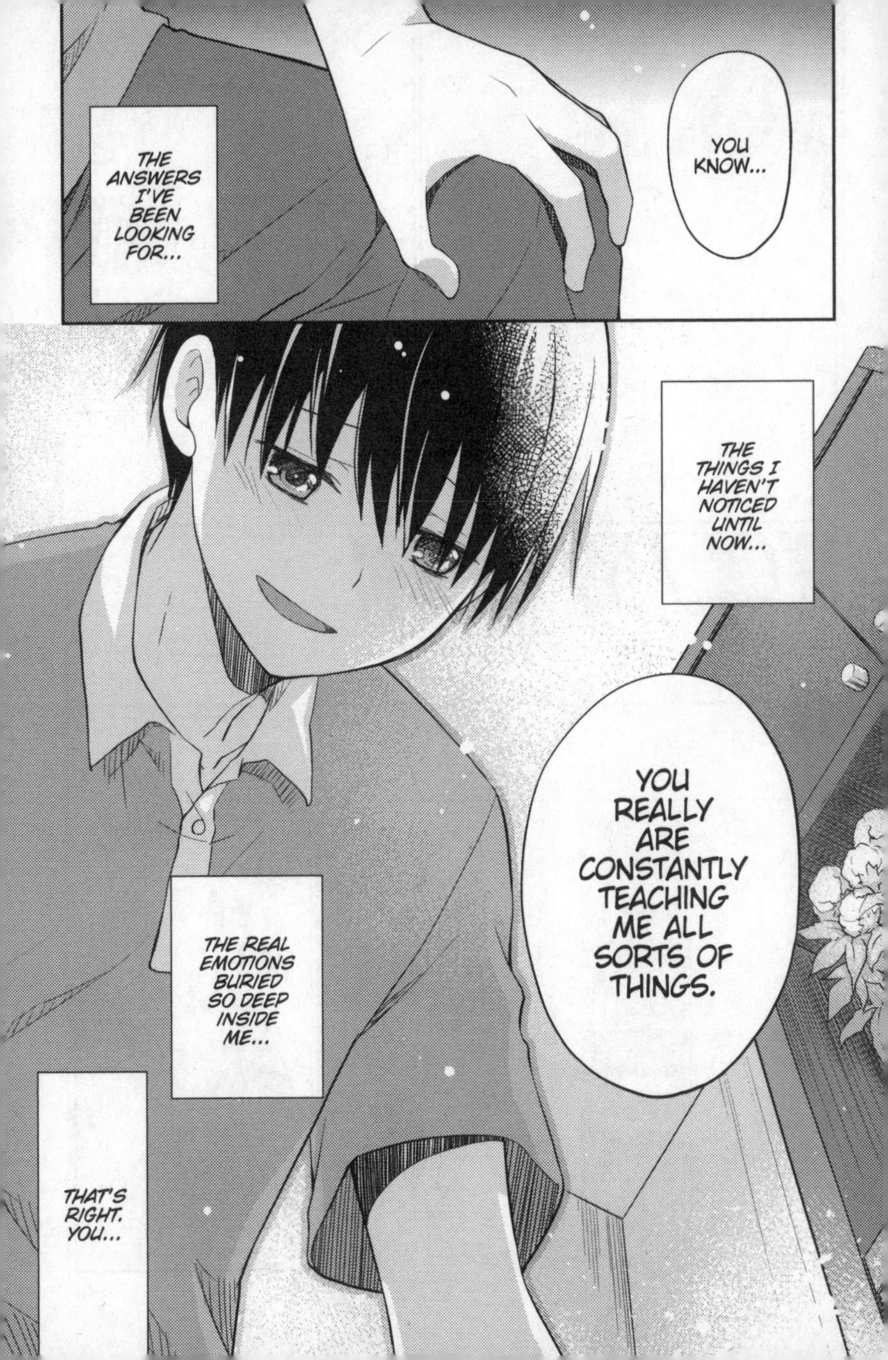
YOU KNOW...
THE ANSWERS I'VE BEEN LOOKING FOR...
THE THINGS I HAVEN'T NOTICED UNTIL NOW...
YOU REALLY ARE CONSTANTLY TEACHING ME ALL SORTS OF THINGS.
THE REAL EMOTIONS BURIED SO DEEP INSIDE ME...
THAT'S RIGHT. YOU...

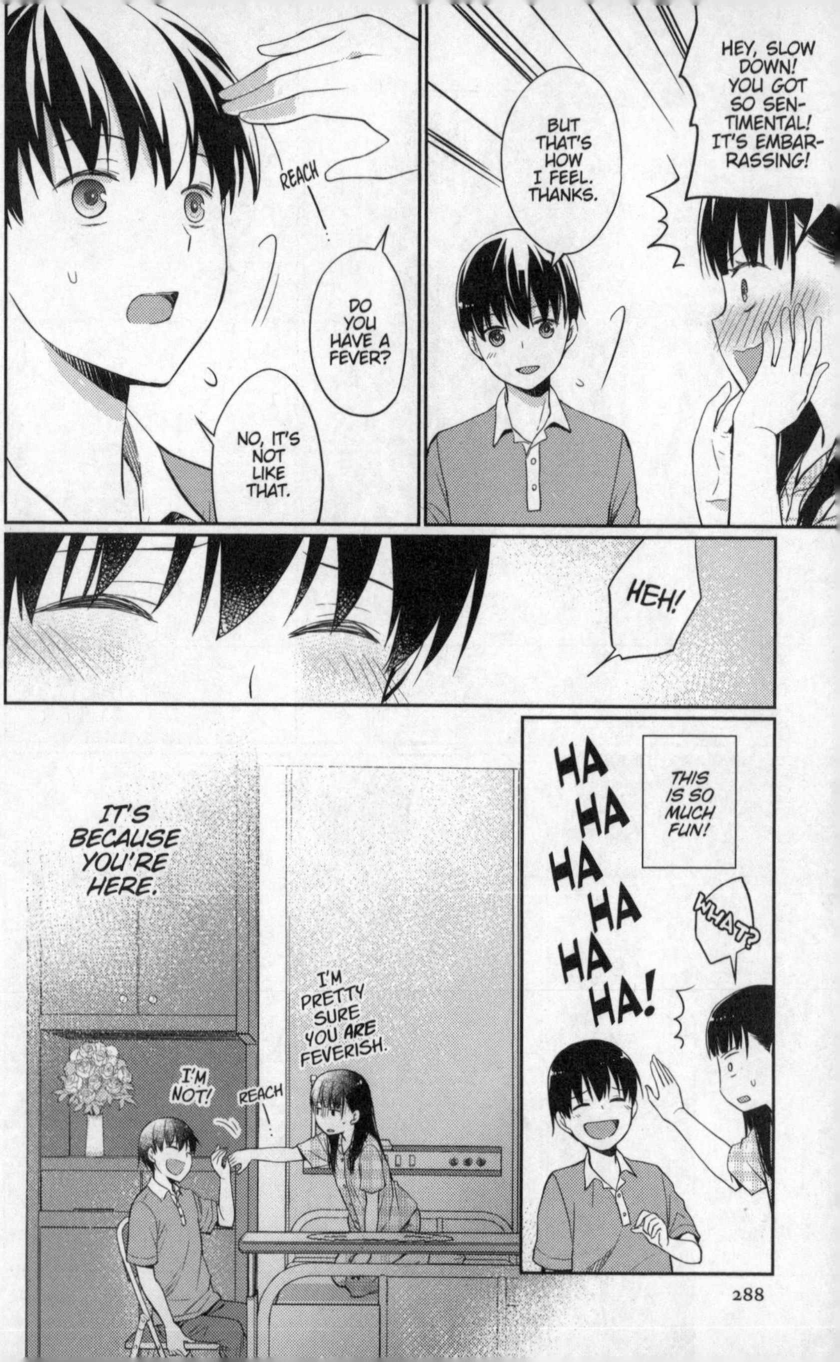

HEY, SLOW DOWN! YOU GOT SO SENTIMENTAL! IT'S EMBARRASSING!
BUT THAT'S HOW I FEEL. THANKS.
REACH
DO YOU HAVE A FEVER?
NO, IT'S NOT LIKE THAT.
HEH!
THIS IS SO MUCH FUN!
HA HA HA HA HA HA HA!
WHAT?
IT'S BECAUSE YOU'RE HERE.
I'M PRETTY SURE YOU ARE FEVERISH.
REACH
I'M NOT!

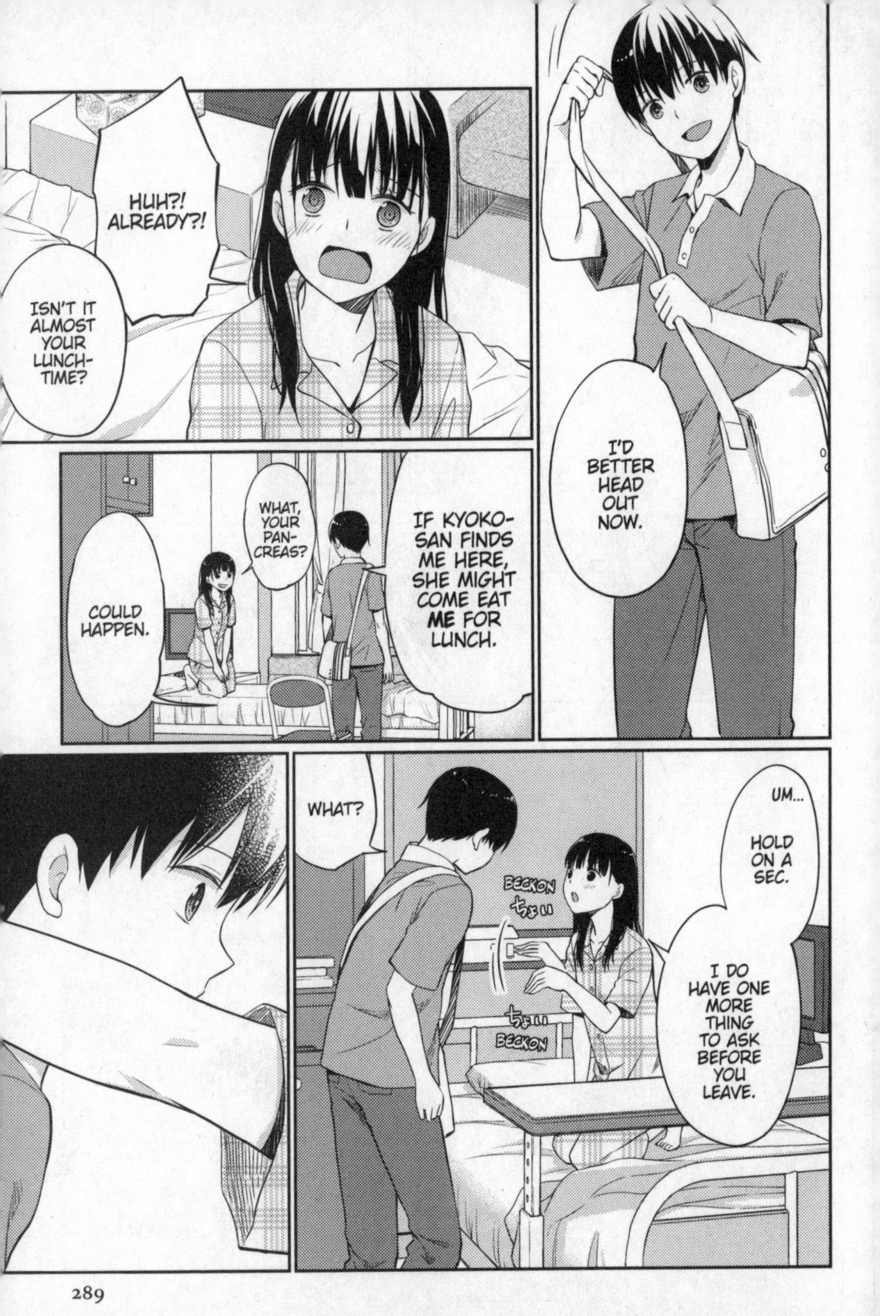
I'D BETTER HEAD OUT NOW.
HUH?! ALREADY?!
ISN'T IT ALMOST YOUR LUNCH-TIME?
IF KYOKO-SAN FINDS ME HERE, SHE MIGHT COME EAT ME FOR LUNCH.
WHAT, YOUR PAN-CREAS?
COULD HAPPEN.
UM...
HOLD ON A SEC.
I DO HAVE ONE MORE THING TO ASK BEFORE YOU LEAVE.
BECKON
ちょい
ちょい
BECKON
WHAT?

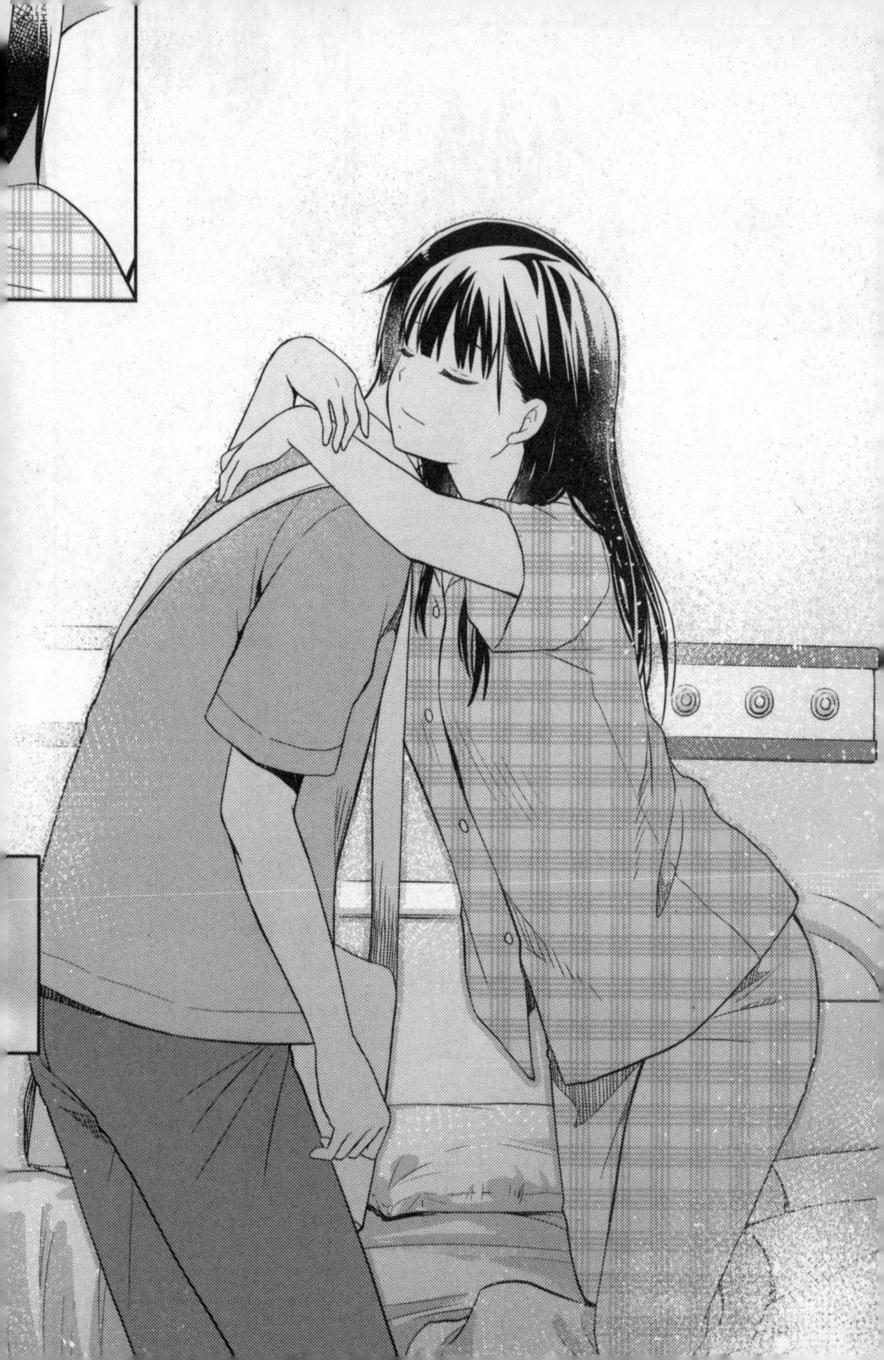

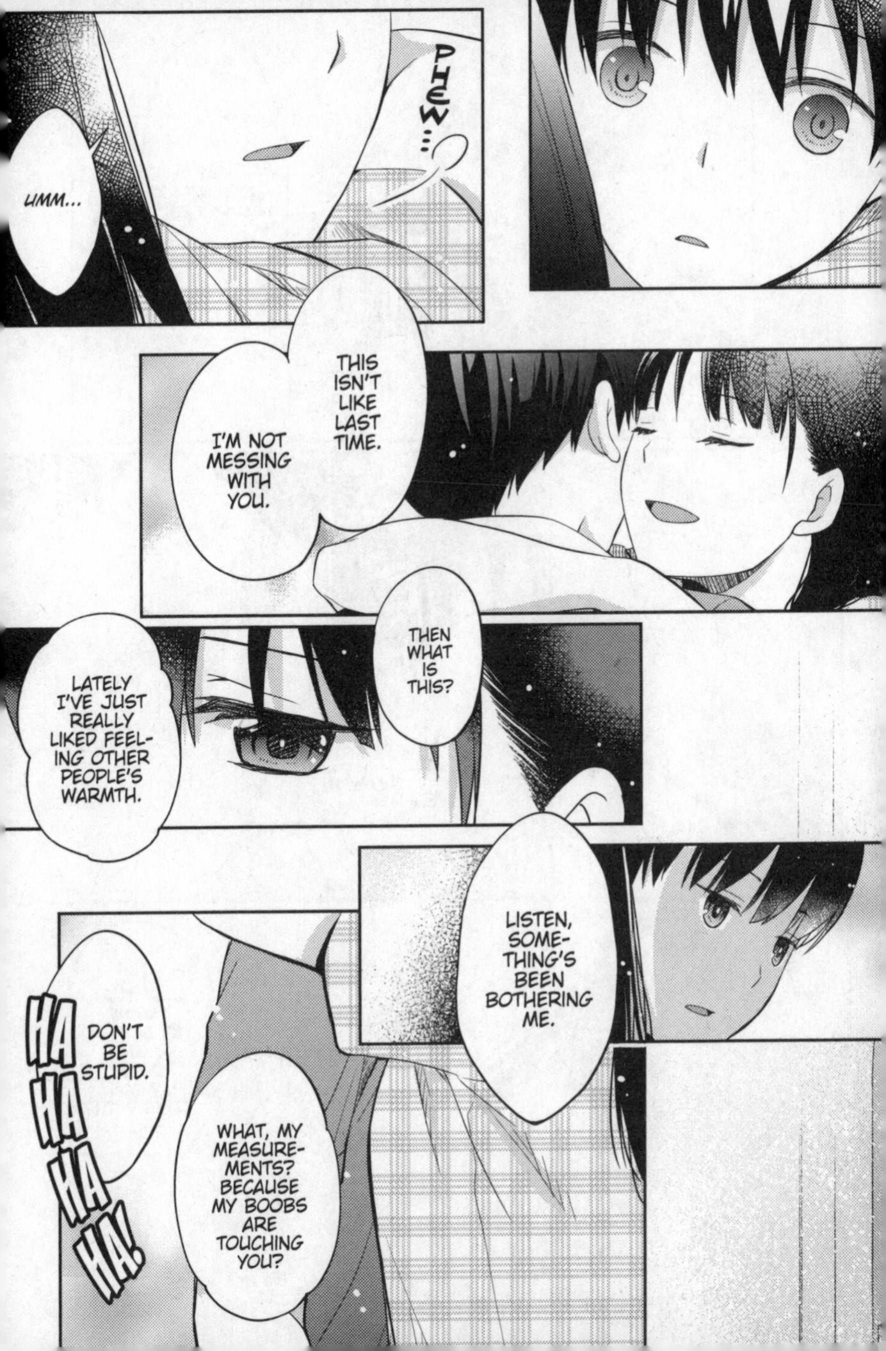
PHEW...
UMM...
THIS ISN'T LIKE LAST TIME.
I'M NOT MESSING WITH YOU.
THEN WHAT IS THIS?
LATELY I'VE JUST REALLY LIKED FEEL-ING OTHER PEOPLE'S WARMTH.
LISTEN, SOME-THING'S BEEN BOTHERING ME.
WHAT, MY MEASURE-MENTS? BECAUSE MY BOOBS ARE TOUCHING YOU?
HA HA HA HA HA!
DON'T BE STUPID.

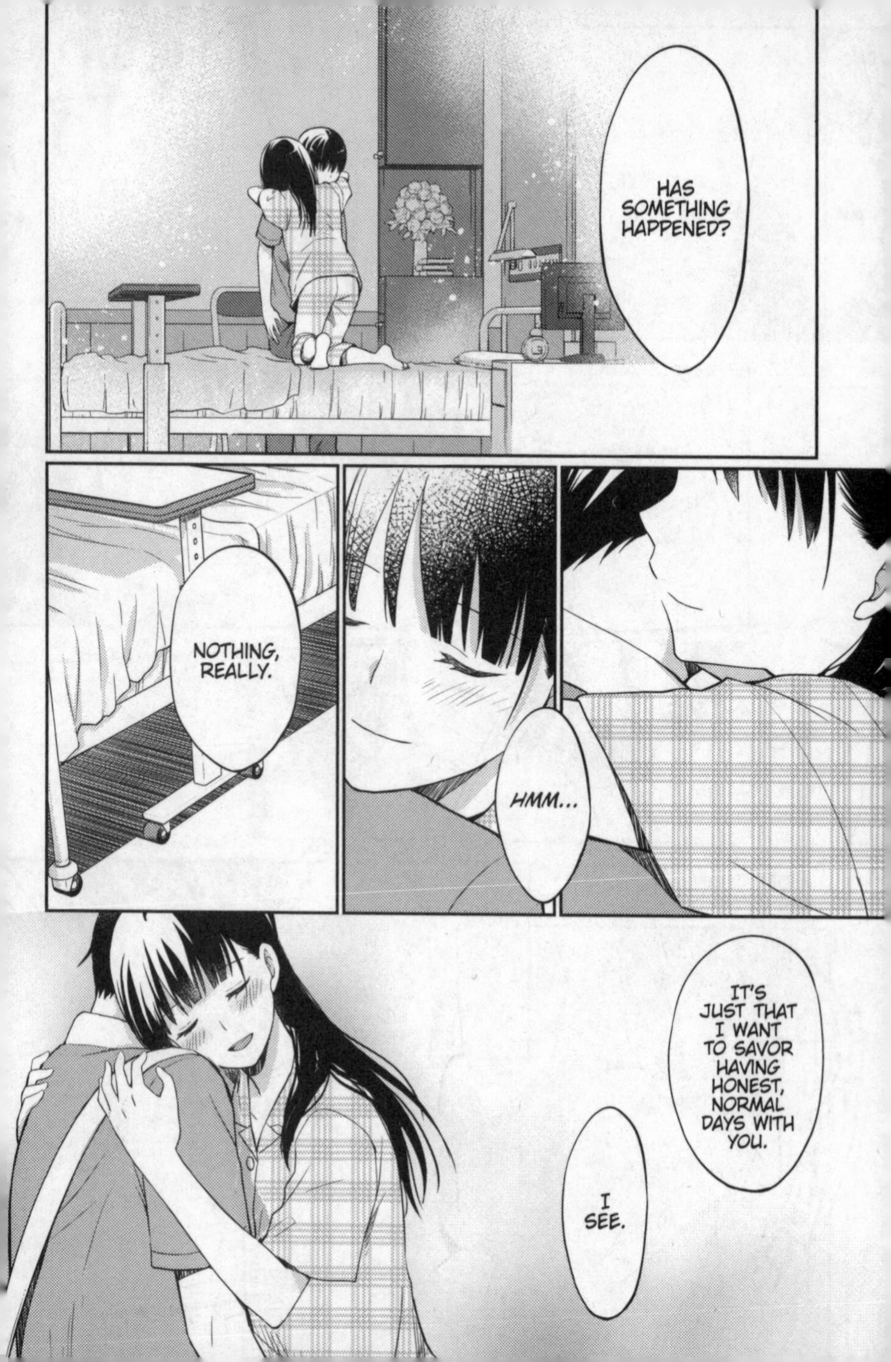
HAS SOMETHING HAPPENED?
NOTHING, REALLY.
HMM...
IT'S JUST THAT I WANT TO SAVOR HAVING HONEST, NORMAL DAYS WITH YOU.
I SEE.

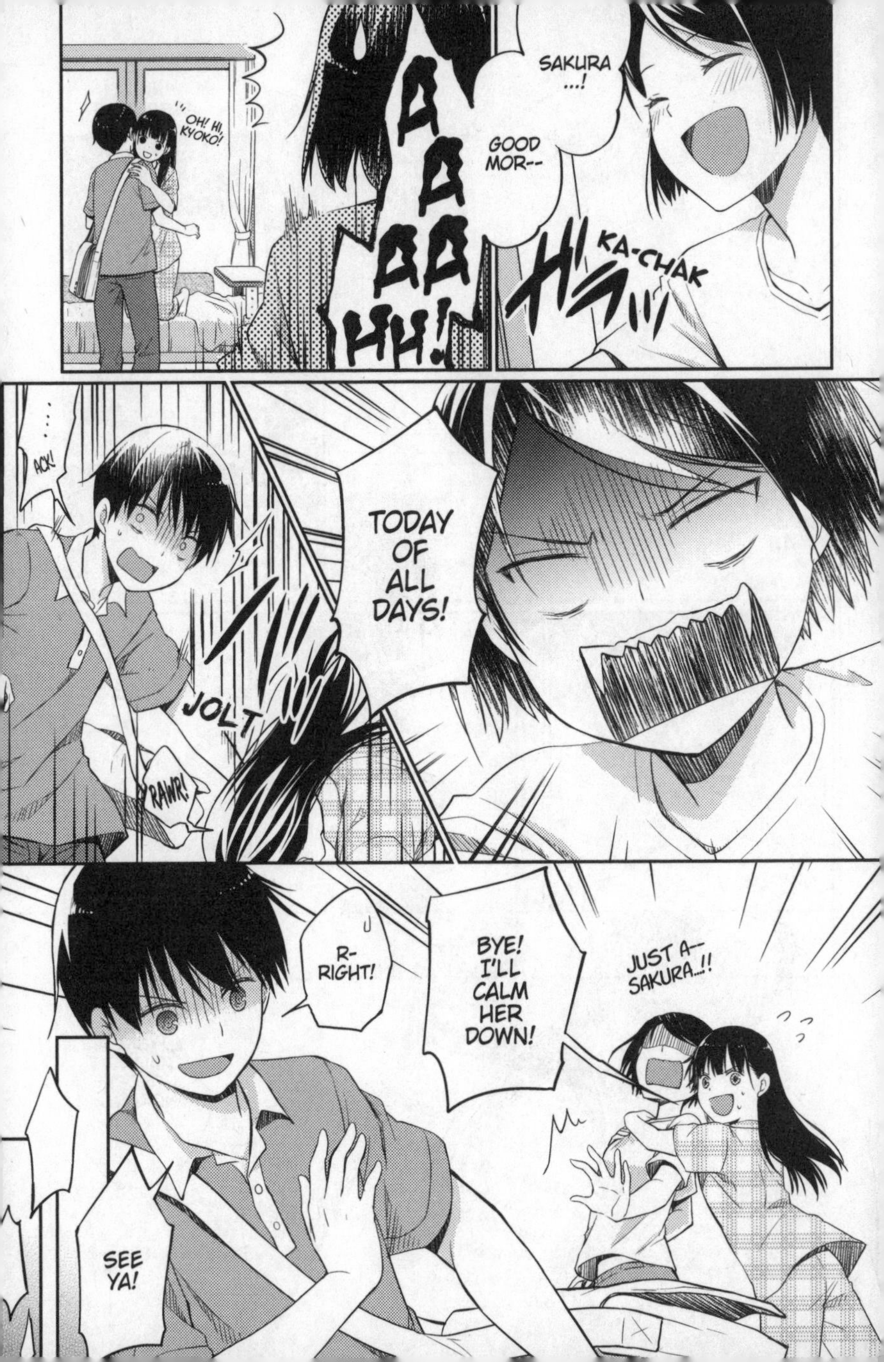
SAKURA ...!
GOOD MOR--
KA-CHAK
AAAAHH!
OH! HI, KYOKO!
TODAY OF ALL DAYS!
JOLT
RAWR!
...
ACK!
JUST A-- SAKURA...!!
BYE! I'LL CALM HER DOWN!
R-RIGHT!
SEE YA!

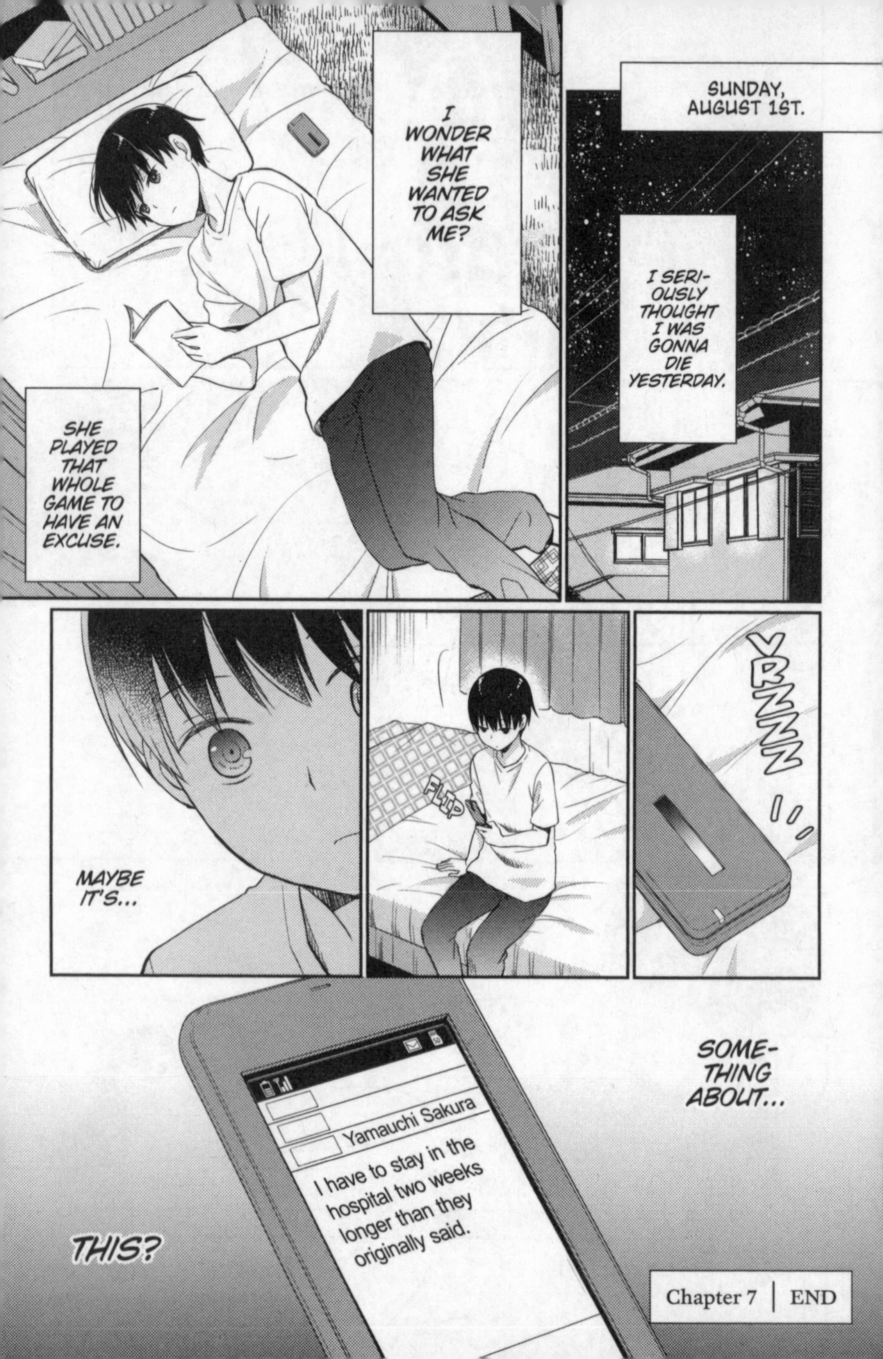
SUNDAY, AUGUST 1ST.
I SERIOUSLY THOUGHT I WAS GONNA DIE YESTERDAY.
I WONDER WHAT SHE WANTED TO ASK ME?
SHE PLAYED THAT WHOLE GAME TO HAVE AN EXCUSE.
VRZZZ
FLIP
MAYBE IT'S...
SOMETHING ABOUT...
Yamauchi Sakura
I have to stay in the hospital two weeks longer than they originally said.
THIS?
Chapter 7 | END

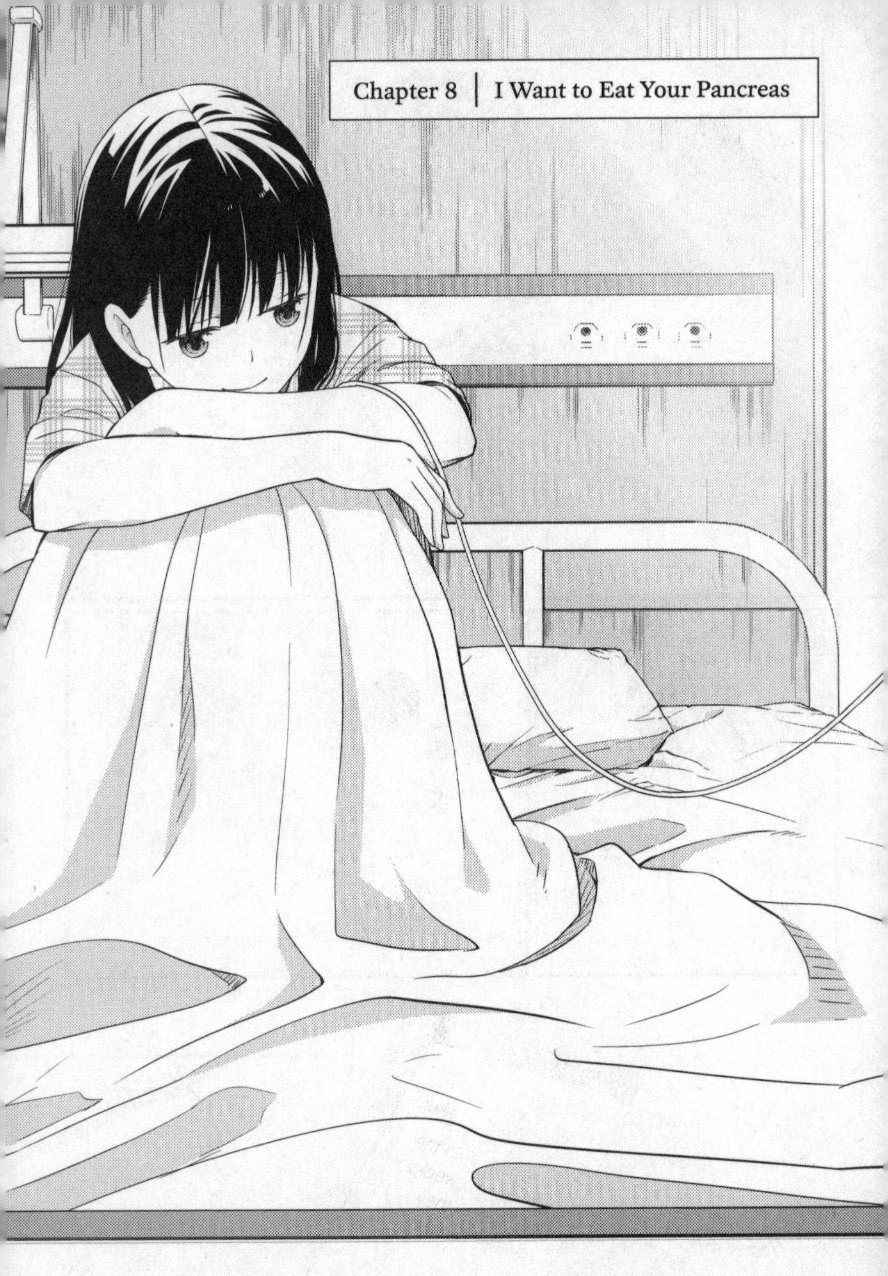
Chapter 8 | I Want to Eat Your Pancreas

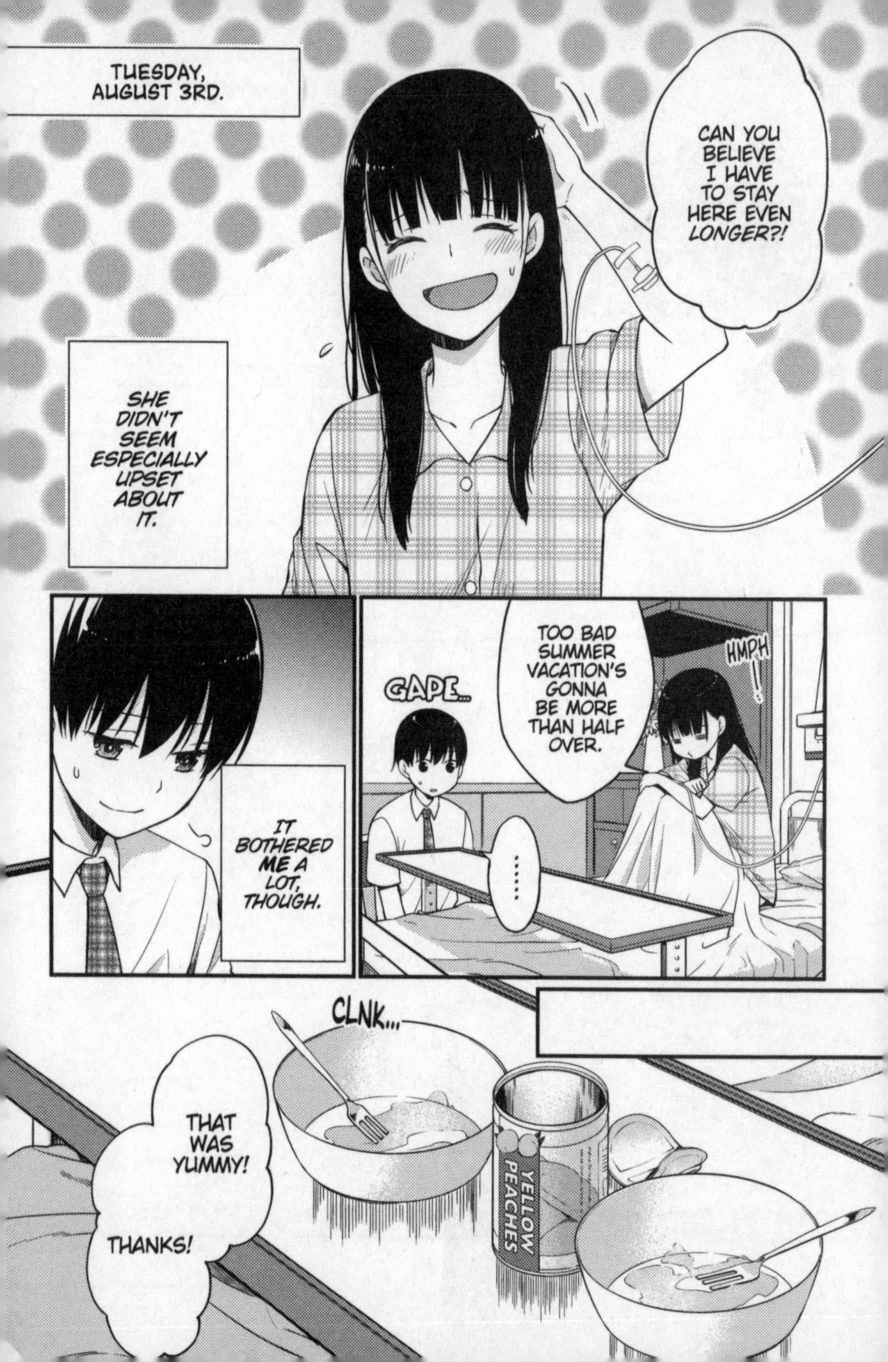
TUESDAY, AUGUST 3RD.
CAN YOU BELIEVE I HAVE TO STAY HERE EVEN LONGER?!
SHE DIDN'T SEEM ESPECIALLY UPSET ABOUT IT.
TOO BAD SUMMER VACATION'S GONNA BE MORE THAN HALF OVER.
HMPH!
GAPE...
......
IT BOTHERED ME A LOT, THOUGH.
CLNK...
THAT WAS YUMMY!
THANKS!
YELLOW PEACHES

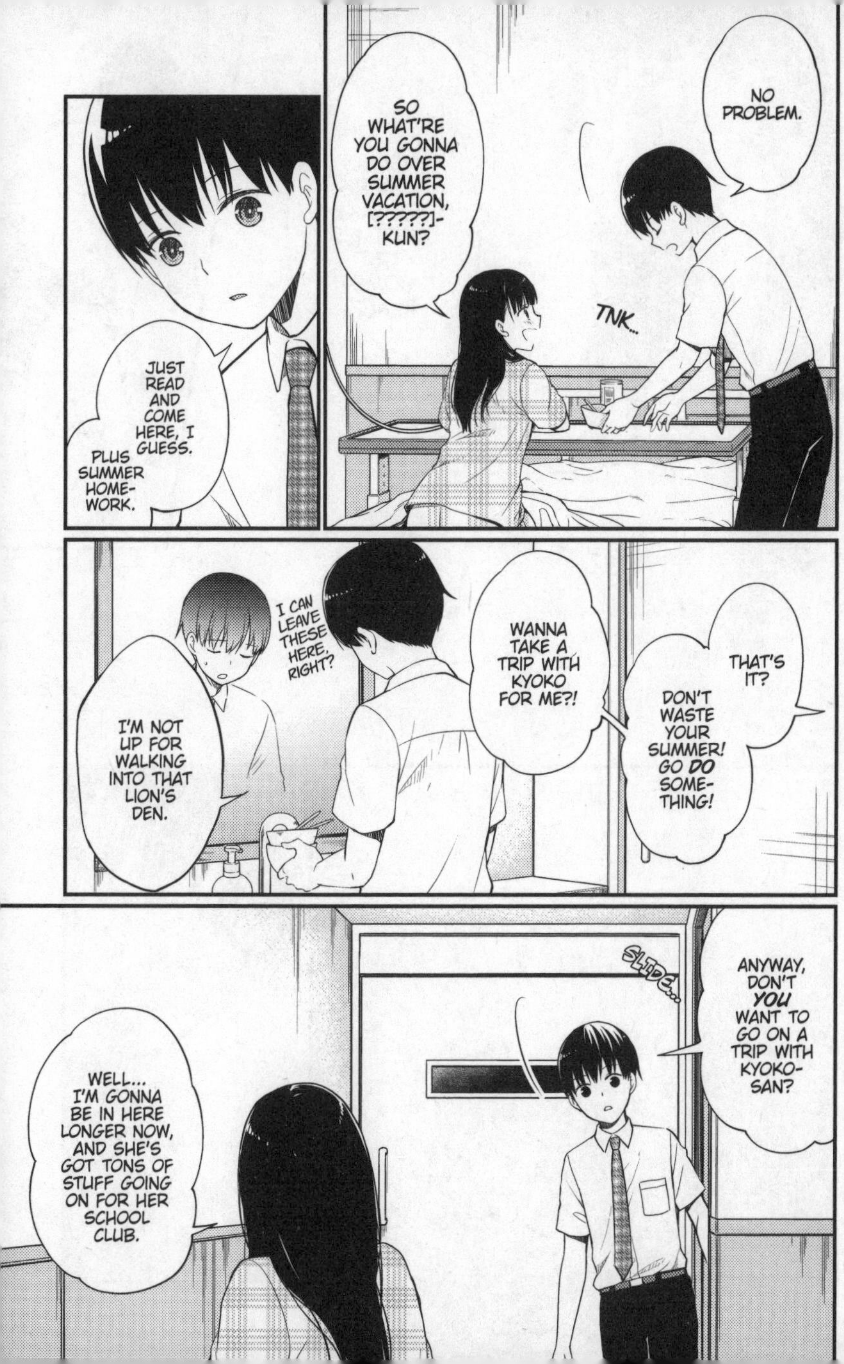
NO PROBLEM.
SO WHAT'RE YOU GONNA DO OVER SUMMER VACATION, [?????]-KUN?
TNK...
JUST READ AND COME HERE, I GUESS.
PLUS SUMMER HOMEWORK.
THAT'S IT?
DON'T WASTE YOUR SUMMER! GO DO SOMETHING!
WANNA TAKE A TRIP WITH KYOKO FOR ME?!
I CAN LEAVE THESE HERE, RIGHT?
I'M NOT UP FOR WALKING INTO THAT LION'S DEN.
SLIDE...
ANYWAY, DON'T YOU WANT TO GO ON A TRIP WITH KYOKO-SAN?
WELL... I'M GONNA BE IN HERE LONGER NOW, AND SHE'S GOT TONS OF STUFF GOING ON FOR HER SCHOOL CLUB.

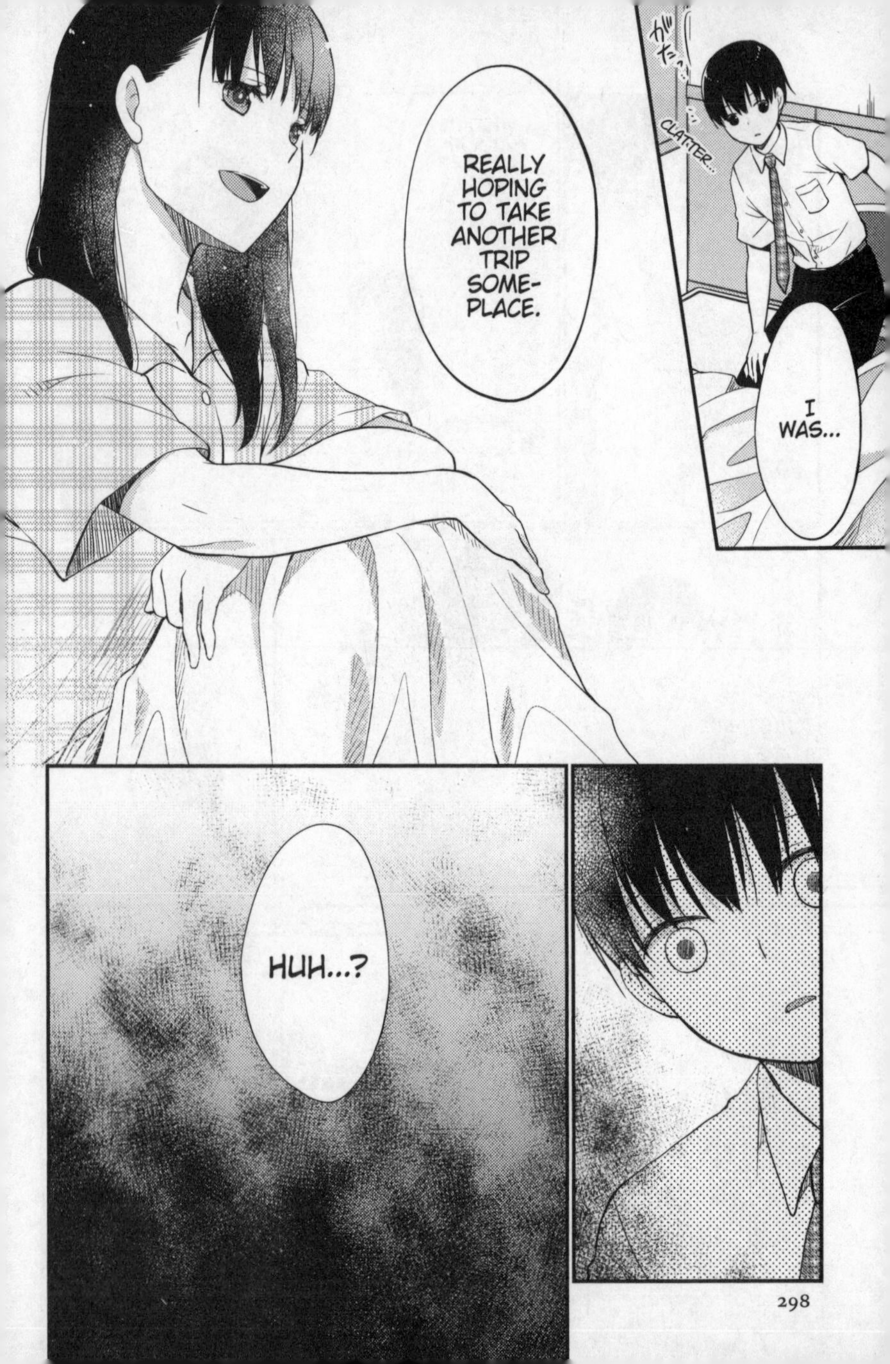
ガタッ
CLATTER...
I WAS...
REALLY HOPING TO TAKE ANOTHER TRIP SOME-PLACE.
HUH...?

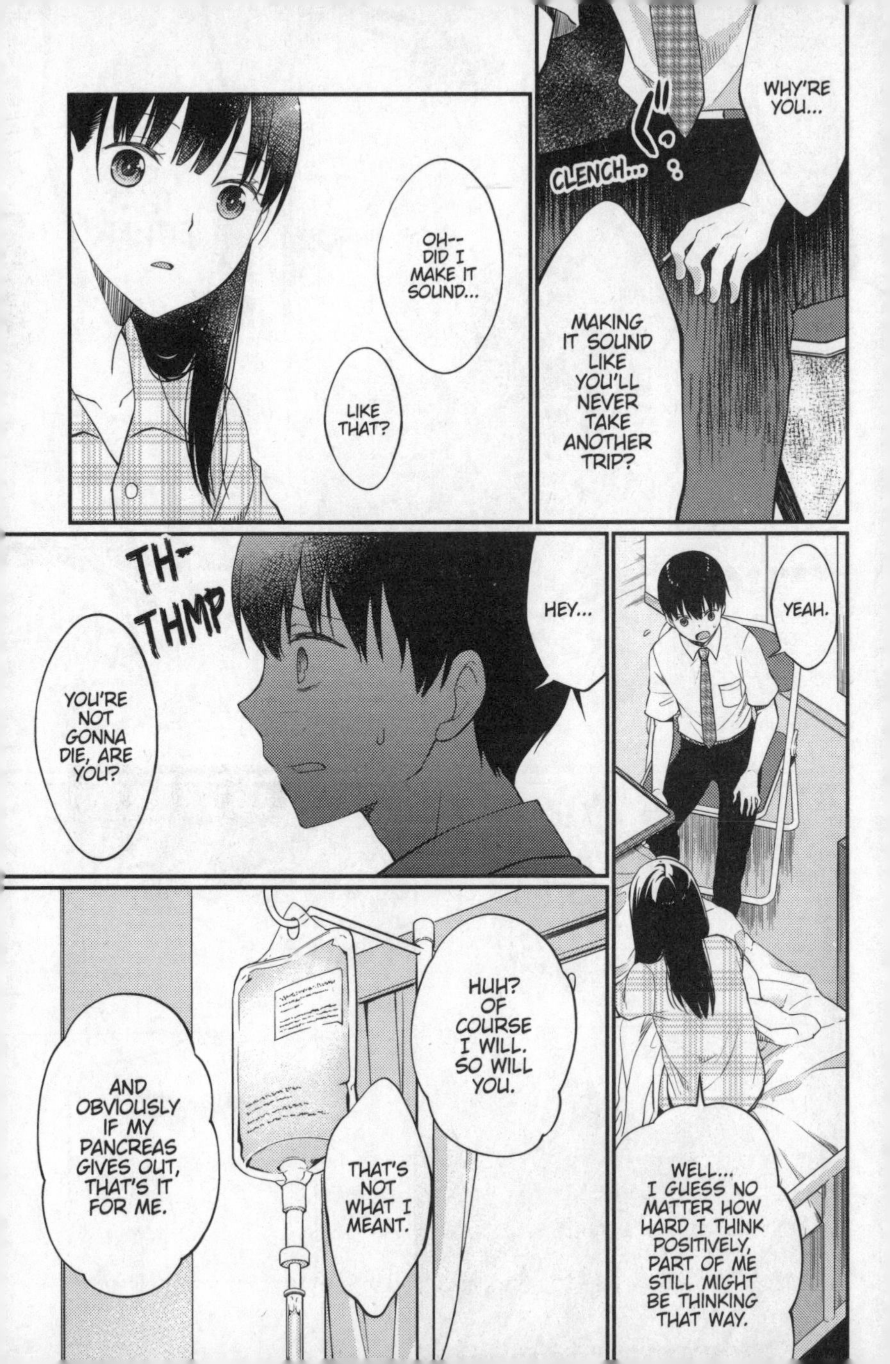
WHY'RE YOU...
CLENCH...
MAKING IT SOUND LIKE YOU'LL NEVER TAKE ANOTHER TRIP?
OH-- DID I MAKE IT SOUND...
LIKE THAT?
WELL... I GUESS NO MATTER HOW HARD I THINK POSITIVELY, PART OF ME STILL MIGHT BE THINKING THAT WAY.
YEAH.
HEY...
TH-THMP
YOU'RE NOT GONNA DIE, ARE YOU?
HUH? OF COURSE I WILL. SO WILL YOU.
THAT'S NOT WHAT I MEANT.
AND OBVIOUSLY IF MY PANCREAS GIVES OUT, THAT'S IT FOR ME.

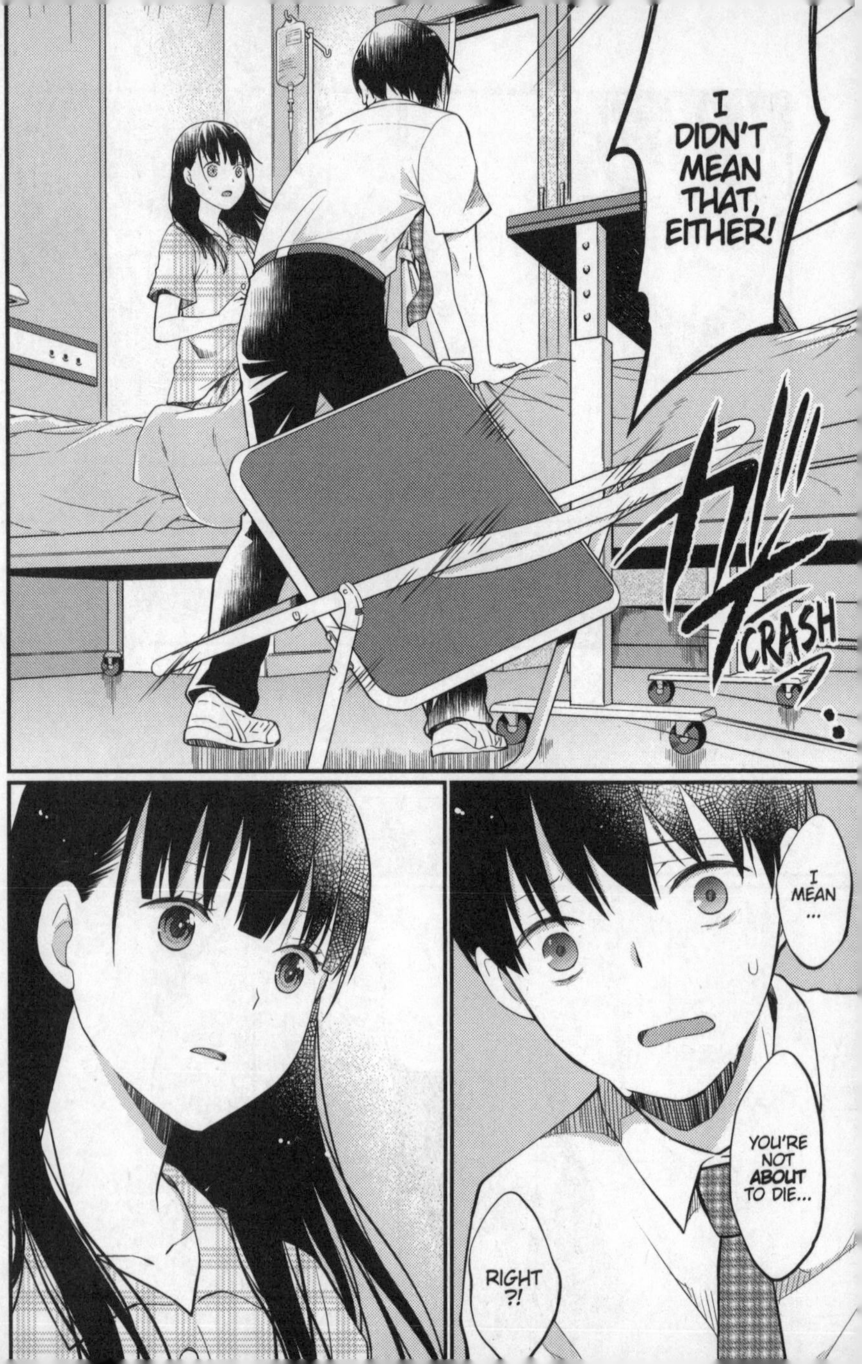
I DIDN'T MEAN THAT, EITHER!
CRASH
I MEAN ...
YOU'RE NOT ABOUT TO DIE...
RIGHT ?!

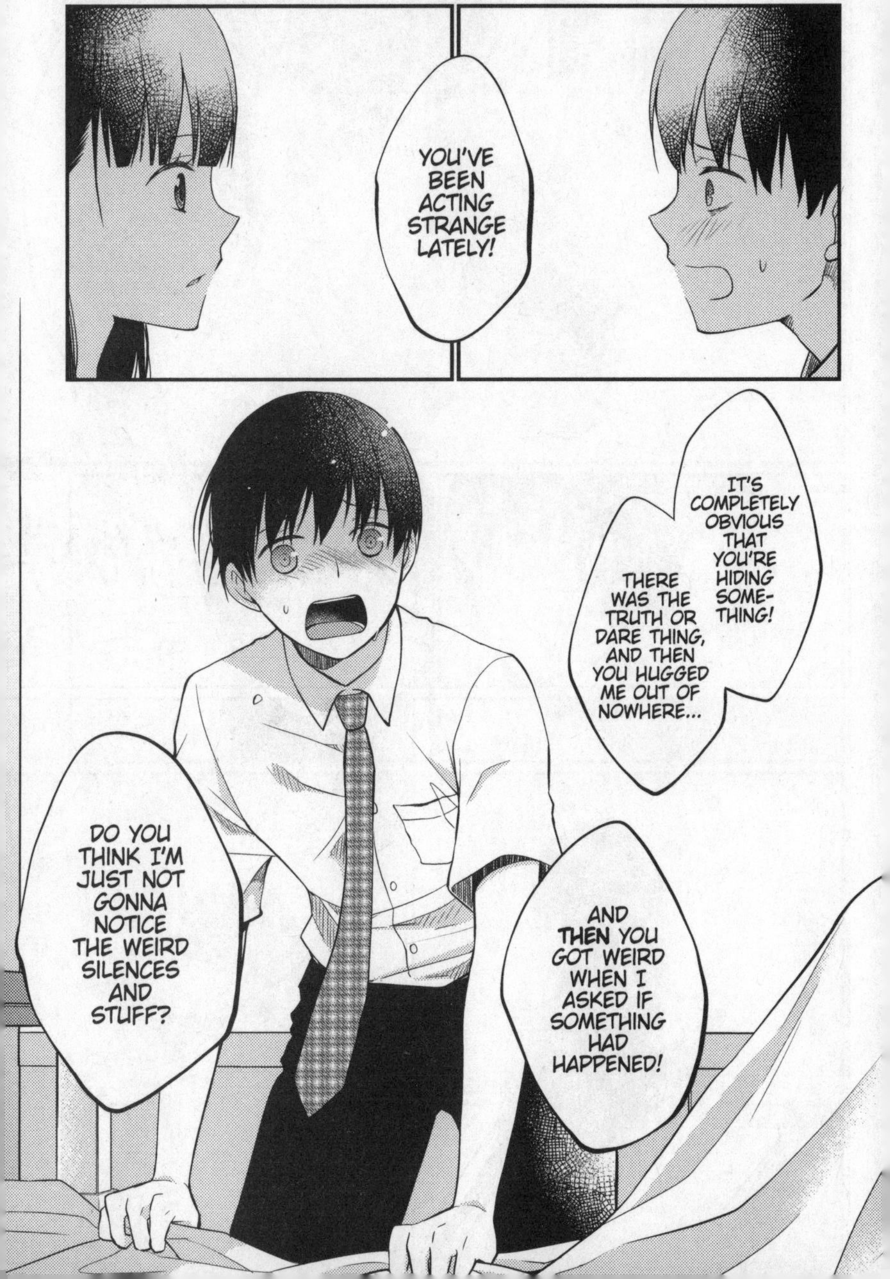
YOU'VE BEEN ACTING STRANGE LATELY!
IT'S COMPLETELY OBVIOUS THAT YOU'RE HIDING SOME-THING!
THERE WAS THE TRUTH OR DARE THING, AND THEN YOU HUGGED ME OUT OF NOWHERE...
AND **THEN** YOU GOT WEIRD WHEN I ASKED IF SOMETHING HAD HAPPENED!
DO YOU THINK I'M JUST NOT GONNA NOTICE THE WEIRD SILENCES AND STUFF?

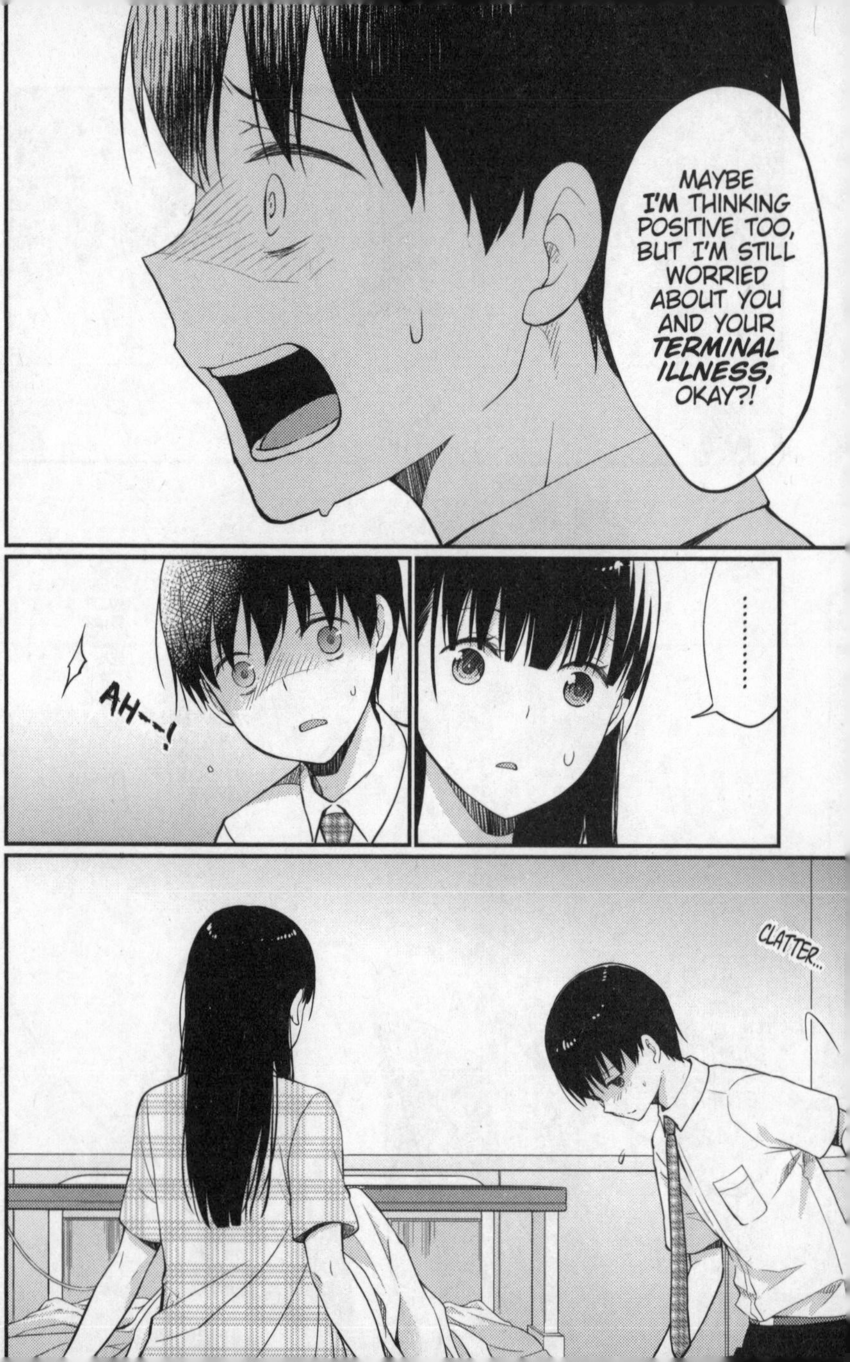
MAYBE I'M THINKING POSITIVE TOO, BUT I'M STILL WORRIED ABOUT YOU AND YOUR TERMINAL ILLNESS, OKAY?!
....
AH--!
CLATTER...

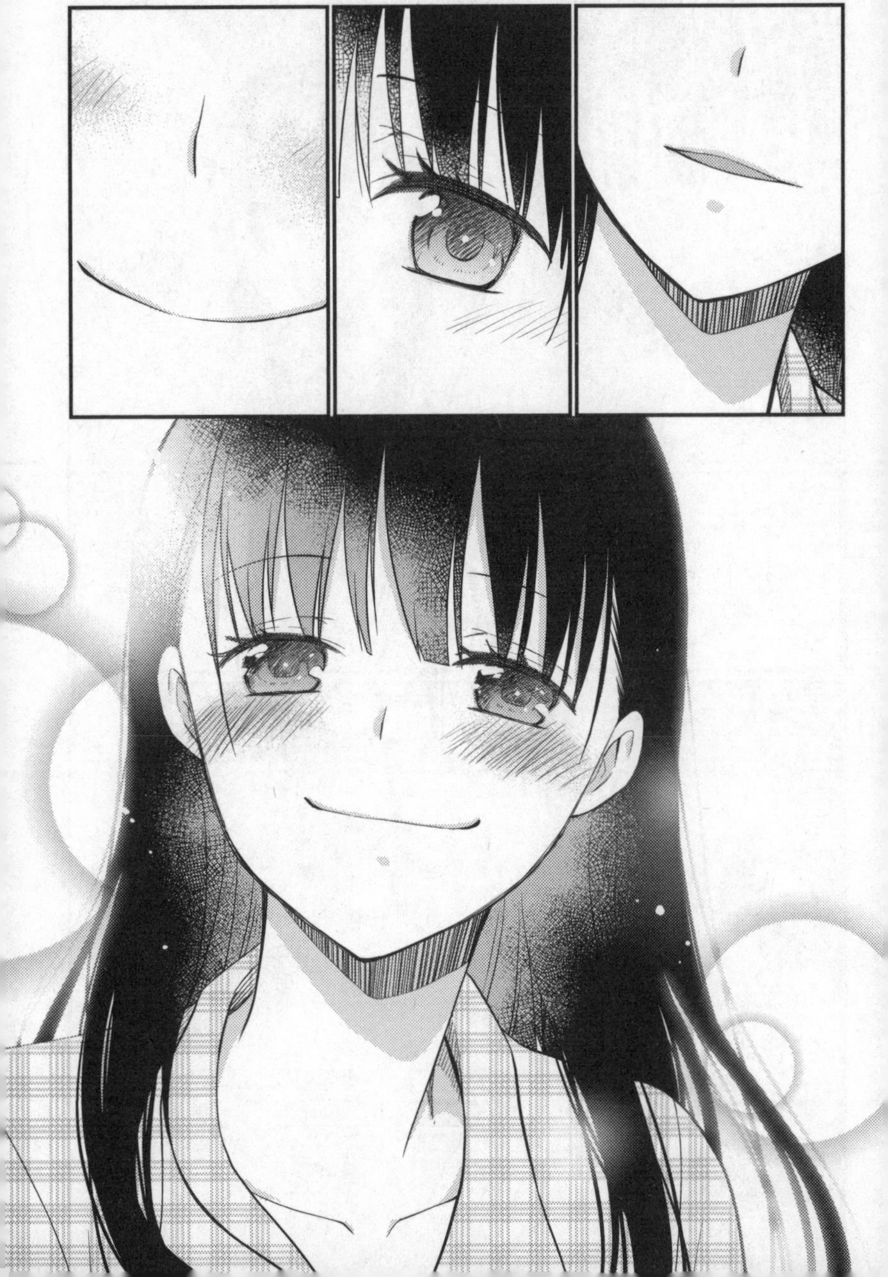

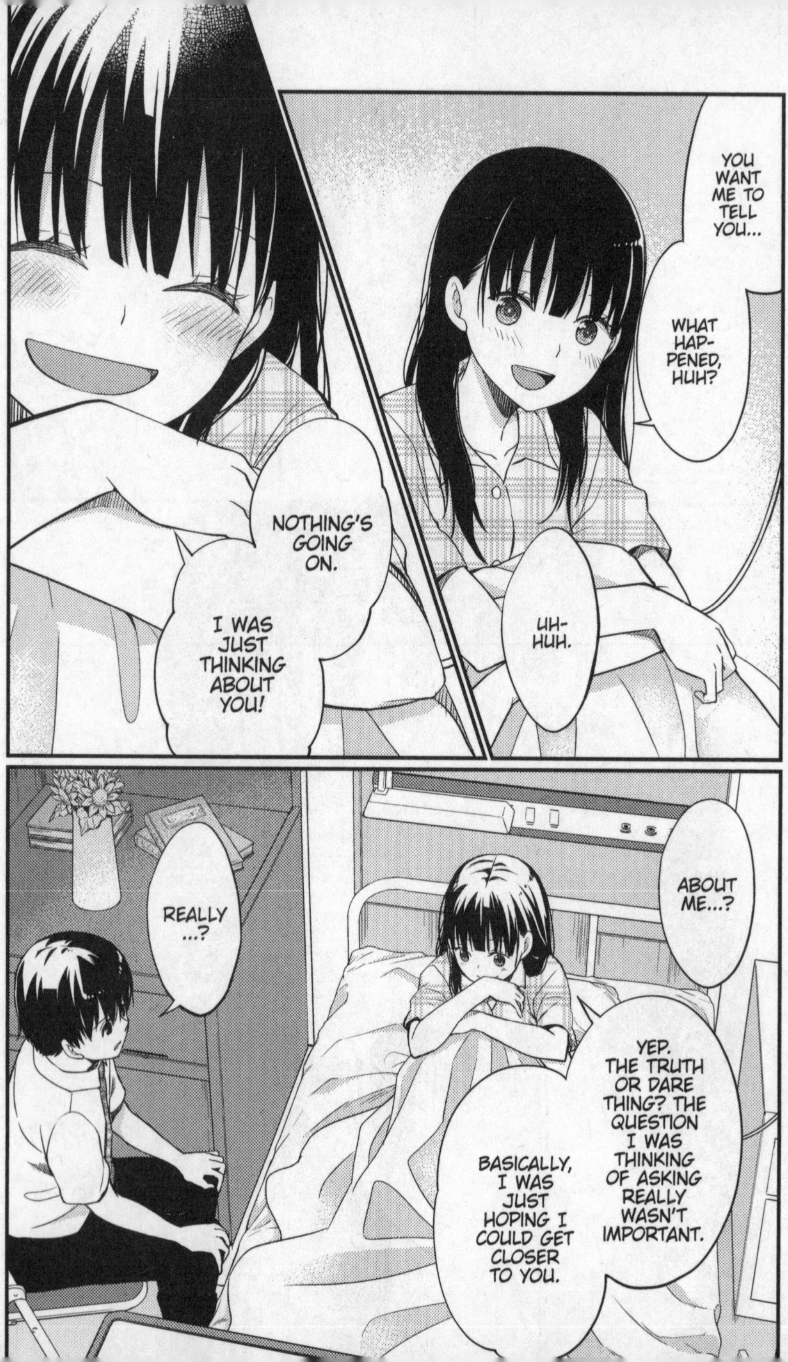
YOU WANT ME TO TELL YOU...
WHAT HAP-PENED, HUH?
UH-HUH.
NOTHING'S GOING ON.
I WAS JUST THINKING ABOUT YOU!
ABOUT ME...?
REALLY ...?
YEP. THE TRUTH OR DARE THING? THE QUESTION I WAS THINKING OF ASKING REALLY WASN'T IMPORTANT.
BASICALLY, I WAS JUST HOPING I COULD GET CLOSER TO YOU.

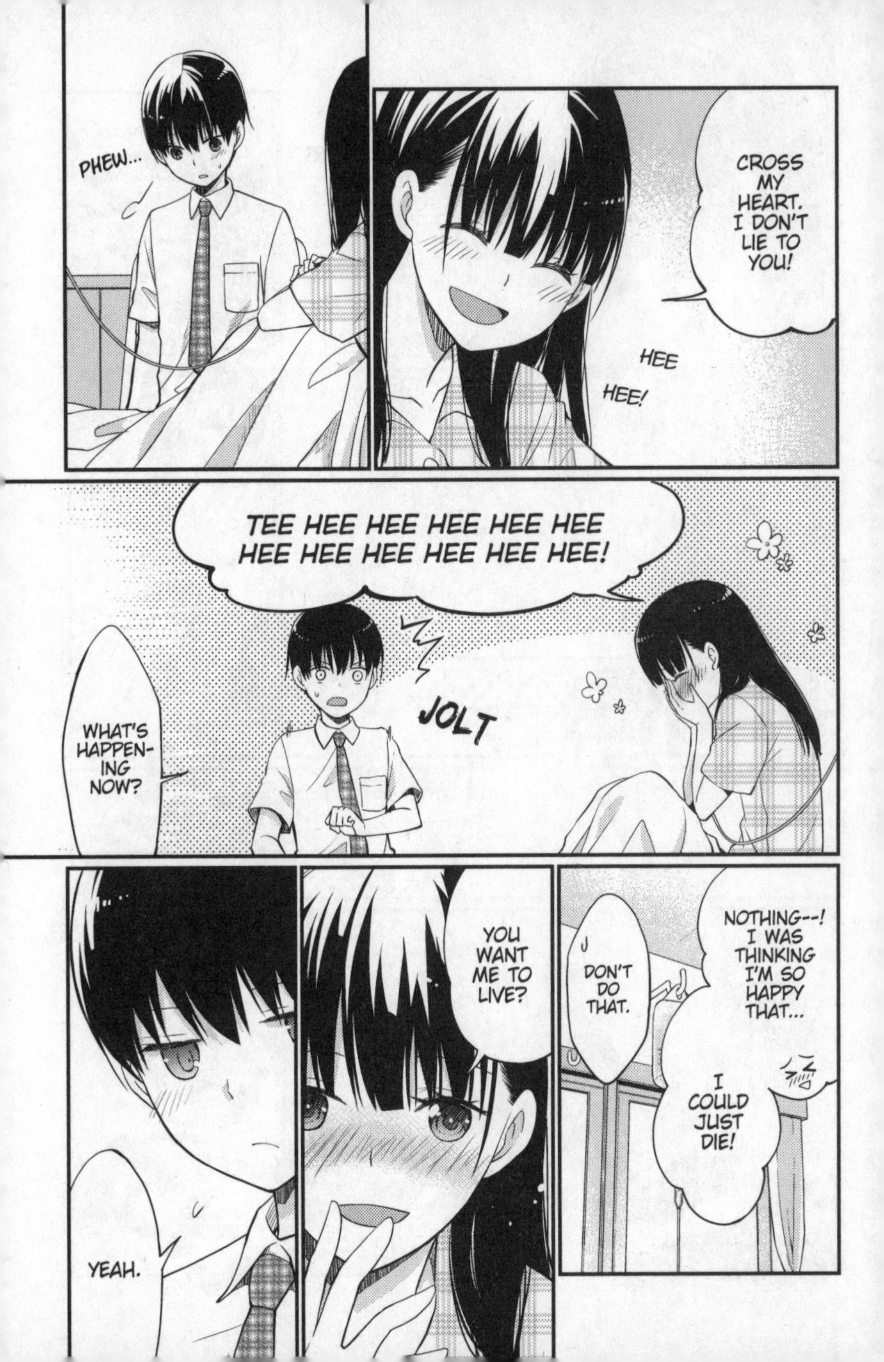
CROSS MY HEART. I DON'T LIE TO YOU!
HEE HEE!
PHEW...
TEE HEE HEE HEE HEE HEE HEE HEE HEE HEE HEE HEE!
JOLT
WHAT'S HAPPENING NOW?
NOTHING--! I WAS THINKING I'M SO HAPPY THAT...
I COULD JUST DIE!
DON'T DO THAT.
YOU WANT ME TO LIVE?
YEAH.

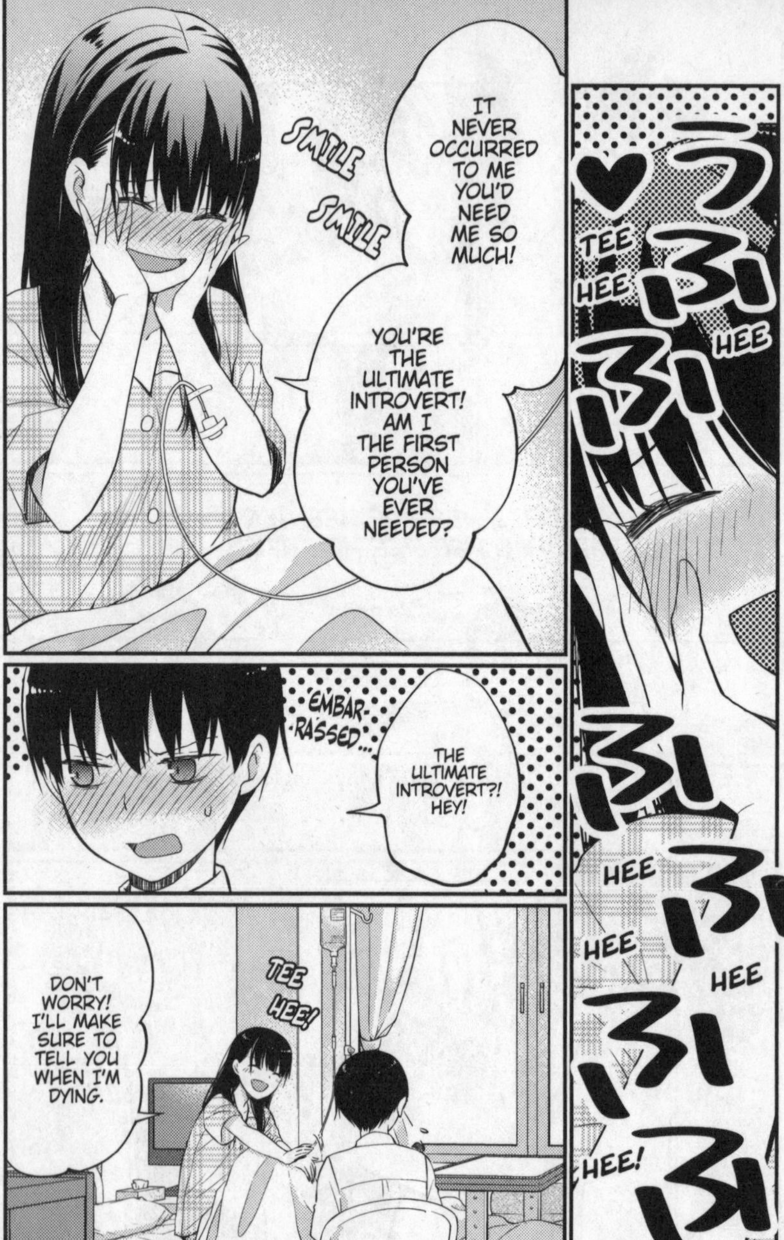

♥うふふ
TEE HEE
HEE
ふふふふ
HEE
HEE
HEE
HEE!
♥
IT NEVER OCCURRED TO ME YOU'D NEED ME SO MUCH!
SMILE SMILE
YOU'RE THE ULTIMATE INTROVERT! AM I THE FIRST PERSON YOU'VE EVER NEEDED?
EMBAR-RASSED...
THE ULTIMATE INTROVERT?! HEY!
DON'T WORRY! I'LL MAKE SURE TO TELL YOU WHEN I'M DYING.
TEE HEE!

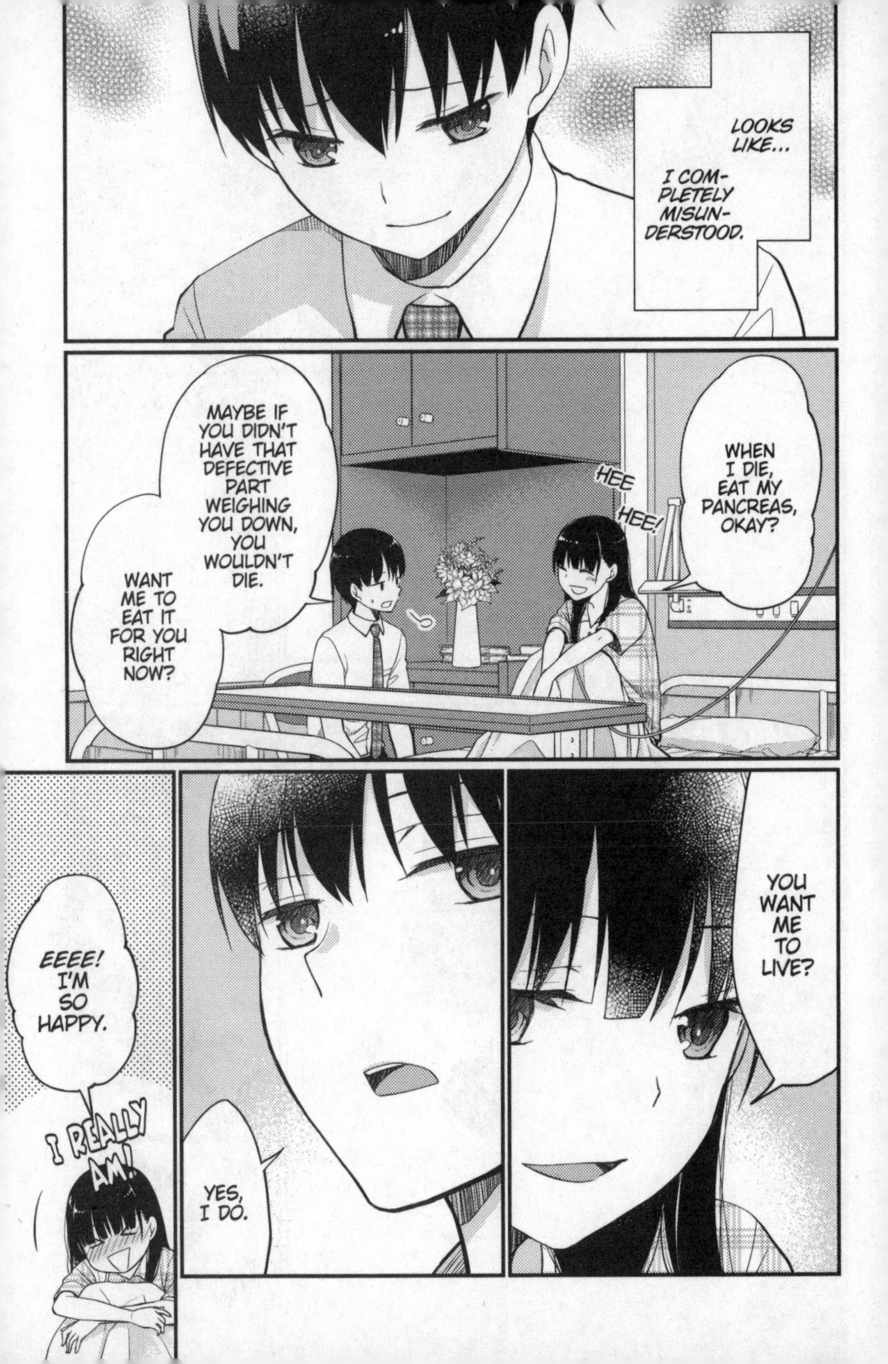
LOOKS LIKE... I COMPLETELY MISUNDERSTOOD.
WHEN I DIE, EAT MY PANCREAS, OKAY?
HEE HEE!
MAYBE IF YOU DIDN'T HAVE THAT DEFECTIVE PART WEIGHING YOU DOWN, YOU WOULDN'T DIE.
WANT ME TO EAT IT FOR YOU RIGHT NOW?
YOU WANT ME TO LIVE?
YES, I DO.
EEEE! I'M SO HAPPY.
I REALLY AM!

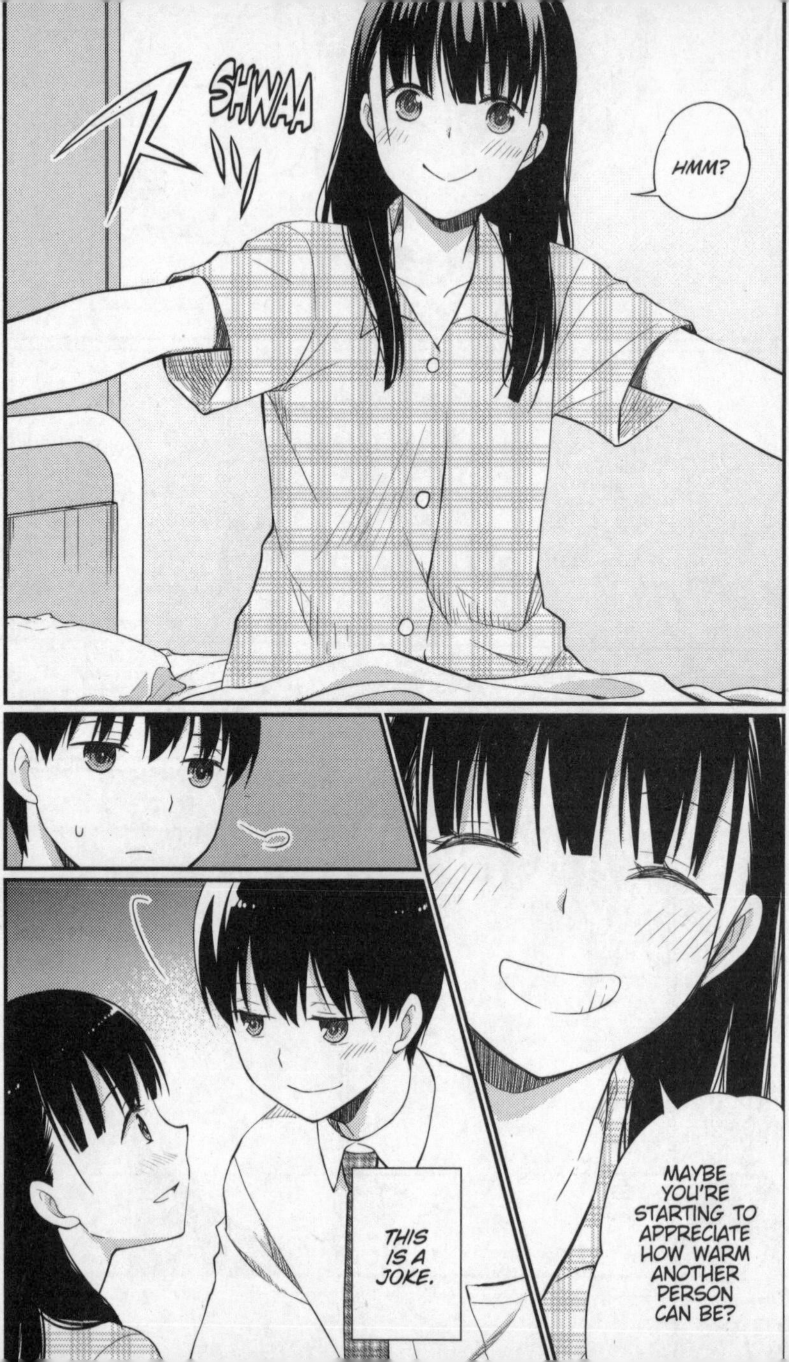
HMM?
SHWAA
MAYBE YOU'RE STARTING TO APPRECIATE HOW WARM ANOTHER PERSON CAN BE?
THIS IS A JOKE.

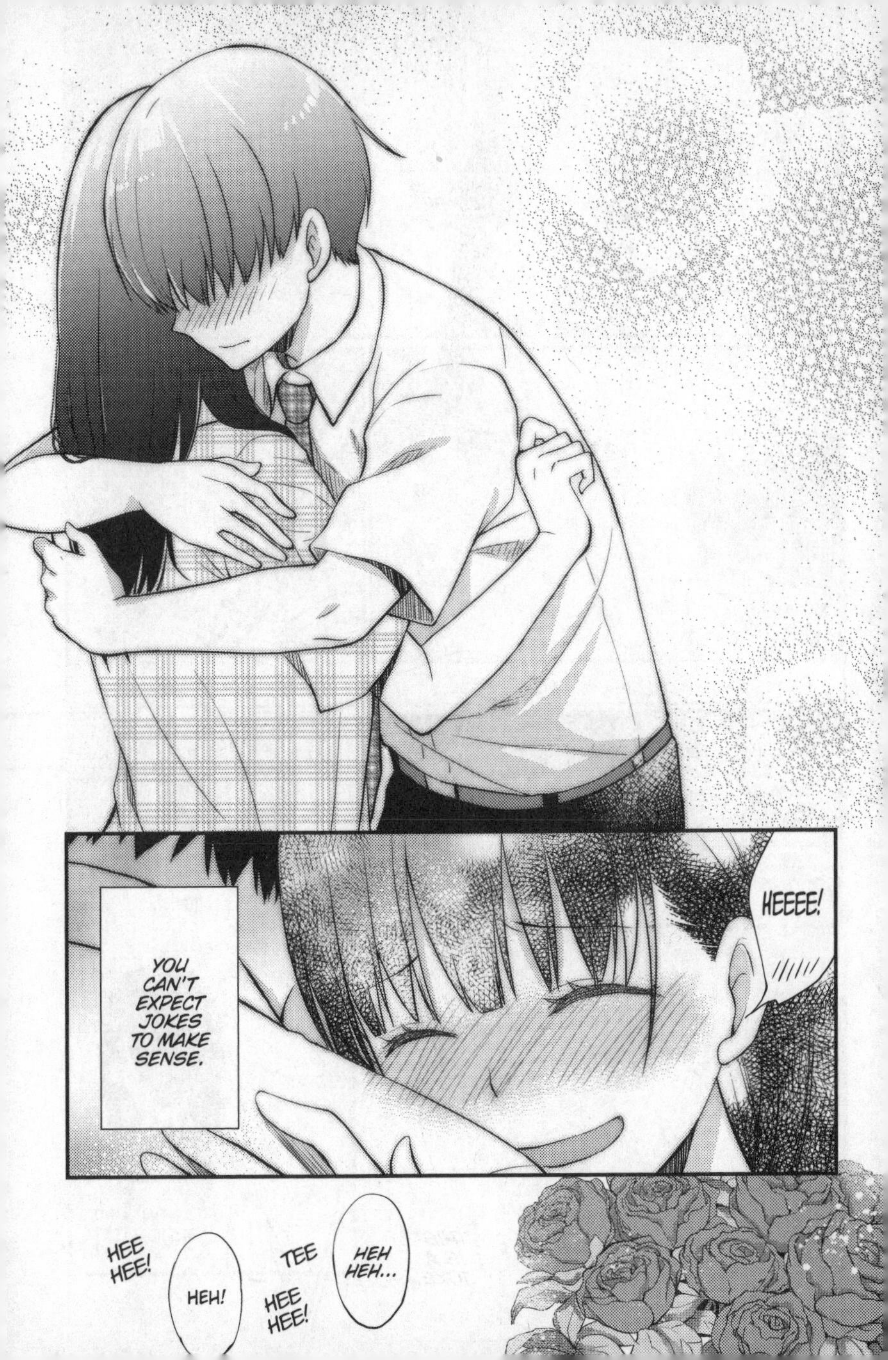
HEEEE!
YOU CAN'T EXPECT JOKES TO MAKE SENSE.
HEH HEH...
TEE
HEE HEE!
HEH!
HEE HEE!

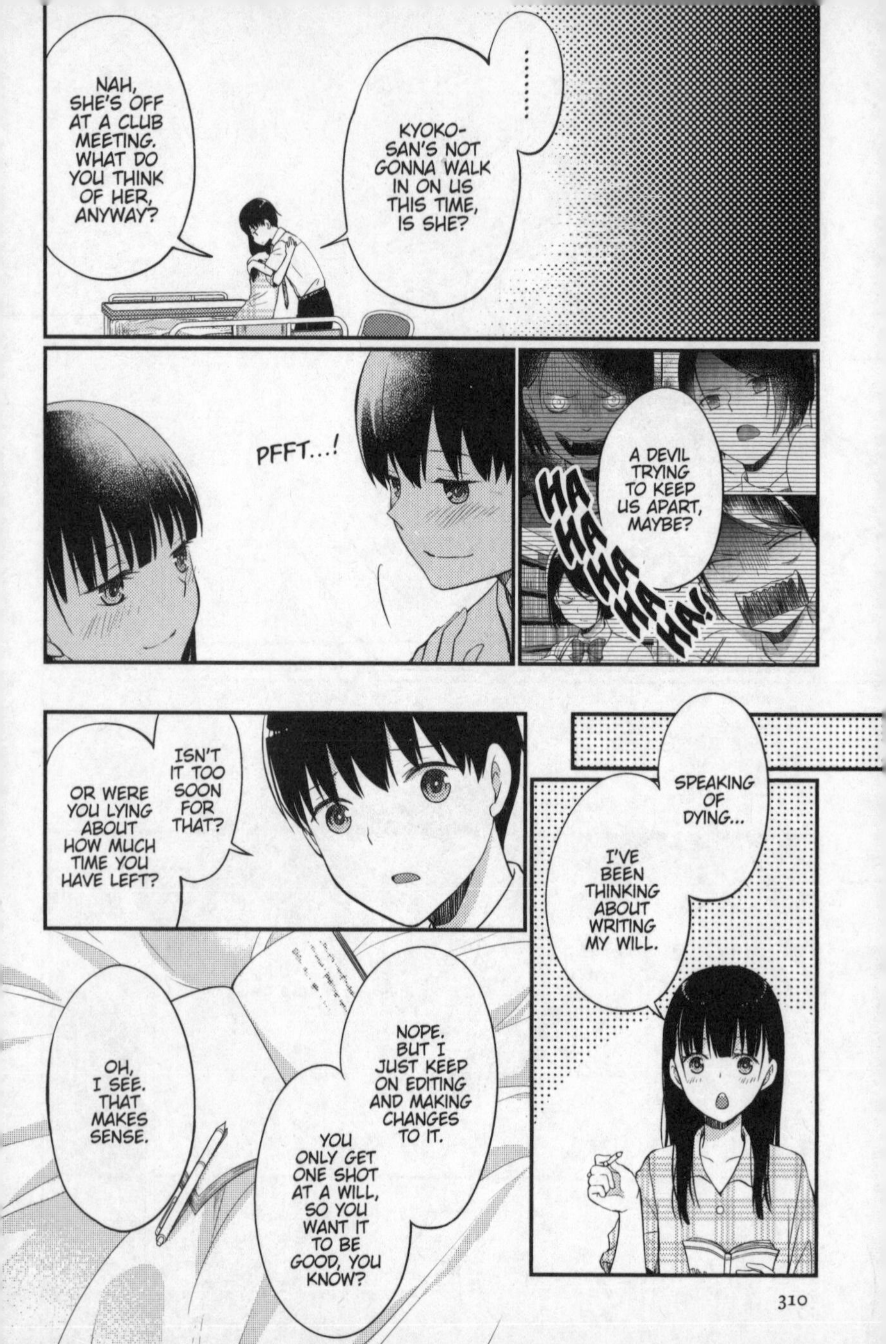
......
KYOKO-SAN'S NOT GONNA WALK IN ON US THIS TIME, IS SHE?
NAH, SHE'S OFF AT A CLUB MEETING. WHAT DO YOU THINK OF HER, ANYWAY?
A DEVIL TRYING TO KEEP US APART, MAYBE?
HA HA HA HA HA!
PFFT...!
SPEAKING OF DYING...
I'VE BEEN THINKING ABOUT WRITING MY WILL.
ISN'T IT TOO SOON FOR THAT?
OR WERE YOU LYING ABOUT HOW MUCH TIME YOU HAVE LEFT?
NOPE. BUT I JUST KEEP ON EDITING AND MAKING CHANGES TO IT.
YOU ONLY GET ONE SHOT AT A WILL, SO YOU WANT IT TO BE GOOD, YOU KNOW?
OH, I SEE. THAT MAKES SENSE.

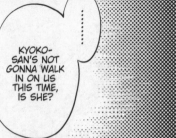

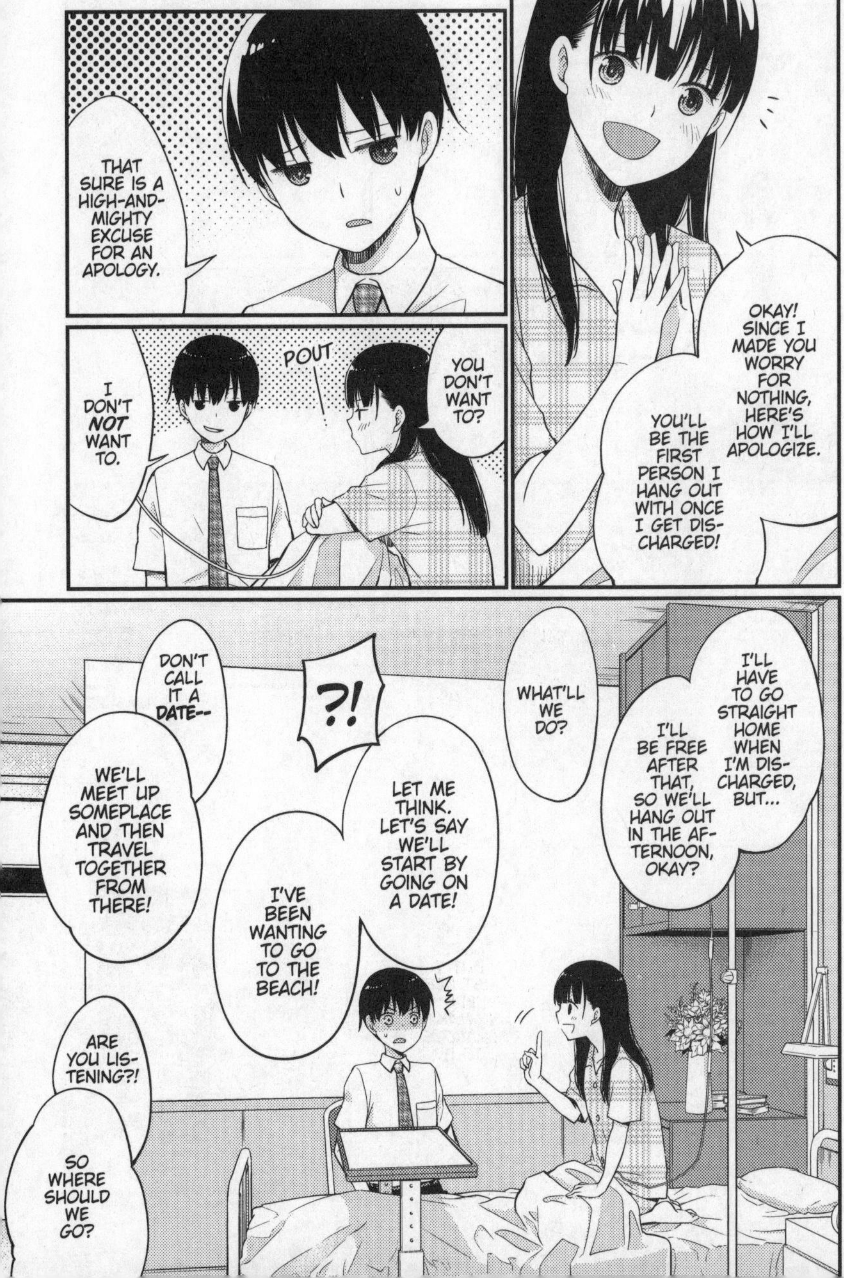
OKAY! SINCE I MADE YOU WORRY FOR NOTHING, HERE'S HOW I'LL APOLOGIZE.
YOU'LL BE THE FIRST PERSON I HANG OUT WITH ONCE I GET DISCHARGED!
THAT SURE IS A HIGH-AND-MIGHTY EXCUSE FOR AN APOLOGY.
YOU DON'T WANT TO?
POUT
I DON'T *NOT* WANT TO.
I'LL HAVE TO GO STRAIGHT HOME WHEN I'M DISCHARGED, BUT...
I'LL BE FREE AFTER THAT, SO WE'LL HANG OUT IN THE AFTERNOON, OKAY?
WHAT'LL WE DO?
LET ME THINK. LET'S SAY WE'LL START BY GOING ON A DATE!
?!
I'VE BEEN WANTING TO GO TO THE BEACH!
DON'T CALL IT A **DATE**--
WE'LL MEET UP SOMEPLACE AND THEN TRAVEL TOGETHER FROM THERE!
ARE YOU LISTENING?!
SO WHERE SHOULD WE GO?

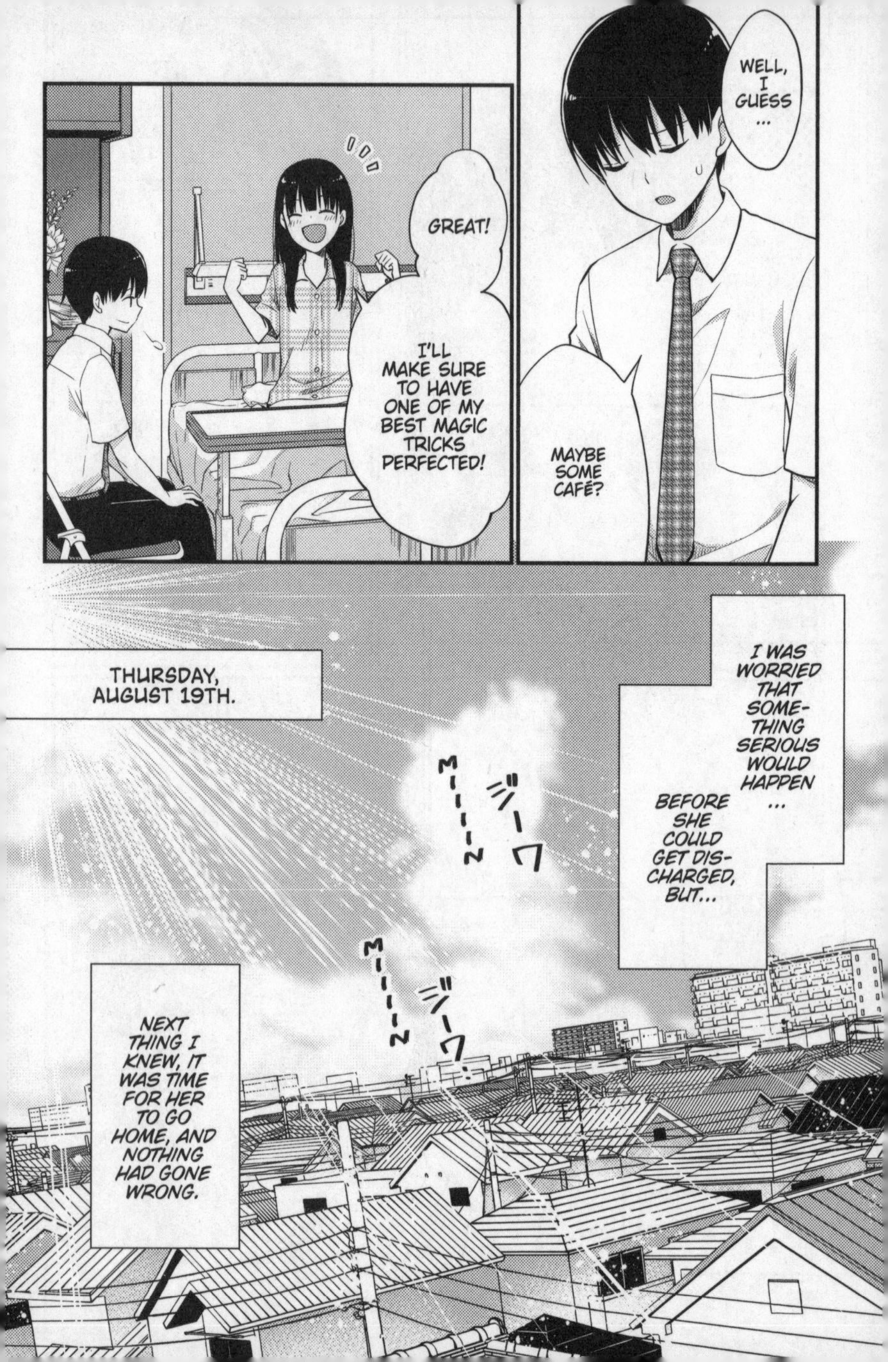
WELL, I GUESS ...
MAYBE SOME CAFÉ?
GREAT!
I'LL MAKE SURE TO HAVE ONE OF MY BEST MAGIC TRICKS PERFECTED!
I WAS WORRIED THAT SOME-THING SERIOUS WOULD HAPPEN ...
BEFORE SHE COULD GET DIS-CHARGED, BUT...
THURSDAY, AUGUST 19TH.
MIIIIN
MIIIIN
NEXT THING I KNEW, IT WAS TIME FOR HER TO GO HOME, AND NOTHING HAD GONE WRONG.

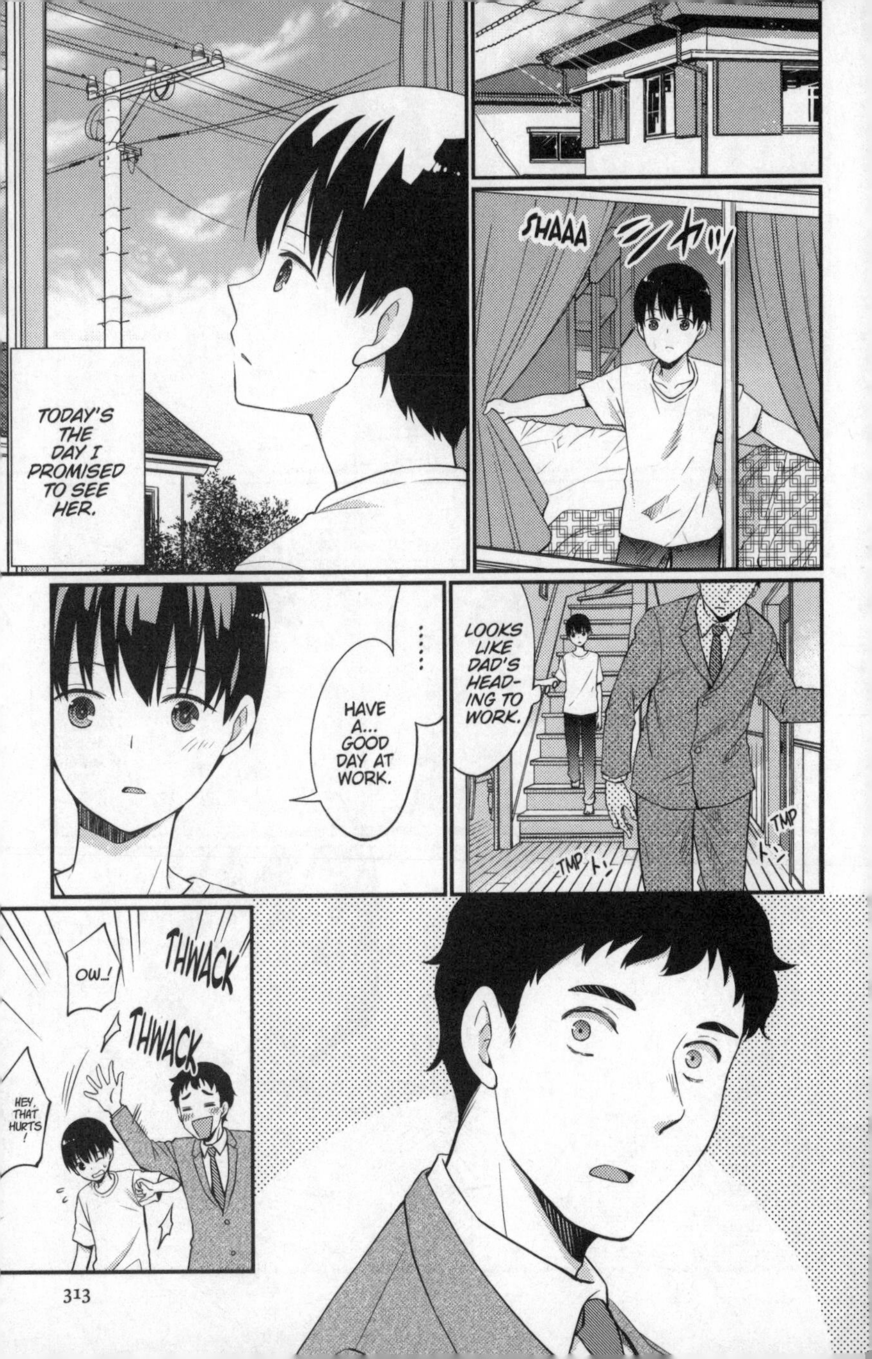

SHAAA
シャッ
TODAY'S THE DAY I PROMISED TO SEE HER.
LOOKS LIKE DAD'S HEADING TO WORK.
TMP
ト
TMP
トン
......
HAVE A... GOOD DAY AT WORK.
THWACK
OW...!
THWACK
HEY, THAT HURTS!

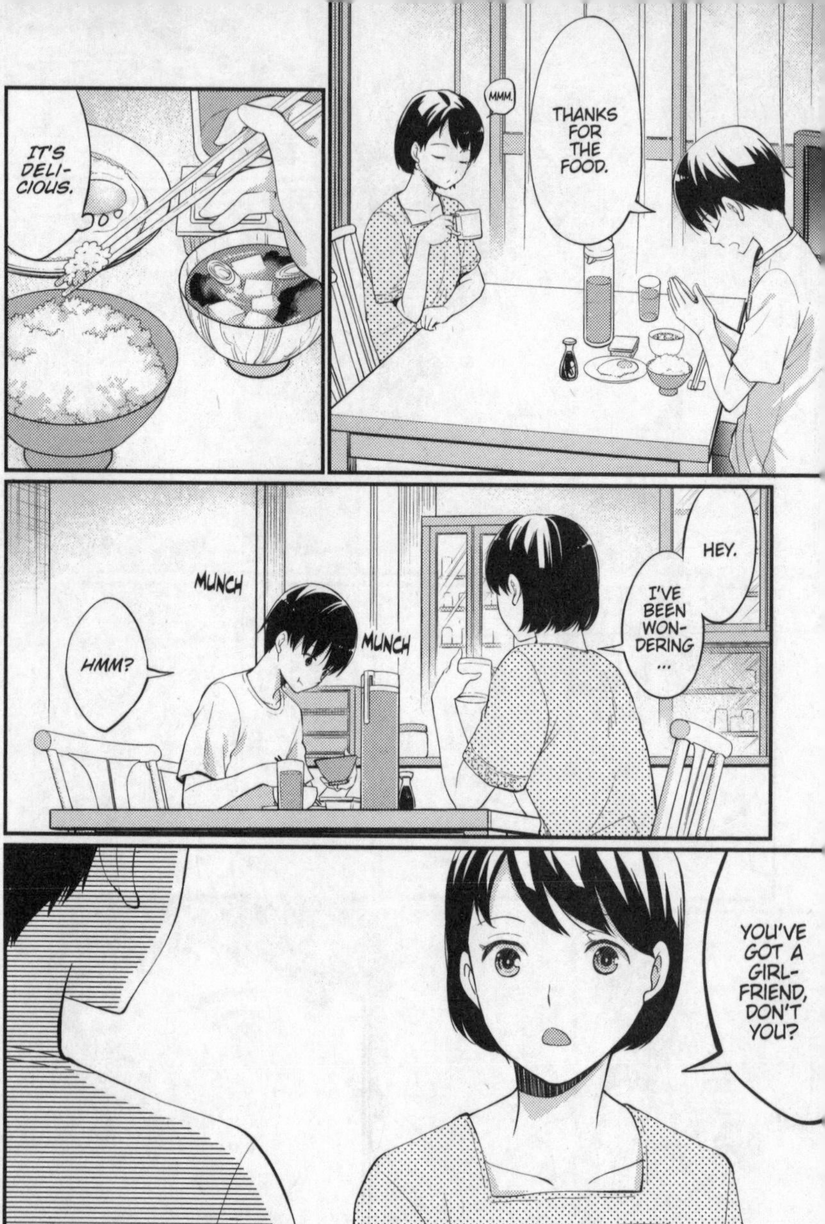
THANKS FOR THE FOOD.
MMM.
IT'S DELI-CIOUS.
HEY.
I'VE BEEN WON-DERING ...
MUNCH
MUNCH
HMM?
YOU'VE GOT A GIRL-FRIEND, DON'T YOU?

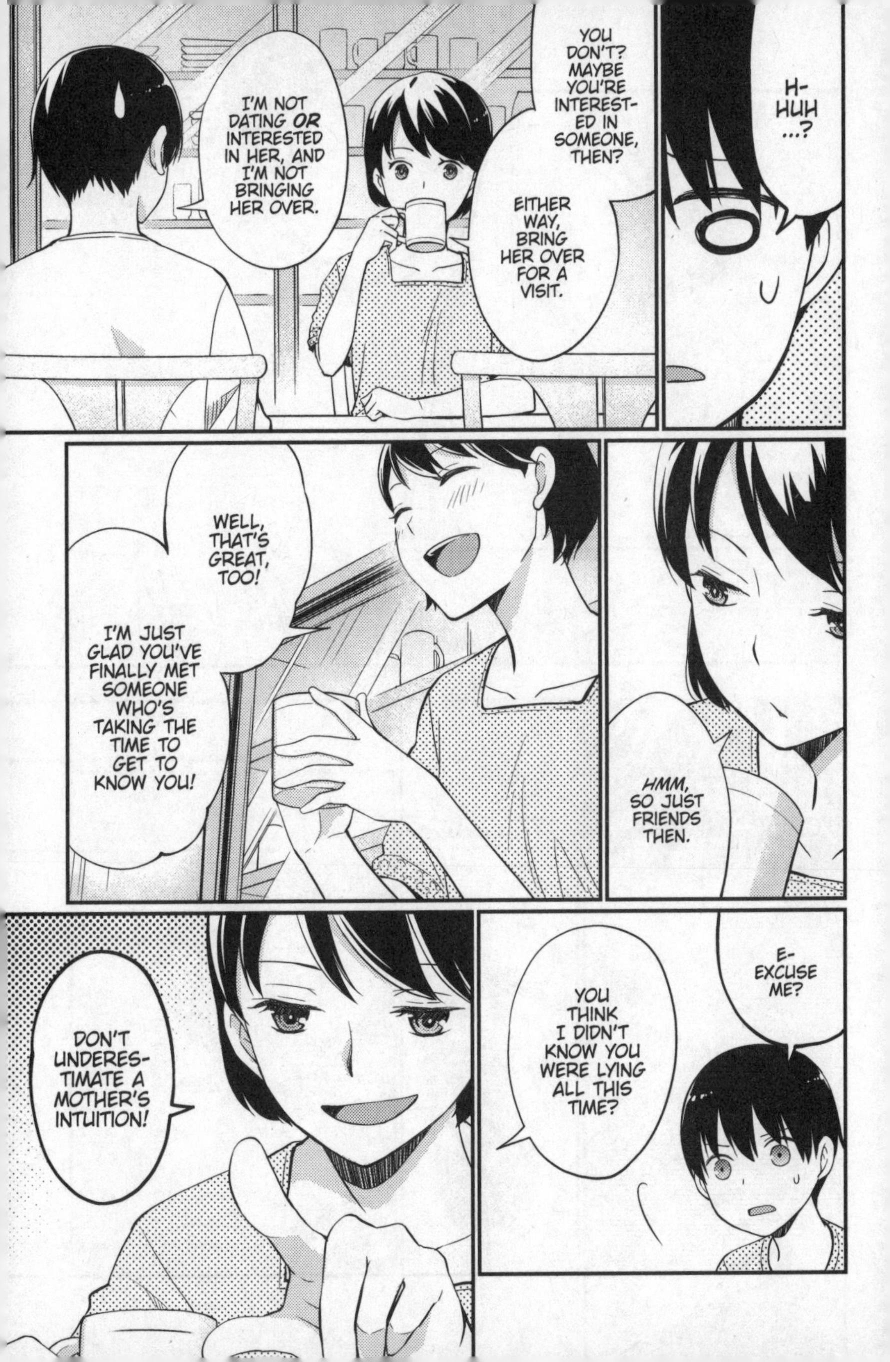
H-HUH ...?
I'M NOT DATING *OR* INTERESTED IN HER, AND I'M NOT BRINGING HER OVER.
YOU DON'T? MAYBE YOU'RE INTEREST-ED IN SOMEONE, THEN?
EITHER WAY, BRING HER OVER FOR A VISIT.
HMM, SO JUST FRIENDS THEN.
WELL, THAT'S GREAT, TOO!
I'M JUST GLAD YOU'VE FINALLY MET SOMEONE WHO'S TAKING THE TIME TO GET TO KNOW YOU!
E-EXCUSE ME?
YOU THINK I DIDN'T KNOW YOU WERE LYING ALL THIS TIME?
DON'T UNDERES-TIMATE A MOTHER'S INTUITION!

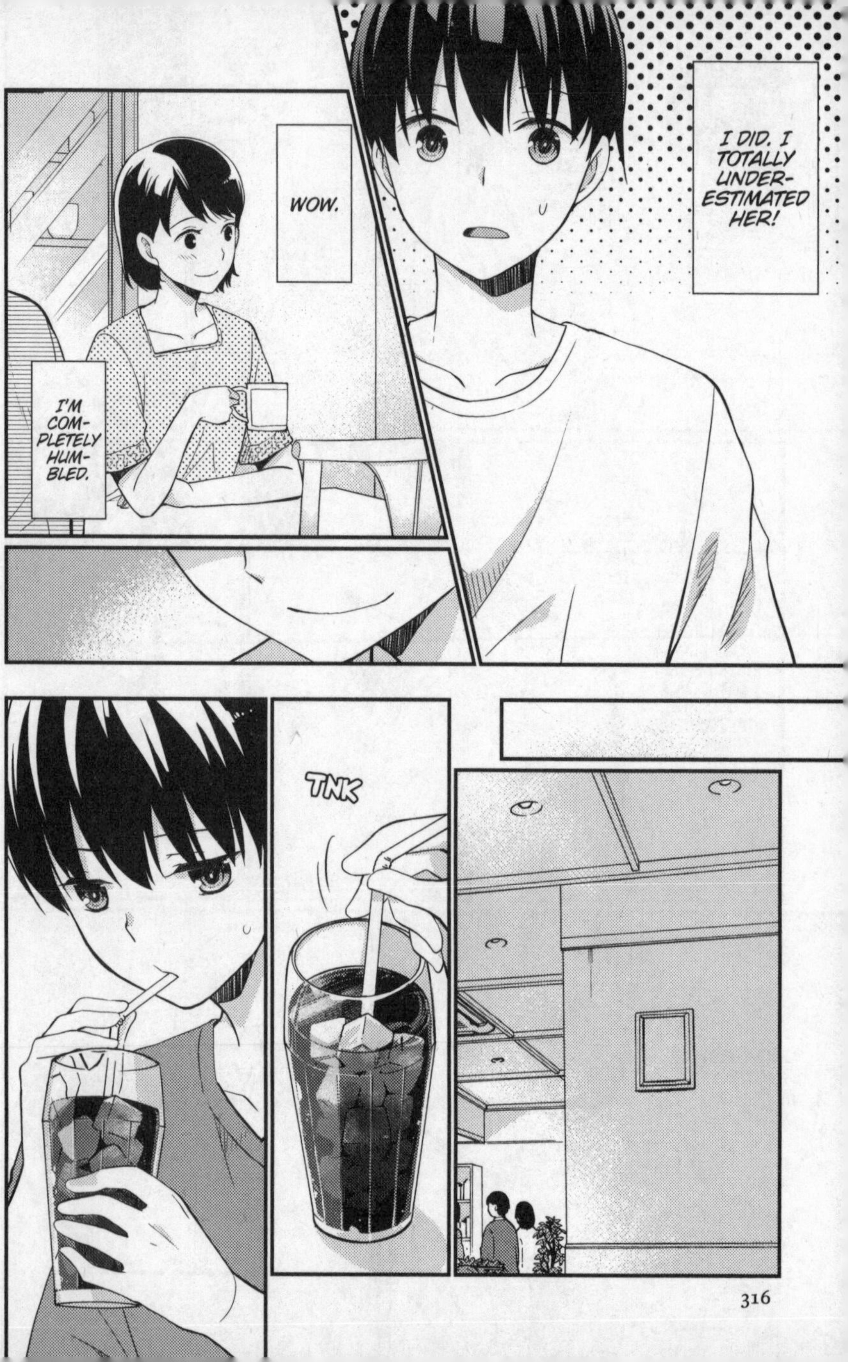
I DID. I TOTALLY UNDER-ESTIMATED HER!
WOW.
I'M COM-PLETELY HUM-BLED.
TNK

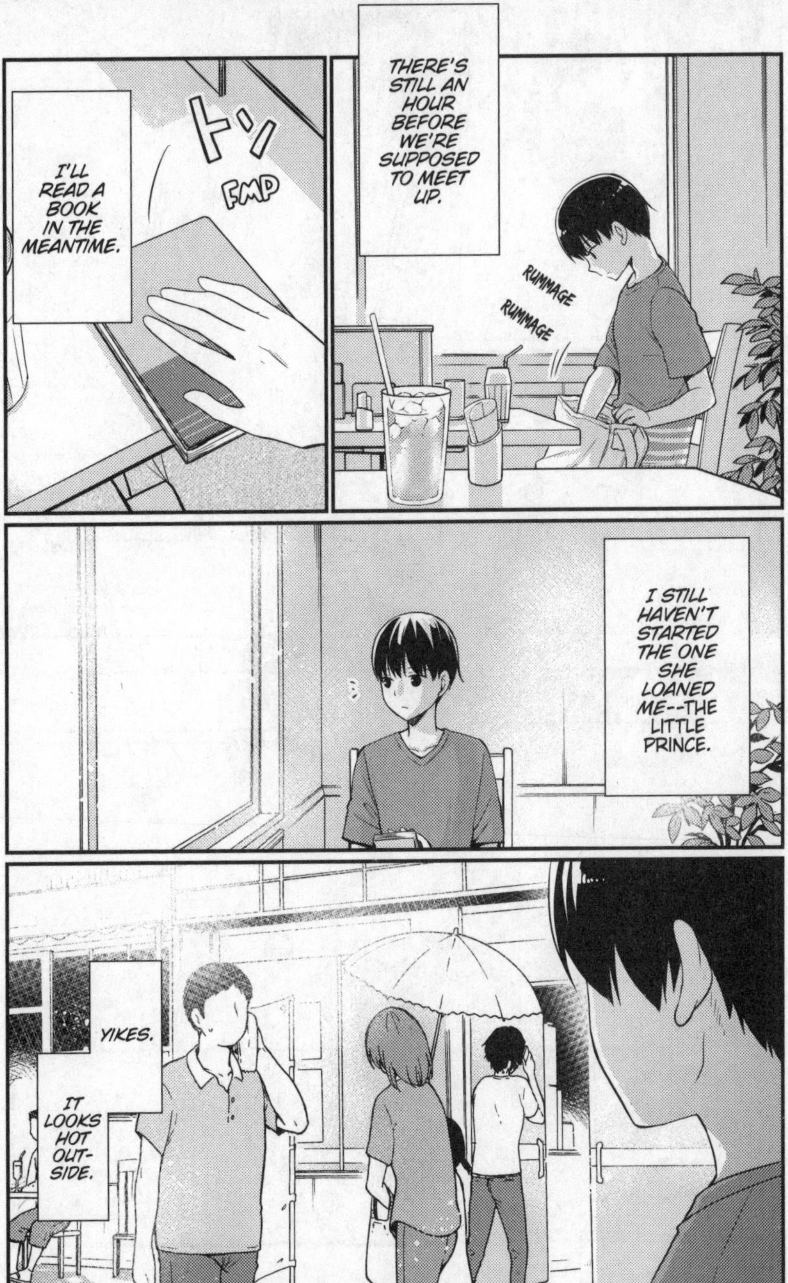
THERE'S STILL AN HOUR BEFORE WE'RE SUPPOSED TO MEET UP.
RUMMAGE
RUMMAGE
I'LL READ A BOOK IN THE MEANTIME.
FMP
I STILL HAVEN'T STARTED THE ONE SHE LOANED ME--THE LITTLE PRINCE.
YIKES.
IT LOOKS HOT OUT-SIDE.

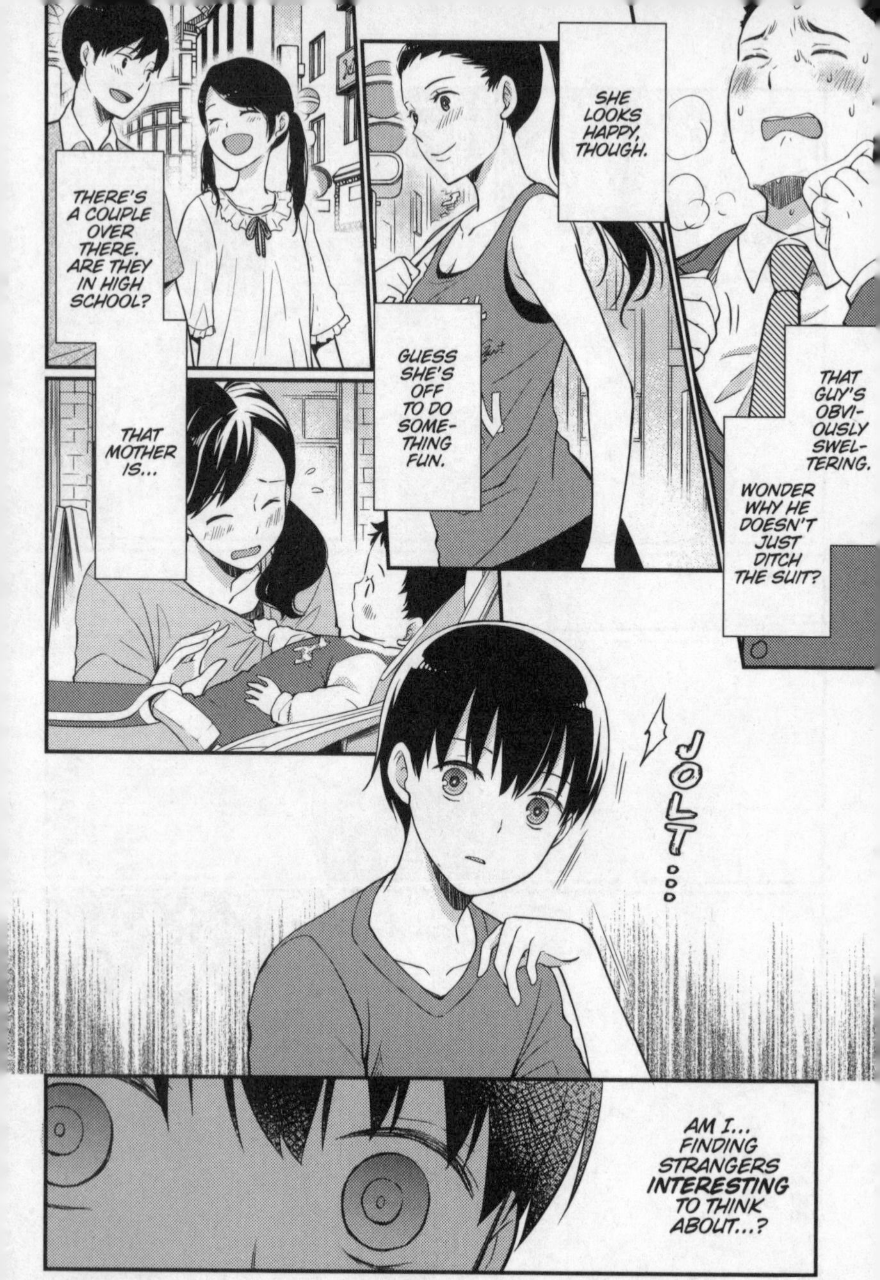
THAT GUY'S OBVI-OUSLY SWELT-TERING.
WONDER WHY HE DOESN'T JUST DITCH THE SUIT?
SHE LOOKS HAPPY, THOUGH.
GUESS SHE'S OFF TO DO SOME-THING FUN.
THERE'S A COUPLE OVER THERE. ARE THEY IN HIGH SCHOOL?
THAT MOTHER IS...
JOLT...
AM I... FINDING STRANGERS INTERESTING TO THINK ABOUT...?

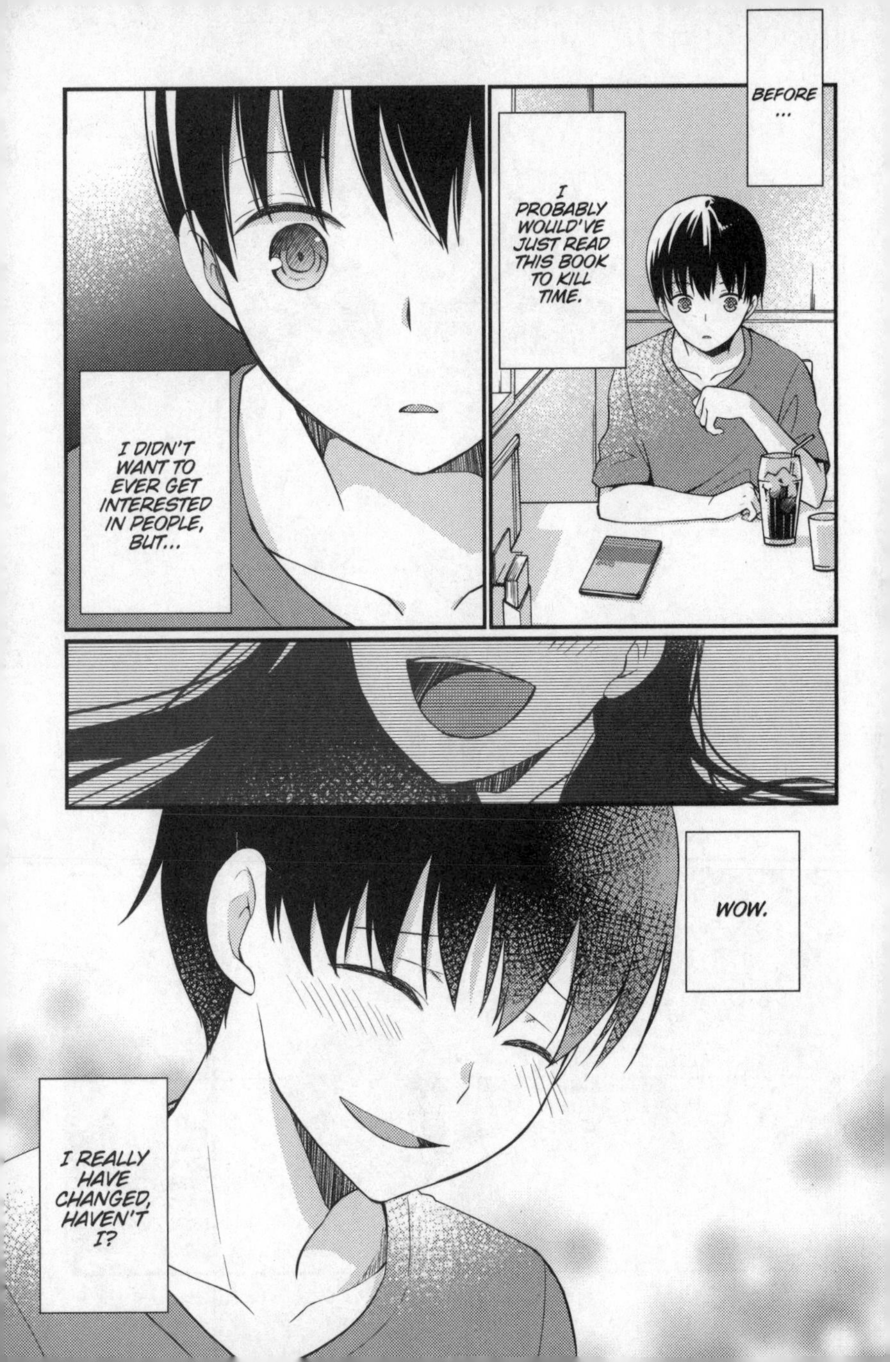
BEFORE ...
I PROBABLY WOULD'VE JUST READ THIS BOOK TO KILL TIME.
I DIDN'T WANT TO EVER GET INTERESTED IN PEOPLE, BUT...
WOW.
I REALLY HAVE CHANGED, HAVEN'T I?

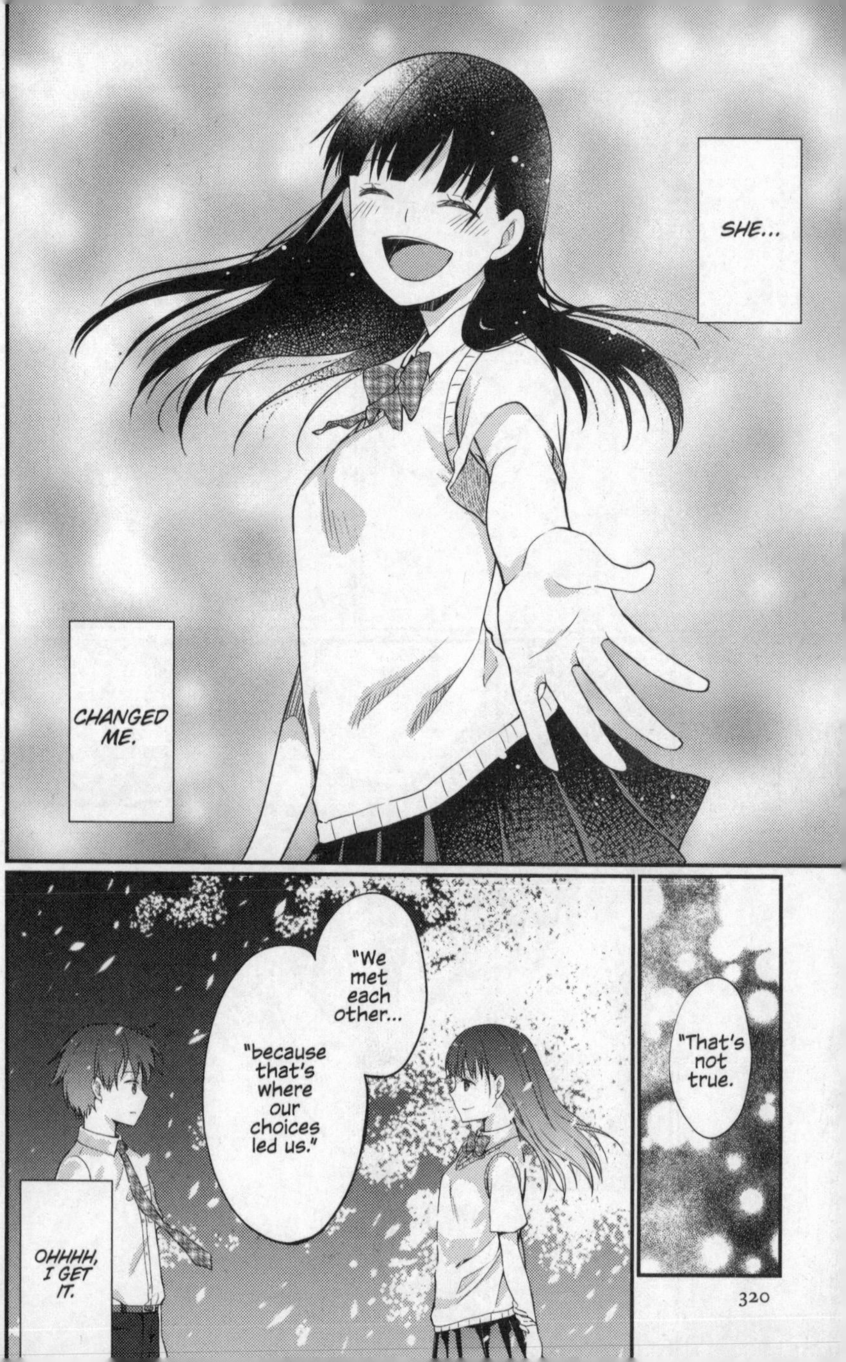
SHE...
CHANGED ME.
"That's not true.
"We met each other...
"because that's where our choices led us."
OHHHH, I GET IT.

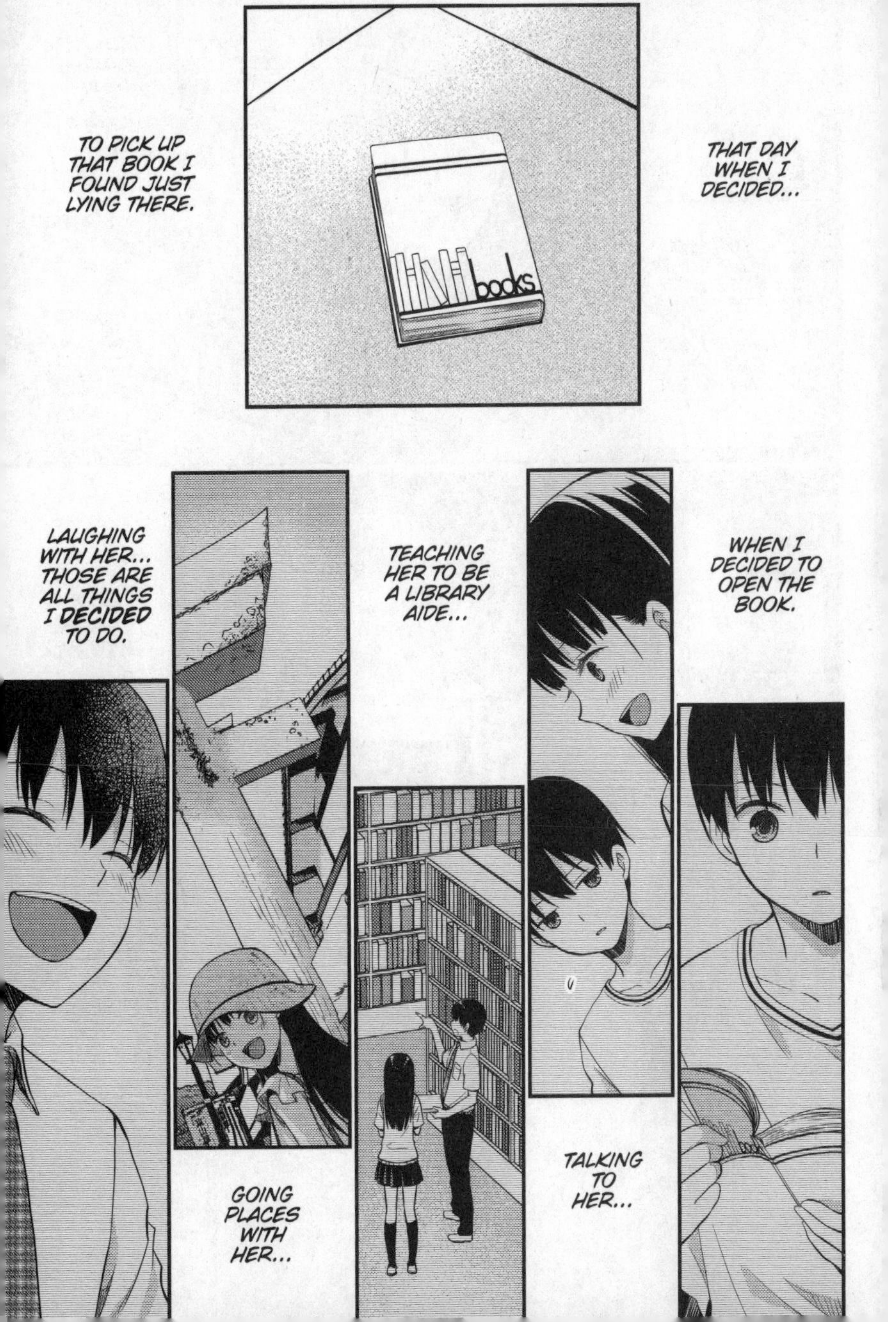
THAT DAY WHEN I DECIDED...
TO PICK UP THAT BOOK I FOUND JUST LYING THERE.
books
WHEN I DECIDED TO OPEN THE BOOK.
TALKING TO HER...
TEACHING HER TO BE A LIBRARY AIDE...
GOING PLACES WITH HER...
LAUGHING WITH HER... THOSE ARE ALL THINGS I DECIDED TO DO.

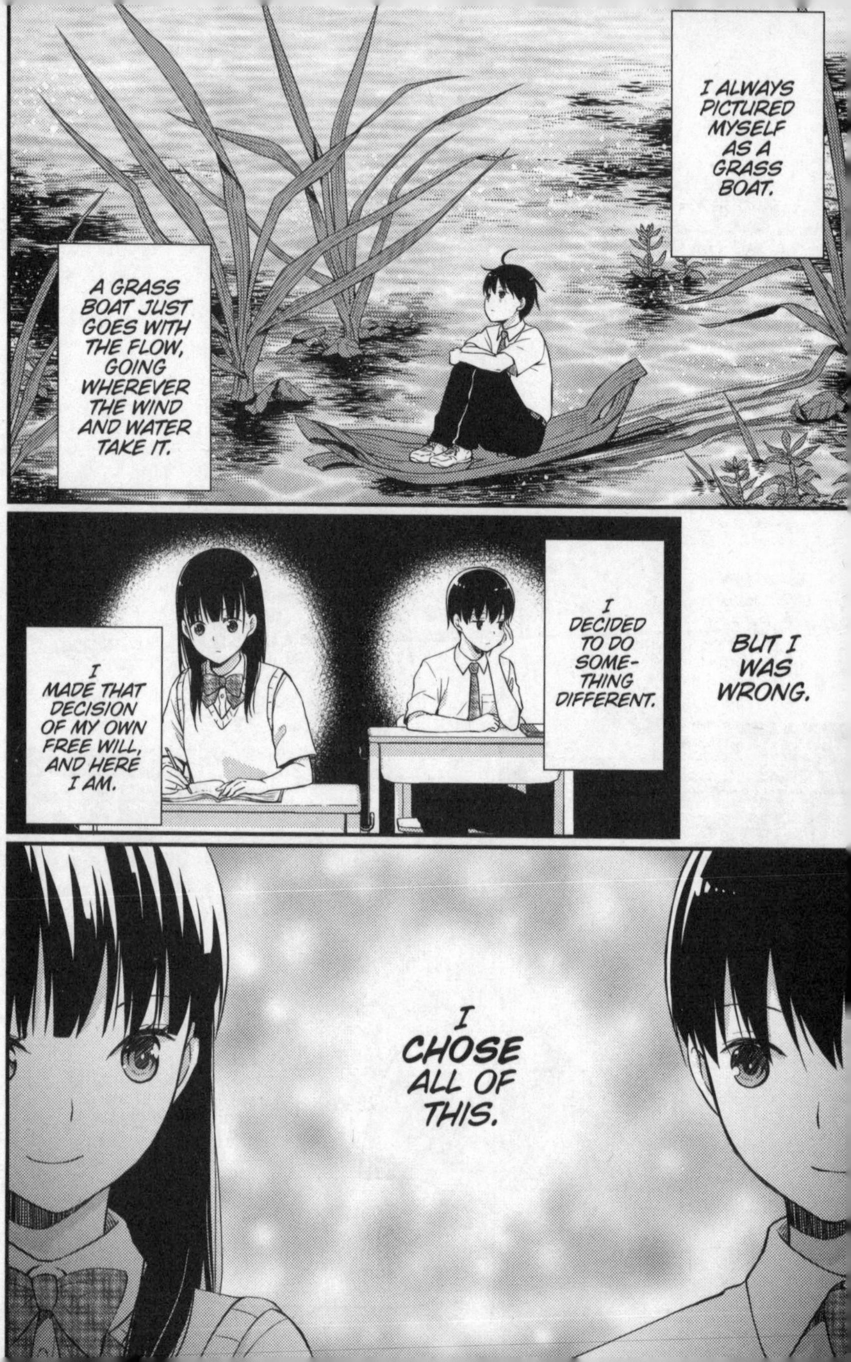

I ALWAYS PICTURED MYSELF AS A GRASS BOAT.
A GRASS BOAT JUST GOES WITH THE FLOW, GOING WHEREVER THE WIND AND WATER TAKE IT.
BUT I WAS WRONG.
I DECIDED TO DO SOME-THING DIFFERENT.
I MADE THAT DECISION OF MY OWN FREE WILL, AND HERE I AM.
I CHOSE ALL OF THIS.

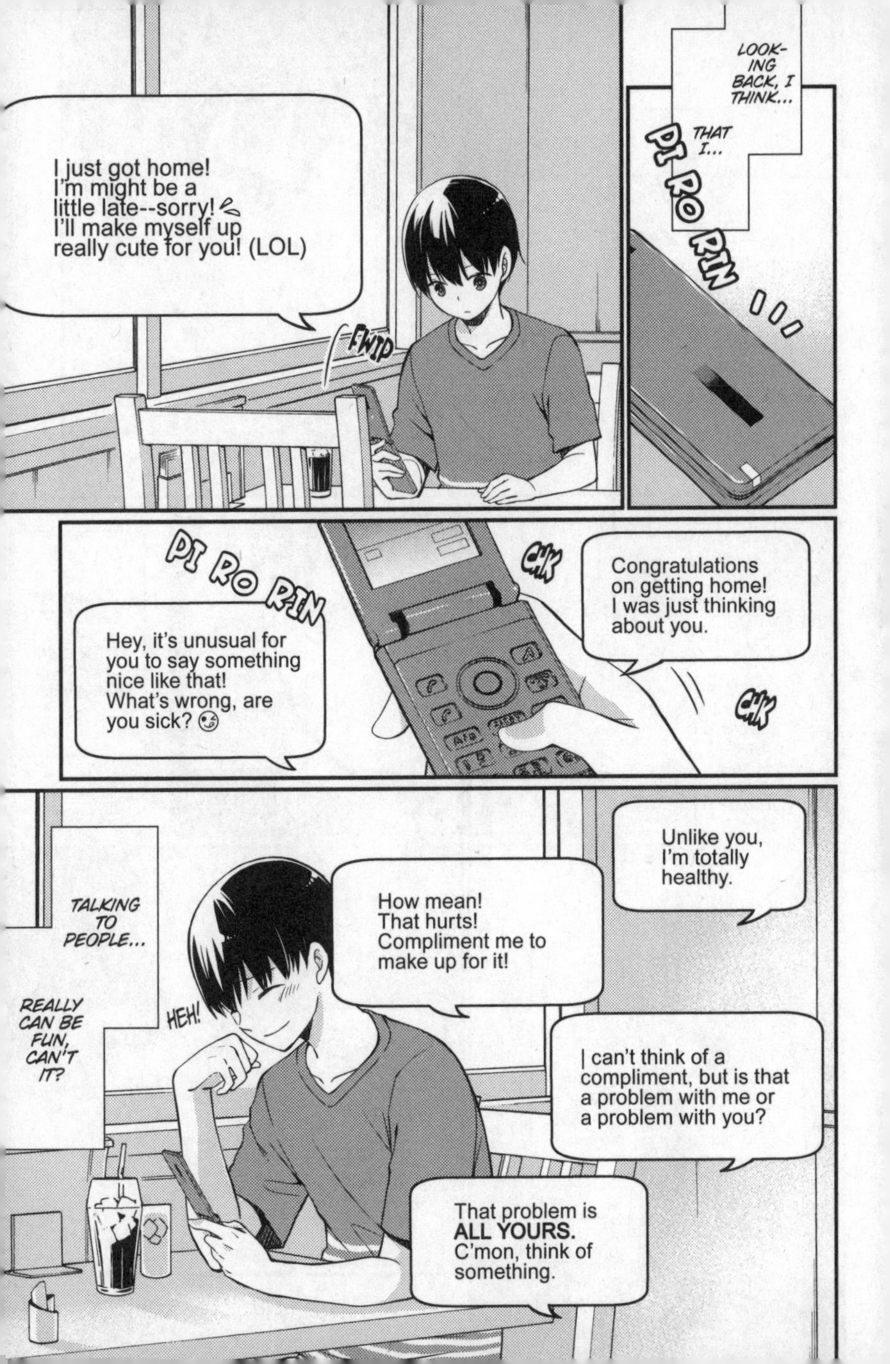
LOOKING BACK, I THINK...
THAT I...
PI RO RIN
I just got home!
I'm might be a little late--sorry!
I'll make myself up really cute for you! (LOL)
FWIP
CHK
Congratulations on getting home!
I was just thinking about you.
PI RO RIN
Hey, it's unusual for you to say something nice like that!
What's wrong, are you sick?
CHK
Unlike you, I'm totally healthy.
How mean!
That hurts!
Compliment me to make up for it!
I can't think of a compliment, but is that a problem with me or a problem with you?
That problem is **ALL YOURS.**
C'mon, think of something.
TALKING TO PEOPLE...
REALLY CAN BE FUN, CAN'T IT?
HEH!

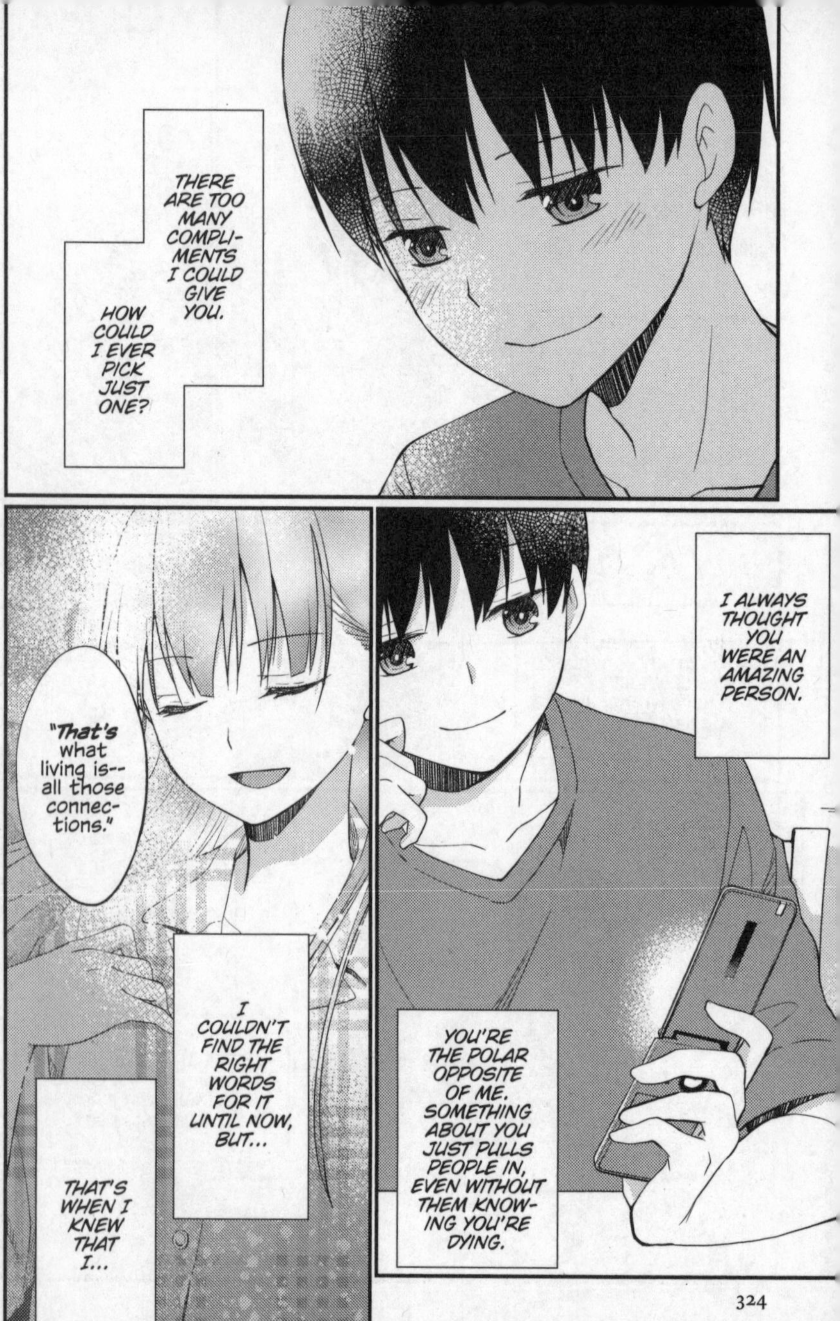
THERE ARE TOO MANY COMPLIMENTS I COULD GIVE YOU.
HOW COULD I EVER PICK JUST ONE?
I ALWAYS THOUGHT YOU WERE AN AMAZING PERSON.
YOU'RE THE POLAR OPPOSITE OF ME. SOMETHING ABOUT YOU JUST PULLS PEOPLE IN, EVEN WITHOUT THEM KNOWING YOU'RE DYING.
"That's what living is--all those connections."
I COULDN'T FIND THE RIGHT WORDS FOR IT UNTIL NOW, BUT...
THAT'S WHEN I KNEW THAT I...

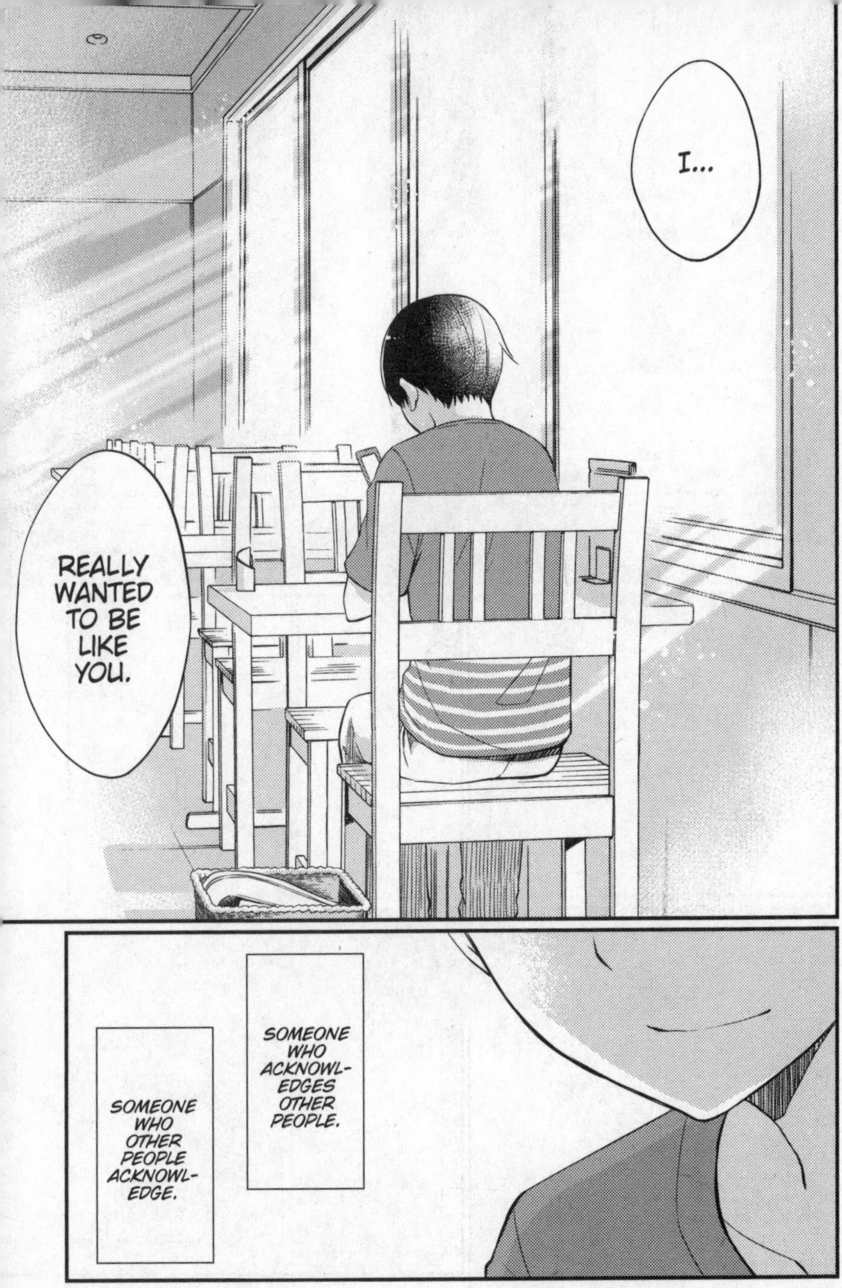
I...
REALLY WANTED TO BE LIKE YOU.
SOMEONE WHO ACKNOWL-EDGES OTHER PEOPLE.
SOMEONE WHO OTHER PEOPLE ACKNOWL-EDGE.

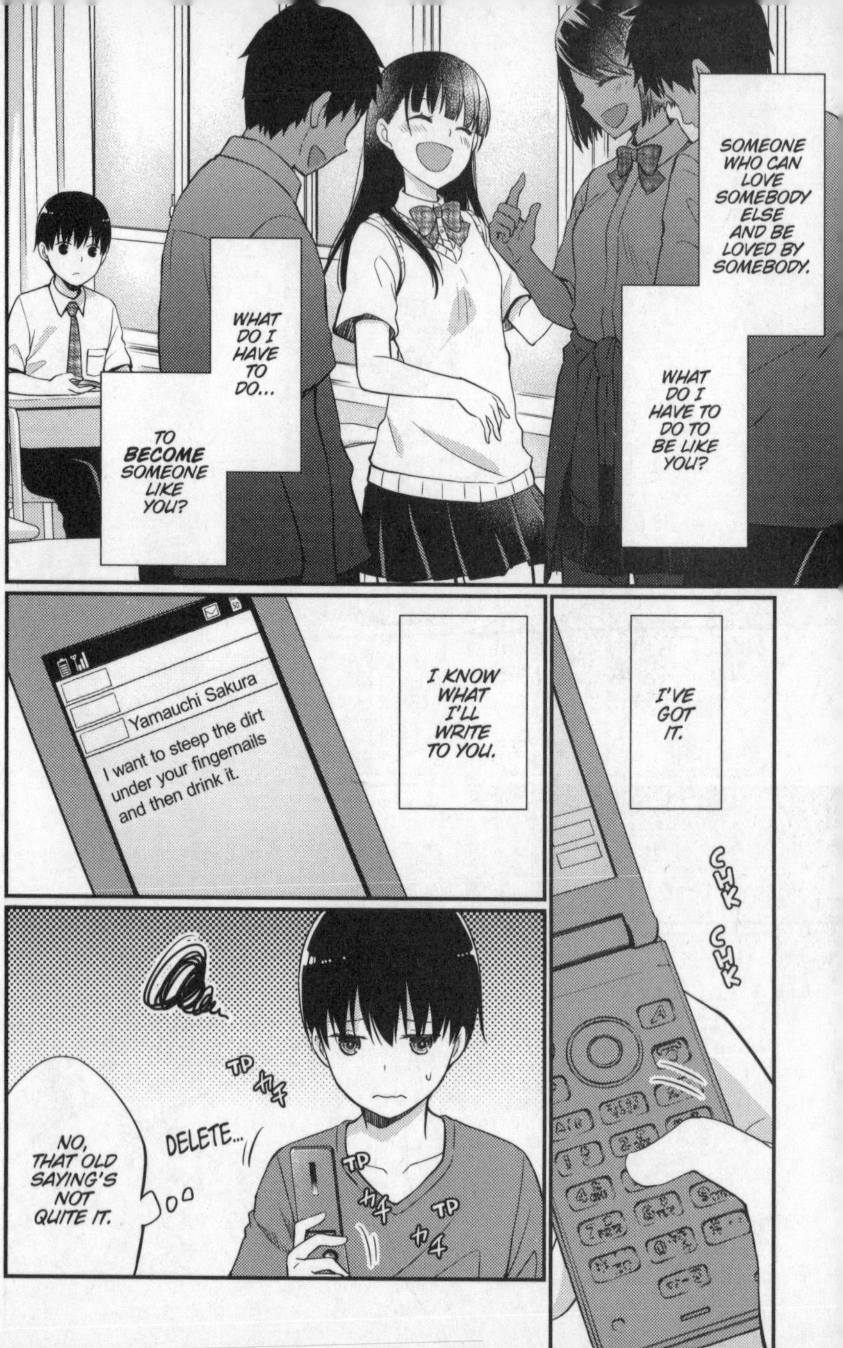
SOMEONE WHO CAN LOVE SOMEBODY ELSE AND BE LOVED BY SOMEBODY.
WHAT DO I HAVE TO DO TO BE LIKE YOU?
WHAT DO I HAVE TO DO...
TO BECOME SOMEONE LIKE YOU?
I'VE GOT IT.
CHK CHK
I KNOW WHAT I'LL WRITE TO YOU.
Yamauchi Sakura
I want to steep the dirt under your fingernails and then drink it.
TP
TP
TP
DELETE...
NO, THAT OLD SAYING'S NOT QUITE IT.

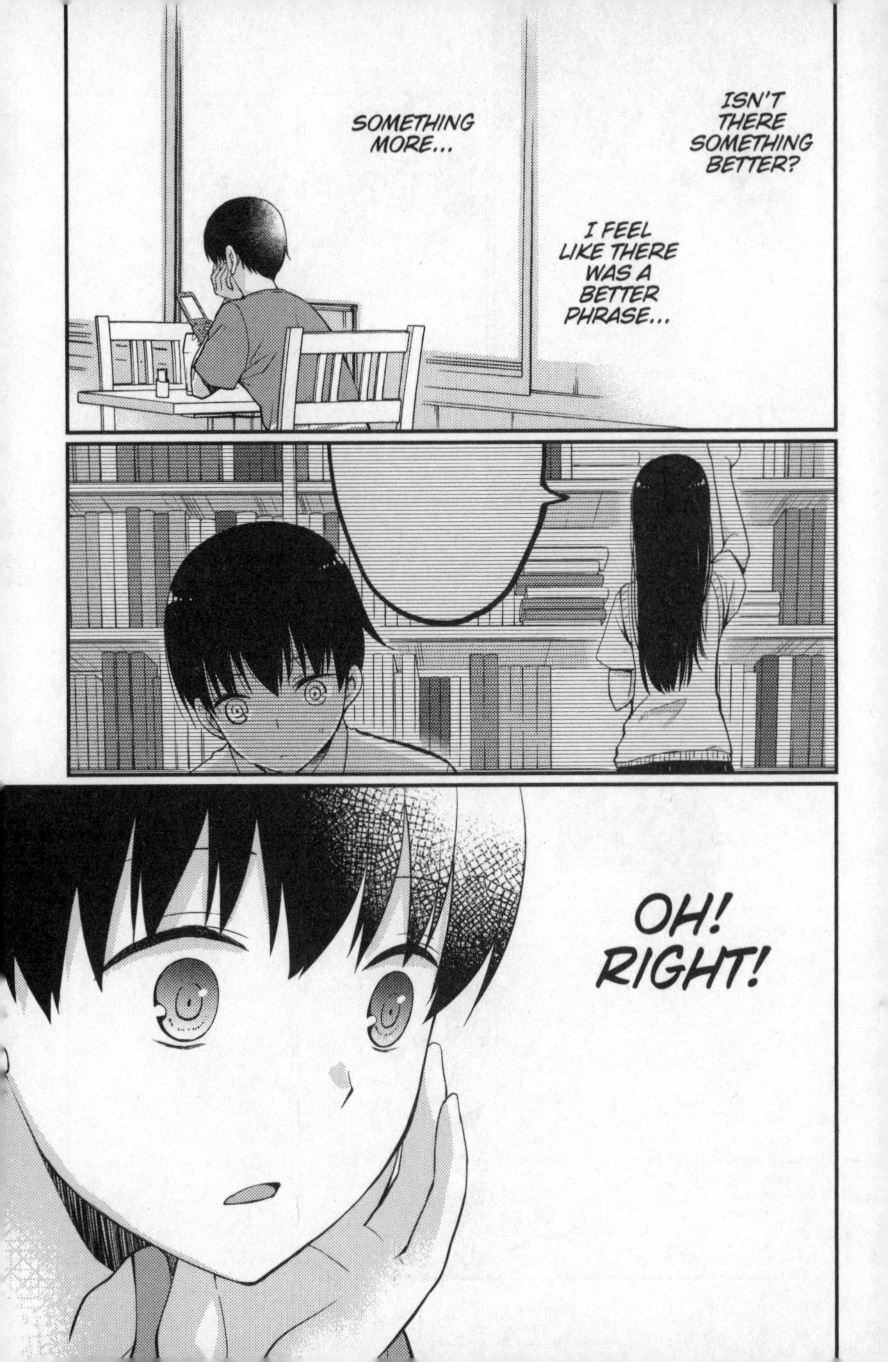
ISN'T THERE SOMETHING BETTER?
SOMETHING MORE...
I FEEL LIKE THERE WAS A BETTER PHRASE...
OH! RIGHT!

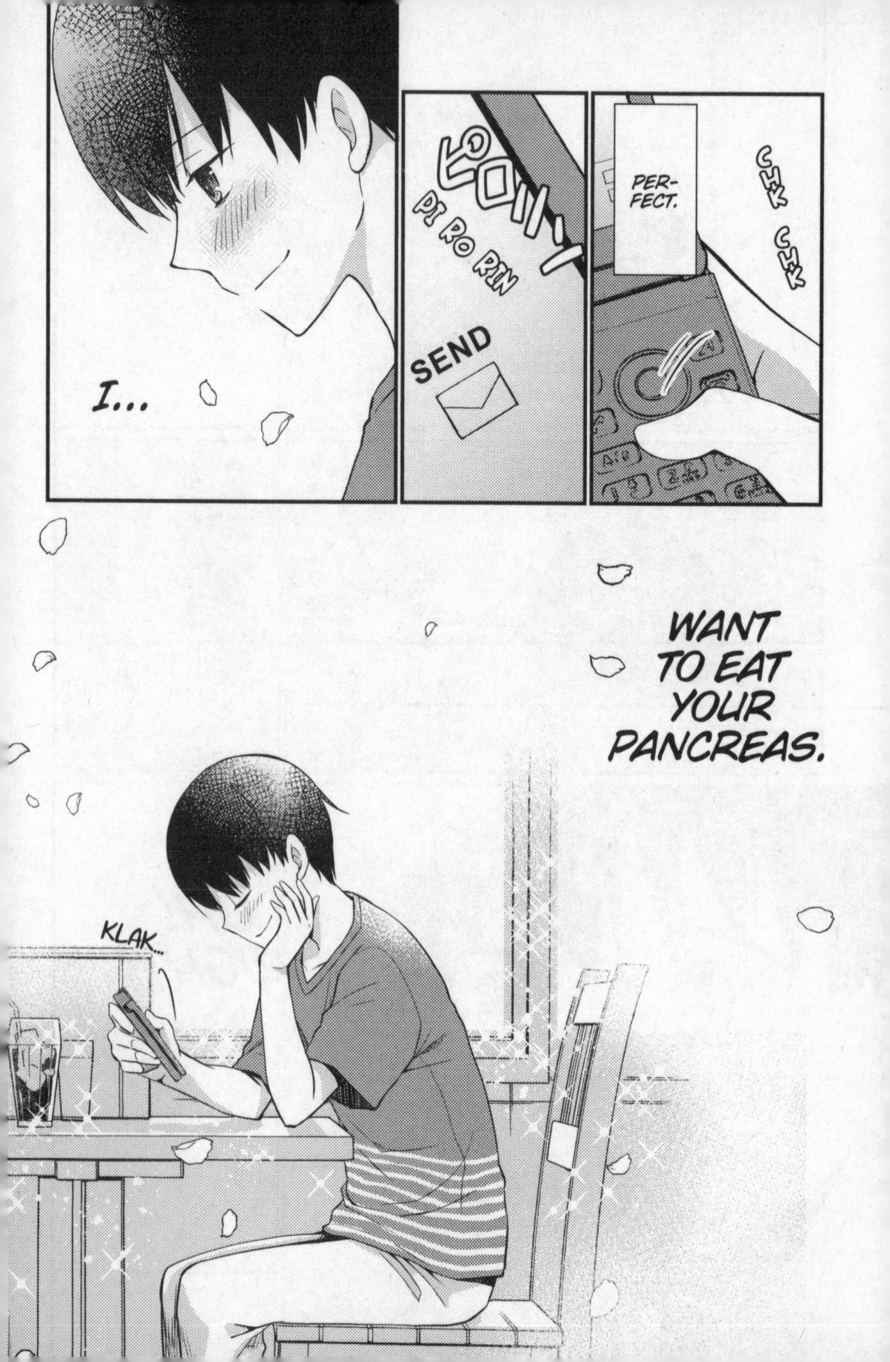
PER-
FECT.
CHK CHK
PI RO RIN
SEND
I...
WANT TO EAT YOUR PANCREAS.
KLAK...

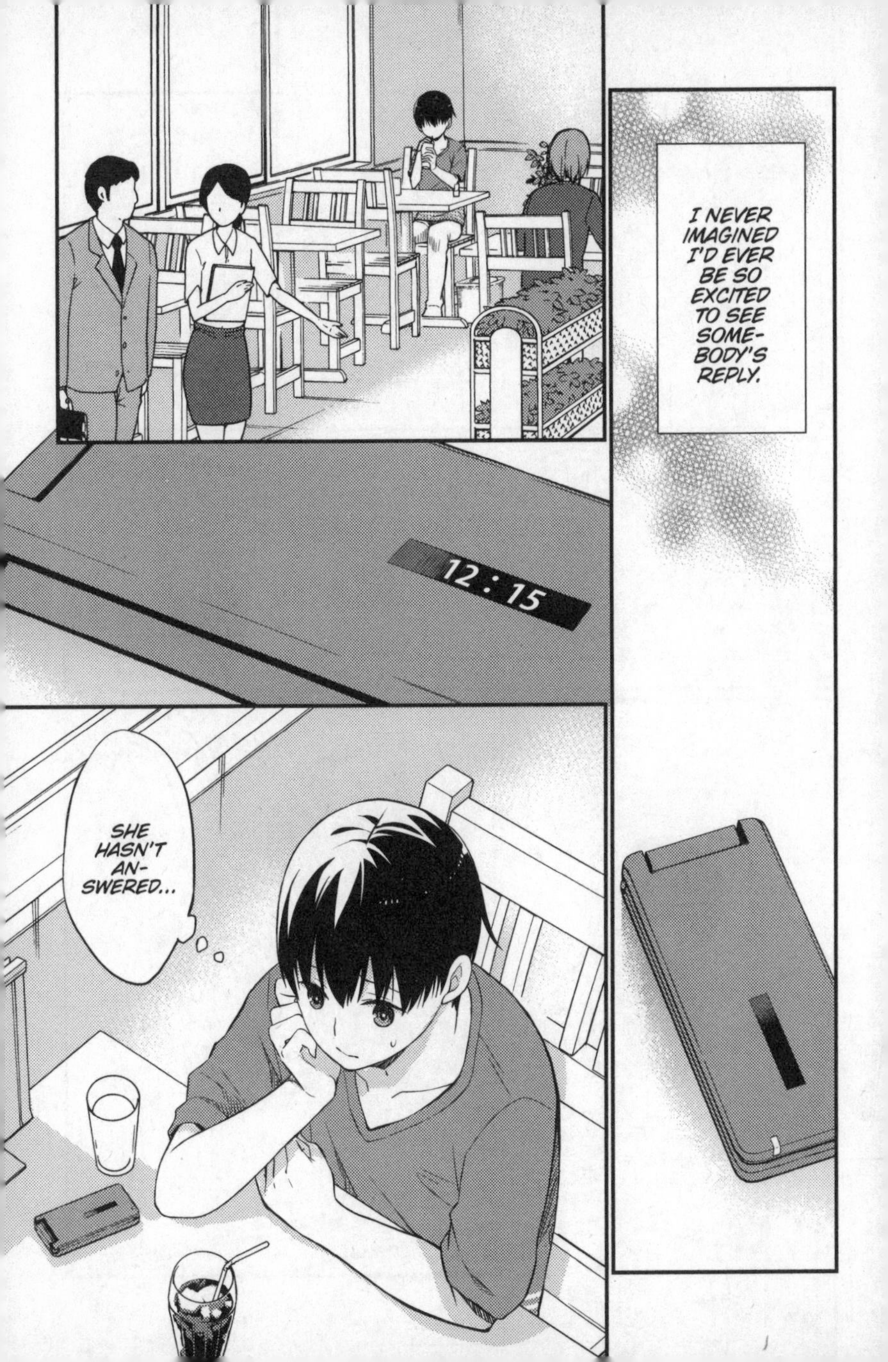
I NEVER IMAGINED I'D EVER BE SO EXCITED TO SEE SOME-BODY'S REPLY.
12:15
SHE HASN'T AN-SWERED...

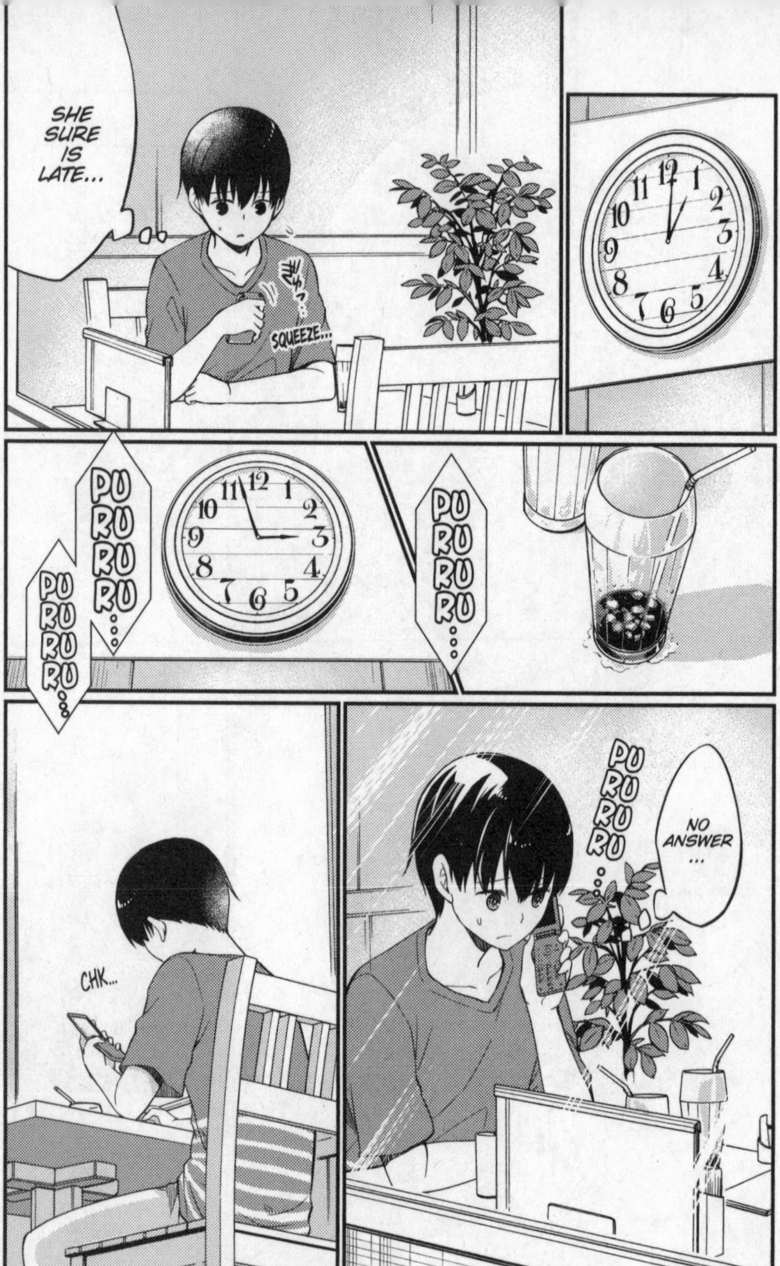

SHE SURE IS LATE...
SQUEEZE...
PURURURU...
PURURURU...
PURURURU...
PURURURU...
NO ANSWER ...
CHK...

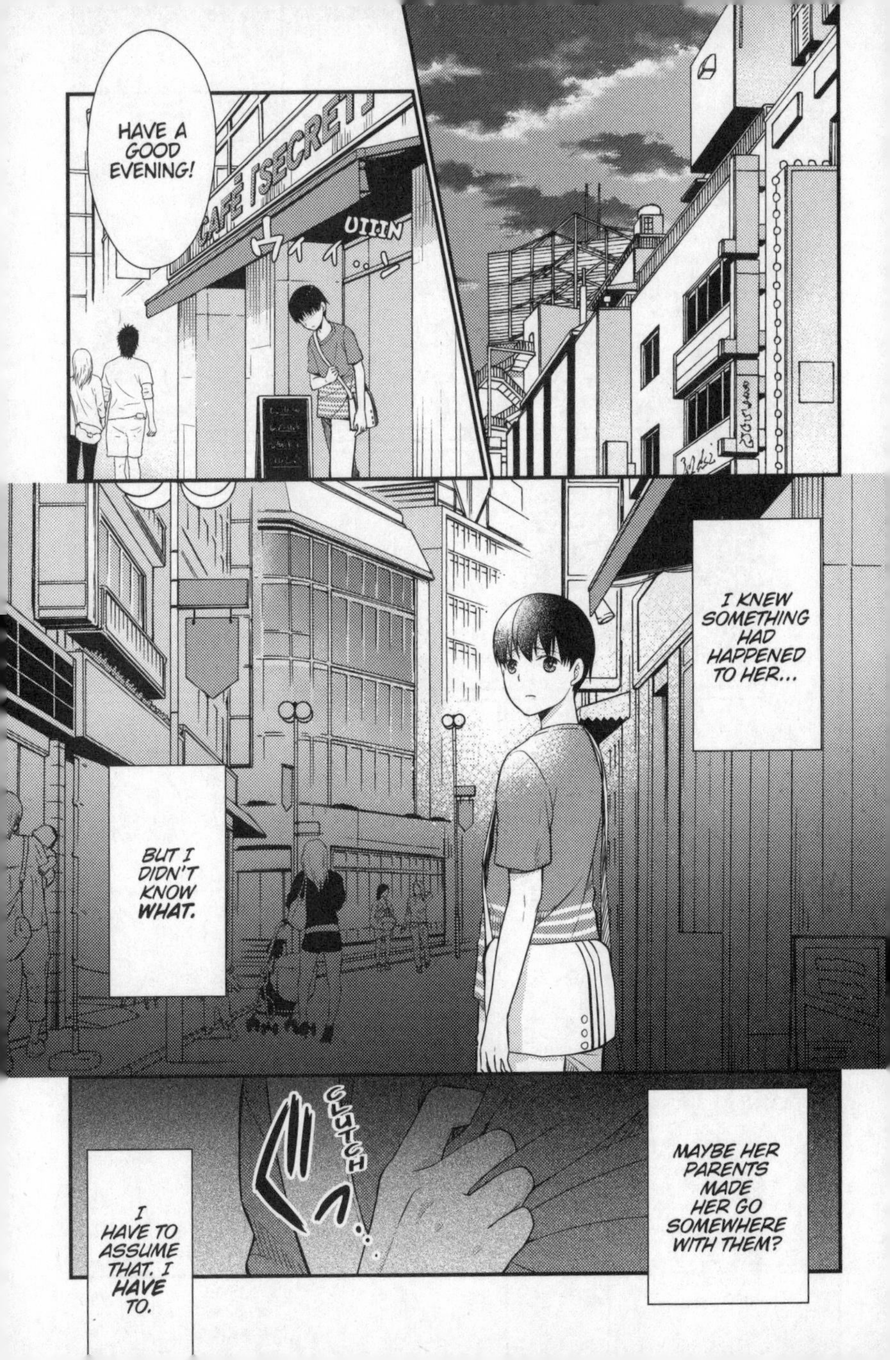
HAVE A GOOD EVENING!
UIIIN
I KNEW SOMETHING HAD HAPPENED TO HER...
BUT I DIDN'T KNOW WHAT.
MAYBE HER PARENTS MADE HER GO SOMEWHERE WITH THEM?
GLUTCH
I HAVE TO ASSUME THAT. I HAVE TO.

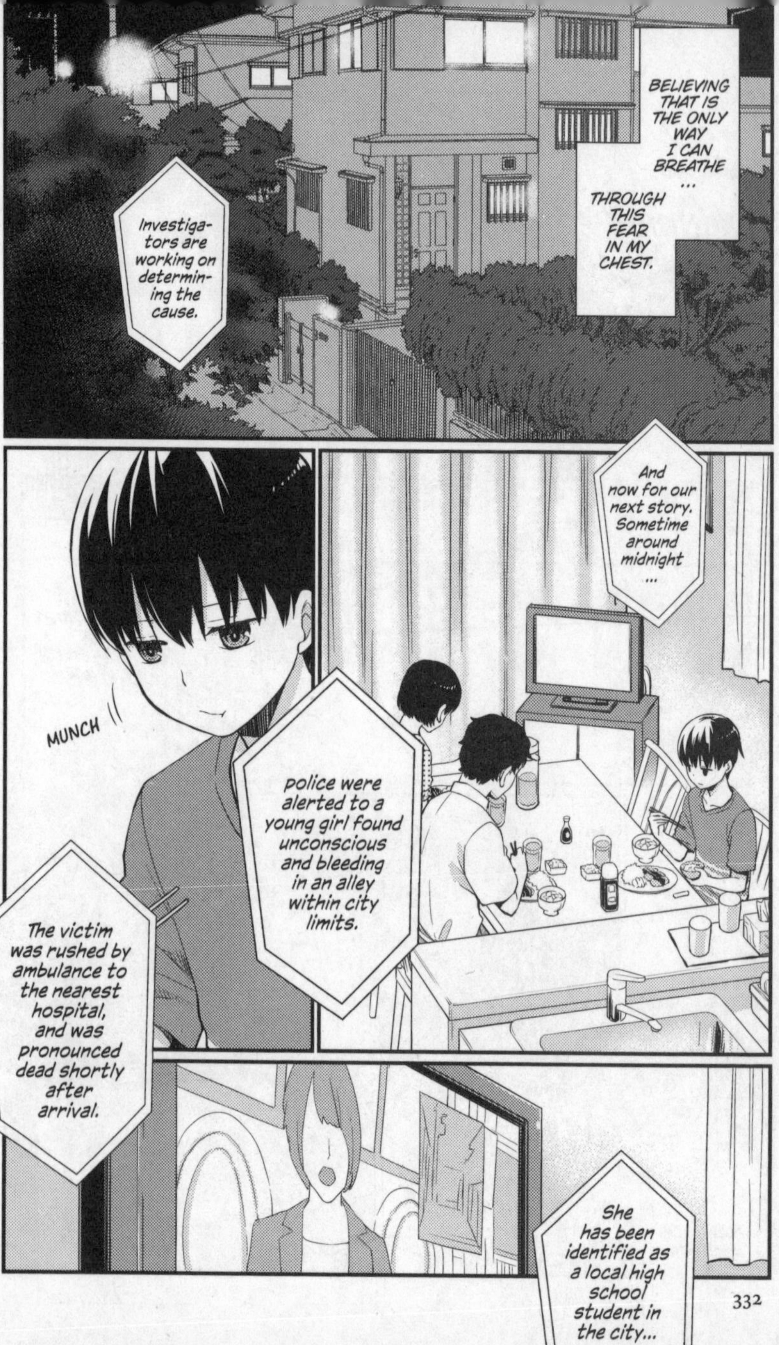
BELIEVING THAT IS THE ONLY WAY I CAN BREATHE ...
THROUGH THIS FEAR IN MY CHEST.
Investiga-tors are working on determin-ing the cause.
And now for our next story. Sometime around midnight ...
police were alerted to a young girl found unconscious and bleeding in an alley within city limits.
MUNCH
The victim was rushed by ambulance to the nearest hospital, and was pronounced dead shortly after arrival.
She has been identified as a local high school student in the city...

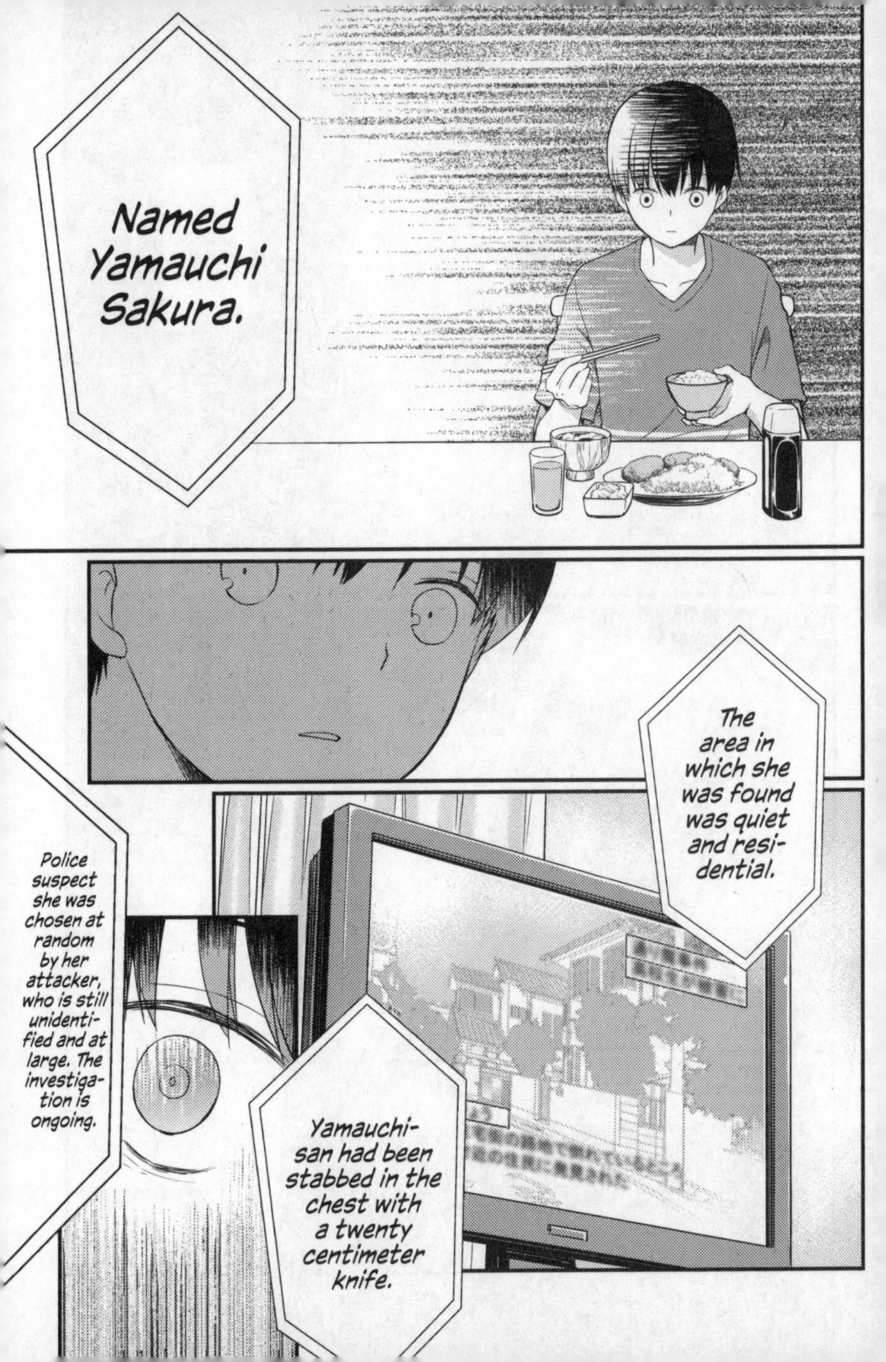
Named Yamauchi Sakura.
The area in which she was found was quiet and residential.
Yamauchi-san had been stabbed in the chest with a twenty centimeter knife.
Police suspect she was chosen at random by her attacker, who is still unidentified and at large. The investigation is ongoing.

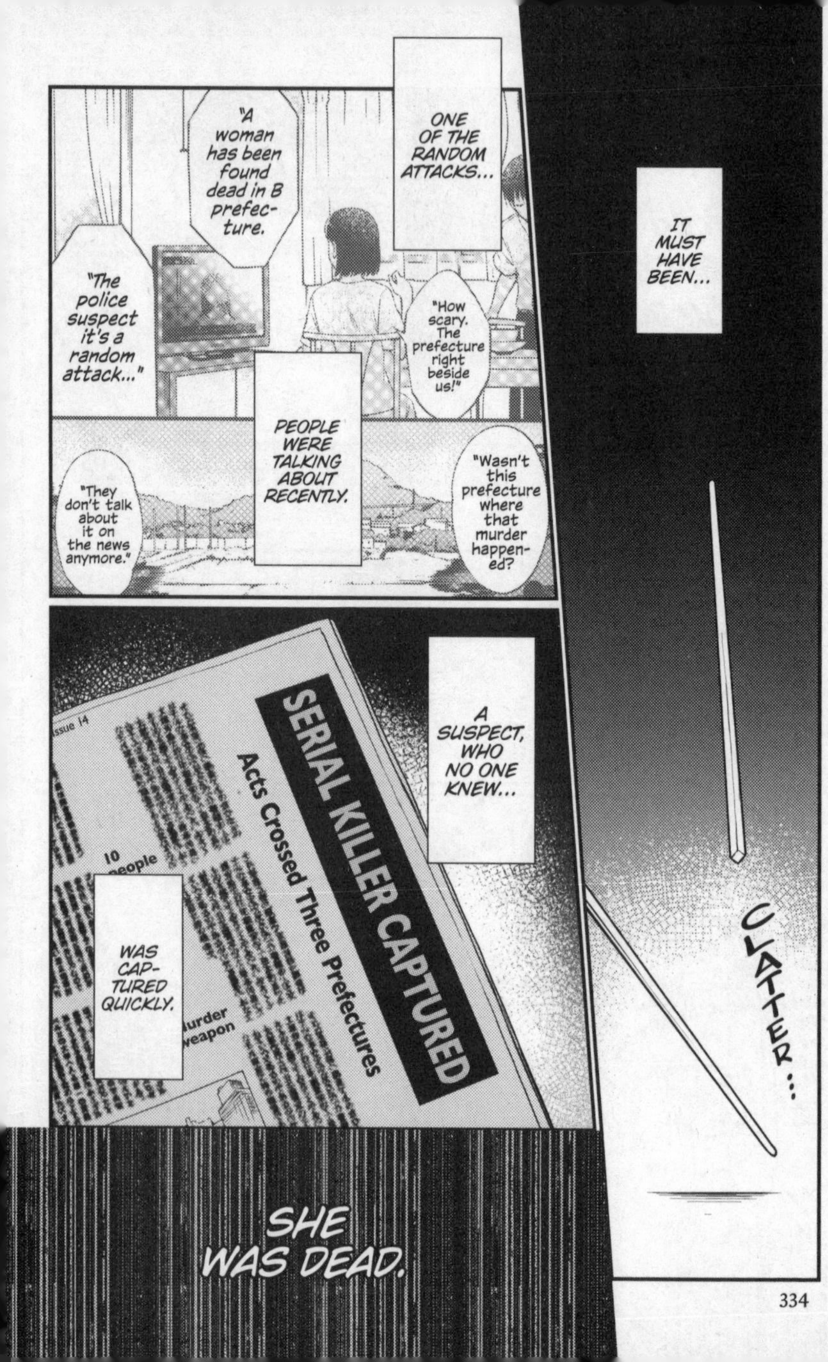
IT MUST HAVE BEEN...
ONE OF THE RANDOM ATTACKS...
"A woman has been found dead in B prefecture.
"The police suspect it's a random attack..."
"How scary. The prefecture right beside us!"
PEOPLE WERE TALKING ABOUT RECENTLY.
"Wasn't this prefecture where that murder happened?
"They don't talk about it on the news anymore."
A SUSPECT, WHO NO ONE KNEW...
Issue 14
SERIAL KILLER CAPTURED
Acts Crossed Three Prefectures
10 people
urder weapon
WAS CAPTURED QUICKLY.
CLATTER...
SHE WAS DEAD.

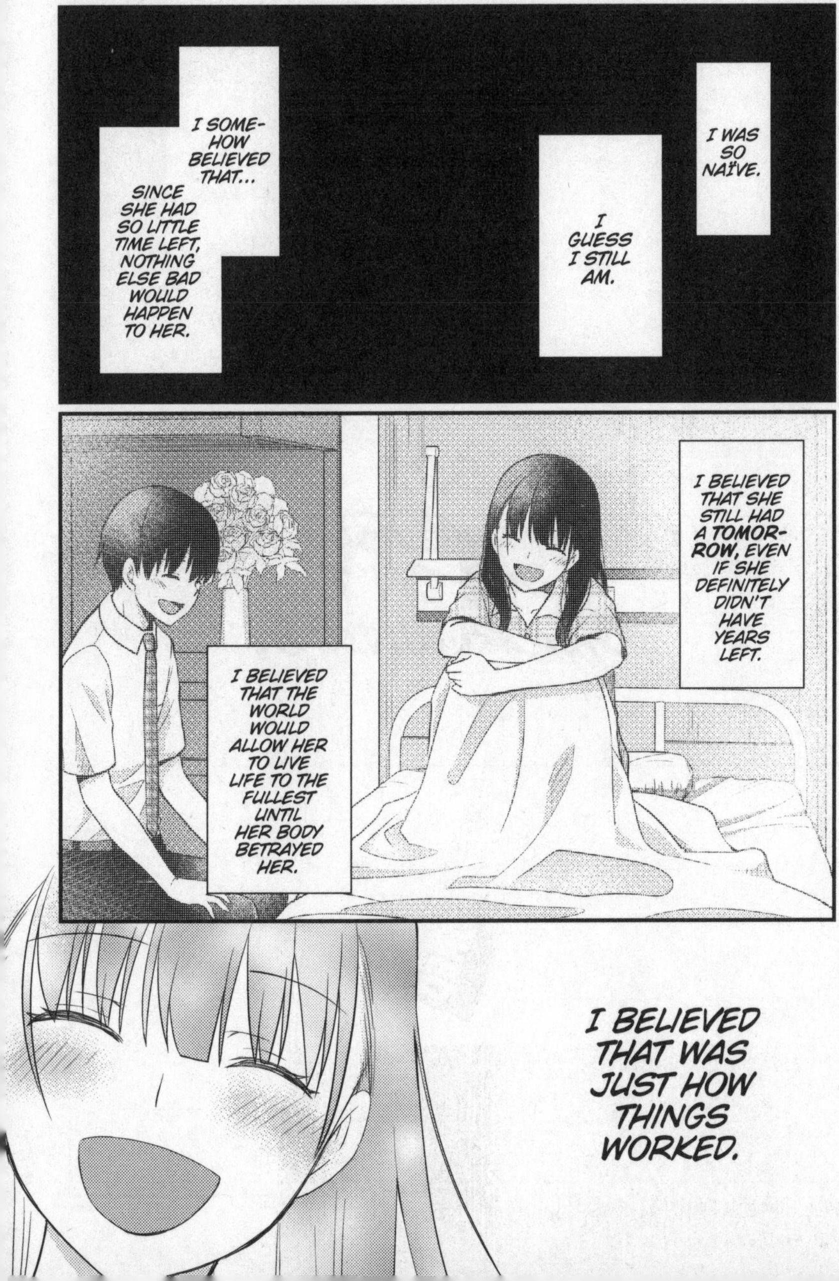
I WAS SO NAÏVE.
I GUESS I STILL AM.
I SOME-HOW BELIEVED THAT...
SINCE SHE HAD SO LITTLE TIME LEFT, NOTHING ELSE BAD WOULD HAPPEN TO HER.
I BELIEVED THAT SHE STILL HAD A TOMOR-ROW, EVEN IF SHE DEFINITELY DIDN'T HAVE YEARS LEFT.
I BELIEVED THAT THE WORLD WOULD ALLOW HER TO LIVE LIFE TO THE FULLEST UNTIL HER BODY BETRAYED HER.
I BELIEVED THAT WAS JUST HOW THINGS WORKED.

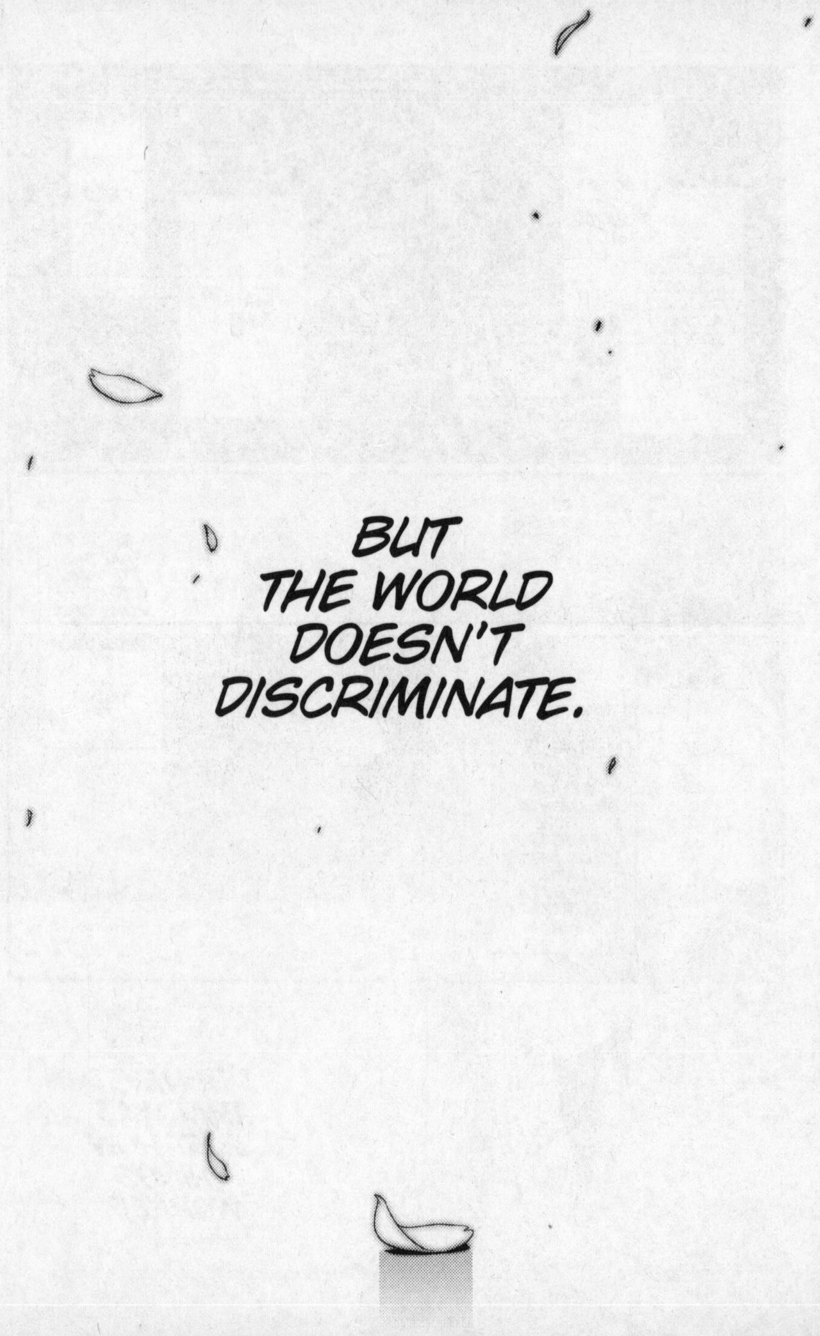
BUT THE WORLD DOESN'T DISCRIMINATE.

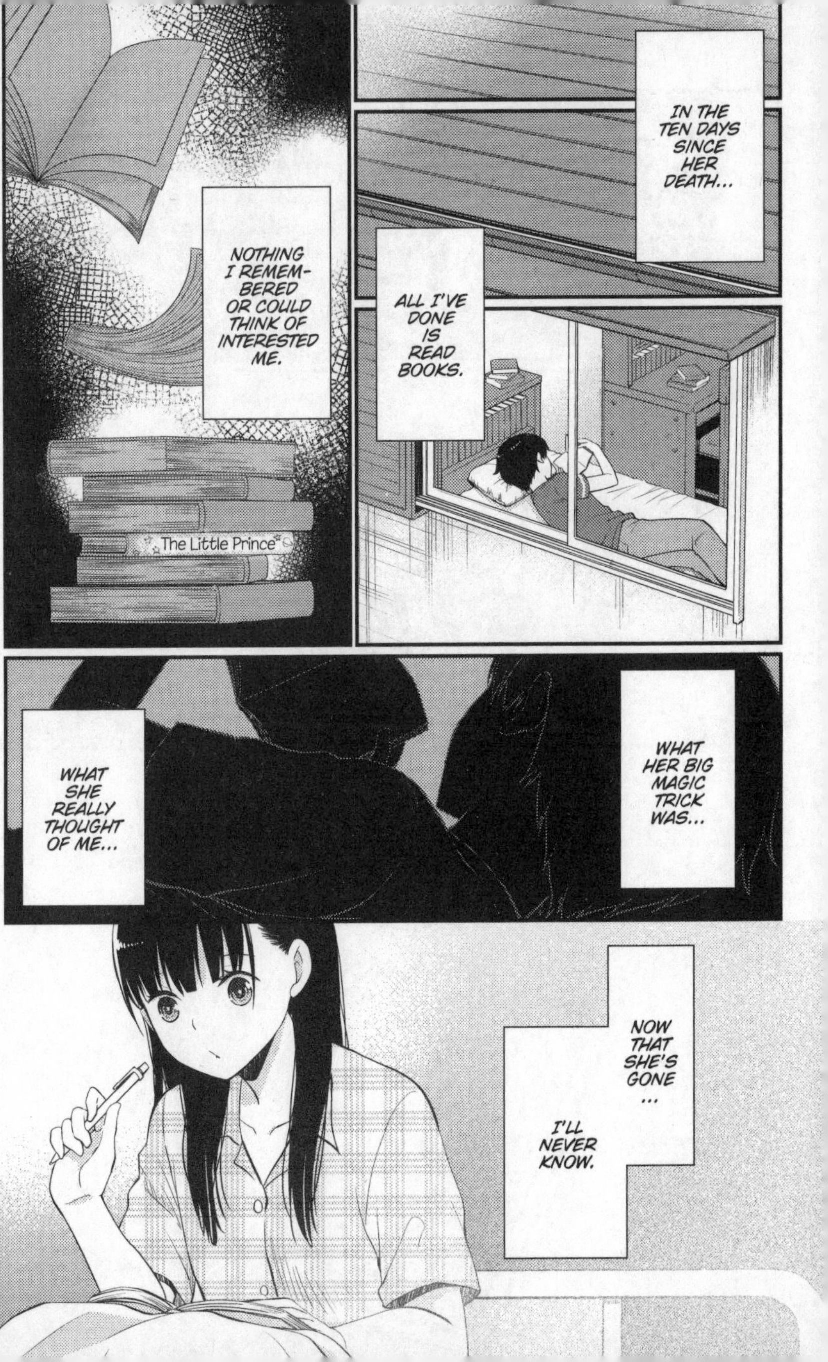
IN THE TEN DAYS SINCE HER DEATH...
ALL I'VE DONE IS READ BOOKS.
NOTHING I REMEMBERED OR COULD THINK OF INTERESTED ME.
The Little Prince
WHAT HER BIG MAGIC TRICK WAS...
WHAT SHE REALLY THOUGHT OF ME...
NOW THAT SHE'S GONE...
I'LL NEVER KNOW.

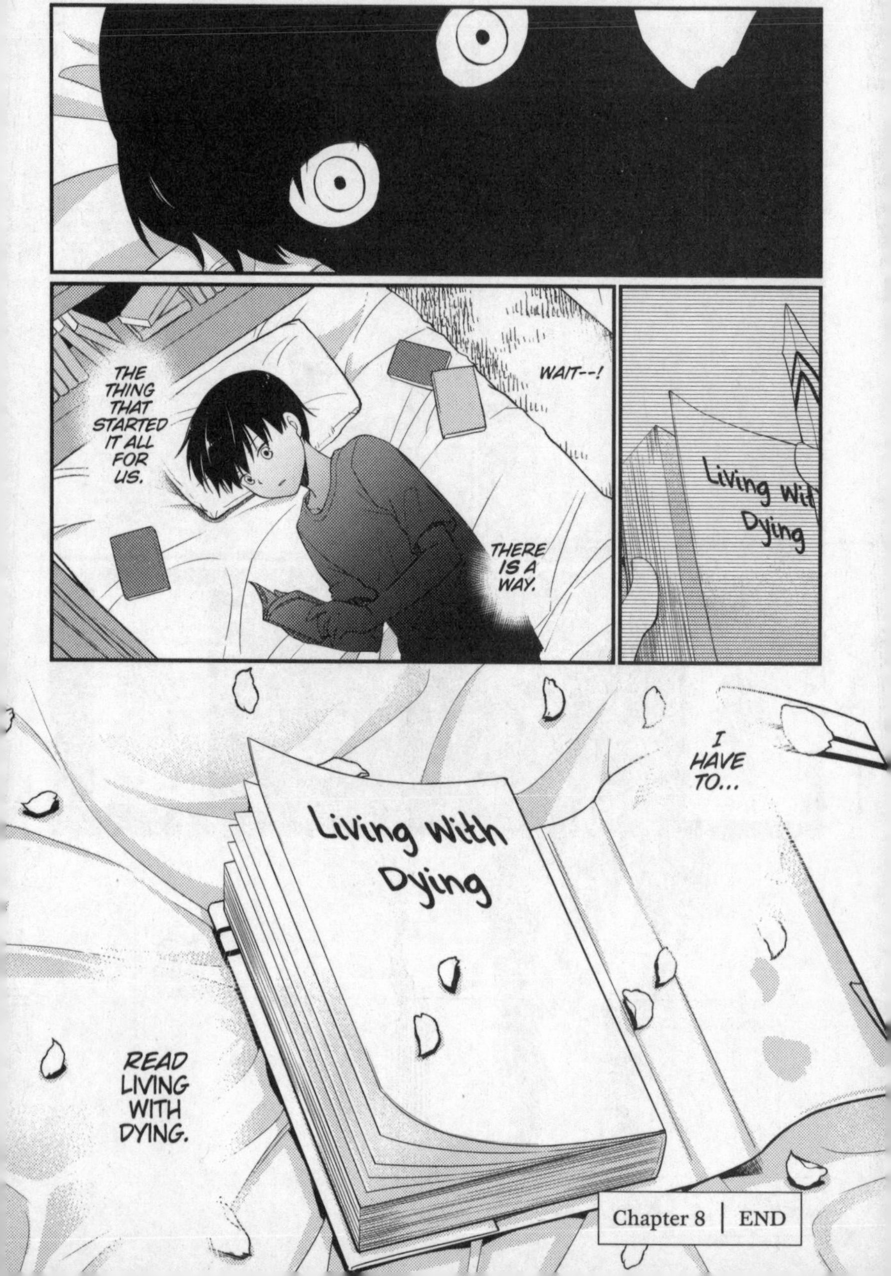

Living With Dying
WAIT--!
THE THING THAT STARTED IT ALL FOR US.
THERE IS A WAY.
I HAVE TO...
Living With Dying
READ LIVING WITH DYING.
Chapter 8 | END

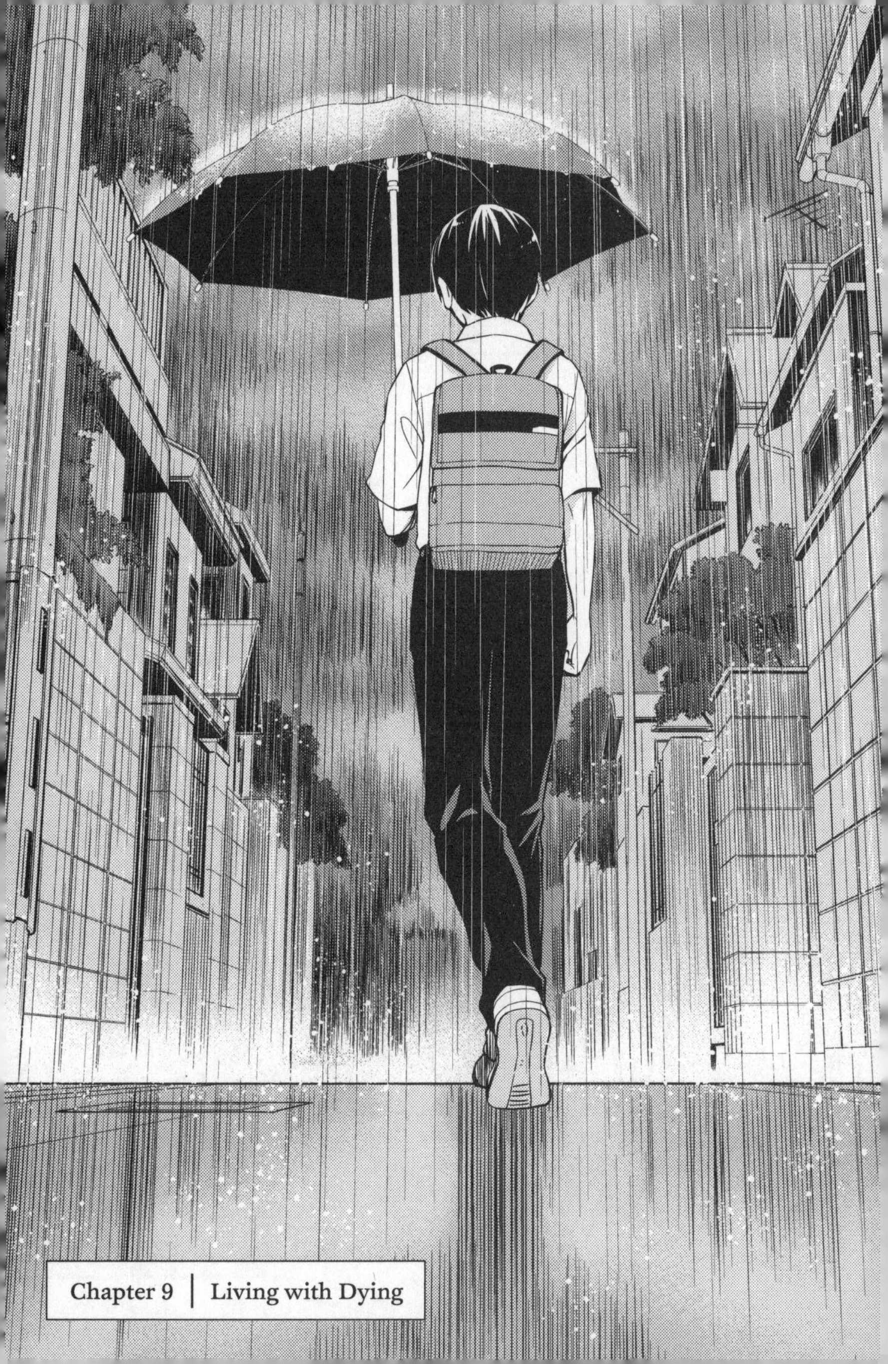

Chapter 9 | Living with Dying

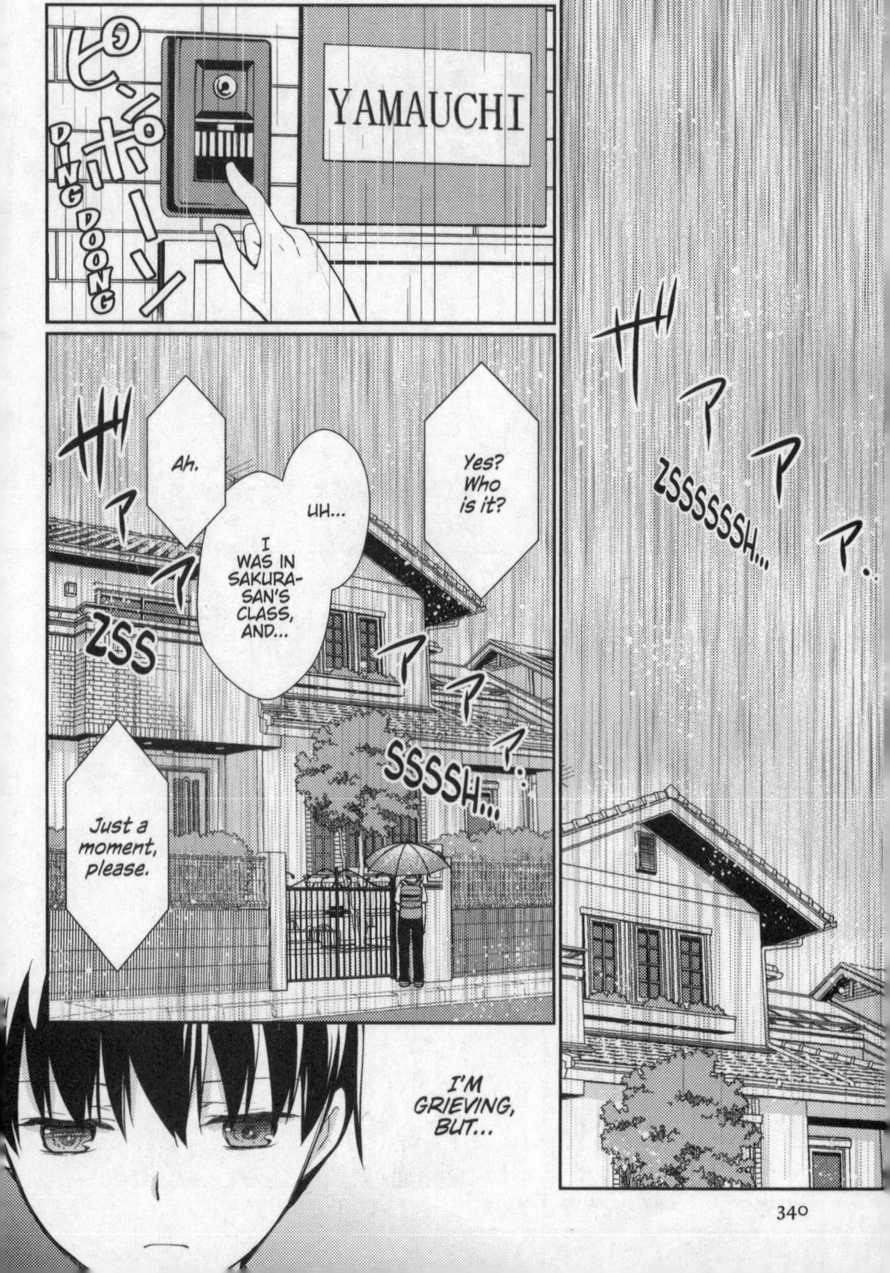
ZSSSSSSSH...
YAMAUCHI
DING DOONG
Yes? Who is it?
Uh...
I was in Sakura-san's class, and...
Ah.
ZSS
SSSSH...
Just a moment, please.
I'm grieving, but...

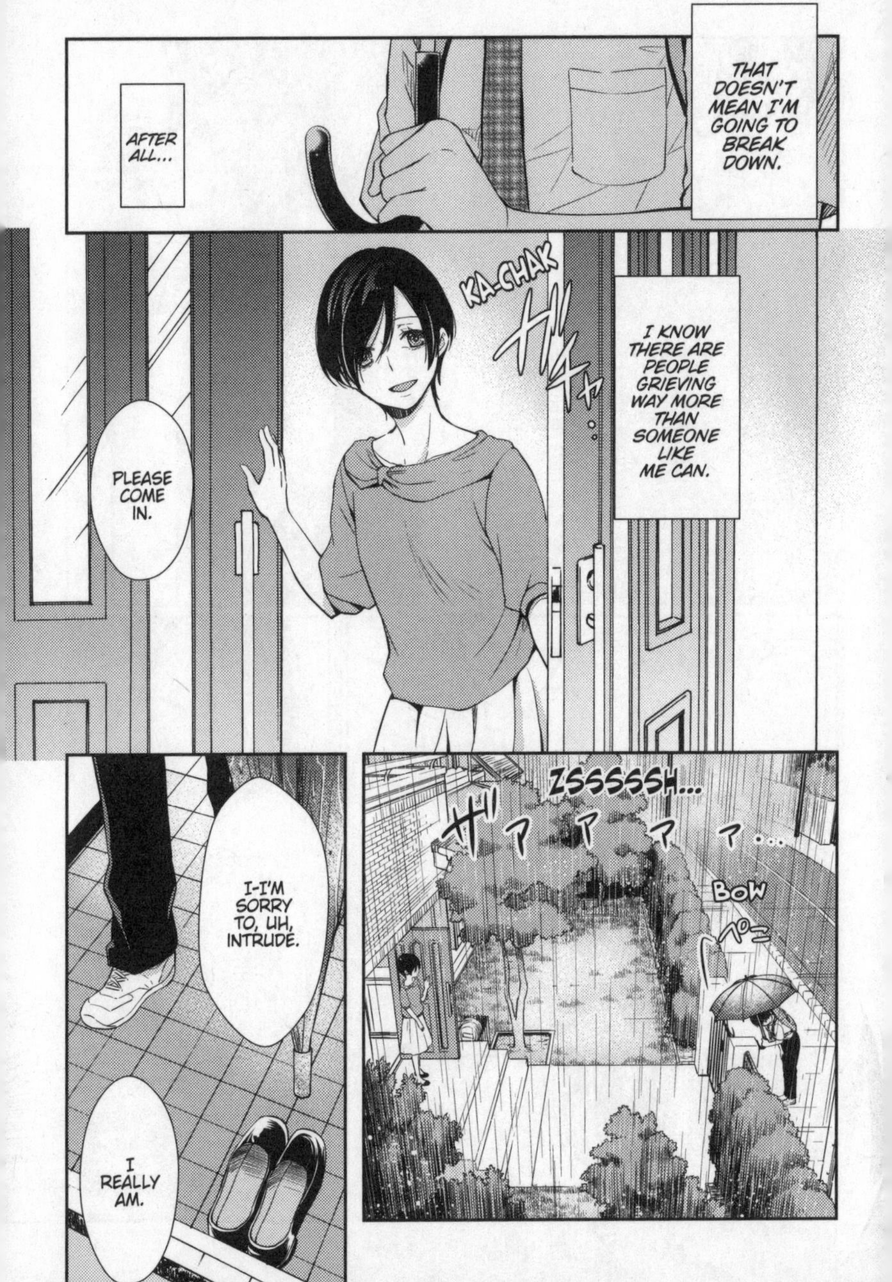
THAT DOESN'T MEAN I'M GOING TO BREAK DOWN.
AFTER ALL...
I KNOW THERE ARE PEOPLE GRIEVING WAY MORE THAN SOMEONE LIKE ME CAN.
KA-CHAK
ガチャ
PLEASE COME IN.
ZSSSSSH...
ザアアアア...
BOW
ペこ
I-I'M SORRY TO, UH, INTRUDE.
I REALLY AM.

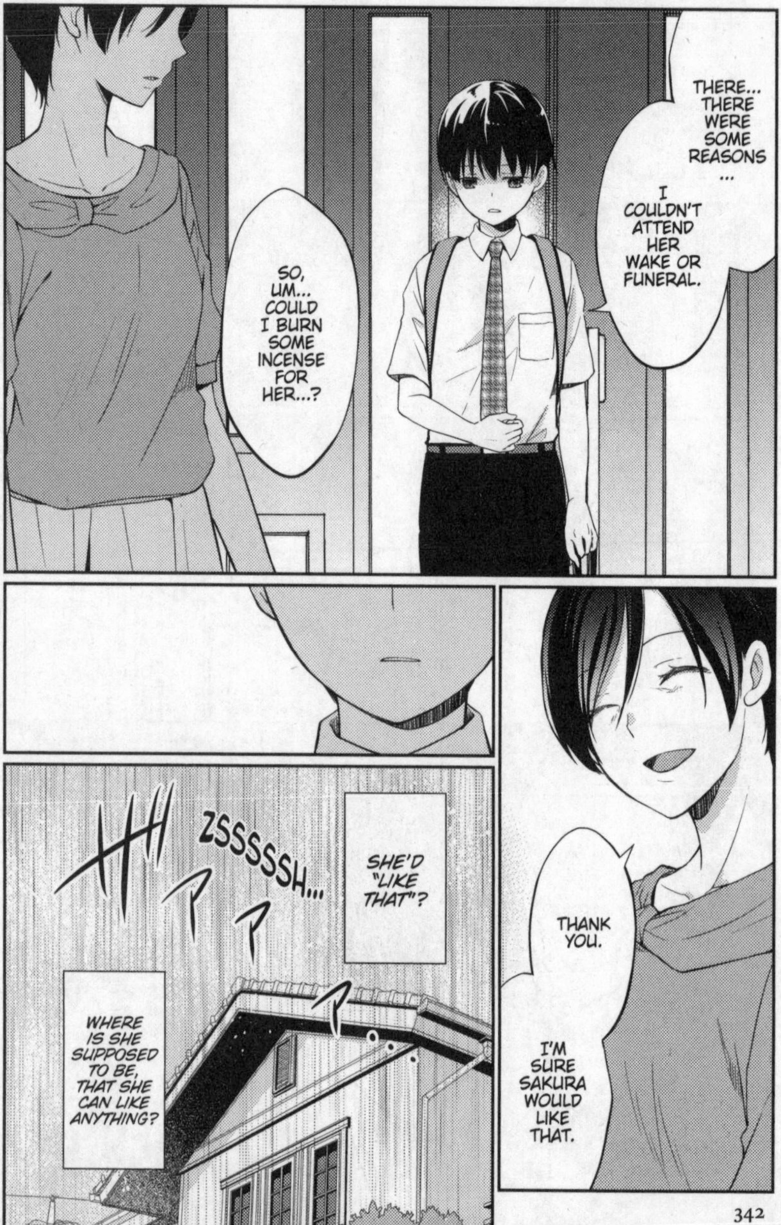
THERE... THERE WERE SOME REASONS ...
I COULDN'T ATTEND HER WAKE OR FUNERAL.
SO, UM... COULD I BURN SOME INCENSE FOR HER...?
THANK YOU.
I'M SURE SAKURA WOULD LIKE THAT.
ZSSSSSSH...
SHE'D "LIKE THAT"?
WHERE IS SHE SUPPOSED TO BE, THAT SHE CAN LIKE ANYTHING?

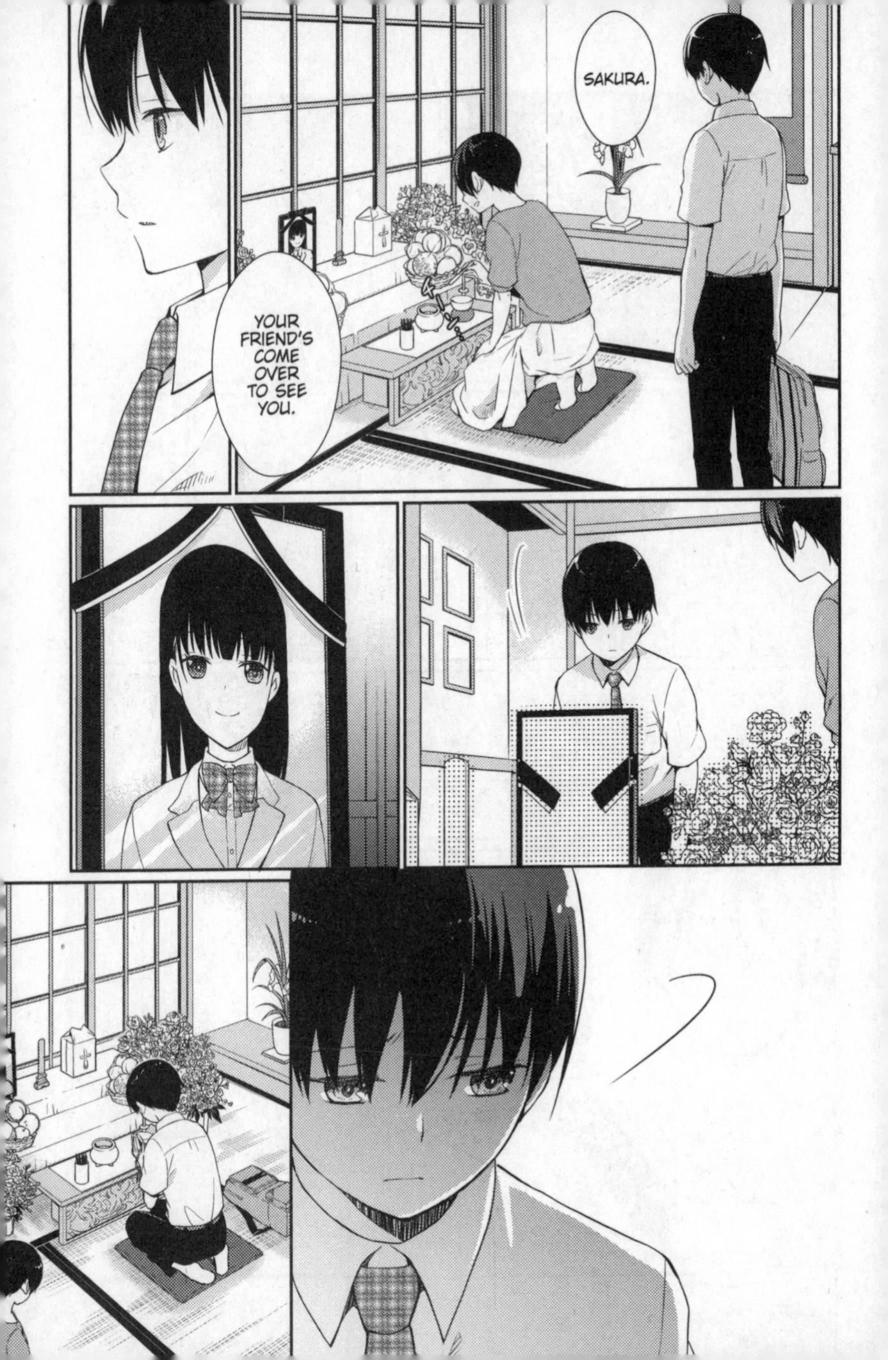
SAKURA.
YOUR FRIEND'S COME OVER TO SEE YOU.

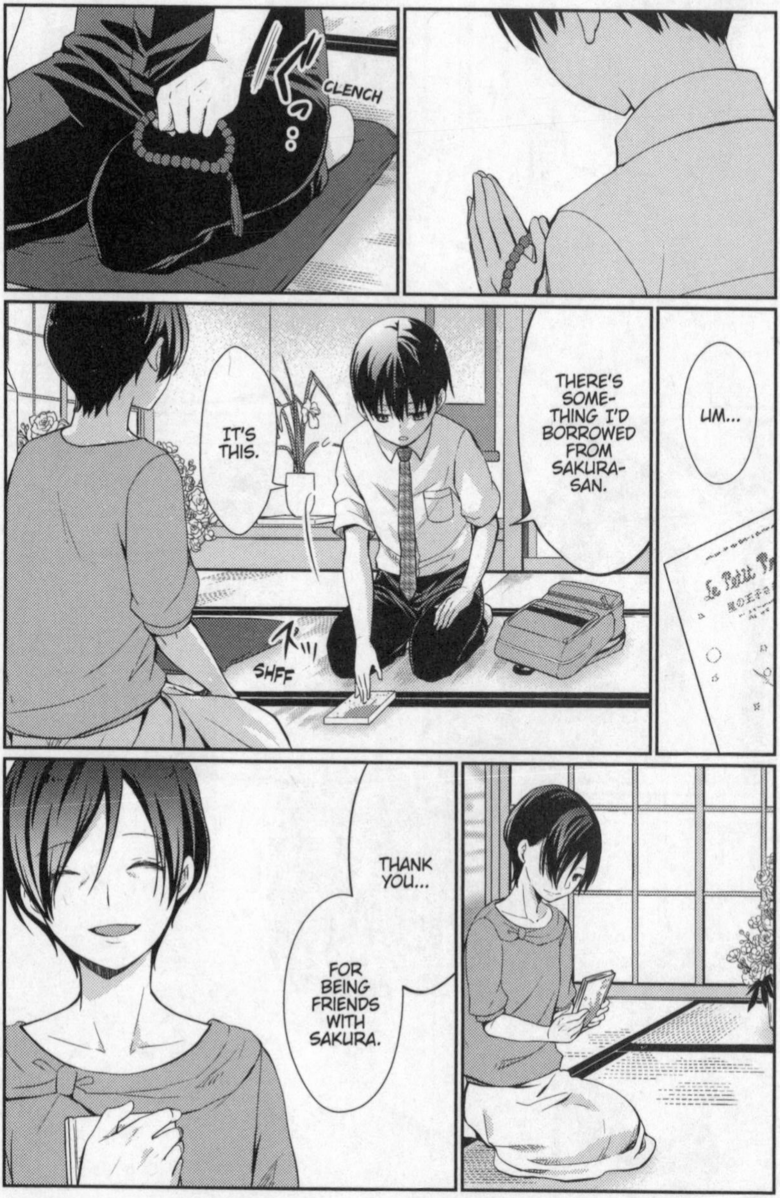
CLENCH
UM...
THERE'S SOME-THING I'D BORROWED FROM SAKURA-SAN.
IT'S THIS.
SHFF
THANK YOU...
FOR BEING FRIENDS WITH SAKURA.

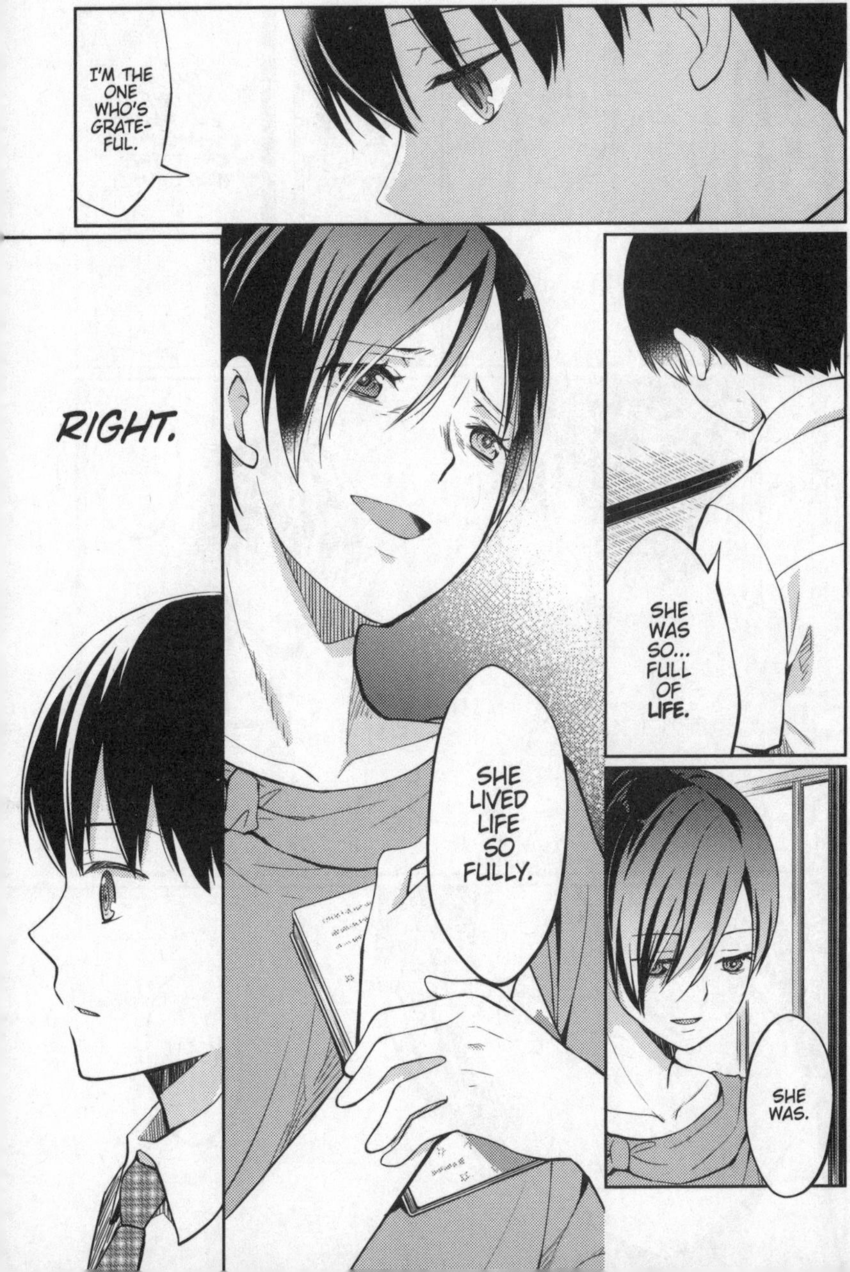
I'M THE ONE WHO'S GRATE-FUL.
SHE WAS SO... FULL OF LIFE.
SHE WAS.
SHE LIVED LIFE SO FULLY.
RIGHT.

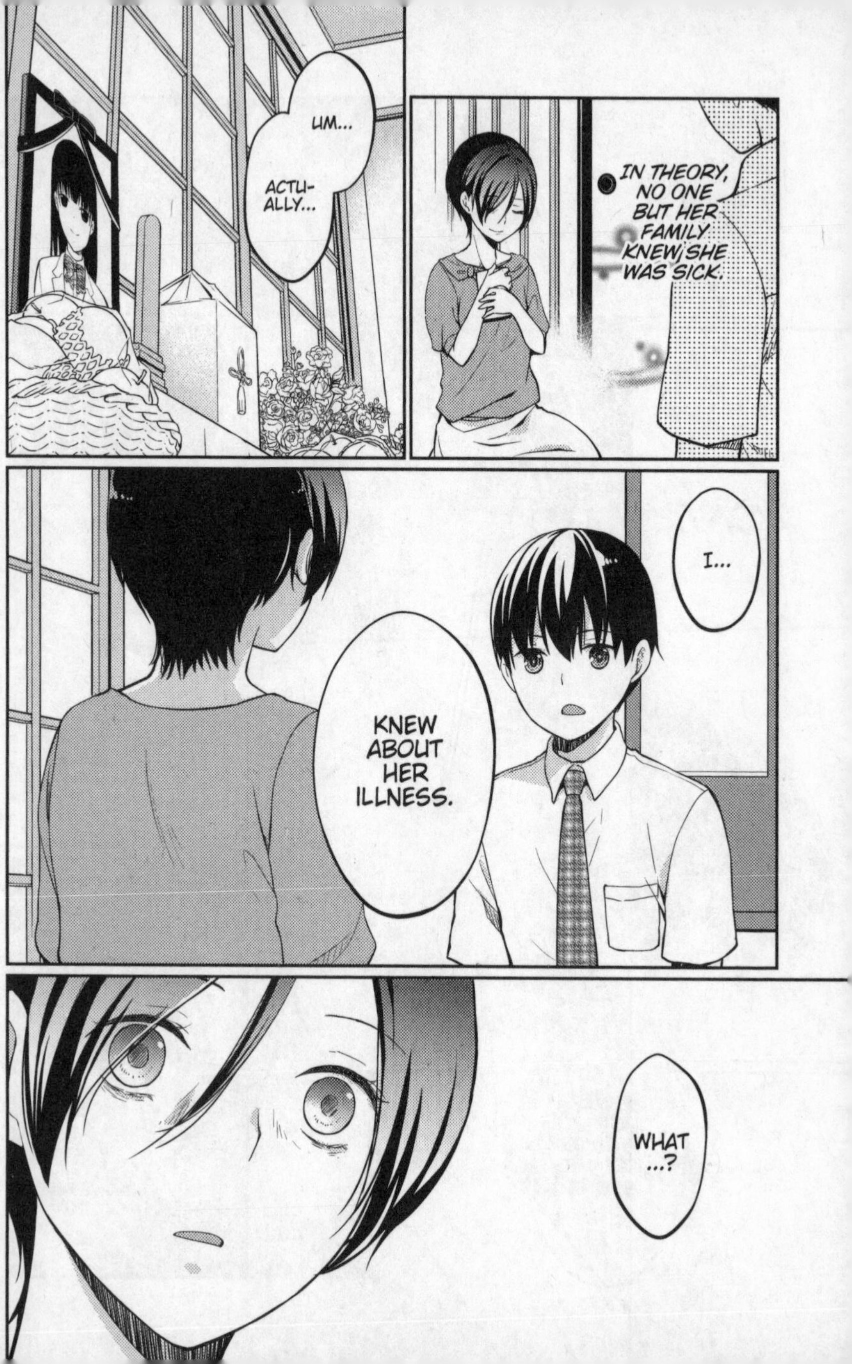
UM...
ACTU-
ALLY...
IN THEORY, NO ONE BUT HER FAMILY KNEW SHE WAS SICK.
I...
KNEW ABOUT HER ILLNESS.
WHAT ...?

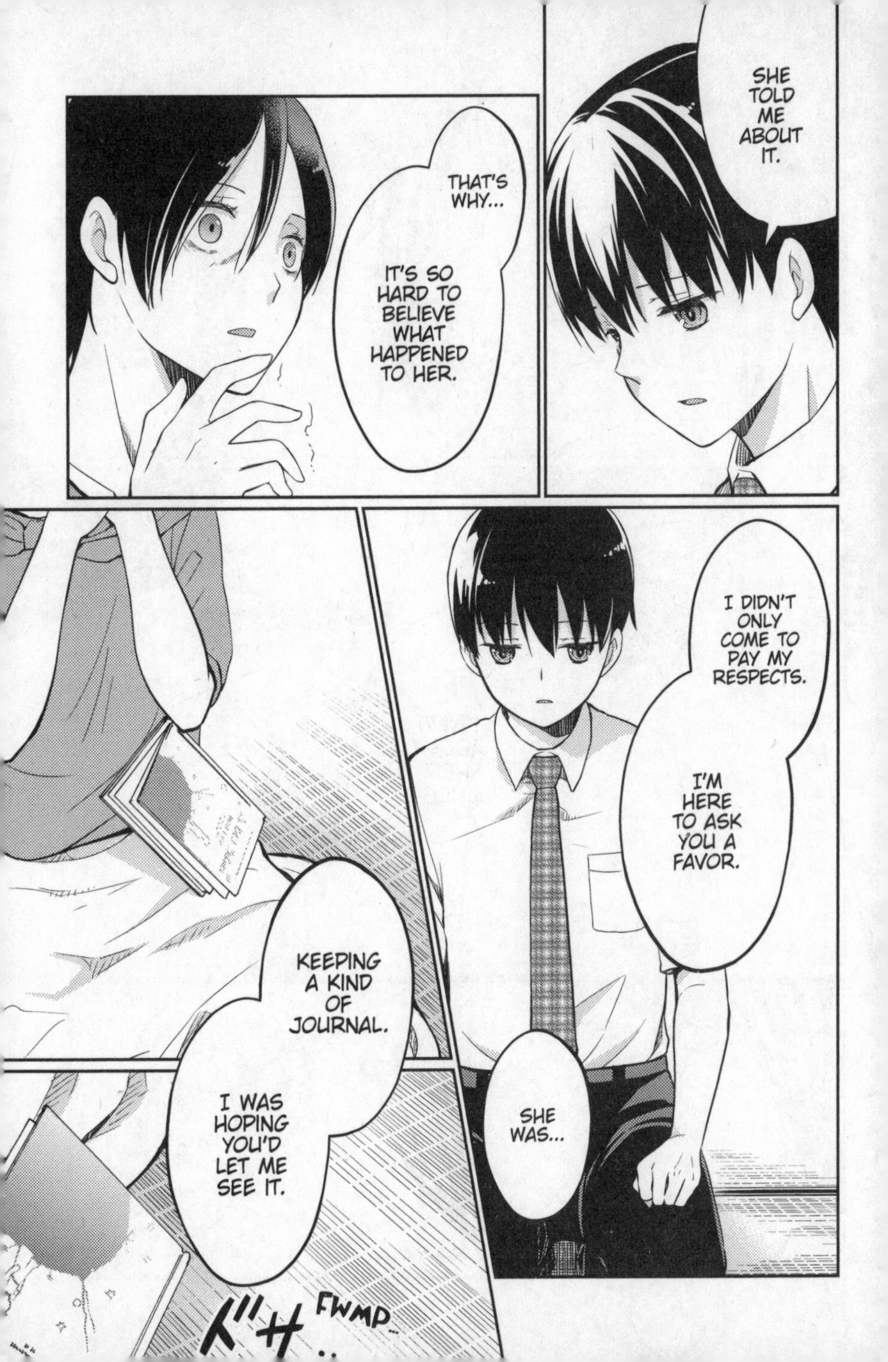
SHE TOLD ME ABOUT IT.
THAT'S WHY...
IT'S SO HARD TO BELIEVE WHAT HAPPENED TO HER.
I DIDN'T ONLY COME TO PAY MY RESPECTS.
I'M HERE TO ASK YOU A FAVOR.
SHE WAS...
KEEPING A KIND OF JOURNAL.
I WAS HOPING YOU'D LET ME SEE IT.
FWMP...

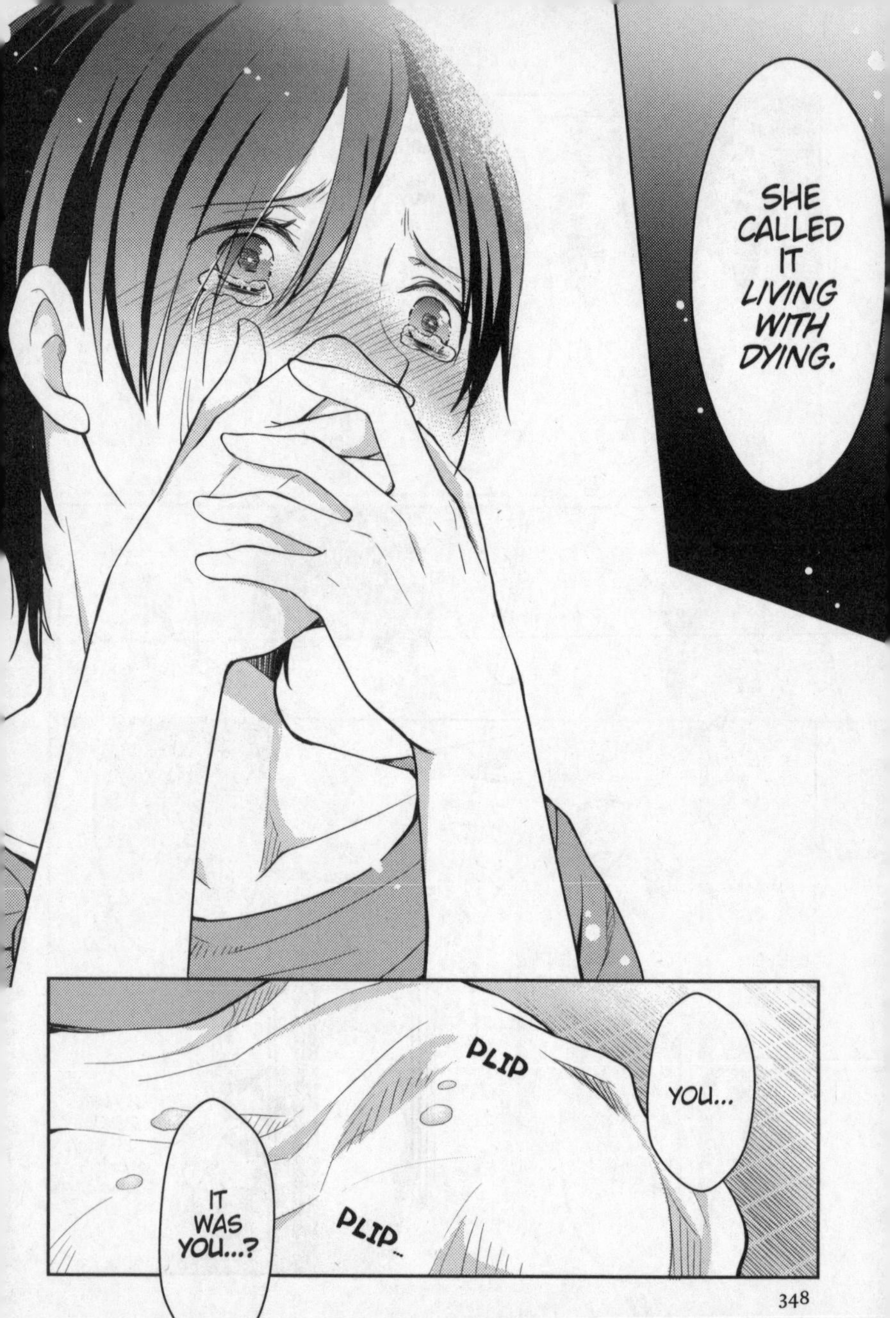
SHE CALLED IT *LIVING WITH DYING.*
YOU...
PLIP
IT WAS YOU...?
PLIP...

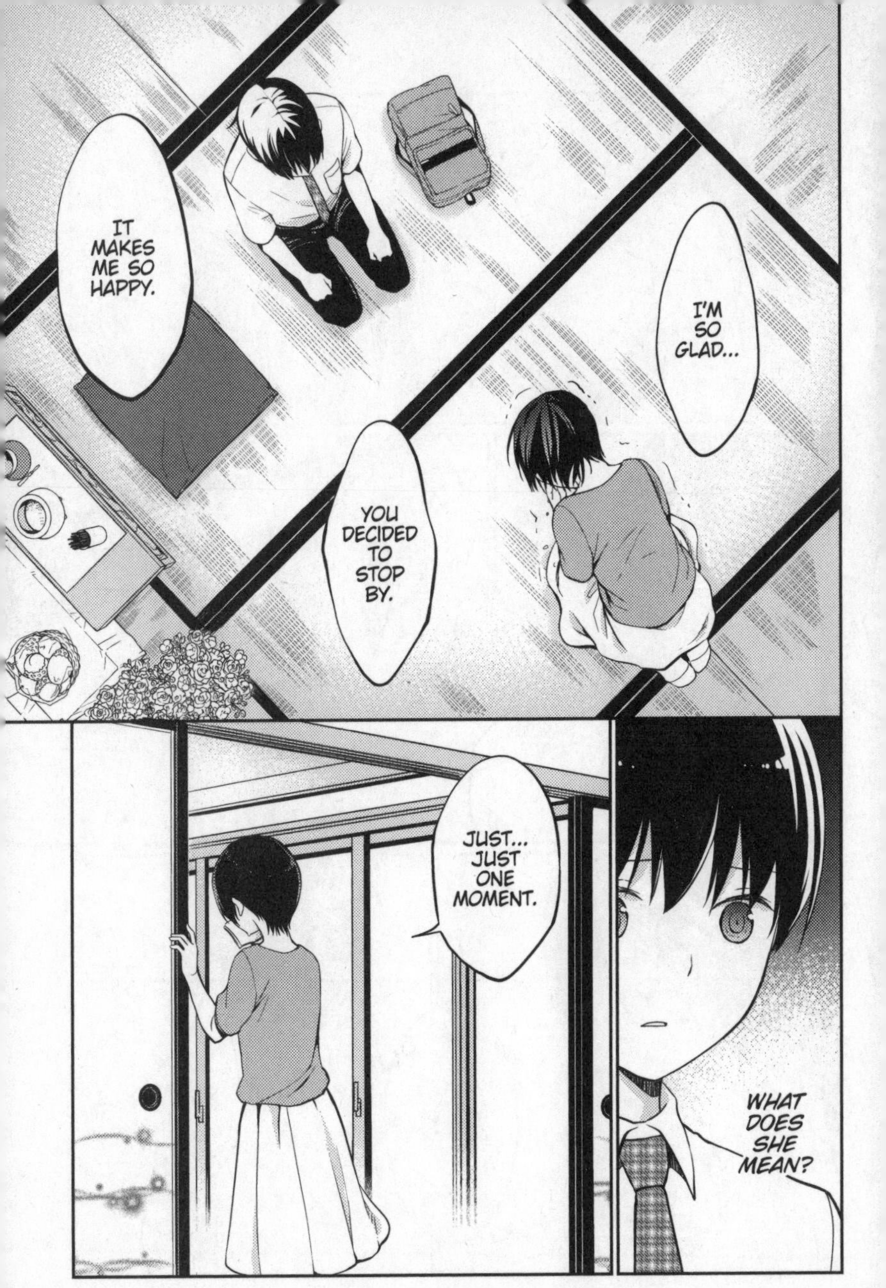
I'M SO GLAD...
YOU DECIDED TO STOP BY.
IT MAKES ME SO HAPPY.
WHAT DOES SHE MEAN?
JUST... JUST ONE MOMENT.

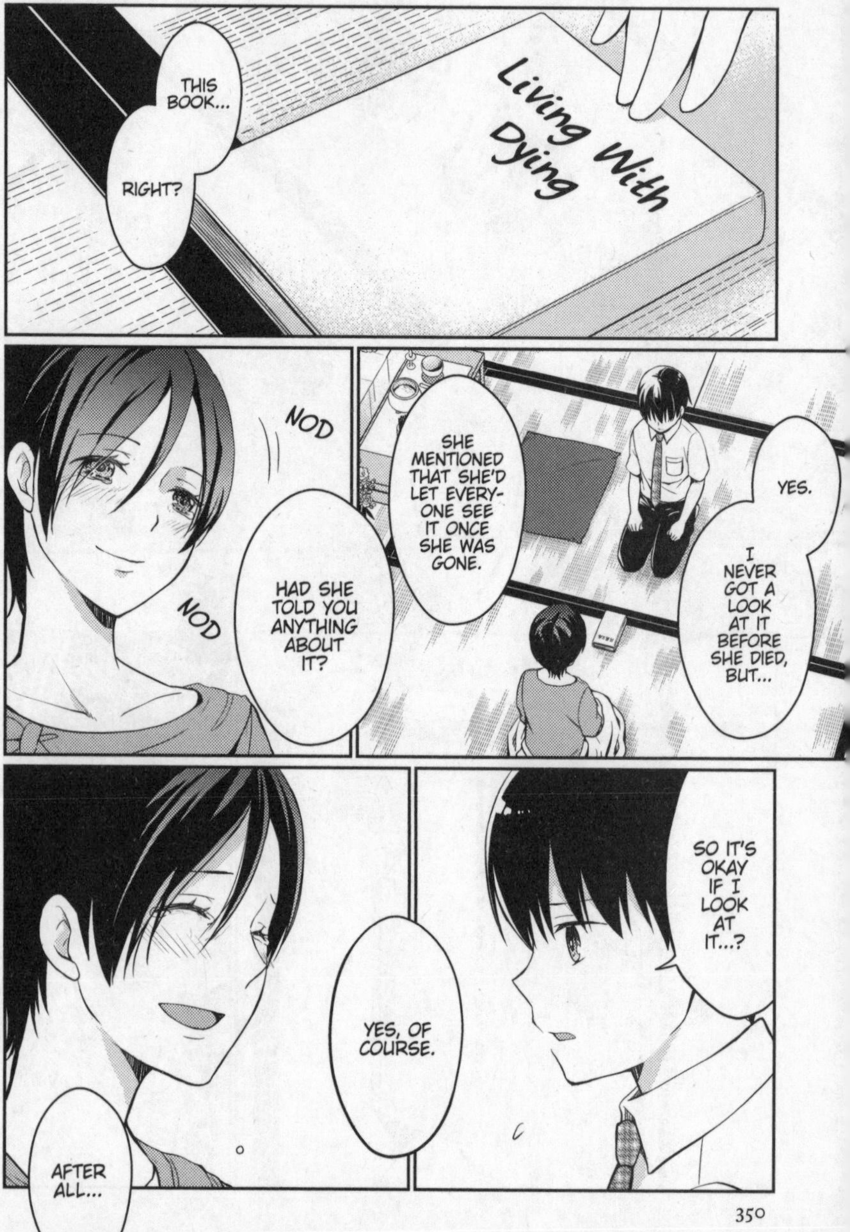
THIS BOOK...
RIGHT?
Living With Dying
YES.
I NEVER GOT A LOOK AT IT BEFORE SHE DIED, BUT...
SHE MENTIONED THAT SHE'D LET EVERY-ONE SEE IT ONCE SHE WAS GONE.
HAD SHE TOLD YOU ANYTHING ABOUT IT?
NOD
NOD
SO IT'S OKAY IF I LOOK AT IT...?
YES, OF COURSE.
AFTER ALL...

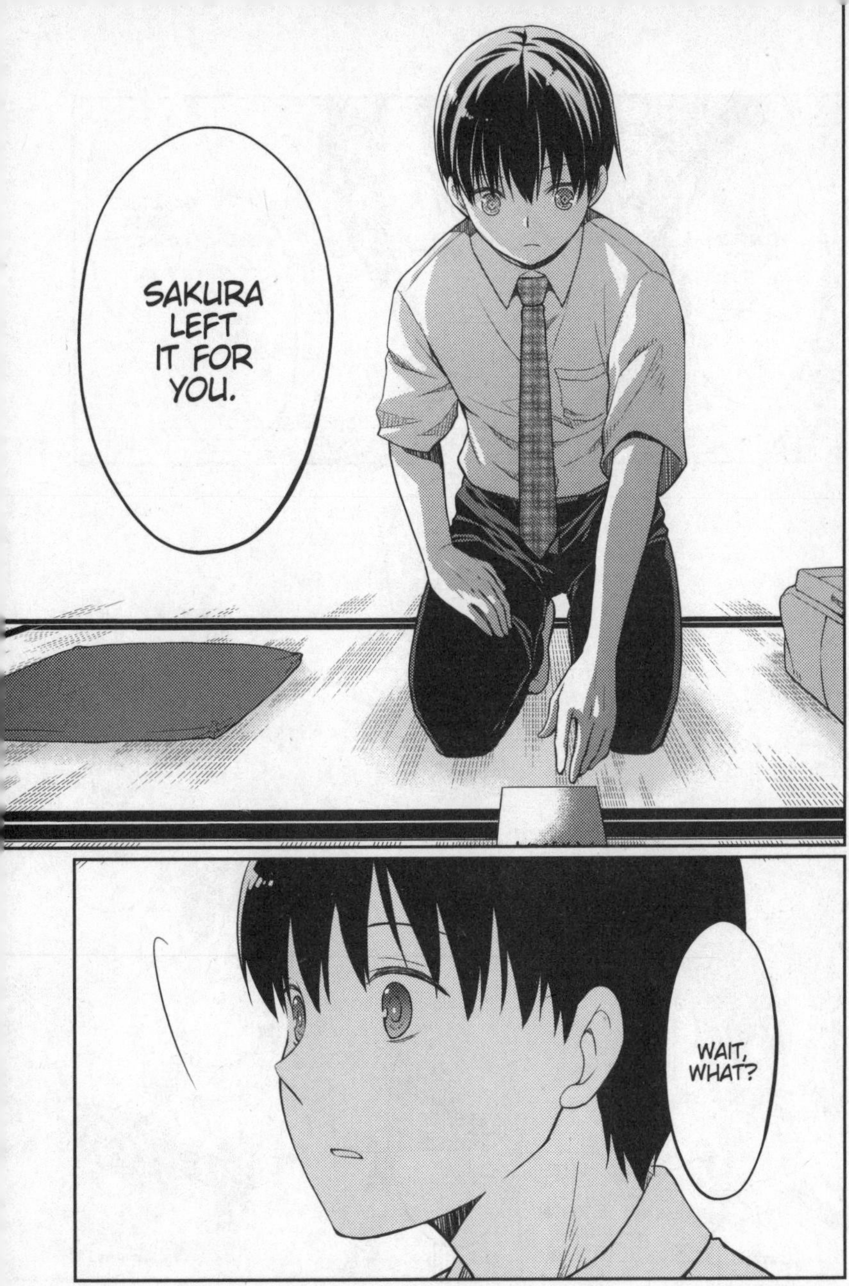
SAKURA LEFT IT FOR YOU.
WAIT, WHAT?

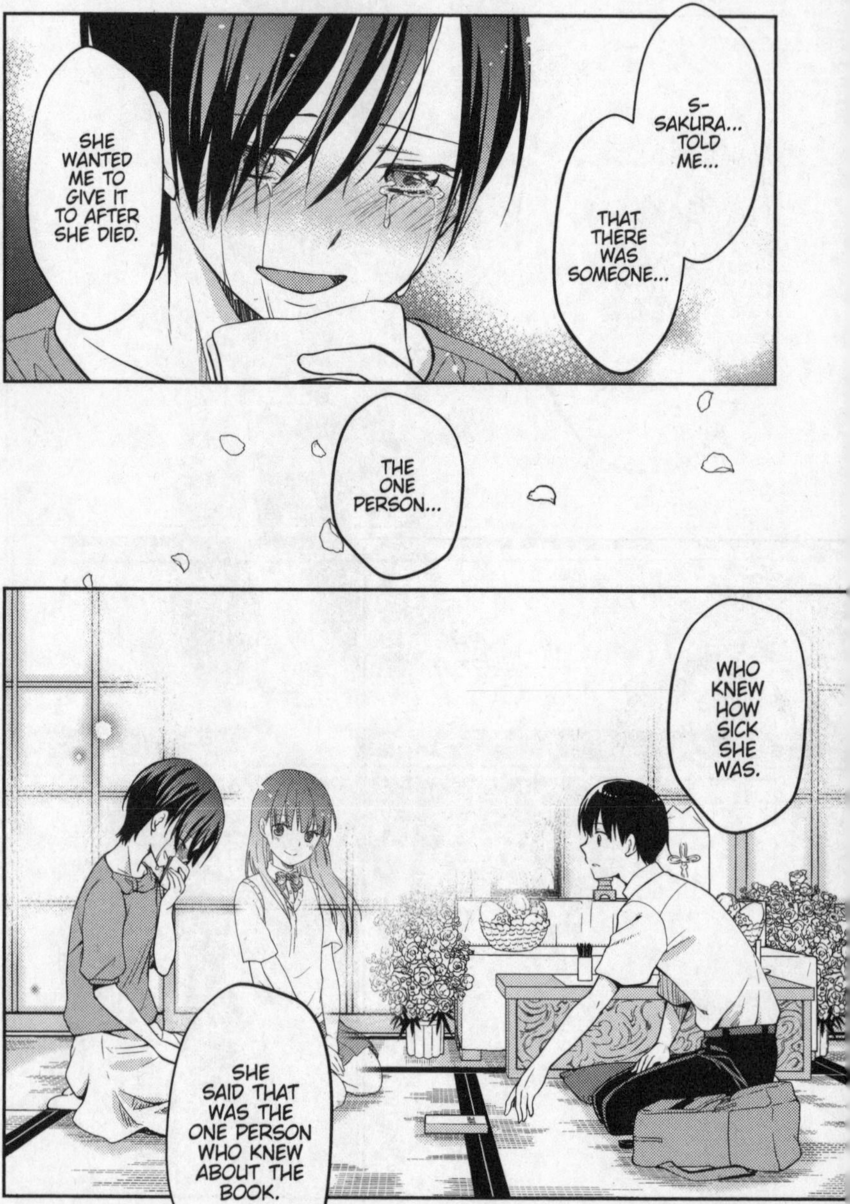
S- SAKURA... TOLD ME...
THAT THERE WAS SOMEONE...
SHE WANTED ME TO GIVE IT TO AFTER SHE DIED.
THE ONE PERSON...
WHO KNEW HOW SICK SHE WAS.
SHE SAID THAT WAS THE ONE PERSON WHO KNEW ABOUT THE BOOK.

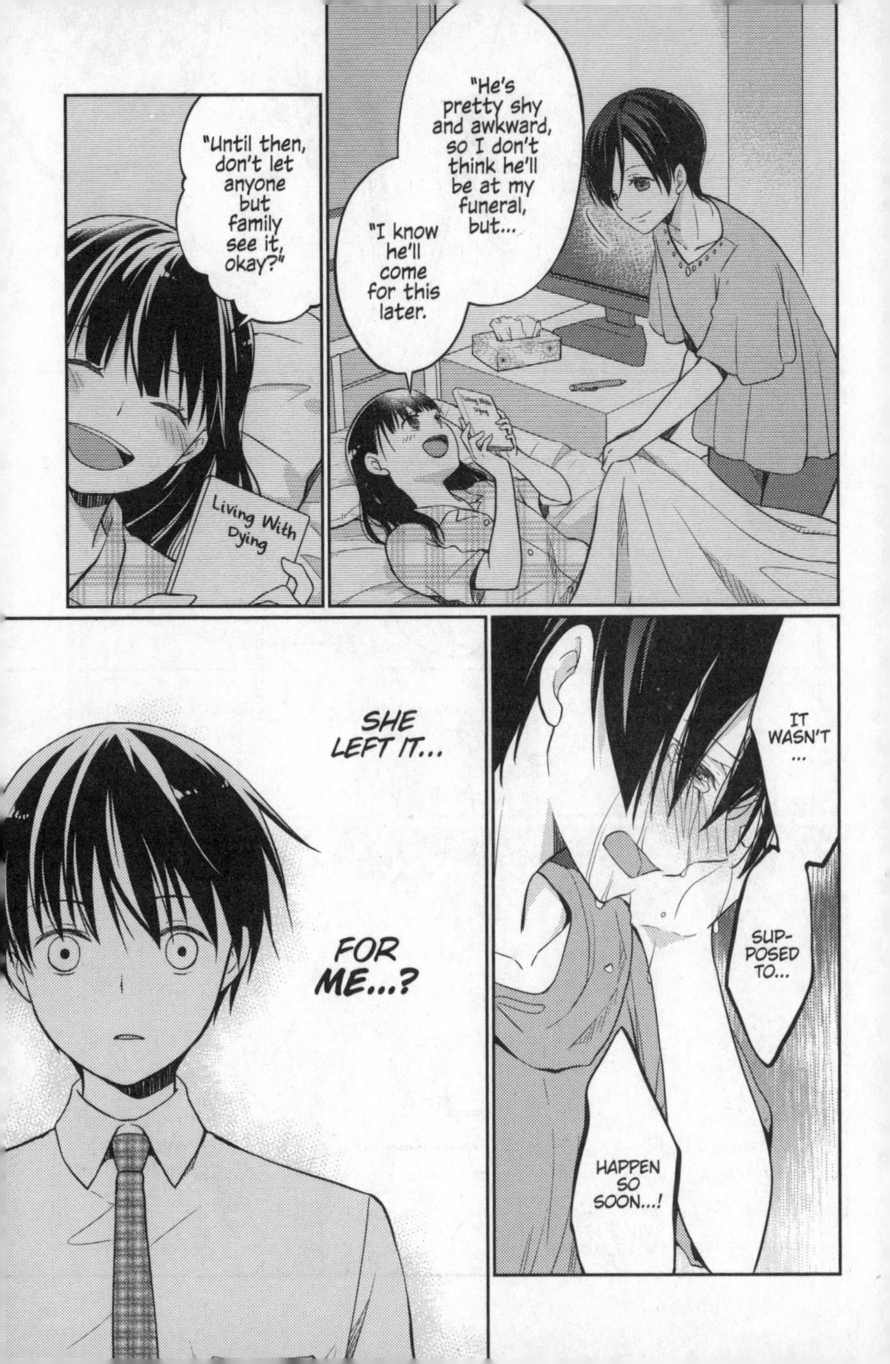
"He's pretty shy and awkward, so I don't think he'll be at my funeral, but...
"I know he'll come for this later.
Living With Dying
"Until then, don't let anyone but family see it, okay?"
Living With Dying
IT WASN'T ...
SUP-POSED TO...
HAPPEN SO SOON...!
SHE LEFT IT...
FOR ME...?

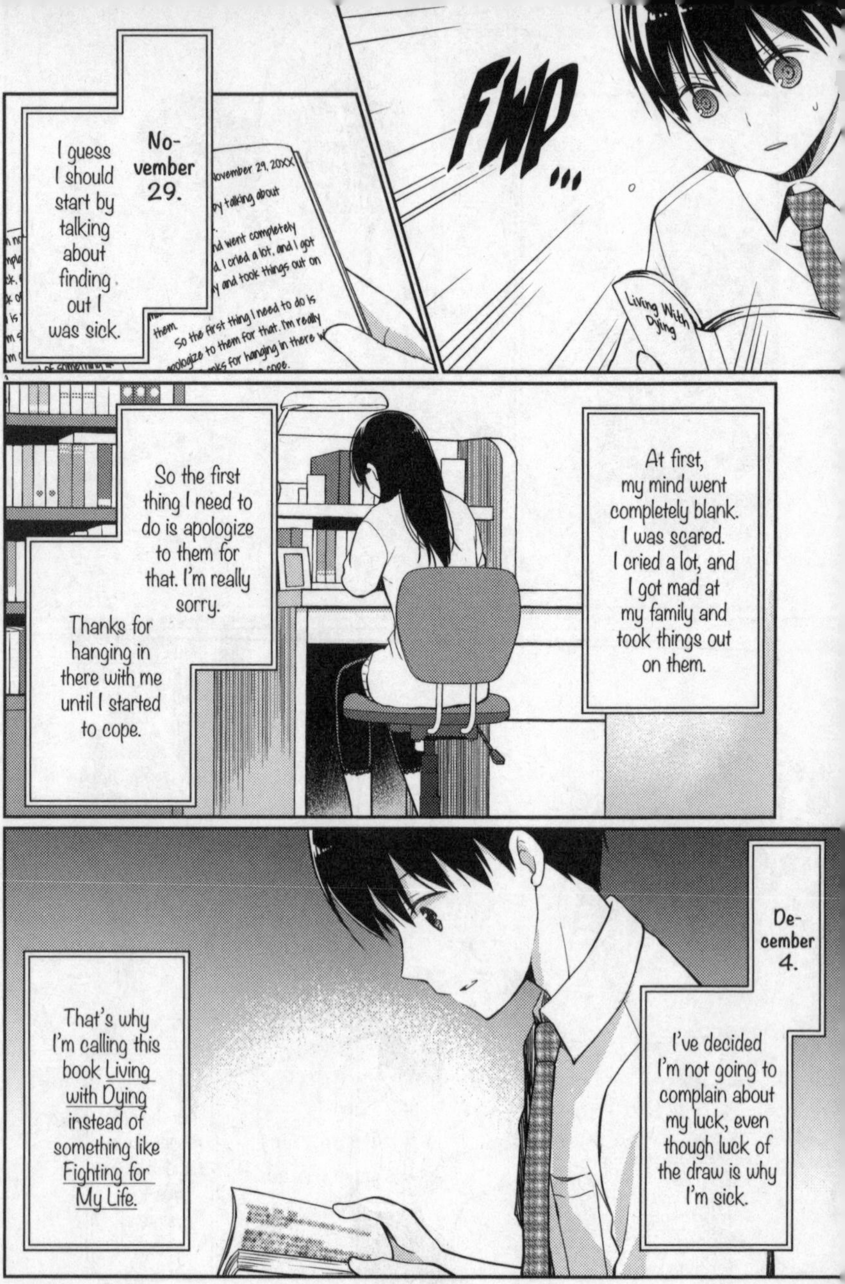
FWP...
Living With Dying
November 29.
I guess I should start by talking about finding out I was sick.
At first, my mind went completely blank. I was scared. I cried a lot, and I got mad at my family and took things out on them.
So the first thing I need to do is apologize to them for that. I'm really sorry.
Thanks for hanging in there with me until I started to cope.
December 4.
I've decided I'm not going to complain about my luck, even though luck of the draw is why I'm sick.
That's why I'm calling this book Living with Dying instead of something like Fighting for My Life.

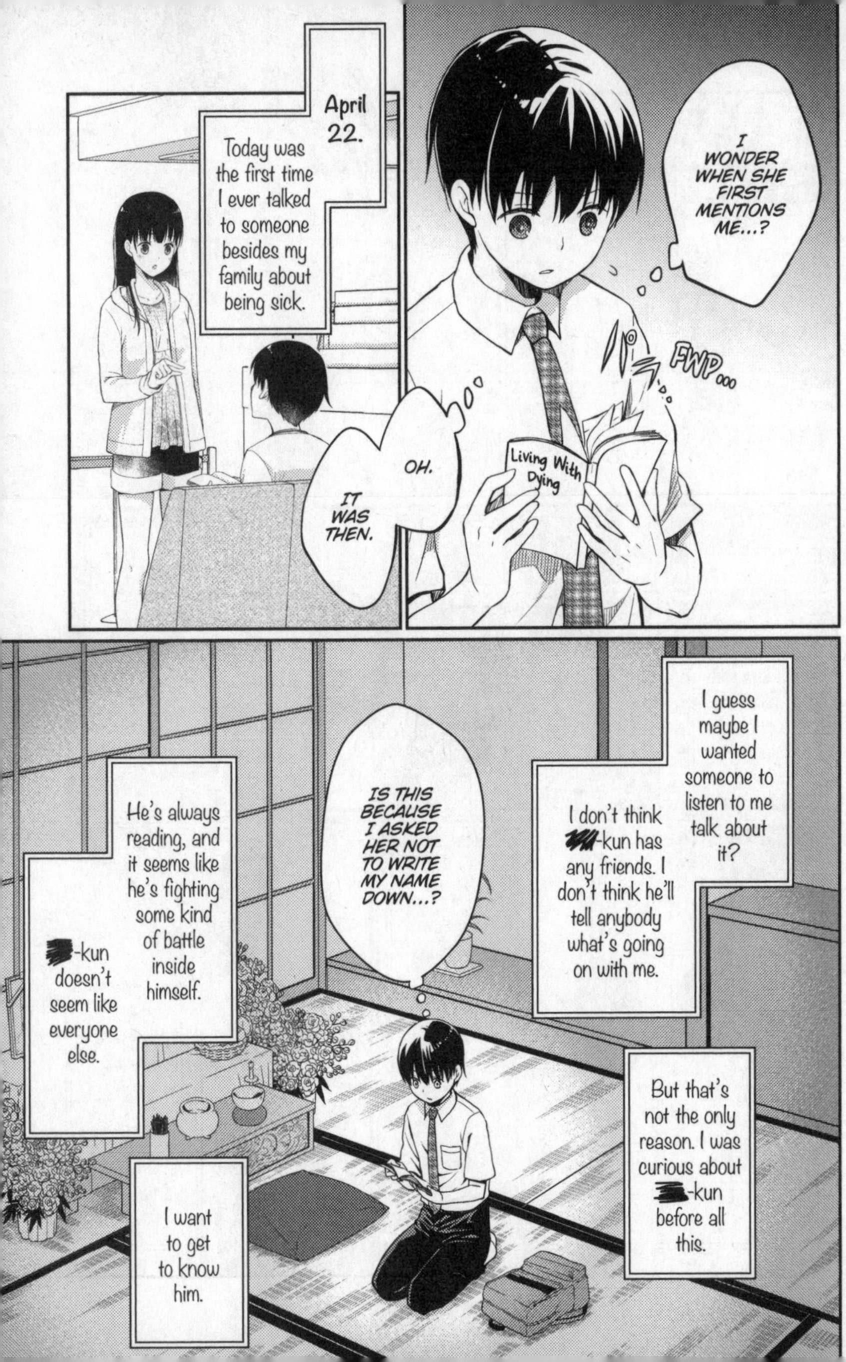
I WONDER WHEN SHE FIRST MENTIONS ME...?
FWP...
OH.
IT WAS THEN.
Living With Dying
April 22.
Today was the first time I ever talked to someone besides my family about being sick.
I guess maybe I wanted someone to listen to me talk about it?
I don't think [redacted]-kun has any friends. I don't think he'll tell anybody what's going on with me.
IS THIS BECAUSE I ASKED HER NOT TO WRITE MY NAME DOWN...?
He's always reading, and it seems like he's fighting some kind of battle inside himself.
[redacted]-kun doesn't seem like everyone else.
But that's not the only reason. I was curious about [redacted]-kun before all this.
I want to get to know him.

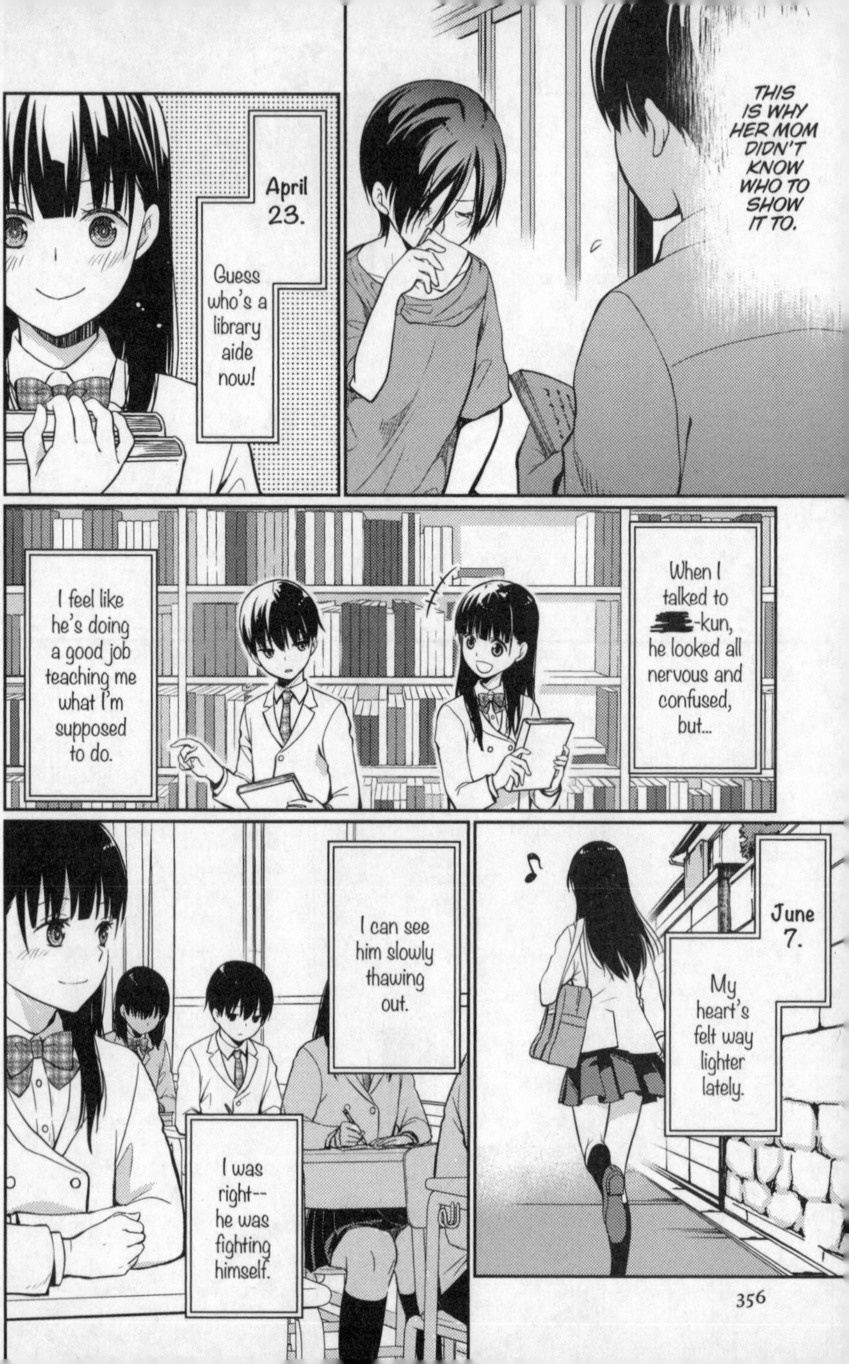
THIS IS WHY HER MOM DIDN'T KNOW WHO TO SHOW IT TO.
April 23.
Guess who's a library aide now!
When I talked to [redacted]-kun, he looked all nervous and confused, but...
I feel like he's doing a good job teaching me what I'm supposed to do.
June 7.
My heart's felt way lighter lately.
I can see him slowly thawing out.
I was right-- he was fighting himself.

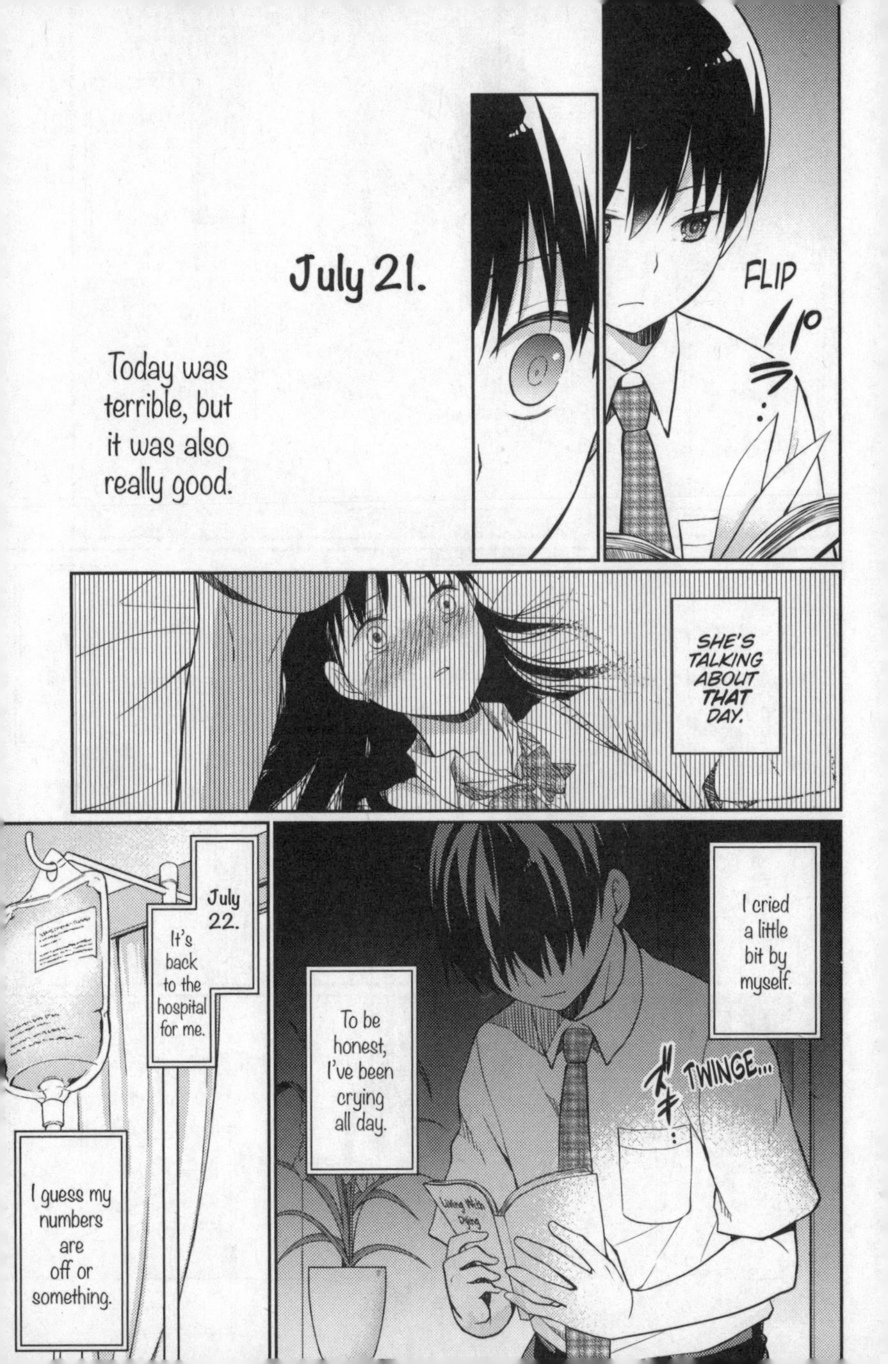
FLIP
July 21.
Today was terrible, but it was also really good.
SHE'S TALKING ABOUT THAT DAY.
I cried a little bit by myself.
TWINGE...
To be honest, I've been crying all day.
July 22.
It's back to the hospital for me.
I guess my numbers are off or something.

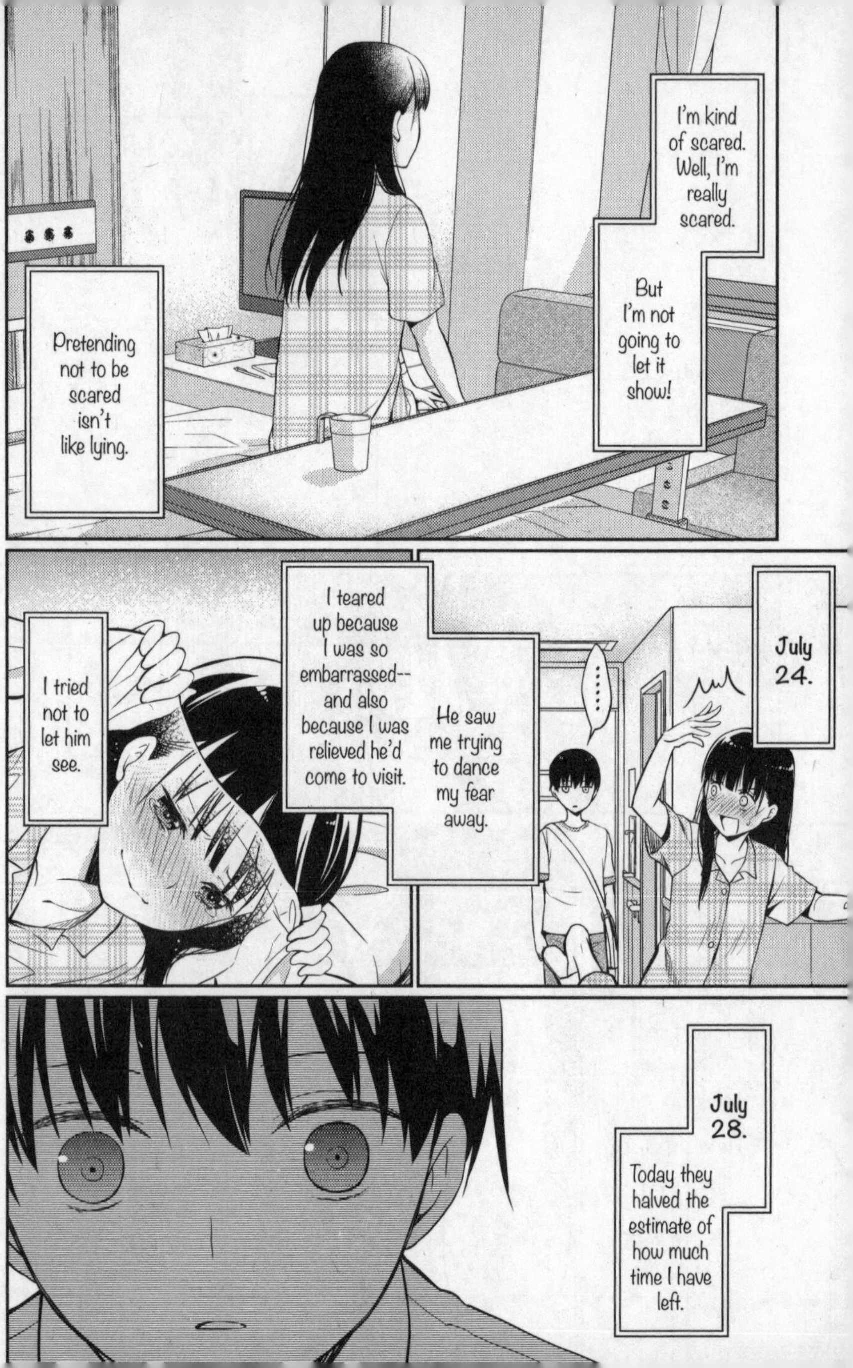
I'm kind of scared. Well, I'm really scared.
But I'm not going to let it show!
Pretending not to be scared isn't like lying.
July 24.
......
He saw me trying to dance my fear away.
I teared up because I was so embarrassed--and also because I was relieved he'd come to visit.
I tried not to let him see.
July 28.
Today they halved the estimate of how much time I have left.

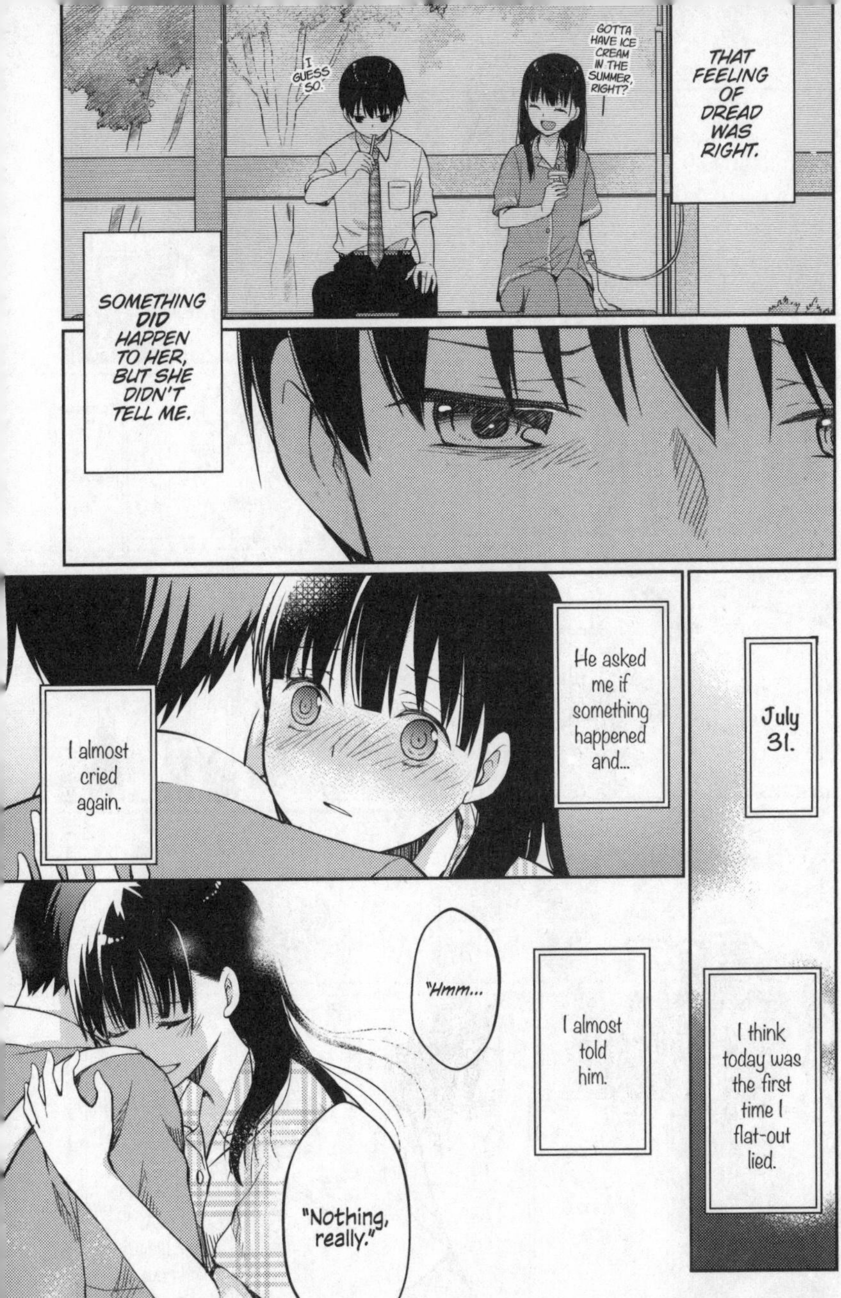

THAT FEELING OF DREAD WAS RIGHT.
GOTTA HAVE ICE CREAM IN THE SUMMER, RIGHT?
I GUESS SO.
SOMETHING DID HAPPEN TO HER, BUT SHE DIDN'T TELL ME.
July 31.
He asked me if something happened and...
I almost cried again.
I think today was the first time I flat-out lied.
I almost told him.
"Hmm...
"Nothing, really."

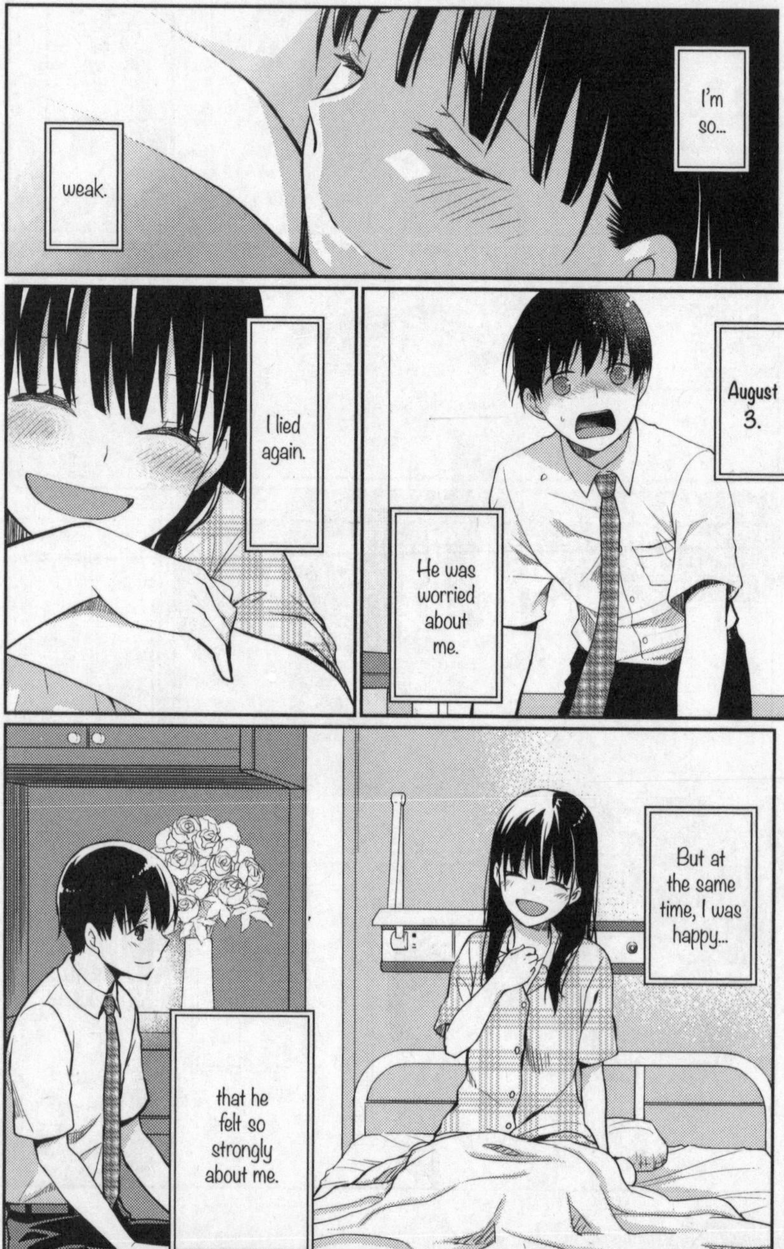
I'm so...
weak.
August 3.
He was worried about me.
I lied again.
But at the same time, I was happy...
that he felt so strongly about me.

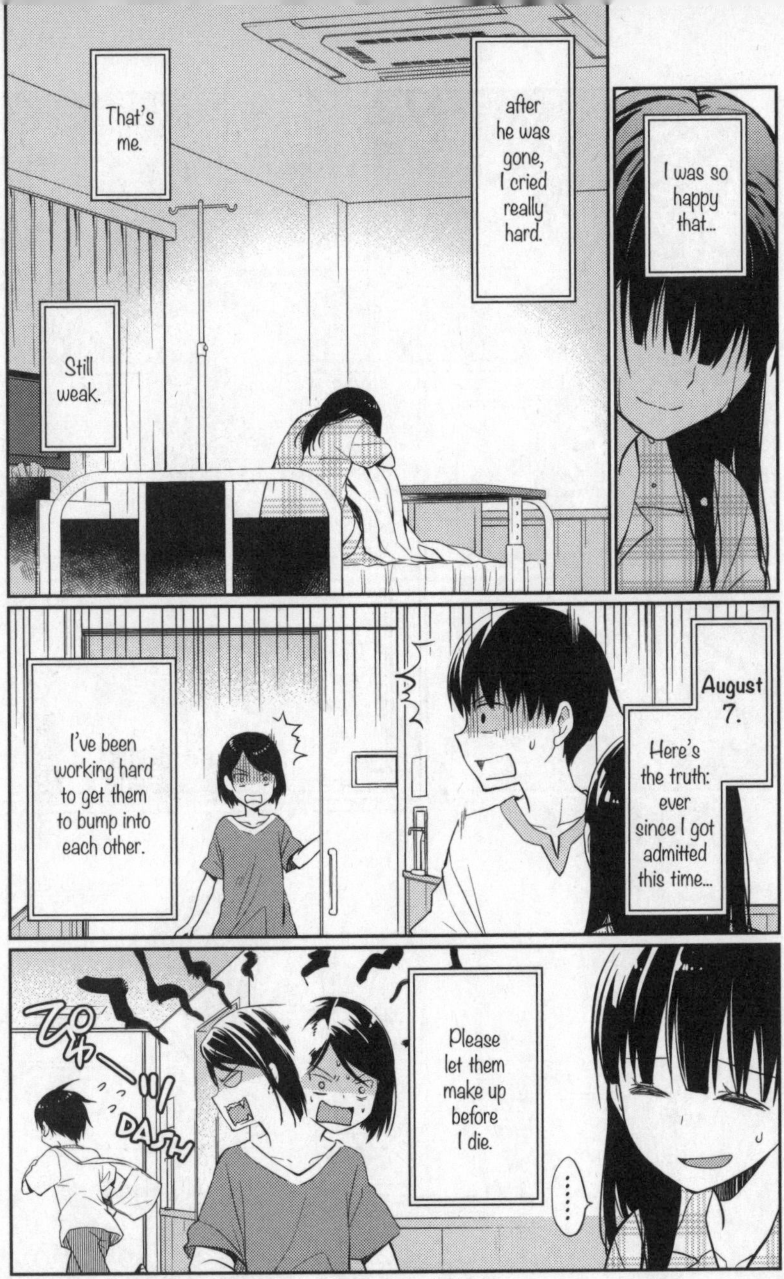
I was so happy that...
after he was gone, I cried really hard.
That's me.
Still weak.
August 7.
Here's the truth: ever since I got admitted this time...
I've been working hard to get them to bump into each other.
Please let them make up before I die.
......
DASH

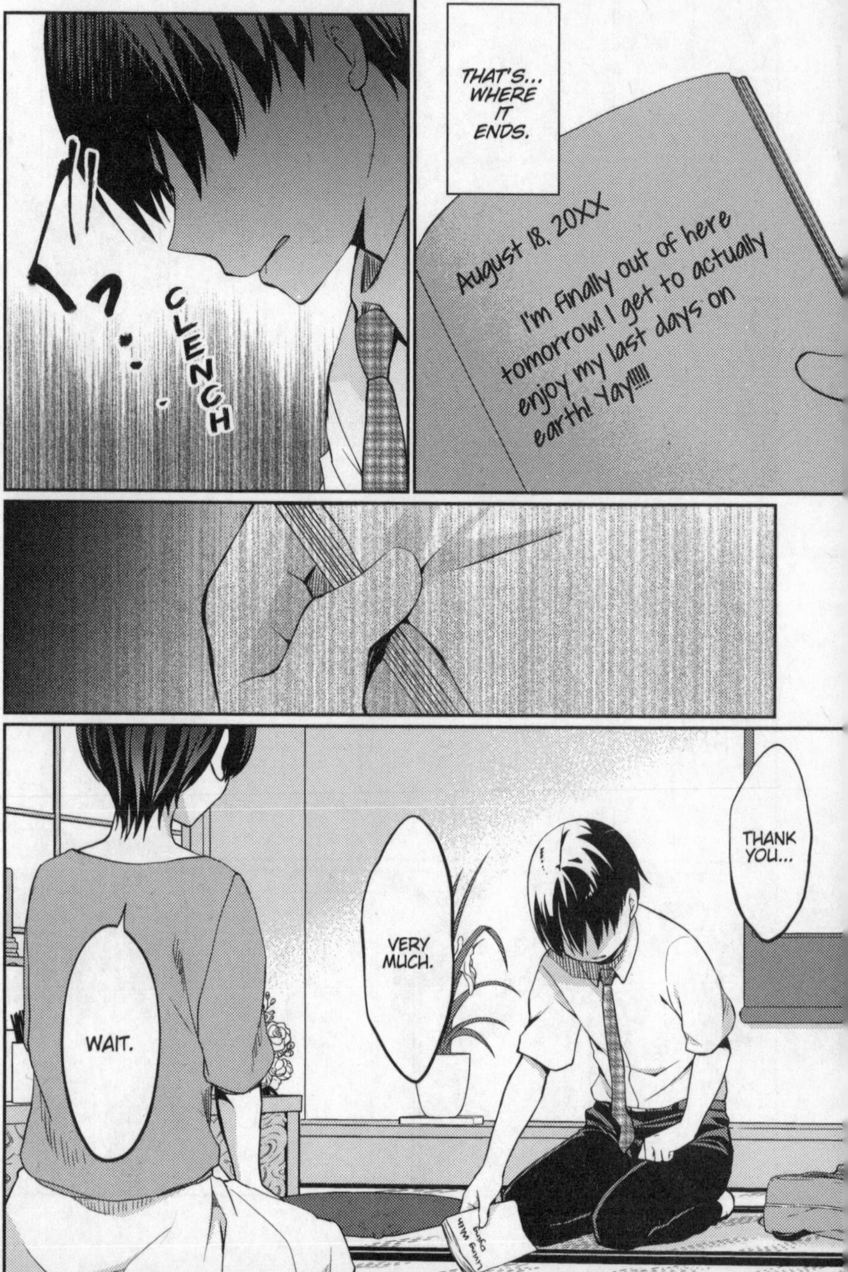
THAT'S... WHERE IT ENDS.
August 18, 20XX
I'm finally out of here tomorrow! I get to actually enjoy my last days on earth! Yay!!!!!
CLENCH
THANK YOU...
VERY MUCH.
WAIT.

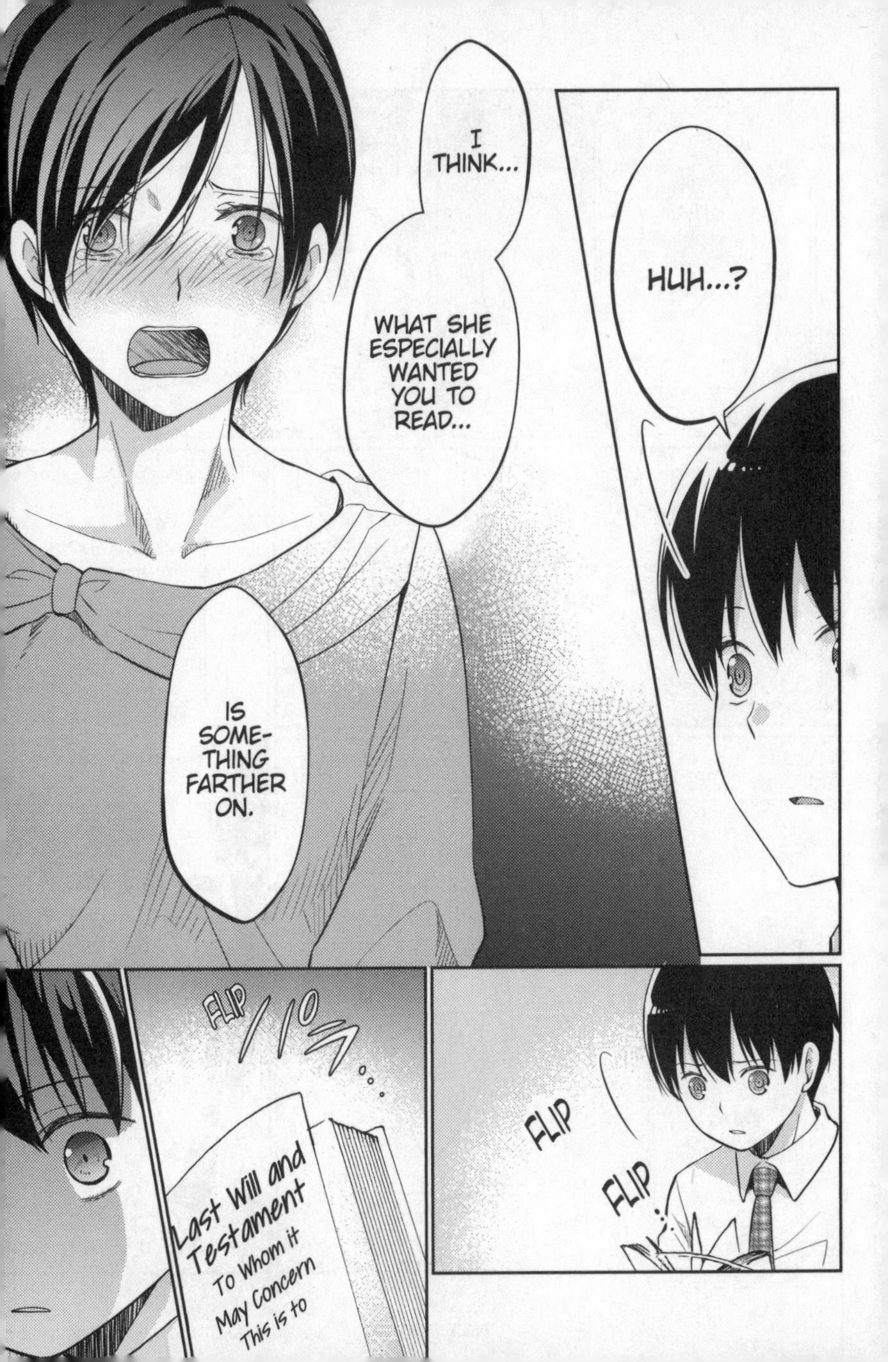
HUH...?
I THINK...
WHAT SHE ESPECIALLY WANTED YOU TO READ...
IS SOME-THING FARTHER ON.
FLIP
FLIP
FLIP
パラ
Last Will and Testament
To Whom it May Concern
This is to

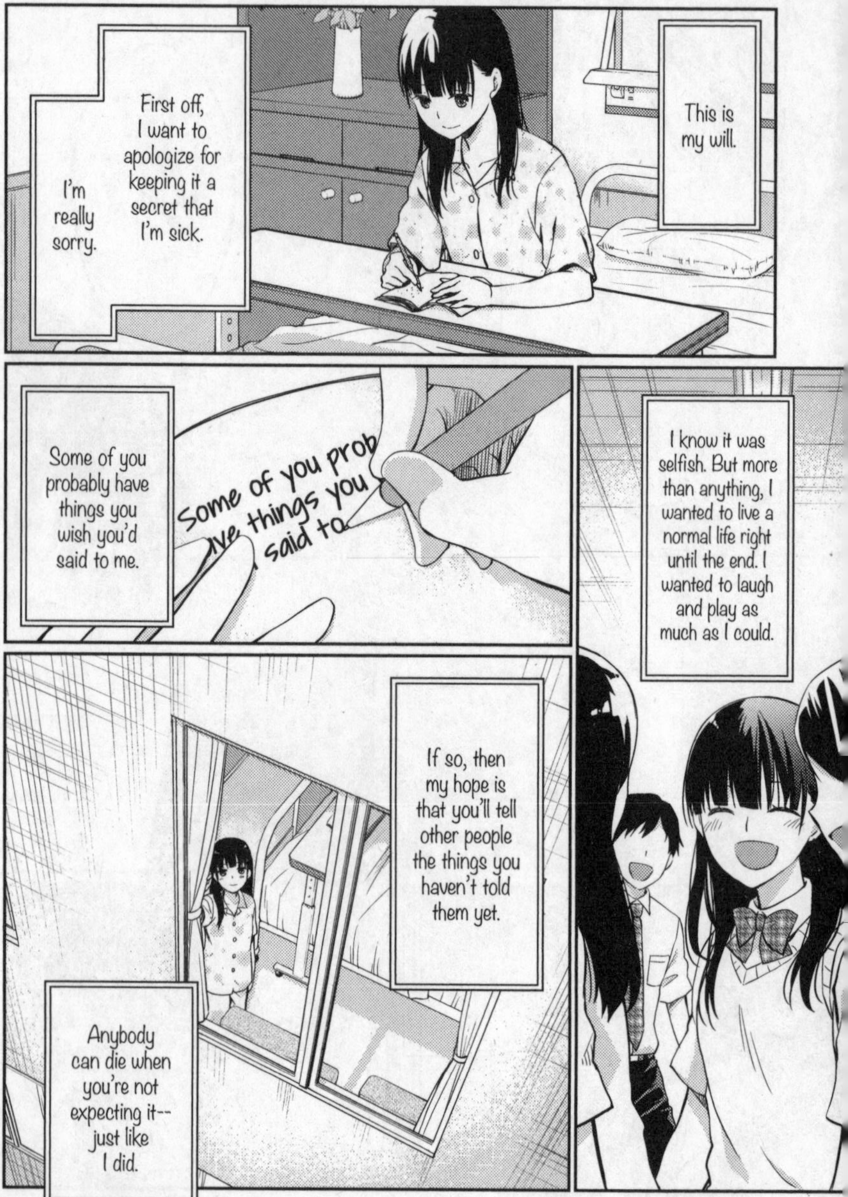
This is my will.
First off, I want to apologize for keeping it a secret that I'm sick.
I'm really sorry.
I know it was selfish. But more than anything, I wanted to live a normal life right until the end. I wanted to laugh and play as much as I could.
Some of you probably have things you wish you'd said to me.
If so, then my hope is that you'll tell other people the things you haven't told them yet.
Anybody can die when you're not expecting it--just like I did.

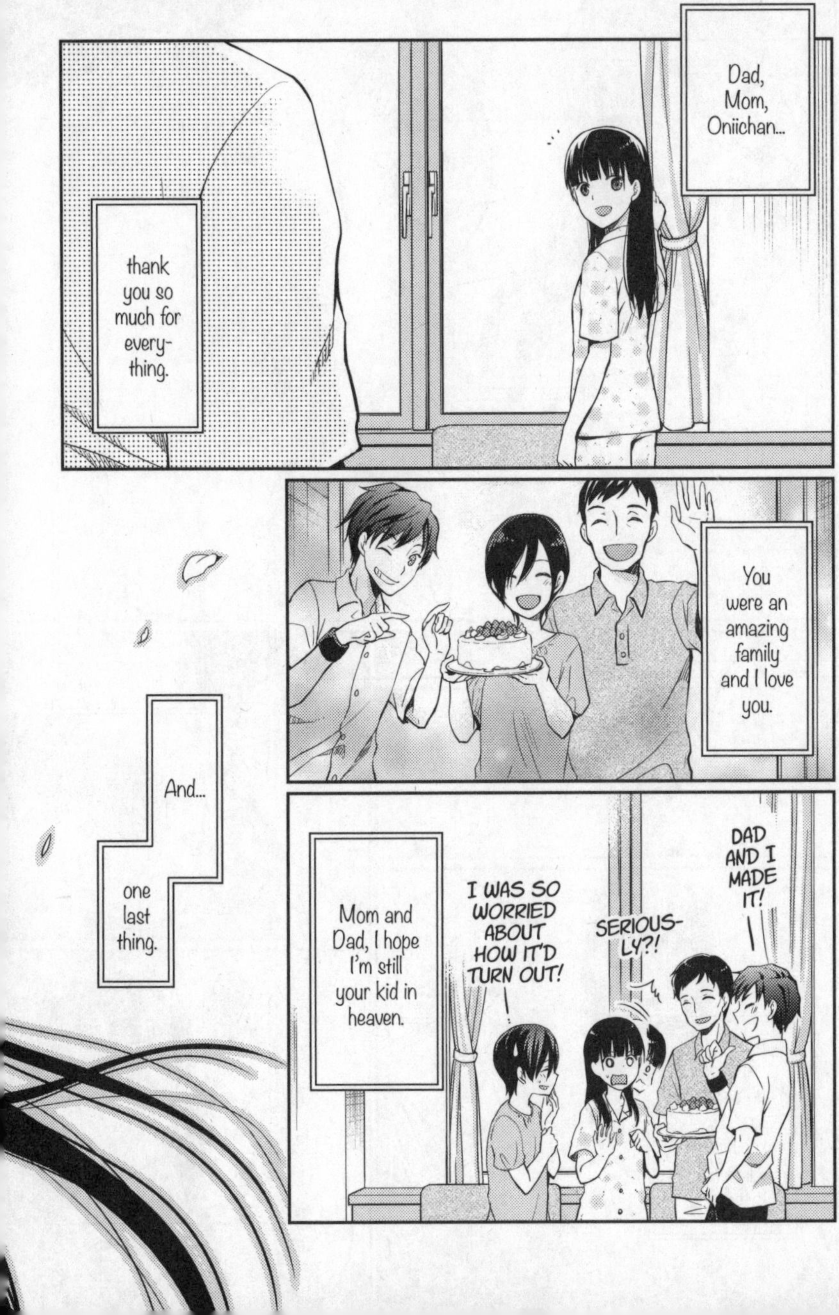
Dad, Mom, Oniichan...
thank you so much for every-thing.
You were an amazing family and I love you.
And...
one last thing.
DAD AND I MADE IT!
SERIOUS-LY?!
I WAS SO WORRIED ABOUT HOW IT'D TURN OUT!
Mom and Dad, I hope I'm still your kid in heaven.

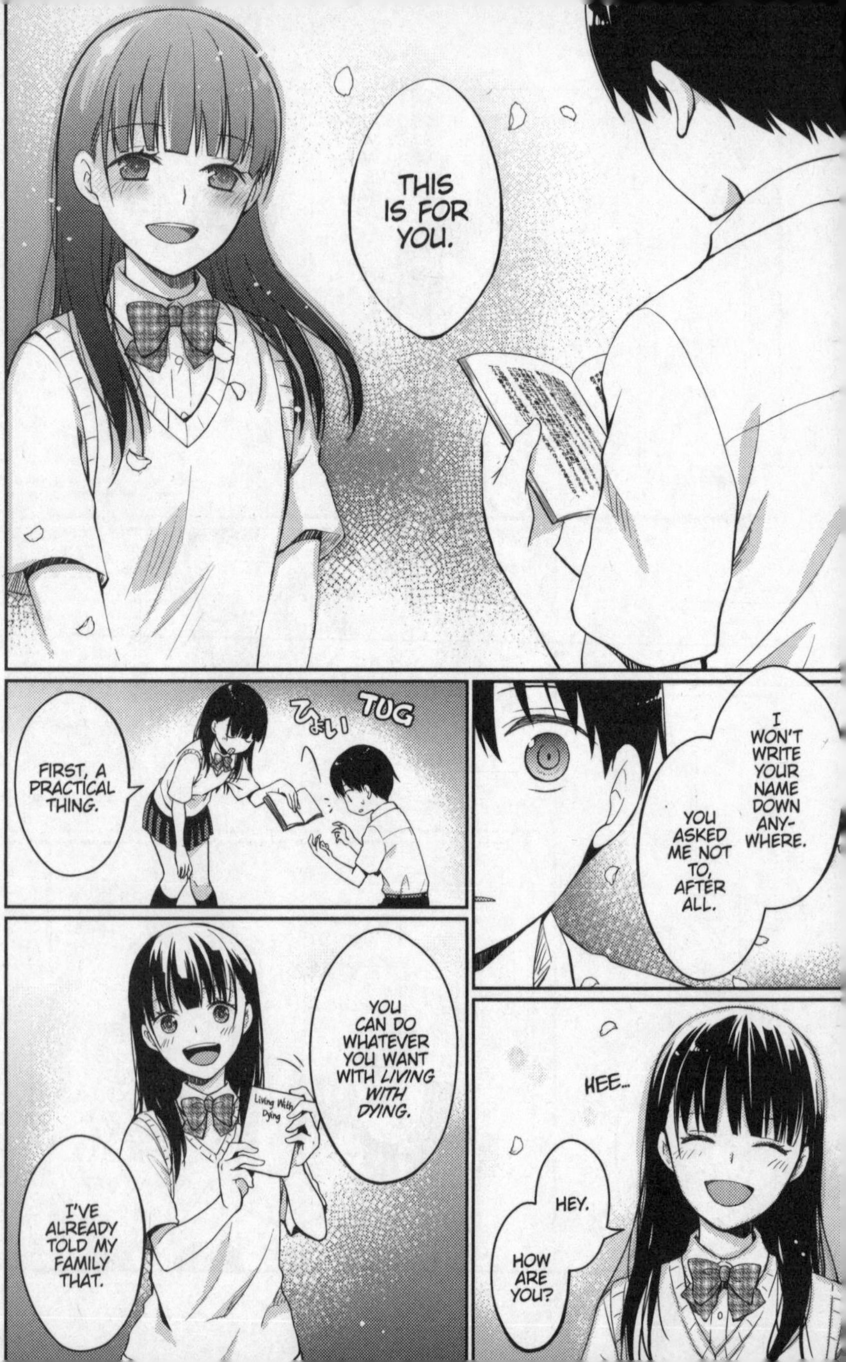
THIS IS FOR YOU.
I WON'T WRITE YOUR NAME DOWN ANY-WHERE.
YOU ASKED ME NOT TO, AFTER ALL.
TUG
ひょい
FIRST, A PRACTICAL THING.
HEE...
HEY.
HOW ARE YOU?
YOU CAN DO WHATEVER YOU WANT WITH *LIVING WITH DYING*.
Living With Dying
I'VE ALREADY TOLD MY FAMILY THAT.

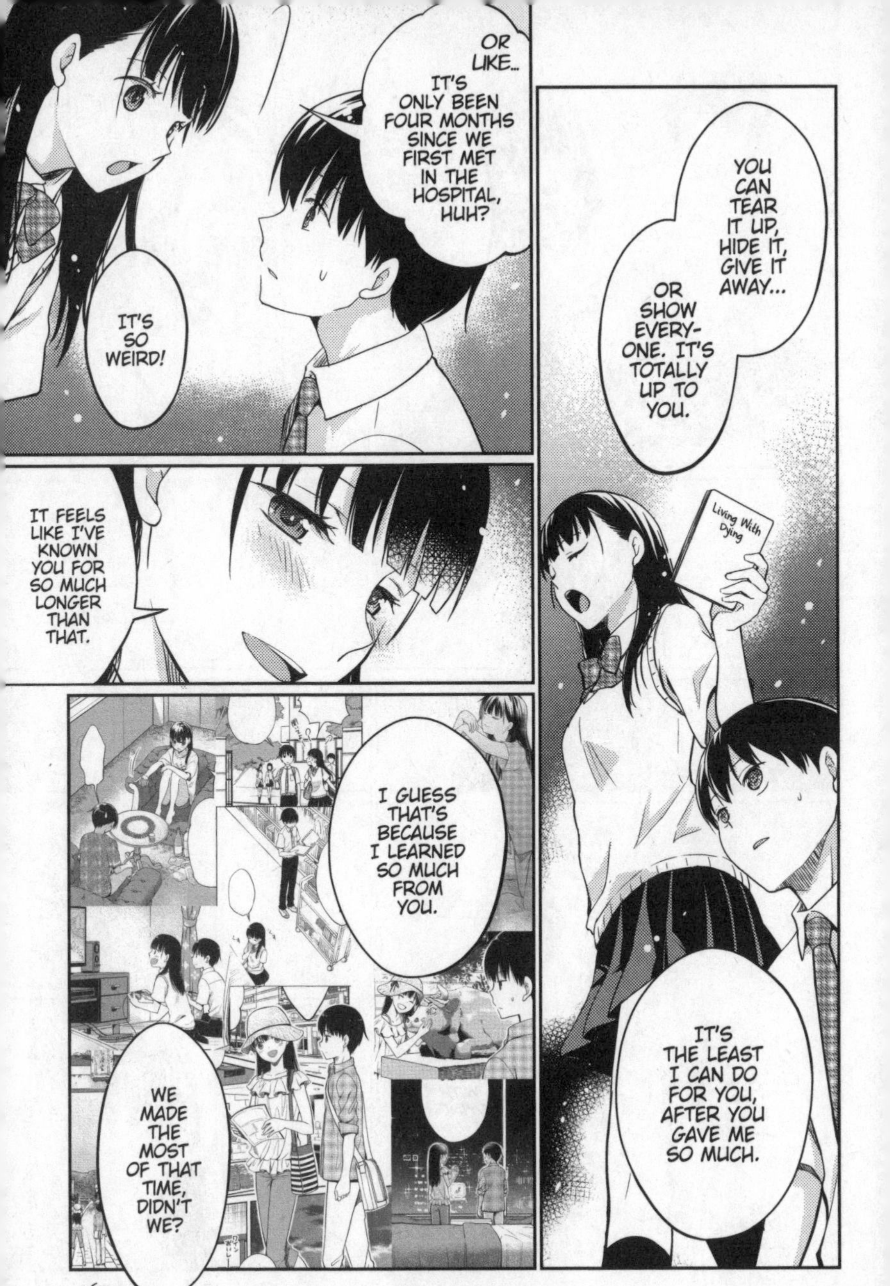
YOU CAN TEAR IT UP, HIDE IT, GIVE IT AWAY...
OR SHOW EVERY-ONE. IT'S TOTALLY UP TO YOU.
Living With Dying
IT'S THE LEAST I CAN DO FOR YOU, AFTER YOU GAVE ME SO MUCH.
OR LIKE... IT'S ONLY BEEN FOUR MONTHS SINCE WE FIRST MET IN THE HOSPITAL, HUH?
IT'S SO WEIRD!
IT FEELS LIKE I'VE KNOWN YOU FOR SO MUCH LONGER THAN THAT.
I GUESS THAT'S BECAUSE I LEARNED SO MUCH FROM YOU.
WE MADE THE MOST OF THAT TIME, DIDN'T WE?

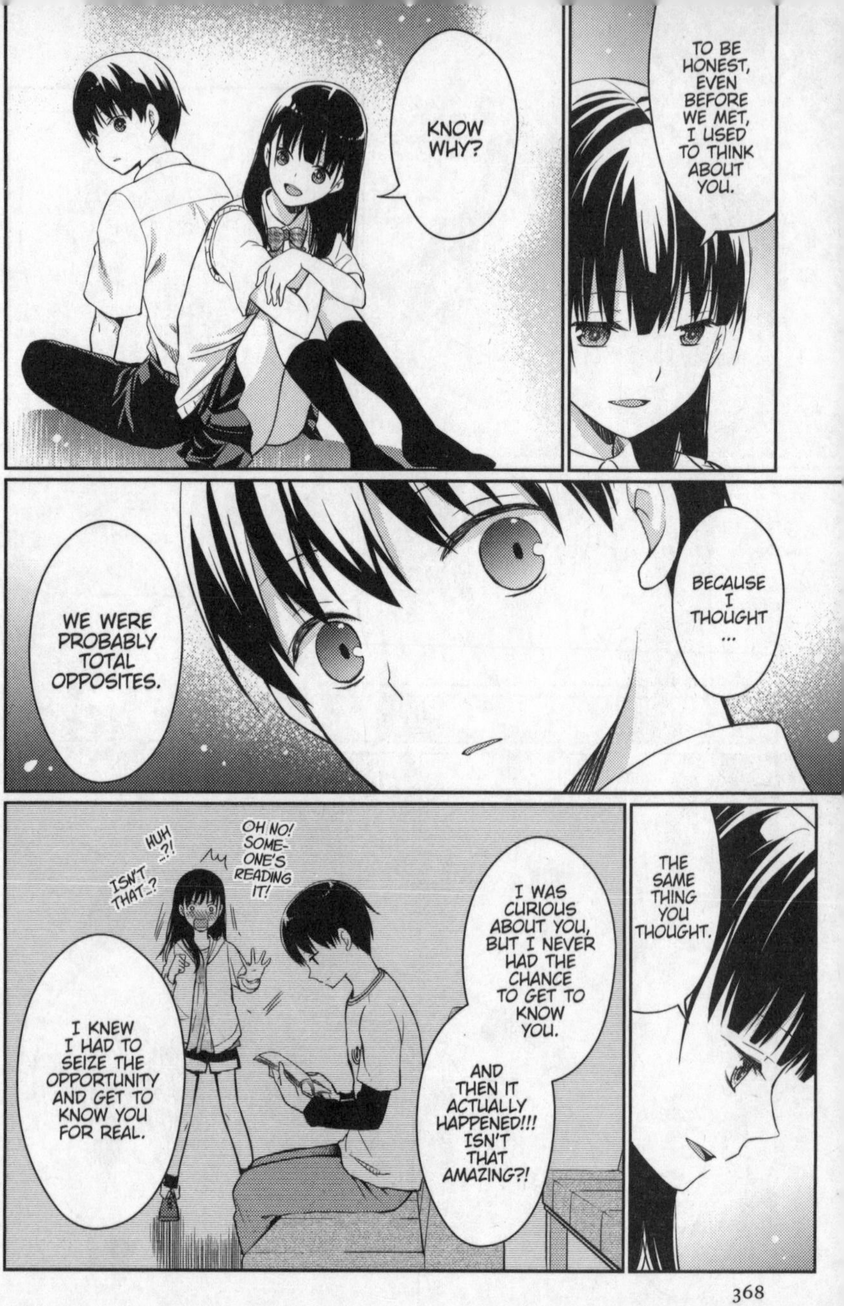
TO BE HONEST, EVEN BEFORE WE MET, I USED TO THINK ABOUT YOU.
KNOW WHY?
BECAUSE I THOUGHT ...
WE WERE PROBABLY TOTAL OPPOSITES.
THE SAME THING YOU THOUGHT.
I WAS CURIOUS ABOUT YOU, BUT I NEVER HAD THE CHANCE TO GET TO KNOW YOU.
AND THEN IT ACTUALLY HAPPENED!!! ISN'T THAT AMAZING?!
OH NO! SOME-ONE'S READING IT!
HUH ...?!
ISN'T THAT...?
I KNEW I HAD TO SEIZE THE OPPORTUNITY AND GET TO KNOW YOU FOR REAL.

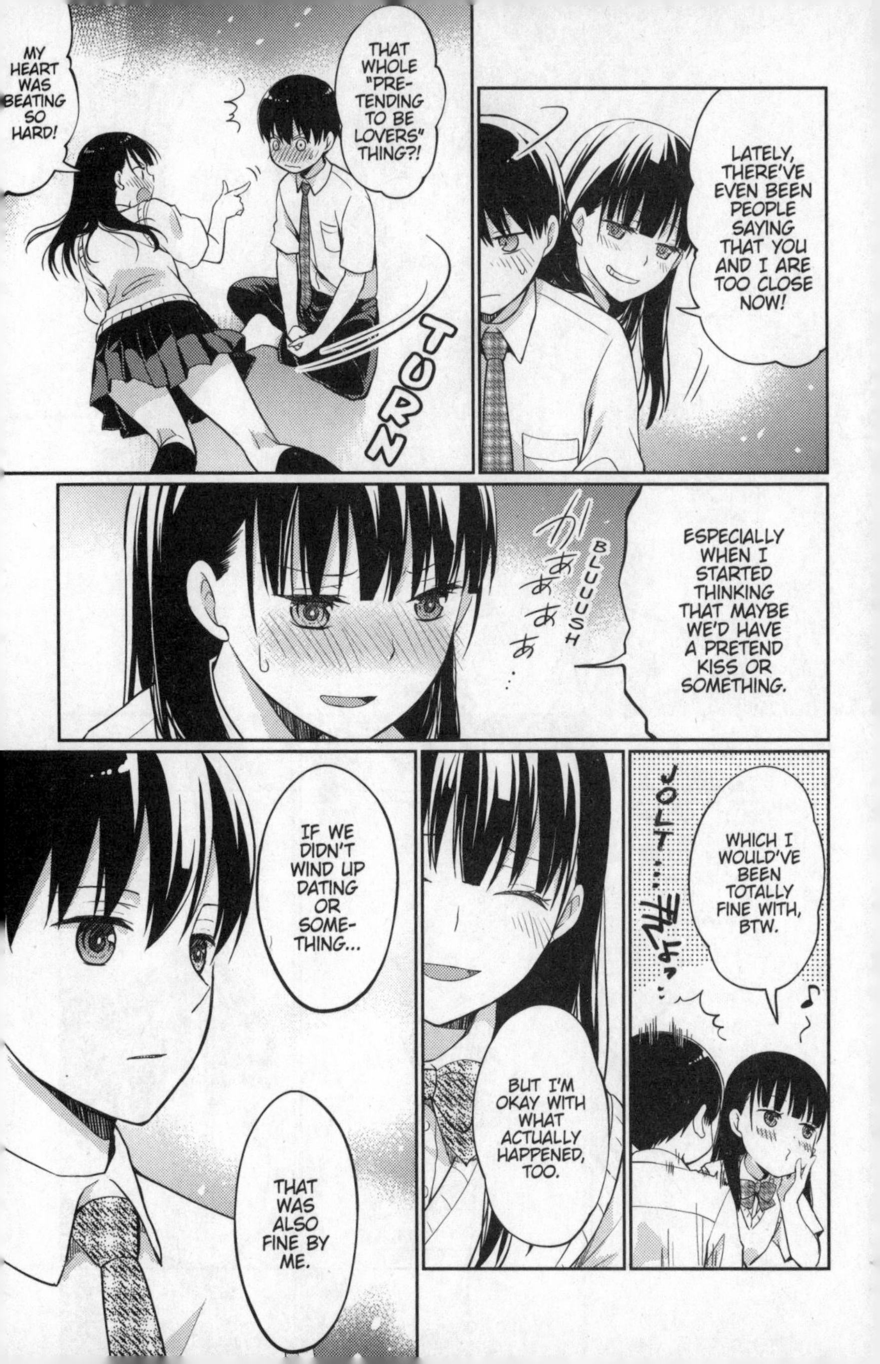

LATELY, THERE'VE EVEN BEEN PEOPLE SAYING THAT YOU AND I ARE TOO CLOSE NOW!
THAT WHOLE "PRE-TENDING TO BE LOVERS" THING?!
MY HEART WAS BEATING SO HARD!
TURN
ESPECIALLY WHEN I STARTED THINKING THAT MAYBE WE'D HAVE A PRETEND KISS OR SOMETHING.
BLUUUSH
WHICH I WOULD'VE BEEN TOTALLY FINE WITH, BTW.
JOLT...
BUT I'M OKAY WITH WHAT ACTUALLY HAPPENED, TOO.
IF WE DIDN'T WIND UP DATING OR SOME-THING...
THAT WAS ALSO FINE BY ME.

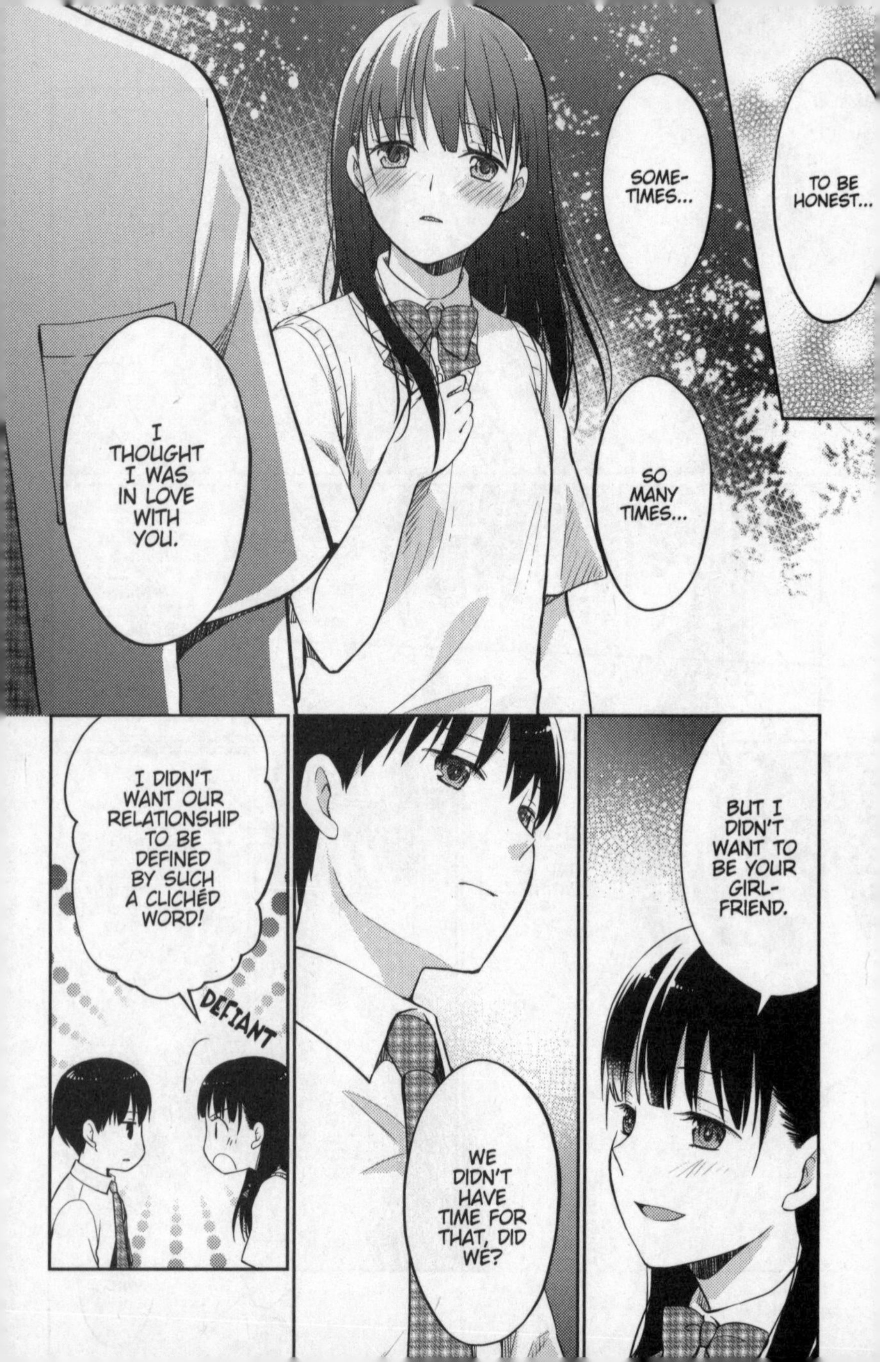
TO BE HONEST...
SOME-TIMES...
SO MANY TIMES...
I THOUGHT I WAS IN LOVE WITH YOU.
BUT I DIDN'T WANT TO BE YOUR GIRL-FRIEND.
WE DIDN'T HAVE TIME FOR THAT, DID WE?
I DIDN'T WANT OUR RELATIONSHIP TO BE DEFINED BY SUCH A CLICHÉD WORD!
DEFIANT

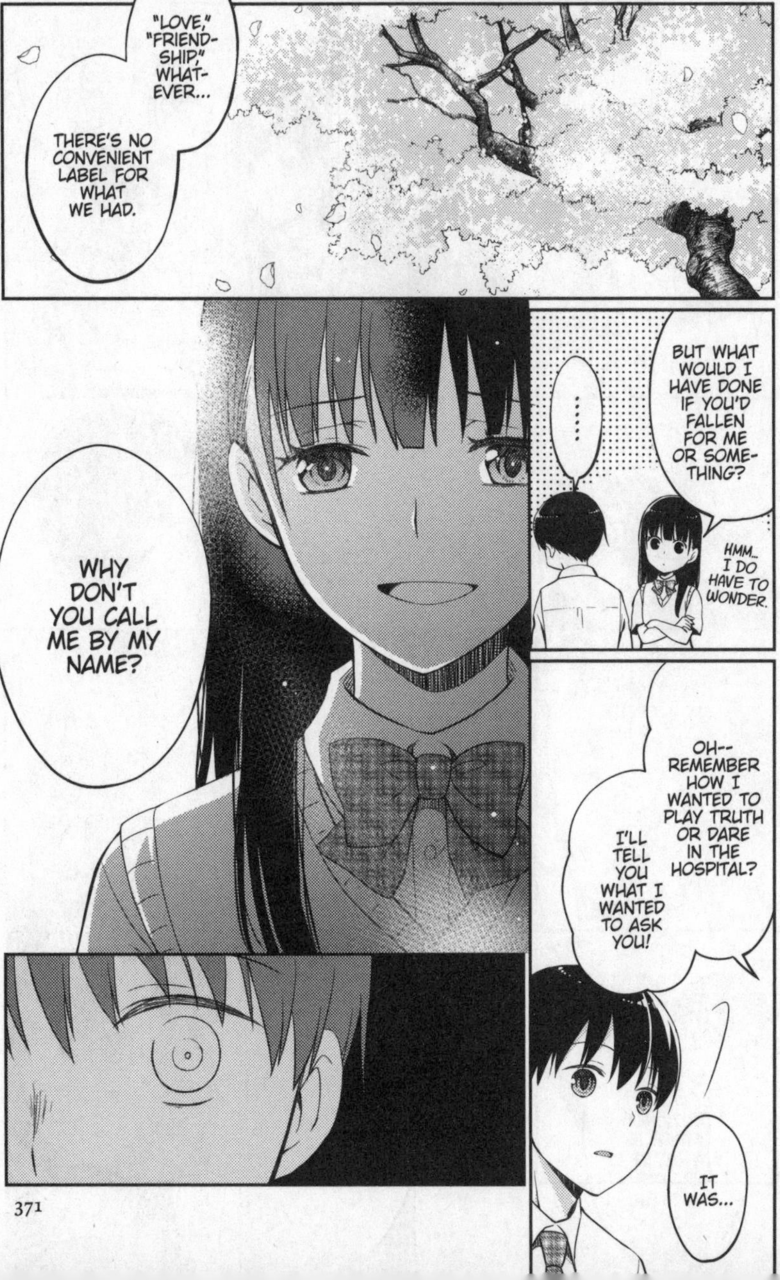
"LOVE," "FRIEND-SHIP," WHAT-EVER...
THERE'S NO CONVENIENT LABEL FOR WHAT WE HAD.
BUT WHAT WOULD I HAVE DONE IF YOU'D FALLEN FOR ME OR SOME-THING?
......
HMM... I DO HAVE TO WONDER.
OH-- REMEMBER HOW I WANTED TO PLAY TRUTH OR DARE IN THE HOSPITAL?
I'LL TELL YOU WHAT I WANTED TO ASK YOU!
IT WAS...
WHY DON'T YOU CALL ME BY MY NAME?

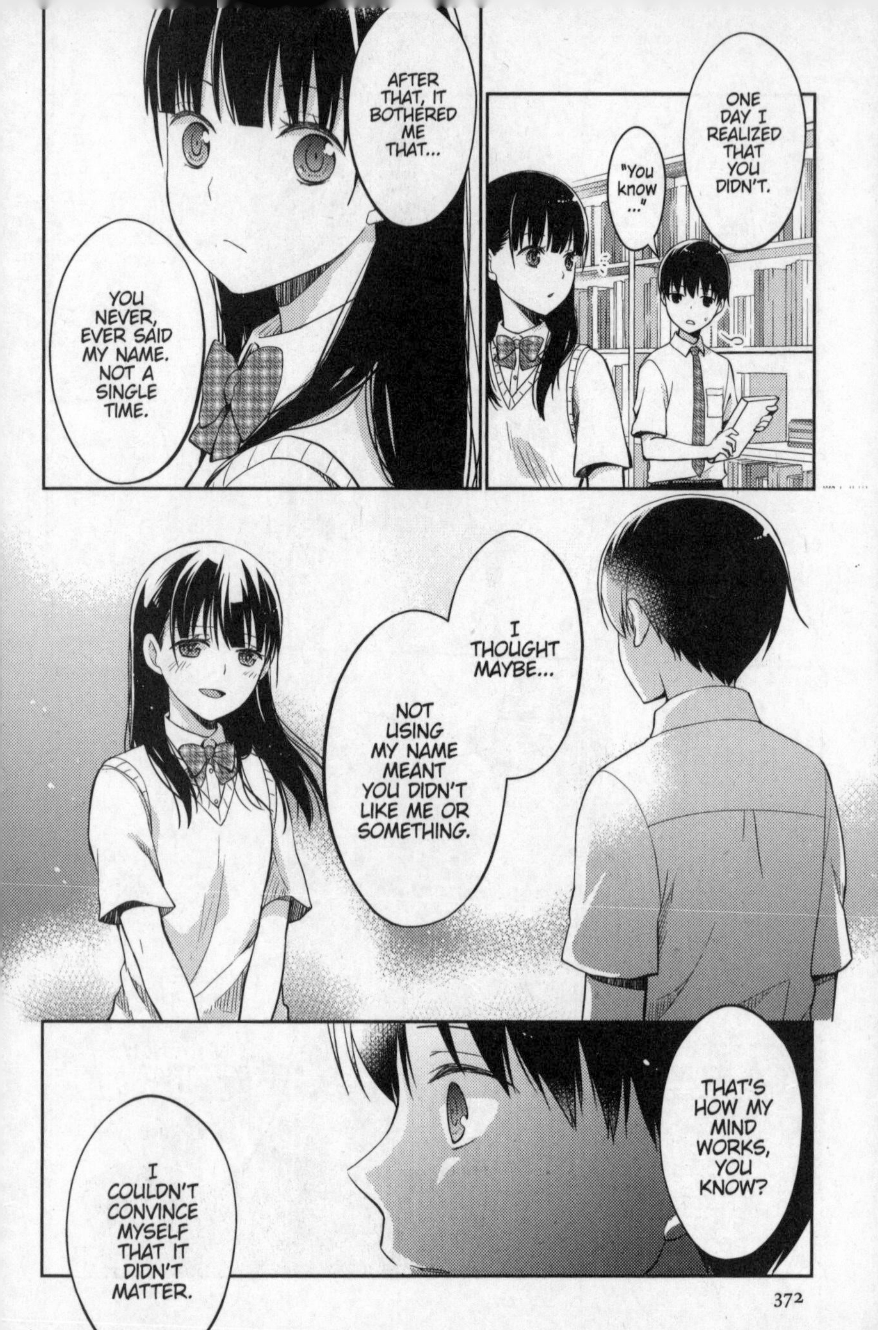
ONE DAY I REALIZED THAT YOU DIDN'T.
"You know..."
AFTER THAT, IT BOTHERED ME THAT...
YOU NEVER, EVER SAID MY NAME. NOT A SINGLE TIME.
I THOUGHT MAYBE...
NOT USING MY NAME MEANT YOU DIDN'T LIKE ME OR SOMETHING.
THAT'S HOW MY MIND WORKS, YOU KNOW?
I COULDN'T CONVINCE MYSELF THAT IT DIDN'T MATTER.

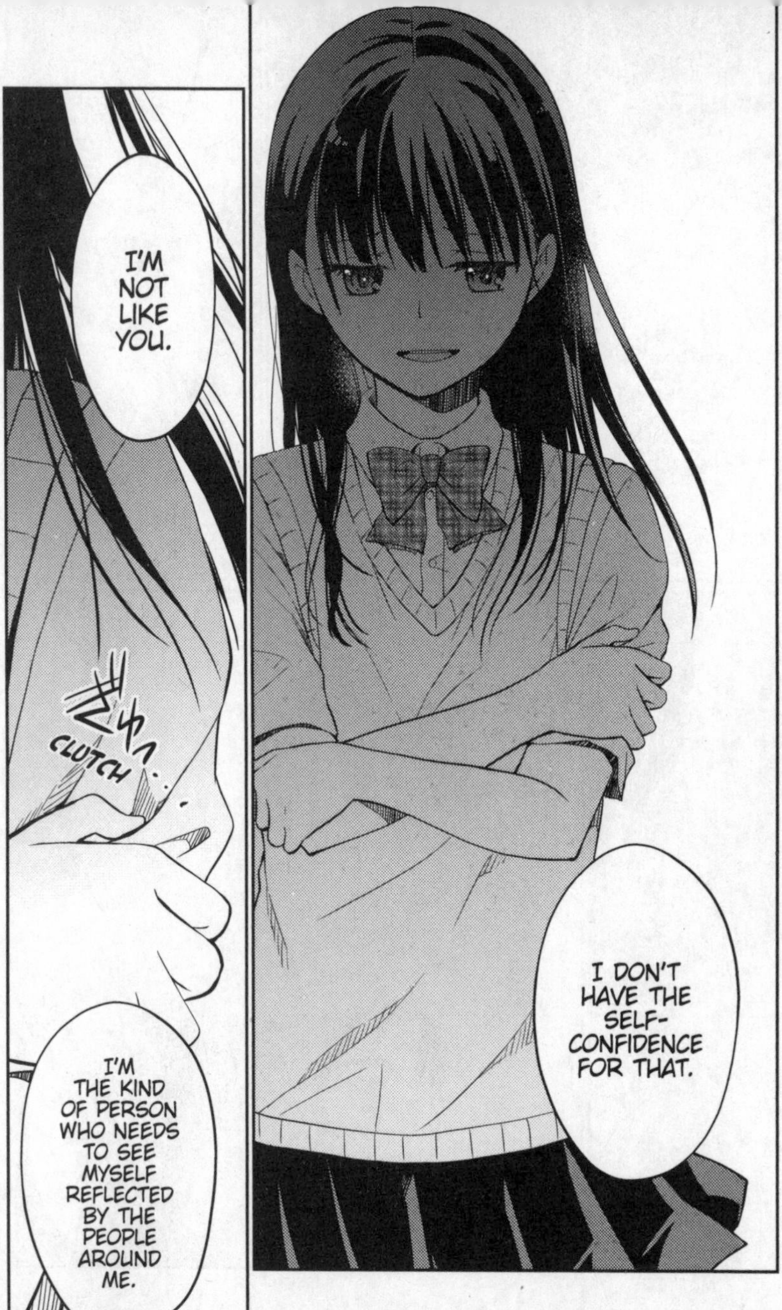
I DON'T HAVE THE SELF-CONFIDENCE FOR THAT.
I'M NOT LIKE YOU.
CLUTCH
I'M THE KIND OF PERSON WHO NEEDS TO SEE MYSELF REFLECTED BY THE PEOPLE AROUND ME.

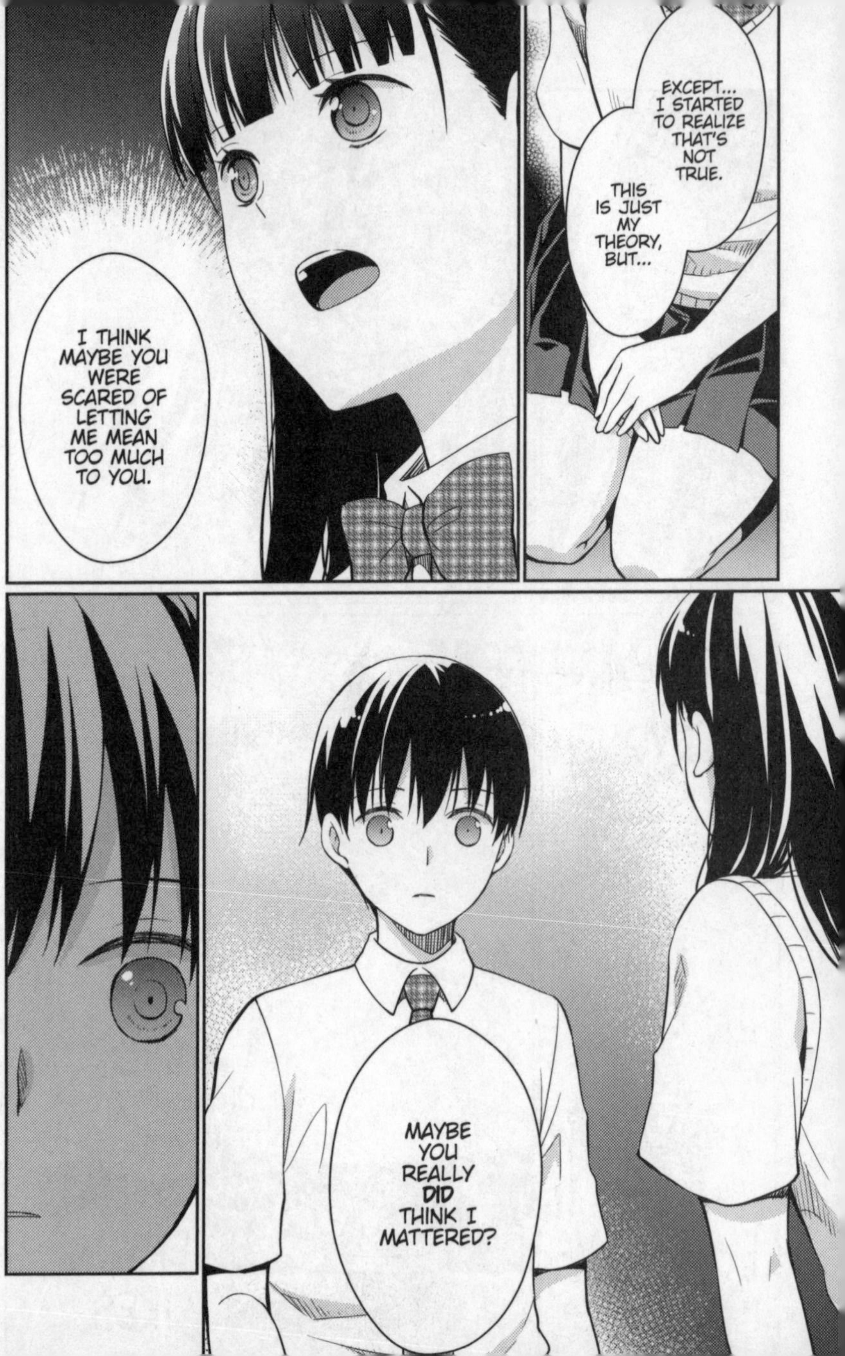
EXCEPT... I STARTED TO REALIZE THAT'S NOT TRUE.
THIS IS JUST MY THEORY, BUT...
I THINK MAYBE YOU WERE SCARED OF LETTING ME MEAN TOO MUCH TO YOU.
MAYBE YOU REALLY **DID** THINK I MATTERED?

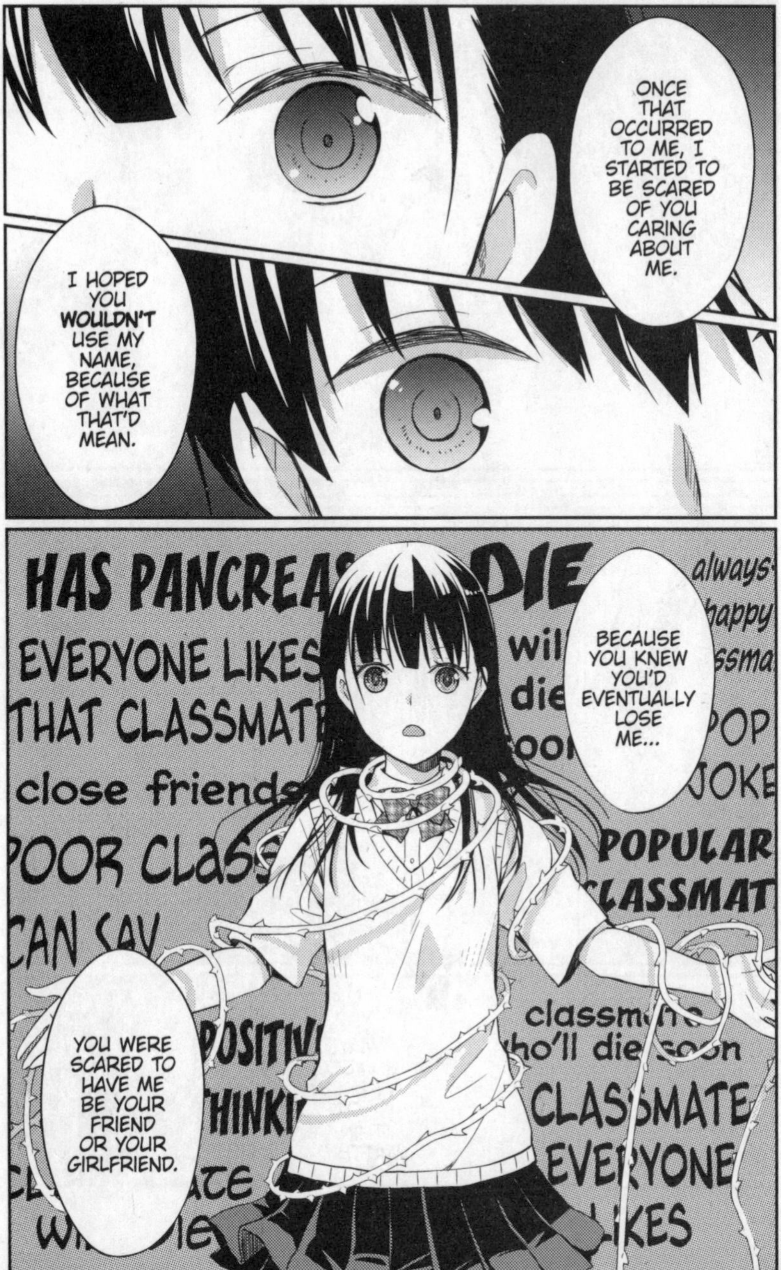
ONCE THAT OCCURRED TO ME, I STARTED TO BE SCARED OF YOU CARING ABOUT ME.
I HOPED YOU **WOULDN'T** USE MY NAME, BECAUSE OF WHAT THAT'D MEAN.
DIE
always-happy
HAS PANCREAS
EVERYONE LIKES
THAT CLASSMATE
BECAUSE YOU KNEW YOU'D EVENTUALLY LOSE ME...
POPULAR
close friends
YOU WERE SCARED TO HAVE ME BE YOUR FRIEND OR YOUR GIRLFRIEND.
CLASSMATE
EVERYONE
LIKES

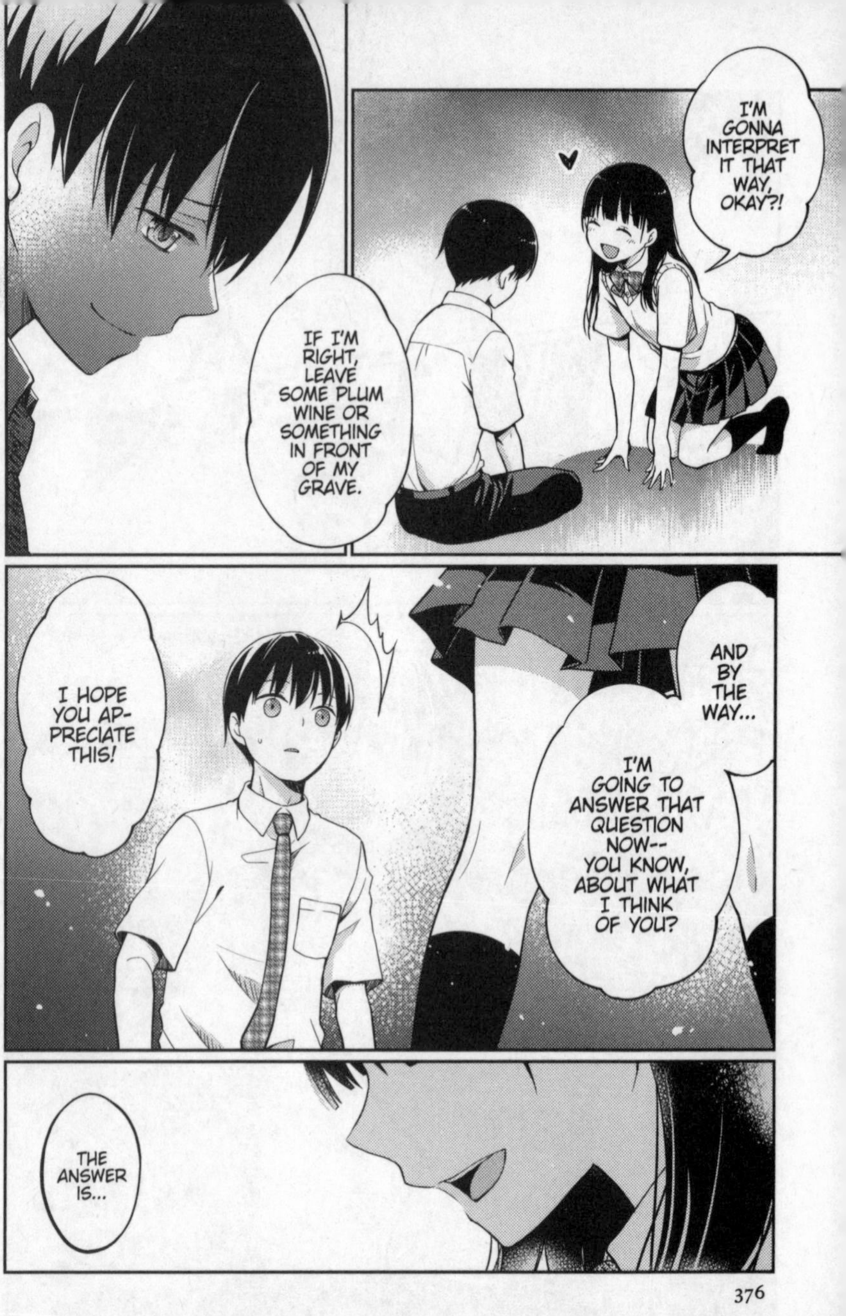
I'M GONNA INTERPRET IT THAT WAY, OKAY?!
IF I'M RIGHT, LEAVE SOME PLUM WINE OR SOMETHING IN FRONT OF MY GRAVE.
AND BY THE WAY...
I'M GOING TO ANSWER THAT QUESTION NOW-- YOU KNOW, ABOUT WHAT I THINK OF YOU?
I HOPE YOU AP-PRECIATE THIS!
THE ANSWER IS...

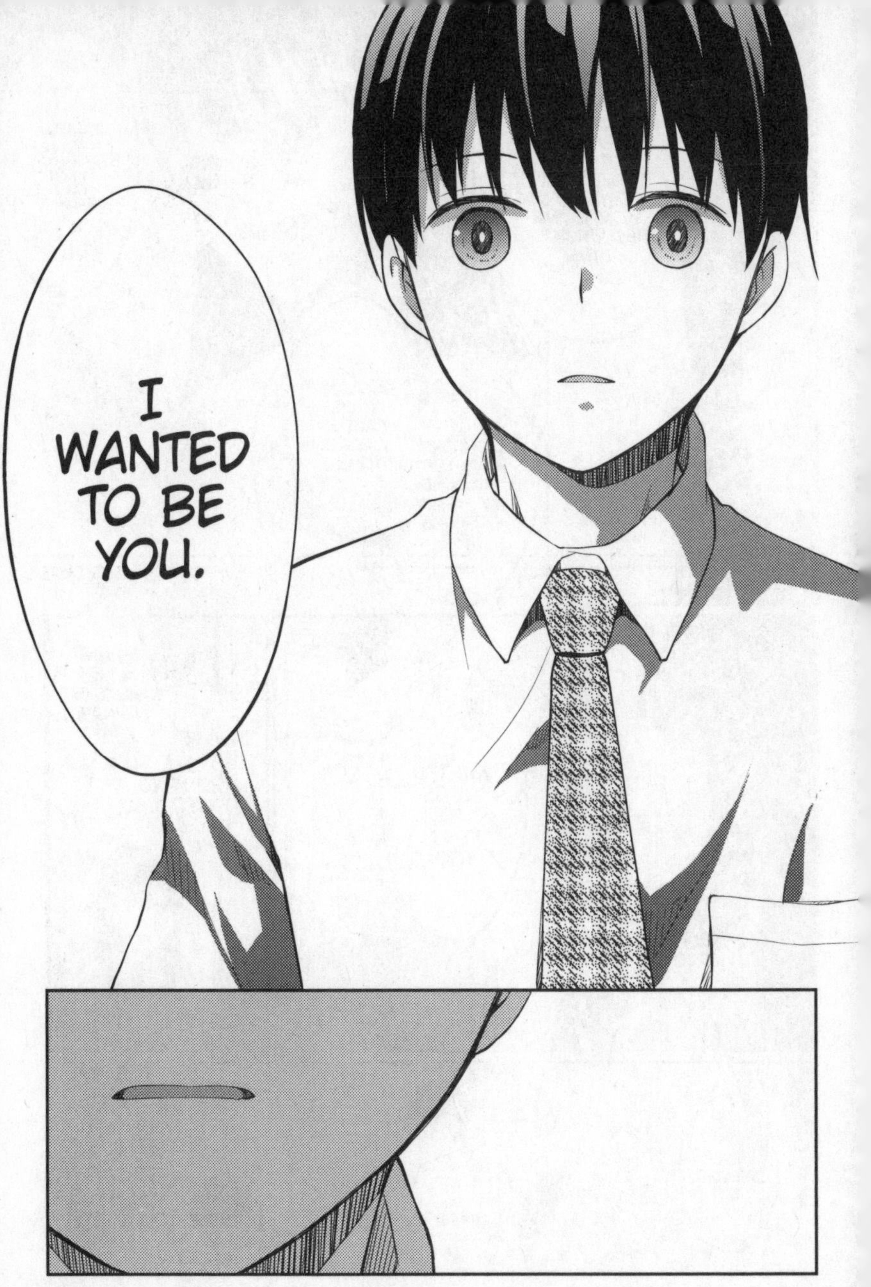
I WANTED TO BE YOU.

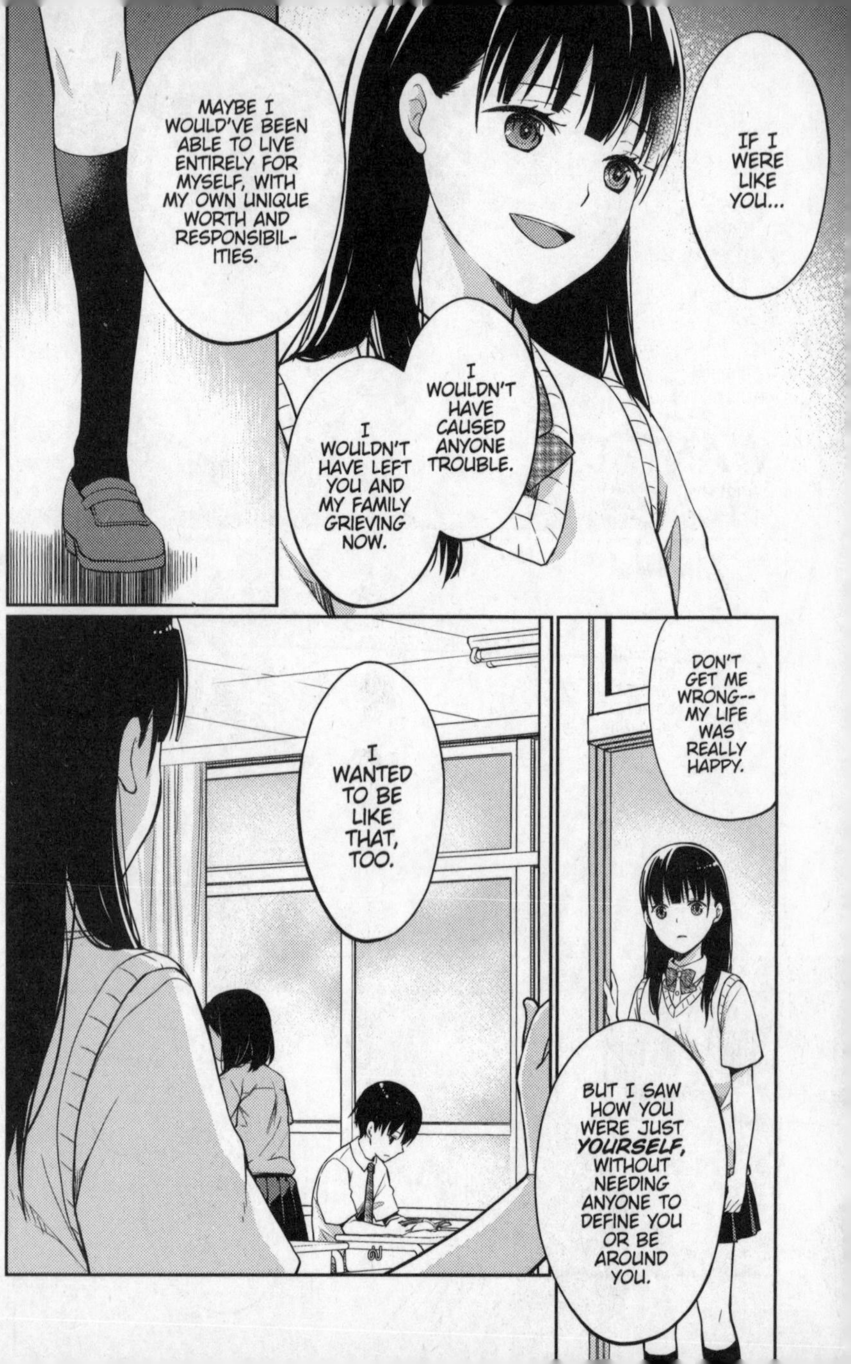
IF I WERE LIKE YOU...
MAYBE I WOULD'VE BEEN ABLE TO LIVE ENTIRELY FOR MYSELF, WITH MY OWN UNIQUE WORTH AND RESPONSIBIL-ITIES.
I WOULDN'T HAVE CAUSED ANYONE TROUBLE.
I WOULDN'T HAVE LEFT YOU AND MY FAMILY GRIEVING NOW.
DON'T GET ME WRONG-- MY LIFE WAS REALLY HAPPY.
BUT I SAW HOW YOU WERE JUST YOURSELF, WITHOUT NEEDING ANYONE TO DEFINE YOU OR BE AROUND YOU.
I WANTED TO BE LIKE THAT, TOO.

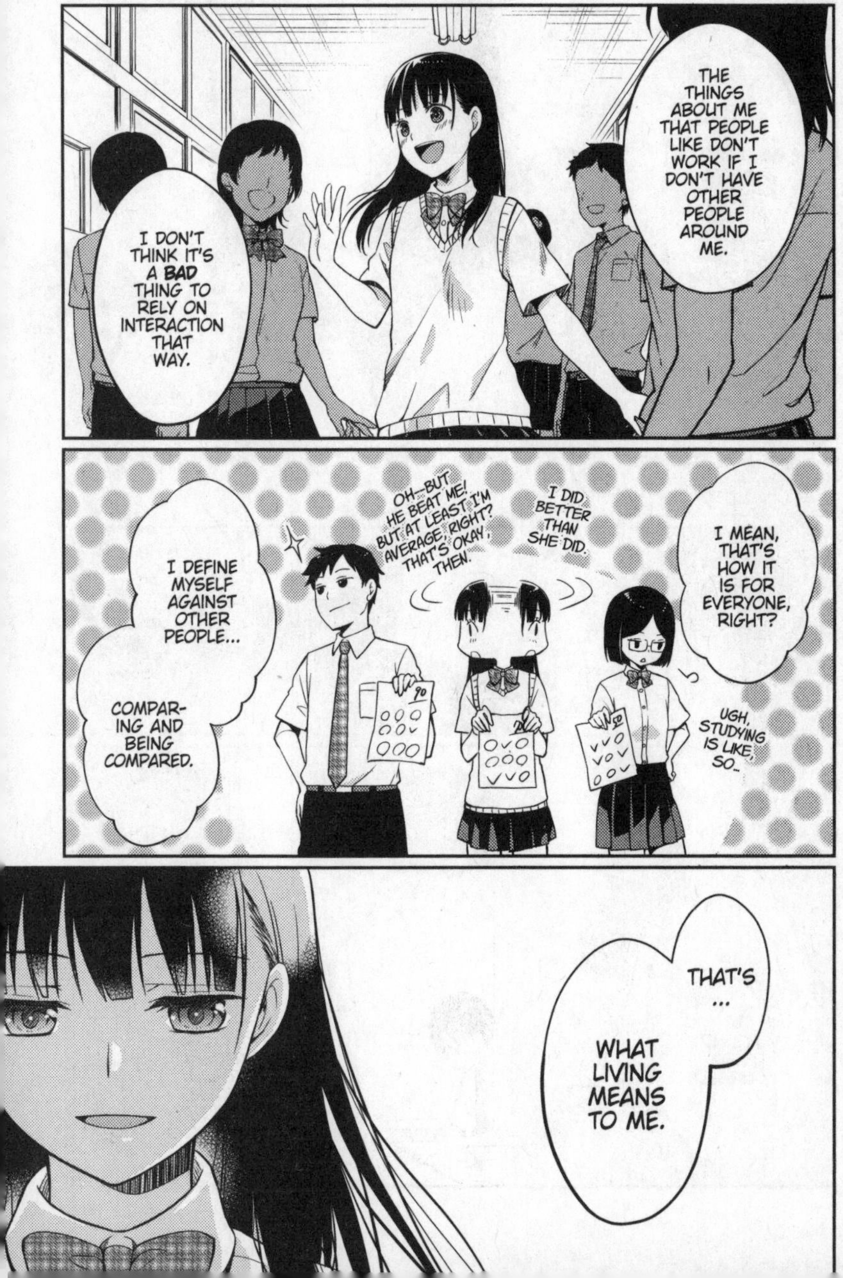
THE THINGS ABOUT ME THAT PEOPLE LIKE DON'T WORK IF I DON'T HAVE OTHER PEOPLE AROUND ME.
I DON'T THINK IT'S A **BAD** THING TO RELY ON INTERACTION THAT WAY.
I MEAN, THAT'S HOW IT IS FOR EVERYONE, RIGHT?
UGH, STUDYING IS LIKE, SO...
I DID BETTER THAN SHE DID.
OH--BUT HE BEAT ME! BUT AT LEAST I'M AVERAGE, RIGHT? THAT'S OKAY, THEN.
90
I DEFINE MYSELF AGAINST OTHER PEOPLE...
COMPARING AND BEING COMPARED.
THAT'S ...
WHAT LIVING MEANS TO ME.

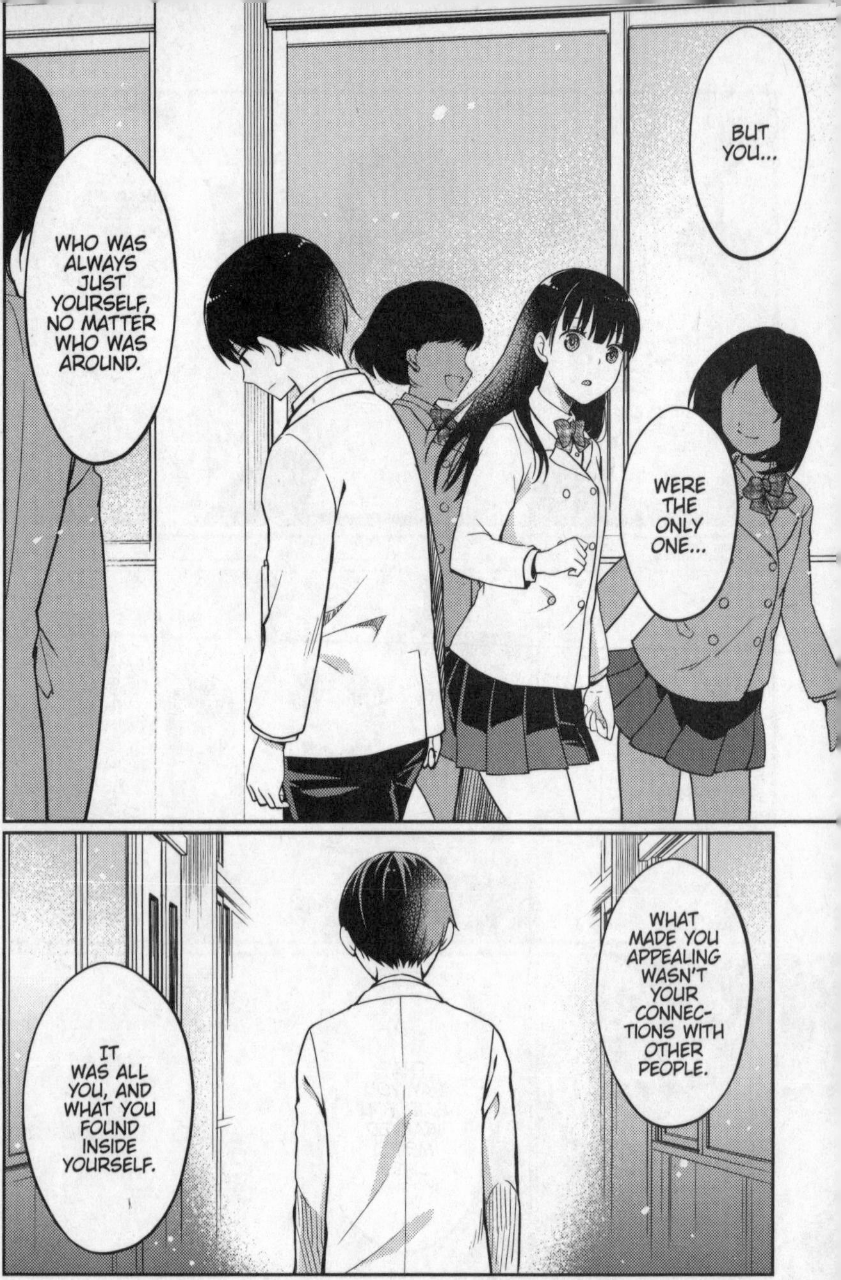
BUT YOU...
WERE THE ONLY ONE...
WHO WAS ALWAYS JUST YOURSELF, NO MATTER WHO WAS AROUND.
WHAT MADE YOU APPEALING WASN'T YOUR CONNEC-TIONS WITH OTHER PEOPLE.
IT WAS ALL YOU, AND WHAT YOU FOUND INSIDE YOURSELF.

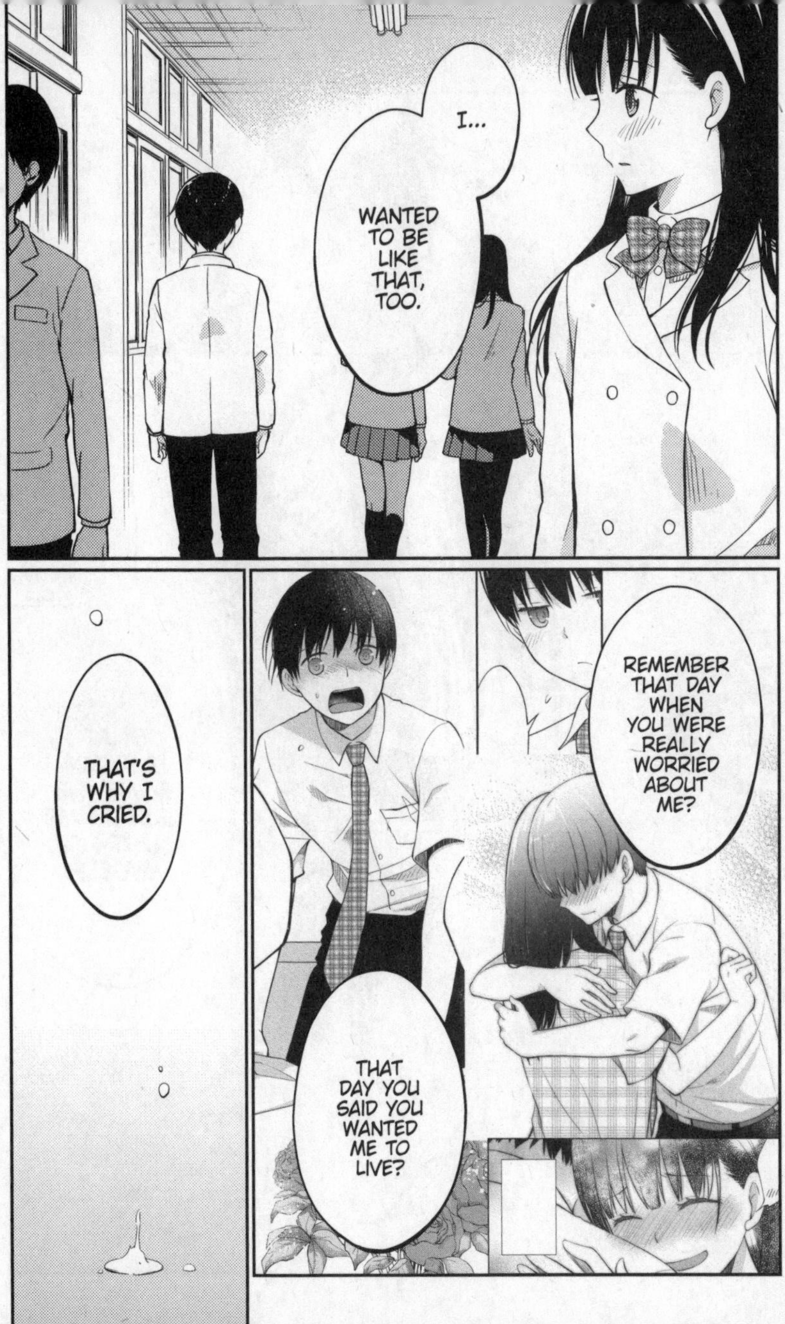
I...
WANTED TO BE LIKE THAT, TOO.
REMEMBER THAT DAY WHEN YOU WERE REALLY WORRIED ABOUT ME?
THAT DAY YOU SAID YOU WANTED ME TO LIVE?
THAT'S WHY I CRIED.

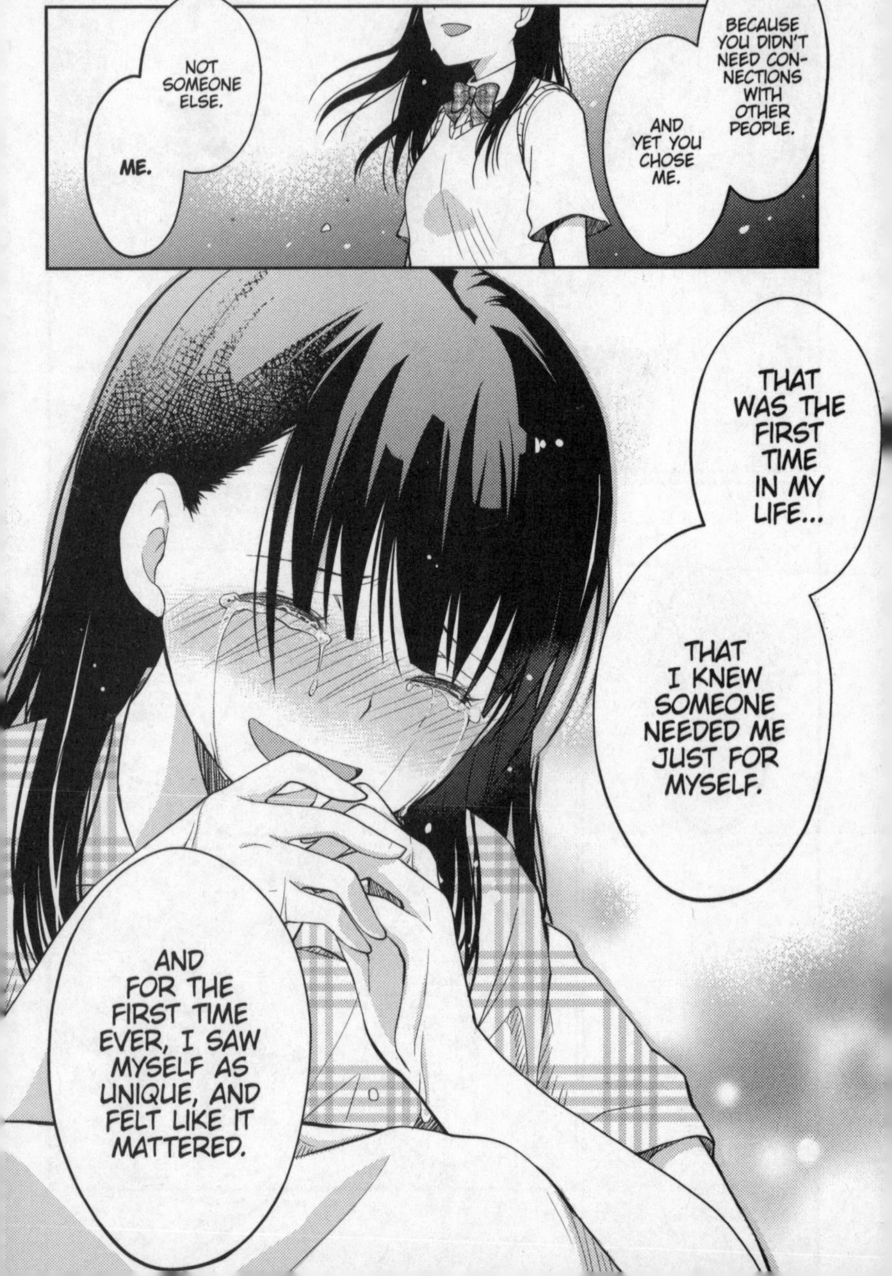
BECAUSE YOU DIDN'T NEED CON-NECTIONS WITH OTHER PEOPLE.
AND YET YOU CHOSE ME.
NOT SOMEONE ELSE.
ME.
THAT WAS THE FIRST TIME IN MY LIFE...
THAT I KNEW SOMEONE NEEDED ME JUST FOR MYSELF.
AND FOR THE FIRST TIME EVER, I SAW MYSELF AS UNIQUE, AND FELT LIKE IT MATTERED.

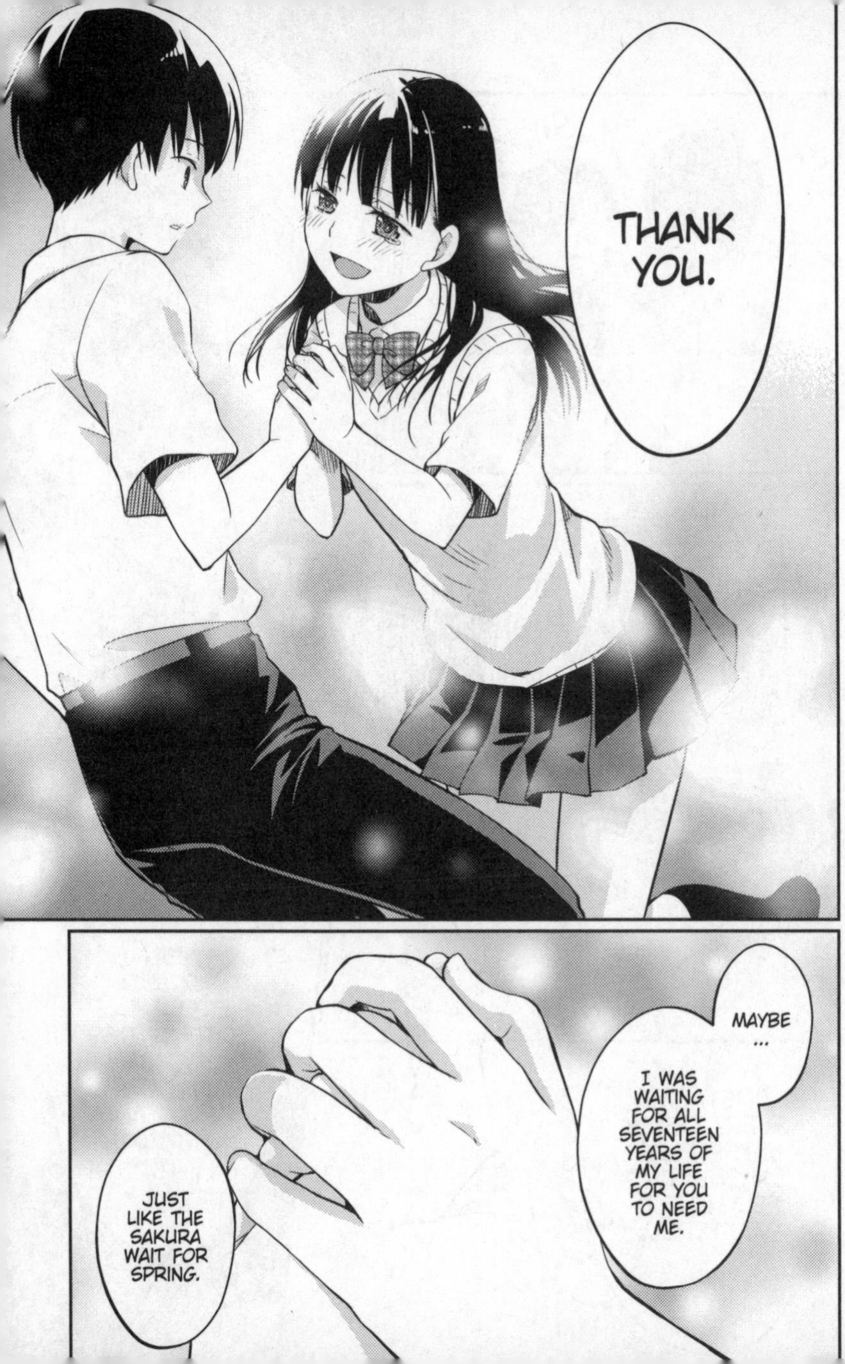
THANK YOU.
MAYBE...
I WAS WAITING FOR ALL SEVENTEEN YEARS OF MY LIFE FOR YOU TO NEED ME.
JUST LIKE THE SAKURA WAIT FOR SPRING.

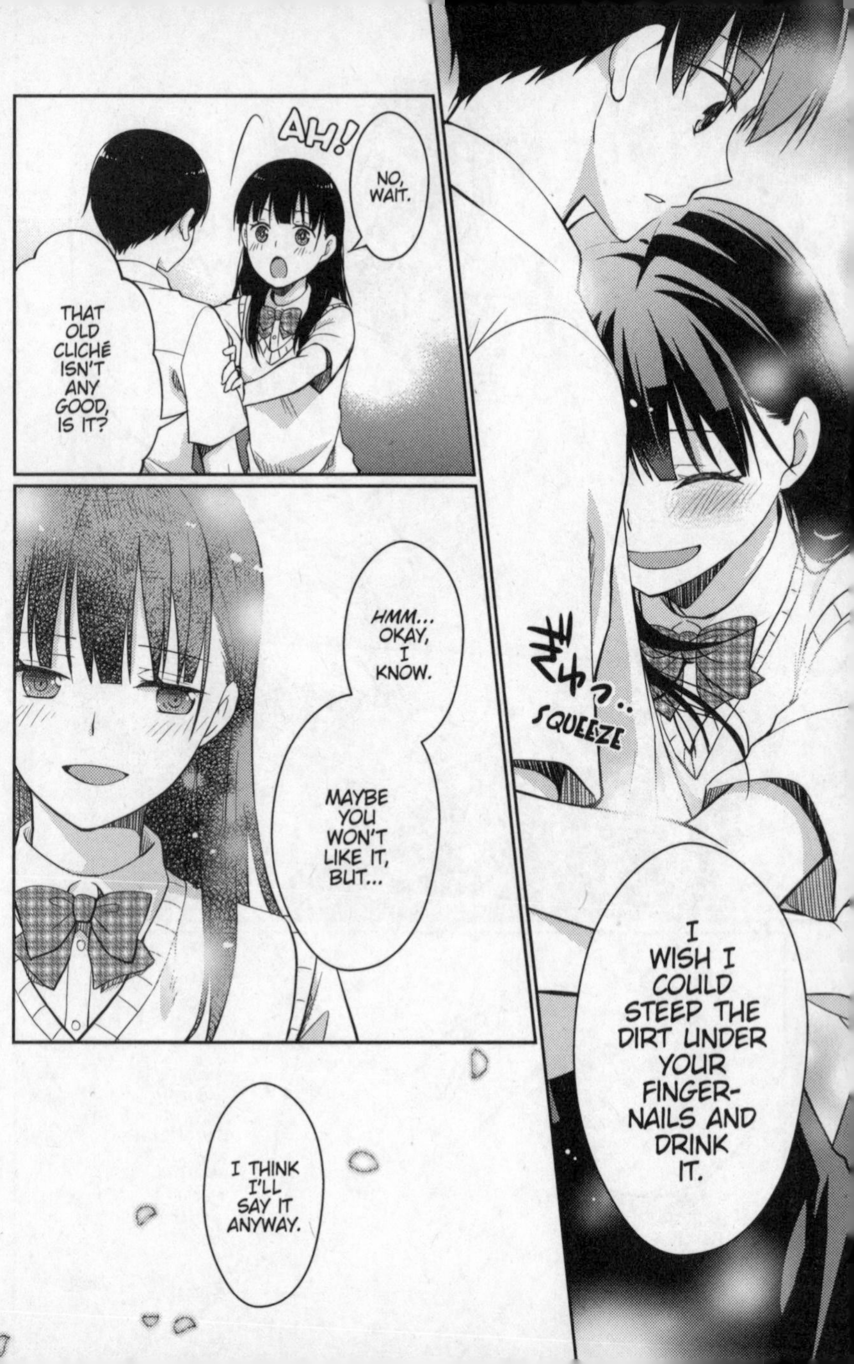
AH!
NO, WAIT.
THAT OLD CLICHÉ ISN'T ANY GOOD, IS IT?
HMM... OKAY, I KNOW.
MAYBE YOU WON'T LIKE IT, BUT...
I THINK I'LL SAY IT ANYWAY.
ぎゅっ.. SQUEEZE
I WISH I COULD STEEP THE DIRT UNDER YOUR FINGER-NAILS AND DRINK IT.

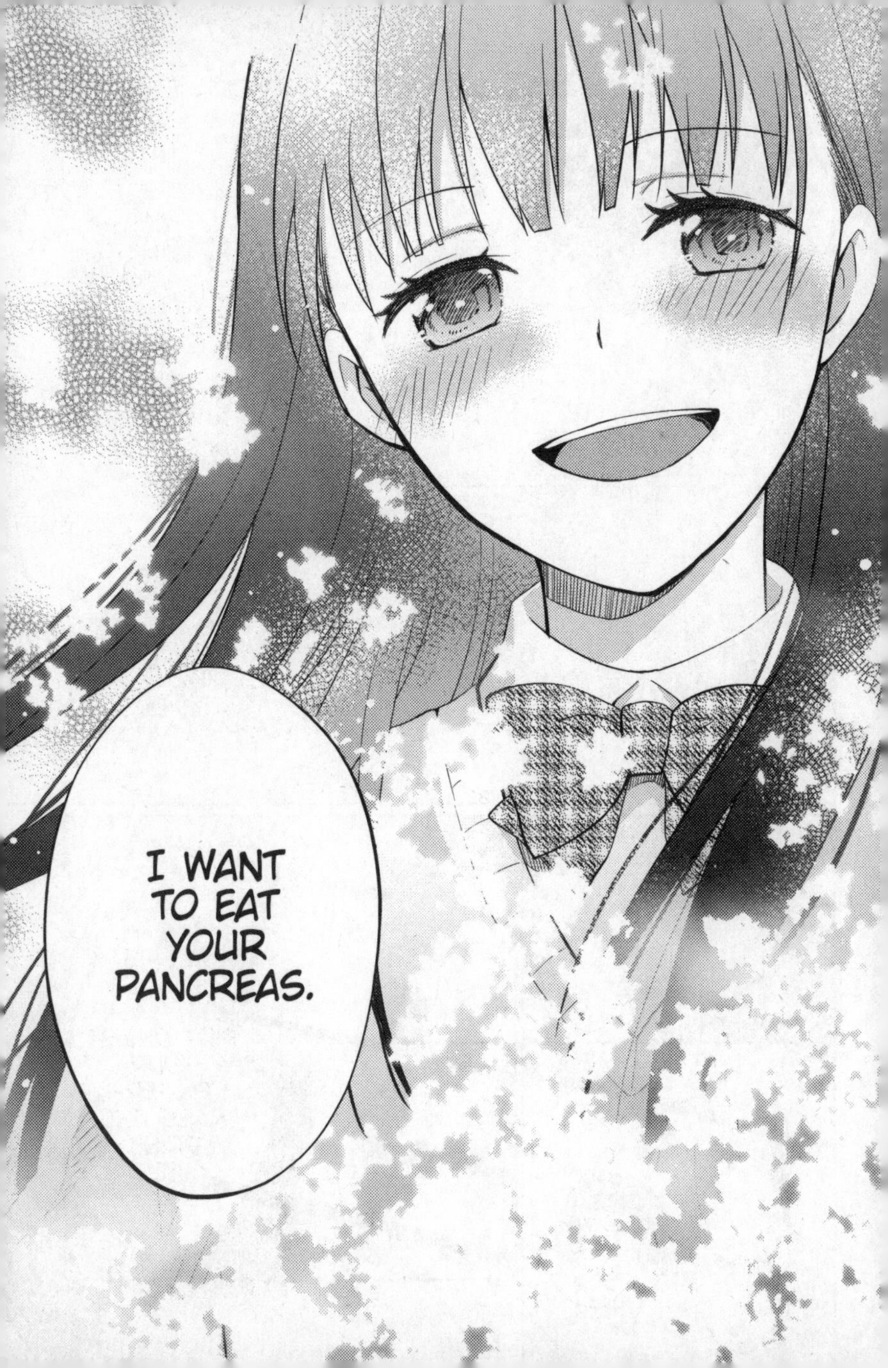
I WANT TO EAT YOUR PANCREAS.

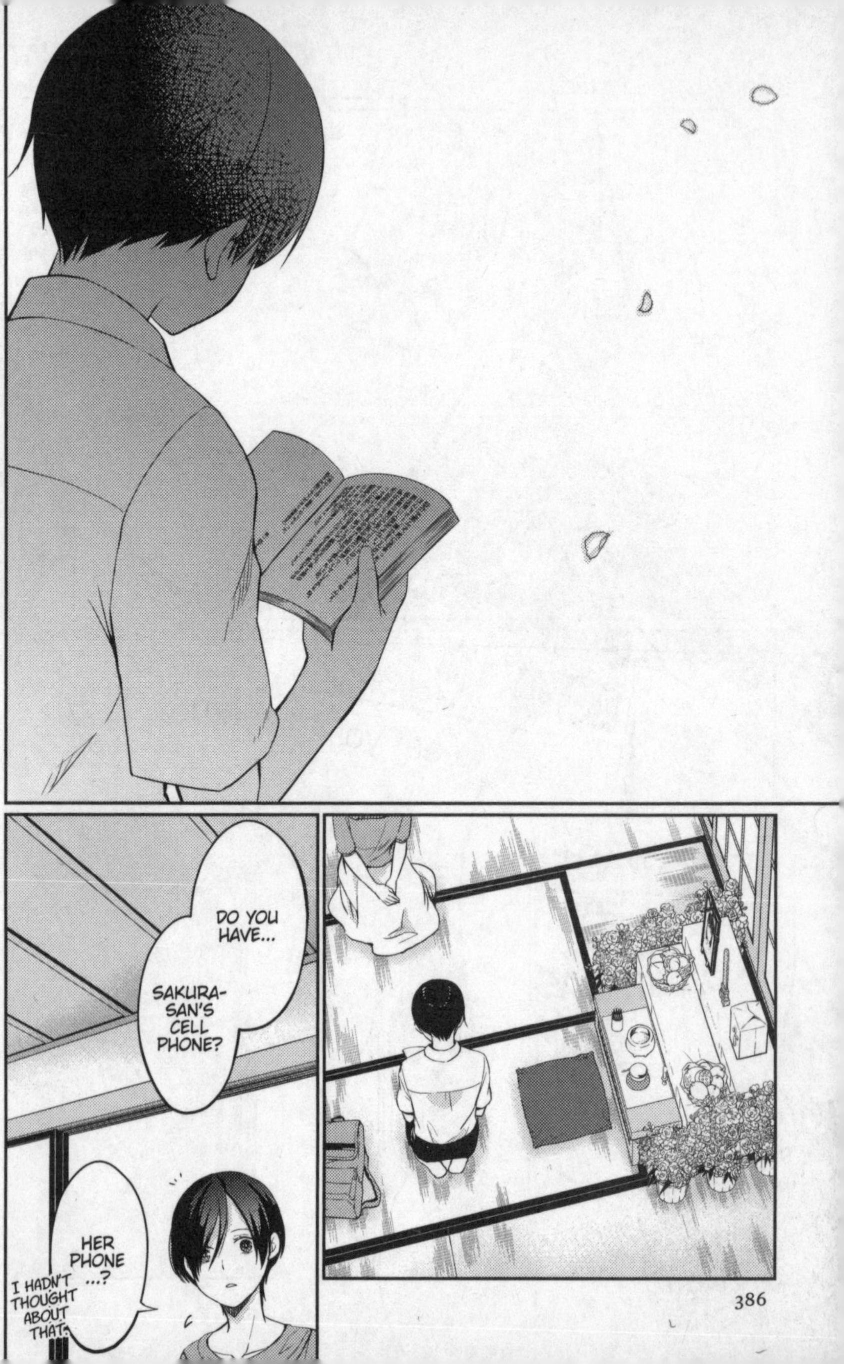
DO YOU HAVE...
SAKURA-SAN'S CELL PHONE?
HER PHONE ...?
I HADN'T THOUGHT ABOUT THAT.

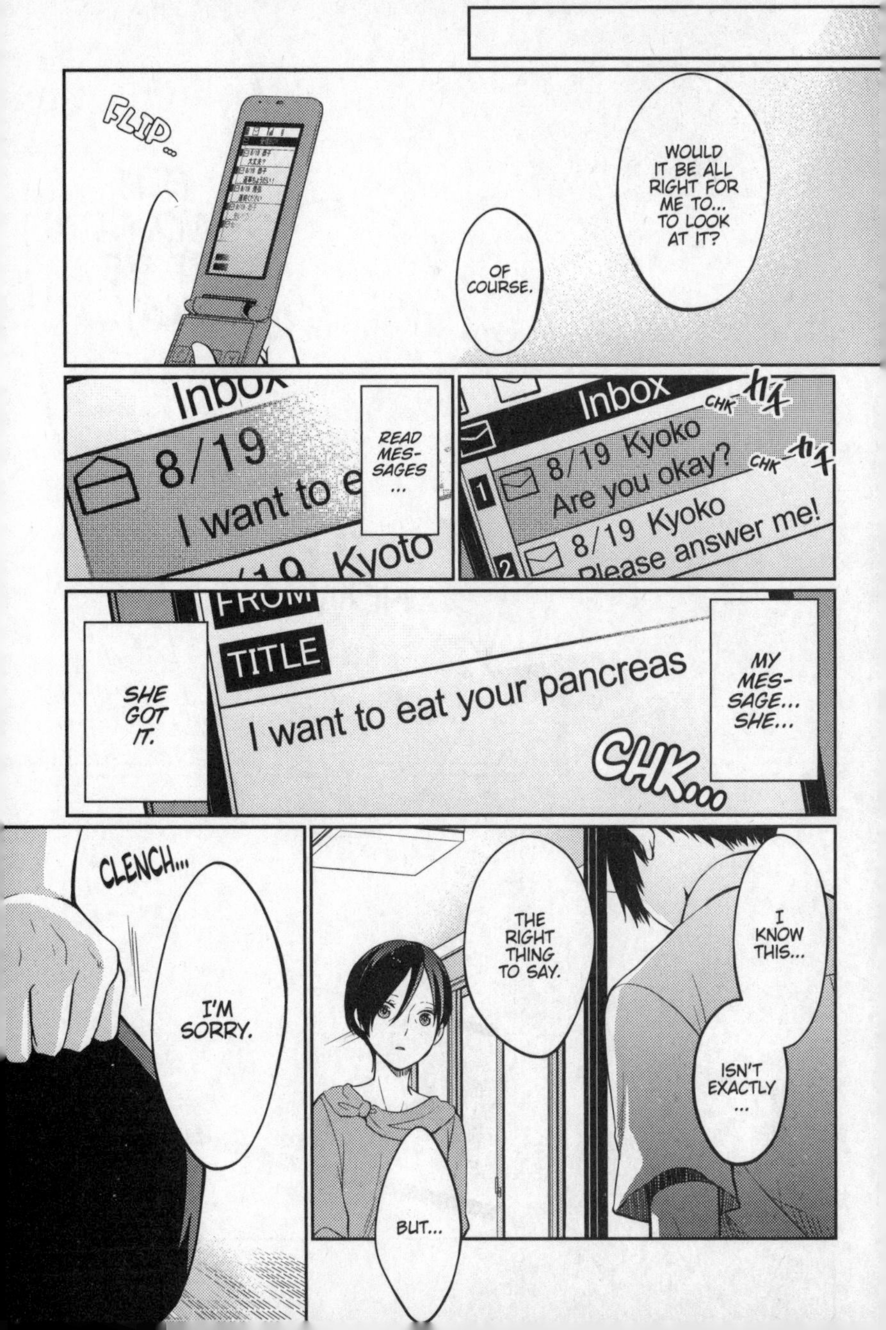
WOULD IT BE ALL RIGHT FOR ME TO... TO LOOK AT IT?
OF COURSE.
FLIP...
Inbox
CHK
8/19 Kyoko
Are you okay?
CHK
8/19 Kyoko
Please answer me!
READ MES-SAGES ...
Inbox
8/19
I want to e
Kyoto
MY MES-SAGE... SHE...
FROM
TITLE
I want to eat your pancreas
CHK...
SHE GOT IT.
I KNOW THIS...
ISN'T EXACTLY ...
THE RIGHT THING TO SAY.
BUT...
CLENCH...
I'M SORRY.

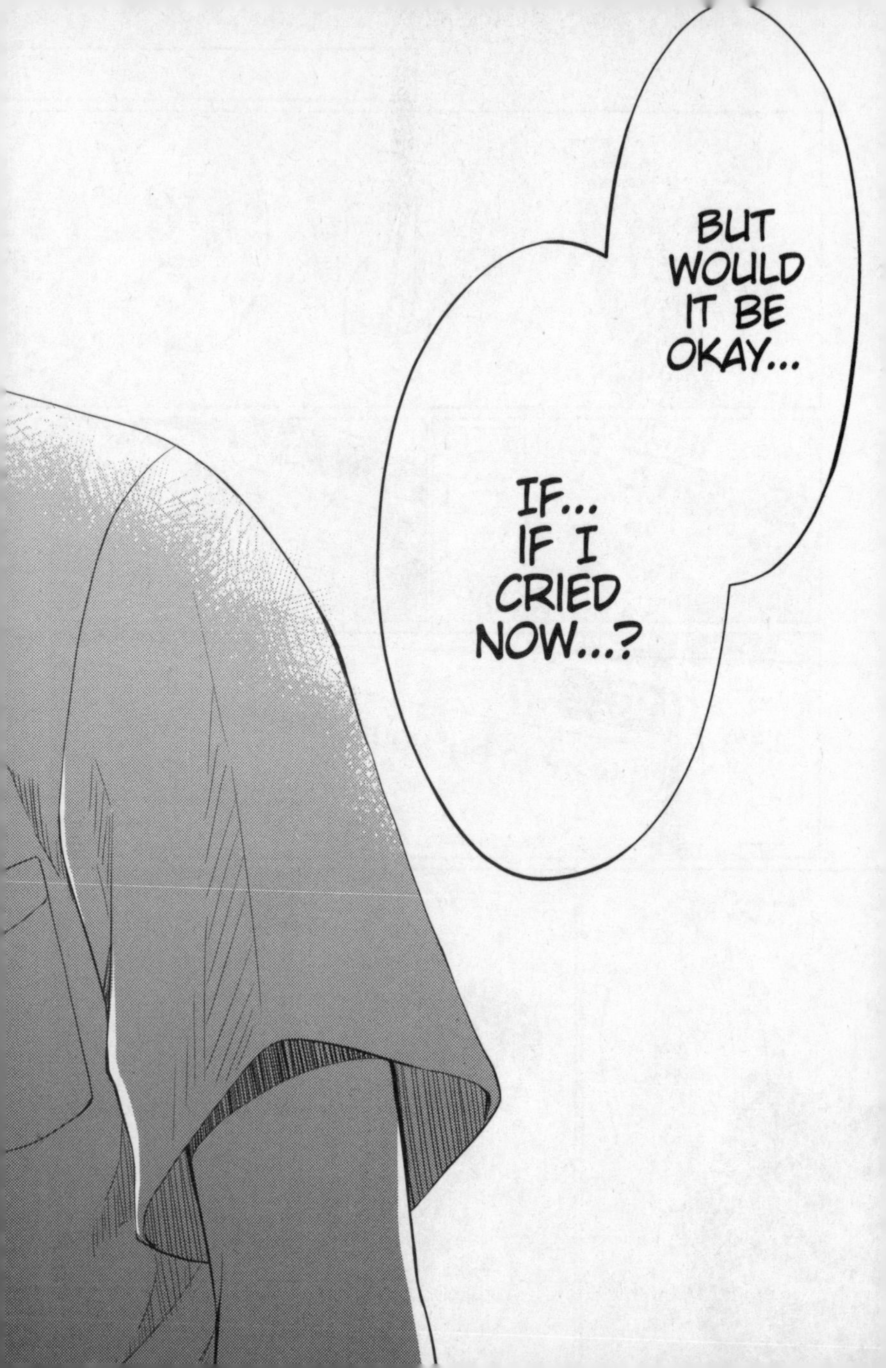
BUT WOULD IT BE OKAY...
IF... IF I CRIED NOW...?

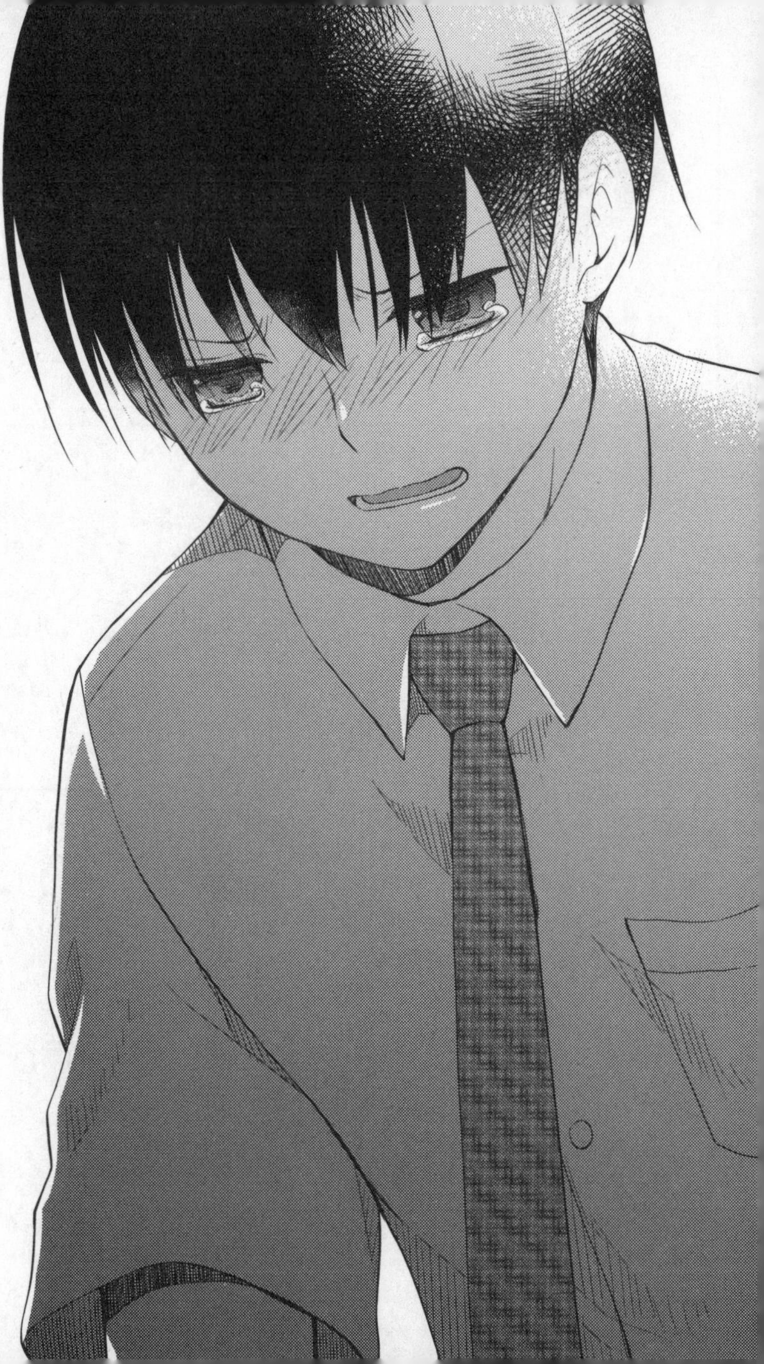

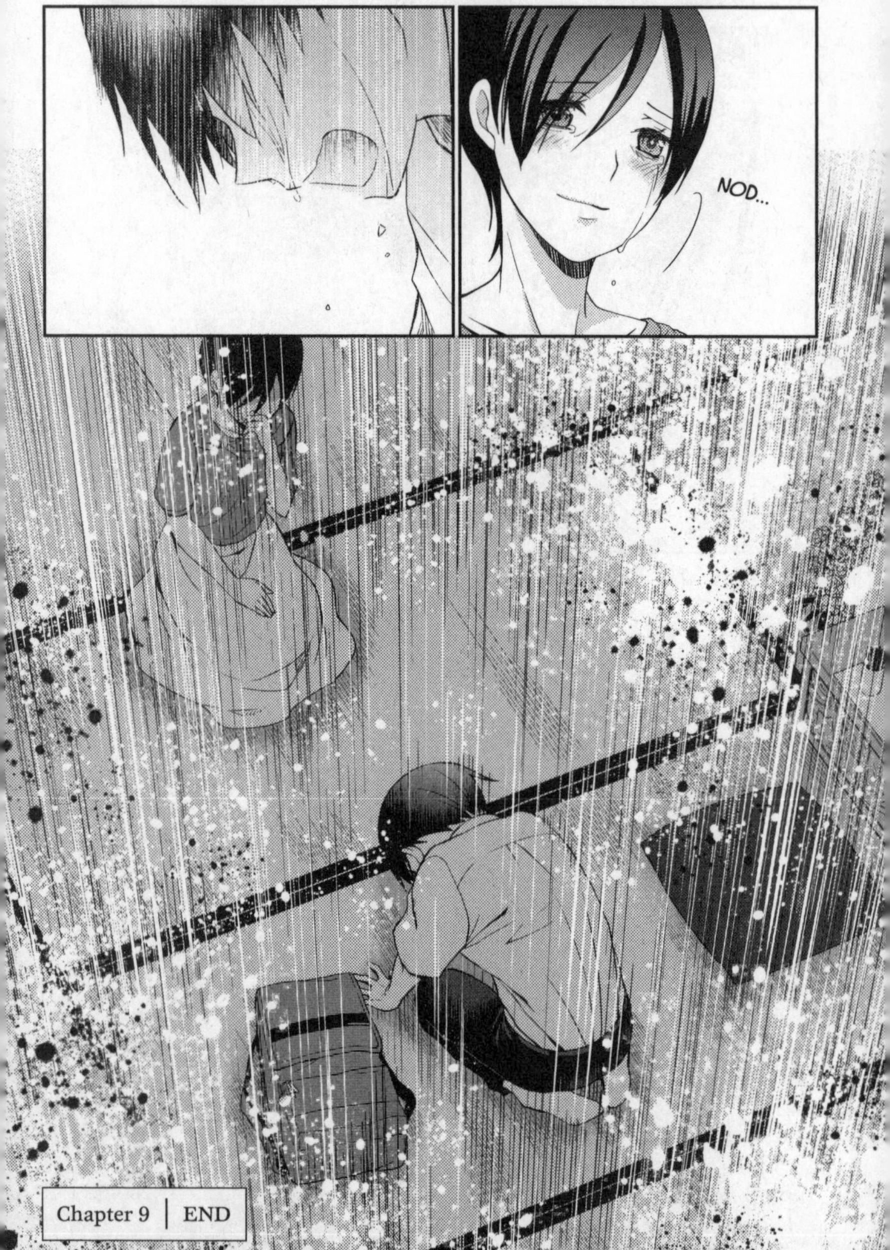
NOD...
Chapter 9 | END

Final Chapter | Walking Down This Road for the First Time

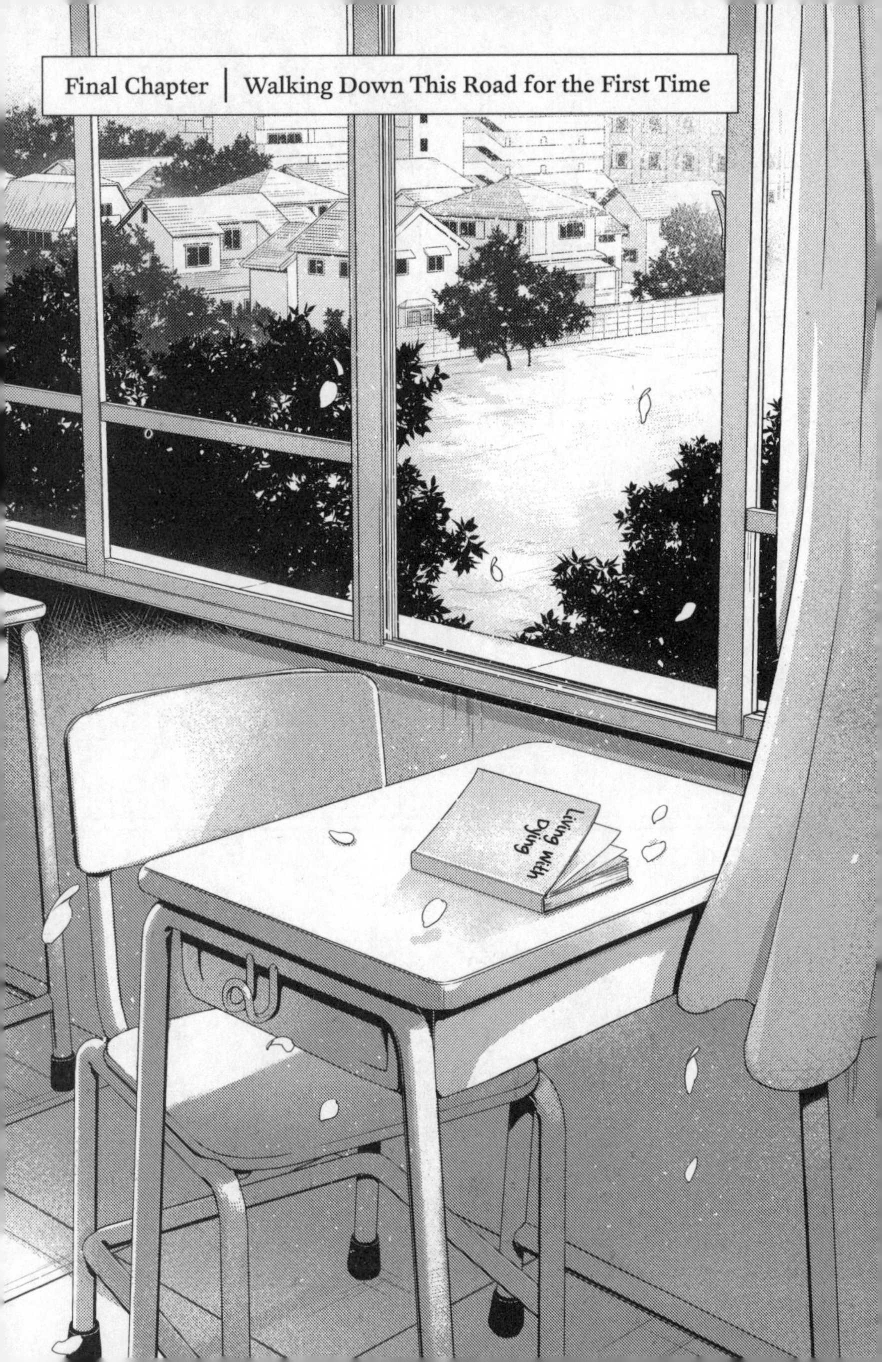
Living with Dying

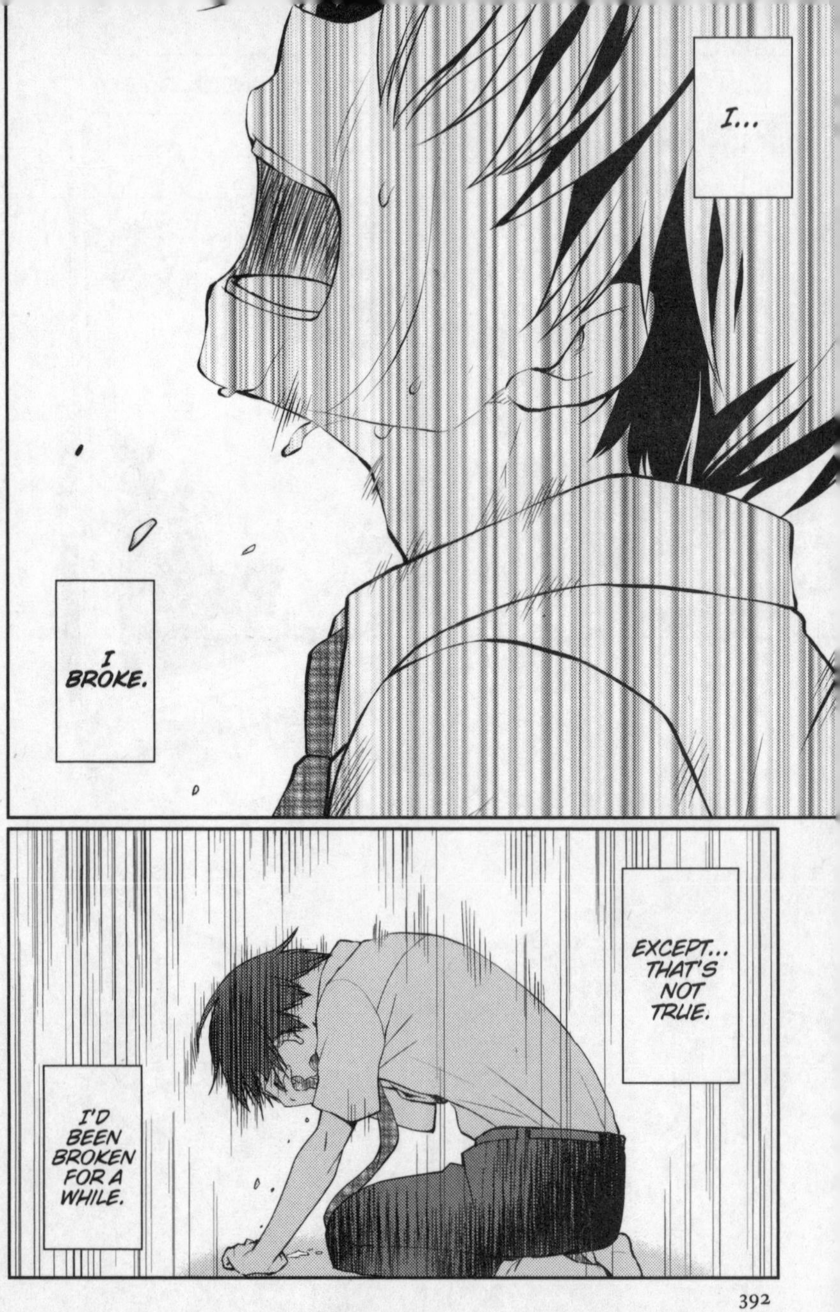
I...
I BROKE.
EXCEPT... THAT'S NOT TRUE.
I'D BEEN BROKEN FOR A WHILE.

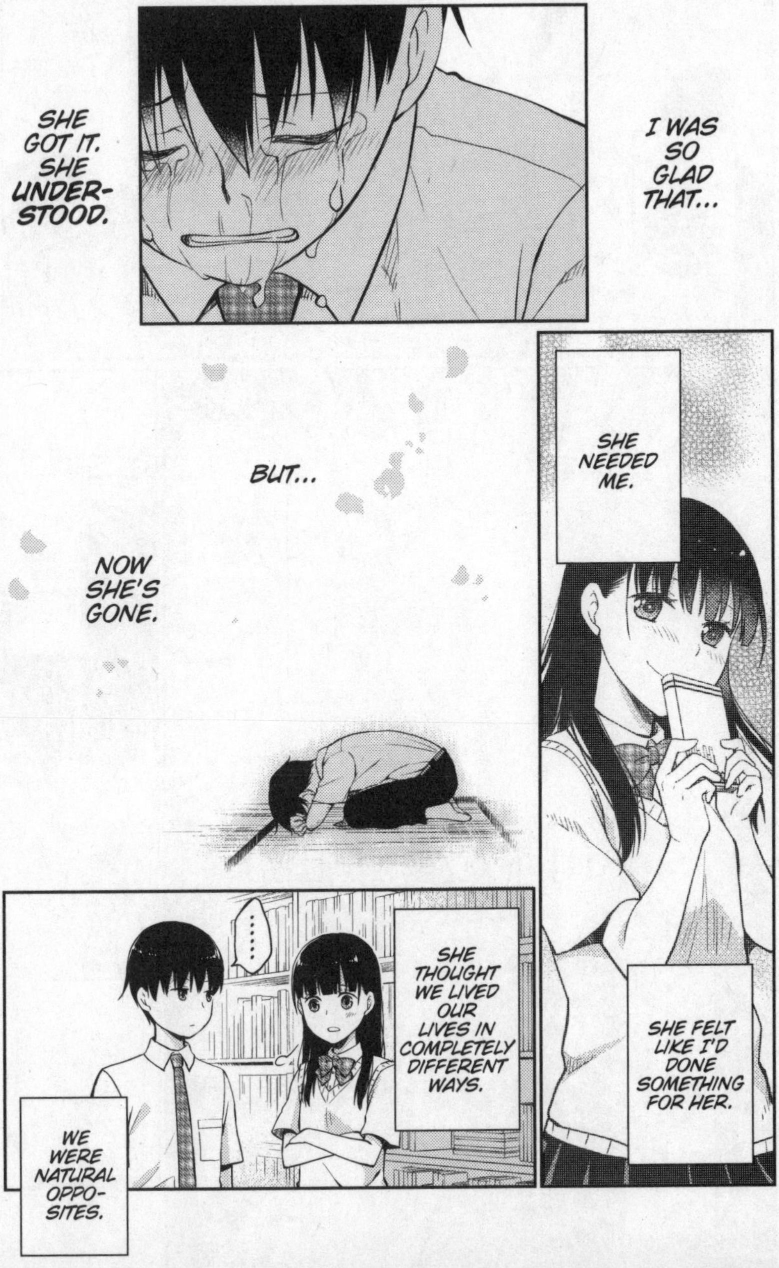
I WAS SO GLAD THAT...
SHE GOT IT. SHE UNDER-STOOD.
SHE NEEDED ME.
SHE FELT LIKE I'D DONE SOMETHING FOR HER.
BUT...
NOW SHE'S GONE.
......
SHE THOUGHT WE LIVED OUR LIVES IN COMPLETELY DIFFERENT WAYS.
WE WERE NATURAL OPPO-SITES.

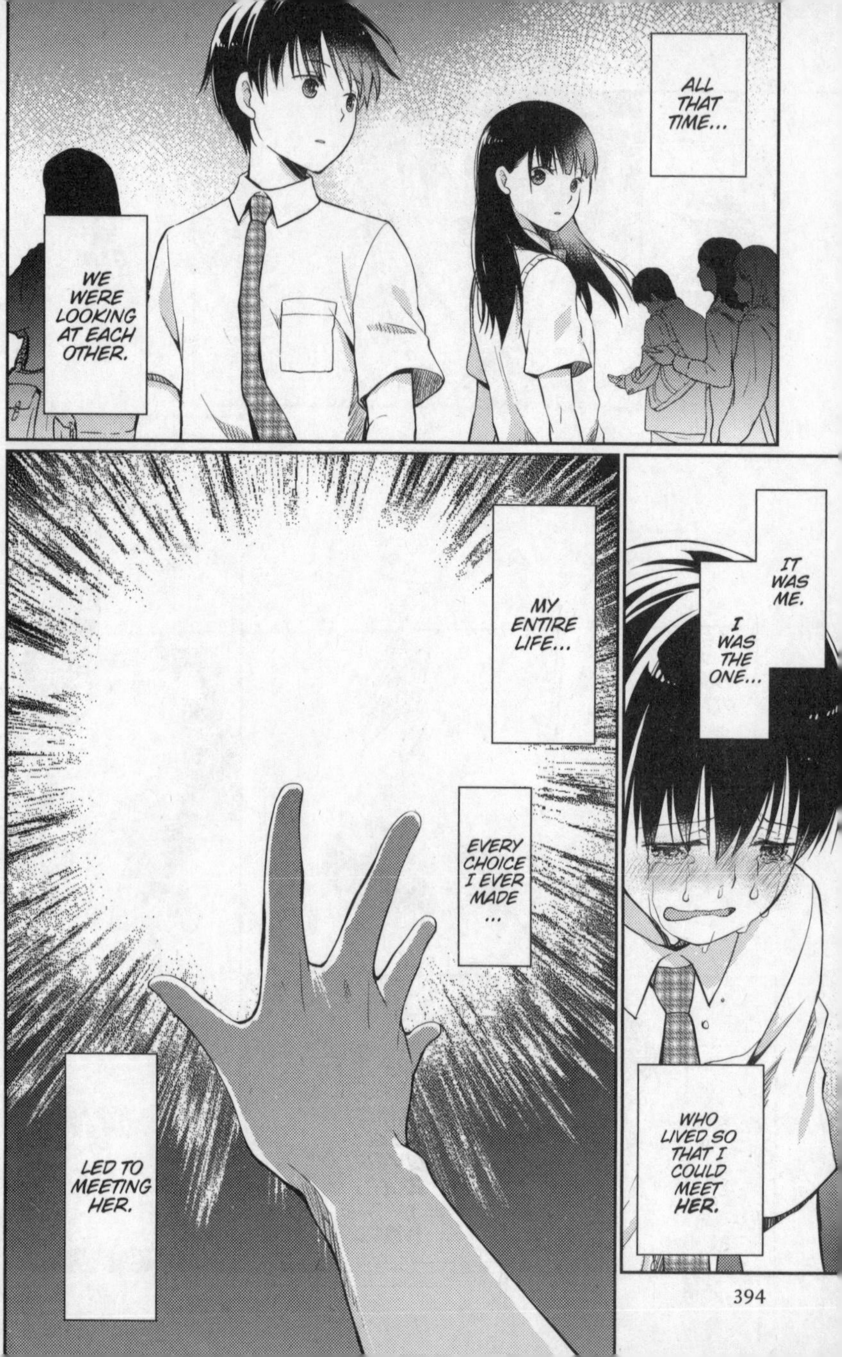
ALL THAT TIME...
WE WERE LOOKING AT EACH OTHER.
IT WAS ME.
I WAS THE ONE...
WHO LIVED SO THAT I COULD MEET HER.
MY ENTIRE LIFE...
EVERY CHOICE I EVER MADE ...
LED TO MEETING HER.

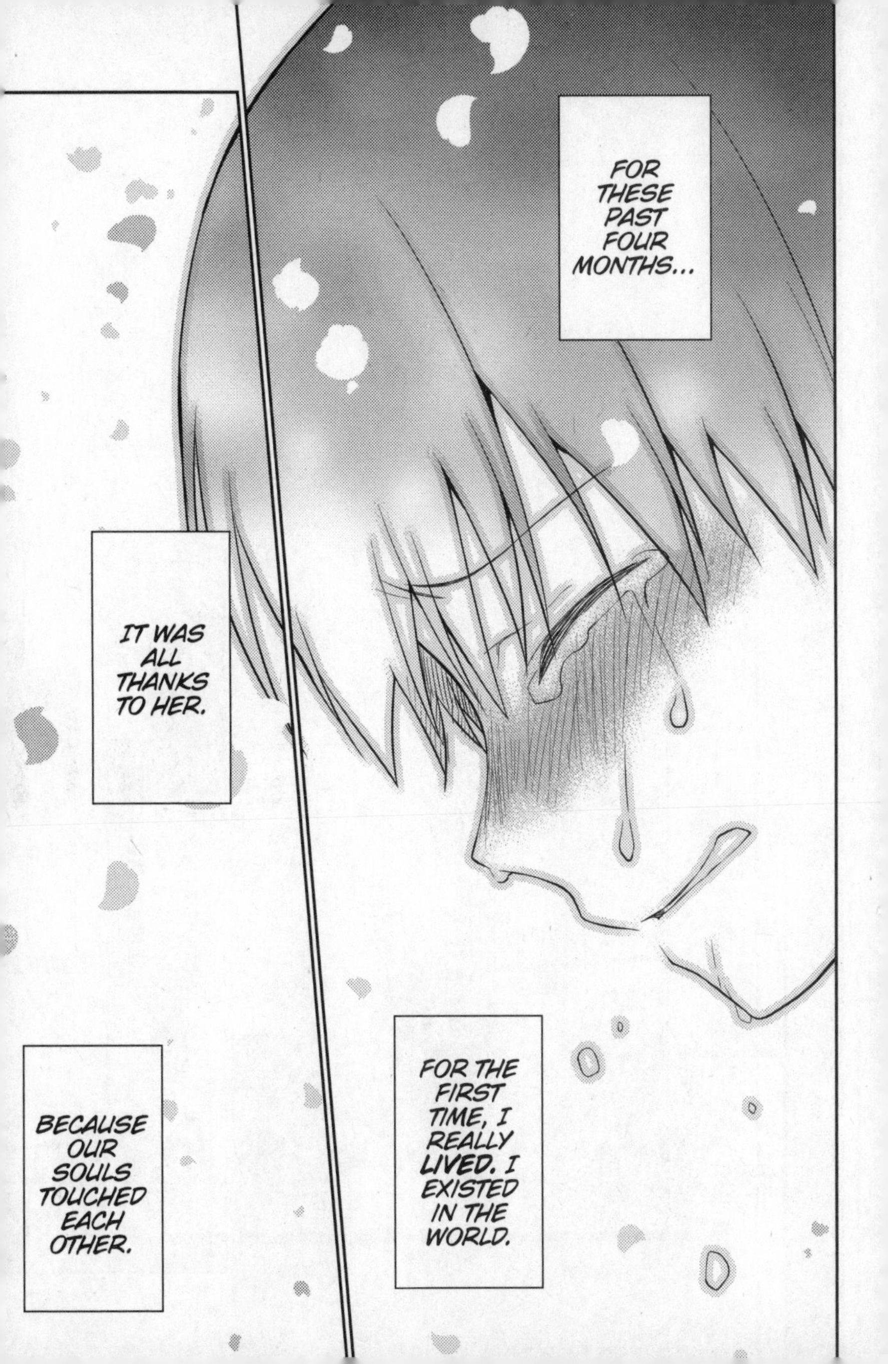
FOR THESE PAST FOUR MONTHS...
FOR THE FIRST TIME, I REALLY LIVED. I EXISTED IN THE WORLD.
IT WAS ALL THANKS TO HER.
BECAUSE OUR SOULS TOUCHED EACH OTHER.

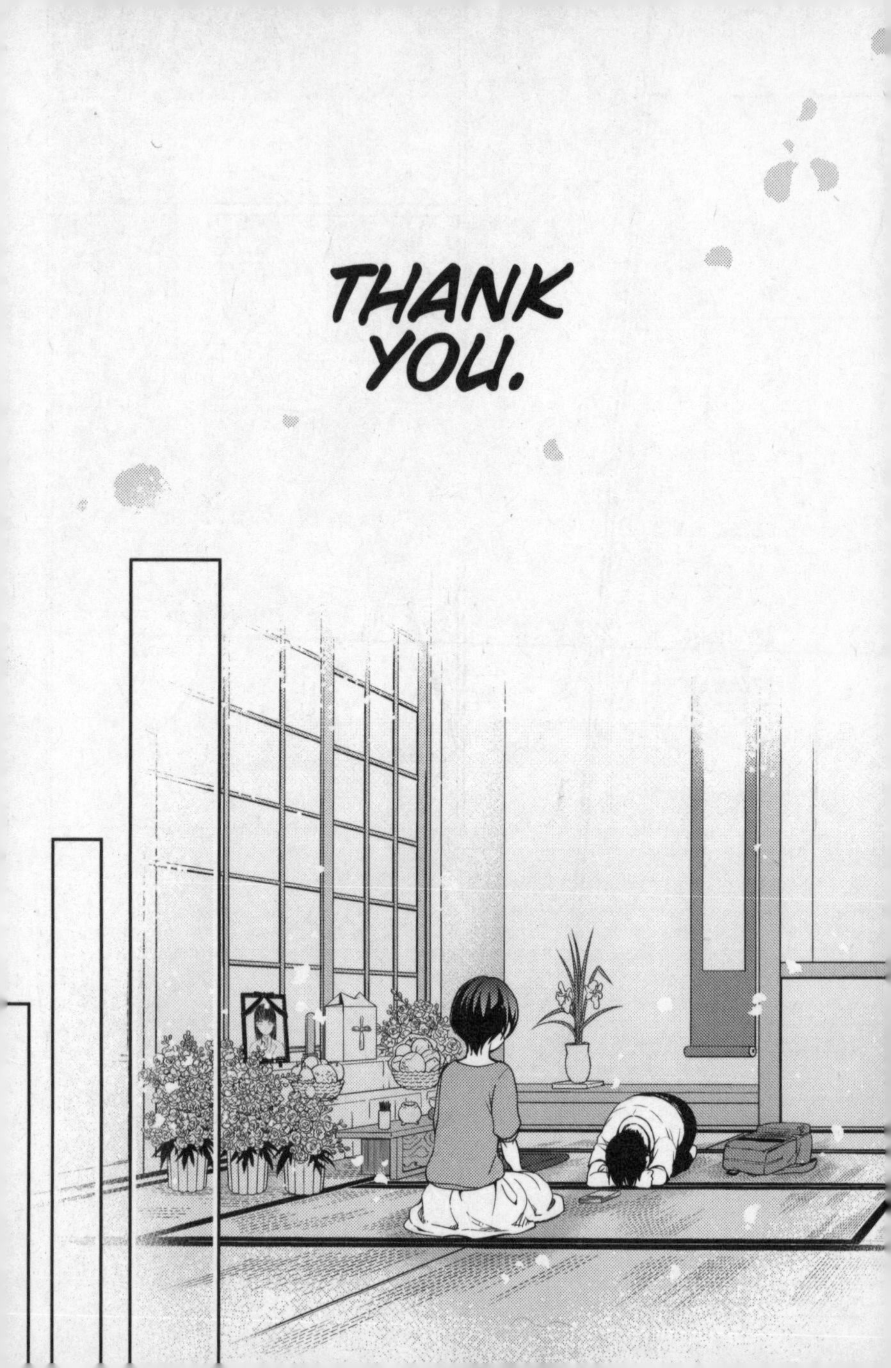
THANK YOU.

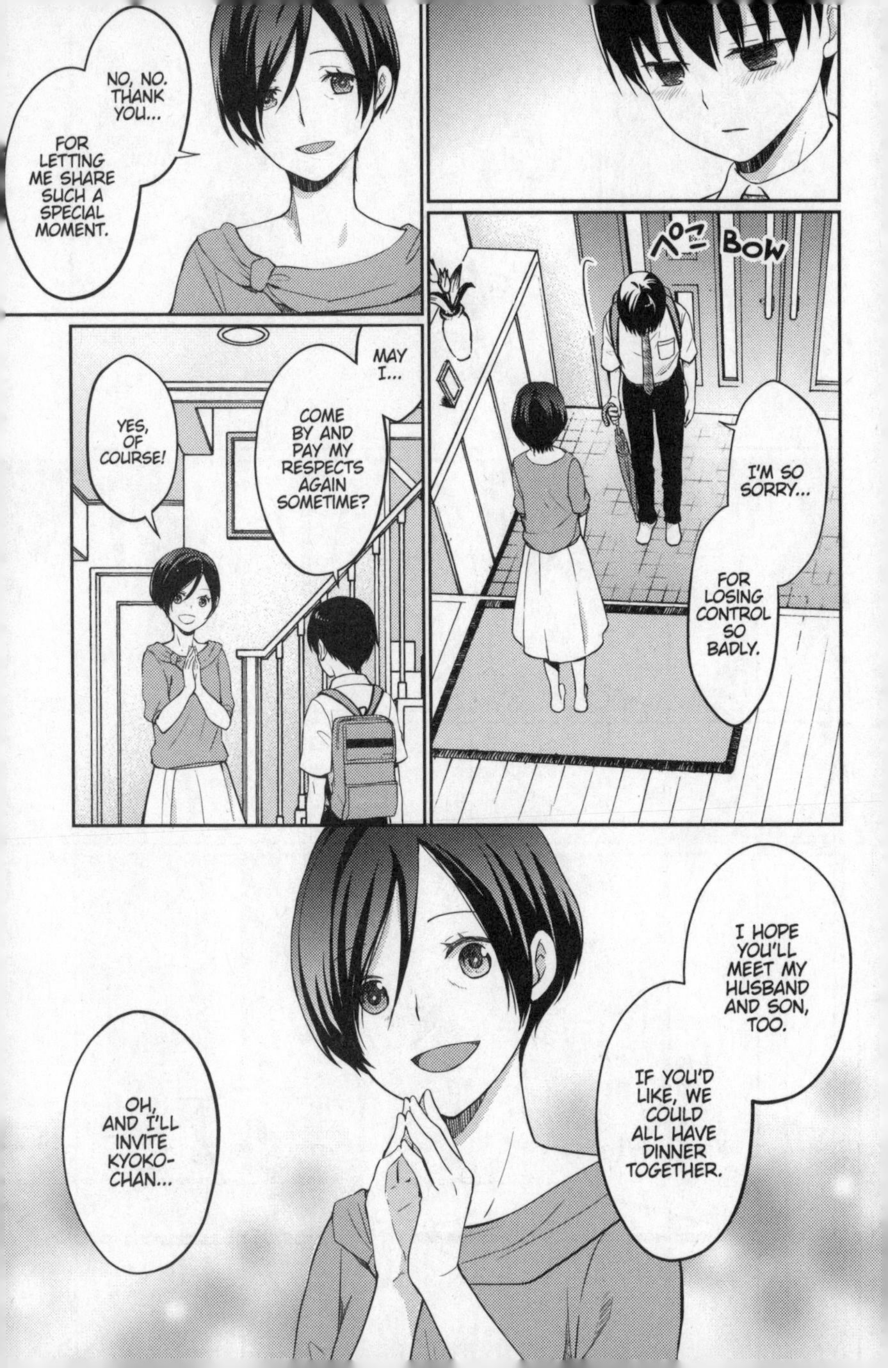
NO, NO. THANK YOU...
FOR LETTING ME SHARE SUCH A SPECIAL MOMENT.
ペコ
BOW
I'M SO SORRY...
FOR LOSING CONTROL SO BADLY.
MAY I...
COME BY AND PAY MY RESPECTS AGAIN SOMETIME?
YES, OF COURSE!
I HOPE YOU'LL MEET MY HUSBAND AND SON, TOO.
IF YOU'D LIKE, WE COULD ALL HAVE DINNER TOGETHER.
OH, AND I'LL INVITE KYOKO-CHAN...

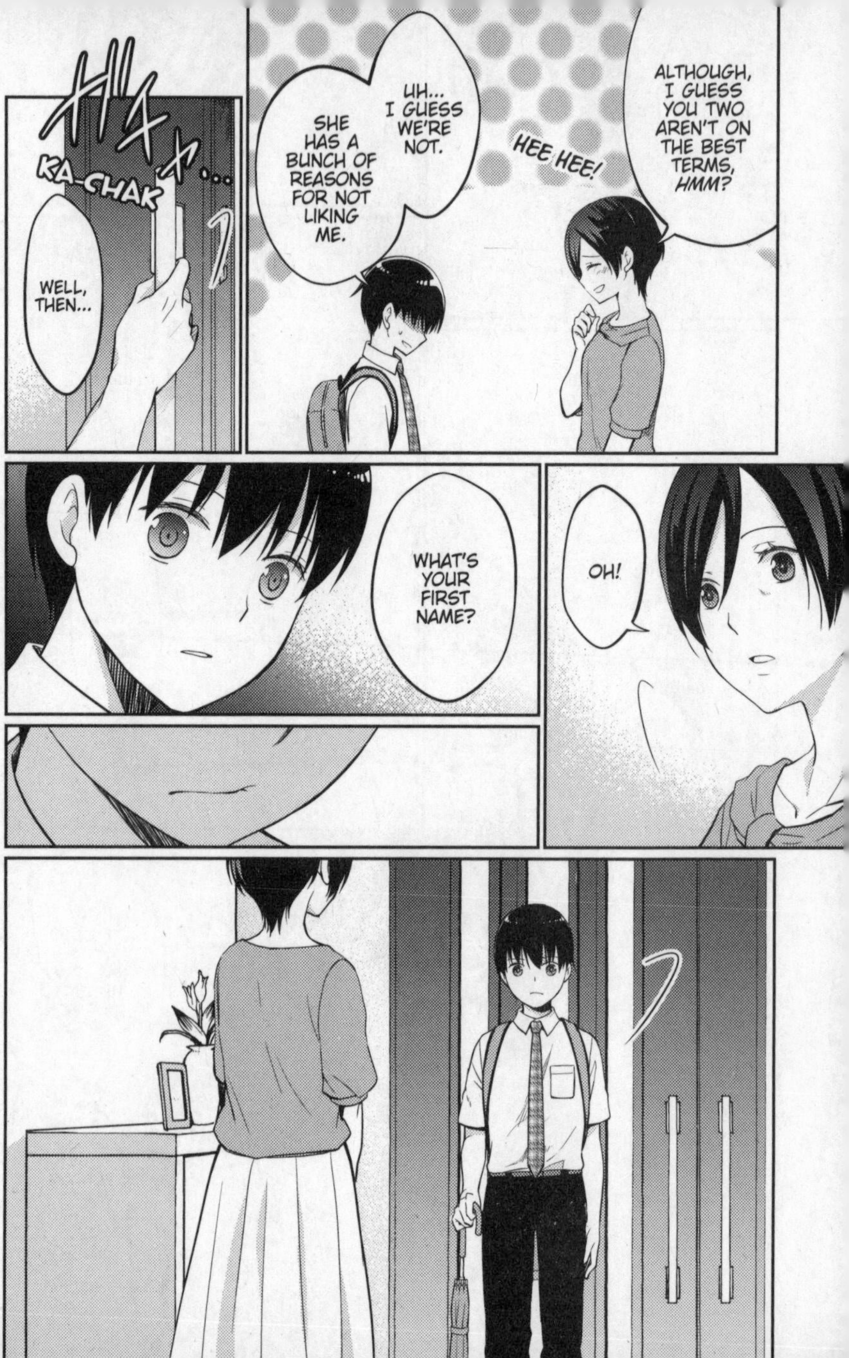
ALTHOUGH, I GUESS YOU TWO AREN'T ON THE BEST TERMS, HMM?
HEE HEE!
UH... I GUESS WE'RE NOT.
SHE HAS A BUNCH OF REASONS FOR NOT LIKING ME.
KA-CHAK
WELL, THEN...
OH!
WHAT'S YOUR FIRST NAME?

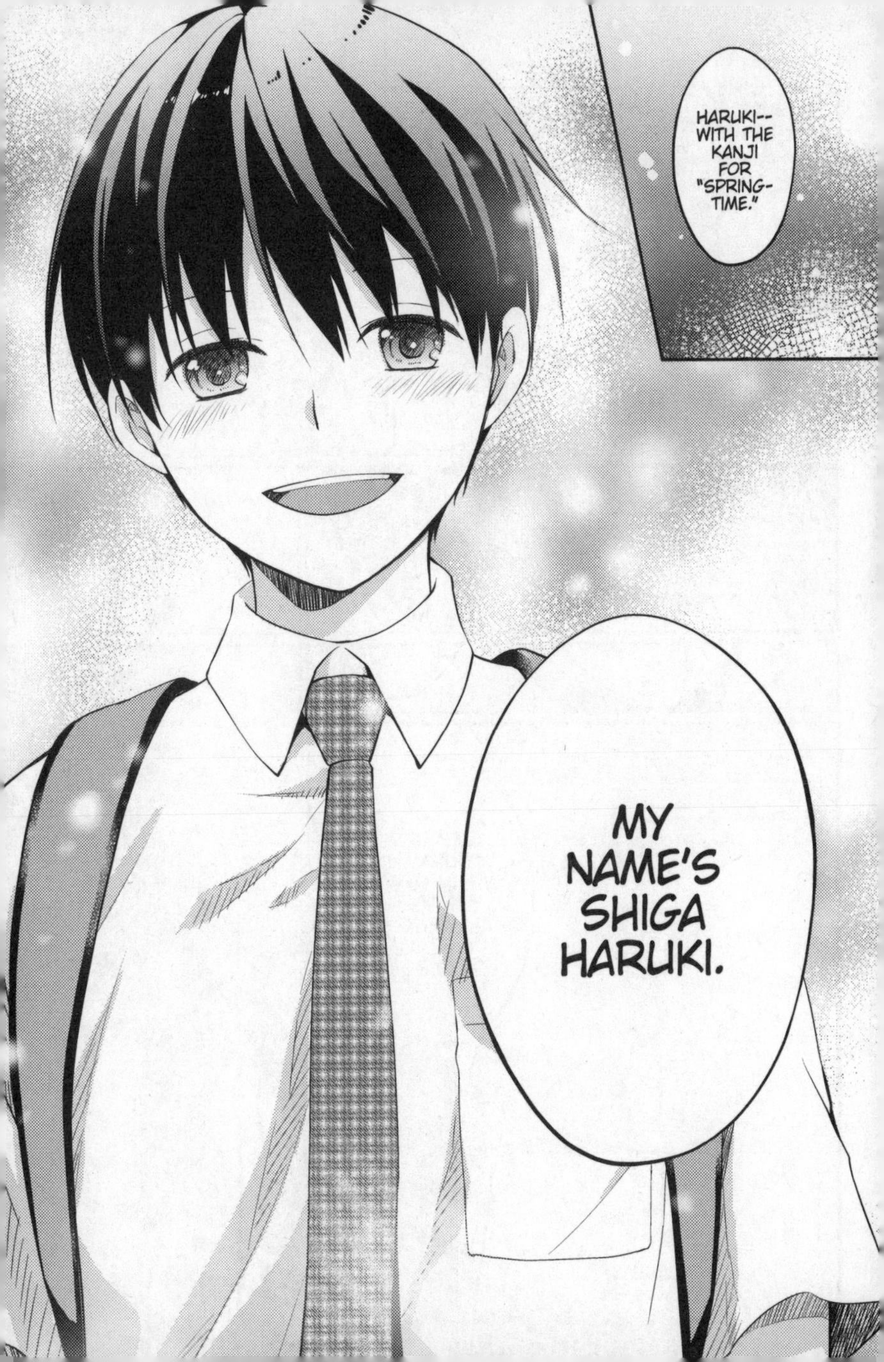
HARUKI--WITH THE KANJI FOR "SPRING-TIME."
MY NAME'S SHIGA HARUKI.

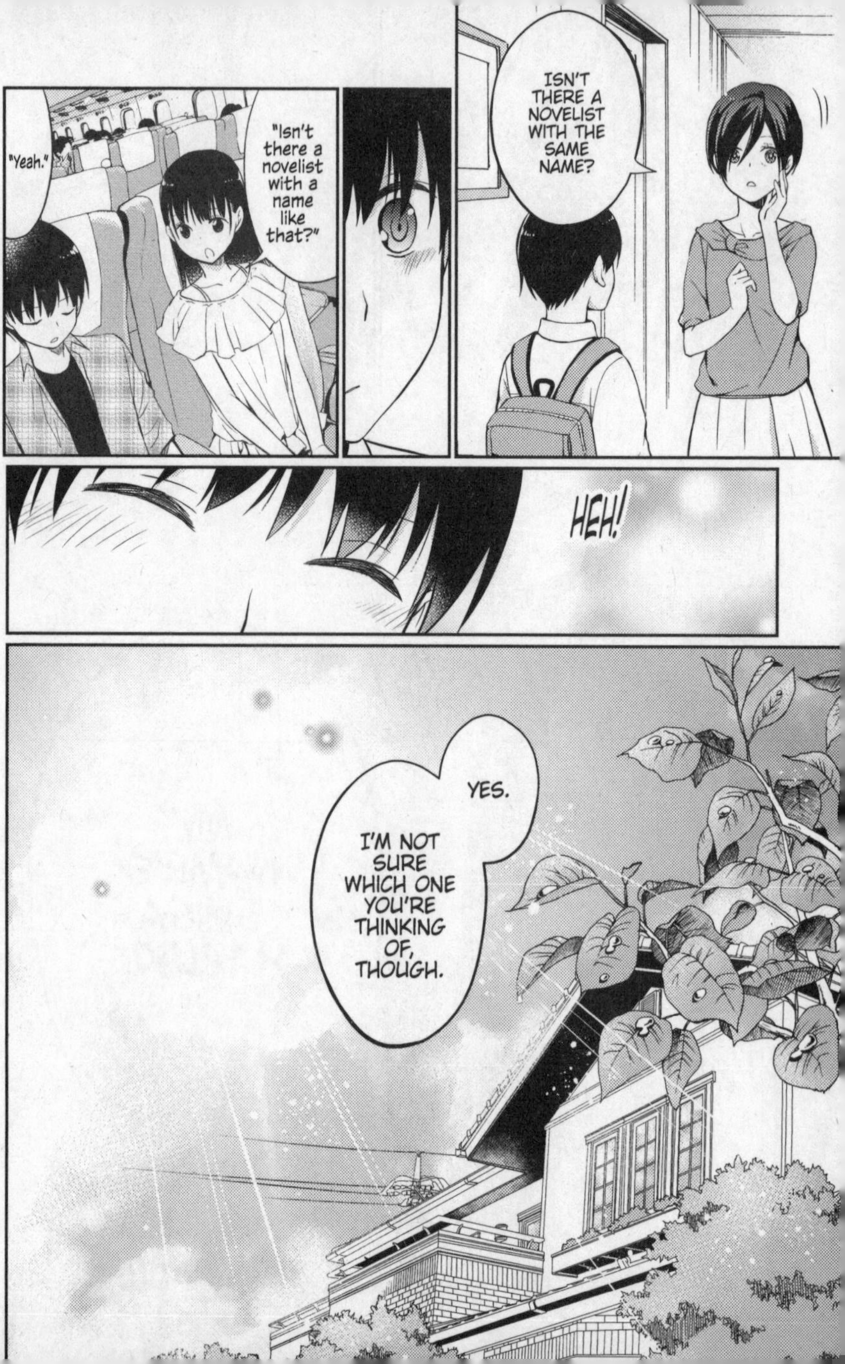
ISN'T THERE A NOVELIST WITH THE SAME NAME?
"Isn't there a novelist with a name like that?"
"Yeah."
HEH!
YES.
I'M NOT SURE WHICH ONE YOU'RE THINKING OF, THOUGH.

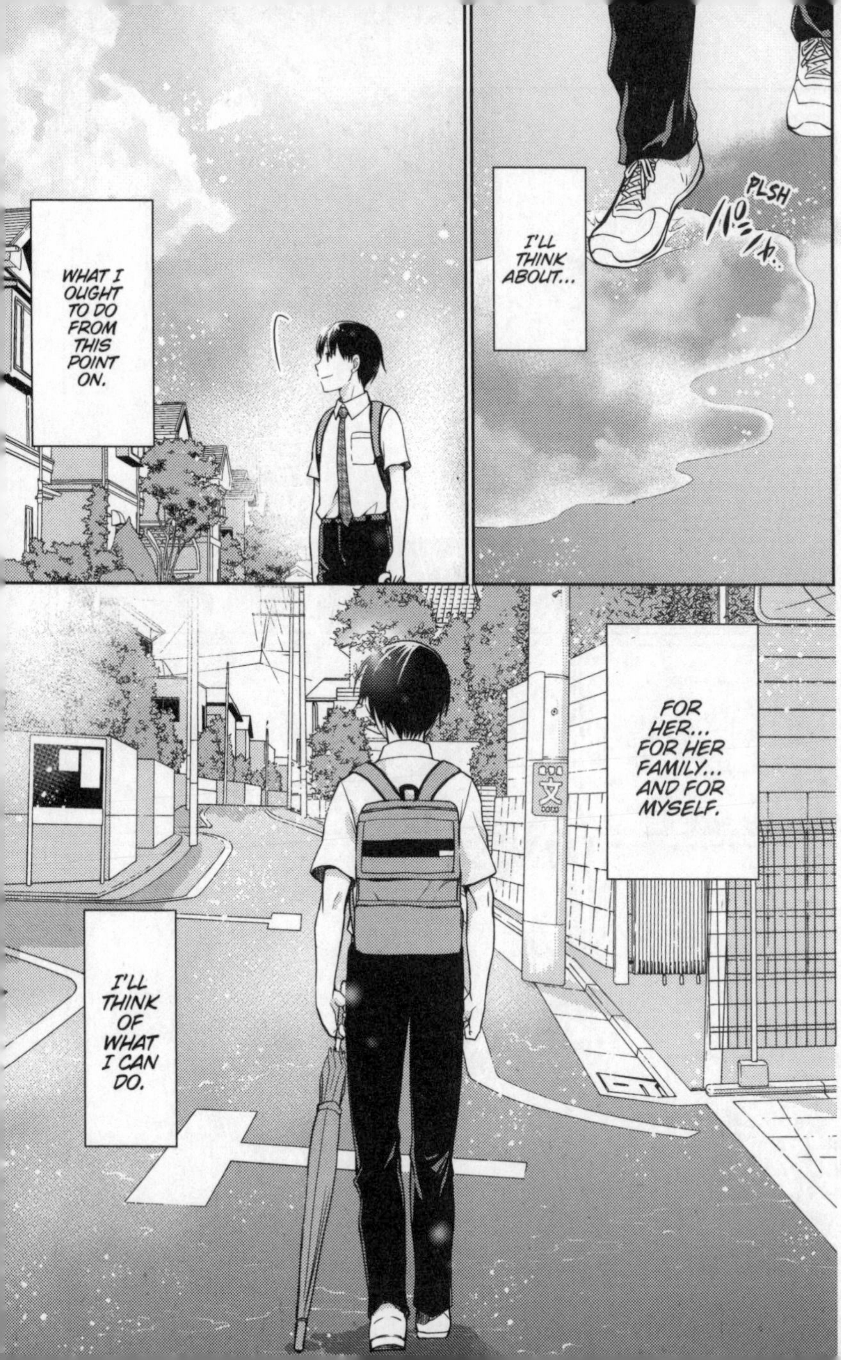

PLSH
I'LL THINK ABOUT...
WHAT I OUGHT TO DO FROM THIS POINT ON.
FOR HER... FOR HER FAMILY... AND FOR MYSELF.
I'LL THINK OF WHAT I CAN DO.

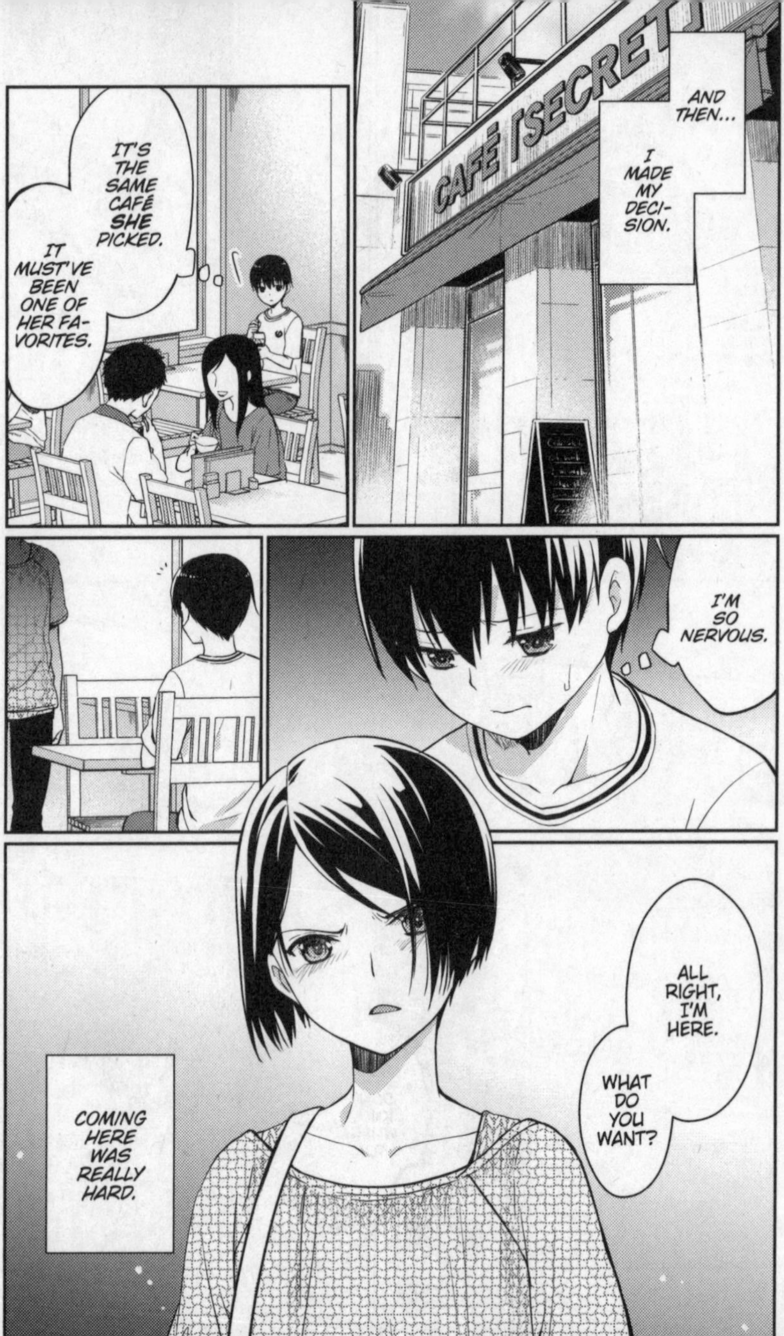
CAFÉ 「SECRET」
AND THEN...
I MADE MY DECISION.
IT'S THE SAME CAFÉ SHE PICKED.
IT MUST'VE BEEN ONE OF HER FAVORITES.
I'M SO NERVOUS.
ALL RIGHT, I'M HERE.
WHAT DO YOU WANT?
COMING HERE WAS REALLY HARD.

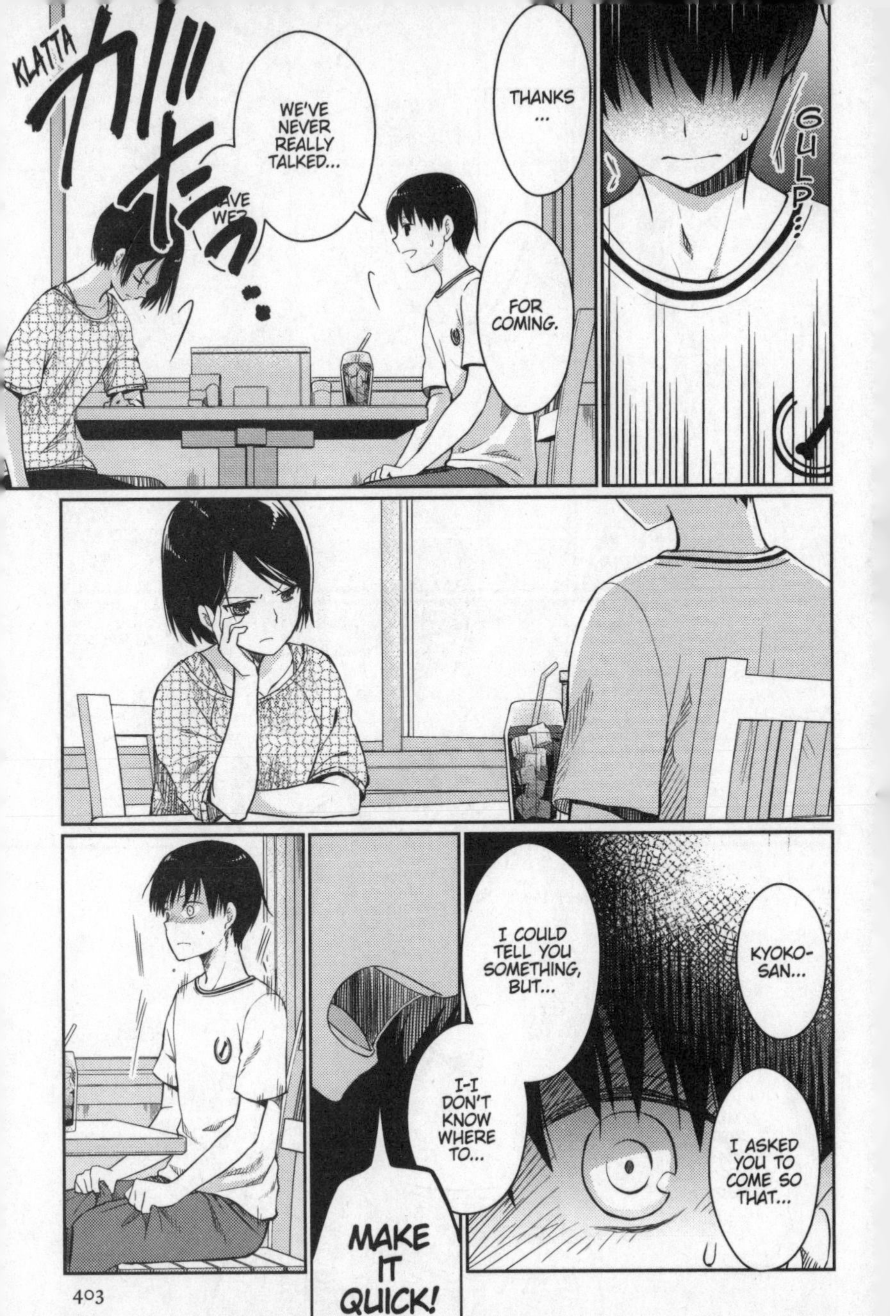
GULP...
THANKS ...
FOR COMING.
WE'VE NEVER REALLY TALKED...
HAVE WE?
KLATTA
KYOKO-SAN...
I ASKED YOU TO COME SO THAT...
I COULD TELL YOU SOMETHING, BUT...
I-I DON'T KNOW WHERE TO...
MAKE IT QUICK!

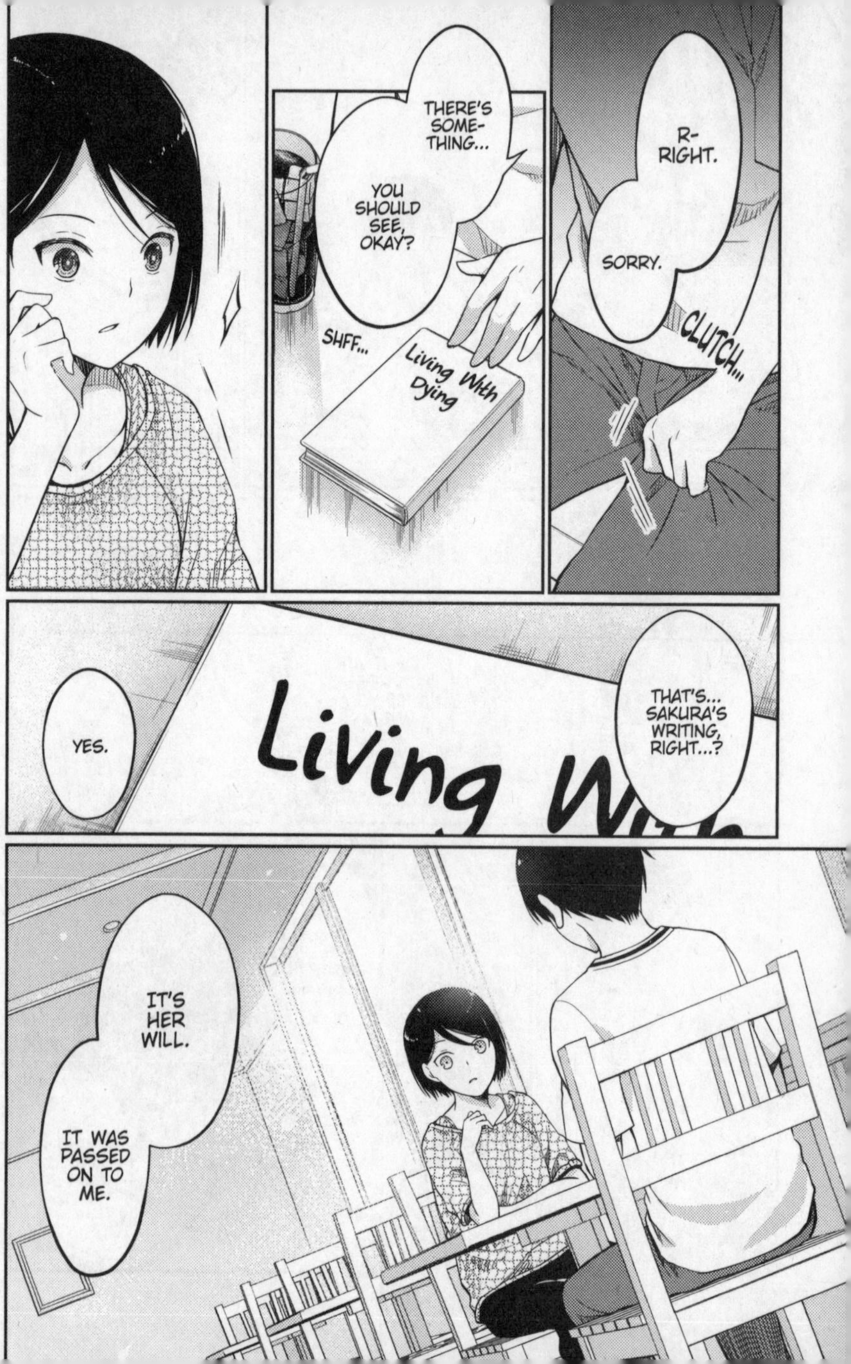
R-RIGHT.
SORRY.
CLUTCH...
THERE'S SOMETHING...
YOU SHOULD SEE, OKAY?
SHFF...
Living With Dying
THAT'S... SAKURA'S WRITING, RIGHT...?
YES.
Living
IT'S HER WILL.
IT WAS PASSED ON TO ME.

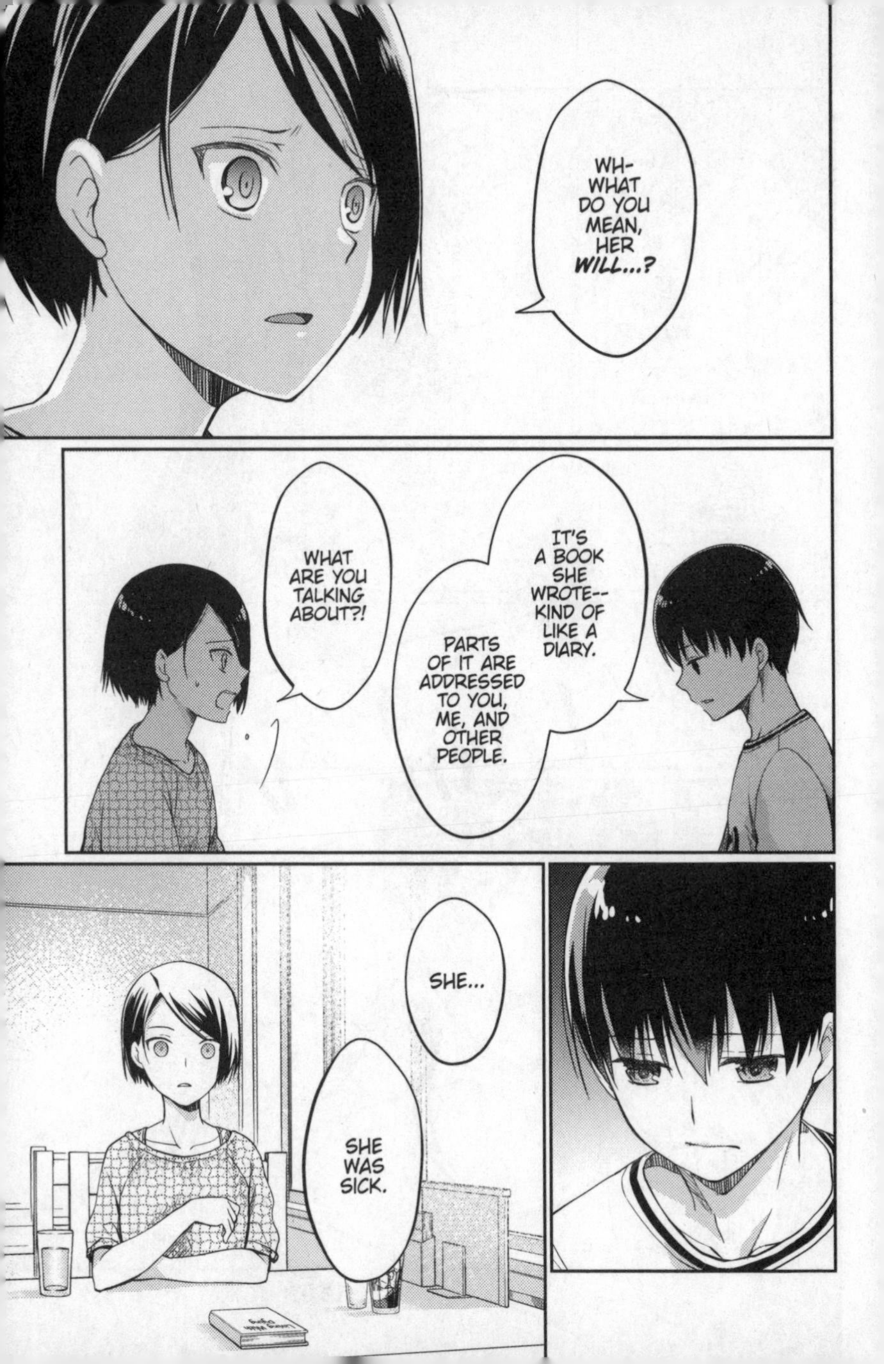
WH- WHAT DO YOU MEAN, HER *WILL*...?
IT'S A BOOK SHE WROTE-- KIND OF LIKE A DIARY.
PARTS OF IT ARE ADDRESSED TO YOU, ME, AND OTHER PEOPLE.
WHAT ARE YOU TALKING ABOUT?!
SHE...
SHE WAS SICK.

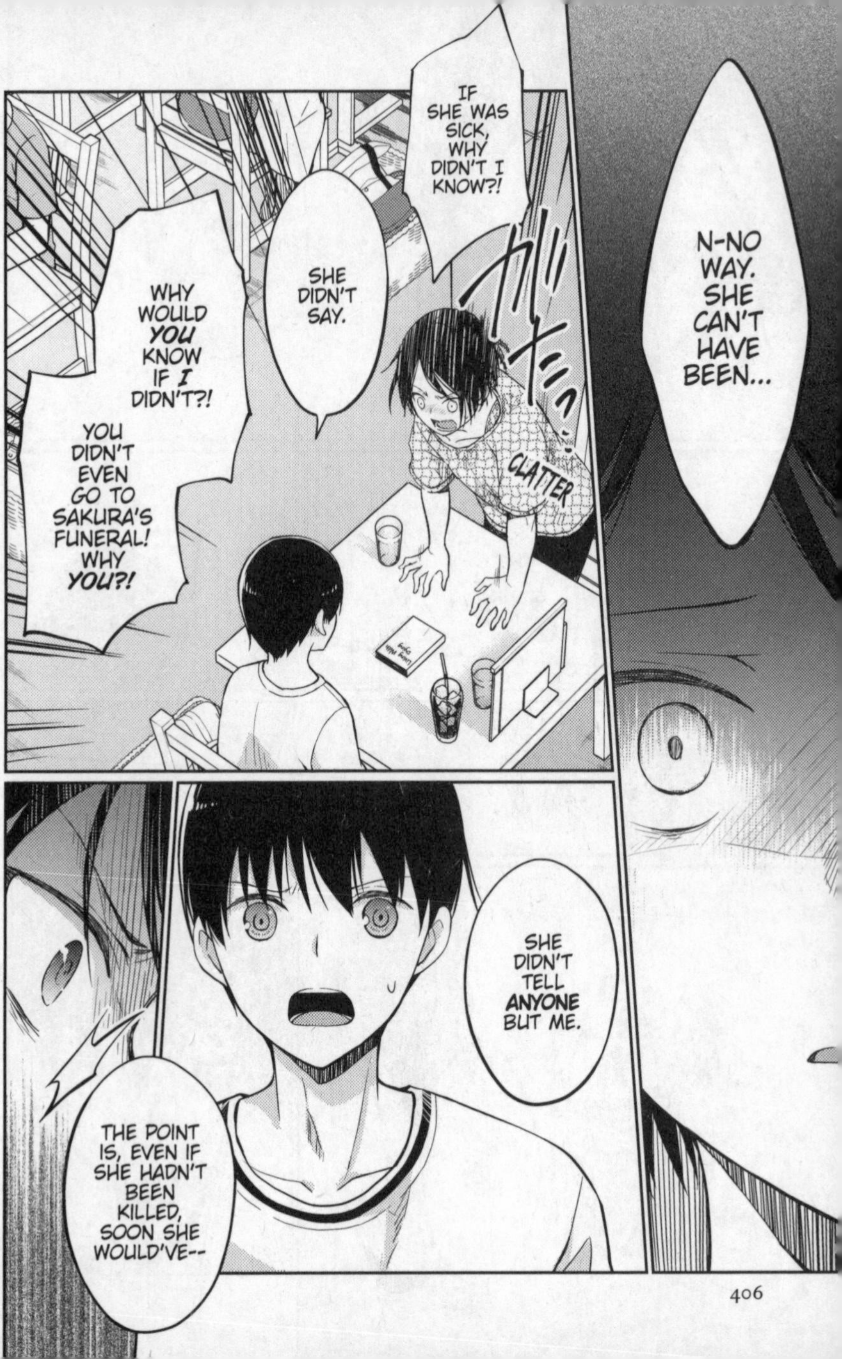
IF SHE WAS SICK, WHY DIDN'T I KNOW?!
CLATTER
SHE DIDN'T SAY.
WHY WOULD ***YOU*** KNOW IF ***I*** DIDN'T?!
YOU DIDN'T EVEN GO TO SAKURA'S FUNERAL! WHY ***YOU***?!
SHE DIDN'T TELL **ANYONE** BUT ME.
THE POINT IS, EVEN IF SHE HADN'T BEEN KILLED, SOON SHE WOULD'VE--
N-NO WAY. SHE CAN'T HAVE BEEN...

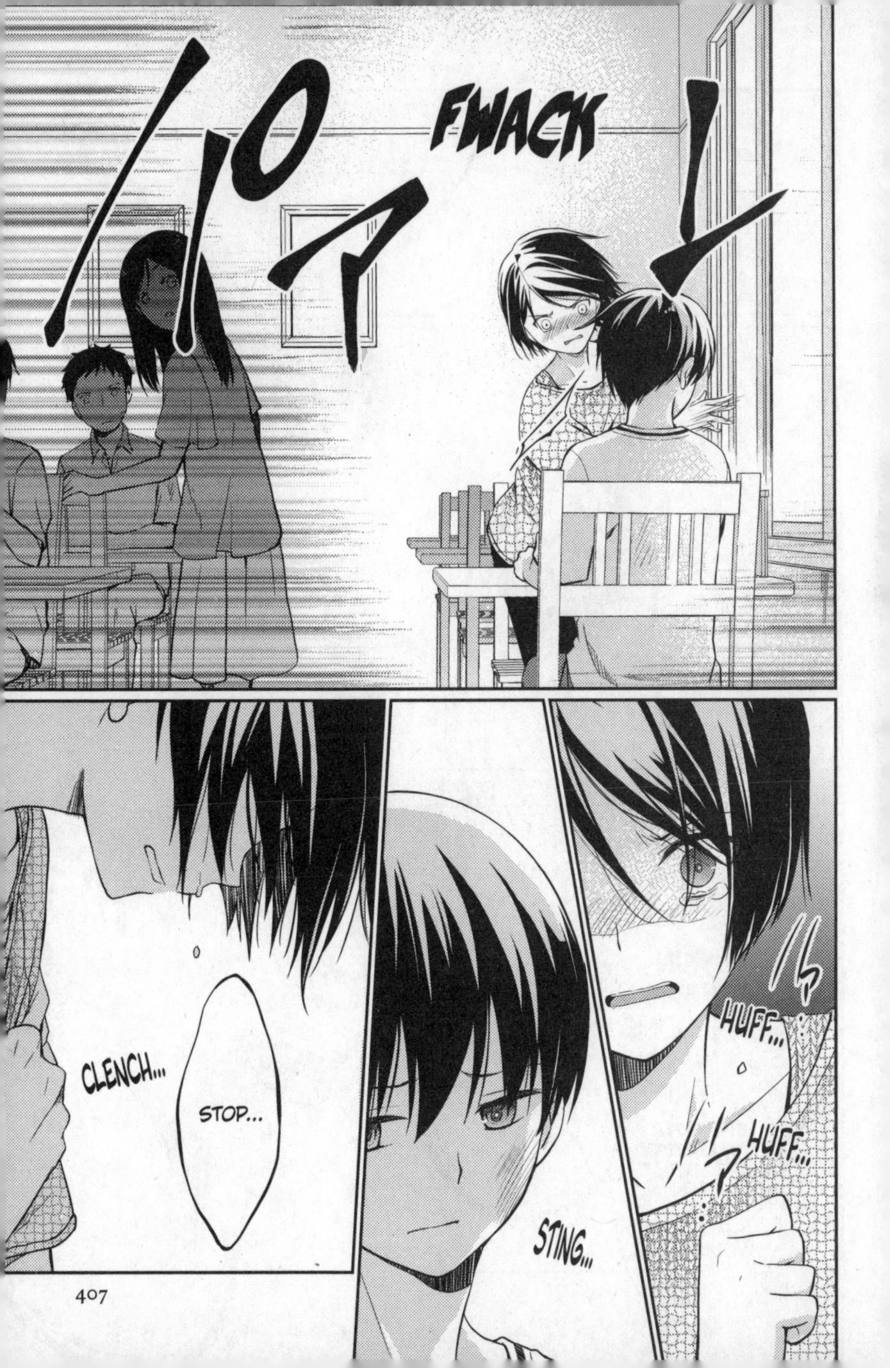
FWACK
HUFF...
HUFF...
STING...
CLENCH...
STOP...

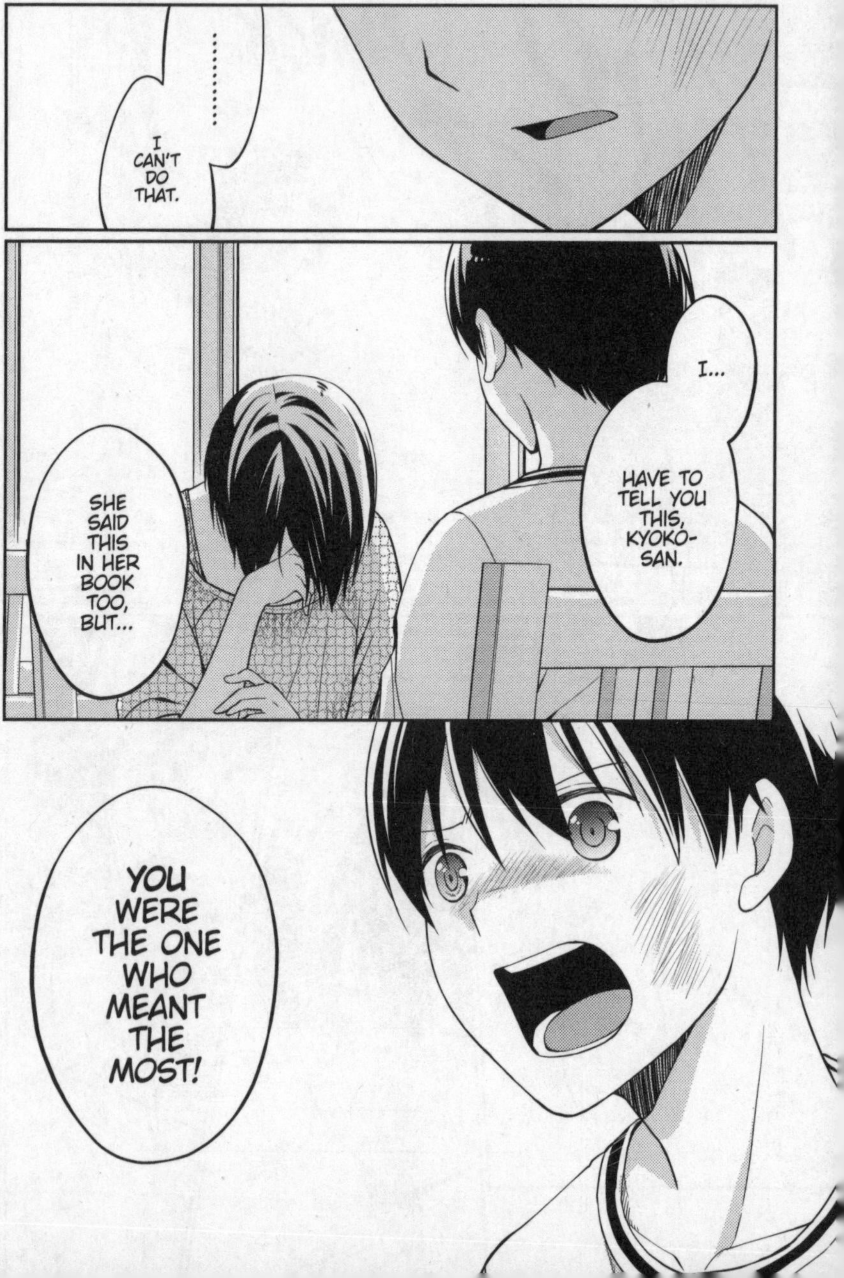
I CAN'T DO THAT.
I...
HAVE TO TELL YOU THIS, KYOKO-SAN.
SHE SAID THIS IN HER BOOK TOO, BUT...
YOU WERE THE ONE WHO MEANT THE MOST!

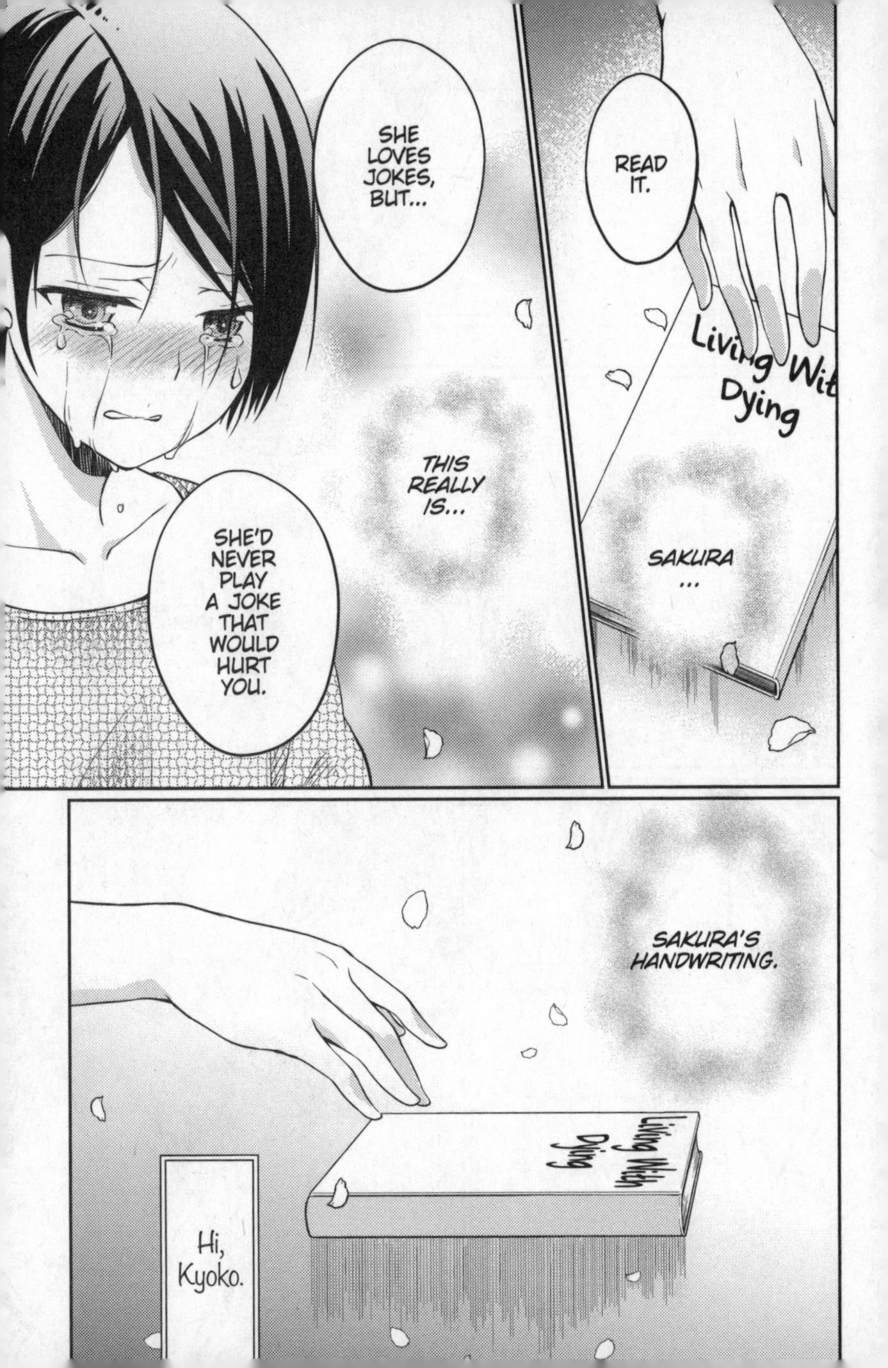
READ IT.
Living Wit
Dying
SAKURA ...
SHE LOVES JOKES, BUT...
SHE'D NEVER PLAY A JOKE THAT WOULD HURT YOU.
THIS REALLY IS...
SAKURA'S HANDWRITING.
Living With
Dying
Hi, Kyoko.

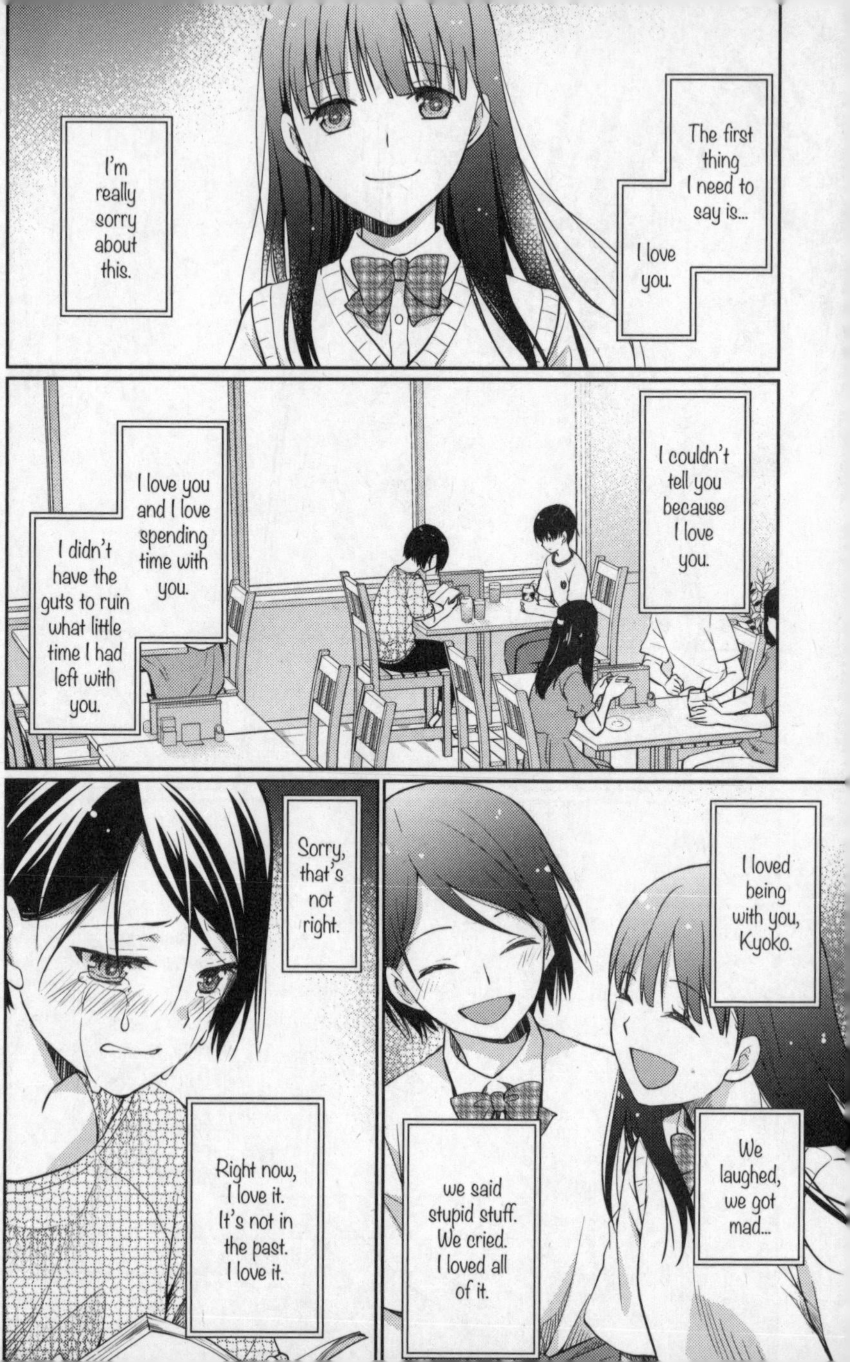
The first thing I need to say is... I love you.
I'm really sorry about this.
I couldn't tell you because I love you.
I love you and I love spending time with you.
I didn't have the guts to ruin what little time I had left with you.
I loved being with you, Kyoko.
We laughed, we got mad...
we said stupid stuff. We cried. I loved all of it.
Sorry, that's not right.
Right now, I love it. It's not in the past. I love it.

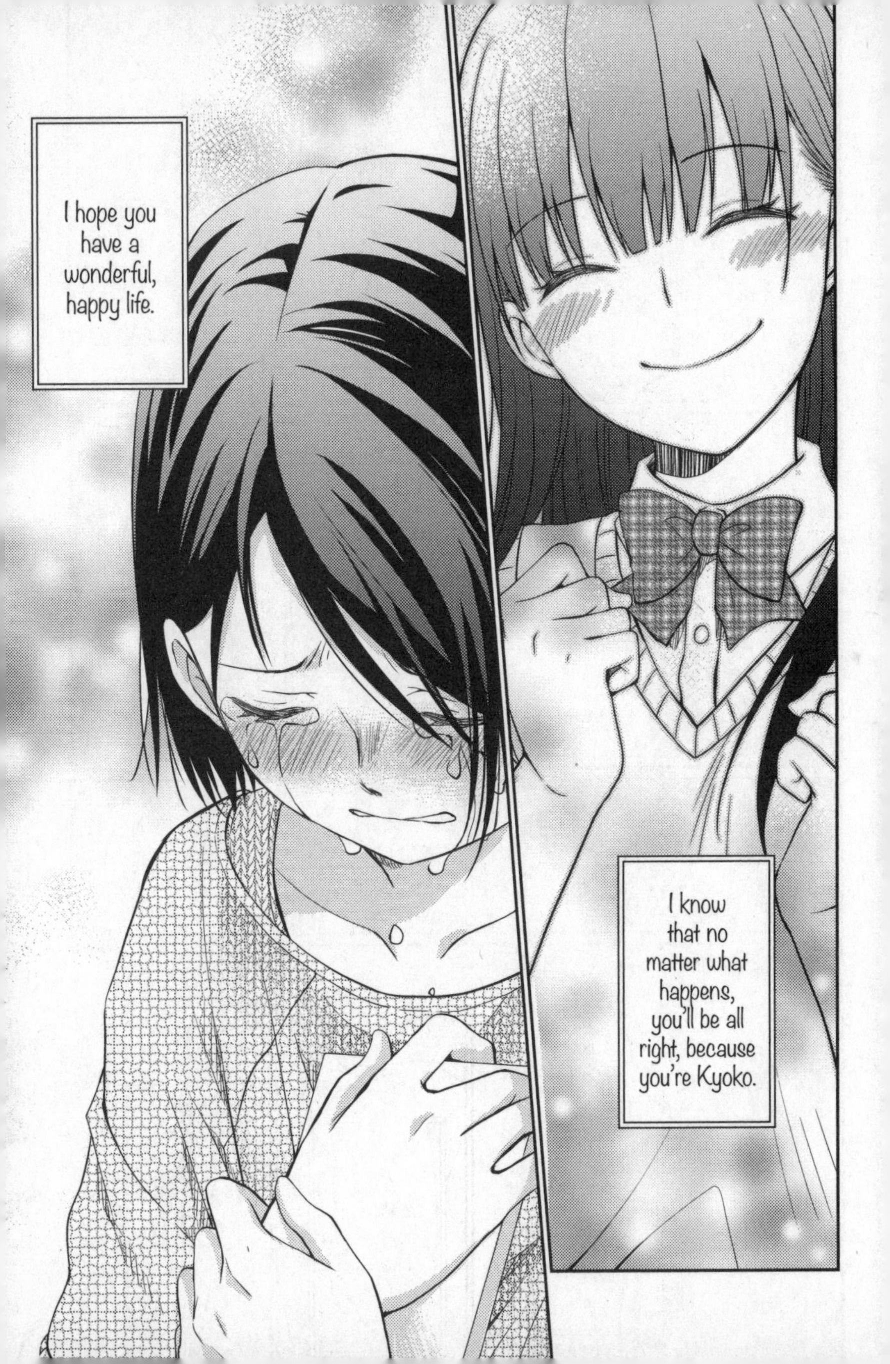
I know that no matter what happens, you'll be all right, because you're Kyoko.
I hope you have a wonderful, happy life.

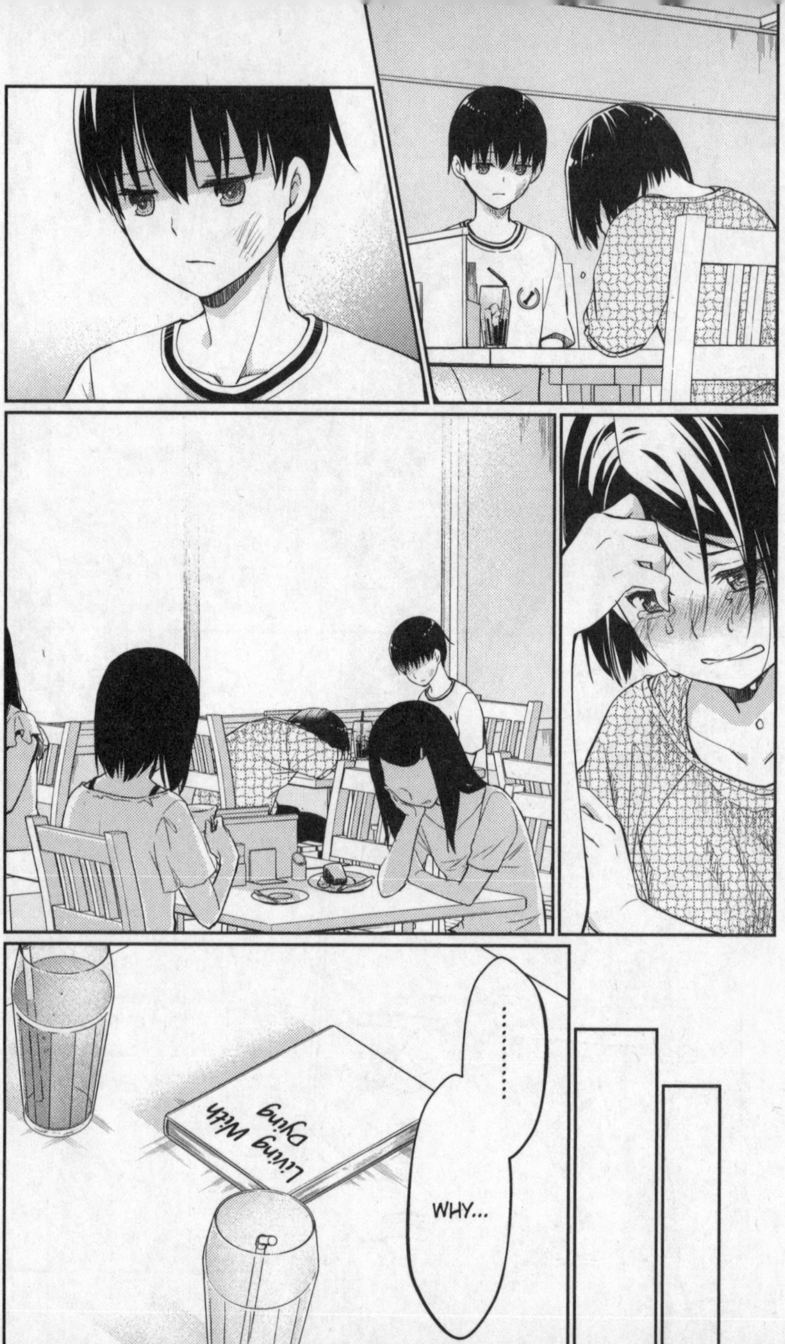
Living With
Dying
......
WHY...

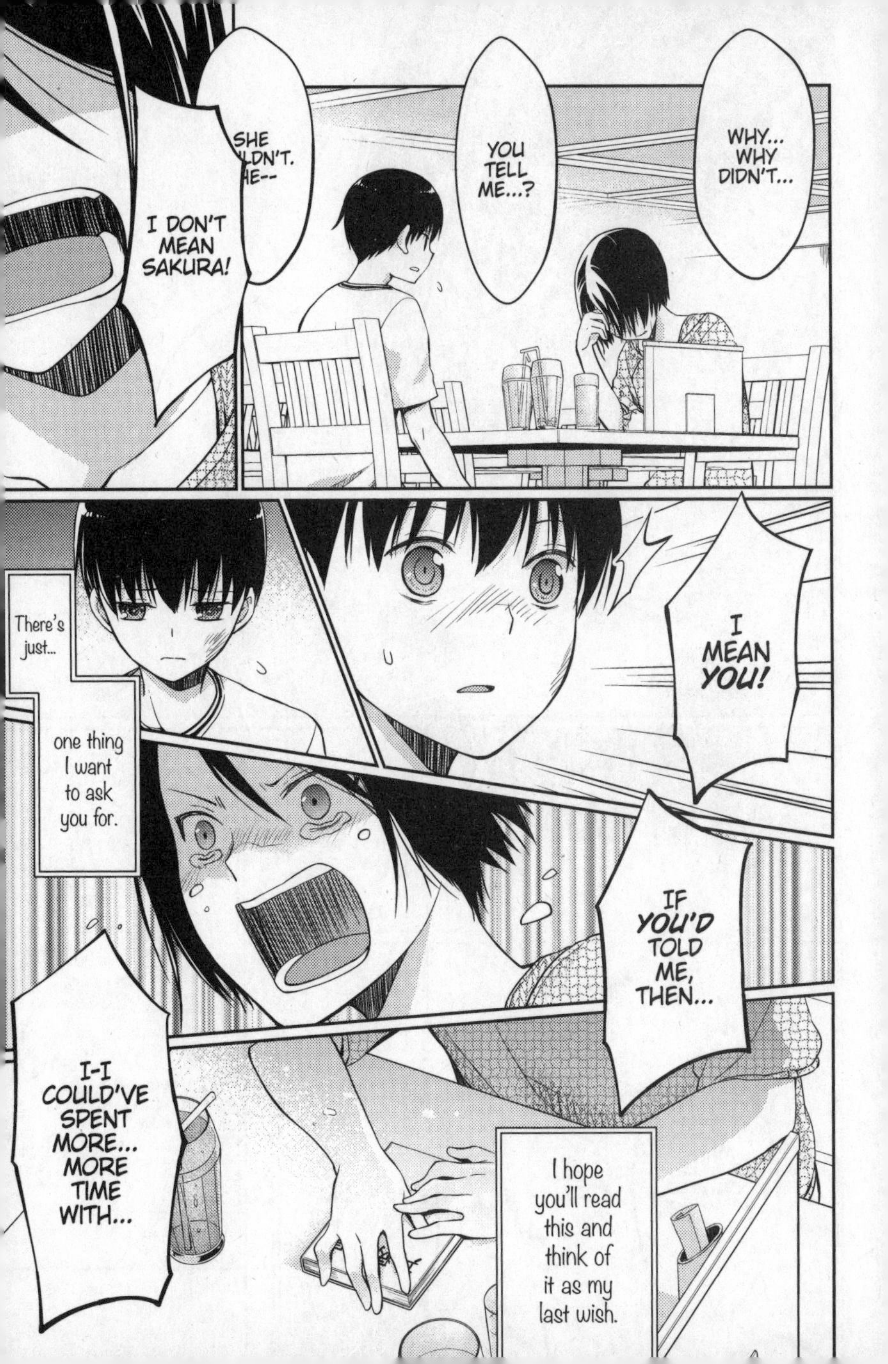
WHY... WHY DIDN'T...
YOU TELL ME...?
SHE LDN'T. HE--
I DON'T MEAN SAKURA!
I MEAN *YOU!*
There's just... one thing I want to ask you for.
IF *YOU'D* TOLD ME, THEN...
I-I COULD'VE SPENT MORE... MORE TIME WITH...
I hope you'll read this and think of it as my last wish.

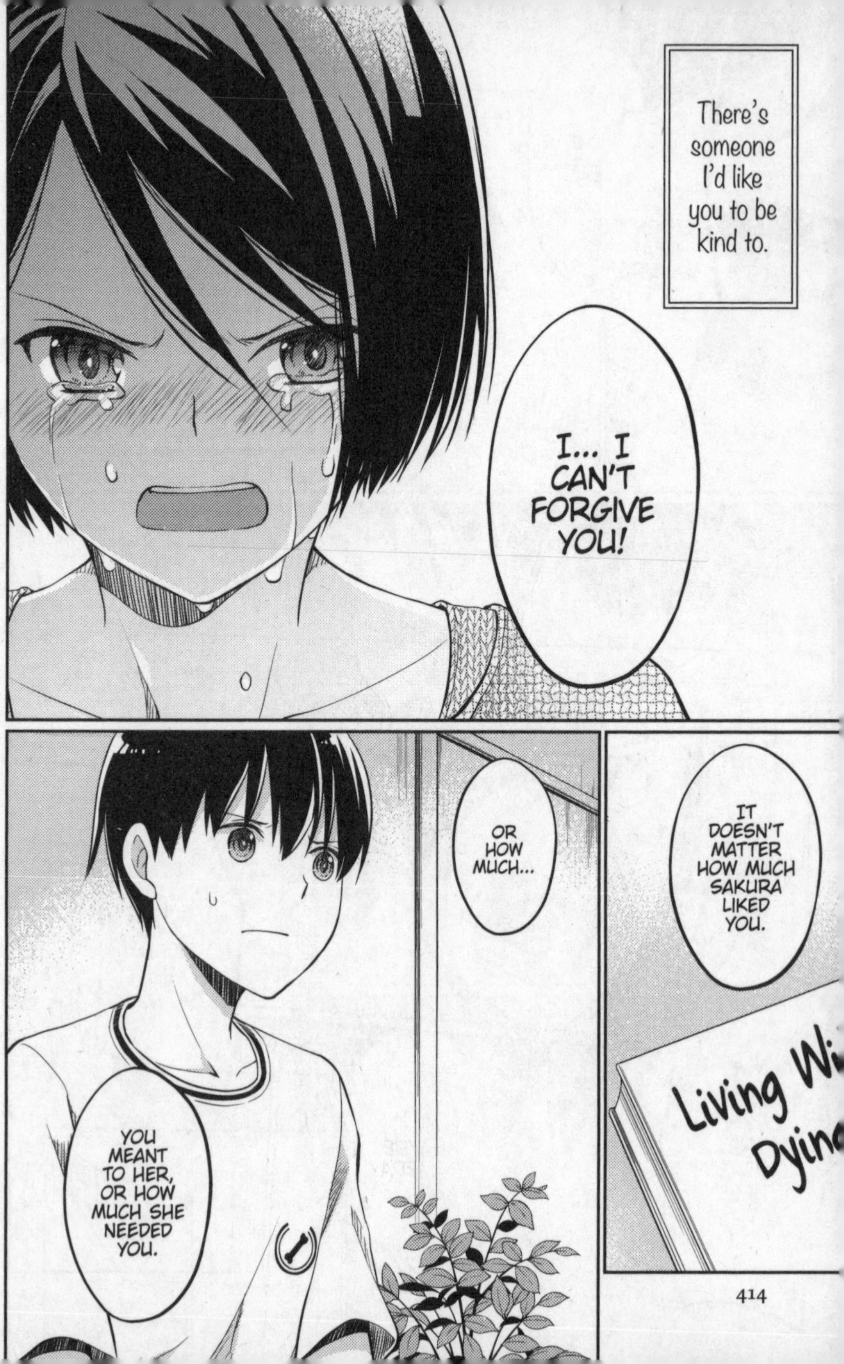
There's someone I'd like you to be kind to.
I... I CAN'T FORGIVE YOU!
IT DOESN'T MATTER HOW MUCH SAKURA LIKED YOU.
OR HOW MUCH...
YOU MEANT TO HER, OR HOW MUCH SHE NEEDED YOU.

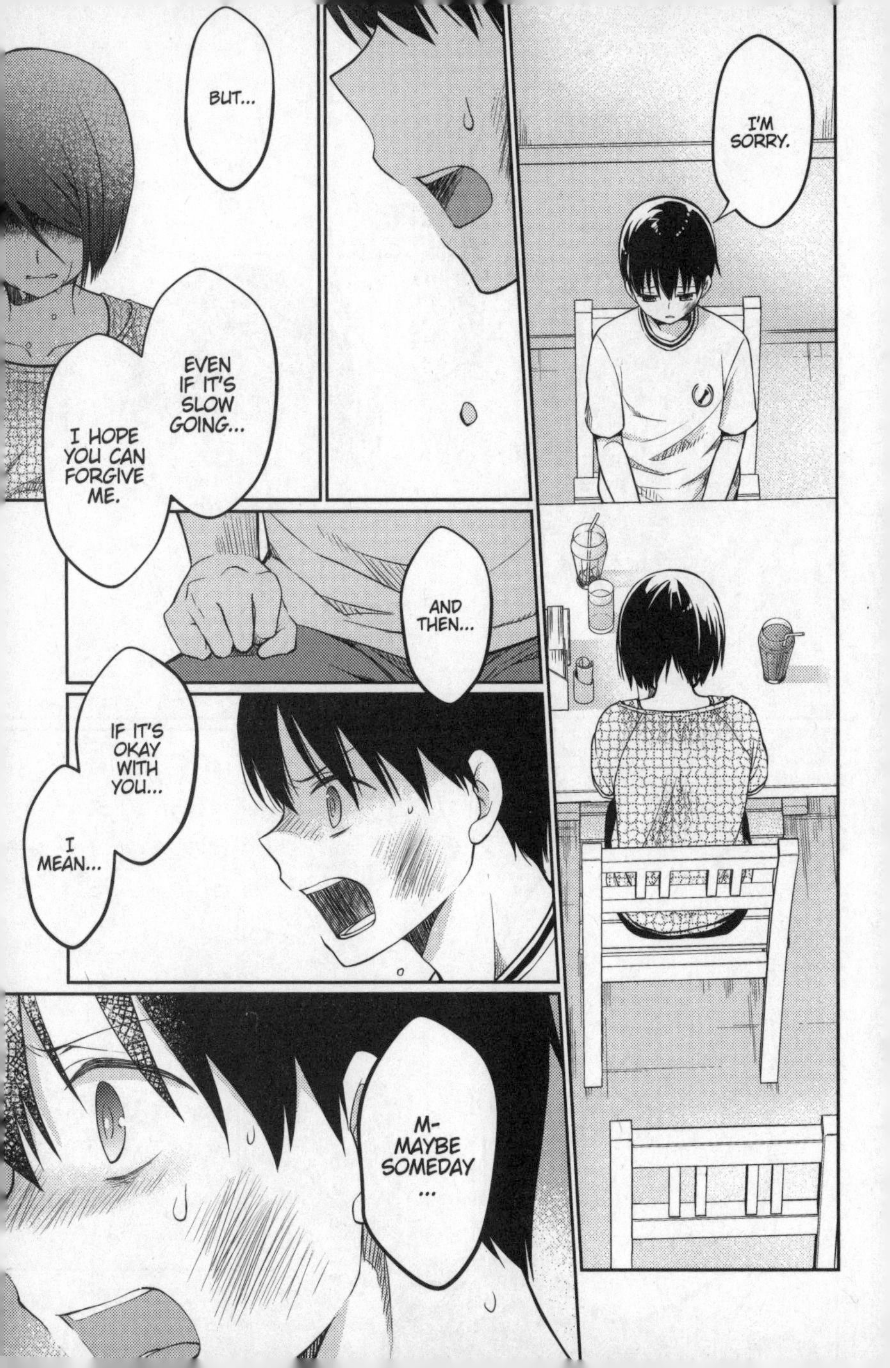
I'M SORRY.
BUT...
EVEN IF IT'S SLOW GOING...
I HOPE YOU CAN FORGIVE ME.
AND THEN...
IF IT'S OKAY WITH YOU...
I MEAN...
M-MAYBE SOMEDAY ...

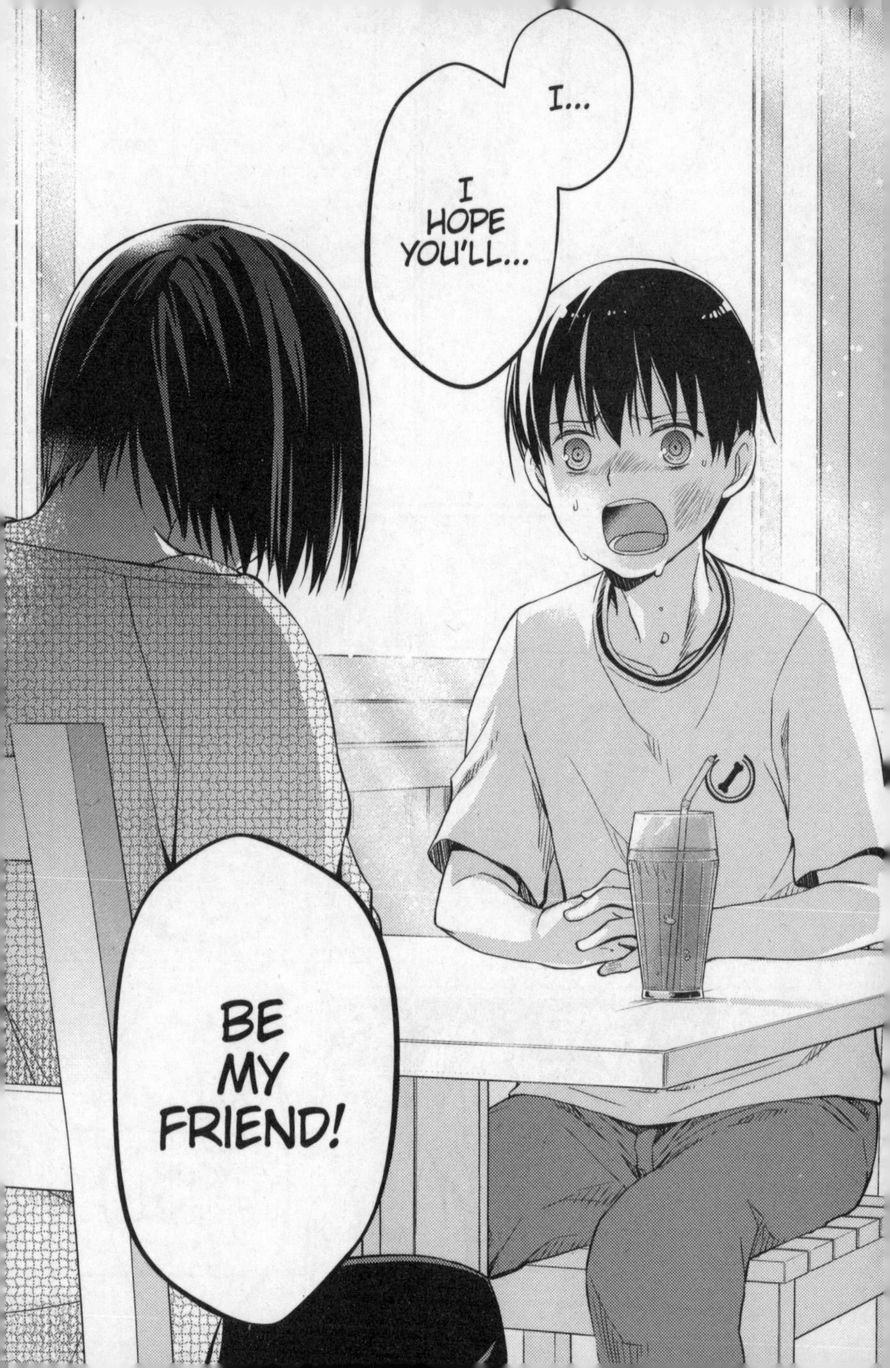
I...
I HOPE YOU'LL...
BE MY FRIEND!

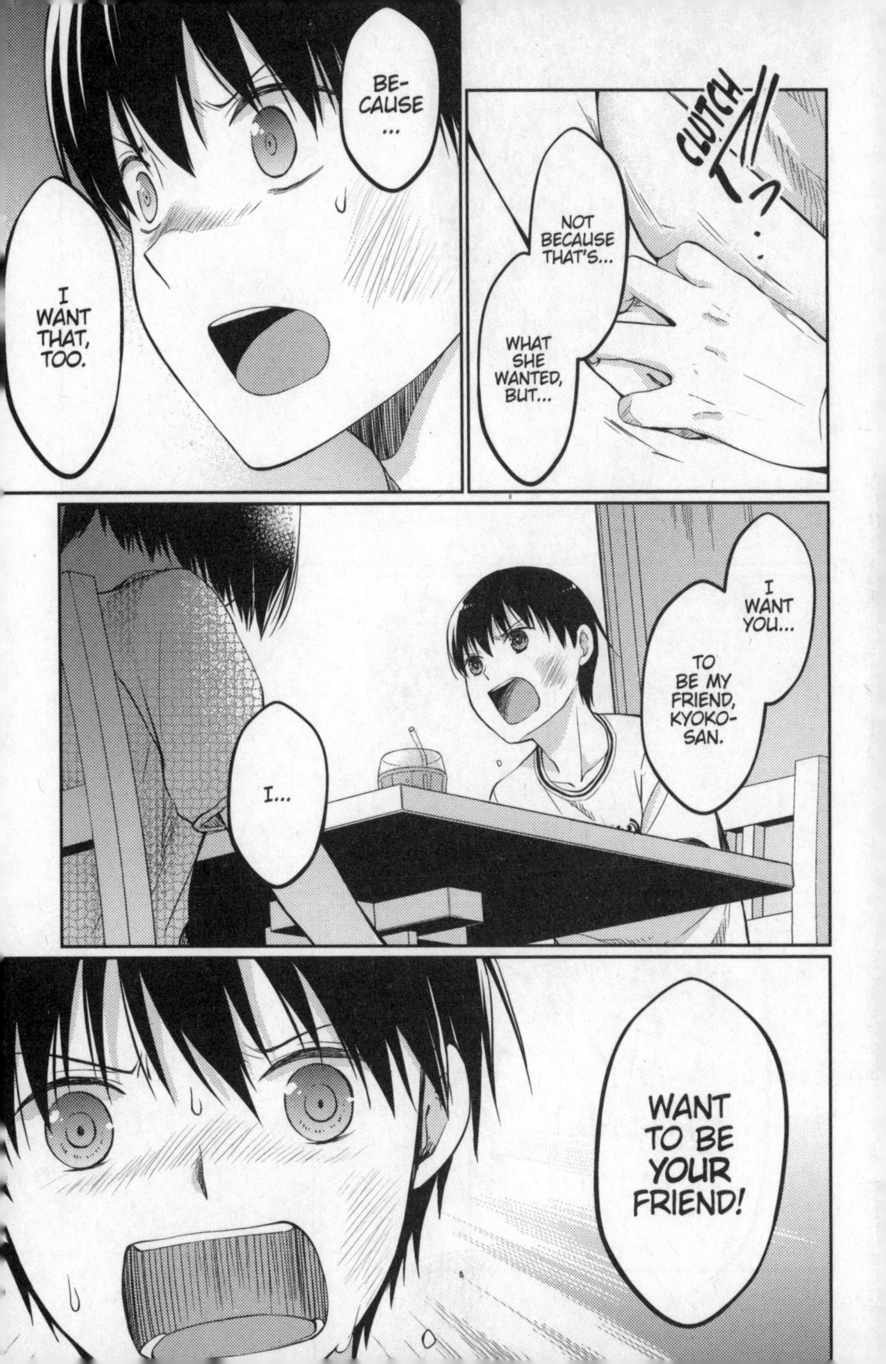
CLUTCH
NOT BECAUSE THAT'S...
WHAT SHE WANTED, BUT...
BE-CAUSE ...
I WANT THAT, TOO.
I WANT YOU...
TO BE MY FRIEND, KYOKO-SAN.
I...
WANT TO BE YOUR FRIEND!

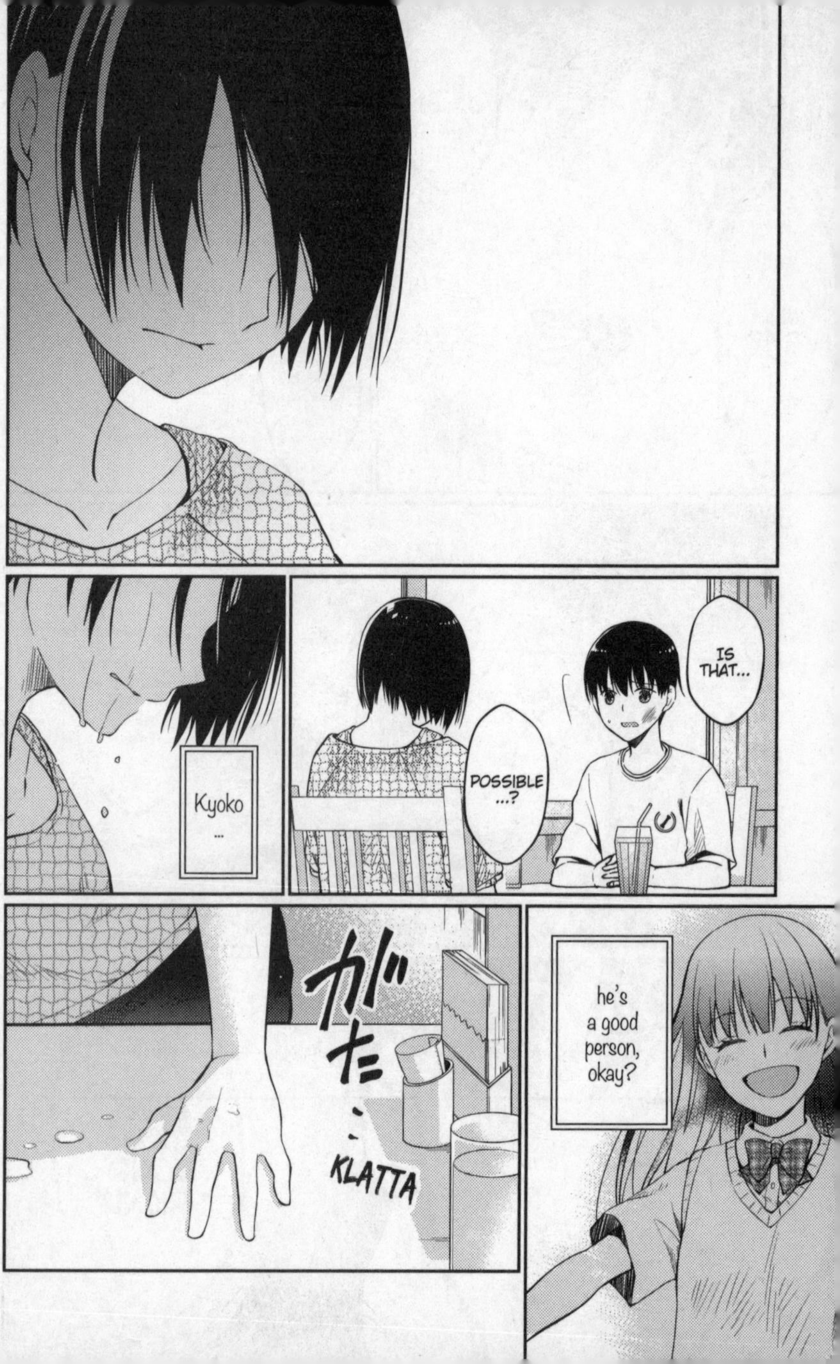

IS THAT...
POSSIBLE ...?
Kyoko ...
he's a good person, okay?
ガた
KLATTA

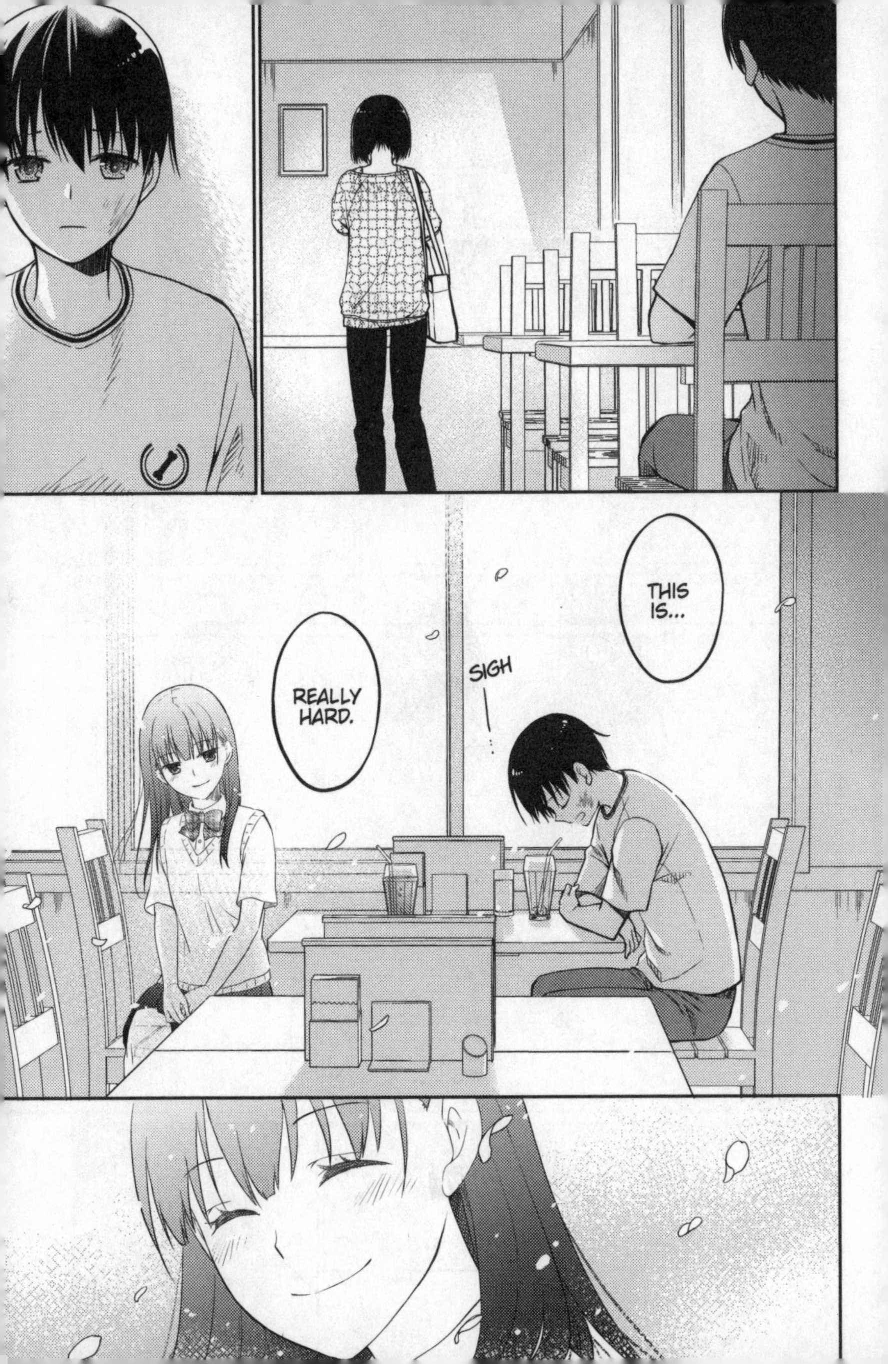
THIS IS...
SIGH
REALLY HARD.

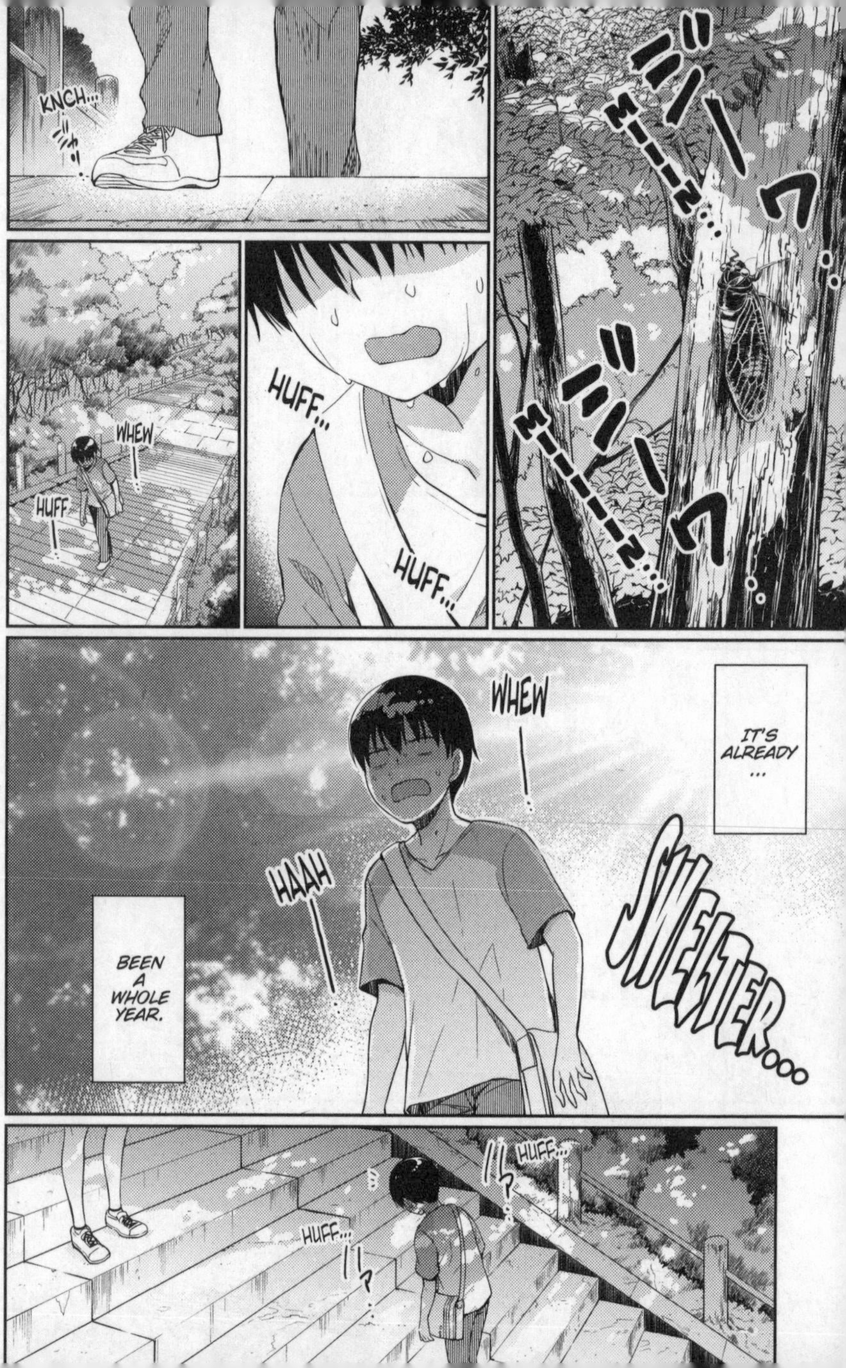
MIIIIN...
MIIIIIIIN...
KNCH...
HUFF...
HUFF...
WHEW
HUFF
IT'S ALREADY ...
SWELTER...
WHEW
HAAH
BEEN A WHOLE YEAR.
HUFF...
HUFF...

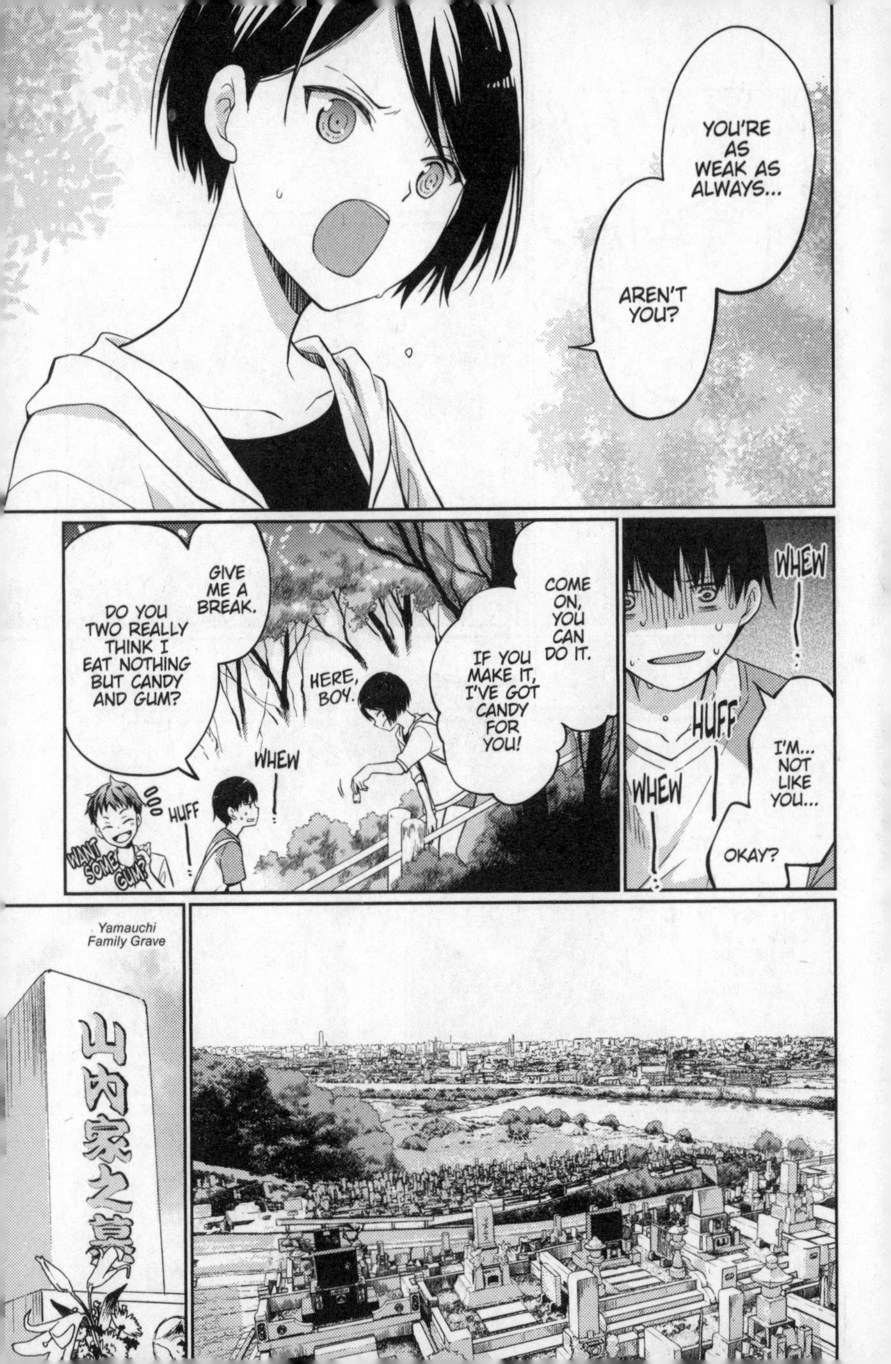
YOU'RE AS WEAK AS ALWAYS...
AREN'T YOU?
WHEW
HUFF
WHEW
I'M... NOT LIKE YOU...
OKAY?
COME ON, YOU CAN DO IT.
IF YOU MAKE IT, I'VE GOT CANDY FOR YOU!
HERE, BOY.
WHEW
GIVE ME A BREAK.
DO YOU TWO REALLY THINK I EAT NOTHING BUT CANDY AND GUM?
HUFF
WANT SOME GUM?
Yamauchi Family Grave
山内家之墓

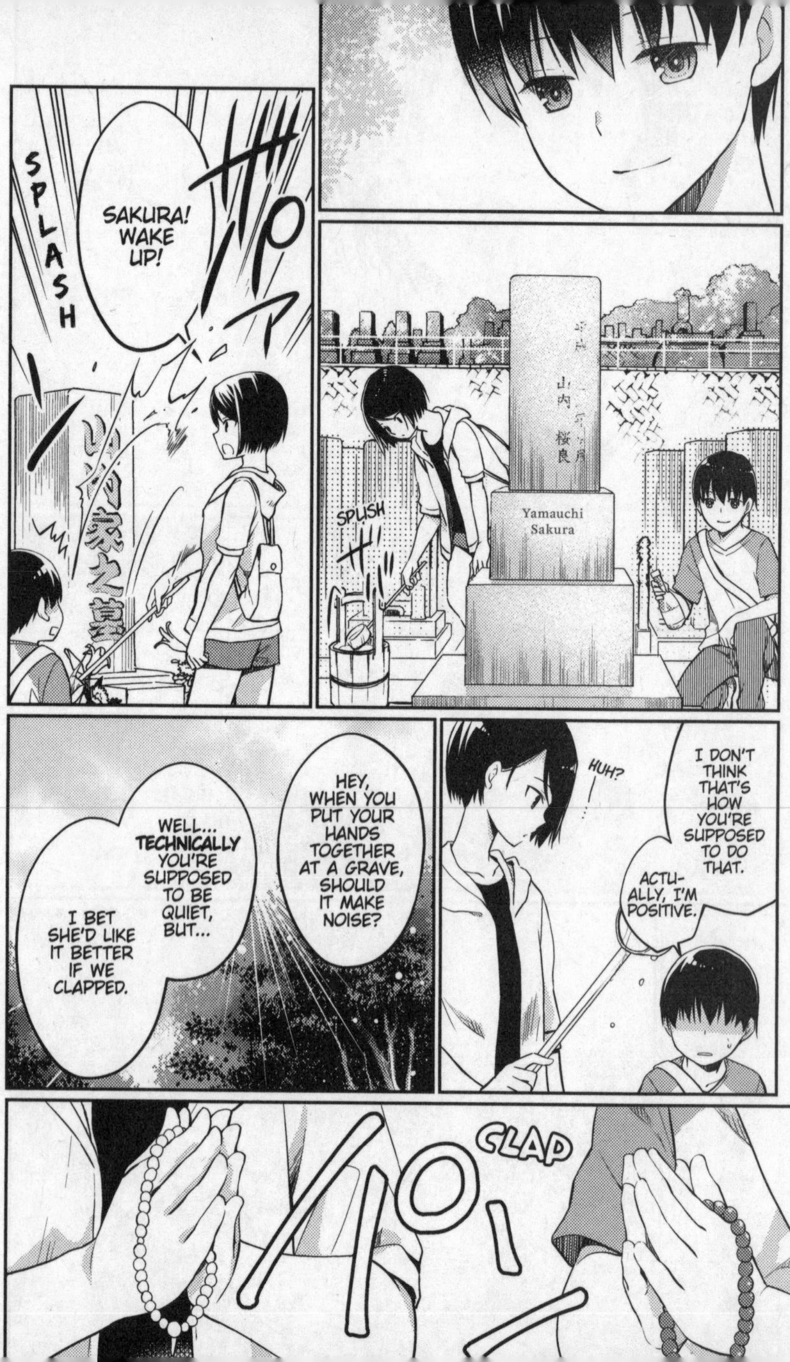
山内 桜良
Yamauchi Sakura
SPLISH
SAKURA! WAKE UP!
SPLASH
山内家之墓
HUH?
I DON'T THINK THAT'S HOW YOU'RE SUPPOSED TO DO THAT.
ACTU-ALLY, I'M POSITIVE.
HEY, WHEN YOU PUT YOUR HANDS TOGETHER AT A GRAVE, SHOULD IT MAKE NOISE?
WELL... **TECHNICALLY** YOU'RE SUPPOSED TO BE QUIET, BUT...
I BET SHE'D LIKE IT BETTER IF WE CLAPPED.
CLAP

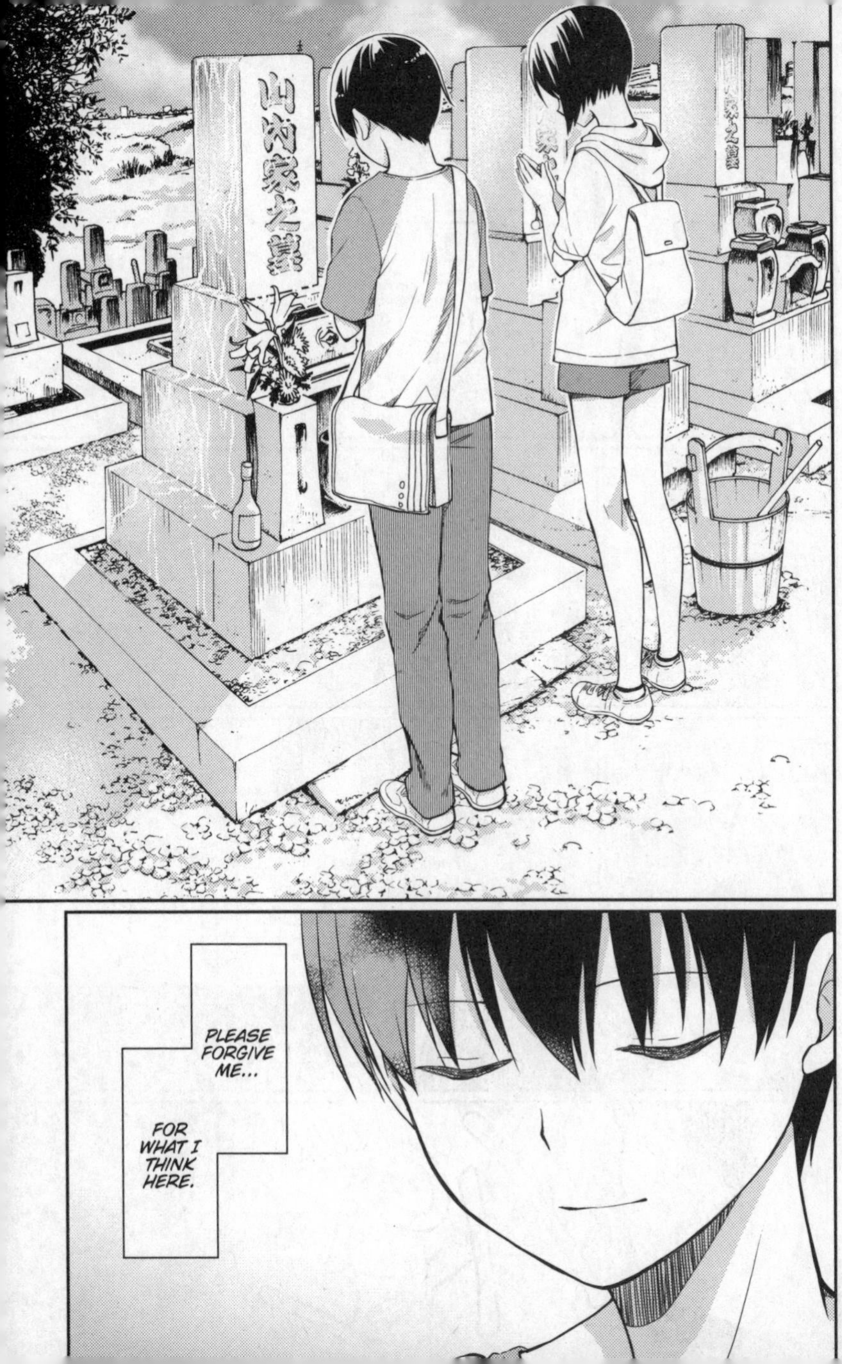
山内家之墓
PLEASE FORGIVE ME...
FOR WHAT I THINK HERE.

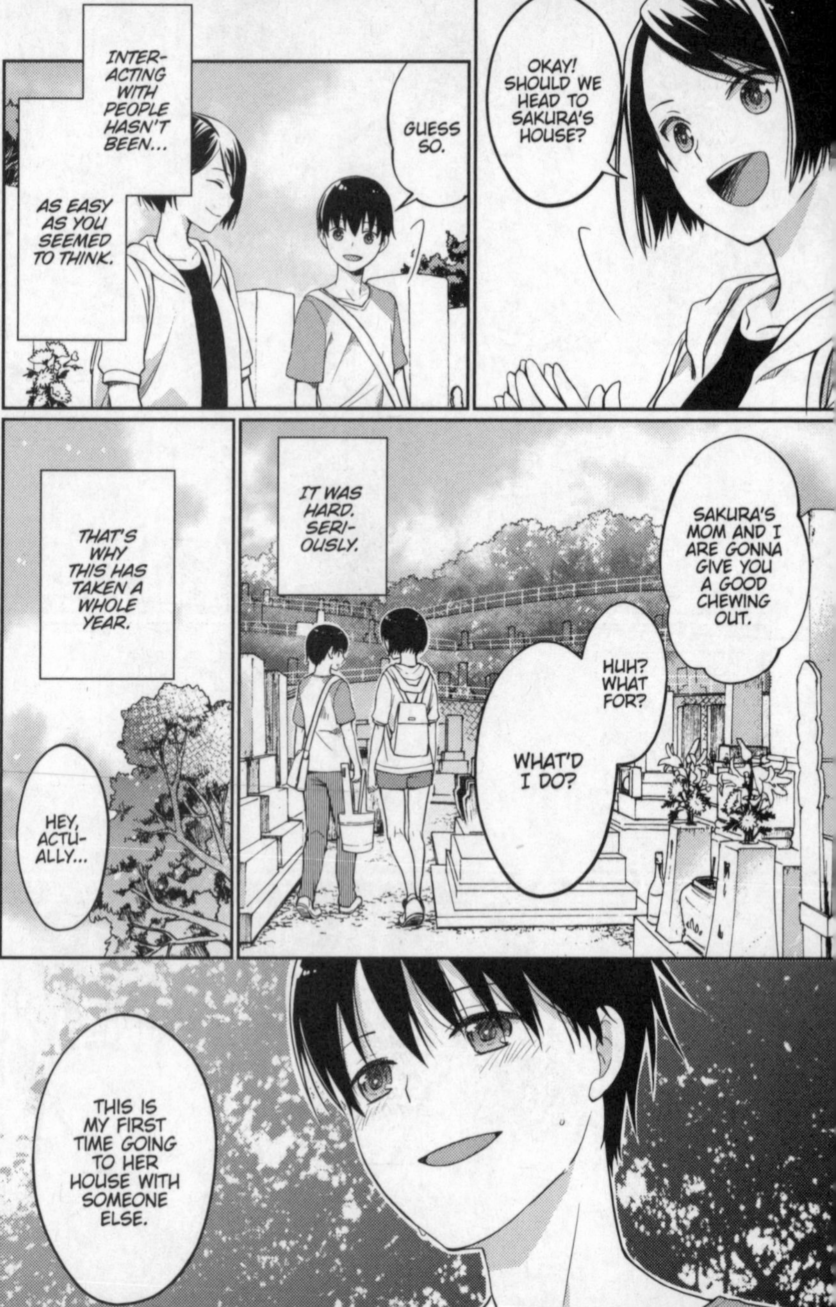
OKAY! SHOULD WE HEAD TO SAKURA'S HOUSE?
GUESS SO.
INTER-ACTING WITH PEOPLE HASN'T BEEN...
AS EASY AS YOU SEEMED TO THINK.
SAKURA'S MOM AND I ARE GONNA GIVE YOU A GOOD CHEWING OUT.
HUH? WHAT FOR?
WHAT'D I DO?
IT WAS HARD. SERI-OUSLY.
THAT'S WHY THIS HAS TAKEN A WHOLE YEAR.
HEY, ACTU-ALLY...
THIS IS MY FIRST TIME GOING TO HER HOUSE WITH SOMEONE ELSE.

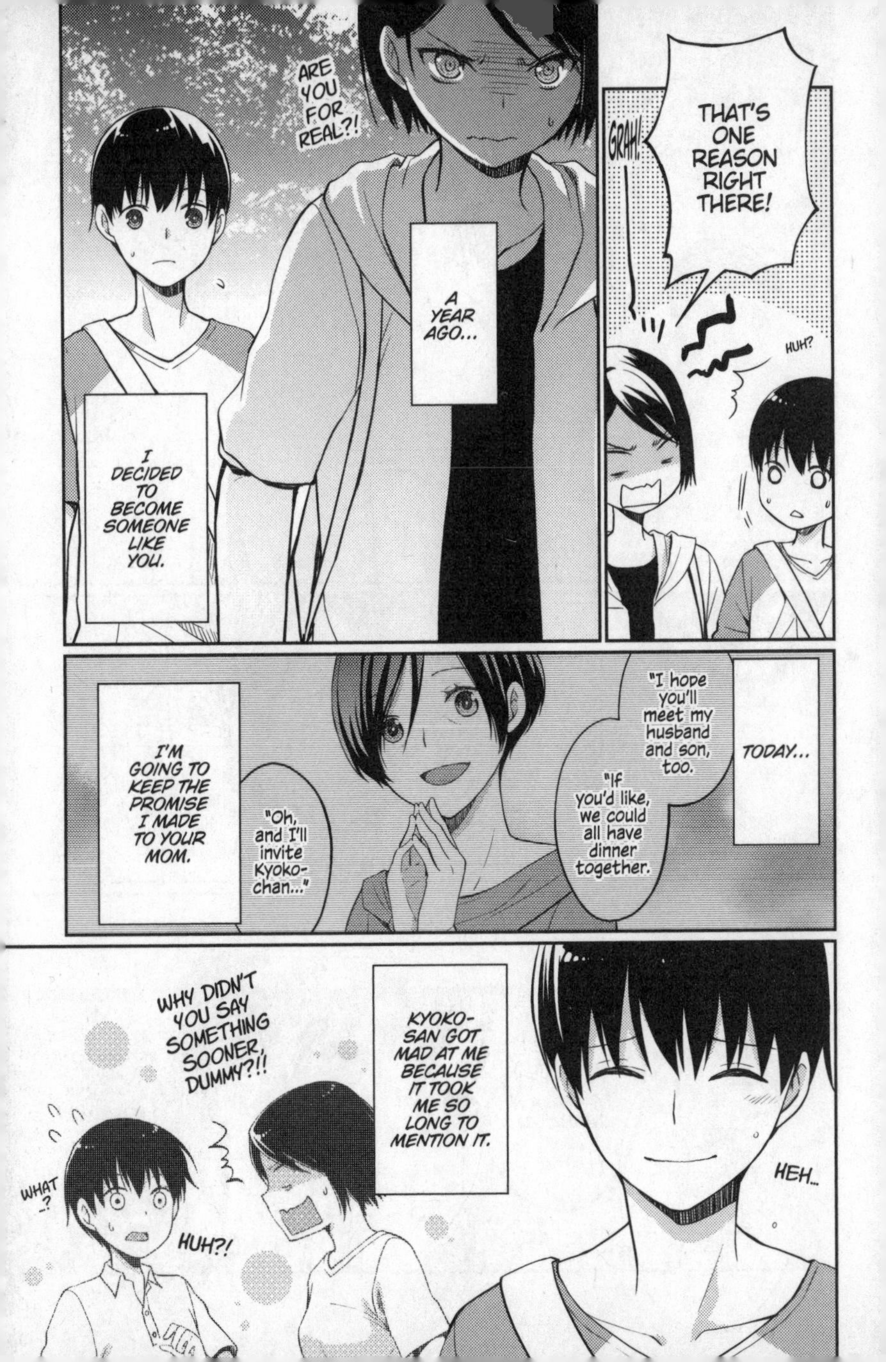
THAT'S ONE REASON RIGHT THERE!
GRAH!
HUH?
ARE YOU FOR REAL?!
A YEAR AGO...
I DECIDED TO BECOME SOMEONE LIKE YOU.
TODAY...
"I hope you'll meet my husband and son, too.
"If you'd like, we could all have dinner together.
"Oh, and I'll invite Kyoko-chan..."
I'M GOING TO KEEP THE PROMISE I MADE TO YOUR MOM.
HEH...
KYOKO-SAN GOT MAD AT ME BECAUSE IT TOOK ME SO LONG TO MENTION IT.
WHY DIDN'T YOU SAY SOMETHING SOONER, DUMMY?!!
HUH?!
WHAT ..?

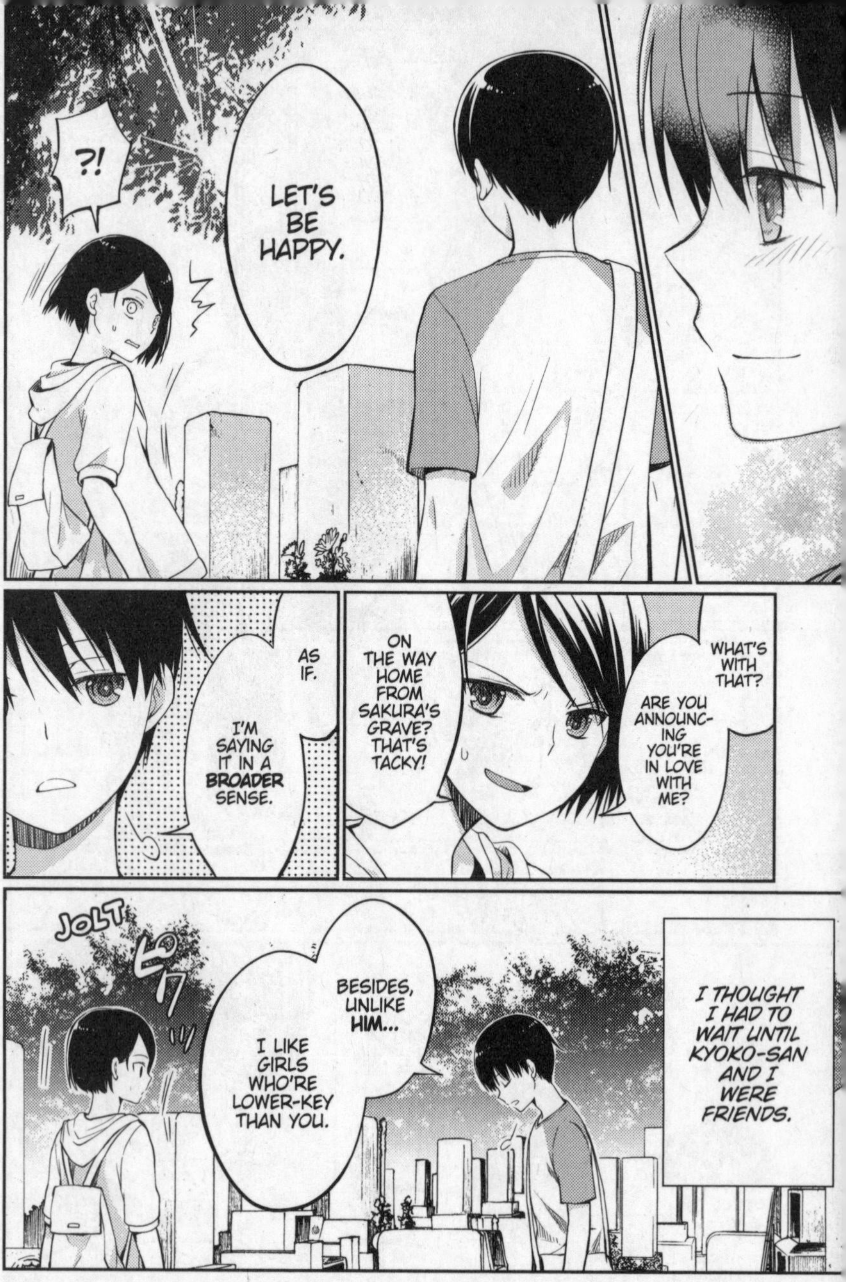
LET'S BE HAPPY.
?!
WHAT'S WITH THAT?
ARE YOU ANNOUNCING YOU'RE IN LOVE WITH ME?
ON THE WAY HOME FROM SAKURA'S GRAVE? THAT'S TACKY!
AS IF.
I'M SAYING IT IN A **BROADER** SENSE.
I THOUGHT I HAD TO WAIT UNTIL KYOKO-SAN AND I WERE FRIENDS.
BESIDES, UNLIKE **HIM...**
I LIKE GIRLS WHO'RE LOWER-KEY THAN YOU.
JOLT

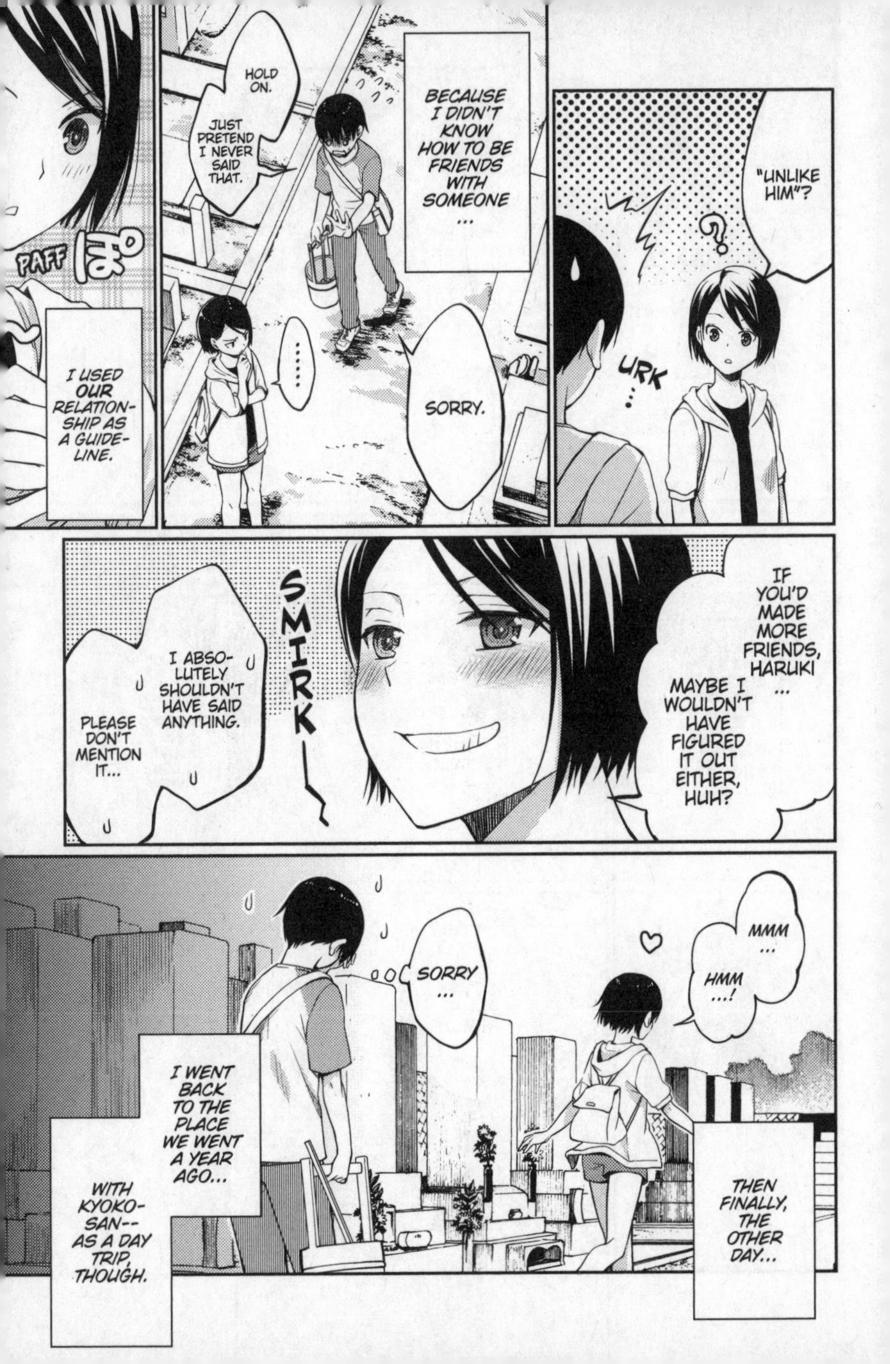
"UNLIKE HIM"?
URK...
BECAUSE I DIDN'T KNOW HOW TO BE FRIENDS WITH SOMEONE...
SORRY.
HOLD ON.
JUST PRETEND I NEVER SAID THAT.
......
PAFF ぽ
I USED OUR RELATIONSHIP AS A GUIDELINE.
IF YOU'D MADE MORE FRIENDS, HARUKI...
MAYBE I WOULDN'T HAVE FIGURED IT OUT EITHER, HUH?
SMIRK
I ABSOLUTELY SHOULDN'T HAVE SAID ANYTHING.
PLEASE DON'T MENTION IT...
THEN FINALLY, THE OTHER DAY...
MMM...
HMM...!
SORRY...
I WENT BACK TO THE PLACE WE WENT A YEAR AGO...
WITH KYOKO-SAN--AS A DAY TRIP, THOUGH.

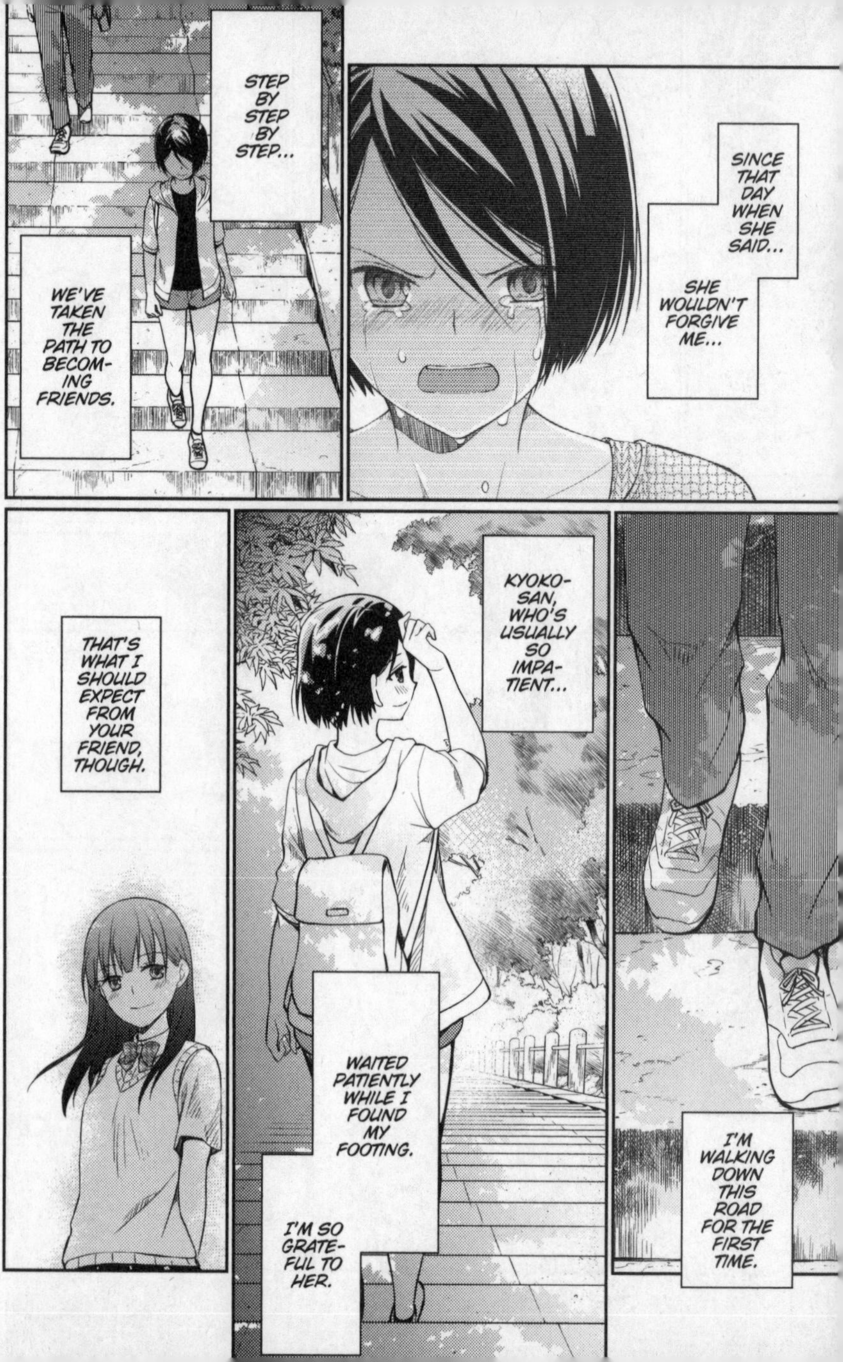
SINCE THAT DAY WHEN SHE SAID...
SHE WOULDN'T FORGIVE ME...
STEP BY STEP BY STEP...
WE'VE TAKEN THE PATH TO BECOMING FRIENDS.
I'M WALKING DOWN THIS ROAD FOR THE FIRST TIME.
KYOKO-SAN, WHO'S USUALLY SO IMPATIENT...
WAITED PATIENTLY WHILE I FOUND MY FOOTING.
I'M SO GRATEFUL TO HER.
THAT'S WHAT I SHOULD EXPECT FROM YOUR FRIEND, THOUGH.

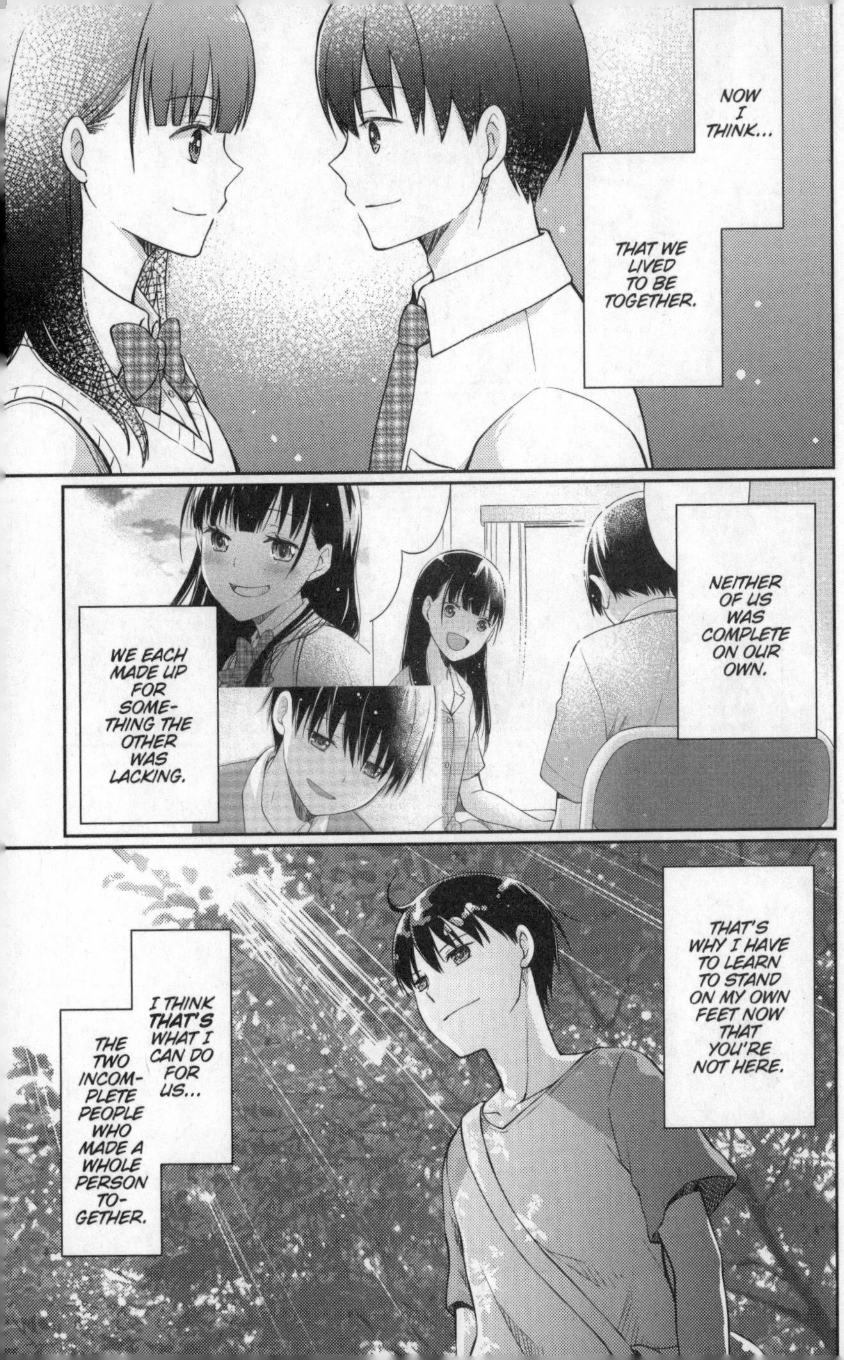
NOW I THINK...
THAT WE LIVED TO BE TOGETHER.
NEITHER OF US WAS COMPLETE ON OUR OWN.
WE EACH MADE UP FOR SOME-THING THE OTHER WAS LACKING.
THAT'S WHY I HAVE TO LEARN TO STAND ON MY OWN FEET NOW THAT YOU'RE NOT HERE.
I THINK THAT'S WHAT I CAN DO FOR US...
THE TWO INCOM-PLETE PEOPLE WHO MADE A WHOLE PERSON TO-GETHER.

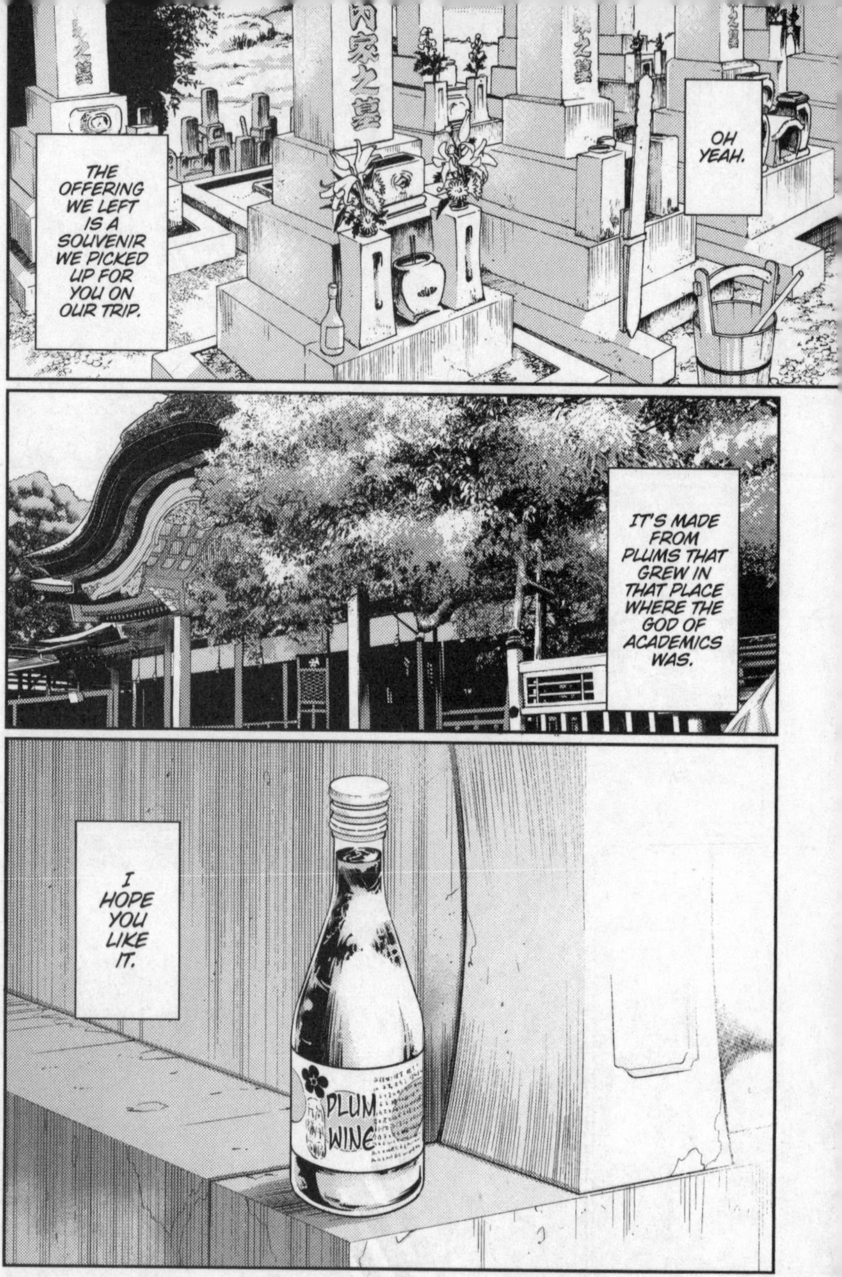
OH YEAH.
THE OFFERING WE LEFT IS A SOUVENIR WE PICKED UP FOR YOU ON OUR TRIP.
IT'S MADE FROM PLUMS THAT GREW IN THAT PLACE WHERE THE GOD OF ACADEMICS WAS.
I HOPE YOU LIKE IT.
PLUM WINE

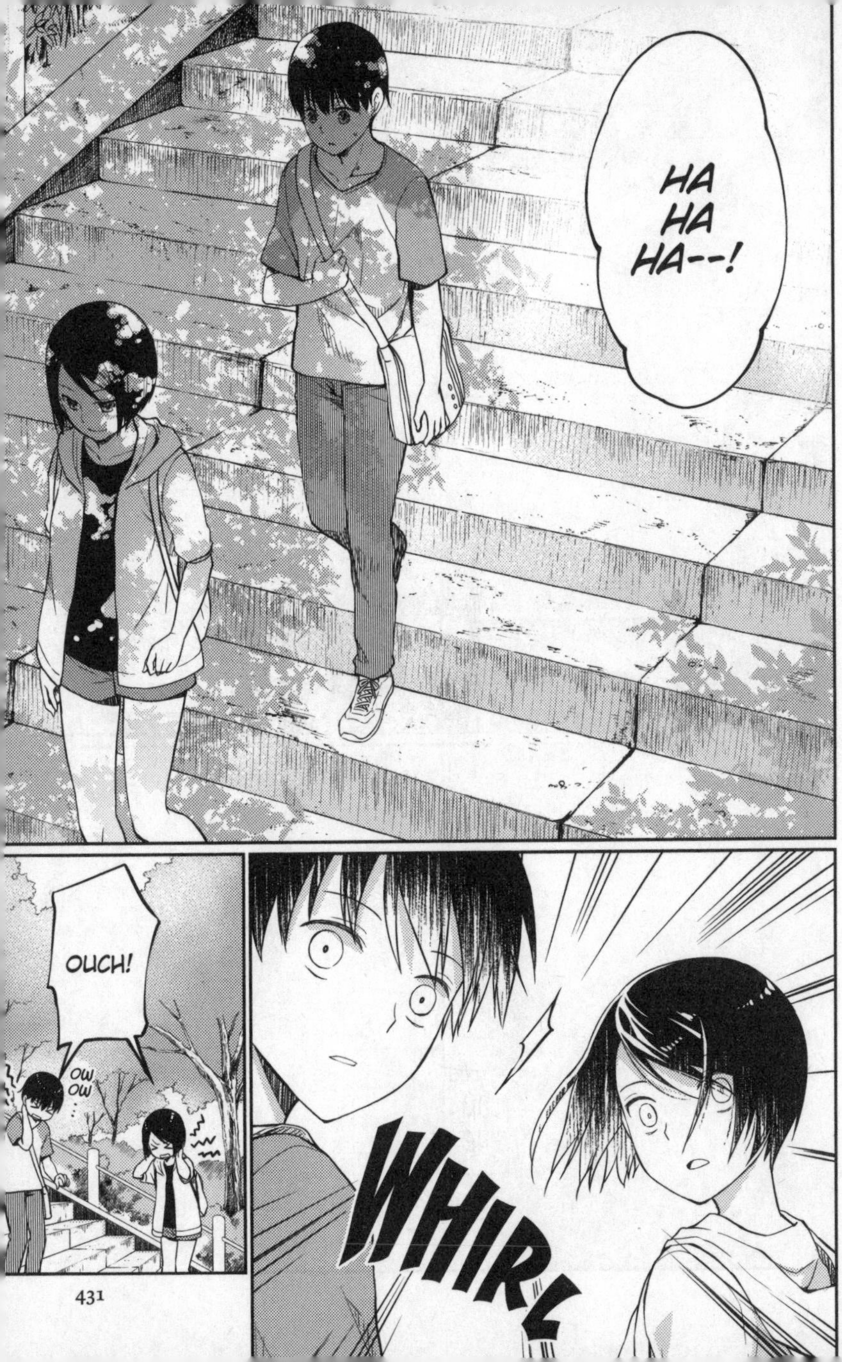
HA HA HA--!
WHIRL
OUCH!
OW OW

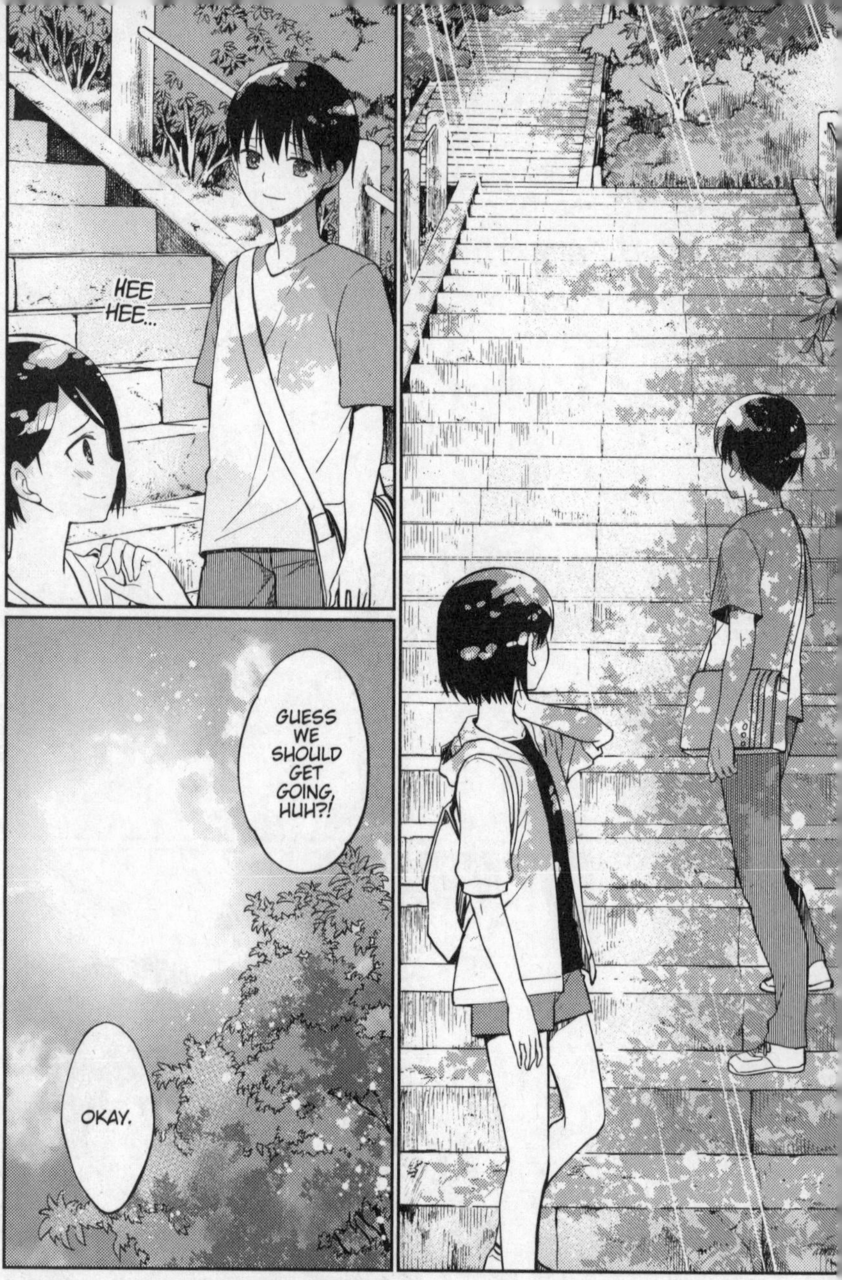
HEE HEE...
GUESS WE SHOULD GET GOING, HUH?!
OKAY.

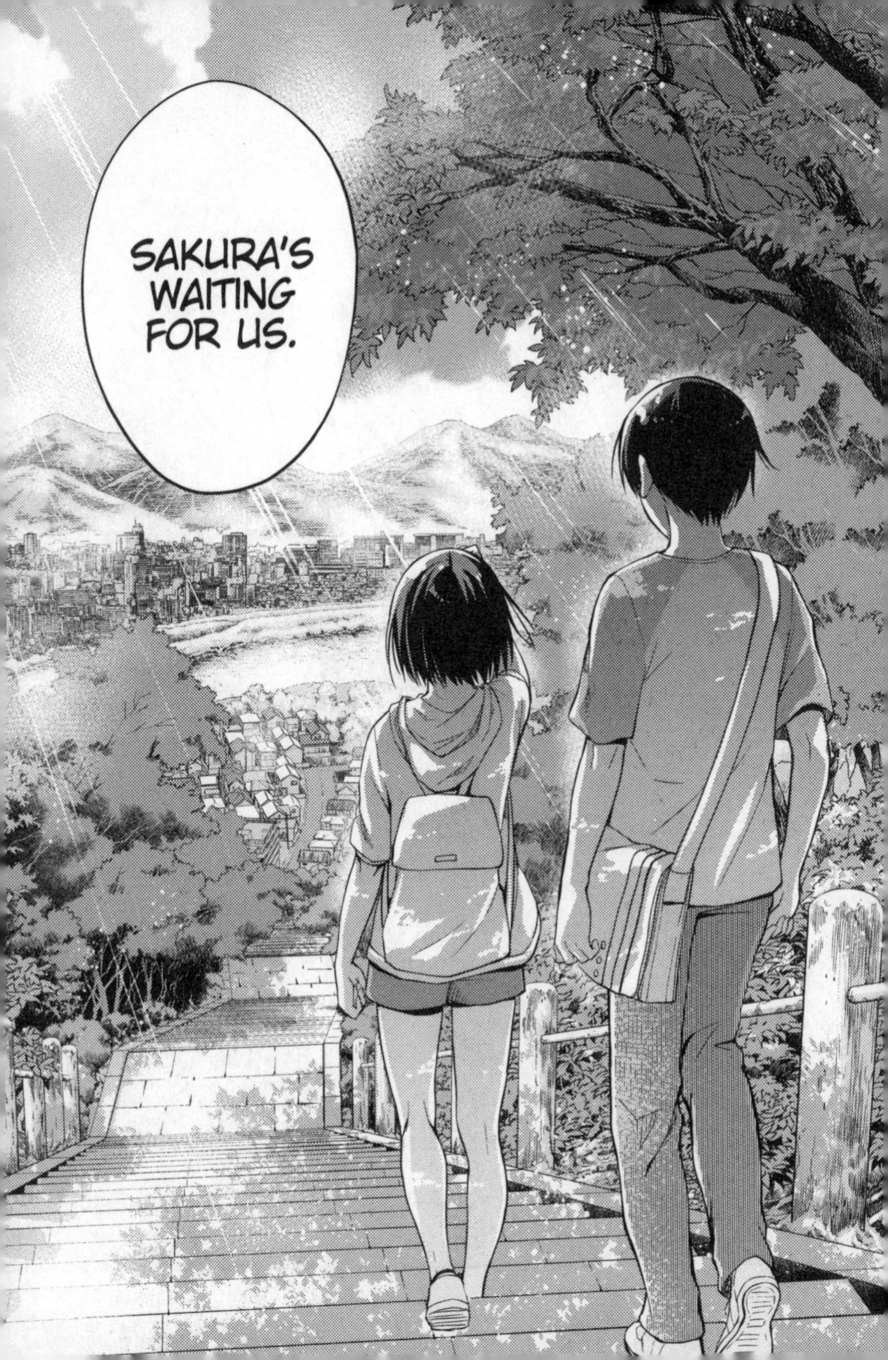
SAKURA'S
WAITING
FOR US.

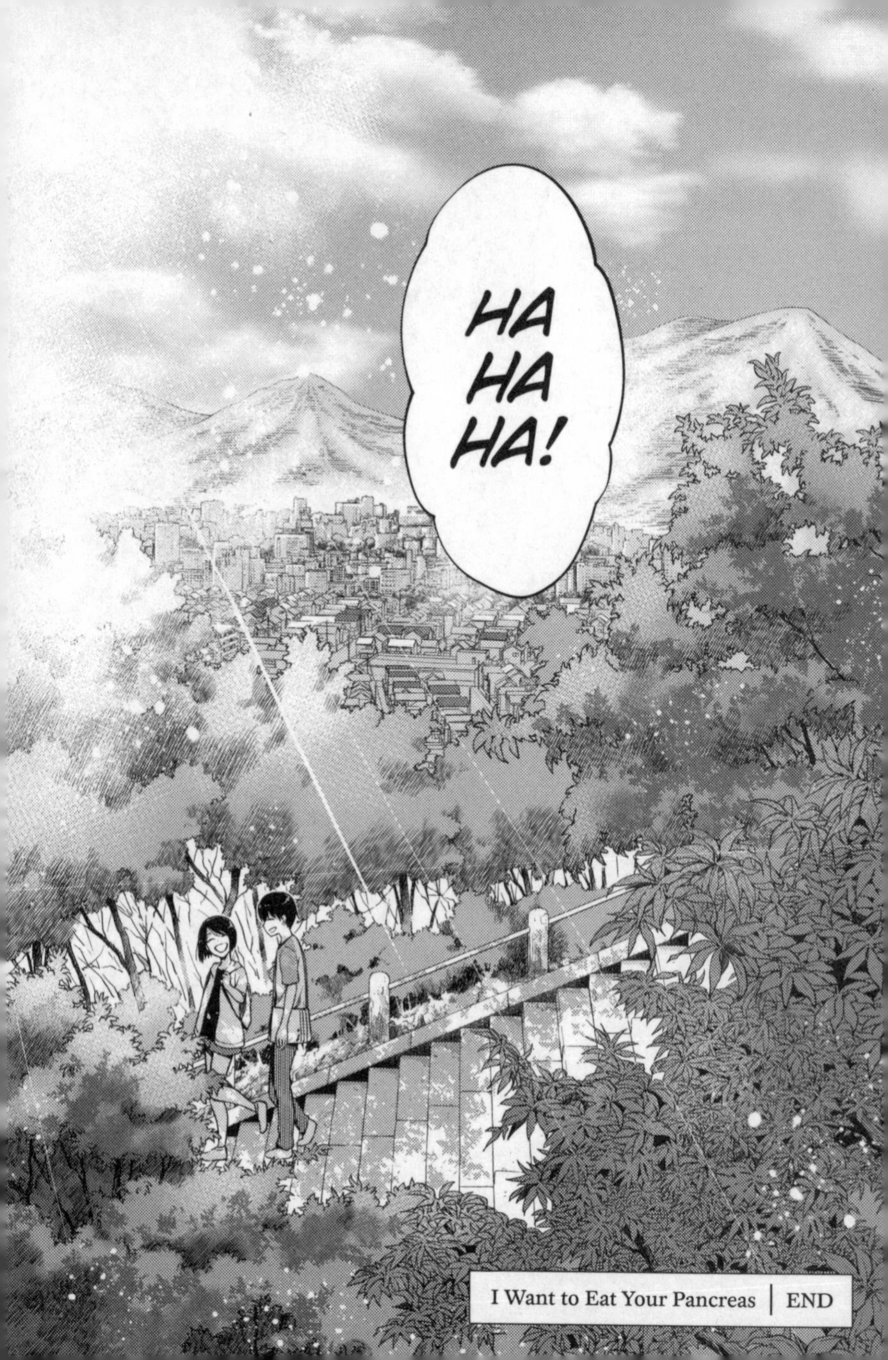
HA HA HA!
I Want to Eat Your Pancreas | END

I Want to Eat Your Pancreas

*I Want
to Eat Your
Pancreas*